FOR

Sir Peter Parker's do

Eat and drink less, and laugh more

Somehow find a way of sleeping twice a day

Do all your sums, look hard, but don't forget you still have to leap

Hire people cleverer than you are and delegate more than you think is good for you

Learn one more language at least; it's never too late

Find things to praise in other people but don't too easily trust yourself about yourself – you're such a flatterer!

If you're in a hanging mood, hang people like pictures, in the best light

One minute of your time could be somebody else's day, good or bad, courtesy or curse

Round tables for meetings do make a real difference

Take your problems home

Organize into the smallest groups you can

Do not ask Frank Sinatra his view on the atomic bomb – ask him to croon

Born in 1924 and educated at London University and Lincoln College, Oxford, Sir Peter Parker's long career has spanned a huge variety of posts, including Chairman of British Rail (1976–83), Shipping Industrial Holdings, British Maltsters, Bookers Engineering, merchant bankers Dawney Day, literary agents Curtis Brown, the British Institute of Management, and Chairman Designate of the National Ports Authority. He has also served on the boards of many organizations such as British Steel, the British Tourist Authority, British Airways, the Royal National Theatre and the Engineering Industries Council. He is a founder member of the Foundation for Management Education; a trustee of the Design Museum, the British Architectural Library and Friends of the Earth; President of the Design and Industries Association and on the Council of the Oxford Museum of Modern Art. Sir Peter is Chairman of the LSE; Visiting Fellow of Nuffield College, Oxford, an Honorary Fellow of Lincoln College, Westfield College, and the Society for Industrial Artists and Designers; and has received honorary degrees from the Open University and the universities of London, Manchester and Bath. In 1983 he delivered the Dimbleby Lecture on BBC television.

Sir Peter is currently Chairman of the Rockware Group, Mitsubishi Electric (UK) and Whitehead Mann. He is married and has four children.

PETER PARKER

FOR STARTERS

The Business of Life

from Sir Peter Parker

PAN BOOKS

in association with Jonathan Cape

First published in Great Britain 1989 by Jonathan Cape Limited
This edition published 1991 by Pan Books Limited
Cavaye Place, London SW10 9PG

9 8 7 6 5 4 3 2 1

ISBN 0 330 31926 4

Phototypeset by Intype, London
Printed in England by Clays Ltd, St Ives plc

*For Jill
and the family*

CONTENTS

LIST OF ILLUSTRATIONS

PLATES

FOR STARTERS

LINE ILLUSTRATIONS

PICTURE CREDITS

The publishers and the author would like to thank the following for their kind permission to reproduce illustrations: Wendy Brammell (p. 198); British Coal (no. 41); British Railways Board (nos 30, 34, 35, 36, 40, 44, 46, 48, 49, 50, 53, 54, 55); *Bromsgrove Messenger* (no. 33); Capital Press, Edinburgh (nos 38, 39); Sir Hugh Casson (no. 45); *Gloucestershire Echo* (no. 17); David Hartley (nos 64, 65); Illustrated London News Picture Library (nos 14, 15); Dennis Keenan (pp. 213, 266, 314); Gemma Levine (no. 31); Marvel Entertainment Group Inc. (p. 205, copyright © 1970, 1989. All rights reserved. Spiderman and the likeness thereof are trademarks of Marvel Entertainment Group Inc.); the Hon. Bill McAlpine (no. 57); Collection of Mr and Mrs Paul Mellon, Upperville, Va. (no. 10); Mitsubishi Electric (UK) Ltd (no. 61); Dr Ohtani (no. 62); Press Association (no. 52); Rockware Group (no. 59); the Earl of Snowdon (no. 63); Wates Construction (London) Ltd (no. 60); Westminster Press Ltd (no. 32). The sketches on pages 221, 223, 227, 286 are by the author.

PREFACE

I have no right to write an autobiography. I had a happy childhood in a happy family – I even liked school, I have been happily in love all my married life, and have been lucky to earn a good living doing things that have fascinated me and may have done the state some service. Also, I can only say 'That's it so far and I'm not finished.' That is one reason this book is *For Starters*.

The second reason for the title is more literal. I admire starters and it is in that spirit that I write. Starters seem to me to come in at least two sizes and styles. There are those people who come to the end of something good in their lives – perhaps with a bang, certainly not a whimper – and they pick themselves up, brush themselves down and start, start, and start again. No regrets. Theirs was a lesson I was made to learn very young and it has stayed with me always.

Then, there are those starters with the blessed ability to be uninhibited by custom and practice; they do what comes naturally – they question and reject and they welcome doing something new or finding a way to do an old thing better. In my career in management and in life at large in the arts, in education, in politics, in sport, I value such people, and in this book encounter many of them again and enjoy them gratefully. Through them I have come to know that efficiency and happiness do not have to contradict one another.

I have relished a spicy variety of jobs in both public and private enterprises, but my time in British Rail was probably the most dramatic in its focus on the demanding need for adaptability, resilience and innovation. This was no longer an option. Either you make a new start or face an abrupt end. It was a fine moment to be on the rails.

My belief is that the world, and particularly our Britain and its ramshackle political system, stands at a moment of that kind. It probably always has done. The difference is that now the hopes that lie before us, if we can react imaginatively and in good temper, are brilliant and enticing, nationally and globally. This, as probably never before, is a time for starters.

I would never have finished this without the sustaining care of a number of colleagues and friends of which there are many more starters than I can acknowledge individually in these pages. I received great support from my former personal assistant, Gwen Cowan, who held my act together over years; and from my invaluable current assistant, Kaye Wilson, with Karen Hunt, who took meticulous trouble in managing my schedule and decoding my scripts. (I handwrite, as Oscar Wilde said, like a man with something to hide.) I am grateful to Barbara Castle and her publishers, Macmillan, for their kind permission to reproduce from her diaries; and to the Hokuseido Press for Blyth's translation of Bonchō's *haiku*. I must also thank Graham C. Greene whose gallant act of faith started me off; Andrew Best of Curtis Brown for spurring me on; Maurice Temple Smith who has been an inspiring friend, goad and counsellor; and at Cape, Tony Colwell for his incisive guidance and Annelise Evans for her elegant insistence during the final stage.

Peter Parker
London
July 1989

1

A Good Start

When I was seven my father lost his job in the slump of 1931. That day was full of surprises. We were living in northern France where my parents had moved after the First World War and my father was an engineering superintendent at a refrigerating plant on the docks of Dunkirk. Because he was a foreigner his job was one of the first to go. He came home early from work, a sure sign something was awry. We were assembled to hear the shattering news. But Tom's own reaction was typical of the man. All his happy, turbulent life his way was not to waste a moment, to be ready to start afresh. He picked up the youngest of his three sons – me. Then he tossed me high into the air and asked the astonished family, 'How would you like to go to China?'

That night in our bedroom, Mickey, Alan and myself debated the challenge in terms we could understand. Alan bounced about his bed chanting 'Would you like to go to China or have ten *cornets d'amour?*' *Cornets d'amour* were the best ice-cream cones in the world, beyond the dreams of lusciousness: we were given them on special days on the *plage*. Not that going to the beach was in itself special. Our big spacious family house was close by the sea and it was only the bleakest of Channel days that kept us away from the family beach hut, at that time one of relatively few at Malo-les-Bains. Cold and grey the waves may have been for most of the time, but I remember those days as golden, days of racing about the long sands, finding thrilling hiding-places in the dunes. The sea was my element and has been ever since – get in there and all's well. And then *tartine au chocolate en famille*, out of the wind, in the hut. On special days, the treat of the *cornet d'amour* . . . So, the adventure of China was put seriously in the balance by us boys. Ten *cornets d'amour!*

We were brought up as French boys. There is a period picture of the three of us in square-necked sailor suits. Mickey, the eldest brother, even looked French, dark-eyed and dark-haired. He went to

1

the Collège Jean-Bart in Dunkirk, while Alan, eighteen months my senior, and I attended the nursery school in our red and white checked *jupons*. All three of us would set off together. We would pass the swashbuckling statue of Jean-Bart, the pirate who harassed British ships in the eighteenth century, but to me in my innocence he seemed a fine fellow, not the old French enemy. I saw the statue soon after the war, and Jean-Bart with his cutlass was still slashing the clouds, but was now pitted and scarred with the bullets of the Second World War. It was a private relief to find he had been fighting on our side after all.

Naturally we boys spoke French most of the time; our friends were French. Tom and Dorothy saw that we spoke English at the table, but they themselves were also living the French life and loving it. I can understand why now. They came from very different backgrounds, and going to France was a new start for them both.

Theirs had been a wartime marriage, in 1917, in Newcastle. Tom was a naval officer engineer; Dorothy, a teacher. Tom was born in Hull in 1888, the son of a tailor who owned a shop in the town centre. As a boy, his signposts were the masts of the ships sailing out of the Humber; he yearned to go to sea, and as a first step he took an engineering apprenticeship at Gray's shipyard. Story-telling for us as children was often about the great 'goings-on' at Gray's shipyard. They were a great saga to him and became so for us. He had never liked the grind of the life there, and the years of dark dawns, had never wanted to be an engineer, but Gray's had been an expanding universe for him as a lad. When he was selected to go to the drawing-office in the main building he leapt at the promotion, but not because of the work: from his new office he had a far better view of the tall ships and of the wide escape route down the river Humber.

I visited Hull for the first time many years later in 1970. I was lucky enough to be welcomed to Hull by the Lord Mayor at a formal luncheon. At that time, I had just become chairman-designate of the National Ports Authority and my earliest priority was to tour the main ports of the country. When the speeches were over, I confessed privately to the Mayor that I badly wanted to step off the white lines of my programme and to visit Gray's. He looked rather taken aback. 'Gray's goes back a bit,' he said. But, still sitting in his grand chair, he whispered to his officials and by the time the banquet had formally ended his car was ready for us. With motorcycle escort, we drove solemnly for some miles, with the Mayor silent and smiling. In a dilapidated part of town, suddenly we swung left towards the river, through a ruined gate with only one tall pillar left standing, and across a bumpy wasteland. There was a small, two-toned, Victorian red brick building, quite derelict. The great car drew up at an overgrown slipway, only about eighteen feet across. 'This was it.' Our playgrounds as children are prairies. It is experience, with its loss of imagination, that reduces them to the size of a pocket handkerchief.

Eventually Tom earned his chief engineer's ticket, which he never really wanted, and sailed the world – his oyster. Then came the war and the Navy, and the good fortune which in a long life of ups, downs and arounds never ran out on him – the love of Dorothy.

Dorothy was one of nine daughters. Her mother's family was rich, part of the John Brown shipping dynasty. I saw my grandmother's birth certificate for the first time when I registered her death. Martha Brown had been 'born off Hong Kong' in 1856 on a China clipper: she was the Captain's daughter. When she grew up Martha defied her own family's disapproval to marry a handsome, brilliant, and finally ruinous, man. Her dowry was her last contact with the Browns. Her young man was a mining engineer with a soaring ability which soon raised him from mines in the Midlands to opulence, advising maharajahs in India and state governments in Australia. 'Golden years and we ate off golden plates,' the old lady once told me. But Martha spent the last years of her life in a small room in the London suburb of Motspur Park, minded by her youngest daughter Mary. Mary was short for Mareba, the name of one of her father's favourite racecourses in Australia. He had reached a stage of such boredom with breeding a family of nine daughters (and no sons) that he gave the last few of the girls place-names. In addition to Mareba, I had an aunt called Pauline Victoria, and Dorothy's full name was Dorothy Sidney. My grandfather returned to England with his excess cargo of young ladies and retired early, and wildly, on what little was left of Martha's money. The tiny, and beautiful, once-merry Martha finally summoned the will to stop his Rabelaisian routine of wine, other women, and song ('I'll say this about him, he had a lovely deep baritone,' was Dorothy's one complimentary memory). Martha gave him money to go abroad. He squandered that in London and was soon back for more. This time, through Thomas Cook, she booked his passage to exile in South Africa.

3

Dorothy, I was told by my grandmother not altogether approvingly, was 'the brainy one'. She won scholarships and prizes, and one of her prizes has survived on my own bookshelves. It is a brick-sized edition of Longfellow's *Poetical Works* in forbiddingly small print presented to her by Rutherford College, Newcastle-upon-Tyne. Page 766 is turned down and marked: there among the hefty rhythms of a poem called 'The Maiden and the Weathercock' the black-haired, serious young student seems to have taken a special pleasure in a dead-pan piece of doggerel from the weathercock:

> When you and your lover meet today,
> You will thank me for looking some other way.

Tom, with his high spirits, handsome in his naval officer's rig, must have been a boon to a besieged band of young women down on their luck. 'I'd never met anybody like him and he made us laugh and laugh.' Dorothy would tell us, still laughing, the story of their wartime wedding: how she had been so nervous setting out for the honeymoon that when Tom had gone off to buy a paper she had hopped into a carriage and hidden while Tom ran up and down the platform. 'What did I think I was doing?' Years and years later that inherited question was to keep springing naturally to my mind when I found myself on the rails.

By the end of the war Tom was suffering from claustrophobia as a result of his experience in the engine-room of a destroyer. Their first son was born, and there was a rough spell until Tom stumbled upon an advertisement for a British engineer to work with a French group, Frigorifique, in Dunkirk. How desirable the one-way trip across the Channel must have seemed to them both. What a relief – the sheer zest of France, the openness, the frankness, the classlessness of their widening circle of friends. Plainly this was, for them both, the best of times.

I have a few photographs from that period in France and there is one of Tom in the Dunkirk hockey team, a light, compact, energetic figure, ready for the off. He had that power of living in the present, and it shows vividly. There is another photograph too, a set piece of Dorothy in the women's hockey team. She was the dashing centre forward, the goal-scorer. We became used to seeing the large silver cup for the most goals scored in the season on the sideboard. My parents seemed a good match, not at all the same, but a match: Tom, wiry, springy, resilient and boyish; Dorothy, stylish and seeking formality in a life of faith and family. Tom was undoubtedly a handful, hard-playing and hard-drinking for some years in France until he became frightened by his lack of fitness. Dorothy took the strain of managing the family, keeping pace with him, but less light-heartedly. He seemed driven by an impulse to keep things moving, to take things on with an eagerness which was boyishly unimpeded by past failure or by what was expected of him. He had a warmth and flexibilty that fitted change better than cold and rigid logic. She had a warmth and flexibility that fitted stability (that is, the little there was to hang on to) better than cold and rigid logic. She would always make the best of things. They both adored the scope of those French years. Gautier has a phrase about one of his characters for whom 'the physical world was very much alive': France was like that for them, and for the whole family. I grew up with the French habit of greeting family and close friends with a kiss on both cheeks. I still do, to a tamed degree. These days the British habit of a peck on one cheek and good night leaves me off-balance, on the wrong foot, kissing the air French fashion to the scrunch of gravel. Anyway, all that kissing had to stop in 1931. There was really no choice. Tom had to find a job. And it was not a matter of China or *cornets d'amour*. Our side of the world, Europe, was darkening into depression, so he set out in hope for the other side of the globe. We took a slow boat to China.

My last memory of France was the house sale. The furniture was displayed on the street for auction: it must have been the custom of the place. Mickey, Alan-and-me (it took me all my adolescence to not say 'Alan-and-me') stood together astonished at seeing the home somehow inside out. As the sale proceeded, prices were placed on familiar treasures, but these amazingly low values had nothing at all to do with ours. Thus ended the first lesson I was to learn about worldly goods: this one was read in French, the second was to be in Chinese. Often in my life since then that point of fierce realism, that street sale, has kept recurring.

Years later, when I was chairman of British Railways, I sometimes reflected on my French connection. Having been born there, on 30 August 1924, I was given the opportunity at the age of twenty-one to become a French citizen, but by 1945 France had become remote in my life and I was in the uniform of the Army, a lieutenant on the joint Staff Mission in Washington. So I said *non* and thanks to the French Embassy for their cordial act of courtesy in extending the hand of friendship over so many years. Had I known that some day I would run a railway – and had I known how handsomely the French treat trains and how great a priority they give public transport – I would have snatched their hand off. It is well not to peer ahead beyond what we can really see. I am sure we stunt our spirits by crouching defensively in anticipation of problems, risks, rebuffs, complications. Look as hard as you like (and sometimes must) you still have to leap. There are moments to defy augury.

Anyway, that is how Tom handled two auguries on the long trip to the Orient, which we made, comfortably and for the most part happily, aboard a small Japanese NYK liner. The first omen was a trapped rat. We had been only a few days at sea when the atmosphere of the boys' cabin was foully polluted, and we had to move out. What had happened was that a rat had prowled irreversibly down the ventilation. One night we saw the glaring eyes and heard the desperate scratchings through the grille in our own cabin, then the rat died, and proved as elusive in death as in life – hence the stench. Tom reversed the omen: we were not being trapped by the suffocating slump, we were sailing clear to Shanghai. And as far as Hong Kong it was plain sailing, but there our second omen, the news of war between China and Japan, was waiting to ambush us. Fighting around Shanghai was reported to be intense. Mickey, Alan-and-me sat on the top bunk in Dorothy and Tom's cabin where the family decision was discussed. There was some talk of abandoning ship in Hong Kong and setting off south for Australia, but Dorothy seemed to find childhood memories of Australia entirely resistible, and Tom's instinct was that in times of turmoil an out-of-work engineer on the spot might be even more welcome. We held our course and in early 1932 we reached Shanghai under fire, just as we were to leave it. Our ship moved into the yellow waters of the Huangpu estuary with bullets pinging on the steel sheets put on the rails to protect the decks. Six years later we were evacuated on a British destroyer slipping out behind a Japanese warship which was shelling the city. The years between were the years that started me thinking, particularly about poverty and politics.

We set up in a house rented cheaply in the Chinese quarter with noisy, bustling, smiling Chinese neighbours, soon to be friends. Tom had to take work as a third engineer on an old ship that sailed the

Yangtze Gorges, a spectacular run through high rocks and fiercely
tidal waters made more mysterious and dangerous by wild mists and
piracy. He would bring us back a thousand and one tales of the
perilous, glamorous views; of the pirates who synchronized raids from
their junks with the hijack of a ship by accomplices travelling among
the swarming passengers; of the cunning plop of opium chests smuggled over the side to sampans waiting in the dark water. He would
return with brilliant vases brought up-country: only one of them has
survived, but it still looks unscathed, elegant and entirely appropriate
in our Kensington flat today.

Dorothy packed us off daily to the Shanghai Public School. It really
was public, a vast multinational comprehensive, with a blazer badge
of many flags. This was in the International Settlement, a breathtaking
piece of Western piracy in its time. Western powers had ripped off
the bits of the China coast that suited their fancy, their navy and
their traders. They had imposed the Concessions, the International
Concession (which combined the American and British Concessions)
and the French Concession. The word 'concession' was itself a flagr-
antly unselfconscious piece of master-speak. The whole of Shanghai
was a glittering mosaic of historical insults to the Chinese. During
the Opium War (as indeed throughout modern history) the Chinese
used the only weapon they had to defend themselves with, their
helplessness. By giving each of the conquerors what they wanted they
at least arranged a degree of separation between the European powers;
then it was a matter of waiting (another art in which the Chinese
excel), and that long and humiliating process would end in the inevitable outbreak of old and reliable hostilities in Europe. Meanwhile
the 'foreign devils' enjoyed the high life in Shanghai. 'Life itself' was
Aldous Huxley's description of the fabled city. 'Nothing more
intensely living can be imagined.'

Only at the end of the first year did our fortunes change. I have
no idea how Tom landed the job of Resident Engineer, overseeing
the construction of the Lester Research Institute, the biggest medical
centre of its sort in the East. Such wide-ranging, technical experience
as he offered on the spot must have been unexpected; normally that
level of appointment would have been filled by expensively importing
someone, family and all, from 'home-side' (England). His simply
being there, having come out on spec, must have surprised everybody.
Also Tom had an unswerving straightforwardness and a trace of

Yorkshire in his accent: that too must have helped in the context of Shanghai. Tom used to say he was brought up Yorkshire. 'Father had his do's and don'ts and nothing in-between.' Shanghai had a lot in-between. China-hands and Shanghai-landers, as the Europeans out there called themselves, lived with a traditional temptation of back-handers, graft, or *cum-shaw* as it was known in the Shanghai dialect.

Whatever won Tom the job, our lives were transformed because part of his terms of employment was that he could build his own house in the grounds. That meant leaving our house in the brawling Chinese quarter, a house of ill memory for me as a child because of one small and violent episode, an indelible black spot. In that house Dorothy had kept the family going, Tom being mostly away and only home for short spells. She had kept body and soul together – her good-tempered phrase for living through hard times – and I learnt the wisdom of it and how much it meant to her. In whatever we did, in success or in defeat, then and later, in luck or out of it, what mattered was keeping body and soul together. And still does. So we managed there well enough – until one thoroughly bad night. The boys had come home to find the house-boy, the servant, shouting at Dorothy. He was a big, stormy Chinese. He went quiet when we appeared, not I imagine because we were any threat to him, but because his quiet could be more menacing. He picked up a chair. Then very deliberately, and suddenly roaring with nasty laughter, he placed it below the box of electric switches in the corner. He got on to the chair and tore out all the fuses. Blackness. I remember a long silence, and he was laughing again, banging his way to the back door. He banged that shut. We went to bed in the dark. Far, far worse things happen to people, but that mad, stark moment stays with me and my thoughts of Dorothy. A long way from home? No, that was her home.

We had years after that of happiness and adventure in Shanghai. Tom built the house and designed much of the furniture, working with an Austrian émigré architect. Tom's idea seemed to be to make spaces for us to grow in. There were spacious verandas where Alan could keep his chipmunks, parakeets and guinea-pigs, and where he and Tom once tried to introduce a baby leopard they had spotted in the Chinese city market on the fringe of Shanghai. There was a long, flat roof where we played roller-skating hockey, and on hot summer nights we slept up there under a light bamboo shelter erected annually as a summer-house. A tennis-court and the formal garden were in front of the house. One day we woke to find one of the half-moon-shaped beds denuded of all its blooms, and none of the others touched. The mystery was soon solved. When we set out for the day – the boys for school, Dorothy to teach at a Chinese school, and Tom no doubt chasing contractors – there outside the gatehouse was a newly erected flower-stall and fresh-cut flowers were offered to us with a smile at a special price. We bought them, naturally, and it never happened again.

Shanghai must have been an outrageously fascinating place for the Westerners, and simply outrageous for the Chinese themselves. For the European it was one of the great cities of the world, a playground with extraordinary parades of all kinds. Parades of opulent power ranged along the waterfront, the Bund, home of the *taipan*, the trading houses of the merchant adventurers: Jardine and Matheson, Butterfield and Swire, the Hongkong and Shanghai Bank, the Sassoons. ('Eve' Sassoon, whose family had emigrated from Baghdad to Bombay to China, was perhaps the most spectacular of stars in that exploding galaxy.) Then there were the parades of Empire, the British Cathedral School, Empire Day, the Shanghai Volunteer Corps which every able-bodied Briton was expected to join in defence of the International Settlement, and which included a detachment of cavalry commonly called the Tight Horse. Then of course there were the parades of just fun and games. There was the Shanghai Club, No. 3 the Bund, a London-style affair but not exactly. The old boy network propped up what was claimed to be the longest bar in the world. There was the Bath Club, and there was the French Club on the Avenue Joffre, the refuge of White Russian émigrés desperately surviving on the fringes of the European and Chinese societies – the men often as bodyguards and riding-masters, the women as hairdressers and mistresses. There was the Race Course, which also formed an exclusive white arena for every sport, and the Public Gardens, with a turbaned Sikh at the gates to see that they were public only for some; dogs and Chinese not allowed. Ironically, the Japanese, during their brief turn to rule Shanghai, were to use Jessfield Park as an internment camp for their Western prisoners. And then there was the *Parade Sauvage* of night-time: here was the Paris of the East, the Whore of Asia, the pleasure-ground of which it was said that if God allowed Shanghai He owed an apology to Sodom and Gomorrah. On Friday nights Alan

9

and I would speed home on our bicycles, down Nanking Road, past Blood Alley, the street of cabarets, usually late after choir practice at the Cathedral School which we had entered when Tom landed his new job. Nanking Road was the most modern in China, an exhilarating kaleidoscope of flashing lights that held the tall, noisy department stores of the Big Four: the Sincere, Wing On, the Sun and the Sun Sun. The road swarmed with crowds overflowing on to pavements and streets, the girls sheathed in silks and brocades, and gleaming in their dresses slit high on the side. We loved the ride home. And we loved our racing-bikes, delightful, light-framed, with low, curved handlebars: we loved them, and we would carry them easily up the broad stairway to our bedroom for the night. We grew up fast, 'intensely living', but secure in a closed circuit of family life and that extraordinary bubble of privilege in the Concessions. J. G. Ballard's book on the bursting of the bubble, *Empire of the Sun*, catches precisely the mood of the Shanghai boy-on-bike, circling the collapse of that crazy, amazing, corrupt, cosmopolitan city. In fact the book opens in the choir stalls of the cathedral where Alan and I sang regularly: it was good pocket-money, and there were two dollars extra (about half-a-crown in those days) for funeral and wedding services.

Between the International Concession and the French Concession was another world apart, the Chinese city of Shanghai. The feudal contrast of conditions made an indelible impression on my mind. Bliss it might have been, even in that twilight, to be alive, and very heaven to be European. But to be Chinese was hell. Teeming poverty and unhappiness are a hot bed for radical thoughts, and it was impossible not to be alive to the loneliness and the suffering all around. Shanghai must have been one of the best schools in the world for revolutionaries. In 1937 over 20,000 homeless people died in the streets, their corpses collected by the fine-sounding Municipal Council of the International Settlement. If I had been a Chinese, and a few years older, I guess I would have done my best to join the Communists on the 'Long March' to resistance in the caves of the Yenan in the north-west. What other choice was there then? Chiang Kai-shek, the head of China, had only marginal control of the country: inland, the war-lords divided up the rest of the chaos that was China. The vast vacuum of power was filled by the imperial ambition of Japan, in two stages. In the Sino-Japanese war of 1931–2 they had lunged over the Great Wall into Hopeh; five years later they were poised for further conquest into Korea, Manchuria and China in their pursuit of a new order for Asia. In July 1937 the Japanese moved into the second stage, with a trumped-up *casus belli*, the so-called Peking Incident. We had our very own Shanghai Incident a few months later in August when the roof fell in. Or rather, it started to rattle.

Alan and I were swimming in the Bath Club at the Race Course, and the bamboo roofing suddenly rattled. Everybody raced to the high veranda to see what was happening. There was a war on. Anti-aircraft shells were embossing the blue sky with black explosions and showering their shrapnel all over the place, including on the roof of our exclusive, sacred Bath Club. Small bombers were diving over the Bund and the Huangpu, angling their bomb-drops with horrific imprecision. Their targets were the Japanese cruisers off the water-front but, as we discovered later, their impact was on the Bund and the populous neighbourhood of Nanking Road. The untouched warships seemed to be charmed at their anchorage in the river.

From the swimming club veranda Alan and I watched the mobs fleeing pell-mell down Nanking Road, and for a moment the surge seemed about to turn in to the pure white precinct of the Race Course, but a reflex of restraint worked even in wretched panic, and the crowd rushed past. During the rest of the day our own family reflexes went on working as absurdly as those of the mobs. In the afternoon, Alan and I, as was our Saturday routine, headed by rickshaw for the Grand cinema, opposite the Race Course: it was there that Dorothy and Tom used to meet us after their tennis at the Club. We had been much looking forward to the film – Dick Powell in *The Singing Marine*. On the way, our world turned over. Streams of lorries filled with jumbled dead and wounded Chinese were roaring and hooting past us. Later we discovered why. Some of those bombs we had seen making their lazy angle of descent, which was so curiously and night-marishly unreal to watch for the first time, had hit an assembly point where five or six thousand Chinese were packed. We made for home, this time to be overtaken by lorries filled with silent Japanese troops, their guns pointing downwards on to the crowded streets. The Japanese had pushed troops into the Settlement and seized the down-town area of Hongkon, but they stayed on the other side of the bridge and held off from occupying the Bund, the centre of the city and the French Concession. Those sectors were to be left, eerily, in a sort of still-life for a few years more and were not completely taken over until Pearl Harbor. And, come to think of it, it was to be some years before I caught up with *The Singing Marine*. For us, that bloody day, the show was over, the roof was in.

Within a few days British women and children were evacuated. Tom stayed on to try to keep the Institute intact, and to wait and see whether the so-called Shanghai Incident could prove to be just that, a passing trauma. In fact, with hindsight, for us it was the beginning of the Second World War – although until the European war began, the West still kept referring to that Sino-Japanese war as simply the Shanghai Incident.

So ended my second lesson about worldly goods, this one in Chinese but the message was unmistakable. The rust and the moth, as the book of Job tells you, my boy, will get it all. Don't love too much those bicycles shimmering up against the veranda doors of the bedroom like the wings of angels. What matters is what you take with you, and that is within you. We stood with Dorothy in the long queues of women and children melting in the heat on the docks, holding the hand-luggage which was all we were allowed to take aboard the British destroyer. The tar was soft; our shoes stuck a little but not enough to keep us there. Our destroyer slid past the Japanese cruisers that were shelling the shore. We could see the gun crews in their asbestos gear, a strange, detached view of such a deadly business, somehow like being behind the scenes; there was a terrible irresponsible excitement among us youngsters. We sailed right down the Huangpu to reach the precise line where the yellow waters of the river meet the blue of the ocean. There a stately white liner called, of all things, *The Empress of Asia*, was ready for us and we were transferred aboard. There was barely cabin room for the ladies and the babies: youngsters, boys and girls had to sleep on deck, and for us, even the youngest of the youngsters, it was a comprehensive education with a romantic fling. We were literally heading into the blue.

We came back to earth in Hong Kong. We were billeted on the university campus, and there we waited for something more to happen. One, two, three months' wait – and Dorothy saw that we made the most of things. We had a lovely time in limbo – the swimming was excellent at Repulse Bay, where the Japanese were to invade so easily only three years later. But the sense of break-up was there too. Symbolically, the island was shaken by the notorious typhoon of 1937: roofs were ripped off, parks devastated, the harbour scoured tragically

12

of junks and sampans with their population of thousands simply disappearing. Big ships were wrecked: the huge stern and propeller of one overhung the big road along the embankment, while another, a passenger liner, was ripped off its mooring and spiked on a rock. This time Tom could not defy augury. He left Shanghai to collect us for what was in theory his home leave in the UK. In practice the day we finally arrived in London, in November 1937, his welcome was a letter telling him that the Institute was not able to keep open any longer and therefore there was no job to come back to. We never saw the Shanghai house – 'the lot' was Tom's phrase – again, including most of the family archive of photographs. We parked in a furnished flat in Wimbledon and took stock. The opportunities for an engineer who had been twenty years out of the country were elusive. I would accompany Tom to the public library to study appointment columns in the newspapers. On these visits I learnt also to study the pink paper, the *Financial Times*, which recorded the rapid decline of the Chinese dollar. Tom was paid in dollars because he had been recruited in Shanghai. He was ruined. He had to move fast.

By now, Mickey had joined the Royal Air Force. Alan and I, having missed one year of formal education, were accepted generously as day-boys by Bedford School, an institution with a staunch tradition of support for overseas-serving families. We rented a newly built, semi-detached house in the Saints area of Bedford, near the park. Carpets were the first household item to be bought and delivered; we slept on them, hilariously, for the first few nights before Tom and Dorothy could get to the sales to buy beds. Tom's hunt for employment ranged around the area. He got on to a second-hand bicycle and found a temporary machinist vacancy in Peterborough for three weeks, but the logic was undodgeable. 'The big game is overseas, in Africa,' he told us in a family parley. The plan was that we should join him once he had made a start there. That never happened. Tom worked briefly in Johannesburg – rough stuff on building sites – then he moved up to the minefields of northern Rhodesia and his luck climbed with him. He was well on his feet in Brokenhill when he sent the signal for us to join him, but it came too late. The war was breaking out, and we were immobilized. I have never been sure how Dorothy felt about the possibility of a family safari to Central Africa. Would she have upped sticks if she could? We had settled quickly into Bedford's ample, quiet bosom: we sat in chintzy chairs in the living-room to write together to Tom to wish him and each other luck. He volunteered to rejoin the Navy but was told that he was too old. 'I wish a bomb would fall on Somerset House and all its birth certificates.' So first distance dispersed the family, then death.

Big brother Mickey was a pilot in Coastal Command and to Alan and me quite an old man. In the RAF he had reverted to his real name, Tom: not Thomas, but by baptism plain Tom, like his father. We saw him a few times on odd weekend leaves. 'Look after yourself, son,' I heard Dorothy call, and young Tom's usual answer, 'I'll do that small thing.' He was killed on 11 February 1940, during the so-called phoney-war period before Hitler's blitzkrieg.

Alan joined the RAF in 1941. He hoped that he would be trained in Africa and come across Tom in the process, and that is exactly what happened: Alan was always supposed to be the lucky one. He was trained to be a fighter pilot in southern Rhodesia, and Tom was working in northern Rhodesia. They had a rendezvous in Durban during Alan's embarkation leave when he was waiting to be shipped north for the Desert War. Tom wrote, 'It was a good night. We said good night to each other, but when I looked out of the window of the hotel room next morning, I saw the troopship had gone – very properly without warning. We never said goodbye.' Alan's aircraft was brought down in the desert but he parachuted clear, wandered lost one night in the wilderness, and met friendly nomads who willingly accepted bits of his clothing and guided him to safety. 'Lucky, it was my birthday you see, Mum,' was his communiqué to us. He returned to the UK to be trained to fly the new Typhoons for the Second Front. By that time I was with the Army in India. His air letters were full of the fun of his visits to Bedford to see Dorothy and Eileen who now lived with Dorothy. Eileen was the girl I had left behind. With more luck than judgement I had fallen in love with her at fifteen and become engaged at seventeen, and on my departure she had moved into the house to keep Dorothy company. She was older than I, Alan's age in fact, and from Alan's happy letters I sensed he was falling for her. It was not surprising: we shared so much. Thank God, anyway, Eileen was there, at home with Dorothy, when the damned telegram was delivered to the front door: Alan was killed on 25 August 1944.

The news hit me in Delhi. I don't believe it is possible to say when one consciously begins to feel an existence as an individual. Joseph Brodsky writes about the act of estrangement which subsumes Marx's dictum that 'existence conditions consciousness'. There is a switching-off, an estranging process that once acquired 'can both condition and ignore existence'. Suddenly I was wandering round Delhi, lost in a blank grief, quite angry too that I had not somehow known before the news reached me that Alan had been killed. We were so near to one another. At one stage of growing up we had even looked alike: grown-up he became the good-looker. I can remember, like Brodsky, my first lie: it was on the slow boat to China. A little boy, younger than us, hung around Alan and me, wanting to be our friend. One day he offered me a sweet but I said didn't I share everything with Alan? Had he offered one to Alan? No, he'd not seen him. 'He's on the upper deck, you go that way – you'll find him.' I sent him the long way round while I nipped up, ruffled my hair a bit, met him and, pretending to be Alan, took another sweet. It became a comic routine between us brothers. I would be taken for Alan and congratulated on, for example, Alan's boxing successes and, less often, the reverse would occur. Once he passed out in the choir-stall, opposite mine; in minutes, mad at myself as I felt myself going, I fainted. How had I not known that he had been hit 300 feet up, strafing a German armed column near Caen; had tried to gain height; was seen struggling to jump; but no time . . . No time.

I came of age in terms of estrangement that bleak, bright Delhi day, and I made some vows. All had to do with what I had been taught so far. The first, to do with poverty and politics and war. I can trace the roots of my radicalism to the East where man's indifference to man was first made plain to me. Of course the West had the same cruel lessons to teach, as the war ruthlessly went on to expose, but East or West, for me poverty is still the beginning of politics. And then, the vow of family. Family was the taken-for-granted joy of my youth. War had split us up and cut us down, but it left the idea of the family enhanced. I regard the idea of the family as the point of transmission of values and energies in my own family, and in my work and my working relationships. In losing my brothers, I began to be aware of the enduring joy of the family. I have been fortunate in that for me such joy outlasted the duration of the war, and has grown with my own family.

As soon as the war did end, my father was able to return to Dorothy. Home again, he again needed money – a rolling stone gathers no pension. He lowered his age by ten years and passed AI into the Iraq

Petroleum Company as a shiftworker on an oil station in the Middle East. Soon he emerged as a superintendent on the line and then Dorothy was able to join him from time to time. He was stationed there by the time I returned to England for demobilization in 1947, and I went to Bedford station to meet him on his first home leave in 1948. About ten years had passed since Alan and I had kissed him goodbye. We had not been given leave from school to go to Southampton to see him off – probably rightly, but we were bitterly disappointed: we reckoned Tom taught us more than school ever could. Now I stood beside the ticket-barrier at the railway station, scanning faces through the grille. The crowds were thinning and I was still looking when I heard, 'Hallo, Pete.' The voice came upwards from below the angle of my gazing. I must still have been looking up at the same angle of our farewell at that gate a decade before. There was Tom, shorter than I remembered, with a big soul and with a tremendous self-starting mechanism. He never finished starting.

2

Inklings

The war years gave me a first inkling of management, the influence that was to be the ruling passion of my career. I served in the Army in India and Burma (1943–44) and in the United States, with Pacific Military Intelligence in Maryland (1945). I was sent into Japan with the occupation forces soon after the surrender, returned to the British Joint Mission in 1946, and was demobbed a major in the summer of 1947. I was twenty-three and rapidly becoming an expert in the art of being managed.

Why should anybody obey an order? That is the question that lies at the heart of managing any human group. Where is the point of sovereignty, the source of power? The question begs its way through recorded history. But when there is war, the answers are made dead simple. As a raw recruit I found myself in the famous cartoon situation: on a massive morning parade, at Wentworth, I dropped my rifle. I was standing at attention, well to the rear, but the roar of the Regimental Sergeant-Major exploding far in front of me almost blew my head off. And the instant answer of the platoon sergeant behind me roared back like an echo; the two roars were as one. 'Take-his-name-Sergeant. Got-him-Sirrr.' As a fumbler with a rifle I was left in no doubt about the drill and discipline for king and country.

But managing a business in a democracy is different from military command: there are no King's or Queen's Regulations to hold the line. It is different also from political power: managers are not elected by those they manage. It is different yet again from religious institutions: there may be many lords in boardrooms, but only very few claim a divine right of management. In reality modern management has to establish its own legitimacy, and therefore it shares with all human endeavour that ancient radical question which throughout history has transformed societies, destroyed tyrannies, shaped our liberties and preserved the dignity of man at work: why should people obey?

17

At a workaday level of consciousness, the answers stream at us in a flood. People do what they are told because of pay or persuasion, fear or faith, greed or duty, honour or glory, lust for power or simply love. A manager tries to blend all these reasons in the magi-mix of leadership. But at another, deeper level, there is less clarity, more significance, more mystery. We obey and conform, or not, for reasons which, as individuals, we may not be able to explain, or even want to – Goethe, a heroic mind, replied to the Socratic 'Know thyself' with 'God forbid'. Our motives, originating from this level, are as individual as fingerprints. The philosophy of a manager starts where any belief starts, at some truly unfathomable depth of being where, like buried treasure, lies the ultimate question of the meaning of life. It is our response to that question that gives meaning to our work, and to our giving of orders and taking of orders. And in the army years, roughly and readily, I learnt something of this – not in any systematic way, but *per ardua ad hoc*.

What I learned first was to speak Japanese. War with Japan had found Britain ill-prepared in so many ways: hands up who speaks Japanese? The War Cabinet's move to correct our language incapability was swift and the results remarkable. Servicemen with some record of aptitude in any language were divided into courses designed to produce interpreters and translators (speaking and writing-or-reading Japanese are separable disciplines). In the emergency some thousand people were trained by 1945 to be proficient in one or the other. But in parallel with the emergency measures there was a wise experiment. It was said to be Anthony Eden, himself an outstanding orientalist, who initiated an imaginative move to recruit schoolboys into the proper study of Arabic and Asian cultures, Japanese, for instance. This meant that there could be a rising generation who were familiar with *Kanji* (the script characters) and *Kaiwa* (conversation). It was long-sighted and civilized of the wartime leadership, under 360° of pressure in 1942, to sustain this small initiative. After all, there would be a need to talk peace when the war ended some day, or as the saying went, when 'the duration was over'. What a good word 'duration' was and is still: in later battles such as the long railway strike I used 'duration' to describe a bad time which, however protracted, you know will end well.

After combing the country for boys who were through the hoops of their main exams and just waiting for the call-up, the selectors chose seventy boys. The 'Orientalists', as we came to be called, were billeted at Dulwich College. The College was having a thin time financially in the war and welcomed the remunerative invasion. Thirty of us were 'Japanese', twenty-five 'Chinese', the others 'Turkish' and 'Persians'. Each day we took the train into London for the morning's intense tuition at London University's School of Oriental and African Studies; then we were left, like university students, to work by ourselves for the rest of the day. It was as exhilarating for us, sixteen and fancy-freeish, as it was advanced in language teaching methods. Our early training was totally on a phonetic basis. Now that method is widespread, but then it was an innovative technique which succeeded with us brilliantly. It set the music of the language in our minds long before we could handle vocabulary; it overcame the fear of the strange noises in our heads, and it gave us courage. I reckon courage is the primary virtue in the learning of any language.

While we were being crammed, we too were cramming the scope of our astonishing liberty with a variety of activities. By definition, or rather by selection, the Orientalists were a community of high standards and voltage. At one extreme, theatre. That boy from Harrow, defiantly long-haired, slinky and solemn, but with wit as cosy as a razor-blade and a half-dozen notebooks filled with plays and songs, was already turning out to be Sandy Wilson of *The Boyfriend* fame. In his revues I had the luck to collaborate with him, to sing his songs and write the odd lyric. At another extreme, sport: we founded a rugby team, the London Orient, of course. With some calibre and more cheek we managed to insert it into the programmes of the well-known London clubs because they were keen to fill the gaps torn in their normal fixture lists by the war. Our compact scrum-half Pat O'Neill was later to become the professor of Japanese at the School of Oriental and African Studies. The wily, aggressive fly-half, with a tough shock of yellow hair like a ventriloquist's doll – bow-legged, his arse close to the ground, beautifully balanced for his dummy runs – became a diplomat, Sir Edward Youde, one of the great Governors of Hong Kong, polished and subtle, those safe hands trusted on all sides in the negotiations over that island's future. The scrum, rough, muddy bums the lot of them, from the point of view of us immaculate three-quarters, were later to be a distinguished array of ambassadors, academics and businessmen.

Those fifteen months were an oasis in our educational lives; we were neither school-fish nor university-fowl and presented Dulwich with an unusual challenge of management. The headmaster, Gilkes, at the outset asked us to organize ourselves, and to elect necessary representation; it became my job to liaise with him on the limits of our new-found freedom. His strategy was unerring: he challenged us to develop ourselves. Gilkes's challenge stays with me: I think of it still in the Eighties, in the midst of the current tidal wave of concern for educating professional managers. There is a swirl and froth of corporate programmes for management development, all well-intentioned and not a moment too soon, but do they force-feed too much – or do they preserve the essential challenge to industrial managers to develop themselves? That personal responsibility must not be swept away in tides of enthusiasm for cloning the good organization man, the ICI man, the BR man, the IBM man. Responsibility is the best teacher, and that was what Gilkes thrust upon us.

The front-line requirements of the war in India and Burma became urgent in the spring of 1943. Six of the 'Japanese' were called up early; I was one of them. I reported to Maidstone for initial training with the Royal West Kents, and as I entered the barrack gates the lock on my small suitcase broke apart to remind me that we are not put on this earth for pleasure alone. 'Joining up' was the popular term for enlistment: I joined up, scuttling around the guardhouse, picking up the scattered bits of myself. By November, after a deal of square-bashing, I was apparently ready to embark, as a private, on the glamorously misnamed, hideously crowded, soon stinking *Reina del Pacifico*.

She was a converted luxury liner, and the 44th and 45th Commandos aboard suddenly found themselves stratified into the class structure of a cruise ship. The pre-war hierarchies of first, second and third class and steerage, with differentials of accommodation and food, were crazily divisive. Our troopship conditions offended against a fundamental custom of command: they must have enraged commanding officers by making such a nonsense of the team spirit of crack troops. Traditionally an officer must see that his men are fed and bedded down before he sleeps – a tradition of good management which incidentally would have had a revolutionary power to transform attitudes in British industry long ago, if it had been applied to company canteens and lavatories. Gradually on the long voyage, I was aware of mutinous thoughts all around me. It was not surprising in the explosive circumstances: tempers were likely to be hot as hell, with portholes at our deck-level shut because of the blackout, producing a stifling fug throughout a trip that included six weeks through the Mediterranean, down the Red Sea, and across the Indian Ocean.

Steaming out of Liverpool we raced zigzag about a stormy Atlantic to evade submarines, finally connecting with a large convoy off Gibraltar. The very first night out was an orgy of seasickness, vomit in the large loos shin-high and slapping the ship's sides as she rolled. We made a human chain up the stairs to convey buckets of it out to the deck and over the side. Our hammocks were slung over the long tables where we were supposed to eat. The second night, in the darkness, I crept out and hid in a coil of rope on one of the decks. I slept a few hours to be wakened by hosepipes washing down the decks and drenching my shelter. There was a fixed bench on the deck which I found myself sharing with another shivering soldier, a Welsh commando who like me was a bad sailor and lacked the stomach to stay below. He was weeping, not crying or sobbing, just tears as he stared through all the shades of grey at daybreak over the heaving ocean. The weeping was nothing to do with what I was quite ready to join him in – a misery of wetness, cold, nausea and self-pity, to mention but a few sea-going woes. No, Haydn was heartbroken because he was a passionate Communist. He had been a pacifist and a teacher, then a conscientious objector, and had only joined up to help the Russians when Hitler attacked them. Then he had trained hard to kill Nazis, but now he was heading for another war altogether, to fight the Japanese, and he wanted no part in that theatre of war at all. 'I've no real quarrel with those silly buggers.'

I failed to cheer Haydn by suggesting that what was happening to us showed fate to be unpredictable. To hell with the determinism of Marx: were we not living, juddering proof that on this ship, man was a bus not a tram? Wild talk, and we talked on and on, and then his Welsh fervour took over and only he talked. He was amusing and erudite as well as desperate and indomitable. I began to glimpse through him the tragedy of that generation of romantic international Communists, trapped by their utopian idealism, doomed by Stalinism. The Thirties' choice seemed to be between fascism and socialism in some form or other – 'unless you were well off'. Democracy was just 'an old bitch gone in the teeth', as that bastard Ezra Pound had said, slumped and resigned to tolerating the stupid waste and unfairness of unemployment. Haydn quoted Dr Johnson, the genius of common

21

sense: patriotism was the refuge of scoundrels. Only later, when we had lost touch, did I come across a poem to quote back to Haydn: actually C. Day Lewis was writing the lines about the time we were pitching and tossing, feeling lost at sea. It was the poet's answer to 'Where are the War Poets?':

> It is the logic of our times
> No subject for immortal verse.
> That we who live by honest dreams
> Must choose the bad against the worse.

If there ever was the slightest danger of my becoming a Communist, my conversion would have come in those quiet conversations with Haydn in the early hours, hoses rousing us from the ropes, the flat rainstorms raking the deck, and our horizon the chaos of the Atlantic. The Military Police aboard, always patrolling the decks in twos, it was said for their own safety, turned a Nelsonic eye to our blatant nightly game of hide-and-seek. But in about a week, weather and course had changed and we had found our sea-legs; we were sleeping below decks as the convoy sailed past Gibraltar and entered the Mediterranean.

Ours was only the second convoy after the victories of the Allied Forces had cleared the North African coast so that we could run the gauntlet of the Mediterranean and reach India through Suez. The Germans launched two assaults against us with their new weapon, glider bombs aimed by radio. Close to the North African shore, their first raids smashed a few ships in our now large convoy, one of which had just joined us when it was struck. It seemed to go mad with fire. We had to sail on, leaving the red ruin making daft circles, foaming, helpless, with hundreds of khaki figures trying to jump clear. Rumour was it suffered eight hundred casualties. But the morale of troops aboard the 'Reina del' immediately rose with the danger. The bombs were at once nicknamed 'Chase 'em Charlies' – and wasn't it good after all that the bloody portholes were kept shut or Charlie would be inside in no time? The gallows humour enlivened the dread deck-shows we devised; we even had the amateur magician who defied the gods with a story . . . The magician is in his routine, each trick more mystifying than the other, but each of his minor miracles is spoilt by a parrot perched on the edge of the cargo-hold and squawking 'That's easy-easy-peasy.' Then, boom! a torpedo strikes and blasts the ship apart. All is blood and confusion, flotsam and jetsam, fish and chips, and the magician struggles in the water clutching a floating spar. Fluttering down from the blue sky, the dishevelled parrot lands on the spar and mutters wearily, 'OK, OK, you win, you win. But tell me, how did you do it?'

Some of the damaged ships in the convoy had to stop off at Alexandria to repair damage; we steamed on through Suez, the mood relaxing in relief. Now we had dances on deck. Wrens and nurses had been put on the ship at the very last moment of embarkation, and accommodating them had made the physical conditions aboard even more restricted for some. But life had its compensations as the journey went on. The benefits were clear to behold during those dances as we came to know those uniformly desirable girls better. Wartime maybe, but plenty of peace and harmony broke out softly on those starlit tropical evenings as we headed down the Red Sea, and the convenient lifeboats saved many a soul at sea without ever touching the water.

The corporal in charge of my table kept up a Rabelaisian commentary on the outbreak of ship romances. He was just the man to do it: apparently he had been a highly paid feature writer, holding the *Daily Mirror* up to nature. 'You waste so much time wooing these girls.' It was true. Hours and hours were spent in heavy-breathing, in flirtations, in dreamy gazing over the rails into dark waters glittering with phosphorus on the bow waves which made gold bows for Cupid, etc., etc. He advised more resolution, much more looseness and licentiousness among the young soldiery. 'I just say to a girl, "Do you fuck?" Once out of ten, maybe, it works and it saves weeks of your long-winded poncing.'

The little corporal was more complicated than this single-mindedness suggests. My hammock was slung next to his, over our table, and swaying through the small hours I listened, as the plot of his own story thickened considerably, or curdled rather. He had fought with the Republicans in the Spanish Civil War. His experience there with armoured cars ensured him rapid promotion when Europe's own civil war, the Second World War, broke out. He had become a captain and had been sent out to Burma, but then, after the retreat from Burma in 1942, he had been reduced to the ranks by court-martial and repatriated. The story, as he told it, naturally did him credit, but it was also credible. In March 1941 his armoured brigade had docked at Rangoon in time to find that the city was collapsing, burning and forsaken. The captain's brigade was told to unload its vehicles, leave them, and start walking out of Burma. And a hard time they had of it. General Alexander himself had realized exactly one day after his arrival in Burma that his mission to hold Rangoon was impossible, and he escaped by a sheer fluke in an episode not much mentioned in the history of narrow squeaks. The future field-marshal was out-manoeuvred; a road-block cut him off. The Gurkhas he threw at it from the west and the Sikhs from the east could not shift it – nor could Hussars with tanks charging straight up the road. Then inexplicably the block was lifted, and the Japanese, obviously unaware of the prize general within their grasp, moved off. The 'enemy's whimsical abandonment', as Compton Mackenzie describes it in Volume One of his distinguished history of the *Eastern Epic*, remains inexplicable to this day.

The retreat proved to be an epic of chaos. Our captain found himself leading an advanced patrol ahead of the retreating columns, and it came to him as no surprise that some Burmese villages had by this time decided that their future was not with the bedraggled British but with the victorious Japanese Zeros flying high above the jungles and the plains. The deadly snag was, he discovered, that the villagers would signal ahead the movements of the routed imperialists. No surprise either that his advance patrols had taken to shooting up villages to prevent their positions being disclosed. Eventually the remnants of the British Army broke back into India, literally in a hell of a way: 'foot and mouth rot, everything – even my gums had retreated.' He'd smile and show fangs. 'But we had to be made an example of. I was court-martialled to show the independent Burmese government that we were sorry about making such a nuisance of ourselves trying to leave their country. Confusing, isn't it?'

Stripped of his rank, he was now the very model of insubordination, and he cheerfully spread confusion like fertilizer over any trouble spots he reckoned to hold promise. 'What d'you think of this tea, Sir?' he asked the young apple-cheeked officer on mess duty. 'Try it, Sir?'

'Not at all bad, Corporal.'

'I think you're right, Sir, in fact, it's marvellous – considering . . . '

'What?'

'Considering the galley crew bathe regularly in these big tea urns. Ablutions in soft water must be a nice change, Sir.'

At once, we could see from our table below an urgent meeting of mess officers' legs gathering on the landing. Then the corporal was called to give evidence. He was dressed only in a battered jock-strap, but he solemnly put on his beret to be properly dressed for the salute. Glistening with sweat he made his shining way upwards, saluting and smiling his black-edged smile. He readily agreed to an identity parade and then went down the line of galley crew, pointing. 'He was in the urn, so was he, and he was waiting his turn to get in.' I came to realize his awful jokes were usually true.

By the fifth week our food and rations had become the focus of the stress and strains of the long journey. I was luckier than most: my diet was varied by a fortunate coincidence. A lieutenant aboard was a school friend and sometimes he would smuggle me manna from his second-class menu (field rank, major and above, were first class). At night, on the dark deck of rendezvous, the recognition call that mattered most to me as a newly engaged – and simply hungry – young man was his whistling of Prokofiev's *Peter and the Wolf*. Together he and I hit on the idea of writing a pantomime for the ship: unbelievably Christmas was coming. Permission was granted, and rehearsals allowed me into the spacious lounges, wearing a jersey to hide the lack of 'pips' on my shoulder. But good humour evaporated fast in the Indian Ocean. One lunch-time after a rehearsal session I was making my way back to my quarters late and I noticed the decks were ominously clear. Downstairs, the atmosphere was hotter and noisier than ever: there had been an outbreak of exasperation when lunch appeared – a square bun and red cabbage. The mess officer on his rounds was asked to sample the fare and suddenly the air was thick with buns being thrown at him for tasting. Then a few bold spirits ventured into the posh first-class dining-room and decorated each step of the luxury staircase with a tin plate of bun and red cabbage. Our table was next to the galley door, and the galley supervisor, a fat, unlovely figure to us, always in a dark blue shirt, would usually stand there grinning. This lunch-time as he stepped into the doorway, a noose swung down, looped from the lintel like a booby-trap, over his head. In the event, there were no serious consequences: flying buns were not a mutiny. Some ringleaders were put on charges – 'clapped in irons' was the buzz. A flare-up, that was all.

Except perhaps for a nasty coincidence. Berthed in Bombay, some had been given shore leave, including crew. A few of us left aboard, sleepless with excitement, were staring over the side at the deserted dock, about two in the morning. A trolley was being pushed along the dock rails, through the ugly pools of pus-coloured floodlights, and on it, sprawled awkwardly, was a fat figure in a dark blue shirt. Knifed badly, it seemed.

My first contact with the British Army in India was unnerving in a different way. The scene: the docks of Bombay, dawn, November 1943. A young officer is inspecting troops who have just landed, showing a dutiful interest as he makes his way down the dim line of soldiers still swaying a little on their sea-legs. He reaches the private on my right, and presumably a touch desperate for small talk at that hour of the day, talks to him about schooling. I hear him ask the private about language ability. 'Some French, Sir.' 'Good.' The officer reaches me and asks, 'Do you know any language?' 'French and Japanese, Sir.' There is a pause: the light is brightening, the suffocating weeks of the smelly ship are over, at last here we are, ready to face the Japanese foe, face anything in fact as long as it is not more red cabbage and square buns for lunch at sea. The officer stares at me thoughtfully. The pause ends. 'How good is your French?' And without waiting for an answer he moves on. For a moment I have to admit to a defeatist flicker of doubt about how the war might end.

My first night ashore ended eerily. We were put under canvas, and I woke to find a razor at my throat. A bearded, turbaned head swung over mine, whispering, 'Sahib, do you want me to shave you?' This was one of many barbers who roamed the camp freely, offering all ranks the treat of a shave in bed before bugle call. In India, even we privates had comparative privileges.

On to Delhi, where my commission came through, and with it a relatively cushy life at an Intelligence headquarters. My work was concentrated in the Lutyens-designed houses of the powerful in the centre of New Delhi, the palaces of the Viceroy and the Parliament. I lived in a tent in the Halifax Stadium which was at the end of a great avenue running straight from the grand imperial complex. The walk up the avenue early each morning was a spacious pleasure between lawns with trees each circled in a dewy mist. The going for a few months was easy, but was not one that gave any contact with the real India. The military services seemed to seal themselves off in the routines of the Mess and within the elegant hotels – Noël Coward described us as 'going through hell at Maiden's Hotel, and sticking

A generation later, with the Japanese where they are in the post-war world, I wonder if we had missed anything in our translation all those years ago: who was taking whom to the cleaners?

But in late 1944 we were winning. It was our turn to invade poor Burma. One familiar sign of changing fortunes was an invitation from a local Burmese headman to have a party. The village feast, lit by a full moon, offered spiced deer meat and *zoo*, a milky concoction of lethal spirit distilled from either coconuts or cannonballs – it was difficult to remember. After the spicy feast, we lolled about in a huge hut, enthralled by an all night, non-stop singing-and-dancing-and-chat show in which the villagers all seemed welcome to take part: men, women, jolly children who puffed on green cheroots and laughed at everything, especially us. Driving away, the low, round moon bouncing along with us, rolling over the rough track through fields scented by the sickly-sweet, seaweedy smell of the dead, I thought about the court-martialled captain. For him, on the run, village visits can have been no such fun at all. Now, less than three years on, our victory was possible.

And for that there were two interdependent reasons: strategy and leadership. I was to glimpse these qualities in two great men, Mountbatten and Slim.

In 1943, the Japanese invasion of India had loomed as a formidable threat, but also it was a slightly mad venture led by the ambitious Lieutenant-General Mutaguchi. Even General Sato, his divisional commander in the field, thought nothing of Mutaguchi and his 'insane' plans. It is something of a shock perhaps to our stereotyped perceptions of the Japanese as disciplined and inscrutable to read in Louis Allen's superb history, *Burma: The Longest War*, that Sato, on the eve of the campaign, gathered his top staff in his jungle headquarters, drank a glass of champagne with them, and instead of the ritual heroic message to rouse the troops, he said, 'I'll take this opportunity, gentlemen, of making something quite clear to you. Miracles apart, everyone of you is likely to lose his life in this operation. It isn't a question of the enemy's bullets. You must be prepared for death by starvation in these mountain fortresses.' He was dead right.

Mutaguchi's grandiose design of conquest came to nothing because our troops sat tight and surprised him tactically by holding out with airdrop supplies. Traditionally we would have avoided encirclement;

we would have pulled back to keep an unbroken front against the enemy. Not this time. Mountbatten switched the 5th Division from Arakan in the south by air – he personally forced this through and the move was a fast and brilliant piece of management. Slowly the besieging enemy was weakened, their lines of communication and supply strained beyond human limits. The besiegers themselves came under siege. Among the British reinforcements were big East African troops. They had been lectured on the way to the battle not to underestimate the fierceness of the Japanese soldier just because he was smaller. But when they arrived on the battlescene as the Japanese attack was broken and withering away, the Africans were bewildered by their first encounter with the formidable enemy. I arrived in Imphal to see them coming back from patrols cradling the starved dead and dying, like wax dolls, in their arms.

Mountbatten's style of command was as daring as his strategy. He had the three essentials of leadership, beyond the professional mastery of his craft. For a start he had luck, the ingredient Napoleon valued as much as anything in his generals. Mountbatten arrived on the scene as the Japanese were reaching the limit of their expansion. Also he knew how to dramatize decisions, for instance the changes of attitude he needed in the management of the South-East Asian Command. He shipped his headquarters from Delhi to Kandy in (then) Ceylon. Moving headquarters is a move I have imitated and recommend to any manager trying to convert defeatist attitudes: buildings can smell of defeat, and literally a change of view can help. Finally, Mountbatten 'connected': he took immense trouble to connect. I was in a group he addressed before he left Delhi. His was a disappointing tale to tell but he told it with dash and excitement. One of the reasons that he, with his naval background, had been made Supreme Commander in the South-East Asian sphere of war was because a seaborne invasion into Burma had been the objective. In the event the Quebec Conference of the Allies had requisitioned landing-craft for the Salerno landing in Italy. He described all this with a direct and, I thought, practised charm – and why not practise? As pep talks went (and we had quite enough of them to be able to judge) this was a right royal command performance. He was a performer and he played the Black Prince superbly. That genius of sourpussiness, the American Lieutenant-General Stilwell who led the long attack into Burma from China, noted once in his diary, 'Louis and I get on famously, even if he does have curly eyelashes.'

Mountbatten's field commander General Slim (later the Field-Marshal) fulfilled that same essential duty of management, keeping his troops in the picture, but he did so in a totally contrasting way. I was with a bunch of soldiers gathered in a jungle clearing when I heard him in action. His message was not rosy either: he was describing the airborne attack being launched in Bhamo, a key Japanese centre of communications. The expedition was commanded by Wingate, who was killed in the course of it. Wingate had the ambivalent reputation of being something of a heroic nut, but he must be credited with almost single-handedly, obsessionally, developing the guerrilla tactics that restored some morale and initiative in our forces after the humiliations of retreats throughout South-East Asia. Slim told us of walking with Wingate round the perimeter of the airfield where our gliders were assembled and debating the risks to the last minute. The raid was very nearly aborted because, immediately before it, reconnaissance of the landing area had shown elephants dragging logs along the fields. Was this normal forestry, simply a concidence of elephants? Or too much of a coincidence? Slim was remarkable in the way he brought us quietly into the detail of the life and death decisions of command. The first wave was sent off. And the very first message, received from a smashed glider, was 'Apple Sauce', the code words for failure. Despite this the second wave was sent off and the landings were consolidated. To this day, when there is bad news in the board-room I think of that. First news from the battlefront is likely to be exaggerated.

Slim caught his audience in the jungle completely. His style had not the handsome charisma of Mountbatten. He was, in fact, a hefty shape, loosely dressed in baggy shirt and shorts and a wide-brimmed hat, stetson-style, and he leant, at ease, on a tall stave. There are so many ways of leading: he created confidence and enthusiasm; he dared to share his problems; he knew from his height of command how to level with us and he took the trouble to do it, to be there, among us. 'Being there' seems to me the stuff of leadership at every level of managing. I cannot pretend to any formula for leadership. Growing up in uniform, I came to know it when I met it, but to this day it remains a mystery to me, because personality is a mystery. The making of a leader is not subject to a recipe. What education and training? Or lack of it? What eloquence? Or lack of it? Courage and imagination are essential ingredients, but how are they bred? Personality? Dean Inge, of St Paul's, the 'gloomy' Dean of the Thirties, used to say there are three mysteries of life: the sense of guilt, of time, of personality.

In December 1944 I was faced with an even more urgent mystery when my small unit reached Kalewa, on the banks of the Chindwin river in northern Burma. I received a message which read, 'Report to Delhi at once for overseas service.' What overseas service? Actually I felt pretty overseas where I was at the time, with prospects limited to the view of a wonky pagoda and a dead elephant. Next day I started to hitch-hike my return to Delhi from an airstrip, earning the first leg of my passage on a Dakota by helping to boot out airdrops over the tangled jungle. The aircraft flew as low as possible for the sake of accuracy, but it was still a hit-and-miss affair. I watched the parachutes relax and bloom over the jungle, and I sensed that their drift was about as certain as my own random destiny. But 'overseas service' turned out to be relatively the lap of luxury: a posting to the British Joint Staff Mission in Washington, DC. It was my first lesson in how Headquarters tend to see things in their own way. 'Overseas', to imperious Delhi, simply meant anywhere outside their vast sphere of control. For me, it meant a New World.

I had to fly to it the long way round the globe, across India, then on by sea-plane, a Sunderland, to Bahrain, Cairo, Djerba on the North African coast. The spacious Sunderland was a superb aircraft, a queen of the air, and what a contrast to the long sweaty weeks aboard the poor *Reina del Pacifico*. The last hop home was over France. 'We have to fly high to keep out of trouble,' one of the crew explained, zipping himself cosily into his teddy-bear suit of leather and woollies. 'You'll get a bit cold. Best of luck, chaps.' We did. One by one, cold and lacking oxygen, we passed out. I can remember trying to keep conscious by dancing a wild jig with a fellow officer and singing about a dolly with a hole in her stocking whose knees keep a-knocking. Then I woke up vomiting over England.

It was a weird, unannounced home-coming, just enough of a stop-over to find out that I had lost my fiancée, Eileen, to a handsome doctor in the US Air Force. We broke an engagement, but nothing else really, and we have been loving friends ever since. The troopship made its way across the old battleground of the ocean without escort, and I felt self-confidently solo too, bleak but free, sailing the Atlantic single-hearted. My first sighting of New York (helluva town!) came miraculously above the early morning mists of the Hudson river, from heaven as far as I could see, the tops of the skyscrapers only. Suddenly everything was different. Food? Unlimited to match my similar appetite: my digestion was wrecked by the change from the dehydrated grub of airdrops and in no time I was in the Walker Reed Hospital with an incipient ulcer. Carbon biscuits settled that for ever. Parties? Lights blazing away all night, and the ratio (crude jargon for the proportion of female to male) was wholly and happily benign.

And work? I found myself one of a number of British working at the Pacific Military Research Centre at Camp Ritchie. This had once been a resort area – dubbed 'the last resort' – on the Pennsylvania–Maryland border, about eighty miles from Washington on the edge of the Blue Ridge Mountain. The centre was run under the command of Americans. It was a crash course for me in the worst and best of American styles of management. There is much between, of course, but the extremes are where the drama lies. The worst was MASH-like, without the fun and wit of that show, but only the mad fury of those oddball colonels. Some of our colonels in Camp Ritchie seemed to come straight from fiction. A pleasant comedy of those years, *The Tea House of the August Moon*, had a colonel of this zany tradition trying to administer unruly Pacific islanders. In a crisis he bawled down the phone, 'I'll make democrats out of them if I have to shoot every one of them.' I recognize the type to this day in American business management, and in British too. For them humour is sabotage – it always is in any bureaucracy, whether military or business. The colonels of management take themselves too seriously: they are too easily self-satisfied, self-promoting, overbearing and over-detailed. When I arrived at Camp Ritchie I had no middle initial. This was not considered to be natural by the masters of rosters, so lists had me as P. E. Parker. A climax of colonels came the day after the first atomic bomb was dropped. Work was paralysed. Certainly I could see little point in my research into defensive cave systems along the shores of the main island of Honshu. What should be done to entertain the troops, before the devil found work for our idle hands? All sections were gathered on a summer's afternoon into a low-roofed hall and a colonel told us he had arranged for a film show. The lights dimmed solemnly and we found ourselves – on Day One of the Atomic Age

– watching a dark blue movie. But there was an even darker, wilder side to the macho style. I heard one of these colonels say in spring 1945, as Germany surrendered, 'We should keep marching.' Hitler had held on desperately in the hope that the Western Allies would get around to saying precisely that.

But the best was there too, a fine style of American management which I have recognized ever since in the way that America works at its best. It is the opposite to the cliché of the Ugly American. It has nothing to do with rank. It has nothing to do with wealth. It has little to do with the Hollywood product of the gen'l'man, the quiet, growling, John Wayne-ish model ready to lash out if the cause is just. Perhaps it is closer to James Stewart, although that is not right either: it is not necessarily Ivy League, with the soft charm of that accent. It is an unwritten code with variations on its theme in all American accents, West Coast, or East, Mid-West, Northern or Southern. It is an elusive and unique equality of attitude which I have found made only in America. I hesitate to say this lest I offend my American business friends: after all, to recommend anybody by describing his gentlemanly qualities is nowadays to lose him the job. But let us face it, the American gentleman does exist – and the American gentlewoman, we have to say. They are alive and well and working all over America, courteous and unsentimental, good-humoured and realistic, energetic and forthright and quite intolerant of bullshit.

I found my first example of this breed of the New World in Camp Ritchie. Lieutenant Otto Graf emerged from a vast basement stacked with captured documents. He was in his early thirties, tall, slightly shambling, dusty and unsoldierly in an apron covering his uniform: he looked like a worn young butler. In the next few months it became clear that our Jeeves was the brains of the outfit: he led all ranks above and below him simply by tireless example. My lifelong good fortune was not only meeting Otto but going with him to Japan immediately after the surrender. Otto had found a base for our intelligence operations in a warehouse in Tokyo Arsenal No. 1, a building which had come through the saturation bombing of the city unscathed while the neighbourhood was in smithereens. We soon had our centre bulging with documents of every possible interest, from the obvious – records of military intelligence, political and public files, prison notes on radicals – to the more exotic, including even mamillary statistics of the wetnurses to the Imperial family.

In terms of intelligence the end of the Second World War was much more fruitful than that of the First World War. In 1918 Germany capitulated, but her central intelligence, her industrial and political secrets, were not taken over by the victors. In the Second World War, everything that was not destroyed before seizure came up for grabs – and the Allies gleaned the battlefields competitively, the Russians and the West racing each other for intelligence spoils. In the Sixties I traded with a German high-pressure hydraulics engineer who had worked on the controls for Tiger Tanks: he told me that when Germany fell all the designs in his drawing-office were requisitioned by an American officer one morning, and in the afternoon another American officer came to requisition them. 'I never found out which American officer was Russian.'

In the Eastern theatre, the surrender and abrupt smash of Japan's military government exposed her secrets; it was entirely possible to piece together a reasonably full story of what had happened, and some of it reads like a thriller – or rather a horror story. The minutes of the 1941 Policy Conference of the Tojo cabinet were discovered eventually in the military archives: here is one of the bloodcurdling 'ifs' of history. For months before Pearl Harbor the Japanese War Cabinet was wrangling over a choice of strategies. The Navy proposed a thrust south into the Pacific to confront the 'bullying' of American and British imperialism; the Army wanted to push north and west, to finish off the resistance in China and to take on Russia. The debate was intense and prolonged until finally the visionary concept of a new order in Asia, establishing 'The Greater East Asia Co-Prosperity Sphere', prevailed. The attack on Pearl Harbor was on. But what if Hitler had taken the slightest care over his remote allies and tilted the balance of the strategic argument? The truth seems to be that the Axis Powers were not geared for the world conflict. Had Hitler encouraged his so-called partners to push into eastern Russia, the Soviet Union could well have been crushed in the titanic pincers of war on two fronts. And the United States might not have been brought into the war at all by Pearl Harbor which, as the records show, was a calculated risk. The Japanese Navy, according to the minutes, warned that beyond the initial success it could put up a good fight for two years but not much more. The expectation of the aggressors was that by then America would have had to come to terms with a world in which the Germans had subjugated Europe and Russia, and the Japanese had imposed their hegemony over East Asia. That terrible, risky hope was an unconscionable time a-dying, but ultimately it had its hellish end at Hiroshima. It was stark dead by the time I landed at Atsugi airfield, outside Tokyo, in October 1945.

Tokyo was autumnal with ruin and rust. We were held up at the airport, for no good reason but, so we were told later, by MacArthur's express order. Anything that hailed from Washington MacArthur always suspected. Even worse this unit included a British element, and that doubled his suspicions. He was ruling Japan and he revelled in it: he had pushed the Emperor off his white horse and climbed on it himself. There is no doubt in my mind that his reign was glorious – and I write this through my gritted teeth. It is hard to praise people one does not like at all. MacArthur's arrogance and vanity were blatant. My frank admiration of what he did is not warmed by any liking for the American Caesar at all. I agree with Truman: 'This pompous popinjay, this courageous outrageous ego, this clever bastard – he set up Japan. On the foundations he laid, the old virtues of Japan rebuilt the nation.' The MacArthur reign, or the 'Macasa Period' as the Japanese called it, endowed Japan with democratic elections; a vote for women; agricultural reform; and radical economic plans for recovery. All these initiatives were inspired by the Supreme Commander of the Allied Forces, a broad title that he relished as it helped him to elude some of the specific pressures from Washington. Some of his achievements, combining military and civil conquests, are unmatched by the two other Western leaders of the time who were converted to political roles. Eisenhower's presidency was unmarked by any originality, and the glories of de Gaulle, which certainly did include a brief proof of his brilliance in the field, even in the defeat of 1940, were militarily not on any scale comparable to MacArthur's scope and success in the Pacific campaigns.

In 1945 and 1946 I witnessed the furious resurgence of Japan, beginning over a harsh winter and an unbelievably lovely spring. The mood of the Japanese seemed to revert to that of the Meiji Revolution of the late last century, arguably the only successful revolution anywhere in 150 years. In the Meiji times, the slogan had been 'Catch up with the West', and that is what post-war Japan set out to do again. Then, a feudal society had been inspired by its controlled outrage at the forced opening of their country by the *kuro-fune*, the black ships of Admiral Perry in 1853. In 1945, their inspiration was defeat and the sacrificial waste of a generation pigheadedly misled by military expansionism, this time it was the controlled outrage at their own humiliating failure militarily and politically that galvanized the country. Since then their sun has risen in triumph and the world has wondered at the Japanese miracle. Studies of it are published galore – surely the secrets of Japan's success are as fully exposed now as the war secrets of their defeat. Behind all the analysis, I keep remembering the evidence of their startling energy and discipline which was showing through the rubble immediately after surrender. As I drove in the jeep to the warehouse, I would see the busy people on the pavements, bustling, scavenging, hammering flat twisted scraps of metal salvaged from the devastation and putting pieces together to make shelters. Otto and I came to be friends with a Japanese family who lived in a house, half Western, half Japanese in its design. They had expected the occupation to be savage. The sweetly smiling mother told us of their family plan of suicide which would be signalled by the conqueror's knock on the door. 'I would have to do the shooting,' she said cheerfully, without bravado. 'The children to be shot first. Then I would shoot my husband – he is a professor and you know how forgetful they are.' Finally she would fling open the door, shoot the invader and then herself. What actually happened was another story: Otto and I were frequently guests of the family in the Japanese half of the house, and ironically the Russians, who fought the Japanese in the very last stages of the war, occupied the other, Western, half.

Otto and I came back from Japan in the spring of 1946 and he left the army to return to his beloved Ann Arbor and the German professorship at Michigan State University to which he had been appointed before the war (he had looked so junior at the time that he had been asked to wear a chain across a waistcoat to age him). Still stationed in Washington, I visited Otto and Sarah, his shining, tiny, spectacular wife, whenever I could. She was sheer delight. She had played her first Beethoven concert at the age of twelve, and she was ever ready to play and sing and dance without the drop of a hint. Otto was also a classical pianist who as a boy had played accompaniment to the silent movies at the local cinema. The Grafs were an odd couple for the Mid-West: they had two grand pianos in the living room and no car in the garage. Through them, I became a little familiar with life on the American campus, and fell for it. Michigan University, although not the huge campus it is these days, had a high, wide and handsome look about it – again, America at its best, ready for anything. I decided then that somehow, sometime, I had to get back to that atmosphere, rare and rich with choice and characters.

More specifically tantalising to me was the discovery of something called management. In Ann Arbor, there was the Group Dynamics Centre, under Kurt Lewin, and the Institute of Social Research, under Likerts. Apparently these were places which studied work and morale, motivation and management, and authority. I found myself foraging amateurishly through the literature, Elton Mayo's *The Social Problems of Organisation* setting me on a long, long trail. Economics, science, psychology, anthropology, law and political theory – they all seemed focused in the study of human relations in organizations and enterprise. A revelation: I was thrilled and shaken. My excitement was in good part confusion, not only over a lot of new words, but over a contradiction which came to shape my thinking.

Here was a world of management unfolding. Here were things called business schools which were proponents of managerial professionalism with a systematic view of work and group behaviours. And despite the occasional radical chic about a managerial revolution, here was a cool world, eschewing the passion of politics. David Lilienthal, the hero-manager of the Tennessee Valley Authority, a masterpiece of macro-management in the New Deal of the Thirties, wrote, 'Politics come in all varieties. Managers, administrators and experts are wise to avoid the lot of them if they want to do a good job.' But I found myself testing the other edge of this bright sword. Did it not cut both ways? It was aimed to reform unimaginative, inhuman management-by-numbers on a basis of social science, I could see that, but how could it swing clear and avoid politics? Did it not cut at capitalism because it argued against the sheer crudeness and cynicism of the model of economic man? That model was not only inadequate, it was an insulting underestimation of the qualities of people at work. A modern manager had a role and a duty in industrial society to make the most of all the assets of an organization, and the greatest of these were people. People are not to be manipulated. People are citizens. People are political animals – certainly I was feeling that increasingly about myself. In fact, in my own work, I was becoming something of a political animal at bay.

On my return to Washington in the spring of 1946, life was a bowl of cherry blossoms, an idyll for any young able-bodied, overpaid soldier. I became a captain, then a major and on our special dollar allowances I could afford a grown-up apartment. Flats were gold-dust but I hit on the only way to get a flat in that crowded city: I came across an American naval officer on the point of demobbing and leaving Washington. He had been born in France as I had been, and in the same little town of Malo-les-Bains, where his father had been the American consul. His christening robes had been borrowed from my mother and were those worn by my brothers and myself. Life seemed to be lucky like that in Washington 1946, full of things like Glady's. With the smooth flat came a smooth maid, a black sophisticated lady who signed her notes to me with an apostrophe 's' – Glady's – and either end of the 'G' coiled like the spring of a watch. When I heard Pearl Bailey in cabaret, in Baltimore, she was the jazzy incarnation of the spirit of Glady's.

1947 was a disenchanting spring. The British officers at our intelligence base on 14th and K Street were ordered to report in mufti: the idea was to make our movements in and out of a building full of American servicemen less conspicuous. I am not sure the tactic worked at all convincingly because the moment the order came through we all dashed to a tailor-shop run by a Cockney with a distinctive London style. All the same, the device was one more sign to me that a new game of intelligence was about to be played.

I was controlling a section of a document centre which handled captured material. We analysed and distributed information over a wide field: military, political, technical and commercial. My section was composed of American, Canadian and British servicemen and civilians, and we formed part of the Central Intelligence Group which was later to become the Central Intelligence Agency. This was therefore about as sensitive a spot as most for a young man to register the realities of peace breaking out between the Allies. Our inconspicuousness, of course, was sensibly devised to avoid drawing the attention of our Russian allies to the exploitation of intelligence material which they would claim was a common concern. Our objectives had switched violently away from the old enemy to a new. The collection of meticulous Japanese maps assumed a new significance: they were now being scrutinized for their rich detail of power stations in Trans Baikal. I recall a senior Western statesman at a summit meeting with the Russians denying the possession of top classified industrial research material from Germany: it was lying thick on the shelves in Otto's room. It is easy now to appreciate the prompt logic of the West in squaring up to Stalin, but then I believe it puzzled some young men wretchedly: it did me. The idealism of the way for one world of peace had nerved us to send convoys through icy storms to Russia, had inspired the gift of a great sword to celebrate the heroism of Stalingrad, had ended with those pictures of the rough-and-ready, huggermugger greetings of happy warriors from all sides when they united at last across Germany. 'We love the Russian people – bang,' Churchill had written about the end of the First World War. Now the same thing was happening again. In my little section I felt the chill of it long before I knew enough to call it the Cold War. This was a political revelation and I hated to take it in. It was too immediate for me. I was not ready for this sad moment when hope dropped like a condemned man through a trapdoor. Peace was not an opening of minds and hearts: the Russians were slamming some doors shut and the Western Allies were firmly closing others.

And within the alliance, we were closing them on each other too. That I could witness going on in my own centre. I detected that key documents and analyses were not reaching us; there was an uneasiness in relationships with senior Americans which I had never questioned before. What had been an Allied intelligence team was coming unstuck. The Americans plainly had their own ideas of creating and running their exclusive show. I could understand something of the background. Churchill had been displaced, and the shock of that rejection was as disturbing to many Americans as the discovery by the British that some Americans loathed Roosevelt (the British thought the only difference between Democrats and the Republicans was that one was in and one was out). Not only had they lost Churchill as the symbol of the special relationship, but they then had to deal with a Labour government which was avowedly Socialist – just how far could the Americans trust the British? Then I began to wonder how far some of the Canadians were to be trusted. Loyalties became strained for some of them who were seeking to stay with the Centre when they left the services.

The ambivalence mattered to me. I had started a secret unit of my own, in the centre itself, to make sure that documents to which the Commonwealth might be losing access would be scanned and even microfilmed. Any ambivalence from any Canadian worried me. And indeed, inevitably, there was a leak, not large, but enough to sharpen

the draughty air in the corridors. There was a distinctly Ustinov-like
silent dialogue going on: I know that you know that I know that you
know – you know the sort of thing. One day I sensed I was being
'fixed up': one of the secretaries accused me of being the father of
her child, a charge that makes the most innocent men feel guilty. I
had to explain to her that she was very beautiful and if I had been
responsible it was highy unlikely such an encounter would have slipped
my mind. But she meant trouble: she insisted that I had taken the
opportunity of the New Year's party, and I could not escape a public
row even if I was to try to escape my responsibilities. For days I was
receiving messages which escalated to threats of reporting my lack of
moral fibre to higher authorities. I was miserable about it all: if the
girl was genuinely pregnant she had to be desperate to involve me,
and I was not able to help because, if she was meant to wreck me,
any move I made to help would set me up for the sucker-punch. And
the discredit of any scandal to my command was bound to accelerate
the deterioration of relationships in the centre. I took a risk. I suggested to her that I was going to ask for a special investigation into
all the circumstances. Suddenly the girl disappeared. My secretary,
to whom I had dictated every shift and turn of event in this possibly
dirty-trick episode, enquired discreetly and was told the girl had failed
her loyalty check and had left. I never heard from her again. I did
learn more about loyalty checks.

The telephone rang: 'Is that Major Parker?'

'It is,' I admitted, and the voice identified itself as that of an
American security officer checking on the loyalty of an American
sergeant in my section, a Nissei (a second generation Japanese, born
in the US).

'Have you any comment, Major, on his loyalty?'

'Yes, indeed, I have: his loyalty leaves a lot to be desired from my
point of view.'

'Any details, Major?' – almost gleefully.

'Well, it's not detail really, it's history.'

'Really?'

'Yes, I reckon that the Americans have lacked loyalty to us British
since the 1770s and Independence and all that.'

Silence. Then, 'God, you're British.'

'And it might be worth checking me out. I support the Labour
government.'

In the late spring I was given a formal hint that perhaps I might like to continue in my line of operation – in uniform or in mufti. But my heart was not in the game any longer. I had gone into the war with no doubts. I was leaving it with uncertainties running hotfoot about my uneducated brain. What were these splits in the world that like geological faults were cracking Allies, industrial societies, my own loyalties? I was not fooling myself with the jejune question of whether it was better to be red than dead: to fight tyranny in any form was always worth the cost. My generation was properly brought up to do that; my brothers had died in that cause. But were we now to keep marching, this time against former comrades-in-arms? Who was giving the orders and why should they be obeyed? At the end of my service I was asking the same questions that I had asked at the beginning of my war. But there was a difference. At least I was growing to know what I did not know. In William Blake's *Proverbs of Hell* he wrote:

> The roaring of lions, the howling of wolves,
>> the raging of the stormy sea and the destructive sword
>> are portions of eternity, too great for the eye of man.

I was reading Blake avidly; he was proving to be the greatest revelation, the revelation of revelations, and he has never left me. Every day I find it enlivening and practical to think of Blake in everything I do. Usually I have some work of his with me, within easy reach, in the car or in the office. I seem to meet his eye. At conferences or negotiations, I need the Blakean directness, a straight look, demanding, searching, looking through the eye not with it. His influence on my career has been immeasurable, but daily and decisive. I have always needed to have the good William around.

I was first conscious of him in the Tamu Valley in northern Burma, 1944, in a small anthology which included one of his poems:

> O Rose, thou art sick!
> The invisible worm
> That flies in the night,
> In the howling storm,
> Has found out thy bed
> Of crimson joy;
> And his dark secret love
> Does thy life destroy.

Bertrand Russell said that in his final term at university, a friend quoted 'Tyger, Tyger', 'in the darkest part of a winding college staircase' and he was overwhelmed. 'I had never till that moment heard of Blake and the poem affected me so much that I became dizzy and had to lean against the wall.' I was stunned by 'The Sick Rose'. Of course I had sung 'Jerusalem' at school, and been taught 'Tyger' but nothing much about Blake. Wasn't he supposed to be cracked? Certainly a little cracked was the judgement of his art by most of his contemporaries, as I later learned. If so – to quote the painter Samuel Palmer who worshipped Blake – it was a crack to let the light in. I caught the light from 'The Rose' and I was dazzled. When I reached the United States in 1945 I found an abundant scholarship on Blake, which started me on an inexhaustible trail of studying his art. His is a unique art, composite in that we can read the pictures and see the poems. I loved the poetry at once, I learnt to love the painting later, and I pursue the visions still.

Blake's vision was of a universe where we can do something about freeing ourselves from the self-imposed 'mind-forg'd manacles'. Imagination was the redeeming reality: 'that called the body is a portion of the soul discerned by the five senses' – this was his dominant idea, the antimaterialism that isolated him in his time. He was a Londoner born and bred; at seventy he died, singing, and was buried in an anonymous grave in Bunhill Fields in 1827. No other of our greatest artists or poets was so cut off from success in his own time, even from an audience. Yet he worked prodigiously, in poverty and in a blaze of inspiration and originality. 'I must Create a System; or be slav'd by Another Man's.' He did. And a century and a half later his bust is in Westminster Abbey and he has a special room for himself at the Tate Gallery; his works are prized all over the world; there is a monumental literature, being continually built up; and his words, and thoughts are quoted and conscripted by a multitude of causes, often contradictory. Why? Not because of this or that poem or painting. Some find his prophetic books are whirling stuff and his paintings strained and unattractively weird: forms wildly contract and expand, proportions are lost in a spin of passion, anatomies get in a twist as people, airborne, fly about desperately separated from their luggage of gravity, faces blank, eyes and mouths agape. But behind everything he did is the vision that gives his works an enlarging relevance in our own time. It is Blake's stature as an artist, a radical thinker, a spiritual presence that is now being recognized increasingly widely in the world. 'A man without a mask,' (Palmer again)' his aims single, his path straightforward, and his wants few: so he was free, noble and happy.' What I read in him was a unity of art and action. He earthed the imagination in his radicalism; his purpose was not to generalize, but to raise the faculties of the individual to action against poverty, privilege, cruelty, inequalities of sex or race, intolerance and above all unimaginativeness. There was nothing vague in his intended disruption of the conventional perspective: his soul-painting was not an exercise in other-worldliness. He was 'full of futurity'; he 'saw' the outcome of a society based on a rationalist-materialist basis as its total truth; he stood prophetically against the satanic mills, his symbols not only for the machine age but also for unbridled scientific reason. His vision was, in the words of Yeats, 'the rise of the soul'. And it was each individual who had to strive to build Jerusalem in the scope of his own imagination and be ready to assert himself against the pomp and circumstance of temporal and spiritual powers – the particular individual. In each of us is imagination, Blake believed, as Jung did in our century. 'All deities reside in the human breast.' We each have it in us, individually, to see the infinite in all things, and in other people. Blake adored the detail of life, 'the minute particulars' – it is no good being kind but in particular, he said. He seemed to say all the things a young man would want to hear: 'Every honest man is a Prophet, he utters his opinions both of public and private matters.' And

> . . . if we raise ourselves
> Upon the chariots of the morning
> Contracting or Expanding Time!
> Every one knows, we are one Family: One
> Man blessed for ever.

In the early summer of 1947, I was nearly twenty-three. I was also obviously in urgent need of education, of what Blake would describe as 'firm and determinate outlines'. In my innocence and experience, Oxford seemed the place to go to next.

3

The Oxford Circus

There seemed only one way to get into Oxford University, and that was to knock on college doors. I did not know the city at all so I bought a map of it at Oxford railway station, a cloth map, very serviceable for what I suspected was to be a long campaign to win an entry. It was already the summer vacation and I wanted to be up for the autumn term. New College, through links with Bedford School, had offered me a place for a year ahead, in 1948, but I was impatient. Twenty-three seemed old. I wanted very badly to get to Oxford and get started. Just what that meant to me, what it could mean to me, I could only guess.

I marked the map with a route which seemed to take me past a number of colleges, including two with which I had some feeble connections. I put a cross by Oriel where an uncle had been, well before the First World War, and a cross by University College, where Air-Marshal Goddard was an honorary fellow – I had done him some slight service in the States and he had suggested that I might mention his name. If an old boy safety net was to be any use that was as far as mine went. But no worry. It was a perfect day. The sun was shining, the Oxford stone was blond and gorgeous and the steeples dreamy. If this was the home of lost causes it looked a wonderful way to go under. The first two colleges on my route, Balliol and Trinity, were politely negative, but from them I learnt a bit of ritual. It was not a matter of asking the porter at the Lodge how to get in: the form was to request a meeting with the Tutor for Admissions. I continued my quick march (I was on demob leave and in uniform) which took me past the Clarendon, the Bodleian, the Camera and All Souls. No luck at Brasenose, nobody home apparently. On to Oriel where the curving wall puzzled me for a moment, and as I hesitated on the kerb I noticed an open door near an arched porch, and a short, chunky, oldish man tugging a large trunk across the pavement towards it. I took one end of the trunk, together we tottered through into a fine hallway, and

45

then both sat gasping at either end of the trunk. As he mopped his face and bald head he asked me what I was doing. I explained that I was trying to find the way into Oriel – was this it? He laughed, 'One way,' and it turned out my new porter friend was the Provost, G. N. Clark, the famous historian. This was his house, the college was through the porch. I showed him my route map, with Oriel crossed as a target area. I explained to him that he was half the sum total of my old boy network. He encouraged me hugely by saying that I should complete my reconnaissance and if I had not gained entry by sundown I should report back to him. Next was University College, and there the Tutor for Admissions brought others into an informal meeting which went well, but I was told that because the Master was absent that day I should not expect any definite decision for forty-eight hours. I strolled on air up the High Street, which struck me as surely the finest street I had ever seen, a broad opening of life. I think so still.

The Mitre had been recommended as the place for lunch. I took a window-seat in the raised back part of the old dining-room, gracious and shabby then, smart and grotty now. The service was leisurely and chatty, and I asked the waiter what I was looking at through the lace curtain. It was the Rector's lodgings of Lincoln College. I calculated that the slow pace of delivery would leave me time between the soup and the meat to nip out and across the road to the Porter's Lodge for an appointment. Two-thirty prompt, Mr Allen, the Dean and Tutor for Admissions. By three-thirty Harry Allen, who became a friend for life, had introduced me to the Rector, and by four o'clock I was in, even in time to catch a train back home. Those were the days, my friend. Nothing like the obstacle course of entry to the Oxbridge of the Eighties.

My mother met me at St John's station in Bedford. She had gone there, unsure of train times, unsure of how the day would go, sure that she should be there anyway. Our long walk home was not really long enough. It was the perfect evening of a perfect day. We walked the long way, by the River Ouse, running greenly, slowly, strongly, full of light, and we were immensely happy. There is no holding the winged joy as it flies, joy has so much to do with the future. Nor do I find myself pinning down past happiness for a butterfly collection of beautiful moments. I believe happiness is a state, as love is. We can be in it, leave it, re-enter it. We may age, our imagination and energy may fail us, fade. But the state of happiness holds good. It is not in the linear time-pattern of a diary of engagements, predictable and pell-mell, running on ahead, piling things on things to do until the last entry and the last day when it ends six foot deep. To be in or out of a state of happiness is nothing to do with time. For me, to be happy is not an event of past, present or future tense. The state of happiness is there, was there, will be there, by the river of life whose spring and ocean are unknown to me. I have never managed to achieve more than a shaky confidence in a religious dogma. All religions are one, Blake wrote. I know delight in the awareness of spiritual life, 'portions of eternity', which are more than the animal, mineral, vegetable world about us, more than this particular, over-ripening vegetable of flesh around me. Dorothy's talk of keeping body and soul together was her 'state' secret. And I suppose that is the great trick, keeping body and soul together, singing in tune, not necessarily in unison but in harmony.

For the next three years I was to discover Oxford to be part of that state, a state of permanent opportunity, where there is the best chance in life to be happy – although absolutely no guarantee that it will happen. I found it to be full of good times, classical and jazzy, and jolly circus music too. There were three rings to my Oxford circus, very roughly one for each year. Each of these linked, of course, with the others, although none linked immediately with the one ring in which I was to spend most of my life, the arena of business and industry.

I arrived at Lincoln College for the Michaelmas term of 1947. I had no clear idea of how Oxford worked or what was going to happen next, but I was aware at once, as everybody else up there seemed to be, that the present was a fine thing. The country was still suffering the war's aftermath of austerity, but the Oxford circus was lit up by a sheer delight in leaving anxiety behind, in being free of uniforms and uniformity. Most of the young men and women had faced years of stress, of combat or bombing or just dreariness. Now here was gladness to be alive and high-kicking and dancing. The air seemed supercharged with energy and expectations. Seven years of the university's annual intake had been dammed during those war years; now it flooded through into every nook and cranny of Oxford's opportunities. Oxford's quality any time is that it enjoys a community of infinite variety and voltage: for the post-war years here was all that talent multiplied by seven. A rising generation of starters was crammed, jostling, under the Big Top, and as Ogden Nash nearly said, nothing pings like propinquity. I was tempted to set off in all directions, and fell for the temptation at once, thank goodness. What saved me from an early death by sprawling was that my first love at Oxford was my college. That kept my sense of proportions intact – almost.

There was no room in the college for me in the first year. I shared spacious rooms in a college residence, Southfields, on the city outskirts. Probably it was a sense of being on the edge of things, of feeling edgy, that sharpened an extra interest in me to become involved in the college's central life through its Junior Common Room. Lincoln is one of the smaller colleges, as the guide-books say. I had not even marked it on my route-map as a possible target. Founded in the fifteenth century, the buildings are on a modest scale but the proportions are fine, with an elegant dining-hall and handsome rooms, particularly the Beckington. There is also an exquisite chapel with its Eastern window full of solemn jokes: Charles I, the Martyr, is made the hero of the biblical tableau of stained glass, Charles playing Adam, Charles playing Jesus – easily identified by his goatee beard. The college's proportion, physically and socially, fitted my frame of mind ideally. The size was just right to sustain a sense of community. At a time when Oxford was bulging with its exceptional population, our membership of 300 had a human scale which larger, grander institutions were finding it harder to achieve. The Junior Common Room became a steadying focus of my friendships and concern. I became secretary, then treasurer, and at the end of the first year, the elected president. To fulfil that short and merry life, it was thought sensible to move me into college, and I was given rooms in the corner of the Chapel quadrangle (which I am honoured to have bearing my name today). The windows overlooking the small and busy quad were my magic casement. From there I had a view of one of the few pieces of organizational dogma which I am prepared to admit to. The small square, 66½ feet by 64½ feet, framed perfectly my first principle of management: organize into the smallest groups you can. I could see, in peace, the living proof and definition of what army experience had given me a feel for but had not formulated. The quad was small but it was the shape of fellowship. Oxford University was a glorious generalization, but this was the particular, this was a ring of reality for me. The university was a mysterious federal system but was no greater than its colleges; the colleges were the parts, which in those days considered themselves greater than the whole.

Later in my life I was to find myself involved in the politics of higher education, and in the hard questions of what universities are for. Should the government, the paymaster, call the tune? None of the complications bothered me then. I simply saw the university as the play, the college as the play within the play and, as far as concerned me, the college was the thing that caught me. The view from the window, the sight of a community at work, has stayed with me in managing anything. In any organization, I have found that groups, as small as possible, create the vitalizing force of recognizable loyalties and understandings and interdependence. From that all blessings flow in enterprise. And the bigger the business the more relevant is that 66½ feet by 64½ feet piece of evidence: that's where real life thrives and prospers. The commonwealth of Lincoln College symbolized the shape of things I would like to come.

In my time, the Rector, the head of the college, was Keith Murray. His impression was as deep on me as on the rest of what I called the Murray-minted generation. Before the war he had come to the college as Bursar; he had become Air Commodore in the RAF, and was soon made Rector on his return to college. His influence on the development of the college, not least its economic affairs, was formidable. He was a subtle achiever, charming and tough as old boots, with a meticulous courtesy that allowed us to have his way. As president of the JCR I saw much of him. I knew he disapproved of my politics: he kept leading me away from any of the invitations which were opening up a political career for me. But quarrels never interrupted our political arguments – then, and even after I had gone down, even in the passionate Suez crisis of 1956 when, to my dismay, he resigned from the board of trustees of the *Observer* because of their criticism of the government. Keith's gift lay in his welcome of variety in the college, of the balance of opinions and intellectual abilities that make up a community of any sort.

I was never as absorbed as I should have been in my academic responsibilities. History was my subject, and I started by taking it much like a sedative. Harry Allen, the Dean, was my tutor and the weekly sessions of one hour with him gradually quickened my wits. At our very first tutorial he handed me the long list of lectures in history at the university that term and said that I was free to go to any of them. 'Go to any you choose, any you'd like to. I have to admit, I never went to a lecture when I was up.' I had just ceased being a major, he had ceased to be a major a year or so earlier. He, in the true Oxford style, was making it quite clear that I was to be a responsible citizen of the academic community, and he was there to tutor, not dictate, not finger-wag. I had come up to Oxford, and now it was up to me. Each week, he set me an essay, and recommended the sources for study on the subjects. I enjoyed the weekly treasure hunt and the writing of the essays that took twenty minutes to read out, and the no-holds-barred wrestling in debate that followed.

I soon discovered that I was selfishly selective about what themes really interested me. Political theory, modern history (which in those days stopped cautiously in 1914), constitutional history, the American Civil War – yes, yes, yes. Anglo-Saxon and medieval history, for instance, was a no-no. I had collected a bric-à-brac of left-wing literature in the war, and my prejudices were simple enough: against empires and against the capitalism that developed them competitively, with the inevitable and regular consequence of wars. Marxist theory provided some rationale for all this but Marxist practice seemed to replace one misrule with another. I needed help, and Harry helped me with his instinctive, Burkean mistrust of formulas. He refined my capacity for doubt, he kept my scepticism intact, he steaded me up sufficiently to take what he called a good second-class degree, and he gave me my head on the issues that were of consuming interest to me and where he knew I would do better. Above all he left me with an appetite for the study of history which, I came to learn, is an appetite for life.

I have never regretted reading history as an undergraduate. It still seems to me to be as fertile a grounding as any on which to start a career managing any organization. It was a car-maker, Ford, who said that history was bunk. The historical conditioning of individuals and their communities is the proper basis of an understanding of their present and future fears and hopes. In Jungian terms, each of us is so old, hundreds, even thousands of years old. History is not what is over and done with, it runs alongside any of us who run anything, reminding us of what the individual can do, of what surprises the unforeseen predictably springs on us, of what a lot of cant clutters our way. I reckon a degree in history ensures a degree of humility: we have to learn that dogmas have their day. Many a board chairman should finish the annual report as one famous historian (who made history himself), Churchill, finished one of his prefaces: 'We have tried to test all documents and authorities at the source; nevertheless we await with meekness every correction or contradiction which the multiplicated knowledge of students and critics will supply.'

I discovered a fascination in the way great men had managed to organize change. Cromwell was a supreme example, with his 'free way' of management. Ever since, I have wanted to relate historical illustrations of what we have this century called management and regarded as a modern phenomenon. There is a Beautiful Book of Management to be compiled: it would be anthological, taking pages of the outstanding modern textbooks of business and counterpointing them page by page with extracts from, say, Homer, Chaucer, Shakespeare, Milton, Blake – with pictures by the great masters too. At last, a book on management one could take to bed and enjoy.

By the end of the first year, I was deep in the life of the college, and from within that ring of confidence, by the second year, I was moving into other widening circles of university life. Politics came naturally, I became an active member of the Labour Club, and editor of its journal, the *Clarion*. My introduction came through a member of the Lincoln community, Bill Pearson. Bill had grown up poor; he had never known his father, who had deserted his mother and left her to scrape a living for herself and her children as a cleaner and by taking in washing. Billy left school at fourteen with no qualifications but a battling good humour and character, which became quickly evident on call-up to the Army. He rose fast to win a commission, and then, on a Dutch dyke, at the Second Front, he lost a leg, blown off by a mine. Somehow during the long months in hospital he came to the attention of Keith Murray, who did what he did for me and many others, and somehow made space for him in Lincoln. Bill had been up for over a year when I arrived for the Michaelmas term in 1947, and bumped into him, first thing, in the lodge. He was in white flannels and carrying a squash racket. Nothing about Bill ever conceded any handicap, a disability perhaps, but not a handicap. This pogo stick of a man bounced over every barrier of so-called disability to become captain of the Lincoln cricket club, president of the JCR, editor and chairman of the Labour Club. I found myself a plodder in his footsteps.

Often Bill and I would meet at Ma Brown's in the market-place for lunch with two merry ex-RAF friends of his. One was a one-legged Canadian from University College: the other Sam Gallop, was from Brasenose and he had no legs. Going about with the three of them, with four legs between the four of us, taught me a permanent lesson to be more numerate about my blessings, to keep counting them. It also taught me that the abilities of the 'disabled' are often wonderfully reinforced by their handicap. Sam Gallop himself is living proof: after retirement as secretary of the Electricity Council, he started a national network of job centres which seek out 'Opportunities for the Disabled'. He has moved tirelessly around the country encouraging employers to make the most of what those with handicaps can still do. His organization now has a small head office in the Bank of England, a national network, a council of which he has made me president, and an unstoppable momentum of goodwill in business which provides assets and sponsors people. As he would insist, this has been only a part of the general advance in the civility of our society towards handicap of any kind. But truly in business we have a long way to go yet; we have only started to make the most of the special abilities of the so-called disabled. In Ma Brown's I had no idea that these occasional lunches with my one-legged and legless friends were part of my management education – or that when I was at British Rail, I would be ready to make travel without handicap a front-line priority in our policies.

Throughout my second year, 1948–49, I was extremely – that is probably the word – active in politics. There was mercifully little doctrinal definition of my own belief in the socialism of the Labour Party then, and the little that was crucial to me was not nationalization, as set out in Clause Four. In the Fifties, that was to become a divisive point of theology, splitting the revisionist from the traditionalist who thought nationalization was an end, not a means. The little of dogma that mattered to me was simple enough but crucial: I wanted the social revolution to come through Parliament and not by its overthrow. Labour was a broad church but not so broad that it could encompass the aims of a dictatorship in the name of the proletariat. Fortunately British Labour was more spacious, more muddled and more syndicalist than dirigiste, more Methodist than Marxist, or at least more Christian than materialist. Marx's own measure of British socialism in its early days, in 1870, was prophetic: 'The English have all the material conditions necessary for the socialist revolution, what they lack is the spirit of generalization and the revolutionary fervour.'

By 1948 the Labour Club had separated decisively from the Socialist Club in Oxford, and everything that was happening in the world outside the state of Oxford reinforced our conviction. Stalin's Communism was already sabotaging the agreements between the victorious Allies that there should be free elections in Poland and Czechoslovakia. Masaryk, the democratic hero of Prague, had been arrested by the Communists: he crashed to his death through a high window of his prison and with him were shattered any reassuring illusions of one world born from the struggle against Fascism. For me the doors of perception – clouded in my days in Washington – were cleansed: the Cold War was as obvious as a kick in the solar plexus. It is probably hard for a post-war generation to appreciate just how sore and how winded some of us were. By now we have grown accustomed to a world divided for so long, to the divisions that have made up the history of almost half our century. We know the outcome and it is hard to remember how little anyone knew at the beginning. At the start of things, as a starter, you only know the start: that is the way history is lived, forwards, although it is written backwards.

So the Labour I delighted in was clear-headed enough to see off the Marxist socialists. We wanted to work and win through Parliament which, in all its ramshackledom, was still the best bet for democracy. The Labour democracy we stood for sounded bold in its visions of democracy, even revolutionary sometimes. But now, 'writing backwards', it seems to have been a moderate, most natural, most consensual period of reform. The new Labour government had come in crowing cockily 'We are the masters now,' but if this was class war, why was the very classy Hartley Shawcross, of all people, leading the singing of 'The Red Flag'? The Labour Party was in an euphoric mood, not unexpectedly, and despite the economic chaos of the peace, it believed whole-heartedly in itself, not in any Marxist version of the inevitability of history. For most of my generation, the war had made sense of slogans about the brotherhood of man; it had illuminated a vision of what the country could achieve in a common effort and what planning could do for the good of all. To me, it seemed only sensible that this was the time for all good men to come to the aid of the Labour Party, the country and the world – and to many of us there was nothing very revolutionary about that. The war had seemed a relatively convincing exercise of consensus to Liberals and Conservatives as well. All were 'socialists', left, right and centre, in laying the basis of the Welfare State. The Beveridge reforms of social security and the Butler reforms of education were common ground in the War Cabinet. And even if that pin-striped revolutionary, Prime Minister Attlee, was going faster than some Conservatives thought wise in transforming Empire into Commonwealth, he had chosen a royal executive, Lord Mountbatten, to get on with negotiating the independence of India. Behind the raucous triumph of the Labour chaos, behind the argy-bargy of party rhetoric, there were the remains of a national unity. Churchill may have smeared the Labour leadership in the election with his wild talk of Gestapo tactics, but in the run-up before it he had met privately with Bevin at Chequers, and had suggested to that colossus of Labour and trade unions that the two of them might go to the country on a joint platform of national unity, above the faction of party politics. That there was even a hint of such a partnership between two of the grandest old men of the century is some measure of the mood immediately after the war. The 1945–7 Hansard records of Parliamentary debates show how surprisingly little controversy there really was over much of the national programme of industrial democracy and public ownership.

So I began in party politics, equipped with little doctrine but heavily loaded with the conviction that much had to be changed if the country was to avoid a repeat of the pattern of events between the First and Second World Wars, producing the Third World War. I believed that our society could be pointed towards more fairness. Whatever the sum of limited resources, I wanted government to allocate more of them towards eliminating poverty and improving opportunities. Social justice might sound now like the Left's equivalent of what, in capitalist America, Galbraith described as the bland leading the bland, but the reality was that Labour, with all its faults, had force enough from its support to virtually eliminate the Communist Party in Parliament and, in the country, to avoid the polarization of extremes. Eventually Labour paid a price for its concentration on the Communists who, ousted from the democratic process of the country, were still able to counter-attack, quietly but more damagingly, by infiltrating the unions and dividing the party ranks from within.

I have stressed the underlying unity of post-war party politics in the country, but at the time it was anything but obvious. In my time as chairman of Labour in the University in 1948, politics were anything but calm in the demonstrations and debates. The collective spirit of the war effort was plainly disintegrating. All the political clubs were intensely active. The Labour and Conservative clubs each had over a thousand members, and every week of term public meetings were held with leading politicians easily attracted from London to address large, often rowdy crowds. There was nothing mild about those encounters. I was chairing John Strachey in the Oxford Union chamber when the opposition cut off the electricity and plunged hundreds of us into blackness. After the short uproar I asked him to carry on and in his reasonable voice he did, arguing brilliantly in the dark. It is a pity that he was only discussing peanuts, that huge doomed venture of the groundnuts scheme in West Africa.

Emmanuel Shinwell, the then Minister of Fuel – surely the wrong job for such a fiery figure to be handling – provoked an even wilder night when he spoke. There had been a horrendous fuel shortage in the previous winter and Shinwell took responsibility for the confusion over supplies but was pugnaciously defensive. Only because Mannie survived to a great old age did he become a Grand Old Man – the British public forgives anybody for anything if they only live long enough. He died as a beloved centenarian, but in 1948 he was deeply unpopular. When I picked him up from the station he warned me that he was under orders to be dull. 'The Old Man [Attlee] has told me to be careful.' A few of us gave him dinner at the Mitre Hotel and obviously there was no way Mannie was capable of being careful, or dull. We had invited the economist Thomas (later Lord) Balogh, who with an outrageous Mephistophelean charm tempted Mannie with tricky questions about government policies.

'Tommie, I can only speak for myself and my own department—'

'But Mannie, you know very well I'm not expecting you to know anything about your own department. You can't, your civil servants see to that.'

'That's rubbish.' Mannie roared with laughter. 'Why that's – that's economics.'

As we dined, a riotous mob had gathered in the High Street and down the Turl to put the Mitre under sieve. I suggested a police escort to lead us to the nearby gymnasium where the meeting was to be held. Mannie shrugged and said, 'Do as I do and follow me.' He had the lights in the lobby turned off, then had the doors opened and quickly walked backwards and unnoticed into the noisy darkness. I did the same, backing in step with this streetwise minister of the crown through the crowd which was baying for his blood. In the packed gymnasium, the rioters went on hammering on the doors and windows, and bringing the best out of Mannie. At one stage rioters came through the skylight and, under a chandelier of dangling legs, he had a ball. He accepted a police convoy to get him out.

Harold Wilson came up on 5 November, fireworks night. He was the youngest-ever president of the Board of Trade, glossy with ambition, full as an egg with ego and statistics. His arrival was delayed, he told us, because he had to finish signing trade agreements with the Eskimos – can it have been he said thirty-two? Despite the brazen vanity, I liked him, then and since: unlike most politicians, he carries most of his faults on the surface. After his display of intellectual fireworks in the town hall, which was full of rapt supporters, he walked down the steps to his official car, and as he did so, a real and sizeable cracker was lobbed over the police protection to explode on the gleaming bonnet. No harm was done: he seemed invulnerable in those days, and on him the burst of the fireworks bloomed like a winner's rosette. Nothing was going to check his journey to the top.

Not all the meetings blew up to those proportions. There were other memorable quieter moments. Attlee addressed us and commanded a respectful attention: he was crisp, masterly, a First World War character, a man of honour. Folk tales make him out to be taciturn to the point of crashing boredom – certainly his style of leadership was unromantic and idealistic – but he did expect the best, and it was fascinating to watch the care with which he dealt with the removal of anything unnecessary in an argument or a situation. And I can bear witness to hearing him tell a story: about a GI in a crowded train. In the GI's carriage was a lady with a lapdog taking up a whole seat. Nobody spoke or moved. Suddenly, the GI let down the window, presumably to help him keep calm. The woman closed it because she said the dog would be in the draught, and this was too much for the weary GI: he reopened the window and threw the dog out of it. A mild Englishman remarked to the GI, 'You're an odd lot, you Americans. You use your knife and fork the wrong way round, you drive on the wrong side of the road and you throw the wrong bitch out of the window.'

A spectacular speaker, in vivid contrast, was Barbara Castle, young, startling and sexy, one of the few women to reach the front line of politics and to keep a broad appeal. I had no notion then of how much of my life was to be influenced by this coppery-bright star. But, chairing the session, I sat close enough to her on the platform to study her techniques for spellbinding. She knew how to make the most of a swervy figure, trim in white blouse, black skirt and aquamarine belt. As she gestured to make her points, as she swung around into profile, this lady with flame hair and dragon eyes may have curved like a question mark, but she had none of its uncertainty. She was more an exclamation mark, and so, I am glad to say, she was to prove later in my career. Perhaps the most authentic traditional speaker in my programme of visitors was the Minister of Insurance, James Griffiths, an embodiment of the movement, father of much painstaking insurance legislation: a craggy, capacious face, a blunt strong shape; a character from the Welsh valleys, self-taught, a natural actor, with a passion that rose up and up like the Welsh mountains. I heard Nye Bevan speak, not at Oxford in my time but later, and there was that same gift of mounting passion, in Nye's case lit by genius. Jim was not a genius; he was a thoroughly decent good man. I got him into the late Friday-night train back to London, and I saw him tug open his fat briefcase the moment he sat down. Opposite him there was a well-known Conservative, who had also been to speak to his faithful: he was opening a thriller, and cheerfully settled down to the trip. Jim joked with him about leisure, 'the fruits of the opposition'. As the train began to move, he leant out to shake hands with me and whispered, 'I don't mind really, you know: you see, it's my whole life, this job.'

But was it my whole life? My job? Was I to go into politics? Certainly I saw politics in my life but not the other way around. I was coming to know younger Oxford politicians close to my own age, who had gone down and immediately set themselves up for a professional political career. There was Tony Crosland, then an Economics Fellow and Dean of Trinity, but already being tipped as a future Chancellor of the Exchequer: he was formidable, handsome, with an intellectual temper edgy with wit and explosive exasperation. Roy Jenkins was already impressive, sleek and determined, effective and generous and difficult to know; he offered to guide me to a constituency if I was prepared to fight one. So did Tony Benn, who had an attractive energy, was fluent and good fun; there was no sign then of today's doomster of the militant left.

Was a political career what I wanted? What should I do? Certainly as chairman of the Labour Club, I was becoming enjoyably and deeply ensconced in the politics scene by the end of my second year. And Labour became even more part of my life when Shirley Catlin, now Williams, arrived on the scene in the autumn of 1948 and started winning hearts and minds – including mine. She was a scholar at Somerville (not that the long black gown did anything for her, I remember thinking the first time I spotted her). She was short and had a lively, rolling way of walking fast, as if she wished she was flying but if that was not what God wanted, then a hop, skip and jump was the next best thing. She had a beauty, a radiant energy in her: shining blond hair and a wide blue gaze with a brightness that made me think of those French women who seem to keep their souls just behind their eyes, and she had a speed and concentration of thought and expression that made her enchanting company and a fine public speaker.

Shirley was bred for politics. Her mother, Vera Brittain, and her father, Sir George Catlin, an academic political theorist, were both busy public figures; both were in the Labour movement but neither of them was making the direct contribution to politics that they probably had desired. Shirley even as a tot was a political prodigy, being forever trotted around party conferences and blessed, I was told, by a pat on the head from the shrewdest of managers, Herbert Morrison. She came through all that and was still her own woman – and is still. But it cannot have been easy. When I visited her in No. 3 Cheyne Row, her handsome family home by the Thames, I came to know Charles, the butler, and the most unobsequious of servants; he proudly claimed as much credit as anyone for bringing her up, but most of the credit, of this I am sure, must go to Shirley herself. In her teens she converted to Roman Catholicism and she pledged herself to the service of others. Everybody recognized a selflessness in her, which has lasted throughout the rough process of a tough political career. Whatever those most against her say about her, they never include that most obvious and reliable of a politician's failings, self-seeking: she probably has too little thought for herself.

When Shirley arrived in Oxford she was an immediate presence everywhere, a winning gold streak around town, very public and very much herself. Her popularity was the mostest. She seemed to lack enemies: if somebody said anything nasty about Shirley you worried not about Shirley but about the poor bastard who said it. I fell for this self-propelled, enchanting, tough-minded husky-voiced politician. We loved each other happily and a bit desperately, as if in our hearts we knew we would run out of time and lose one another in our rush of ambitions. Which is what happened really.

Certainly it always seemed to me that politics for Shirley would be her whole life. She had supreme qualities for it. Many of us thought of her as potentially the first woman Prime Minister: actually the girl who made it was up at the same college and at the same time, but relatively unnoticed. The public images of the two women provide misleading contrasts: one of groomed and lacquered chic, twinset and pearls, the other a slightly worn, unselfconscious teddy bear; one stiff-featured, stern, unlistening, assertive, the other soft-mannered, wide-eyed, her features over-expressive to show she cares about what is being said. But these powerful, very different women, have much in common. Each can electrify an auditorium with her oratory, and each adores applause. Each has an instinct for being where the action is, exocets attracted by the heat. Each has a delight in overworking. Each has a swift reaction to nonsense in an opponent's argument. Each can attract loyalty and affection. The real contrast is, I suspect, less obvious. One is more expedient, more populist, more hungry for power. The other, Shirley, is less changeable, more reflective; she has pursued her principles so singly it has led her to a lonely eminence – how much more convenient to have stayed in the Labour movement and not broken away. I see little difference between them in toughness or ambition. Once, during the Heath government in the early Seventies, Shirley and I were discussing the weakness of Tony Barber at the Treasury. I was suggesting that Heath should make Keith Joseph Chancellor. Shirley disagreed: she said that if she were in Heath's job, she would choose Margaret Thatcher from among the Conservative front bench. Margaret is famously not cosy. Shirley, in reality, is no cosier, is determined and devoted to her cause. Perhaps the greater difference is not in strength but in quality of mind. Recently I met Dame Janet Vaughan, a most distinguished woman who, as a don, had known Margaret Thatcher and Shirley in their Somerville days. She said, 'Margaret has never changed, she's a ruthless administrator. But she hasn't got it here, you know.' This great dame stabbed at herself with a forefinger. 'Not here, you see, not here,' stabbing insistently. I suppose most people would guess that she was pointing at her heart, and they would be wrong. She was pointing to her brain. 'Shirley's got it here, she can see issues all round.'

The second year of Oxford was for me exactly what the storybooks say it should be. The second year for most undergraduates is the most free of the three. I have never had more time to enjoy myself in my life. There was none of the nervousness of beginning, and the shadows of exams had not started to creep about the quad. Life was in the brightest colours. Politics and Shirley were primary, but there were many other colours running into the picture. My diary was a kaleidoscope. A dawn raid on the academic work was the first thing: work on the essay theme, and reading. Early morning is still for me the best time for work, 'the moment in the day that Satan cannot find' (Blake, of course). Mornings began with a scramble of political and other committees, and after ten-ish came tutorials and taking notes in the Radcliffe Camera. Nights were for theatre, politics, debates, and delights. In between, in the afternoon, raining or shining, the sporting life, mostly rugby and swimming. Of all competitive sports I had always rated boxing as the most attractive – to do, not to watch. In school-days a boxing team provided the most democratic of activities; other school sports were roughly grouped by ages, but in boxing the spread of ages and seniority from flyweights to heavyweights disrupted the hierarchies of any school establishment. Seniors and juniors trained, toured and fought as a group. Nerves are a great leveller. But the unique excitement for me in boxing was the miracle of the eyes: at a miraculous speed, somehow two fighters see through each other's eyes everything that is happening, fists, feet, shifts of the body, shifts of the spirit even – all in splits of seconds. Eye to eye is all: lose eye contact and all is lost. Nowadays there is a repellent sleaziness and crookedness, a brainlessness and heartlessness about the professional ring. The ideal of the noble art is ludicrously remote. But as a boy I felt it not so: it was the best of sports. When I reached Oxford my boxing days were over, but rugby was still a joy. I played on the wing – and in those days of innocence, there used to be three-quarter movements and the ball actually was passed down the line to the winger, a rare occurrence in the modern game. I had begun to play serious rugby for the Bedford town team and then for the East Midlands. At Oxford I trained and played with the university side, became a Greyhound, but not a Blue: the Oxford side in those years was packed with many Internationals. I was finding sport a real necessity, both in terms of keeping sane and fit, and in economic terms. University vacations were long: part of my formula for finding my way through them lay in rugby tours, either with the college side which I captained or with the Oxford XV. Sports plus political conferences, plus theatre, made up the full formula.

As I entered the third year I was enjoying myself hugely in the third ring of my Oxford circus, the theatre. In his book, *O.U.D.S: A Centenary History of the Oxford University Dramatic Society*, Humphrey Carpenter describes the work of post-war Oxford theatre as a golden period. Undoubtedly the names of many involved in it have become famous and even well regarded in drama, films and television. A selection of these is impressive: Lindsay Anderson, Anthony Besch, Michael Codron, Michael Croft, Nigel Davenport, Peter Dews, Robert Eyre, William Gaskill, Robert Hardy, Frank Hauser, Norman Painting, Tony Richardson, Robert Robinson, Glynne Wickham, David William, Sandy Wilson. The normal annual intakes, added to the late arrivals delayed by the war, made these vintage years. Carpenter suggests that it was the maturity of students, many of them ex-servicemen, that explains this flowering of talent. To an extent that was true. Yet the most exotic bloom of that flowering was not an ex-serviceman, and was never an ex-anything: Ken Tynan. He was a prototype of starters. He had come up two years before me, and was very young, startlingly funny, inconceivably arrogant, and lived extravagantly on five bob a week. Physically he was both golden and macabre, very tall and thin, with a skull of a head and large rolling eyes, a stammer that gave a twist to his mouth, an explosive emphasis to his ideas, long extravagant fingers that gestured incessantly, and gold satin shirts and purple suits which he wore most of the time. He could switch on intellectual brilliance like a floodlight. He surrounded himself and his friends with tremendous laughter. He was unreliable about money, women and politics, and unsure of his own identity outside the spotlight. People who knew him then, friend or foe (and I was both), will still say after all this time, 'I was up with Ken,' and will feel they have something special in common. Our relationship was only brief but in its complexity very special indeed.

In my first term, Sandy Wilson, whom I had known during our time together learning Japanese, suggested I join him at a casting session of the Experimental Theatre Club. There he introduced me to Ken Tynan who offered me the minor character of the Hobo in *Winterset* by Sherwood Anderson. I jumped at it. It was a tiny ten-liner of a part, literally a mumbling shambles of a character, but the production was to be presented after its Oxford opening at the Theatre des Champs-Élysées in Paris. That tour would dovetail exactly with the Oxford University XV's tour of Wales: my budget for the Easter vac was settled.

Much more was settled really, had I known. At the casting session I entered a competition to perform two extracts. In the first, as the Duke in *Measure for Measure*, I played opposite a stunning Isabella, Rosemary Boxer, Marc Boxer's older sister, a girl as beautiful as she was intense. As Claudio there was Harold Hodson, later to be the famous and original cartoonist, 'Haro'. (At that time Haro also wrote poetry and I read some of it on the radio. Poetry reading for the BBC, at one pound a minute, was to become a most pleasurable and profitable experience.) The second extract was from *The Idiot*. Russell Enoch (William Russell became his acting name) played Miskin, I the burly Rogozin. From this exposure came the chance to take Ulysses in *Troilus and Cressida*, an outdoor production in Halifax gardens. I was given an all-black Elizabethan costume to wear, just what I wanted. Ulysses is usually played grey and foxy; I wanted him to be a dark, elegant fixer.

That production changed my life. Sitting in the preview audience during a dress rehearsal was the best part of my destiny, a beautiful girl, way, way at the back: I was going to marry her three years later. Also Ulysses brought me and Ken together. He saw the opening night and next morning there was a note from him in my pigeonhole in Lincoln Lodge. It said, 'I never knew you had legs. You could play Hamlet.' Apparently the shabby rags of the Hobo had been obscuring assets Ken needed for his next venture, the First Quarto *Hamlet*, not done since Donald Wolfit's performance in the Thirties. And athletic legs are more significant in this tougher, vigorous version of the melancholy Dane. The 1503 text was probably pirated, pieced together from shorthand prompt copies and actors' memories. It runs about two and a half hours, 2,200 lines compared to the 3,200 of the good Quarto, and it rearranges scenes. The lines are cruder but the directness and the compact force ring true to what might well have been the original box office attraction. For instance, the 'To be or not to be' soliloquy comes (sensibly in my view as an actor) immediately after Hamlet sees the ghost. No messing about. Hamlet says:

> To be or not to be, ay – there's the point,
> To die to sleep, is that all? Aye, all.

This Hamlet is more Burbage-shaped, more Wolfit-shaped than the slender, aesthetic Folio figure we have come to expect. Wolfit came to our revival at the Cheltenham Festival in the summer of 1948, and wrote an approving notice. So, that winter, on we went to London; we were a motley crew but remarkable in retrospect. I had two Horatios, Lindsay Anderson out of town, and John Schlesinger in London. Robert Hardy, the most professional of actors in my time at Oxford – and probably since – was the Player King; Jack May played Polonius, called Corambis in the First Quarto. Ken himself played the Ghost, and I found him the hardest man to share a stage with. He sucked attention towards himself always, on stage and off. He could have become an actor or a director with as much elan, if not as much distinction, as he later won in theatre criticism, and I only wish he had done more performing before he settled for confining his restless genius to paper. The fun in him thinned and his last years were frayed and hellish.

The book by his wife, Katherine, is brave, and a more clinically admiring portrait of the greatest theatre critic of his generation than I would have thought a wife could draw. But it's saddening. His gifts as a director were humour and passion. We recruited an army from the text of Hamlet: there were shouts from Ken as strange names and ranks emerged from the lines – Marshal Stalk, General Air, Sergeant Death, Corporal Air, Privates We – but god's sake, where's the Captain? Robert Hardy, doubling as Fortinbras, suddenly had him: Captain Go-Greet ('the King of Denmark etc.'). There was even a small oriental gardener, Ho, to keep the parade-ground tidy. Ken could not resist the swooping extravagant touches – wolfhounds pulling Gertrude on for her first entrance – and he ached to shock his audience, to change them and thus to have life reflecting theatre. He was more in everything he did, and with that versatility went a looseness. He borrowed money unscrupulously, but then was generous with it; he found a joke, worked it up, exploded it and stunned hostility into admiration. His appearances in the Oxford Union outraged a majority who then voted him to be an august officer of that self-conscious institution. He was the only real whiz-kid I have met: his opinions, wit, passions, likes and dislikes, loves and hates, eyes, arms and legs, really, really whizzed. Sometimes in those days he was enraging to me when he whizzed politically, from right to too far left. When we were working most closely and hardest together he was editing a very short-lived fascist journal called *Vanguard*, and I was editing Labour's *Clarion*. By the mid-Fifties he had whizzed way over in the other direction towares Brechtian convictions, and wore khaki guerrilla jackets at parties with Princess Margaret. But why should one expect a genius of the theatre to be sound on politics? It is a muddling media habit, asking someone eminent in one field to pontificate about another. Do not ask Frank Sinatra his view on the atomic bomb: ask him to croon. Ask Ken to write about plays and performances and he would carry his pen superbly like a lance. Ask him to champion the cause of theatre and he campaigned ceaselessly for what he (and I) regarded as the most exalted of the arts.

For over a century nothing had come of earlier campaigns but in October 1963 the National Theatre finally happened. Ken as much as anybody helped to tilt British ambiguousness in favour of the concept. He once described a critic as a man who knew the way but couldn't drive the car, but this critic drove hard for the idea of a national centre of risk-taking where classical work and new plays might thrive together. The British hesitated so long for a number of reasons. There was the Puritan hangover from the seventeenth century, when acting was regarded as a form of clothed prostitution. Also, Ken argued, there was a lack of interest from our rulers, in particular from royalty. And parallel with that, a prevailing lack of trust in government action: if government could not back winners in industry, a theatre with politicians as the 'angels' backing the shows was surely going to be a loser. Who wants faceless men in power using the taxpayers' money to pay for something the punters should decide on for themselves? It was a powerful line of argument. And is. I am on the board of the Royal National Theatre now, the royal name being granted after twenty-five years of trial. With the pendulum swinging one way only these days – towards the ideology of the market-place and away from subsidizing anything, let alone play-acting – there could well be another day soon when we will wish for Ken's lance. At his best, and that is the best moment to value people, he made defeatism impossible and danger a delight to relish. In Ken's world taking risks was the proper thing to do.

We saw little of each other after Oxford. When, almost twenty years later, I was asked to be chairman of British Rail for the first time, Ken interviewed me for a television profile, and told me he thought of an actor's life as stupefying. He congratulated us both on our escape from it. Asked for a comment on me, he was reported by the *Observer* as saying, 'Peter played Hamlet as if he badly wanted to be king.'

The strange, happiest link between us, that neither of us could have known at the time of *Hamlet*, was that with our totally different lives and values, and at different times, we both wanted to marry the same girl – that very same girl sitting, way, way back in the audience on that lovely, chaotic afternoon of the dress rehearsal of *Troilus and Cressida*. She had been brought to see the preview by Frank Hauser, who was in my judgement the clearest director at Oxford in my time (he was to be my best man). Even at a distance she seemed irritatingly uninterested in the play. She just sat there, black hair shiny and drawn straight back, wearing a flared, brown cotton dress with a boat-shaped neckline, bare arms dangling a wide-brimmed straw hat with a long ribbon. She was Jill Rowe-Dutton.

That evening Frank and I had coffee at her flat with her best friend Marie Woolf, the niece of Virginia. They were both medical students at the Radcliffe hospital, and Jill had been at St Anne's for three years before that. 'Jill absolutely shattered her boyfriends,' was Marie's comment, recalled in Katherine Tynan's biography of her husband. Ken's first sight of Jill had been as compelling as mine. 'One morning, outside the Playhouse Theatre, Ken saw a tall girl with dark hair and a long equine face like a Chardin – her nose slightly upturned suggesting wistfulness rather than pertness.' Kent sent a message immediately asking her to tea – 'A presumptuous note, for no doubt he knew Jill's reputation in Oxford as a travelled sophisticate, daughter of a diplomat, considered a femme fatale, with a string of aspiring lovers. Jill, on the other hand, thought of herself as a family-orientated country girl.' Ken and Jill had had a fabled life together during 1947, engagements were announced, Ken solemnly arranging the formal document to be signed allowing her to marry as a minor. But as Jill was to tell Katherine years later, 'I felt there was nothing about the country in Ken at all, not a blade of grass.' Their love was tested to destruction

65

by a summer vacation in Donegal and soon after, both tearful and angry, Jill put an end to it. When Ken published his first book, *He That Plays the King*, it was dedicated to Jill, and the frontispiece, a picture of the bust of Nefertiti is astonishingly Jill-like, with tall neck, finely poised head, hair back, and the expression in repose sweet and daring. We came closer and closer, always without a commitment, always in a relaxed mood. She was neither in politics nor in theatre, but she was always about, glittering and good fun, always somehow with time for what Keats calls 'heart-easing things'.

In the summer of 1949 I was at the start of my last year and still being drawn deeply into theatre; the art of it forced me towards an imaginative truth I have found nowhere else. The religious nature of drama has faded from our theatre, but still it is where people can go to seek the truth of character in action in an unpredictable world. Drama is central to community life. It has been so since the earliest records of those Dionysian rituals of the ancient Greek communities: in profound thanks and in fear they symbolized the seasons, the fruits of spring, and the tragedy and comedy of the human predicament. Theatre is only natural, acting is only natural. I have never felt the art of acting to be unnatural: I am therefore I act, and that does not mean playing false. It is natural for people to act, they are doing it almost all the time. There are a very few aspects of social life when we are unconscious of others, even ourselves, and those are most intimate. But on the revolving stage of everyday there is a real sense of performance: the rituals of routines and manners, the ordinary greetings and farewells which are standardized into those low-key, dramatic forms we call habits. There are more spectacular habits, of course, the ceremonies of institutions which we perform with an elaborate self-consciousness to symbolize what it is we are up to: the pomp and procedure of the opening of Parliament; church services with gorgeous vestments; the court wigs and costumes of the law; the political showbiz of annual conferences on an operatic scale; sports rallies with bands and parades, flags and flames, and the set tableaux of posed photographs of the Star with the Cup. In the business world, there is more and more theatre and pageantry as the influence of television begins to prevail. Media experts about to make heroes of management into their own PR image, to see that the chairman knows the script word-perfect, to see that the angle of the spotlight gives a halo effect at the right time and place. Corporate advertising dramatizes the company's performance: through it the actors can write their own reviews, or rather instruct their advertising agency to act as their sophisticated pedlars of self-praise. We know precisely what we are doing: we actually talk of 'putting the act together', of the 'role' of management and the 'role' of the unions. Management styles and costumes, too, are meticulous: there is recognizable typecasting with the aid of refined status symbols of title, rooms and furniture, clothes, cars and secretaries. The symbols tinkle away and sometimes clang – it is pure theatre. But this does not mean play-acting or pretending. I have never thought of acting as pretending. It is like all other arts, a search for the truth in this character, that situation. For me, the chance to explore Shakespeare's art from inside some of his characters was a marvel, a permanently amazing experience. To take any part is to be forced to learn, willy-nilly, about oneself. In the smallest part, the Hobo, with only a few lines, I found myself walking around the inside of my head before I walked on. Of course, the glories of the great parts that came my way were well beyond my straining, untrained grasp, but what is Oxford for? I found myself entertaining the idea of a professional career.

I played Lear at the Fortune Theatre in London. Again it was a doctored version of the text: I was turning out to be a player of quack Shakespeare. This time it was the adaptation by Nahum Tate, the Restoration poet and playwright, which had been performed for about as long as the genuine article has been. When Nahum Tate edited the text in 1685, Shakespeare's play was reckoned to be unplayable. He civilized it by giving it the Hollywood treatment. He smoothed out some of the noisy infelicities: 'Blow winds and crack your cheeks' became 'Blow winds and burst your cheeks.' He introduced sex and romance: Edgar loves Cordelia. He left in the gory bits, such as the horrific blinding of Gloucester, but with one major switch of plot he ensured a happy ending. Simple really: Cordelia wins the battle and the tragic last act never happens. Edgar marries the girl, and together they ascend the throne which Lear abdicates to take himself and Gloucester off to some 'quiet green cell' and live happily ever after. That new *Lear* was accepted as the acceptable and tolerable *Lear* and it played right through the eighteenth century. That was what Garrick was doing in the well-known print (which I mimed for the publicity shots). Charles Lamb complimented Tate on his achievement well over a century later; Tate he said had 'put a ring through the nose

of the Leviathan'. Not until 1843 was Shakespeare's *Lear* resurrected
when, greatly daring, the solemn, early-Victorian star, Macready, had
a go at the real thing. Nobody thought of Nahum Tate after that –
until we put it on at the Fortune. It was generously received, but
intrigued as I had become with the part, I was even more frustrated:
this was Lear Interruptus. I remember one night near the end of the
run when, scraping off whiskers and paint after the show, I imagined
the true development of the awesome plot. I was sweating and shaking
as if with fever. It was truly fear and yet I yearned to try the real
Lear. That would finish acting for me, I thought. I enjoyed acting so
much but knew that it could not be my whole life. What would I do?

There are said to be two judgement days in one's life; one is finals
and the other is far more important. Finals, the final examination of
three years, concentrated my mind on what I really wanted to do –
return to the States to study management. I had to catch up with
myself and my original purpose. I was no longer living in college and
had taken a room in Wellington Square, very cheap and decorated
tastefully with coffee stains splashed on the walls with passion by my
predecessor. I did my poor best to buckle down to my history books,
my stepping-stones toward a visiting fellowship to an American university. The Oxford circus had every ring but the one I wanted to get into
– the industrial arena. Lord Halifax, the chancellor of the university in
those days, told me a story of his finals. As a student, he stood
commiserating with friends on the steps outside Schools, where finals
are taken. The history paper had been a stinker. But they were
confounded by one cheerful examinee who went on and on about a
brilliant answer he had written on that seventeenth-century villain,
Titus Oates. Halifax's depression deepened – but checking on the
exam paper he said, 'Steady on, there was no question asked on
Titus Oates.' 'Ah,' said his friend, totally untroubled, 'I noticed the
omission.'

There was no question on industrial affairs at Oxford. From my
college window there was a magic casement opening on to careers in
politics, state services, the arts and professions, academia. But a future
in industry was not on the cards, and though my mantelpiece was
cluttered with dozens of programme cards from different clubs, none
of them had anything to do with business or industry. I did discover
a Cambridge club which had commercial connections and it quaintly
called itself the Magnate Club. Oxford took industry for granted, or

THE FORTUNE THEATRE

(NEXT DOOR TO DRURY LANE)

Managing Director PRINCE LITTLER   Controller FREDERICK LLOYD   Licensee D. A. ABRAHAMS

July 8th & 9th and the week of July 11th
at 7 p.m.

Matinees Tuesday and Friday at 2.30 p.m.

(BOX OFFICE OPENS JULY 4th.   TELEPHONE : TEMPLE BAR 2238)

THE HISTORY OF
KING LEAR

With the Happy Ending and Romantic Sub-plot as adapted from William Shakespeare's Tragedy by

NAHUM TATE

Based on DAVID GARRICK'S production of 1742

Produced by WILLIAM PATRICK and JENNIFER RAMAGE

With PROLOGUE and EPILOGUE specially written by Mr. NEVILL COGHILL

Jillian Palmer   Micheline Patton

Michael Vowden   Charles Lepper

William Patrick   Michael Godley

Peter Parker

and

The Oxford University Players

took the effectiveness of industry for granted. Economics and politics were matters of intense research, teaching and debate but these were all in the spirit of the great Oxford School of Literae Humaniores – Lit. Hum., or Greats. There were none of the special facilities for the education of businesses which another chancellor of the university had once urged at the start of the twentieth century. He wrote a memorandum to voice his mighty concern, even in those days, that business men were saying that Oxford gave the wrong sort of training. As evidence of their criticism he pointed to 'the large financial contributions which the merchant princes are in the habit of making to the younger universities as compared to Oxford and Cambridge.' The chancellor's suggestions came to nothing, or very little. The opposition came partly from those who claimed honestly that the university was too profoundly ignorant of business to teach it, and partly from those, like the Warden of New College, who thought 'it would be a pity if too much of the brains and vigour of the country were attracted into a business career and the more important and more ennobling careers of the clergyman, the student, the man of science, the lawyer, the doctor, and even the public servant, should be neglected.' Others added that 'the wealth-amassing career of commerce or business had an ignoble and sordid taint and the University would be degraded if it undertook to direct young men into such a career.' The chancellor at the time was Lord Curzon of Kedleston, the date 1909. There was a welcome for industry as a benefactor and through the tradesmen's entrance, but it was isolated from Oxford's culture. There was an appointments office in the university which was run efficiently and provided an exit to those graduates desperate enough to have to head industry's way, but the office was an outpost. The calamitous implications for British society of this refined resistance of higher education to the needs and values of enterprise were not as obvious then as they were to become. Thanks to my previous experience in the States, I had come up with management in mind: the pursuit of management was still a mounting passion with me. But in Oxford, in those days, it was a love that dared not speak its name.

In 1950, I launched a spring offensive of applications for fellowships which would take me back to research into industry in the States. My main target was a Commonwealth Fund Fellowship, a kind of Rhodes Scholarship in reverse, awarded to applicants between twenty-five and forty-five from all over the Commonwealth and in a variety of fields.

The Fund was founded on the Harkness railway fortunes in America and its grants are now called Harkness Fellowships. The interview for it was the eeriest of my life – the only ghost story I know. I almost missed it because, the day before, I had been carted off a rugby field to the Radcliffe Hospital with an injured knee. There my leg was cased in plaster to the hip and pointed up to God. I was frantic. The next day, deviously, I slipped out of the harness and into my clothes and, dragging the leg, lurched by taxi and train to Portman Square, London. The trip was a clumsy business. With both hands I had to hold my trouser-leg to stop the weight of the plaster crushing my foot. My entry to the interview panel was bent-backed, a hobbling, ungainly mess. About six interviewers were at the table, chaired by Sir Walter Moberly with Lord Halifax on his right, the old grey face looking like canvas pitched on the top side of a thin mountain. I had checked out the names of the panel and as the talk developed I ticked them off in my mind . . . and at the end of the table there, saying nothing, looking like an unfrocked bishop, was Sir James Fitzjames Duff, Warden of Durham University. I thought I recognized the technique: it was his turn, presumably, to be the observer, not to worry about joining in the discussion but just to watch the inter-viewee's reactions. But after about half an hour Moberly went round the table for final points from everybody and then Sir James spoke: he had two questions, one was technical about the paper I had written, and we dealt with that. The other was personal: had I a brother who had been at Durham University in 1941? There was nothing at all in the documents to link me with Alan, who had been nineteen when he went to Durham on a course for six months before joining the RAF. Alan had been an athlete and had that bouncy walk: eight years later, aged twenty-seven, I had entered the room, hooped over and dragging that cursed leg. How on earth had he recognized Alan in me? I felt my mouth fall open; I needed to breathe. I failed to ask those intelligent questions I knew I was supposed to volunteer when the chairman gave me the last word. I just wanted the hell out of that room. I picked up my leg and walked as fast as I could. Next day a message reached me from Sir James. 'Sorry to ask that question, I don't know where it came from. You reacted like a man shot. I owe you a drink.' We met and were amazed together at what had happened. He said it was something in my eyes, as I was coming into the room, and he had a sudden memory of the back view of Alan bouncing off

71

to the squash courts swinging a racket. He had not known Alan very well. One young man on a short RAF course, in the teeming river of life and death that flowed through Durham during the years of war and peace over eight years ago:

> What a little thing
> To remember for years –
> To remember with tears!

James and I stayed amazed and became good friends, and years later he became godfather to my second child and first son, Alan. I was lucky with the fellowships: I collected a few. The most important was from the Commonwealth Fund, and I was told it was first ever in the industrial field of studies. The good news came in the last weeks before I left Oxford.

As a boy on a ship coming through the Suez Canal, years and years before, I had been startled by the cry of the newspaper sellers coming aboard shouting 'News of the Next World', Oxford had been a world in itself for me, brimful of chances and hopes and love and longings, so much so that it actually overflowed and ran into the next world. A theatre company was created to tour America in the summer months of 1950, with *King Lear*, this time the real *King*. I was given the role, exactly fulfilling my last ambition on the boards. The production started with Tony Richardson as director, then David William. I shake when I think about it. The tour was a harrowing success. I ended the run exhausted, roughly on my hands and knees, feeling every aching minute of Lear's three-score years and ten. We had whirled through Chicago and the Middle West to Boston, down the East Coast's summer stock theatres and into New York. The cast was powerful in its promise – Ron Eyre as the Fool, Peter Dews as Gloucester, John Schlesinger, and Robert Robinson in small roles. Shirley had been an utterly believable Cordelia. We parted at the end of a wonderful run, in the most unlikely setting of an off-Broadway theatre. Shirley went back to England with the rest of the company; she had another year to go at Oxford. I headed off to take up the industrial fellowship at Cornell and Harvard. Neither of us was aware the parting was really goodbye.

4

The Dynamics of Labour

Jill called me from New York, taking me as ever by surprise. For two months I had been working flat out at the New York State School of Industrial Relations at Cornell University in Ithaca, upper New York State. This was late autumn 1950. The American 'fall' is the better word for what happens there: the trees go down in flames of leaves in the small abysses all over that unique campus. Ebenezer Ezra, the founder, was inspired to start a university 'high above Cayuga's waters' in the words of the Cornell song: it took a lot of nerve and countless bridges, like lace-work, across the ravines. It seemed to me the perfect setting for a venture into new academic territory.

I hustled happily to lectures and seminars which took me across my own chasms of ignorance. I was into a new world of social science, law, economics and politics – all elements of management education, and of the 'human relations' approach. My fellowship was described as research on 'the Dynamics of Labour'. Unsure what that meant, I still felt the better for it, and inches taller. Then came Jill's voice, a snake-charmer's, the telephone rising and swaying:

'How is it going, Peter?'

'Fine, fine, but what are you doing?'

'I'm on an obstetrics research fellowship at this New York hospital, Brooklyn No. 1.'

'Doing what exactly?'

'Balancing a taxidynamometer on mums' tums, measuring the consumption of oxygen during childbirth. This is a Puerto Rican quarter and there are a lot of mums here.'

I was not keeping up.

'Really? Sounds complicated.'

'Certainly is, Peter, and I have to admit, I'm not too sure about it all myself. But, you know what the authorities here call it? Research on the Dynamics of Labour.'

I began to realize that there would be no escape, we were obviously fated for one another: it was a marriage made in jargon.

Over the next few months I found myself driving fast and regularly out of Ithaca, down the Catskill mountains, bright with snow and then with spring, to New York, and Brooklyn Hospital No. 1 where Jill was waiting. I moved for three months to Harvard, particularly to meet two management gurus of the time, Fritz Roethlisberger and George Homans, and to study at the Business School. The climax of the Commonwealth Fund's generosity came in the provision of a grant for each Fellow to buy a car to tour the States, and so I did, right round over six weeks: across the north to Oregon, the handsomest of states; south along the golden Pacific coast edged with tough oaks crouched against the wind, towards San Francisco and its startling self-confidence; through awesome New Mexican deserts, and into Texas, where I met Eileen, my first fiancée – she was now happily married and going Texan, thinned by the heat, rangy, drawling and smiling-slow. On to New Orleans, like 'Frisco another self-contained, self-confident city, still just about unspoilable, and then into the straight, heading for Jacksonville, Florida, to the airport to meet Jill's plane landing at midnight from New York. Two weeks, easing through the southern states, days sunlit, nights starry, and certainty growing like a bone. We wanted to marry. We went to Washington where Ernest, Jill's father, was a governor of the International Monetary Fund and of the International Bank. Remembering my attempt at acting Lear he asked what I had felt like with three daughters: he had three daughters, he explained, 'two of whom at any time are Regan and Goneril'.

1951 was proving to be a year of decisions. The second most important of these was emerging from the pursuit of my thesis, my studies in management and my particular interest in the human relations school. I decided that rather than go on fizzing with theories about work and management, I must return to gain some practical experience on the job as a manager. Two reasons compelled me homewards. I was not cast by nature to be an academic, a non-participating observer. And I was like a manager possessed. I believed in management with a new-found faith. In my year of study I had learnt that management mattered just as much as I had guessed it did, and I felt the excitement of a pioneer. By continuing my thesis on the Human Relations School, which was the latest frontier of management thinking in the States, I had stumbled onto a scene that was fraught with confusions and possibilities. To find my way through it I had first to puzzle out for myself the meaning of management.

Management is a peculiarly American word, and multipurpose. It defines a job and also those who do it. It is a field of study, a discipline, and also a power position in social and commercial structures. For the American school it seemed that any institution known to man, business or non-business, involved management. I took the only path through the semantic minefield that I had been trained to take – historical – and I was daunted and impressed by what I learnt. At a New York party I met, by chance, the leading man of Mae West's latest show, *Catherine Was Great*, played on a stage converted into an enormous bed. I asked him the sort of question that anybody would ask and he gave the perfect answer: everything you've heard is true. So it was with management. It lived up fully to my expectations.

Of course managing has been going on as long as human history; somehow the human race has managed. But with the evolution of the industrial age, the process started to receive special attention. The nineteenth century had its managerial prophets. At its opening the French economist J. B. Say gave the good word which is all the rage at the end of the twentieth: he invented the 'entrepreneur' as the man who stood between the assets and the market and was able to bring them together to make the most of them. Two other Frenchmen, Fourrier and Saint-Simon, had the vision of managing systematic structures for the productive use of resources – and Marx hated them for their romantic humanism. These utopians, as he scornfully described them, denied historical inevitability as an outcome of patterns of production. America also had its nineteenth-century spokesmen of the future: Alexander Hamilton with his *Report on Manufacturers*, Henry Clay later with his *American System*.

All those were great theorists, but for me it was two islanders who were the most prescient. Both were practical businessmen though they were a world apart, and each saw the scope of the management role in a way that was fundamentally ahead of his time and is still challenging. One was the Scottish mill-owner, Robert Owen, who saw the interdependence of prosperity and social policies, of productivity, profits and people – and the responsibilities of managerial leadership. The other was a Japanese of the Meiji period, Eiichi Shibusawa. He understood the reciprocity of enterprise and national purpose, of

FOR STARTERS

enterprise and personal values: according to Peter Drucker, who has been a managerial prophet of this century, 'Shibusawa envisioned the professional manager first.' The detailed making of a manager and of management as a distinct function was another story, an invention of the twentieth century. Yet we can still see the messages of Owen and Shibusawa writ large in the growth of the huge organizations they had only been able to guess at.

In my attempt to understand the history of management theory I divided the story into an old and a new testament. Into the old testament came genesis, the *Principles of Scientific Management*, published by an engineer, Frederick W. Taylor, in 1911. His doctrines on the pursuit of efficiency have some claim to be America's most substantial contribution to Western thought since the Declaration of Independence. His teachings had a worldwide impact, waves of management history begetting economic history, begetting social history, begetting political history, and rippling to the farthest shores. He did something nobody had done before him. He studied the organization of work, analysing and timing the man on the job.

In that same decade, others were spreading their research from the workplace to include the systematic study of organization itself. Henri Fayol, with his mining enterprise in France, and Elihu Root revolutionizing the United States Army, were structuring the performance of the individual tasks which Taylor illuminated. Germans began exploring *Betrelswissenschaft*, the science of management: Eugene Schmalenbach, Walther Rathenau, Hugo Muensterberg, German-born and working in America, were all, before the First World War, advocating the functionalizing of management, and setting it into its social context.

The old testament was mostly written before the 1920s. These are the early gospels of scientific efficiency, but some of them, such as Rathenau, were touching on the questions of the new. What is the place of the large enterprise in a modern society and in a modern nation? What impact does it have on them? And what are its fundamental contributions and responsibilities? The advent of Taylorism at the turn of the century set the standards and established the methodology of management, but by the Twenties there were clear signs of a challenge to the classic, near-tyrannical doctrines of efficiency. Taylor and his followers had done remarkably well in raising productivity by time and motion studies but, as is often the case, their

76

strength was reinforced by amputation. They cut out so many variables from their analysis: one above all, was human nature and its unpredictable and irrational tricks. Man is not a calculating machine that scientific organizers can rely on, not a cash register either, nor a standardized unit on an assembly line. Man is not that reasonable, that isolated, that reliable. Hamlet thought him a perfect piece of work, but for scientific management he is not that well designed.

The reactions to Taylorism built up slowly and inevitably, from academics who were exposing the limited logic of its approach and from workers themselves who were subject to speed-up systems. There had been some brilliantly original work done in Britain during the First World War, in which careful scrutiny of the effects of tea-breaks showed that output was improved by the interruption. The Medical Research Council investigated the significance of tea-breaks and confirmed that they improved productivity; but the implications of the research, the reciprocal effect of the researchers on the researched, both involved with each other during the process of work – all this was undeveloped. It pointed the way to a breakthrough, but in line with one of our dreariest of British traditions the research was not exploited – neither in the intellectual nor in the industrial marketplace. It was left to a team from Harvard, led by Elton Mayo in the late Twenties and early Thirties, to herald the New Beginnings, as they were called.

The work of that team, the Hawthorne experiments, produced five years' worth of reports which became the texts of what was, for me, the new testament. Originally the team was brought into the Hawthorne plant of the Western Electric Company (part of the Bell Telephone System) to advise on working conditions. What emerged was that the working conditions were important, of course, but not as important as some other influences less easy to measure. Better lighting, for instance, raised output. Then the tough-minded researchers asked what would happen if the lights were dimmed. Output kept going up. The interest of the people at work had been roused; they felt that they were participating. The work at Hawthorne Electric took years of gruelling investigations, during which twenty thousand of the forty thousand workers on site were interviewed, and on that solid foundation the Human Relations school of management thinking was founded. But the obvious needed to be proved. Social and psychological factors not only had to be taken into account, they had to be so refined and defined that they could be removed from the realm of opinion and turned into stark facts to be reckoned with by the efficiency experts of Taylorism who had ruled over-confidently and too long.

The school of Human Relations was founded on the solid work of Elton Mayo and Roethlisberger. From then on, the concepts of formal hierarchies, as set out by the organization chartists, would have to allow for the equally important concepts of informal groups, which establish themselves naturally in any structure of people at work. Organizational trees can be drawn; less visible, but vital, are the roots of the trees spreading out into the human ground in which they must live. The fragmentation of work, the atomization of incentive schemes, the classic divisions of labour, could be seen to be contrary to the sheer human need of a worker at any level, from shop-floor to boardroom. Everybody in a working community is in the business of fulfilling not only the common aims of the organization but also their own.

The pioneers of Human Relations deserved all credit for exposing the limitations of Scientific Management. They were a liberating power in the managerial world, and their work provided the most prominent thrust in the post-war period of management in America. So many of the features of any modern management today derive from their originality. So much of their influence is permanently at work in the method and vocabulary of modern management: the management of human resources, group consultation and divisions, communication, education and training, counselling – these are common demonstrations of success in enterprise. On the other hand, like many pioneers, they were unwilling to recognize the limits of their theory. To the pure spirits of Human Relations even trade unionism could be regarded as a consequence of malfunctions in the organization, and this put me on my guard. I admired the new approach – but from afar. That is why I was keen to study in the States. I went there as a pilgrim and came back a sceptic. I had convinced myself that the Human Relations school was invaluable but inadequate. The major objective of my fellowship was to test my untutored proposition that this new school was too restricted in its explanation of what made people work, or rather want to work. Had not the painstaking research at Hawthorne been suspended because of conditions of trade? That made my point. Their magnificent piece of pioneering in the study of a working community had not included the relationships of that working community and the larger community outside in which it operated and which it served. A slump in trade was the rough reminder that the life of an enterprise is not self-containable. No management is an island. The concept of the social setting of work came naturally to me: it is what a student of the Left would think.

I devoured the works of the prophets, Mayo and Roethlisberger, Chester Barnard and Herbert Simon, and all the starters of the New Beginnings. Mayo was the most daring of visionaries. I was wrong about him. He was not restricted to factory limits, even if the researchers at Hawthorne had been. His belief in the relevance of social skills knew no bounds at all – and that I found as much of a problem as the over-concentration of studies of the workers at work. Mayo's optimism seemed to stop at nothing. He strode from improved productivity to thoughts of improved civilization, social peace and universal welfare. I could only follow him so far. If the social and psychological needs of the workers were better appreciated by entrepreneurs, then, I could agree, surely society would be better off. But Mayo went on a bit: 'If our social skills (that is, our ability to secure co-operation between people) had advanced step by step with our technical skills there would not have been another European war.' Mayo obviously felt that management with a human relations policy could make the world go round. I never did.

I found myself weighing the ambiguous blessings of Human Relations. It was a definite and necessary antidote to the so-called Scientific Management. It brought common sense to bear on the economic process of organization. It was essential, vigorous, humane, stringent. But there were growing doubts which I had to face; two were widely debated even then in the early Fifties, the third was my own. The first and most cynical worry was that Human Relations could be converted into a tempting, manipulative technique for undermining the spread of the unions. The Wagner Act of the Thirties, which established a new legal framework for industrial relations in the US, had protected the unions: they were there to stay, so 'a humanized management' was a way round their new legitimacy. The trade unions were already referring to a human relations policy as 'moo-cow-sociology', and there was no doubt some truth in this criticism: the adjustment of 'malfunctions in the organization which produces unions' was a tempting line of initiative. Aldous Huxley had written another introduction to his *Brave New World* in which he admitted that he had made an error: to subjugate people, there was no need to cow them or drug them – just keep them happy. But this cynical line of attack was not conclusive in my mind: after all, a good idea can be used or abused. The Left might criticize management with a human face as camouflaged capitalism, but if the outcome was that people at work were in fact going to be treated more like citizens that, for me, was progress, and better than management with the face of a stopwatch.

The second seam of doubt, however, began to bother me. Human Relations put its emphasis on understanding, not doing. It seemed, in all its humanity, not to admit the awkward reality of command and action, time and surprises, and the tempests that blow away the best laid plans – like the slump that halted the Hawthorne research in its tracks. Managers cannot for ever passively chew the cud of consultation while precious time goes by and decisions have to be taken. So it could not be a matter of either Scientific Management or Human Relations: it must be both. Decisions are the steps, but commitment is the dance, and there is abundant research to prove that decisions are more effective if people who fulfil them have had a share in taking them. Or feel they have.

My third and most important set of doubts rooted back to the questions that I had brought with me to the States in the first place: surely the divisions in the working community could be traced through to the splits in our industrial society. To understand the working situation I felt I had to explore the no man's land between industry and the community. It seemed to me too much to expect from any management, however 'human', that it could cope with a range of issues beyond it. So much was out of its control, and crucial: the worker's education, the health of the family, housing, the environment, all these were matters of social policy and were decisive. And was government to be the sole trustee of these priorities? What was the social responsibility of enterprise? I was stuck with that question – for life.

Just at the right moment of doubt I found the right woman, Mary Parker Follett. She was one of the earliest of the bold standard-bearers in new management thinking. This bony, plain Bostonian, who had died in 1932, had for me the most persuasive vision of them all. She transformed the ideas of management into human proportion and into terms of community. Mayo made me uncomfortable, he strove to be universal; she was earthy. He moved grandiosely from the particular to the general; she came from the general to the particular. That was the pattern of her career. When she was still a young woman in the States, her books on government, on grass-root democracy, and on education had put her reputation high in academic and national affairs. During the First World War she became involved in wage arbitration, and the judging and nudging of bargaining rituals fascinated her: 'each side hoping to win by keeping the whole problem hazy'. She found she enjoyed the vitality of businessmen. 'I have been asked several times why I am studying management,' she wrote. 'First of all, it is among businessmen (not all, but a few) that I find the greatest vitality of thinking today, and I like to do my thinking where it is most alive. Another reason is because industry is the most important field of human activity, and management is the fundamental element in industry.' This prophetic woman was speaking my mind the year I was born. In 1924 she published her *Dynamic Administration*. There it all was for me, the united analysis of work and social organization. Mary Parker Follett denied the old classic lines of responsibility drawn between those who manage and those who are managed: 'strand should weave with strand and then we shall not have the clumsy task of trying to patch together finished webs.' It follows that no individual function is an island in enterprise. Leadership has power, that is 'simply the ability to make things happen, to be a causal agent, to initiate change'. Authority is 'vested power'. Naturally there will be conflicts; conflicts are normal and constructive in any organization. But their resolution best derives not from the domination of a boss, although sometimes there can be no other way, nor from the compromise that changes too little: resolution should come from both sides following the logic of the situation towards something new for both sides, a gain for both. I have tried to live by that. Whoever was the father of modern management, I have no doubt about who was the mother. Frederick Taylor died with a stopwatch in his hand: she should have been holding a compass when she died, in Britain. Studying her, I have felt steadied on my course. I decided to go back to Britain and learn management from the inside.

Jill and I sailed back on the *Queen Mary* and our ship came in just as Attlee called the General Election of 1951. I rang the local Labour candidate for Bedford, my home town, to find that she had been rushed to hospital for an operation – would I stand in her stead? Naturally, yes. My plan had been to find a job, marry Jill, enter politics when I had managerial experience to offer and the wherewithal to be my own man. Life as usual came the other way round. The political tide was changing. Bedford had signalled a swing in the 1950 election when Labour lost to Christopher Soames, Churchill's son-in-law. The post-war Labour leadership was weary and worn out with office. Every time I stood on the platform I could feel the sands of its time running out between my toes. But I was furiously proud of the Labour government. It had laid the foundations of the welfare state, which with all its faults was to make Britain a fairer and happier place for the vast majority. Also it had not just talked about the rights of man, but had done the magnificently decent thing, unprecedented in history: Britain was dissolving its empire and giving back to people the right to make or muddle their own destiny. Of course, not every-body was agreed then. One night I spoke about the independence of India. The platform was stormed and the microphone ripped away from me: the general idea of the opposition was that I should go jump in the nearby river. Then, as abruptly as it flared, the violence evaporated and there was cheering and laughter with the booing and jeering. I discovered that I enjoyed campaigning.

And there was nothing really vicious in the electoral battle. I felt, and I think most people felt that, whatever our differences, we were all ridding ourselves of the burden of the past. We were in a fighting mood not because of the past but because of the possibilities of the future. The fierce experience of unity in the war still held me and many others in its spell. In the cursed period of the Twenties and Thirties, with its misery and poverty, politicians had said it couldn't be helped. Well, we thought it could be helped, if we would help ourselves, as we had done when the enemy was more obvious than inequality of opportunity, loneliness and suffering, racial absurdities and injustice. An old Labour voter attacked me after one session: he accused me of being too ignorant of the realities of the pre-war unemployment. 'Those times made me a thief,' he said. 'I stole milk off doorsteps in your district.' In one of Shaw's letters there is a sentence which describes the condition of my mind then: 'To me living in a world of poor and unhappy people is like living in hell.' That was true for many in that post-war phase, and it was not a romantic aberration. I take it that the capacity to admit a sense of

1 Tom Parker, 1943

2 Dorothy Parker, 1937

3 The Parker boys in France: *(right to left)* Tom (Mickey), Alan and Peter (aged four)

4 *Above* The Shanghai *Bund* in 1938, a skyline almost unchanged fifty years later

5 *Left* Peter (aged eleven) on the flat roof of the Shanghai house with his father's gun, just before the outbreak of the Sino-Japanese War

6 Learning Japanese in 1942: the London Orient XV. In the front row are Peter Parker *(centre)*, Peter Bates, a future chief of Plessey Electronics *(third left)*, the future Sir Dermot de Trafford, industrialist *(second left)*, Pat O'Neill, future head of Japanese Studies at the School of Oriental and African Studies *(far left)* and in the back row *(far left)* is Ted Youde, future Governor of Hong Kong

7 Peter's brother Tom *(standing)*, 1939, in the Royal Air Force. Killed in 1940

8 Peter in 1939 with mother Dorothy and brother Alan *(right)*, killed in 1944

9 *Below* Dorothy Parker and Eileen, then Peter's fiancée, in 1943

10 William Blake: Peter Parker's first sight of his art was at the Chicago Art Gallery in 1946

11 *Below* Peter Parker's identity card

12 *Below* Washington, with Sarah, wife of Otto Graf. The Grafs opened the young Peter Parker's heart and mind to the American scene

13 Professor Otto Graf at Michigan State University

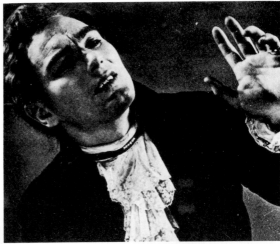

14 *Above left* Ken Tynan, as Second Player in Oxford University's 1948 production of *Hamlet*, which he directed

15 *Above* Peter Parker in the title role of Hamlet

16 *Left* Peter Parker as Lear with Ronald Eyre as the Fool, on American tour in 1950

17 Shirley, a perfect Cordelia

18 The Oxford University Players in *Hamlet*. Among the cast are Peter Parker *(centre)*, Ken Tynan as the Ghost *(in the niche)*, Robert Hardy as Player King *(standing, far right)* and Lindsay Anderson as Horatio *(sitting, right)*

19   Jill Rowe-Dutton, 1950, in New York

20   *Below* Jill on her wedding day, 15 December 1951, with her father, Sir Ernest Rowe-Dutton (Robert Hardy in the background)

VOTE FOR

PETER PARKER
THE LABOUR CANDIDATE
OCTOBER 25th 1951

Published by G. W. Baker, 34 Alexandra Road, Bedford, and printed by Stonebridges, 4 Midland Road, Bedford

21 and 22   Electioneering in
Bedford, Peter Parker's home town

23   Jill and Peter Parke[r] with their children, *(left [to] right)* Alan, Lucy, baby Nathaniel and Oliver

24   *Below left* Dorothy with a firm hand on grandson Alan

25   *Above right* Tom with his gift of a bicycle to grand-daughter Lucy

26   The new Parker boys: Nat, Al and Ol

moral obligation for others is to be reckoned as part of the normal human disposition, as real as and at least equal to its competitive instinct. Without it the human race's chance of survival would be wretchedly slim. The Labour Party which we fought for then had made its act of faith: it built on the assumption of that moral potentiality in each individual in his community. That was the bet we made. A generation on, Thatcherites are betting more on the individual, not, as we did, more on society, to promote the individual. It is ironic that the personal dignity of the individual as a citizen, once the battle-cry of the Left, is now that of a triumphant right.

The first weekend of the three weeks' election campaign was spent cleaning out the Labour Party headquarters – literally washing it down and painting it up. Labour's organization was abysmal: there was a part-time, underpaid officer who was untrained and not at all well. Bedford was a rambling constituency covering the town and the rural suburbs. I was scheduled to be in two or even three places at once. Jill, innocent of politics, brought up as a strict civil servant's daughter, was occasionally drummed into service to cover for me. 'Just talk about what you know about,' my faithful followers advised her, 'about babies and orange juice, that sort of thing'. And she would then find herself facing an audience of square-shaped farmers, sitting impassively, hands clenched on their sticks and chins galore squashed on their hands, just waiting for Jill's baby-talk to dry up so they could ask grumpily, 'What about the price of pigs, then?' Jill used to plead with the cheerful supporters who escorted her from pubs to clubs not to unnerve her with their loud 'hear, hears!'

Elections force a candidate to make speeches all day and well into the night: the main aim, it seemed to me, was to poll one's strength, not to convert votes. The halls were packed with my supporters and enlivened by the trained hecklers who followed me around, but after the first week it was noticeable that while most meetings were welcoming, some were surging with enthusiasm. I sensed the surges the moment I entered: I had only to ride the wave and I would be carried home and dry. I checked to see who had preceded me at each venue and discovered that each of those sensational meetings had been warmed up by the same speaker. I asked to meet him, to thank him. He was the unprepossessing caretaker of a Bedford dancehall, a stubby, limping man, his shoulders tilted oddly, and he had an angular humour to go with his shape. He said it was easy for him, he'd been coached to speak by a master, Oswald Mosley, whom he had followed for a short while when Mosley broke from Labour to form his own party. I invited him to join me at all my big meetings and on the Eve of Poll, to speak first. The technique was startlingly effective. His Goebbels-like lack of attraction vanished as he leaned towards the audience, and drew it to him with challenges. Why are you here? Because you want to whatever-it-was. Isn't that it? He screwed up the tension with silences. Well, isn't it? Gradually the responses would come and grow into a chorus. And then he would turn the enthusiasm towards me as candidate. That's what he's fighting for. Isn't it? Yes, and he'll fight and fight and fight again. Hugh Gaitskell came up to speak for me, and heard him. I always have wondered if the oratorical rhythm echoed in his mind: he certainly used the incantation to famous effect in the Labour Party's debate on nuclear power in the mid-Fifties. The events of the election were to put me in touch with the Labour Party leadership and organization; for the next two decades and more I was a member of the Labour Parliamentary Association.

The agenda of the 1951 election was noisy and forgettable: at my level it was mostly peanuts, vermin and petroleum. The disastrous Groundnuts Scheme in West Africa was a heckling nag the whole time. Vermin was what Nye Bevan had called the Tories, and this lack of taste upset a lot of the voters in fur coats. Petroleum was the most substantial issue perhaps, and the nationalization of the Iraq Petroleum Company by the Prime Minister, Moussadeq, who had tormented the few months of Herbert Morrison's tenure as Foreign Secretary. Morrison could do nothing about it. It was a nasty moment of British history, when the British were forced to see through themselves to the fact that they were no longer a great imperial power. The heckling teams taunted us with comparisons between Morrison and Anthony Eden. Labour had been outclassed by world events, that was their line, and if only Eden had been there everything in the Middle Eastern garden would have been lovely. Wasn't Eden the man to sort out the Middle East? Within five years, Suez gave an answer to that in another nasty moment of self-realization. But mostly in 1951 it was domestic issues that dominated the outcome. The electorate was generally fed up with its wartime regime and Labour was seen to be the party of boring rationing and planning regulations. Their continued existence infuriated a people who had fought nobly, had come through the siege of the immediate post-war reconstruction, and as I had heard regularly on the doorsteps, were now buggered if they knew who had won the war.

When the count came, it ran a closer finish than we had a right to expect. Bedford was one of the very few constituencies where the Labour vote rose. But on the day of reckoning, at the count in the town hall, there was old-fashioned good temper between the three candidates. Mary Soames sat with her knitting, her knitted hat, her calm and charm; she really won it for her husband Christopher. He was a good deal more anxious and uncomfortable, still newish to politics and some way from the powerful reputation he was later to win in a wide range of offices of state. Indeed he was nervously called Captain Soames in the party propaganda prepared, I imagined, when the Labour candidate had been a woman and before I had come on to the scene. The Liberal, an ambiable schoolmaster, strolled with me around the tables busy with the vote boxes. If he had known, he said, that Labour in Bedford had a real chance he would have asked his followers at his Eve of Poll rally to vote for me – perhaps shades of the Alliance were even then closing round the growing boy? In fact, at the end of the day, Labour lost by less than the total Liberal vote. A friend from the Blue Mist neighbourhood of my home, the very same thoughtful friend who had slipped me snacks on the deck of the troopship going to India, appeared from the crowd at the announcement of results. 'Why didn't you stand as a Conservative? We'd have got you in all right.' And as he said this he was tapping me on the chest as if I were a barometer and my needle was stuck.

Our marriage was a few weeks later, on 15 December 1951, at the Queen Anne church on Kew Green, with the reception also on the edge of the green, at the exquisite Queen Anne house, No. 22, where the Rowe-Dutton family lived. It was a fine day and full of friends. I remember the shock of seeing the Other Family's friends for the first time: the Rowe-Duttons' network linked politics, the City, Whitehall, Fleet Street, Eugene Black, the President of the World Bank, was there, and so was Louis MacNeice. Parkers' friends were from Oxford, Bedford neighbours and the Bedford Labour Party. Jill's wedding dress was ravishing, made up from pale lilac brocade and the entire Rowe-Dutton family clothes rationing books. We honeymooned in Brighton, which was empty and beautiful and cheap.

The snag was that I was broke and still out of work. I had studied work but now badly wanted some of my own. No. 22 Kew Green became my base for the frustrating job hunt. My track record read pretty unconvincingly to potential employers: a failed Labour candidate and an aspiring manager with a business education from another world. Something rum here. One night I was desperate, juddering back to base on the No. 27 bus. I had been rejected on two applications in one day, and one was a job I had particularly wanted – manual work on the night shift at the Firestone tyre factory on Westway. It would have paid well and left me with plenty of time to search for better prospects during daylight. No luck, I think that they suspected me of being a journalist infiltrating for a story. When the bus stopped at Kew Green near No. 22, it was the end of its run, and I felt a bit like that myself, at the end of the line. I had my forehead pressed against the steel rim of the empty seat in front. I had thought the bus totally empty at the last stop, and I saw no harm in cooling my brow, but as I looked up to go I saw Ernest, Jill's father, getting off ahead of me. I knew he must have seen the back of my head, and reckoned I was either at prayer or in a poor way. It was a low moment. When I got in he said nothing about it, but the wonderful man did have a very large whisky waiting for me.

The high moment came a week later at Victoria tube station. I was depressed and down to basics, and I did the simplest thing. I looked up 'industry' in the telephone directory in a kiosk, and trawling through, I came across the name of the Industrial Welfare Society, 48 Bryanston Square. I took the chance and rang, and asked to speak to somebody in charge. I was put through to John Marsh, the director. He suggested I go round and see him; Bryanston Square was not far. I did and he rescued me.

John Marsh was an original, a man of spirit and more good ideas than he had time to deal with. He had been a Japanese prisoner of war on the infamous railway; his survival astonished and inspired him for the rest of his life. He was permanently urgent, hustling and bustling with things, people, ideas, as he was to prove in his leadership of the Institute of Personnel Management and of the Industrial Society, and later as Director-General of the British Institute of Management. He was always starting something. That day he started me off in industry by putting me in touch with Philips, the Dutch-based electrical group which was one of the great international companies of the world, and as an international, untroubled by my little local difficulty as a Labour man. It was easily able to make sense of my confusing record. I was to work two years for them before John Marsh came into my life once more. Those years were to give me my industrial bearings, and I was to enjoy the nearest thing to routine that I have ever known.

But first we had to find somewhere to live. Ernest had retired from his directorships of the World Bank and the International Monetary Fund, and in January 1952 sold No. 22 (for £6000: it came on the market in 1988 for more than half a million) to buy a house in County Wicklow in Ireland. Jill and I started looking for rooms. We hired a handcart, loaded on to it a tea chest of books, odds and ends, and the large white suitcase which Jill had been given for her honeymoon, and pushed it down the King's Road, looking at adverts offering accommodation. It grew late and we were still trundling about when an address in Walpole Road gave us hope. The landlady, huge and wholly knitted, had drawn the curtains in the funereal living-room in which she interviewed us. She warned us that there was 'an umbargo' on guests, and as she intoned her taboos, bits of the room seemed to be flying apart – there were several cats, leaping and prowling in the dimness. But we had to settle. As she let us out to collect our bits and pieces under canvas on the hand-cart, the light through her front door lit up the hall and revealed a drawing of a ravishing, thin woman with swooping Marlene Dietrich eyelids. 'That's an Augustus John,' the lugubrious lady said, 'of me.' We had to pay a week in advance but we made off after two 'umbargoed' nights. We found a studio flat off the Fulham Road, one large single room with a large single bed and pipes coiled weirdly around the place, a sort of third-floor basement.

In the spring of 1952 Jill had become the first woman medical officer at Unilever House, with a salary twice mine. Her decision to do this was an act of marital generosity because about all that really interested her in the work was that it meant regular hours for us. Now both of us were on a routine. I would set out at sixish in the morning to catch a bus to Victoria and the bus ride made or unmade the daybreak. It was a lesson in the power of personality. The magic difference was entirely in the character of the bus conductor: a lively character could transform the passengers into the semblance of a dawn outing; a grim one turned us all into doomed travellers in a tumbril. (Years and years later in BR, a Travellers Fare steward of the Western line was on the Queen's Honours List, and every passenger who knew him and had been served by him knew why he had the MBE. They were delighted at the celebration of his style: one of them said to me it was the best thing I had ever done on the rails.) From Victoria to Mitcham in Surrey I became a counter-commuter, riding against the floodtide coming into town: my train was caught by only a few hungry people, jockeys heading for Epsom and myself.

I worked in the personnel department of the Mitcham and Mullard works, which formed a complex of four thousand people, a community the size of a largish village, without a village green. Mullard produced electronic valves, while at the Mitcham works complete radios and television sets poured off the fearsome mass-assembly belts that made visitors flinch at the sight of them. The personnel offices were set apart, symbolically perhaps – personnel is a staff not a line function – but our responsibilities took us into the interstices of the village life, into every aspect of operations: recruitment and training, records and statistics, health and safety, welfare, pay and productivity, involving incentive schemes and bargaining, communications and consideration. This was a passport to every department. At last I was learning something about industry that was not in a book.

On the first few days of my orientation, I was taken by a seasoned supervisor around the mass-assembly plant and taught a lesson. He gave me the view from an overhead walkway, looking down on the assembly lines, long centipedes with human arms for legs. He had sized me up as a young man needing a good talking-to about the dangerous lack of discipline 'down there'. As Personnel I would see, and probably become part of, the processes that rotted the power of the foreman. Consultation and staff experts were to blame. Sounding like Charles II in exile, he lamented, 'But some day we'll come back into our own again.' In simpler, earlier times he had been the gaffer. Now consultation committees with unions, the experts in time and motion studies, the personnel officers counselling on the personal problems of 'his people', the planners – the bloody lot of them had sapped the strength of his line command. He had been the boss, the foreman: the word had originally depicted the bowman to the fore of the other bowmen. That had stood for something. Now nobody knew where he stood. And that was the truth of the situation. I agreed with that, and still do: a history of our decline as an industrially effective nation could well be called the Decline and Fall of the Foreman. Modern management has to see that supervision is the flashpoint of successful management. The supervisor, he or she, is the spark that must cross the gap from management to action on the shop floor.

Lesson Two was related to this story: on industrial democracy. I was naturally hot for certainty in matters of joint consultation with the unions, and I attended the committees which were pyramided from departments to the top of the organization where the convenors of the shop stewards and the managerial chiefs would meet regularly. There were plenty of arguments at these encounters, but there was also a distinct chumminess, a cosiness and a chattiness about test scores and holidays, a swapping of Christian names. I saw the top management drawing closer to the union leaders than to some of their middle and junior managers. At this genial forum – only advisory, of course, not executive – the communication at summit level was direct and convincing. It was the reporting back to the constituent parts on both sides that so often failed. Supervisors would hear the news from their shop stewards, about business results or even about the dates of the holiday shut-down. At the other end of the consultative procedures, I sensed numb indifference. Union members were not switched on either, their leaders were often out of touch. In our rather complicated system of representation one of my duties was to collect the votes for the election of representatives, and I would hump the cardboard ballot-boxes around the shop floor. Nobody was particularly glad to see me or to be bothered. 'I work here, for Christ's sake, do I have to get more involved?' The keenness to participate was crushingly low. If industrial democracy was to mean anything, it had to be more than committee life. The trade union representatives on joint consultation were not properly trained to represent, nor to appreciate the economic facts of life or death in enterprise. The trade unions themselves saw their role as protecting their members' interests by improving pay and conditions: efficiency and profitability were not their business. I had come light years away from the New York State School of Industrial Relations at Cornell where I had studied business management alongside American trade unionists of my own age ready to grapple with the realities of competition.

So to Lesson Three: communications. There had always to be more, up and down an organization in and out, sideways, round about – don't stop. The personnel department under John Ross (father of Nick Ross of television fame) believed that. We started orientation courses for all new recruits with tours around the works, and we found people who had been years in a department and never been to the one next door. We also promoted education and training schemes designed for all levels of the community. Philips encouraged us to innovate. For instance, I remember taking an expedition of apprentices to the Royal Academy where they could enjoy comparing notes with Leonardo da Vinci: there was an exhibition of his drawings which included his miraculous and meticulous technical inventions. (What would that genius have done if he had had computers?) Another example was the plant journal I was able to start, *Ariel*, written and roneo-ed and sold by volunteers. It was a new angle for me on many things. The rough, tough convenor of the engineering unions turned out to be a gentle champion, a breeder of canaries.

Informal contacts in the working community proved to matter as much as the formal. Communication in industry at one level is simply technique; publications, word of mouth messages, consultative procedures all play a part in it. But without trust in the relationships these add up to little. In turn, trust depends on having a sense of how people think and feel. Once upon a time, a poster was displayed in the engineering shop showing the annual results of the enterprise. The various items were symbolized conventionally: there was the cake and one large slice was for investment, another fat one for pay, and a criminally small slice for dividend. But it seemed that the workers didn't eat cake, so next year the results were shown in glasses of beer: foaming tankards for the amounts of investment and of pay, a thin sliver of amber at the bottom of the glass showing the relative amount of dividend. The shop steward took off his coat and made for the door of the machine shop. The foreman shouted, 'Where d'ya think you're going?' 'I'm off to buy the poor governor a drink!'

A communication policy without trust as its premise is not credible. Fortunately, the personnel department was conducting motivation research directed by a remarkable man, Hubert Somervell. Hubert was wealthy and wise, sad and funny, a businessman and an artist: he loved music and painting. Born in the industrial purple, he had lived in the family shoe business as a young man and became the managing director of it in his late twenties. He chucked it all after a few years, passing it over to his twin brother while he was ordained into the Church of England. Then his sense of vocation slipped again. He threw up his life as a priest and gave himself to industry. He wrote a remarkable book, *Industrial Peace in Our Time*, and worked with the

National Institute of Industrial Psychology; their two important studies on joint consultation and the role of the supervisor owed much to him. Among Hubert's many delightful virtues was his adoration of Jill and her love of music; Jill was an oboist, and the only regret of those years was that when we felt particularly broke, after the first baby, Jill decided to sell the oboe. Hubert became godfather to Lucy, and something of a godfather to me. He helped me hold to the vision of a working community as intimately interdependent, a social unit whose purpose is to serve the community through its prosperity.

That appears high-flown and abstract, but I was not in the business of theory, there was really no time for that. We were engaged in a highly practical enterprise, and one major project in Philips during my second year there was the introduction of a form of work study. This was becoming all the rage at that time, replacing time and motion study. Its exponents, the new evangelists of efficiency, based the system on standard timings of movements, the fractions of a second it took to grasp a screw, say, lift it, insert it, release it. I did some of the timing tests myself and wondered how is it that we refine the worker's life into minute proportions and motivate by the minute – and still expect behaviour to be in terms of the year's results and long-range strategies.

Lesson Four: the banality of mass-production work. Next to my small glass-windowed office was that of old Doctor Fuchs, an Austrian who had been blinded in the First World War. A prisoner of war, he stayed in Britain, and developed a reputation for training blind operatives. In a smart white coat, he tapped his way about the works with an awe-inspiring confidence, jerking his arms away from any cautionary hand. I was fascinated by his success in preparing blind and disabled operators for the demands of life on the moving belts of the assembly line. He told me that to do some automated work, it can be much better with one sense less, more efficient and more tolerable. Actually the women sitting at one of those 'bloody great wheels', testing valves, putting on one unit with the right hand and removing another with the left, told me that they 'never thought about it much', and 'it never bothered them much', but there is not much comfort in that really. Human nature is just too infinitely adaptable. In industry we tend to get used to our 'mind forg'd manacles'. Therefore, let us pray: 'O Automation, in abundance bring forth thy robotic blessings and quickly, quickly exterminate, exterminate such drudgery and slavery of the spirit.'

I was, and am still, impressed by Philips. The corporation was profit-minded and open-minded; it was not clumsy; it was still able to think small, 'in particulars'. Indeed, one of the basic principles of Philips then was evident in the vast parent plant at Eindhoven in Holland. The working population of over 20,000 was as far as possible organized into small groups where people could know and trust each other. As a starter, I was privileged to be witness to the imaginative intelligence of Philips at work. Their actions were my hopes as a young man. I owe them much.

I left them in autumn 1953 when John Marsh came back into my life. He called to tell me that HRH the Duke of Edinburgh had just agreed to preside over a conference on the problems of industry as they affect the individual and his community: could I help? I really did feel called – vastly out of my depth, but called.

John brought me into the Industrial Welfare Society (now simply the Industrial Society) as head of its Overseas Department. Despite the old-fashioned, cracked ring to its former name, the IWS was one of the most advanced institutions in the country in the field of organizational and particularly personnel practices. Its membership included most of the leading companies and was spread throughout the country. It provided a touchstone for good ideas and practices, a platform for conferences, an education and training service, and practical consultancy on everything from canteens to corporate philosophy. The post-war growth of the international companies, coming to and spreading from Britain, had opened up a new market for the IWS's energies and experience, hence the Overseas Department.

When I arrived, the department was embryonic, tadpole-shaped, all head and no body. But it was to be the ideal base for me, not only for the work itself but for the equally embryonic Duke of Edinburgh's Conference. The IWS had a non-partisan stance, and the drive and courage to inculcate new thinking. The society had been started in 1918 by the energetic Reverend Robert Hyde. I met him only as a benign and silvery old man, but in his prime he had been a crusader and a radical. I suspect that, like the Reverend Sidney Smith a century before him, he would have preferred Five Articles and Thirty-Nine Muses rather than the other way round. His advice to employers was that a fitter, happier worker is a harder worker. Welfare was a crusading slogan in his time. The society was instituted to provide a centre of exchange of good practice, and he took a practical line whatever the problem. Graffiti? Provide a notepad to hang in the lavatory and save the walls from the scribbling.

One of his suggestions to the IWS's patron, the young Duke of York, later to be George VI, was to hold annual camps for industrial apprentices and young people from all walks of life, and these had been a popular feature in the Thirties. When George VI died in 1952, Prince Philip was invited to take over as patron of the IWS and his reply, in crisp monosyllabic naval style, was yes but what could he do that was of use? John Marsh, who had succeeded Robert Hyde as director, elaborated on the idea of the camps in Britain and suggested that Prince Philip hold a conference of young people of the Commonwealth and Empire. Walter Monckton, the Minister of Employment at the time nodded Homerically. It seems most unlikely that he had thought about it deeply or about the complications. It transpired, too late, that a conference was being agreed without anybody being at all clear what it was to be about. The bandwagon began to roll too fast, and the press were on to it. On the day of John's call to me, there was an editorial in the *Evening News*. Prince Philip was committed publicly. Yet the precise aim, programme, membership, funding and organization were still dangerously undefined. I was set to work drafting a programme, feeling like the boy on the burning deck, with flaring tempers and tensions crackling round us.

To the left and right, there was trouble. The Trades Union Congress leadership was aghast at what they suspected was the unprecedented intervention of royalty into the minefield of negotiations. Arthur Deakin, the leader of the Transport and General Workers' Union, was the most upset. He had the only face I have known that could roar without the mouth opening. The mildest, quotable part of his description of the conference proposal was that it would be the greatest tragedy in the history of industrial relations in this country. Some of the employees in the Federation of British Industry, the CBI of its day, were more moderate but no less devastating, and this was made imperfectly clear at a meeting in Buckingham Palace in July 1956. I had entitled the draft programme 'The Social Responsibility of Industry' and that was a mistake to start with. It was suspect; I was suspect. In a critical profile of me in the *Evening Standard* I was labelled as a leftie adviser to royalty. This managed both to exaggerate my role and emphasize my sinister radicalism; fortunately it rather defeated its own intention by quoting what I reckoned to be the most bland, Ramsay MacDonald-like chunks of my speeches, full of on-and-on and up-and-up, hardly the stuff of the barricades.

On the big day at the Palace, the meeting itself opened with the FBI president reading a prepared statement, concentrating a barrage of pompous platitudes on the title. Were not the implications critical of industry? And that word social: that sounded socialistic. The pin-drop silence was broken by a brilliant stroke of chairmanship by Prince Philip. He was sitting at the centre of the table. His equerry, Michael Parker, and I were behind him and we could see him stiffen. This was his first formal, and formidable, encounter with the industrial establishment and all was not going well. But he kept a relaxed tone, looked down the long thin table at the speaker and apologized, 'I am sorry I must have missed something, I couldn't altogether follow that.' Then the *coup de grâce*. 'Do you mind saying it again?' The next time round, the case did not sound good at all. But it was not logic that we had to counter: it was not what was being said but who was saying it. Philip had won the point but if the FBI were not happy the title still had to be changed. By the finish of the session, however, everyone there had become aware of the grip HRH was taking on a big, new venture, and also the grip the idea of the conference was taking on him. He wanted to do this. The day would have been lost without that conviction. And that day's victory was to be a lifelong interest of his and a boon to the rising generation of Commonwealth leadership all over the world.

Not that anybody would have guessed all that at the end of the meeting when the arrangements for a press release came to be debated. We had prepared two, one for failure, one optimistic. The first announced tersely that there had been a gathering of industrialists and trade unionists at Buckingham Palace, nothing more, omitting even a reference to Prince Philip being in the chair. The other went into confident detail about the proposal for a conference, stated that Prince Philip had taken the chair of the meeting, and confirmed the authority of the occasion by listing the chieftains from all sides who had attended. Across the table to us sat the great shopkeeper, Sir Simon Marks. So far he had not spoken, but when the shorter state-ment was beginning to find favour, it was too much for him. He spoke straight to the chair: 'We can't leave out your name from whatever we say – that would be taking the guts out of it . . . ' and he paused, seemingly surprised at his own vehemence in the royal circumstances. He looked around the scarlet and gold decor and, picking his way too carefully, went on, 'It would be like playing Hamlet without the Prince.' More stillness. Prince Philip chuckled, 'A lot of people prefer Hamlet without the Prince, you know – a very unstable fellow anyway.' In the relief of laughter all round, we agreed the longer statement. It was obvious that Philip had started something.

The relief in my own mind at that moment was that the outline programme had come through the ordeal unscathed. The title had to change but not the content. In fact the tensions on all sides had strengthened the logic of the conference's scope. One piece of common ground that was shared by all, royalty, employers, unions, was that the conference would not deal with matters that came within the normal scope of collective bargaining. Therefore, we were forced to find a theme that could provide the neutrality that would allow HRH to take part. The 'No Trespassing' sign on the well-ploughed field of industrial relations meant that we could only go where I really wanted to go, up to the fresh high ground of management which so much needed to be thoroughly mapped. This was what had been my major study in the States: the relationship of industry and the community. Neutrality was to be found in the domain of the unexplored. Here royalty would not be in danger of interfering; here being neutral would be positively useful; here we would talk not of bargaining relations but of human relations – and on challenging scales.

The agenda would have to cover those factors that make for efficiency, satisfaction and understanding both inside industrial organizations and in the everyday relations between industry and the community around it. We were being driven towards the central question of industrial societies which had not been asked before: how to reconcile the imperatives of industrial and technological developments with the needs of the individual and the community? Industry and social life interact at every point: it follows they can only be studied intelligently as a whole. Answers to questions of industrial peace and efficiency are not to be found within the four walls of a factory, nor can the community be immune from the effects of industrialization. Well beyond the negotiating table, this was the challenge of change which was embracing the communities of Commonwealth and Empire in every stage of economic development. So 'Social Responsibility' gave way in the title and we came to a less catchy twenty-one words, 'His Royal Highness the Duke of Edinburgh's Study Conferences on the Human Problems of Industrial Communities within the Commonwealth and Empire'. But the same challenge held firm. Bernard Shaw used to send a hundred titles when he was going to speak: 'Choose any title, the talk is the same.'

Once over that perilous wobble of will at the first meeting, there was no weakening in any quarter. A council was formed from those attending, and a chairman of council appeared, Sir Harold Hartley, seventy-four years of age, moving very slowly because of an injury in the First World War, but still the fastest mind on the scene and acting with Prince Philip's full confidence. They had come to know each other when Harold had been the president of the British Association and handed the presidency over to Prince Philip. Their friendship saved our conference. Harold himself turned out to be the prince of fixers. He interviewed me over luncheon at the Travellers, his club in Pall Mall, and he had the high old style of the Edwardian age, courteous, careful, deadly in attack. His great age amused him. Did I realize his father, as a child, had met Lord Brougham who had said to him, 'Remember, you've met a man who had a nanny who knew someone who had been at the execution of Charles I in 1649'? I hung in there, wondering how on earth the conversation would link into any current interest. He went on about his time in Oxford: he had got a First in chemistry and a fellowship at Balliol College in 1900. My Second in history did not impress him at all; he brushed it away but cheered up visibly with the mention of my Commonwealth Fund Fellowship. The came the First World War, in which I later learned he had won a Military Cross. All he told me about was working in the Chemical Warfare Department, 'spoiling war as a sport' as he grimly put it, and incidentally blowing himself up and damaging his legs. Between wars, one of his achievements was to be made vice-chairman of the London, Midland and Scottish Railway where he developed and directed research policies and built the foundation of the world-renowned BR centre of railways technology at Derby, a monument to his far-sightedness.

Gradually he was steering the talk to the contents of my draft programme, and to the industrial concerns which had sprung naturally from his career. Above all he was concerned that there were limits to the earth and that society should cherish our natural resources. One aspect of the social responsibility of industry was surely to act from a disciplined respect for nature. The old man turned out to be wonderfully up to date, singing from the heart about an issue at the heart of our agenda for the conference. When it happened, in 1956, his 'Two partnerships – Man with Man and Man with Nature' was to be a centre-piece speech. At the end of my fascinating interview, or rather his, he said that he would recommend me to Prince Philip as the secretary of the new and separate organization which had to be started to run the conference. His first move was to try to quieten the industrial politics around us, and I had to prepare letters introducing him to the few key industrial potentates of the day such as George Woodcock, who had just become General Secretary of the TUC. In my draft, the dense paragraph I had written on Harold's past and present distinctions was rather creamy; Harold, however, had a delightful, rightful vanity and seemed to lap it up. He checked me on only one detail. I had a sentence covering his presidency of the World Power Conference and his former chairmanship of BOAC and of BEA. He corrected that reference. 'I was chairman of BOAC and creator of BEA,' he said mildly.

I worked for him for the next two years – a risky joy on a long tightrope, every step of the walk watched by the hobbling ringmaster's eagle eyes, every moment concentrated, exhilarating, high above complacency. My organization built up in the roomy basement of the IWS building in Bryanston Square, but we were separated from the IWS and reported straight to the conference council through its chairman. The conference was to have a life of its own, and the staff expanded explosively to keep pace with the ambitious objective we had been set. We were to design a Study Conference to be held in July 1956, attended by three hundred members drawn from business and trade unions all over the Commonwealth and Empire. There were to be three weeks of plenary sessions and discussions based in Oxford, and study tours throughout the UK. From the date of my own appointment, July 1954, a new member entered my team about every six weeks over the two years of preparation. The functions articulated rapidly to cope with finance, selection of membership, co-ordination of studies, public relations, transport, recreation and social activities, office skills and special duties. The council took infinite care to see that the organization gave this extraordinary experiment (Prince Philip's word for it) every chance; and the details are matters of life or death in a conference on this scale. For instance, in raising the funds, it was vital to gain widespread support from companies so as to avoid any one big-brother donor. My appeal letter was exquisitely improved by an ex-Treasury council member, Sir John Henry Woods, who below my ranking of contributions suggested the elegant sentence: 'We would be glad to know into which category you wish to promote yourself.' The money rolled in.

The details of membership and of the programme of studies were both, of course, supreme priorities. Prince Philip had made it a condition of his involvement that 'the members of the conference should be people who appeared likely to be the next generation of leaders so that when the time came for them to take important decisions they would have the benefit of what they discovered here to help them.' We settled on the band of twenty-five to forty-five years – a detail I borrowed from the Commonwealth Fund Fellowship at that time. And the members had to represent nobody but themselves. There were to be no mandates and no flourish of trumpeting resolutions at the finale. The single purpose of the conference was to add to the experience of the individual attending it.

Details of the pioneering programme were put together by Guy Hunter, the co-ordinator of studies. He became the Toscanini of the conference themes, giving coherence to the speeches and the background papers. There were twenty-four in all, written from India, Africa (South, East and West), the Caribbean, Canada and Australia, as well as those home-grown in the UK. Another detail: he had trouble with finding an author for one of 'the impact papers' (impact was the fashionable word then, I can't think what word we use now). Our special problem was the impact of industrialization on religion. The Archbishop of Canterbury had decided he would rather preach a sermon on the second Sunday than write a paper, and I was invited to a tea-break at some episcopal rally at Church House to hunt a bishop, any bishop. I was passed from bishop to bishop in stirring Shakespearian language: have a word with Gloucester, see Coventry, speak to Exeter, try Bristol. 'Ah,' said Bristol, 'I tell you what I'll do, I'll write the prayers for the Archbishop's service.' Spiritually it seemed we were stuck. I thought I would try a different tack. I wrote to T. S. Eliot. The next I knew was Prince Philip asking me pointed questions only a few days later: how was I getting on with the paper on the religious aspects of industrialization? I mentioned my latest desperate fling. 'T. S. Eliot? Deep, but narrow.' I think that was the most surprising remark I have ever heard him make. Lord Louis Mountbatten reading a poem was imaginable, but Prince Philip deep in *The Waste Land*? By chance, as a regular reader of the magazine *Encounter*, I came across a short story about a funeral in black Africa. There was a cortège with tribal chiefs in native dress and top hats, and aircraft flying overhead: bronze age to jet age in one generation. We wrote to the author, Asbodieh Nicol, who proved to be Dr David-son Nicol, the Beit Memorial Fellow for Medical Research at Cam-bridge, brought up in Sierra Leone and Nigeria. He sent a brief postcard of agreement by return, and later an original and fluent exposition of 'The Impact of Industrialization and Science on Morality and Religion' came in exactly on time, handwritten on the back of handwritten scientific text in what looked like hieroglyphics. It took its place eventually in the fine two-volume history of the conference, published in 1957 by the Oxford University Press.

The range and originality of some of those conference papers are still impressive. There were, for instance, Hugh Casson on 'The Look of Industry', Fraser Darling's 'Thoughts on Ecology', Sir Harry Pilkington on 'Community and Enterprise'; these were among the earliest expressions of themes so crucial today– design, the environ-ment and business in the community. I believe the record of the study programme presented the first extensive definition of the long and irregular frontiers of social responsibility in industry in developed and developing economies. Those who seek a definition of the elements of social policy for enterprise will find them there.

We sent the papers to each member three months before the event. Also three months before, we organized the three hundred members into small groups of fourteen and we chose twenty from the UK managers and trade unionists to be group chairmen. We had a pre-conference for these twenty, whom I regarded as the hinges of success for the plan, so that they could become familiar with the aim and methods of the conference. Arrangements were made for each of them to walk the course of their study tours. Each study tour was individually organized in one of twenty city centres around the UK, spending about half the time in factories and on an industrial topic and the other half on such social priorities as housing, education, community life, health, travel to work and voluntary services.

Finally, it happened. In his welcoming letter to the members, Prince

Philip had written, 'It is no good wondering what is going to happen at the conference because something like this has not been attempted before. Nobody quite knows what is going to emerge.' The conference members gathered at Oxford. I watched them streaming out of the buses. We held our breath and wondered whether even this intricate ambush was enough to cope with the complexity. The inaugural assembly in the Sheldonian Theatre presented a daunting spectacle of variety: there were contrasts of colours, cultures and creeds, costumes, jobs and geography. We had worked and looked hard at the details but now – the leap.

At 9.15 on the morning of 10 July 1956 I shut the big doors of the main hall in Rhodes House as the first sessions began. I stayed outside, leaning on them, alone in the empty lobby. At least I thought I was alone, but the Warden of Rhodes, Bill Williams, was watching me from his drawing-room at the very end of a corridor. He paced slowly and solemnly towards me, his hands behind him, said nothing but came right up to me. Silently from behind his back, he handed me a large gin and tonic and paced off to his own chambers. Bill, a brigadier with Montgomery, was given a great deal of the credit for the victory of the Battle of Alamein – and I can see why. Three weeks later, we all knew the conference was a victory all round, everybody had won. Of course we had solved nothing: life is a riddle to be solved by a riddle, Emerson said, and certainly life in any industrial society will never be free of problems. But after the conference we were all seeing our problems in a new light. For all the contrasts of Commonwealth and Empire our similarities were more important than our differences. In the last speech at the closing dinner in Christ Church Hall, I spoke of Prince Philip's reference to the conference as a bonfire, 'which the brighter it burns the more darkness it shows up, the more mystery, the more ignorance, the more challenge is left to us after our three weeks' work.'

The challenge of social responsibility in industry was taken up next in Canada, six years later, in 1962, with their own Commonwealth 'Conference across a Continent' as the book about it was called. Then Australia, in 1968, and every six years since 1956 there has been a Duke of Edinburgh's Commonwealth Study Conference hosted by the UK, Canada, Australia and, most recently, India. The conference of 1956 has proved the model for the series: each has been a three-week variation on the theme of business and society, each with a mixed membership of unions and managers in private and public organizations, each with study tours to compare theory and practice, each organized into the smallest groups (twenty with fifteen members) and each presided over by Prince Philip. The next will be in 1992 in the UK and I have the nerve-racking privilege of being vice-chairman of the conference trustees, with the Duke of Kent as chairman, to be responsible for its preparation. Prince Philip intends to preside over the seventh of the great experiments.

Outside the conference circles, his extraordinary performance as president has not been widely recognized. Yet I find it hard to think of anything he has done in a royally busy lifetime which is more his own achievement. He started it and is devoted to it. The records of the conference, far too little known, show his summings-up during the final days of reporting back at every conference, his comments always impromptu, public, vivid, uninhibited, revealing and sharply to the point. More than 2,500 of his own generation have been involved, and felt the reality of the man's views and concerns – and these have all been people up-and-coming in their careers, by definition, by selection. The Who's Where of membership is a benevolent network, criss-crossing the globe, culturally and commercially; and with our island drawn inevitably into a more European role it would be wasteful and short-sighted to undervalue these Commonwealth connections at the end of the twentieth century. At the very end of 1956 Prince Philip said, 'You unlike myself will go back to put ideas into practice.' The frustration of a man of action was movingly obvious, but history will show that he put the idea of the conference into practice, over and over again, and it has worked. I was given a slot to speak at the conference in Melbourne in 1986: I spoke on 'The Manager as Citizen', and over dinner that night, under the dramatic multicoloured glass ceiling of the banqueting hall in the Melbourne Art Gallery, we admitted to our surprise that the formula of 1956 had remained unchanged. 'But why change something that works well?' he said. I lifted my glass in a silent toast to the ghost at the feast, Sir Harold Hartley, GCVO, MC, FRS, born 1878, scientist, industrialist, manager *extraordinaire* – certainly the Grand Old Man of my life.

Three men from the 1956 conference shaped my life. One, Prince Philip, simply because, as he puts it to this day, he gave me 'my first real break'. The second was the GOM, Harold. It was a labour of love to do anything for him, but a baffled love. He was a puzzle: a

101

fastidious scientific brain and yet wildly romantic about royalty. For him Prince Philip could do no wrong. I sometimes gagged at the adoration. What impresses me about HRH has nothing to do with princely qualities. But Harold was happily and always bowled over by the thought of the throne and being so close to it. I used to notice how much Harold, famous for objectivity, adored the ritual and had a shrewd eye for the presentation and display. Certainly a puzzle, and in all our time together he never gave me the clue that would have explained so much to me of the nature of the man. After parting from him, and taking time off between jobs, I stumbled on it. I was browsing – a passion of mine – in a second-hand bookshop in Notting Hill Gate. There on the very top shelf (where else would a Harold Hartley find himself?) was a book called *Eighty-eight Not Out*: it was his father's autobiography. All was revealed. Harold's father, born in the year of the Great Exhibition in 1851, became one of Britain's biggest exhibitionists in the late Victorian era. He had begun humbly with a 'Pure Water' company, brought almost accidentally at an auction to help a friend. It seemed a good idea to provide food to help him sell his drink, and through a tobacconist in Whitechapel Road, Salmon and Gluckstein, he made contact with a certain Joe Lyons. They and Lyons were to be the greatest names in catering for the next hundred years. Together they won a contract for the opening ceremony of the Imperial Institute in South Kensington. They prospered sensationally and developed their market by inventing great occasions where their food and drink would be sold. So they started the famous exhibition halls of Olympia and Earl's Court, creating the Disneyland of their day, and making their fortunes. Father Harold had lived to be a famous collector of art and of great names, the more royal the better, and his autobiography at eighty-eight was lavish with royal portraits. I could see that royalty ran in the Hartley family, and so did a genius for putting on a tremendously good show.

Harold died in 1977. I had just joined BR and on my early tours of the system I found his reputation still very much alive, especially on the Midland Line. I heard that he was unwell, and thought I would visit him to report to him about his and my railways. He was lying in bed in an over-furnished room in an apartment block close to Olympia. His long hands waved over his form. 'It's a great thing to be dying from the feet up, Peter, death's nò way near my head yet. I must finish my history of the Royal Society,' and another wave to the pile of reference books at the bedside. *Salut*, GOM.

Of all bosses I have admired, Harold was both the closest and the most remote. My next was to be far the most fun. My third man of the conference was Jock Campbell, chairman of Booker Brothers McConnell Ltd. He offered me a job before the conference was over. My star was dancing.

5

Time to Build

At last, in 1956, I had a job that I felt I could put my arms around and call my own. Running the Overseas Department of the Industrial Society and acting as conference secretary for the Commonwealth Conference over three years had been exhilarating, but administrative and advisory. Advice is advice, business is business. People ask advice but seldom want it, and in fact only go on asking until they get the advice they would like to have. I wanted to be in business. I felt it was time to build a career there, on the bottom line, working for a proper return on the capital employed.

And to provide for the growing family. Jill, the main provider, earning twice my salary, had lost her job as medical officer at Unilever House because she had to take maternity leave for the second time to have Alan, following Lucy. Unilever had managed to cope with one baby but two was over-production, even for the most civilized of companies. Nowadays that could not happen; business has to behave more caringly about women at work – by law. Even so, there is still a long way to go in stretching management's imagination to make the most of women in business. It is a matter of being less unthinkingly chauvinistic, and waking up at last to the lunatic waste of talent that ignores the resource of half the population.

In my case maternity was the mother of invention. I had to get on, and Jock Campbell gave me my chance just when we needed it. We had found the dream house. Late on a spring evening, there it was, framed in cherry trees at the bottom of Brunswick Gardens in Kensington, a tall, thin, white house with a tilted Utrillo look about it which the survey explained was the result of bombing in the district during the war. Strange how definite the genius of a place can be. This one said at once, 'This will be fine – no halfway house. This is going to be home.' And it lived up to its promise. We were there twenty-five years, and our four children still think of Brunswick Gardens as home although we had to sell up in 1976. My son Alan called the business he started in 1986 The Brunswick Group. 'It has the right ring about it somehow,' he said. I try not to pass that corner, even now. It is too tempting to step through the gate when the camellia we planted is in red flower – would one be missed? Oliver and Nathaniel, the third and fourth babies, were both born there. Nat very late. During that overdue springtime, a friend telephoned Jill to draw her attention to a lovely photograph of our house on the back page of *The Times*; there it was, idyllic, with trees of cherry blossom foaming either side. Those were the days when *The Times* featured daily a single large photo on its back page, and on the front, in dense, small print, were advertisements and announcements of marriages, deaths and births. Jill's answer was that in all the circumstances she was far more interested in being on the front page than on the back.

We had lived in furnished flats before Brunswick Gardens. To have a house was a thrill and a shock. It was so empty – bare floors, five of them, stairs, landings, and more stairs, and all those windows – bliss, but unfurnished bliss. And just as there is no such thing as a free lunch, I have still to find such a thing as a real bargain in furniture. We had bought a vast sofa from the Ancient Mariner's grandson, Gilbert Coleridge, who had been a neighbour at Kew. It cost one pound, and fifty times as much to have it moved, re-stuffed and swung into No. 35 through the windows. For ten shillings we bought an oceanic double bed, but then the mattress cost the price of a small yacht. My father and I became weekend painters and decorators for years. One Saturday, Jill introduced us to a lady she was hoping would be a home help; we stopped hammering, nodded politely, too mucky to shake hands. Afterwards, as they were going upstairs, we heard her congratulating Jill on finding workmen who seemed nice enough. Six months were to pass before Jill and I woke up to the realization that our second-floor bedroom, front-of-house, still had no curtains, and I suppose we were the last to notice.

Settling into the neighbourhood – London is made up of villages – was entirely Jill's achievement: we became much more respectable when she joined the local general practice partnership. She began, part-time to start with, in 1957. It was a two-partner NHS practice in Palace Gardens Terrace, with a patient list of 4000 in a catchment of Kensington and Notting Hill Gate. It worked from a house which was white-stuccoed, early-ugly Victorian as ours was, but I discovered that the incomparable Max Beerbohm had been born there and the

London Council Council agreed to give it the distinction of one of their bright blue plaques. It was a delight to have Jill working so close to home, and the children grew up trotting in and out of both houses. There was a long, thin garden at the back of the practice which abutted at right angles on to the long, thin garden at the back of our house. I could see the light on in Jill's surgery, and she could check my signal that I was back.

On Saturdays shopping with Jill was something of a mystery tour for the family. Smiles, nudges and muttered consultations were quite beyond the rest of us, and sometimes beyond Jill too. 'Ah, doctor, now, those pills you gave my husband were no good, shall we try some others?' It was difficult enough for Jill to remember the patients out of context, let alone their relatives. We would eavesdrop in amazement. 'Right, I'll bring my knee in to see you.' I am still amazed at the life which demands that the GP must somehow manage to be freshly and conscientiously concerned with what it is to be human and ailing, with humanity in its particulars, individual by individual, not with humanity massed and rolled into political or industrial platitudes. Comparing notes at the end of the day, my problems have always seemed relatively puny.

More than thirty years later, with the much enlarged practice now moved to nearby Holland Park, Jill is still with them, part-time again, two and a half days and two nights a week. She had found her vocation in the late Fifties. Those were blessed years, the fortunate Fifties: we were building our home, raising our family and getting down to business.

The business that I was joining in autumn 1956 was an international enterprise, Booker Brothers McConnell Ltd. The management called itself Booker Brothers, and that, to the credit above all of Jock Campbell, was the spirit of the enterprise. I had become convinced by the work of the conference that the international company was going to be the decisive institution in business in my time. More clearly than any other business, the internationals had to define their purpose; they had to explain themselves to the countries in which they operated and from which they drew profits – sometimes, like oil companies or like Bookers, literally from the earth. Who worked for whom and who got the two dollars? What is this thing called social responsibility, let me hear it again? Jock and I had wrestled with these questions during the conference, especially over the paper he was to give called simply 'Why does man work?' During our debates he said that he wanted to set up a social policy unit at the centre of Bookers rather than a conventional personnel department. Also, it emerged that he judged too many of Bookers' assets were in the combustible areas, the Caribbean and Central Africa. The group was therefore beginning to diversify. There was no desire to desert those regions, but the group had to become less dependent on them for profit, and quickly: the fuse of independence was lit all over the Empire and the bangs were imminent. Engineering in the UK was one area of possible diversification: would I join the party as executive director of a new holding group? Of course the parallel challenges were irresistible.

Jock, as executive chairman, wove round himself a bright circle of young managers, not a pyramid, and their mission was to convert a ramshackle empire of colonial-style companies into a profitable and coherent international. Jock was in his mid-forties and midway through his unstoppable strategy of reform. Half was done: the reorganization of the group into clear functions. That had been a formidable task: pre-Jock, there was about as much order in the business as in any file marked 'miscellaneous'. The other half was still to be done: there had to be a better balance geographically and commercially.

Bookers was an organizational happening, its history reflecting uncannily in microcosm the rise and fall of the British Empire. In 1815 the earliest brother, young Josiah Booker from Liverpool, had waded ashore carrying a sea-chest to seek his fortune in British Guiana. The country was a chip of Europe's colonial history high on the right-hand shoulder of South America. Britain had seized control of it from the Dutch in the Napoleonic wars, but only Dutch courage and skills had made the coastland habitable by colonists in the first place. This was 'the land of waters', where the Warrau Indians along the coastline lived in houses on stilts, and when the Spanish explorers had arrived along the shore to the north they had given the place the name of Little Venice, Venezuela. Since the end of the sixteenth century the swamps and jungle conditions had defeated the Spaniards and even the best of the British, Sir Walter Raleigh, who envisioned this land as El Dorado. Its promise obsessed him tragically: his final voyage with a thousand men failed to fulfil its false prospectus and he sailed back to be tried and executed. On his headless body was found a small idol and a nugget of gold from the Orinoco. The Dutch did better. They brought with them their tradition of irrigation, dams and drainage. They built a sea wall and to this day it defends the arable land, which at high tide is below sea-level. To grow sugar there was a grim enough task, but when the British took over they eventually made the planters' life grimmer still by the abolition of the slave trade. The freed Africans mostly drifted into the towns and some banded together in communal settlements – like the one called Buxton, after the abolitionist, where they had a saying, 'Never let the sun go down on a white man.'

Josiah Booker by then had become a plantation manager, but times were desperate. The planters faced ruin. In 1837 one of them gained permission to import coolies from India (he was one of the wealthiest and strictest and was the father of W. E. Gladstone). The coolie labour was almost slavery by another name. It saved the sugar industry but also permanently guaranteed Guianese society a tangled destiny of Indian and African tensions. Meanwhile, Josiah was showing that entrepreneurial quality of counter-thinking which makes the lucky ones millionaires. In the economic troubles many plantations came up for sale cheaply and he bought steadily. Nothing succeeds like being on the spot. His two brothers joined him and they began to put together the group of Booker Brothers.

Over the course of a century the company spread from sugar-growing and refining into distilleries and cooperage, wholesale and retail shopkeeping, shipping and stevedoring, drug manufacture, printing works and newspapers, engineering workshops, gold and diamonds in a minor way, even fish glue – which might at least have helped keep Miscellaneous Unlimited together. Mergers gradually expanded the conglomerate into other parts of the Caribbean and also into Africa.

One of the mergers brought Jock's family firm into the brotherhood. Jock had been born rich in this rich tapestry, John Middleton Campbell. Young Campbell went to Eton and graduated into a bit of a tearaway with fast cars and fancy-free ways. He had a wild temper and a stammer that can only have fuelled his rages. Half Irish, he never lost a rebelly-boy look about him, ever. Then he was sent to British Guiana and had the shock of his young life: his romping life of plenty had been based on the poverty he now saw. Those were the hard times of the Thirties when a ton of sugar sold for as little as the price of a cricket ball. All Jock's abundant energy was converted to a faith that Bookers had to mean something in a new deal for the West Indies and for black Africa. Demerara was his Damascus. And the stammer disappeared, almost completely.

During the Second World War he became a leading figure in the establishment of the Commonwealth Sugar Agreement which revolutionized the economics of sugar by establishing a firm price structure for sugar producers – thereby stabilizing the economies of those developing countries living at the unreliable mercy of cane crops. Immediately after the war he came in at the top of Bookers and put in hand the first half of a strategy for reform. His premise was a humble one, sensationally so when I consider how seldom it is admitted by top businessmen. He started on the unusual assumption that he was only human and not superhuman. The task he inherited, he declared openly, was beyond him: only a superman could do it and he did not believe in supermen. Therefore the organization must be chopped into human proportions that could be delegated to and managed by mere mortals. Jock reshaped the historical muddle of businesses into a functional federation: sugar, estates, shops, shipping, liquor and industrial holdings, each with its own board and bottom line. Responsibilities were devolved as far as possible and the groups within the group were set clear, attainable aims. Organization was made to fit people – and Bookers thrived.

The next half of the strategy, diversification, was starting when I arrived to join the evolving engineering group. Bookers had found a natural entry through the acquisition of a Derby business, George Fletcher and Co. Ltd, a well-respected supplier of sugar machinery. Its chairman, Cecil Murray, was feeling his age and wanted to see the company and its community of seven hundred people in safe hands before he left it. 'I went to Jock – I'd known him since he was in knee-pants,' Cecil told me, and it had been an agreeable deal to both sides. I was set to understudy Cecil.

At least I was to try, because in reality it was impossible. Not because I could not be at home with the technology: obviously that was a deficiency, but I have always kept my own nerve, in an excessively mobile career, by believing that a manager is a manager is a manager, and one of the basics of the job is to recognize what you do not know. Your art and craft lie, above all, in your capacity to select other managers who not only make up for your deficiencies but whom you also find revealing and fun to work alongside. What was impossible to reproduce in my generation was Cecil's First World War style. He had been a fighter pilot and won the Air Flying Cross when the RAF was in knee-pants too, as the Royal Flying Corps. He had a squirearchical mastery over the business; he paced about the seven-acre site of darkened Victorian red brick, his authority straightforwardly that of a gentleman manager of another era. Actually he was pacing slowly and painfully when I first met him – bad gout. But he still kept up his shrewd, courteous contact with overseas customers, reeling them into the business with a cunning and charming line of tweedy, quiet chat. I followed his trail all over the world. Everybody in sugar knew and trusted old Cecil. He was a model of simplicity. Keep faith with your customers when they need help, then they'll be friends, and whatever anyone says these days, that's something. Watch the margins on turnover, for Pete's sake, or you'll find what I used to find landing my fighter – until you touched down you didn't know the undercarriage was shot to hell. Mine was the classic management casebook problem: to introduce a modern management into a back-of-the-envelope operation and to replace a brilliant, seat-of-the-pants flying entrepreneur with a recognizable chief executive. Cecil did pass the chair to me but he kept a beady eye on the new order as president. As so often happens, stopping was fatal. He was putting on his overcoat one frosty morning, heading for the old, timbered office we had for him at the works, and he crashed down dead at his front door.

Over the next few years the new management settled well into its stride. Fletchers bought an old rival, Duncan Stewart, another of the great names in manufacturing, and the British suppliers were rationalized to two, ourselves (now named Fletcher and Stewart) and S. W. Smith, the Tate and Lyle subsidiary. Modernizing the management was vital, but modernizing the machinery was equally urgent. On a visit to our Indian markets I was told how solidly our equipment performed. A Fletcher sugar-mill would last a hundred years: the only problem was that when it arrived it looked as if it already had. It was essential to bring our designs up to date. The German competition was offering sleek, clean lines to the casings of rollers, and their use of colours was vivid and appealing. It's just cosmetic, Cecil would grumble; our mills are just as good. All the same, once the German competition had caught on to the value of design, we had to catch up. My generalized concern for design was brought down to earth with a bump. Ever since, I have believed that design is not decoration but at the heart of competitiveness. Fortunately, Fletcher and Stewart had a proud record of exporting. The world had to be its home market, for over ninety per cent of our products were sold to sugar-cane estates overseas, and we were among the earliest winners of the Queen's Award for exports. But orders for capital goods like ours tend to be in large lumps, and it was a feast or famine existence. We needed to diversify.

We pointed ourselves into three new directions. Firstly we decided that our strength in some of the markets of the Commonwealth and Empire would weaken perilously unless we invested in them. India in particular was disappearing. One of Cecil's legacies was a friendship with the Sawhney family, who were great growers and traders in the sugar industry of India, and with them we formed a fifty-fifty partnership, more often than not a fatal formula based on the friendliest intentions. At first the going was good. Triveni Engineering Works was built near Allahabad and was the biggest factory in southern India. I saw the machinery being grouped in. The local Indian labour, dressed as they had been in the fields for centuries, swarmed happily over the glittering capstans and huge lathes, and adapted themselves in a marvellously short time to new skills and disciplines. But both partners underestimated their problems. The Indian family had to adapt its hierarchical habits of age and seniority to the managing of a meritocracy, which is what a modern management must be. We Western managers had to recognize there was more to communicating know-how than putting a load of drawings into a crate and sending them abroad: the only way is to put experienced men on the ground who are prepared to take their coats off on the factory floor and be ready to work at the machines to show what the drawings mean, if necessary. We grew together, but not without pains. Eventually the Bookers interest was bought out, but to the credit of both partners there is now in the centre of India a highly profitable Triveni engineering works with a manufacturing programme extending well beyond sugar machinery.

But not only had we to make the effort to hold on to our former sugar-cane markets; we had to open new ones. Our search in this second new direction brought us into another partnership, this time with Vickers, the well-known engineering group, who had experience behind the Iron Curtain. Together, Vickers and Bookers had won a huge order for the construction of two beet-sugar factories in the USSR, each on a bigger scale than anything built *de novo* in the UK. Shostakovitch might well have turned to what followed for the inspiration of one of his solemn symphonies – Contract and Contradiction perhaps?

Our factories were to be part of Khrushchev's massive programme to renovate the Soviet refining industry and increase the supply (there were cartoons of the plump Khrushchev, like some Santa Commissar, stretching out his arms to give bags of sugar to the people). The negotiations in Moscow and London were long and hard, and at times hilarious. We seemed to hang about for days in the Ukrainya Hotel, a blond but boring version of St Pancras. More details were constantly requested: the French and the Germans had provided more information about the weights of the evaporating pans, surely the British could match them? Gradually it dawned on us that really what was happening was that they were playing for time. They were wretchedly overworked and needed more time to analyse and digest the information they already had from us. There were many such meetings where Oblomov, that arch procrastinator of Russian literature, could have been keeping the minutes.

Occasional parties were more illuminating. One summer evening, in a banqueting room with its heavy curtains drawn against the light, presumably to concentrate us all on the pink vodka and Georgian champagne, we settled to a dinner. I was placed next to a rugged figure introduced to me as the Boilermaker of Russia, a short, powerful blob, the shape of those legless toys that rock and rock but never fall over. Try to clear him up, my team had said to me. I had evoked only grunts over the first two courses. When I was asked to speak about my impressions of Moscow, I said one of them was of a city redesigning itself; there seemed to be a horizon of construction cranes wherever I turned. The woman interpreter had hardly completed the thought when, with a hefty grunt as he pushed his chair clear, my stumpy boilermaker somehow made his way to the curtains, pulled them apart and gestured an invitation for me to join him at the open window. We gazed out to a delightful, clear summer-evening sky, not a crane in sight. The boilermaker had totally bowled me out and this chuffed him enormously. He clasped me to his bosom, and by the end of the night we could hardly be disentangled, we had crisscrossed arms so often in toasts to a new Moscow.

London had its moments too. Eight sugar technologists were brought by the central negotiator to Bucklesbury House in the city, then our headquarters. They sat stiffly, opaquely, as if their faces were pressed against very thick plate glass. They brought their own interpreter, an attractive lady whose name I remember as 'Miss Mouvemovemova', who seemed too good to be true. She had a bubble haircut, a white blouse and a tunic dress that had wide epaulettes and a broad belt with a round, bright buckle: the whole ensemble and the sparkle in her eyes made me think of one of those pre-war Bentley sports cars with flaring mudguards and a strap across the bonnet. The central negotiator and his woman interpreter, in a contrast to their companions under glass, were lively and amusing at the negotiating table – and under it. I was between them at the head of the table and found my legs tangling with those of the lady tangling with those of the head of the delegation.

It was late evening when the delegation left. I escorted them to the portico of the building leading to the Wallbrook, where three large, black Russian sedans with dim windows awaited them. Their leader and the lady shook my hand and got into the first car, the posse of technologists disappeared into the others and the cortège glided off, leaving that heavy smell of Russian petrol fumes. To my astonishment, the happy couple were standing on the other side of the portico: they had walked straight through the car, as they do in the movies. I went across to ask them what I might do for them. They asked, was there anything to do in the city at that hour? Nothing really. So I had the unique pleasure of sending two Russians to the Tower. They wandered off down Cannon Street hand in hand, reds in the sunset.

Finally the contract was signed. We celebrated long into the night at a nudie cabaret of their choosing; they stayed even longer after we had crawled off home. According to the conventional wisdom of those who dealt regularly with the Russians, once the hard bargaining was over the rest was strictly and fastidiously reliable. So it was with us, to start with. Then the reverse. A plague of minor complaints began to break out like a rash. Their inspectors found fault with extraordinary cussedness. This line of paint around the tank was two-thirds of an inch, not half – as if shipment should be delayed on such a fraction of a decorative line. Or the packing cases, hitherto always perfectly adequate anywhere, were not strong enough: we found ourselves making cases to the specification of expensive coffins. And then stories

113

started to come back from the cargo ship's captain, reporting that our deliveries were piling up on the quays of the Russian ports. What was happening? Castro had ousted Batista in Cuba and had had to turn to Russia for trade. The island had been the sugar bowl for America for over a century and was the greatest single supplier in the world; now suddenly Khrushchev had access to as much sugar as he wanted and he was in no hurry to erect our factory to process beet in the Ukraine. Painfully we completed the deliveries and sure enough the payments came through.

The third new departure of Fletcher and Stewart was the search for new products to make. George Fletcher, the founder, had put his hand to many things, from penny-farthing bicycles to mining gear – and pretty ladies too. It was said that the sweet, brick cottage built snugly into the boundary wall, well away from the offices and with a door on to the road outside, had once been the seraglio of the exuberant Victorian phenomenon with his phenomenal moustaches. We revived only his mining interest; we launched into the new market for hydraulic roof supports which were transforming the life of mines underground. Dowty's, the engineering company which had originated the sophisticated pit-props, and Huwoods, their only serious rivals, were the giants in the field. But there is usually room for a little 'un and we joined the fray for the National Coal Board's attention.

As often happens, we made sound profits from not being the first, but by the mid-Sixties there were other little 'uns, Sutcliffe and Wild, and the competition was pell-mell. This was the time of the Industrial Reorganization Corporation, formed by the Labour government to accelerate mergers which seemed vital to the competitiveness of the country. The motor-car and electrical industries were prime targets, and British Leyland and the General Electric Company were to be the focus for the near-monopolistic powers in their sectors. Soon we were made aware of the NCB's plans to tidy up the brawling competition at the coalface; their plan seemed to aim at concentrating on the two big 'uns and letting the little 'uns go in with them or go under. NCB computers were beginning to phase us out of their purchasing programmes. I set out to put an alternative future to the NCB, the IRC and any members of parliament concerned: we could form a third grouping with Sutcliffe and Wild to keep Huwood and Dowty on their mettle. A commando operation on these lines appealed to the common sense of Lord Robens of the NCB and Sir Charles

Villiers of the IRC. And someone must have spoken to the computers, because from then on our newly formed company was given every chance to quote for a fair slice of the NCB action.

Understandably, sugar machinery was a foundation of Bookers Engineering when I arrived. For less obvious reasons, just before my arrival, Bookers had ventured into the unknown field of electrical equipment by picking up a small manufacturer of potentiometers, Reliance Controls, in Walthamstow. The factory of some fifty-odd workers was worn out, the founder-entrepreneur was retiring, but everyone else in the industry was racing ahead with the electronic age. Technologically little Reliance had no resources to compete: we had to fatten it for sale at the right moment. A first essential step was to move into new premises and introduce brighter management. We decided on a special-purpose factory unit to be built in Swindon, and this was the first factory building for which I had responsibility. I consulted James Stirling, who at that moment was building in Leicester University, and since has gained world renown. My project was too small for him, but he suggested that I make contact with a partnership called Team 4, two young architects and their wives. Their ideas proved both innovative in design and materials, and economic. This was their first factory building, too, but when the plant was up it immediately won one of the first Financial Times Awards for industrial architecture. I had been lucky enough to strike future gold medallists of the Royal Institute of British Architects, names which individually were to become among the most famous in the world – Richard Rogers and Norman Foster.

But a few years with Reliance were enough for me to find one iron law of nature in any holding company: you spend about as much time with the problems of your smallest subsidiary as you do on your larger, more profitable, headaches. The right moment came and thankfully we were able to merge Reliance with a high-tech American group, and I was able to concentrate on the larger strategy of Bookers Engineering. Through Lord Rochdale, an industrialist I had come to know as a council member of the Duke of Edinburgh's Conference, I met Lord Piercy of the Industrial and Commercial Finance Corporation. ICFC had been invented to fund and encourage smaller-scale enterprise, and once any of their protegés reached a certain size then ICFC would tend to bow out. Lord Piercy had reached just such a stage with Sigmund Pumps, a company with a five-hundred-strong workforce in the North-East of England, in the Team Valley Industrial Estate in Newcastle. I went to meet the Czech founder of the company, Mirka Sigmund, and knew at once that here was a lion of a manager. He was about fifty, heavily built, with a large head and lined Slav features, heavy nose, heavy hands and the brightest, shrewdest blue eyes. The meeting convinced us both there was a match of interests. He brimmed with energy and plans for expansion which were more than ICFC's criteria could cope with; we had to take the plunge into something sizeable outside our traditional scope.

Mirka had an extraordinary story to tell. He was the youngest of three brothers who had inherited the great Sigma corporation in Czechoslovakia, one of the biggest specialists in pump manufacture in Europe, employing 4000 or more people. As the invasion of their country appeared imminent, a mere few days before the sell-out by the Allies in Munich, the brothers drew lots, one to stay in Sigma and face the Nazis, the other two to take what technical drawings they could carry and flee, one to France, the other to England. The eldest, who stayed, was taken from the factory one day after the assassination of Heydrich, the Nazi gauleiter of Czechoslovakia; after months of horror he was murdered. The other brother had only just time to start up a small operation in France before the Germans invaded in 1940. Mirka, twenty-seven, with his staunch and lovely wife, Huberta, reached London, with his drawings and no English to speak of. He was advised to try the North-East where the experiment of the Team Valley Industrial Estate had recently begun. There, in 1938, he made his start, making small and large fire-pumps of a quality for which Sigma had been famous. In no time the Second World War and the blitz made fires a roaring market. Sigmund produced the ubiquitous stirrup-pumps which in the air-raids seemed often to be the only civilian weapon we could put up against the Luftwaffe. When the news of his brother's death reached him through the Red Cross, Mirka began to make Bren guns as well. By 1945 this young manager employed 2000 people – then suddenly the business of war collapsed and he was struggling again to sell fire-pumps. ICFC stepped into support him and at the time of our acquisition Sigmund Pumps covered a fine range of products for industry and municipal markets.

We were able to build on that. With Mirka's formidable drive reinforced by the security of Bookers' backing, we could attract management for him in a way he could not as a small company, and this freed him to follow his entrepreneurial spirit. Together we thoroughly enjoyed the new scope opened for us. An old competitor, about our size, Pulsometer Pumps of Reading, was acquired and Sigmund Pulsometer Pumps was formed. We took over the neighbouring site on the Team Valley and developed a central heating company. Mirka had spotted a small circulating pump at an engineering fair and bought the licence to manufacture it in Britain. 'This little thing will change the British way of life,' he said, and it did. The Thermopak, as he called it, proved to be the secret of small-bore central heating. Economic and easy to install, it replaced the old gravity systems with their expensive clobber of huge radiators and pipes. The Thermopak led the revolution in comfort and its early success tempted us into making the steel radiators and new boilers to go with it.

And then the inevitable happened. Mirka met me over dinner and admitted sadly that he could not stand corporate life any longer. He had decided to resign and start off again on his own – not in competition; in fact he wasn't at all sure what to do next. Holding companies, boards, corporate plans and group policies were not his idea of entrepreneurial heaven. This was not totally unexpected. The ritual slaughter, sometimes self-slaughter, of the entrepreneur is a familiar, saddening pattern within a few years after acquisition. I had argued originally for ten per cent of the company's equity to be left with Mirka, but that was a fairly messy formula and not enough to hold him. He was too much his own man, the lion was not tameable. I missed him terribly. He had that primal quality of courage without which all other managerial virtues are leaderless.

The diversification of Bookers was proceeding apace and fairly consistently. Parallel to the push I was making into the basic areas of engineering and capital goods, our shopkeeping group was growing into the basics of distribution in the UK, beginning with wholesale food. But there were some surprises. There are some businesses which live by the corporate plan, and die by it. Not Bookers. One Monday, Jock came in with the question, 'Read any good thrillers lately?' Over the weekend he had been playing golf with an old schoolfriend, Ian Fleming, and perhaps he had gone too far. During the round at Huntercombe, at the fourth hole, Ian had interrupted play with chat about his wealth and health: both were presenting problems, the first growing almost uncontrollably, the latter wilting gravely. Everything he was writing was turning to gold, and everything he was doing was in flagrant defiance of his doctor's orders to slow up. It seemed Ian enjoyed life too well, he simply had no brakes and must have known he was skidding into a fatal collision with time's winged chariot. Jock listened to all this, a little impatiently. He badly wanted to get on with the game – he was murderously competitive about all games; word-games, croquet, golf, squash, ping-pong, these were matters of life and death. He made a brisk proposal. Ian should set up a company to own his books, then sell part of the company and with the capital gain organize his family affairs accordingly: meanwhile the business of golf could be resumed quietly. At the end of the round, and heading back to the clubhouse, Jock was brought to a halt by Ian saying 'Right then, let's do it. I'll do my bit and you'll buy the company, will you?' He had cast Jock as some sort of supremo in business, as 'M' among managers. At the Tuesday board meeting, Jock formally put the proposal to the board. Not all were in favour: was Bookers not supposed to be limiting the group's risks in the face of the increasing tensions overseas? However, most of the younger directors had a few Bonds under their belt, and were intrigued; they argued that not much money seemed to be involved. We went ahead. For £100,000 Booker bought a fifty per cent share in Glidrose Ltd, which Ian had formed to hold the assets of his writings. Sadly, Ian Fleming did die soon after, but the flourishing business of Bookers Books had begun. We found that we had stumbled onto a tax formula which attracted successful authors who could capitalize the assets of their written works. The tax window has now been closed but the list of authors was impressive and then so was the profitability. The annual Booker Prize grew out of this, a celebration of creative management as well as creative writing: I always think of it as the touch of Jock's gold fingers as well as Ian Fleming's.

Our diversification policies were racing against time. It was impossible to know precisely when independent status would be given to or taken by the combustible peoples of British Guiana, Northern Rhodesia and Nyasaland, but it was bound to happen. Bookers faced the uncertain future openly and sympathetically. As a demonstrative part of our policy for change, Jock set up the Social Policy Committee when I joined the company and made me chairman. This was where I wanted to be. The engineering company was UK-centred, but the committee was my opportunity to be involved with international management at last. My remit was to stimulate and co-ordinate our group policies in personnel, welfare services, education and training, community relations and public affairs. The jargon makes all this sound bland and pappy, but these elements were truly fiery particles of management in the society where we operated. In the early Fifties there had been spectacular riots in British Guiana. How were we to run our enterprise in a way that reconciled the legitimate interests of the shareholders and the legitimate aspirations of national fervour? No company in its right mind would have consciously committed itself to the extent to which Bookers was stuck in British Guiana, but there we were, where history had put us. Jock once said about our suvival in the most awkward of physical and political conditions, 'The wonder is not that life is not utopia, but that life and production can exist at all.'

Of course, any company anywhere is both an economic and political entity. An international, however, operating in the less developed countries, has to be wide awake to the priorities of social policy – wider and earlier awake than enterprise has tended to be in the advanced economies. The appalling rate of unemployment and the sporadic riots on our doorstep have recently focused business minds on their responsibility in the community as a whole, but until the last decade social policy has hardly featured on the agenda of companies in the UK. The international was well ahead. It had to be. An international like Bookers has a high degree of visibility, and the host country watches its every move. I soon learnt the truth of Disraeli's comment that sugar is politics.

Jock's personality had kept Bookers in touch with the politics of the business: as a businessman he talked politically and was completely unafraid to do so. When I came to tour abroad I met some of the political leaders and they would speak of him as if he were a friend in the next room. He understood their idealism and was idealist in return; he reckoned that to be idealist was the only realistic thing to do in the circumstances. Idealism and realism had better learn to live together, that was his line, and I tried wholeheartedly to follow it. The Social Policy Committee had to declare a bold way forward. We were given our head, and ample headroom; even in the Bookers Annual Report to shareholders we were given a page for our report, a highly unusual feature in the Fifties, although now such matters as communication and consultation have become an obligatory reference.

In the report we stated our economic aim: that we worked for profit, profit not only for our shareholders but also for the employees and the community. Profit was the best measure of our effectiveness in the service of the community in which we operated. Our aims for social policy were to widen participation in our enterprise and to serve the community. The company as we saw it was an educator, we had a responsibility to advance education and training facilities inside and outside Bookers. We had to stand for the principle of making careers wide open to talent at all levels of skill. In the communities outside, we sought to widen opportunities for local investors by making markets for our own shares in the host countries: we promoted house ownership at peppercorn rates, health services, sports and arts. Put like that it sounds pat, or even worse, paternal, an updated upbeat colonialism. In fact, that was just what we were trying to avoid: we had to keep out of the trap of uninvited benevolence which ends in tears: why do you hate me so much, I was never kind to you?

The prooof of the Booker pudding was to be in the eating. Shareholders' assets survived the independence of Guyana, of Zambia, of Nyasaland: deals were done with the new governments, and Bookers was gradually able to be well and profitably in the clear. The Booker Group of today is unrecognizable, but it would not be there if Jock had not had what Adam Smith of all people called 'sympathy'. He was the master and manager of the art of the unexpected; there was a humanity in all he did. That did not mean he was easy to work with. He was far better to you when you were winning, not so good when you were down. He drove people hard, himself hardest, but life was exhilarating when he was around, hard, sharp and funny. He had a needling banker's brain (his grandfather had been governor of the Bank of England) and he was amazing with words, delighting in the choice and play of them (Torquemada, the grandest inquisitor among setters of crossword puzzles, left Jock his papers to edit for the Cambridge University Press). He could contradict himself in a Walt Whitmanly way, and his adopted name of Jock was one of those contradictions. Neither by appearance nor nature was there an ounce of Jockiness in him, yet when he was knighted he sought permission to be dubbed Sir Jock. When he took a life peerage from Harold Wilson, he insisted on being a cross-bencher; later he moved to sit with Labour; later still the rebelly boy was back on the cross-benches.

Before that, in the mid-Sixties, when he was still head of Bookers, his health cracked, and he recovered only to decide to retire. None of us expected him to do that, not at fifty-five: he hated the end of anything, hated the idea of dying. But he pulled out because he felt that he had done all he could. That struck me as a piece of dazzling self-awareness, an act of grace rare in chairmen, who tend to act like Lear even at full retirement age, mouthing the intention to abdicate but still wanting their hundred knights. He diversified himself thereafter. Among many other activities he was chairman of the *New Statesman* and a trustee of Chequers, but most of his time went into the chairmanship of Milton Keynes, a satellite new town which he helped to turn into a star in its own right. Busy diaries have separated us but we have never lost touch nor he his unexpectedness. During my time at BR, when my name and that of Ian MacGregor, as chairman of Steel, were both prominent, and a well-known contrast in management styles, Jock dropped me a note to say he had dreamt his first-ever punning dream: he was at Chequers saying to Mrs Thatcher that Ian MacGregor and Peter Parker had much in common.

'Really?'

'Yes, they both fire people with enthusiasm.'

Could I interpret this please?

Those Booker years brought two main influences to bear on me as a manager. First, the understanding that good management, whatever else it was, could also be good fun. Secondly, I was able to explore the meaning of international management at the right moment, when it was taking on a global significance. The oldest form of international operations (and Bookers was a fine specimen) was that of the colonial conglomerates which had grown up Topsy-like, running slightly wild over the imperial gardens of British history. They were an endangered species. The newer models were self-conscious structures; they had their origins in the late nineteenth century and were powered by a desire to secure export markets and raw materials. Their credo was summed up by William Lever who started Lever Brothers and who said it all in 1882: 'When the customs duties and various restrictions hinder sales into a country, it's time to build there.'

Time to build there: that could have been the motto of international management. A century ago that spirit of 'building there' was what stirred the Bayers of Germany, the Nestlés of Switzerland, and the Michelins of France; while in parallel, to secure the primary sectors of industry, the nations of Europe were grabbing handfuls of Africa for gold and coffee, nickel and cocoa, and of the Middle East for petroleum. The internationalizing of business was slowed by the Russian Revolution and the two World Wars – the Thirty Years' War, as Paul Johnson has called it – but developed again afterwards with new intensity.

The reconstruction of Europe and the dawning of the consumer society provided a gigantic temptation for American banks and industry: they evangelized Europe with their exports. Gradually the Europeans staggered to their feet, and just as the East had copied the West, the Old World began to copy the technologists and management of the New World. Then the time came inevitably when the Americans had to reckon it was 'time to build there'. They moved in massively with investment, at first to hold on to their markets, and after 1957 to make the most of the widening European market. The eagle had landed among the pigeons. By the end of the Sixties there was a famous call for a European counter-offensive, by Jean Jacques Servan-Schreiber in his book, *The American Challenge*. Passions were roused as they have been since by the Japanese penetration. If Canada was an American attic, Europe took no joy in the possibility of becoming an American outhouse. It is not difficult to understand why. The onrush of entrepreneurial exuberance from the New World seemed overwhelming. It was steered by professional management of a kind that did not exist in Europe. It was supported by corporations with central resources of research and technology, with marketing strategies and information systems well beyond us. We Europeans were having a taste of what Africa, the Middle and Far East, and South America had to swallow when the West expanded in its heydays of the nineteenth and early twentieth centuries.

In these unnerving circumstances, we did not count our industrial blessings in Europe. We underestimated our strengths. Of *Fortune*'s list of the hundred biggest industrial manufacturing companies, fifty were multinationals and twenty-five of those were European. In Britain there were, and are, world leaders such as ICI and BP and, with the Dutch, Shell and Unilever. Also we were underrating the European investment going into America even then. Since that time, the ratio of the stock of European investment in the US to that of US investment into Europe has come into balance: so, in the event, Europe was to give as good as we got. This perspective should be some reassurance to Europe, obsessed as it is currently with the invasive competitiveness of Japan, although Japan will have to become a great deal more accessible if the analogy is to be telling.

I found myself in the thick of the international management world because by 1960 I had joined the British Institute of Management and had taken the chair of its Overseas Committee, which later became its Overseas Council. BIM corporate members with international operations were intensely interested in exchanging ideas and experience about organizational problems, recruitment and training, pay and conditions; but while we were looking hard at our front wheels and pedalling frantically uphill we seemed to have no time to research the social and political implications of international business as a phenomenon. This was a bewildering blank, but the blank began to fill up with some alarming numbers. I quoted some of them in a paper I delivered to an international conference on automation and management, held at the Hebrew University in Israel in 1969. My sources were two distinguished and threatening gurus, Professor Perlmutter and Dr Steiner of the University of California. Perlmutter forecast that by 1988 the economy of the free world would be dominated by 300 companies capable of most of the world's industrial output. For those daunted by such figures of concentration there was some comfort from Dr Steiner, whose vision doubled: he prophesied 600 by the same year.

Actually, in 1988, things have not turned out quite as simple as that. Nor, I suspect, will the millenarian views about the growth of multinationals which are now being projected towards the year 2000 – and they are on very much the same lines as those of twenty-five years ago – come to pass. What has been happening in reality is a much more complex process than the simple concentration of fewer and fewer giant corporations. The growth comes from an increase not a reduction in the number of companies becoming international, particularly in oil, nuclear power, electronics, chemicals. Of the fifty largest multinationals in 1955, twenty-three were top of the list twenty years later – the Seven Sister Oil Corporations; the motor giants like Ford and General Motors; the chemical manufacturers like Dupont or ICI; food giants like Nestlé and Unilever. But the rest of the fifty were newcomers. Of those who slipped out of the top fifty, only five were 'concentrated' (that is, taken over); the others, mostly manufacturers of aircraft, steel and auto accessories, just slipped. The significant trend is not so much the looming dominance of fewer giants:

what matters is that the global business is proving indispensable to the quality and growth of the living standards of the world.

That will be the reality for the next century, and I find it enlarging and encouraging. It will transcend the competition between the nations and the regions of the European Community, Asia and the Americas. Already we are living with the logic of international trade, we work with it, we play with it. Read the names advertised around the major sports arenas of the countries in the OECD (Organization for Economic Co-operation and Development): the evidence of brand internationalization is there. The enterprise that bases its future only on its own country is likely to be pushed to the tariff wall; that will provide brief temporary protection but if the company cowers there too long the 'unilateral' will die as surely as if it were shot up against it. The multinational pattern of competition is here to stay. Global vision will surely become the average vision of the professional manager in an advanced industrial society.

Of course with that is posed the political challenge to any host country, though this may be exaggerated. At a time when I was thinking of this, 30,000 feet up at breakfast time, the stewardess offered me a choice of cornflakes: they were the same brand but the packets were different, one produced in the US and the other in the UK. It is hard to work up a patriotic passion about that: I doubt any Western country is likely to lose its sovereignty because a foreigner has the power to put the crackle-bang-pop into its cereal bowl in the morning. More often than not these days European countries are competing for the favour of foreign visitors. Loss of some sovereignty is tolerated as a sensible trade-off if it brings the benefit of increasing technology and jobs to the host country. Different parts of our little island vie with each other in offering dowries to seduce the visitors: there was cutthroat competition between the Scots, Welsh and English for the pleasure of the company of Nissan. The desired internationals thoroughly enjoy the new sport. They call it 'dowry-hunting'.

Nevertheless, even presuming the best will in the world markets (a tall presumption if ever there was one), genuine issues of sovereignty are bound to arise. These are not necessarily at the extremes, such as in the interventionist role of ITT in Chile, but in the more normal course of international business. It must be so if some multinationals have profits larger than the gross national product of the smaller countries of the world; or if IBM is a key component in NATO defence; or if national tax systems are thought to be outmanoeuvred by the subtle internal pricing of companies operating cosmetically; or if the devolution of powers to subsidiaries and 'local' management is seen as a sham because total accountability needs must go back somewhere – Detroit or Tokyo or London, some place must be boss. The multinational can be in danger of being Big Brother; it tends towards secrecy and towards centralization, which is becoming both easier and so much more tempting with the advent of high technology. What's good for General Motors may be good for America, but it still may not be good for the world, or even some part of it; but then who is going to say so?

These are long-term, background factors of multinational politics, but there are also more abrupt issues that hit the headlines daily. Cable and Wireless fight a way into the Japanese market; Toshiba is said to sell strategically sensitive propellor technology to Russia; IBM and Coca-Cola leave India rather than concede that local shareholders can have at least fifty-one per cent of their Indian subsidiaries; America insists on 'voluntary agreements' with Japanese exporters of cars and electrics; oil companies and tankers in the Gulf are the stuff of international crises; those least emotional of institutions, international banks, finally decide to withdraw from South Africa; the politics of mergers in the Common Market maddens ministers of the member states. These issues are no longer a crude case of the Third World being exploited by the club of the rich; South Korea, Singapore, Taiwan are in the club too.

By the early Seventies various codes of conduct began to appear in an effort to calm the relationship of governments and multinationals. First, in 1972, there were recommendations from the International Chambers of Commerce; then from the OECD in 1976 came guidelines to raise standards of disclosure of information, competition, financing, taxation, science and technology, employment and industrial relations. Meanwhile codes have been adopted by the United Nations and by the International Confederation of Free Trade Unions dealing with social policy. I believe that we are only at the start of understanding the new economic and political balances that will have to be struck within Europe: we are still struggling in the toils of a new European company law. Certainly the manager of the international in future will have to expect life to be more complicated than the dear, clear old simplicities of the nineteenth-century joint-stock company which

existed only to make profits for the shareholder. The internationalization of business is going to need more watching than that of the
shareholders' interest alone. As new standards emerge for global
business, the quality of the professional manager, the heart of the
enterprise, will be crucial day to day, on the spot where the action is.

Back in the Sixties, I was finding myself more and more concerned,
through Bookers and through the British Institute of Management,
with the making of international management. It had then, as it has
now, a vested interest in surmounting barriers of culture as well as
tariffs and political frontiers, and that seemed no bad thing. Over a
generation, there had been a remarkable converging of management
methods in advanced and advancing economies. Britain was a prime
example. Immediately the war was over, the Atlantic was almost flattened by boatloads of trade union and management teams dashing to
and fro to see how the Americans 'did it'. Patriotism and Productivity
were still a common cause, and the British Institute of Management
was started on the initiative of a Labour government (Sir Stafford
Cripps, the Labour Minister for Productivity, was the godfather).
About that time, the Administrative Staff College was also established,
an independent venture into the no man's land between higher education and enterprise – actually a piece of beautiful, rolling parkland
at Henley. But vital as Henley was, not enough of industry wanted to
do business with education. Industry's reaction was that of my daughter Lucy when a kind aunt gave her a pin-cushion. Lucy said, 'Thank
you very much, I've always wanted a pin-cushion – but not very much.'

However, short courses in management began to proliferate, mostly,
I noticed from my base in the Industrial Society, as weekend exercises
at seaside resorts – a bracing breath of fresh air and a whiff of new
techniques, really not much more. That was why in the mid-Fifties I
joined with a half-dozen managers to form a small war-party to start
to fight the case for management education as something at the back
of other university disciplines. Most of us had experience of the
American business scene and their professionalism based on business
schools at universities. The party included Sir Hugh Tett, chairman
of Esso; Neil Salmon of Lyons (echoes of Harold Hartley and his
first encounter with Salmon and Gluckstein, in Whitechapel); Sir
Noel Hall, the first principal at the Henley Staff College; Sir John
Rogers, the MP for Sevenoaks; and another brand-new MP, Sir Keith
Joseph of Bovis (in those youthful days, Keith was glowing with

enthusiasm, so keen a keeper of the minutes it seemed he could hardly wait for the meeting to write them). An entrepreneur, John Bolton, took the chair; and of that set of crusaders he was the most original of managers. I cannot think of a businessman who has worked harder for the cause of management education in Britain in his time: he chaired all the key centres of initiative, the BIM, the Business Graduates Association, the Foundation of Management Education. In business he was a pioneer in the sunrise valley of electronics, setting up his own company there in the early Fifties, straight from his Harvard Business School training. His name only went public in the Sixties when, as chairman of what came to be called the Bolton Committee, he championed the cause of small businesses, years before it was fashionable. And, not incidentally, it is saddening that John Bolton has never received that full public recognition he deserved long ago.

Our war-party began to lobby the universities directly. Because two of our members were MPs we could invite them to the House of Commons for dinner, and we ate our way through two years' worth of vice-chancellors – pretty tough going as most of them were bored. There were two redeeming exceptions: Sir Charles Morris of Leeds, and his brother Sir Philip Morris of Bristol, who pulled out a draft plan for a new business school faculty from his pocket at the dinner table. Philip had attended the 1956 Duke of Edinburgh's Conference as its summing-upper; his was one of the most memorable pieces of speaking, a summary three hours long of a three-week-long conference. I found myself comparing it with trying to write the Lord's Prayer on a pinhead of time. There was also John Baker (later to be Lord Baker) of the Engineering School at Cambridge. This blessed academic trinity said they were ready to try if we could raise some funds. So we sweated and strained to do so. Industry's response was polite and distant. Wasn't this an American idea? And wasn't management education being made to run before it had shown it could really walk? I recall a breakfast with a tycoon: the breakfast was spartan, the views over Green Park sumptuous. He listened patronizingly and then explained that he could not be expected to do more for industrial training than he was already doing. He had given £500 that year to encourage engineering apprenticeships. Obviously, the concept of management education as an intellectual discipline at the level of higher education was not plugged into the power lines of British business.

We had to make a beginning among ourselves. John Bolton put in £5000 of his own money, Esso £2000, Bookers £1000, Bovis £500: slowly we clawed our way towards our modest target of £30,000. My former head of college at Oxford, Keith Murray, had become the czar of education as chairman of the University Grants Committee; I consulted him and he walked me round the moonlit quad after a Senior Common Room dinner at Lincoln College. He told me that if we reached £30,0000 he would top it up with £10,000, and that would prime the three universities showing real interest, Leeds, Bristol and Cambridge. That total might have remained mere moonshine if we had not reinforced ourselves by inviting a silvery magician retired from the board of Shell to take a lead for us. Jim Platt proved just the elder statesman we needed. The country has an amazing resource in top managers retiring from Shell: their directors step off the board but are sustained by keeping their offices and services, and this fall-out of managerial stars over Britain is supremely benevolent. The individual directors are usually an imposing silver grey; silver-grey suits, cars, chauffeurs, secretaries and, sometimes, as in Jim's case, silver tongues. Jim made the most of his contacts and parleyed up our funds to the critical point, and delightedly we split the small spoils between the three willing universities. We were even emboldened to request the appropriate Ministry to register us with a somewhat grander name than perhaps we deserved, but with the luck of the green (which is what we were) and the blue (which is what he was) John Rogers had meanwhile become a Minister at the Board of Trade in the Conservative government. In 1960 he had the satisfaction of signing the necessary approval for the creation of the Foundation of Management Education. We were off.

Within months, ripples from our pebble thrown into the still waters of the academic pond started to widen beyond our wildest hopes. You can nearly always tell when a radical idea begins to be acceptable in Britain: you're winning when it comes under criticism for being too small. In my experience, that has been true about the Channel Tunnel and about the way that management education was gradually adopted by British business and by the universities. Vice-chancellors began to twitch into life again, revived as if by smelling salts by the scent of some money, though admittedly not very much. And employers' associations and big corporations showed their interest in our little experiments by declaring that if something was to be done it should be done properly, not in our pathetic penny-packets scattered around a number of campuses. Quite right too, we agreed, that is, if more pennies are forthcoming. And that now seemed possible.

At about this time another group of industrialists, closer to the Federation of British Industry, formed to advocate the setting-up of 'a Harvard-type business school'. Imagine the gentle curl of British upper lip and slight lift of eyebrow which might have greeted a cry of such naïvety from the other side of the Atlantic that America should start an Oxford-type college. For one thing, cultural transplants are not a simple matter. For another, Harvard had begun to grow its business school at the beginning of the twentieth century; and for yet another, historically, American education has grown up relatively at ease and on good terms with commerce. Similarly, in continental Europe, commercial life integrates into the national systems of education. Not so here. In the Fifties our higher education was hopelessly out of joint with commerce, and even in the Eighties Britain needed a Year of Industry to remind itself of its weakness: that we are an industrial society with an anti-industrial culture.

The tension between an embryonic Foundation and the new and welcome enthusiasms became critical. Inevitably a national voice was asked to pronounce on how this new national priority of management education should be handled. Lord Normanbrook did what national voices of this high order usually do. He said mostly what we all wanted to hear. There should be two major centres of excellence, at London and at Manchester, but smaller-scale initiatives should be encouraged wherever possible. The movement of management education in Britain as it was later described in a report of the Ford Foundation had begun in earnest. An appeal was launched for three million pounds from industry, and the government gallantly promised to match industry pound for pound to that amount. Staggeringly, the response from industry was more than double the target. Seven million pounds poured into the Foundation which, thanks to Jim Platt's business diplomacy, had become the chosen instrument for the funds. This huge sum plus the government's three million pounds was a measure of the new interest and hope.

That was the good news. Less cheering to those of us with some idea of the timescales involved in management development was the vagueness and the greatness of the expectations. Some disappointment was inevitable. Almost at once, ominous doubts were circulating about getting value for money, ominous and ceaseless; over the twenty-five years, doubts have been a condition of life at the business schools. Too theoretical, too elitist, too angled towards careers in the City – and anyway, what was it Shaw had said about teachers? Those who can, do; those who can't, teach. And sometimes those clichés of criticism have seemed nothing but the truth. I have had interviews with some of the polished products who have emerged as business graduates and discovered that they are not a bit interested in production. They sit there with immaculate conceptions of marketing, financial controls, organization, and are plainly only interested in starting their careers as vice-chairman, and that probably only part-time. But I remain a believer. Rather than an obsessional nagging about that weakness, we should be concentrating on one of the main problems – that they do not produce enough graduates.

Thirty years after our war-party began I was chairman of the British Institute of Management, and I was visited by one of the early warriors, Sir Keith Joseph, who was then Secretary of State for Education. He came to Management House for a meeting with the BIM and the CBI in 1986. Keith was in one of his *mea culpa* moods. He expressed a saintly despair about the results of the business school movement which we both had had a share in starting. Now all we could share was a rueful perspective. 'Peter, what have we done?' The decline of British competitiveness had not been checked, where were the entrepreneurs? Keith's colleagues in the Cabinet seemed to me thoroughly to enjoy their own brand of zealotry. Not Keith: his sense of past political sin seemed always to sit on his face and squash his good nature. I agreed that we were guilty of not doing enough, or enough right, but I argued that he took too pessimistic a view of what had been achieved. It was too early to judge the movement: only now are the business graduates of this generation reaching positions of power. There was an annual output of over a thousand graduates, and even if that was far too low, still they seemed to be highly desirable because their rewards were high. Surely there was a need to improve the schools, but just as surely the need was for more not less of a national effort to develop management education.

From differing standpoints we reached the same decision: to commission a review of the provision of management education, development and training, both in educational institutions and in companies. This was put in hand at once, with the then director-general of the BIM, Dr John Constable, in charge of the review body, which consisted of the BIM, the CBI, and the Department of Education and Science. Two years later the review was published, simultaneously with the Handy Report from NEDO, the National Economic Development Office, which provided international comparisons. Already both have proved to be turning-points. Both urged a major upgrading of the effort to make British management more professional, and in doing so, argued for more flexibility in the attitudes of client and supplier, of businessmen and educators. The excessive optimism of the founders of the Foundation of Management Education was that we had hoped to introduce the concept from the top down. But there was no infrastructure of relationship between industry and education at schools and colleges. Learning about business is not natural in the British educational system. In our urgency to create the business schools, all we were doing was to pop a maraschino cherry on the grapefruit – nice to have it there but it was not an organic part of the fruit. However, an integrated response is now at last being made, linking business and education at every level of growing up. The business schools in higher education will have something to build on for the next century.

There was another misjudgement we made, equally serious but not so obvious even now. We were not able to include two priorities into the frame of our vision. Both were lessons I had learnt from my experience at Cornell University, and I kick myself still that I failed to be convincing about them in the early days of the war-party. I had seen at Cornell's School of Industrial and Labour Relations the possibilities for business studies at the undergraduate level, but I had not been able to keep that in the frame of possibilities in the early stages of our campaign. Perhaps it was as well after all. We were rightly focused on one objective, the ascent of management studies to the highest points of education in the country so that we could bring the best minds to the challenge of managing better. We were fighting desperately in the Fifties to get a toehold on the Eiger face of complacency in business and universities. To have diffused the debate into the validity of undergraduate studies in management would have been tempting providence. Thank goodness now, a generation later, undergraduate courses are well in our sights, as business is much closer to the world of education at every level.

Alas there has been no such progress in the other priority which I failed to establish. At Cornell, I had also witnessed the involvement of young, brilliant trade unionists as members of the business school. In Britain the trade union leadership never showed the slightest interest in the Foundation of Management Education. Nor did the Labour Party. By the 1959 General Election, the Conservatives had seized the significance of educating managers; it even had a mention in their manifesto. Simultaneously, I had also suggested to the Labour Party that improving efficiency through better management in industry was worthy of reference in their manifesto. But the answer came back in a limp letter from Austen Albu saying that the Party was emphasizing the importance of industrial apprenticeship. Five years on, the Wilson government sustained without questioning the Conservative government's commitments to fund the education of managers pound for pound, but the party faithful were either not bothered or suspicious. The business manager was still considered to be a gatecrasher in the Labour Party.

There was to be little progress on the trade union scene. I wrote to my friend, Victor Feather, general secretary of the TUC, on their centenary celebration in 1968 to suggest that the TUC might make a historic proposal: why not a college at a university devoted to the study of industrial relations, and the expanding theme of industrial social policy? The cost would be relatively small, and government should be persuaded to join in pound for pound. This could bring together a rising generation of trade unionists, managers and civil servants. Philip Nind, the first and brilliant director of the Foundation of Management Education, proposed we might call it Bevin College. The intellectuals of the party, in true Oxbridge style, had been bred with at best an indifference to how industry worked, or at worst a contempt, and the trade unions saw the manager as a mere bargainer on the other side of the table, or as the steward of capitalism, a Malvolio figure of no fun. Efficiency and competitiveness were problems remote from this pantheon of the movement's gods; distribution was their issue, not production. Both intellectual and unionist questioned the motivation of the manager. What were managerial values? Only money. What was a manager worth? I was soon going to run head-on into the jaws of that very crude, very good question.

I knew how much Victor had loved Bevin, but his final response to our proposals was to make a face and say, 'We'll have to wait another hundred years, Peter.' I began to sense a clash between my managerial values and my hopes to serve the Labour Party.

6

Minding Our Own Businesses

'Nationalization is a constitutional outrage.' Who said that?

Astonishingly, Nye Bevan, over thirty years ago, and he surely was one of the experts on the subject, one of the architects of the Labour government's great programme of nationalization from 1945. What worried him, specifically and prophetically, was the muddle between the chairman of the public sector industry and the Minister responsible for it in Parliament. Was the Minister the champion of the industry, jousting for it in the government, or was he its scourge, championing the tax payer? Whose side was he on? And was the chairman of the board of the industry (say mines or railways) the agent of his political master, or was he in business, competing, taking risks in the market-place, in research and development? Was he thinking ten or twenty years ahead, in contrast to the politician for whom five years is eternity? This confusion has often proved a built-in, self-destructing component in the performance of public enterprise in Britain, and it has much wider implications. It reflects a weakness in the industrial policy of Britain since the war; the unfruitful coupling of politics and industry, of Parliament and business.

I believe that government is involved inevitably in the prosperity of the economy in any advancing, technologically based society. The degree of involvement has been the stuff of politics in post-war Britain. Butskellism, an uneasy faith in the mixed economy, lived unhealthily and finally died in the arms of corporate consensus in the Callaghan government of the late Seventies. Thatcherism may not die in anybody's arms – but its longevity will depend on how long it can preside over its pell-mell privatized economy. History provides the evidence that Nye was right: Labour failed to think through its nationalization policy, while the Conservatives' failure could prove to be that privatization was as ill-thought-out as nationalization. Ultimately there must be a vision that gives coherence to nationalization or privatization. Neither is an adequate substitute for industrial strategy. I agree with Michael Heseltine, who in the current Conservative Party emerges as the rich man's Nye Bevan: he insists that it is no longer arguable that we do not need an industrial strategy, just as it is no longer credible to claim that we have one. That is the voice of a manager.

The weakness of political parties is the lack of managerial experience of industry in Parliament. This seems to me sadly unavoidable. Politics has become a full-time job. All the more important, therefore, for thought to be given to the straining links between government and business. Privatization will change the strain, not remove it. The control of monopoly may not be much less of a headache than the control of unruly and turbulent chairmen of publicly owned corporations. It is in that context that some cautionary tales of the Sixties may be relevant. They press a most sensitive spot on the long front of the politico-business battleline – the appointment of the chairman of a nationalized industry. Suddenly all sorts of awkward questions are brought into painful focus.

In the spate of nationalization legislation under the Attlee Labour government the question of who was to run the public business was not seen as a matter of much moment, *pace* Nye Bevan. The minding of our own businesses was passed mostly to senior civil servants and soldiers, with the odd trade union peer, like the great Lord Citrine, proving an exception to the old Whitehall rule. When the Conservatives took over for the Fifties they seemed to have plenty of other things to think about. The act of nationalization that came to obsess them was Nasser's annexation of the Suez Canal. But by the end of the decade the effectiveness of public ownership was brought into sharp and painful focus by the Select Committee on Nationalized Industries. A bright-minded Conservative back-bencher, Toby Low, now Lord Aldington, chaired the committee's investigations of the managements of coal and rail, and found them wanting.

Then one of that rare breed, a businessman in the House, an accountant and roadbuilder, Ernest Marples, bustled on to the scene as Minister of Transport. He created a Special Advisory Group to look into the organization of the British Transport Commission, which included the railways. Four businessmen were on it. 'I wonder,' enquired Alfred Robens, the chairman of the National Coal Board, a Labour MP who was later to be made a peer by a Conservative government, 'I wonder whether these four businessmen realize that they may well have been brought in to be the handmaidens of government policy.'

A year later, one of the handmaidens with a small moustache, the stoutish, steady-eyed one on the right, was to be offered the chair of the newly separated British Rail, established in January 1963 – Dr Richard Beeching. Marples could not have picked a better man to fulfil his purposes, which he made icily clear in the government's White Paper, *The Financial and Economic Obligations of the Nationalized Industries*. Management was to achieve a break-even position over a five-year period, and to meet defined rates of return on investment. The ice was clear but terribly thin; it was bound to crack and indeed it did, pretty quickly. Gourvish, in his masterly history, *British Railways 1948–73*, wrote, 'Beeching was appointed to give effect to government intentions for its largest loss-maker by a Minister bent on redirecting resources into road transport.' He went on to do a magnificent job with the wrong terms of reference, and thank goodness he stopped before he finished the job. The railway system as a whole could not be made a profitable enterprise; nobody now pretends it can be, though parts of it may. To have gone on 'Beeching' the rail system would ultimately have been as futile as Peer Gynt peeling the onion to find its heart.

However, it was the Mountie-like determination of Marples to get his man that broke the long, discreet spell that had been cast over pay and rewards in the public sector. Beeching was given a five-year contract on terms equivalent to those he had enjoyed as technical director in ICI, at £24,000 a year, and this was twice as much as his predecessor, General Sir Brian Robertson, had received. (The General had also been chairman of the overlording organization, the British Transport Commission, at £10,000 a year, and when Churchill had appointed him he had compared his position to that of a viceroy.) Beeching's rate was also more than twice that of the chairmen of the Coal and Electricity Boards at the time, and more than three times that of the Parliamentary Secretary who was on £7,000, which incidentally was what the average executive member of a nationalized company board received. (The word 'member' is, as Churchill described an MP called Bossom, neither one thing nor the other. Why not 'director'? Presumably because a public corporation is not a normal business, but then neither does membership imply anything as jolly as joining a club.)

Marples's deal for Beeching was realistic but the contrast between rewards in different parts of the public sector made the headlines. The question was forced into public debate for the first time: was the management of a public corporation to be thought of as minding a business or was it simply administration? Beeching had no doubts about what he was doing. He brought in some forty top and senior managers from outside BR and paid a price for them in the competitive market of good management. The mistake he made was in not closing the gap of differentials between the old guard and the new. The traditional management were left to feel they were second-class citizens. This was true within BR and among the other nationalized industries.

Marples had at least made a start, but in 1964 it was the Labour government's turn to face the awkward question of exactly what value to put on a manager. Beeching resigned, a great man much misunderstood by the Left, Right and Centre. From the Left he appeared an axe-man: from the Right, from the road-hauliers' viewpoint, he was a threatening, questionable shape, a neutrally minded manager who would stop at nothing to achieve his cost-based analytical ends. Why, it was even possible this objective fellow might expose the economies of road as he had done rail and the unfair tilt of advantage to road-planning would be there for all to judge. From the Centre point of view, which included that of the ineffective, nice new Labour minister, Tom Fraser, Beeching's going was regrettable because with him went any hope of reviewing the whole complex of inland transport, not just railways.

Beeching's departure created a fresh opportunity to value a top manager in public enterprise, and Labour muffed it completely. Beeching had recommended one of his vice-chairmen, Stanley Raymond (later Sir Stanley), to succeed him. Raymond was a tough, decent manager whose remarkable career had begun as a Dr Barnado's boy, but the self-discipline that had brought him so far had left him short of the flexibility which the very top job needed. What is more, he was wrongly rewarded. Nothing had been achieved by the Beeching breakthrough on pay for those already on the public pay scales. Poor Raymond was hailed by the press as the Half-Pay Rail Chief.

The next chance to make management in the public sector more competitive with the private sector came with a bang: the nationaliz- ation of the steel industry. Once again, the unreadiness of Labour for the task of minding their own business was embarrassingly obvious. Richard Marsh became Minister of Fuel and Power and one of his immediate priorities was to nationalize fourteen steel companies. It was probably the most complicated take-over in British industrial history, and he found that no thought had been given to how it was to be done. (Two decades before him, in the advent of the Labour government in 1945, Emmanuel Shinwell had suffered a similar shock on becoming the Minister responsible for nationalizing the shambles of the mining industry after the war – he found that no plan existed to implement the policy which generations of Labour had yearned for.) In particular, in 1966, Marsh discovered to his astonishment that 'after years of argument about steel nationalization, no thought had been given to the potential chairman of this vast new undertaking.' Once again, management was the missing link in Labour's thinking.

This was the moment I first met Dick. He invited me to join an organizing committee which he was setting up to steer the giant merger; we were to work in parallel with the legislative process in Parliament, and to be ready, when the Act was passed, with our plans for a new corporation. We were to settle its long- and short-term policies for finance, marketing, production, industrial relations and technology, as well as its management and organization – all within a year. Dick was at his best on this first encounter, utterly relaxed and frank, one leg swinging over the arm of the easy chair in his enormous office. 'I'm about to make my reputation by cocking-up the steel industry if I'm not careful. I need help.' He had no illusions about his hazardous mission. His own Cabinet colleagues were divided about the case for nationalization. Woodrow (now Lord) Wyatt particularly had exposed this half-heartedness in his merry, ruthless fashion during the fierce debates in the Commons over the Bill. If only the steel barons had taken the initiative by rationalizing their fragmented industry for themselves, a settlement with the Labour government would have been feasible. But the barons were more used to compet- ing with each other than pulling themselves together, and Dick's view was that Conservative politicians had discouraged any moves towards voluntary collaboration. On the Labour side, any compromise was felt to be confusing, and since Wilson's 1964 government had a tiny majority of three, the political battlelines had to be kept clear for the imminent election. In 1966 Wilson was returned with a comfortable majority, but by then the barons were themselves in confusion and their industry in the gravest economic difficulties.

The story of steel is one of the saddest of many examples of adversarial politics putting its curse on the performance of British industry. Dick Marsh himself was not doctrinaire, and certainly no crusader, but he became convinced that the Act was the only way to make something happen in an industry paralysed and unprofitable. I thought his handling of any situation would be deft and I was wrong. It was masterly. He had an attractive openness of mind which surprised the steel leadership; his laid-back wit and self-mocking lack of pomp disarmed opposition, or at least shook it. This flexibility made him many friends in the industry, but not in the Labour Cabinet. His winning trick was his first: his appointment of Julian Melchett, an unexpected and superb choice. Julian was that rare bird, a merchant banker with an eagerness to be close to industry, a financier who behaved as if working people mattered. He had no experience of running a big organization, he had never tangled with politicians or Whitehall, never wrestled sumo-style with the fat, slow-motion unions, and this freshness was his strength. He was delightfully unencumbered by experience of the industrial world and moved the swifter for it. With his quick brain and humour there was a sturdiness of will which only emerged as troubles thickened. Steel entered his body and soul, I felt his sense of purpose became overwhelming; it made him impatient not with others but with himself, and it shortened his life.

In the early stages of the committee, Julian and I had a talk about the crushing workload. He was anxious because his committee members could not spare time to help him in depth, and I was anxious because I, like the others no doubt, had a diary six-foot deep with duties in the job for which I was being paid. I suggested that we had to get away for a clear weekend: surely he had some large house in the country in which to corral the lot of us? No, but he thought a friend would help.

The friend's place was Upton House in Oxfordshire, a many-splendoured mansion bought by Lord Samuel, from the founding family of Shell, and teeming with beautiful things. There the Organizing Committee crystallized its strategy in a weekend session. Capitalism was the generous host to a bunch of businessmen and trade unionists plotting their advance up a so-called commanding height, unlikely revolutionaries in an unlikely setting of grandeur and treasure.

Not that I knew about the wonders of the place at first. I arrived on the Friday night, dropped my bags at the palatial doorway and, without entering, followed the butler's direction down the drive to the wing where the meeting was assembled. We got to work at once but hours later, when there was a pause for a natural break, Sir Michael Milne-Watson and I took a prowl. We were tempted down a pitch-dark corridor, guided by our fingertips, intrigued by the feel of the velvet walls. Going up a few steps I touched a light switch. A huge room glowed with masterpieces, gold-framed against green-velveted walls. There was Breughel's Seymour Triptych, and there the sombre shock of his black and white 'Death of the Virgin', and Bellini's 'Last Supper', and much else – masterpieces were all over the house. I slept with a Goya in my bedroom. It was in this sumptuous context that the committee of captains of industry sat solemnly to settle the ways and means of fulfilling the old, almost fading, socialist dream of steel nationalization.

The next evening, the Minister and his posse of civil servants joined us, and even in the relaxed and constructive atmosphere I smelt the first whiff of that fire and brimstone issue; what should be the salary structure for the management of the new corporation? The fourteen companies all had their separate and different systems of pay and rewards for their managers, but they shared the reality that they were international businesses, and as such they had to hold their own in competitive worldwide markets for their products and their people. Steel traditionally paid high salaries and its managers had high expectations. It would have been ludicrous to expect that all these salary structures could be crushed together and crammed downwards to fit within the low ceilings of pay in the nationalized industries. Yet the Labour Cabinet would certainly not accept the logic of market rates for management: what was the world coming to if the principle of public service was to be corrupted by these commercial standards? Surely it was grotesque to talk of such selfish priorities at a time of economic crisis in the country when wage restraint was what was really called for.

One senior civil servant suggested a simple solution. Our problem became complicated, his argument ran, because statutorily board membership was a public appointment made individually by the Minister, and therefore the salary was published as a matter for Parliament. His suggestion was to have a wholly non-executive board, at inoffensively low fees which would be publicly known. The board could then proceed to pay the executives whatever it liked, and this could cause no political embarrassment at all because it would be entirely the board's business. This tempting piece of fudge was, of course, inedible. We had fourteen companies-worth of executive directors, most of them proved, competent, tough managers, annealed by lifelong experience of the industry. It would be vital to involve them in the policy formation of the new corporation, to give them a say in their own destiny, but ultimately the board had to be in charge, and how could a non-executive, part-time board be a credible authority over that lot? All the same, the wily suggestion was very revealing. It was the traditional administrative reflex to a business problem, and it measured the distance between the realities of the world and industry and those of Whitehall. It illustrated the sophisticated habit of avoiding that difficult issue, the value of management. Ten years later, on the British Airways Board, I witnessed Sir Henry Marking, as chief executive and a board member, with some 150 people in his organization paid more than he was. In my first year in the chair at BR, I appointed from outside the railway a general manager for pensions, and he was paid more than the chairman's rate.

We left Upton House sensing that a formidable row was brewing. The controversy escalated to the Chancellor. A small war-party of Julian Melchett, Ray Brooks (chairman of GKN and later Sir Ray) and I were summoned at 11 p.m. one night to No. 11 Downing Street. The Chancellor, Jim Callaghan, had just returned from the Queen Elizabeth Hall where he and Audrey had been to a concert, and a mood of harmony prevailed. Jim Callaghan had Dick Marsh on his left and Fred Lee on his right. We presented our case: steel was an international business; we had to compete in the recruitment and retention of good managers; our proposed salary structure compared sensibly with that of other sizeable corporations; and it would be unwise to demotivate the existing managers now when we needed to make the most of them. We said that we would have to resign if the rates paid to members of the coming corporation were set unrealistically. Dick Marsh recorded later: 'The impact on public and probably foreign confidence, of three leading industrialists saying that they were resigning from the Steel Board because they believed that it was being treated frivolously by the government, would have been considerable.'

By midnight Jim was nodding, convinced, and saying that he would put the case to the Cabinet personally the next day. He closed his file, and looking up, not at me, he said, 'Well, Peter, what does it all add up to, d'you think?' I looked blank because while I had been arguing about levels of average salary, any idea that I add up the total could not possibly make sense. But a voice from a shadowed alcove behind the Chancellor said something I couldn't hear, and in a moment people were on their feet and that was that. We eased off over a drink. I then discovered that the Peter who had answered the question I had not even understood was a Peter Baldwin. He was a civil servant working in the Treasury, and it was to him that the Chancellor had put the question, throwing it over his shoulder, checking on Peter's general reaction. Peter in his crisp, reassuring style had said fine. I was to come to know that style well. Ten years later, when I met him again, he was the Permanent Secretary of Transport for six of my seven years in BR, and was a godsend to me.

Cabinet approved the recommendation and Dick summed up the No. 11 climax in his autobiography: 'It was one of those occasions which demonstrated the ultimate role part-time non-executive board members can play if they have the courage . . . This was one of the few occasions when the government was faced with a serious challenge from the part-time members of a nationalized industry.' It taught me early on that the best hope for good management in the public sector is a strong Minister who can hold his or her own in Cabinet and a strong board which can hold its own against the Minister.

The Organizing Committee formed the nucleus of the board for the new British Steel Corporation, and this was my first membership of a board in the public sector. I served on it part-time from 1967–9, while continuing to work for Bookers. But before that, at the start of the Sixties, I had found myself drawn into the vacuum between government and industry. The FBI (now the CBI) had a working party on economic development, and I was part of that. There was a mood of frustration in industry. The stop-go routines of government policy were baffling managers, and our national competitiveness was faltering just as the newly equipped nations of Europe were hitting their stride. We persuaded the Conservative Chancellor, Selwyn Lloyd, who seemed similarly baffled, that some form of industrial strategy was sensible; and it was a Conservative government that inaugurated the National Economic Development Office in 1961. Neddy was born, and from it a litter of little Neddies followed, each a committee dealing with a main industrial sector of the economy. We were all planners then. Some attended the christening with new hope; others simply to see what the little bastard looked like. The first years of Neddies were messy. The company representatives on the committee were chary of blunting their competitive edge by too much exposed consultation; the unions were chary of being active in support of a Conservative administration. There was a lot to do and too little enthusiasm around the table to do it. Still, something was stirring, and some enthusiasts, like myself, felt strongly that an open partnership of government and industry, both employers and unions, was the best chance we had to make a success of the mixed economy. Neddy has lasted twenty-five years but now, in the heady confidence of the third Thatcher government, it is being cavalierly reduced by Nigel Lawson. It is almost a ritual of new administrations that Neddy is criticized and cut down, then cautiously encouraged.

I served on the Mechanical Engineering Neddy in the mid-Sixties. I was chairman of Bookers Engineering by then, and the group was expanding. The necessity for modernizing the manufacturing base of Britain was starkly obvious, particularly to somebody manufacturing basic equipment like pumps and mining equipment. I threw myself into the British Pump Manufacturers Association, of which I became chairman, and was staggered to find there were over 150 trade associations in the gnarled old British engineering industry. Most were arthritic with the pride and prejudice of their trade, many were run by senior citizens sitting on the edge of their pensions. Some rationalization was vital, but only slowly, slowly did it happen. It was not until the Seventies that the Council of Engineering was established, although by the end of the Sixties we had made a start, when twelve associations joined the British Mechanical Engineering Confederation. I persuaded Ray Brooks (with whom I later worked in the formation of the British Steel Corporation) to be the first president, and I succeeded him. The history of Britain's ramshackle array of trade associations is an industrial tragedy, a powerful cause of the downfall of our manufacturing. Competing nations had streamlined their processes of industrial representation, but in Britain manufacturing did not have a coherent voice as the crunch of competition came on us. The CBI was an employers' lobby, but too large, too full of contradictions, trying to cope with the conflicting interests of suppliers and customers. In all this muddle, engineering got itself lost.

It was in the year following my recruitment on to the British Steel Board that the next round of cautionary tales about the relationship of government, civil service and enterprise began. On Wednesday, 8 November 1967, I was at the board of our central heating group on the Team Valley Estate, Newcastle, when a message arrived from Barbara Castle at the Ministry of Transport: could I meet her at six that evening? There was no explanation, but the urgency was underlined by the detail that a car would meet me as I stepped off the plane at Heathrow. When the plane touched down, sure enough I was picked out for special treatment, ushered down the steps, and instructed to wait there. It was a drizzly, grey evening. Our small flight had been parked on the edge of the world, it seemed to me. The rest of the passengers marched past me to their bus; soon the deck and cabin crews stepped off, the steward smiling reassuringly at me, and they were driven away. I stood there, getting wet. Eerily, nothing happened, nobody was about. I just got wetter. I decided that I had better pick my way through the huge parking lot of glistening aircraft toward the nearest well-lit warm building. I started walking, then trotting and cursing, holding my briefcase over my head against the rain. By the time I found shelter and a phone, I was soaking and boiling at the same time. No, the Minister was not available to take my call. I explained that I had been literally running late – what the hell was happening anyway? Ah, yes. The Minister had had to cancel my meeting, hadn't that message reached me? No – but it had certainly reached the car that was supposed to meet me; it never arrived. Only the rain got through to me.

The incident at the airport was on the Wednesday. I heard no more about it through Thursday. The aborted meeting, I reflected, must have been related to the work of the committee for the Review of London Transport in which I, with Sir Anthony Burney, had been cast as the external minds. I strongly suspected that, before the Committee had ever met, the Ministry had decided that the chairman of London Transport should be changed, and I concluded that they were now arranging an elaborate cover. The Minister wanted me, as an external member of the firing squad, to be involved in the decision. That at least seemed the most likely explanation of why I had been called so urgently. A couple of months previously I had spent an hour with Barbara Castle and her private secretary, John Gunn. We had touched briefly on the possibilities of all change at London Transport, but not in any depth. Our talk had been wide ranging, spirited and inconclusive. It was bound to be, though Barbara was in her most decisive and dazzling prime. The Prime Minister had put her there to give the Ministry of Transport some drive – 'I must have a Minister who can act' – and that brief was red meat and champagne to Barbara. I left her feeling uplifted, feeling that somehow I had just been measured for my uniform, though there had been no mention of exactly what branch of the Salvation Army I was to serve in. However, all that had been months earlier.

On the Friday morning, 10 November, John Gunn rang at the crack of dawn: the Minister wanted to see me during the morning. I said that I had to go a memorial service at Blackheath. The Minister was hoping to go to it as well, but it would not be possible to talk in public, so we fixed on nine o'clock at her office in the Commons. As I walked alone through the echo-filled corridors of the House, I could not resist thinking how pleasant a place it was – when empty.

Barbara was brimming with energy and exulting in decisions – 'something cheerful to do with my metabolism'. She sat at her desk, fiery hair back-lit by the bright window, turquoise-blue suit, copper bangles. A shrewd beauty. I remembered my brief encounter with her on the platform of the Oxford Labour Club.

We got down to business immediately. She had it mind, she said, to offer me the chairmanship of British Rail. Straight on: she warned me that the press was unlikely to react favourably, because of my age and politics. The top railwaymen were not going to welcome any outsider, either. Her directness was impressive. I tried to respond as straightforwardly. I was honoured to be trusted with the job. The press reactions should not concern me at the outset, but the support of the BR Board was essential. I explained that on boards I chaired, it was normal to ask at least two senior members of the board to give a preliminary assessment and recommendation of any new appointment: could I meet some of the BR Board? The Minister said, 'That is the very issue. I spoke to Bill Johnson, the vice-chairman, on Wednesday afternoon and he objected strongly to the proposal of an outsider. I did not tell him your name.' Then, we agreed, he should be told and I had to meet him: 'We must take the risk at once.' That was the beginning of what Barbara Castle described six weeks later, in her diary entry, as 'the famous Parker case'.

On Sunday, 3 December, the morning session with Bill Johnson opened politely and tensely. Johnson, at sixty, made no bones about his opposition to an outside appointment. Railways needed a rest from political interference: that was the attitude of the railway managers. They were fed up with outsiders coming in, getting a gong and getting out. No railwayman could get to the top through the scramble of politicians, civil servants, consultants – and 'outsiders'. I interrupted, genuinely puzzled, 'What about Sir Stanley Raymond?'

'He's not a real railwayman, he's only been with us for ten years, he came from the buses.'

There was a moment of silence, then Bill started to chuckle at himself and what he had just said. 'I know, I know – we're all in the transport business, but that's what we railwaymen feel.'

We went on to examine what I saw as the crux of the argument: the excruciating degree of political interference. To a degree, it was inescapable. Politics had become part of the permanent way of life on the rails. The ticket office and the voting booth are only semidetached in the mind of politicians. One role of the BR Board was to strive to see that the political relationship did not confuse the living daylights out of the managers responsible for the service day to day. If an outside appointment could help to clarify the expectations that government and railways had of one another, then that was a bull point in its favour. Together Bill and I analysed the weaknesses of the political links. This was an issue bigger than BR. Politicians had no time for serious business experience in their careers. Neither did civil servants, but their influence had continuity. Ministers flitted through the corridors of power and out at the far end: the civil servants had the staying power and the brains. The last hope was to see that a board was created strong enough to hold its own under these pressures. New appointments to it would have to be made and a new deal defined for BR, one which clarified its strategy and scope. It seemed unrealistic to expect much to happen differently if the same old guard turned up round the table and went into battle for it. For two hours Bill and I were at it. When Maisie, Bill's wife, appeared with coffee Bill said simply, 'I think I can make this man into a railwayman.' We had talked ourselves into a possible partnership.

Bill became a friend and an ally over the next few weeks. We had no secrets from one another from that first day. In my notes of the encounter, I found myself reaching a long way back for the right words to describe Bill: 'sterling worth', 'straight as a gun barrel', but really his were the ancient virtues – simplicity, honesty, courage – and the good humour not to make them a bore. The one combustible issue which we had not anticipated at all that Sunday morning was the one that blew up and blew us off course. When I was reporting on my session with Bill to Barbara on the Monday evening, 13 December, her room was overcrowded with advisers. I said that I was confident that the way was clear to go ahead: in engine-driver language, the lights were green all the way. Barbarba Castle describes what happened next in *The Castle Diaries 1964–70*:

His answer therefore was yes, he would take the job. I then broached the question of salary. We were reviewing salaries in all the nationalized industries but it would take a little time to complete. Would he start at Raymond's salary of £12,500? He looked at me squarely and said quietly and steadily, 'No, that would be my first mistake as Chairman.' It soon became clear to me that getting nationalized industries more in line with private industries was a key principle with him. 'Look,' he said unhappily, 'I want to help. But as a lifelong Socialist I believe we simply cannot make public ownership work by starving it of talent. A man like Johnson, for instance, as Chief Executive ought to get at least £15,000 and I won't take the job unless he does. I shall have failed unless in two years' time we have a first-class Railways Board. How on earth am I to recruit them under a ceiling of £12,500? I couldn't get a financial director under £18,000. I don't mind paying him more than I get myself, but we must begin an upward movement in salaries for all key staff and to do that I must have headroom. Why, they offered me £15,000 just for a board job in steel! The Chairman of BR ought not to get a penny less than £22,000. I am prepared to come for £17,500, provided Johnson gets £15,000 – and that's not the professional salary. But it is not the money that I worry about for myself. After tax it will only make a few hundreds difference anyway. But I must have room to move up the men under me – it's the only way to get that upward boost in morale. I fought this battle on steel and my first job as Chairman must be to fight it on railways.' I was very impressed by his manner and, as for the argument, I was already convinced, having backed Dick Marsh over the steel salaries. All I could do was to say that I would do my best – and tell Gunn I wanted to see the Chancellor and PM right away.

Two days of intensive and secret talks followed. In Bookers I had to make plain the proposition before me and the stand that I was taking. In government, Barbara was lobbying 'like a fury' – though lobbying was not one of her strongest points. Two civil servants came over to see me to vet details of a paper to be sent to the Cabinet. Their memorandum on the Monday sermon checked accurately with a minute I had drawn up for myself (I was glad to see it, though sad to have to admit that it was far better written). We relaxed over coffee and talked over the likely timetable for Thursday. Barbara was pushing the item up in the Cabinet agenda, there was a good chance that a message would reach me mid-morning. Meanwhile I was to pass over personal objects and photographs for the press release that afternoon.

On the Thursday morning I was chairing a Booker Engineering board. I warned my colleagues that it was likely that I would be catching my train between ten and eleven. That hour passed. So did eleven to twelve. And twelve o'clock too. We sat down to lunch and still no call. A few minutes after two the message arrived: I was to see the Secretary of State, but could I approach the building inconspicuously and make my way through the side-door. She met me at the door of her office. 'We've won in principle, we've just lost in timing.' I said that was about the most political remark I had heard for a long time. She explained that they wanted me to come in on the tariff rate; my own recommendations would be implemented later.

I had to say no, and at once. I could see myself with a new Minister of Transport in no time; me sitting here and the new Minister saying over that very desk, with polite concern, 'What exactly was the arrangement?' Then Barbara pitched into me. A shrewd beauty all right but a rough, menacing fighter. My reputation would be ruined if I failed to do my public duty because I was not being paid enough. The Government had clout with the press, what had I got? In the secrecy of the past week, the code-word my office had used for her had been 'dragon eyes', and the dragon eyes blazed away. In a pause, I asked if she meant to frighten me into changing my advice: surely if she succeeded this would only prove she had the wrong man. She sighed grimly and said to her personal secretary, the good John Gunn, sitting in on all this, 'I told the Cabinet that is how he would react. Now you have him.'

John led me off to a solitary confinement for ten minutes. Then I was told that I was to see the Prime Minister in his rooms at the House. Wilson met me courteously, thanked me for my (in fact, small) part in a television broadcast during the election, then sat me beside him at the long table. Barbara was on my right and said nothing during the next ten minutes. The three of us sat in a row as if we were already at the press conference that was to open in half an hour. Actually the talk was quiet and genial. Wilson was, as ever, calm: halfway through he put his feet up on the table. We got nowhere. He addressed his feet through a cloud of pipe-smoke in front of him. At one stage, gazing through the incense, he mused, 'I think I'll have a word with J. C. about this.' For a flash, I couldn't help wondering if he really had to go quite that high – but of course, he meant Jim Callaghan.

With hindsight now I must admire the self-control of his perform-ance, a courageous show because he had much mightier matters than myself and railways on his mind. The interview must have been trivial, enraging in the context of his day, which had begun with a disastrous Cabinet that morning. But he gave absolutely no sign of that Thursday being the worst Thursday of his government life, as I was only to discover some days later. On reflection, perhaps the strain on him showed in a degree of excessive informality which puzzled me at the time. I had some difficulty finding where his sentences ended – he was playing it too much at ease. But his meaning came through forcefully enough: my proposition on pay structure was neither timely nor acceptable, the economy was under strain, pay rises at the top would be a bad example when restraint was called for. What would the unions make of it? Or the other chairmen in the public sector?

I told him that I could make my recommendations only within the limits of the task I was being set. If there was to be change on the rails, it must be through a commercial approach, and our dealings with managers must be commercial too. Labour should not keep the managers of public enterprises as second-class citizens compared with the private sector. Plans for the strengthening of railways management were already published, and they openly declared the need for four appointments at board level; this meant recruitment from outside into the railways, and it would be impossible for me to promise that I could recruit and retain the top people needed unless there was a realistic and competitive salary structure. Surely the public would respect a prompt, realistic decision. The value of management in public enterprise was a professional issue: if it was faced in a business-like way at last it would be to the credit of a Labour government determined to improve efficiency in public services. I had taken the trouble to consult my touchstone, Vic Feather of the TUC: Vic reckoned everybody getting over £2,500 was overpaid anyway but he had gone robustly on to say that it was a matter for government and the government should pay the market rate. 'They're confused, the dogs are on 'em, Peter,' he had said, but had added that the trade unions believed in paying the rate for the job. As for the current chairmen of the nationalized industries, the senior of them, Alf (now Lord) Robens, had been telling me emphatically that the time had come for a new deal over the anomalies of public and private pay; he had even complained that I was wrong to pitch the level as low as I had.

Wilson heard me out gamely enough. He was a much nicer man than ever he gave himself credit for. He was not the hard, sharp character he sometimes wanted to seem, nor was he a soft do-gooder; he was a tough think-gooder. He pulled his feet down and stood up and said sorry that he couldn't help. That startled me. I said I was sorry that it seemed I couldn't help either; any outside appointment would stand where I stood, and if my first recommendations were not sensible then they should go for the good 'insider'. And I headed round the table, for the door and out.

Barbara did not move, but she broke her silence to ask me to hang on outside for a moment. I was surprised to see in her diaries that Wilson had said after I left, 'He's impressive.' I felt I had not made the slightest impression. The day had risen with the highest hopes until high noon, and then had crashed, literally within minutes of their realization. I felt bleak; I ached to do the job. Not to do it was to be at odds on all sides – with government, with Labour, with the media and the public. And in the long run, of course, even with Bookers. There my colleagues had been kept in the picture and had been staunch in support throughout the week, but after all this, it would be obvious that I was loose in the socket of my Booker job.

Barbara came out and we spoke briefly. Would I hang on a few days more? Of course, but I wondered what good that could possibly do. She was crying a bit. She dabbed at her face and said she had to go and tackle the press conference where everything was ready to launch me – photographs, releases, the lot. I went home, the place which, as the poet Robert Frost once put it, 'when you have to go there, they have to take you in'.

Jill and Tom, and Lucy, now fifteen, talked with me into the night. I knew that I was landing them in the worst of public troubles, that is the confusion of two rights. I had a public duty to the government, though that meant one thing to them and another to me: I thought I had to hold my ground for the sake of the railways. It was only an outsider who could argue this case for them, and for the whole public sector. It was obviously in my interests to be convenient but it would also destroy my effectiveness in doing the job and so my credibility with the board. 'A bloody difficult day,' said Tom, and it was not like him to swear. Just how bloody and difficult for the government I, with the rest of the nation, learned on the Saturday and the Sunday, when I listened to Wilson's famously ambiguous broadcast on devaluing the pound in people's pockets.

Barbara rang me immediately afterwards to fix yet another meeting on the Monday. She filled in the background for me. The Cabinet on the previous Thursday had been overwhelmed by the debate on devaluation; the railway appointment had originally been the early point on the agenda, after Parliamentary business and overseas affairs, but it had been pushed down to a sub-committee which had stalled her. She gave me also the full story of the months of discussion over the choice of chairman. Apparently she had decided on me after our first encounter two months before but the Department and her advisers had headed her in other directions. Headhunters had been let loose for a wider search, the first time this had been done on this level of appointments. My age, forty-two, had been against me; and so, paradoxically, had my Labour credentials. I had not run a big 'name' organization, and was I tough enough? (Barbara had later discovered that the very adviser who had raised the doubt about my durability had himself nursed an interest in taking the chair.) Now, she commented wryly, considering the roughness of the fight we were in – which I had started – toughness was the least of her worries. She swore that never again would she use headhunters. (Never my

151

view: I think that, used wisely, they are invaluable. But then, I would say that. Nowadays one of my keenest interests is the chairmanship of Whitehead Mann, a leading British search organization with world-wide connections.) Barbara asked me, where did I stand now? Of course, devaluation changed things. I answered that as far as I was concerned I would take a cut of twelve and a half per cent; in fact, she could pay me in washers, but Bill Johnson must be at the £15,000 level to give me a chance to bring in top management from outside at competitive rates. Fair enough, she replied. But over the next few weeks she could make no progress. Barbara and I agreed to hang on together in the swirling water around the wreck of the government's economic policies. Devaluation had stopped George Brown dead in his tracks: he was the chief architect of growth planning at the Department of Economic Affairs but his Declarations of Intent had proved to be only a pavement to hellish disappointments. He moved into the Foreign Office, raging with frustration. Callaghan lost his grip on the Treasury and slipped overboard, into the Home Office. Roy Jenkins moved into No. 11 Downing Street.

In those next troubled weeks two main points became clear to me. Firstly, the Railway Board were solidly in support of the case I was arguing. Secondly, if I was not to take the chair, undoubtedly there was a reliable alternative in Bill Johnson, and I said so to the Ministry. The ensuing press headlines of 'the Parker thing' were not a pretty sight for the family. I was in the pillory and pelted with fruity adjectives such as unpatriotic, selfish, insensitive to the honour of public service. Newspapers who had never had a good thing to say about nationalized industries were most severe in their condemnation of my refusal of such an honour. But it was the disappointment of Labour friends and colleagues that isolated me most. I could understand that well enough. The ideal of the Labour movement was brotherhood, fellowship, community, the sacrifice of self-interest for the common good; and I had never taken the expression of these values to be mere sentimentality, starry- or even bleary-eyed. The war had shown what a commonwealth of free women and men could do with that ideal, working together each according to his ability for the enrichment and happiness of all. I believe that finding a cause larger than one's own is civility. My own ideal, William Blake, had talked of casting away the Sceptre of Selfhood. 'Damn the money,' Blake said, and in his long poem *Jerusalem*, 'Lo! We are One, forgiving all Evil, not seeking recompense.' Yet there I was, cast as someone in the thrall of the Sceptre, behaving disgracefully, selfishly showing concern above all else with my own reward. It was Managerialism versus Socialism, with a vengeance. Business friends were mostly relieved: 'You're well out of that.' Jill received sympathetic calls from several of them, one solicitously saying, 'The job would have killed him, you know, it's impossible.' Actually Jill was only worried that not doing the job would crack me.

When the call finally came for me to meet the new Chancellor, Roy Jenkins, I happened to be standing by my bookshelf at home, eye-level to *The Pursuit of Progress*, written by Roy in 1953. I pulled it out to flick through it. My habit then was to rename a book if I had become very interested in it: it was a crude device I used to register the book's theme in my memory, or rather, my view of it. The title that I had scribbled under Roy's was 'Socialism versus Managerialism'. Even more relevant was another scribbled reference to page 178:

> A rational policy for wages, salaries and other personal incomes must be worked out. It is hypocritical to talk about greater equality and fairer shares unless this is to be applied between different industries as well as between different social groups. Those who work in profitable industries must remember the claims of those who work in industries such as the railways which are unlikely ever to be free of financial difficulty.

I reminded him of this in the heat of the hour or so we spent together at the Treasury the next afternoon. He began by saying that he had to be the Iron Chancellor, and that we should be able to clear the issue in twenty minutes. I said that my case gave him the opportunity to be that, to take a firm line, to prove that Labour was committed to efficiency and to bring the Labour Party into the managerial age. He showed an unhesitating welcome for the idea of my being chairman, 'We can settle this quietly and quickly. Do it Peter, and you'll be in the centre of things – centre-stage,' (an unexpected phrase from him, though it wouldn't have been from me, I suppose). He said that we could sort out the pay strategy for BR management in a year or so. I realized, finally, that Barbara had been only half right. Certainly we had lost in timing but we still had not won a victory of principle.

Roy and I were neither of us at all pleased with one another by the end of what had been fixed to be a twenty-minute meeting. We had taken an hour and twenty minutes and were standing angrily at the end. We were both due at the same dinner party and had to change. When we met there at dinner I asked him, 'Will you tell her or shall I?' He replied shortly, 'I've told her already.' I could tell that I was damned in his estimation. Barbara records in her diary the message reaching her at work the next day, and by teatime she rang me at Bookers to say she had offered the job to Bill Johnson at £12,500, and he had accepted. He wanted a word with me. 'I'd have been happy either way,' he said.

The next year I was in political purdah, a non-person, but I hardly had the time to notice. Our Booker engineering businesses were struggling for orders at home as the domestic economy went through Roy's wringer of deflation. Exports were more than ever vital to us, and we were scouring the world on sales missions. A sugar-factory order was extracted from the Philippines through an agent who then operated from a single room and now has a building in the centre of the City of London. It was a big but bizarre bit of business, negotiating through the jungle of presidential relatives, a sleek top-cat society glittering and phosphorescent with decay.

Another long hunt was in East Africa, for a vast agricultural development contract in Uganda. Corruption there was more formally institutionalized, and contract terms would solemnly propose a contribution to the Milton Obote Fund. There was the inevitable series of rendezvous on dark verandas outside Kampala, and there were sometimes more exotic moments, like the midnight dance in the Police Commissioner's gardens, attended by ministers and also by the Uganda dance group, which was about to set off for a tour of Britain. I can just remember shaking a lance with a spectacular topless beauty while the Commissioner beat the drums. But we lost that deal to traders from behind the Iron Curtain who, we were told later, seemed to have found the way to the appropriate Minister's heart through a Swiss bank account. I had met this Minister and had not wished him well: he was a young, elegant economist, stupendously arrogant, in a trance of vanity, a dream of avarice. Within six months he had disappeared but not at all according to the plan he had no doubt prepared for himself. The money must have turned his head, which was then screwed even looser by the attractions of the wife of a cook working in the State buildings. The affair had not been conducted discreetly.

A black ministerial Mercedes parked regularly most afternoons outside the cook's shack in a slum area naturally became the subject of some talk. One afternoon the talk reached the cook. He took an afternoon off and cycled home to catch the Minister in flagrante. Later he cycled to the local police station and reported proudly that he had stamped on a Minister's balls. That night the Minister, wrapped in bandages, was bundled out of the country.

Business with Castro's Cuba, on the other hand, was clean as a shark's tooth. We tried to land a whale of a contract there for sugar machinery and irrigation equipment, and I made two trips there in 1968 and 1970. The first was with Jill, which of course, as always on a business trip, halved the social strain and doubled the fun. As a doctor she was impressed by the classlessness in the hospitals she visited there. Once she was being taken round wards by the hospital director, a surgeon of international reputation, when they passed a little old lady sitting desolated by the empty bed where her husband had died during the night. The doctor took her out to sit with him on the fire escape, to talk with her, to try to give her some comfort. Would that have happened under our own hospital conventions?

The hospital was understaffed, underequipped, undermanaged, but also mercifully unhierarchical compared to the traditional and stratified medical institutions of the West. This was roughly the story of Cuba as a whole. There was a puritanical mood of dedication. The Revolution was just nine years old. Nightclubs were shut and ice-cream seemed to be the order of the day, served in a rainbow of varieties and all over the city. I saw for myself the young people working in the fields, not a newsreel camera in sight, and heard them singing happily. I went to the Isle of Pines, renamed the Isle of Youth, and saw there the horrific round prisons of previous regimes being converted by the young workers into youth hostels and polytechnics. I discovered Castro had stuffed his political prisoners into the even older, rotting gaols around Havana's harbours. It struck me that here was a genuine revolution caught in the trap of Marxist communism. What had begun as an 1848-style uprising against tyranny had been doomed to end as a wonky, unreliable cog in the Russian Cold War machine. I was never convinced of the thoroughgoingness of Cuban communism. The nature of the people, their gaiety, their uncontrollable vitality is surely the best insurance against that withering credo. And it was not Communism that started the rising against Batista's long and brutal dictatorship. It was more a madcap courage and a murderous fury. When Castro's tiny revolutionary force landed in 1958 it was ambushed, and only about a dozen survivors scrambled through swamp to hide in the mountains. Within a year, that is all, they were riding in triumph through Havana, swept into power by a people's revolt. The early days of victory had been chaos, not a Communist take-over. I was told of a noisy session of the revolutionary committee when the guerrilla leaders were dividing the Ministries among themselves. 'Who is to take finance?' asked Castro, shouting over the hubbub, 'Who's an economist?'

'I am,' cried Che Guevara, thinking that the question had been 'Who's a Communist?'

The United States, who had cynically backed Batista, had no policy to cope with these adventurers. All they tried to do was to bully the new Cuba back into its old shape as the sugar bowl for the North American continent. Their subtle negotiating tactic was to hammer the US price for Cuba's sugar. Castro retaliated by expropriating the American-owned sugar plantations, but the break with the US forced his hand. He had to find another customer for Cuba's only tradable asset, its huge sugar crop. Interestingly enough he turned to China first, not to Russia, and Cuba filled up with Chinese experts who were to help diversify and industrialize the island. But the Chinese revolutionaries patronized the Cubans with their experience and bored them with their ideology. Castro went on the radio one night and ordered the Chinese to leave within twenty-four hours, the lot of them; any left over would be arrested. (What if they had got on well as partners – would Cuba have opened up as China did?) Russia was the only alternative customer of sufficient scale to deal with, and the Russians forged their trade agreements like manacles. They insisted on Cuba concentrating its efforts on the historic priority, sugar, dispelling the dreams of diversification and reducing the role of the revolution as standard-bearer for the Third World. Cuba was to be a sugar bowl again, this time for the Russians.

In disgust and broken-hearted, Che Guevara left Cuba to seek more revolution in Bolivia, and the Russian planners moved in. I would see them at the Havana Libre (formerly the Havana Hilton), sitting po-faced on the edge of the swimming-pool, dabbling their toes in the shallow end, and pondering no doubt over their impossible mission: how to make Cubans good bureaucrats, filling up forms efficiently. Efficiency was not the strong suit of the Cubans: enthusiasm certainly was. I kept finding my letter-box crammed with letters addressed to Wesker. 'Half right anyway, wasn't it?' said the smiling porter. Arnold Wesker, in black shirt and black jeans, was in Havana to attend the première of his latest play, but of course only half his scenery seemed to have turned up. I had tried to help with the funding of the experimental theatre, the Roundhouse, in London, so we knew each other. He had enthusiasm to match that of the Cubans. He described sitting close to Castro during one of those lengthy Castro speeches. 'Messianic, of course.' I pressed him for more detail. 'The beard's surprisingly wispy, though the photos make it look massive.' After a moment's thought, 'You know, I think he must be Jewish.' The greatest compliment from Arnold.

I met Castro myself for four hours on the second trip. My team of negotiators had been accommodated in one of the 'protocol houses' on the edge of Havana. These had once been a millionaires' row of airy mansions, spread sumptuously along the gold beaches and bright blue seas. Our negotiations were intense, but we dressed relaxedly, and melted into the water as often as we could. On the fourth day, Quesada, the central planning executive in charge of the negotiations, surprised me by asking me to wear a suit for a tour of visits to Ministers who would all be dressed smartly in their air-conditioned offices. I came back in the late afternoon to find Quesada hopping about anxiously on the steps. 'You must take that suit off quickly. The Commandante is coming for a surprise visit. If he finds you in a suit he'll think I've warned you.'

Castro actually arrived hours later, about ten at night, in combat uniform, boots, peaked cap, and driving his own jeep, with his Sten-gun-toting aide alongside. When he entered the conference room, his aide exchanged the gun for a Swedish calculating machine which he immediately plugged in close to Castro. Throughout the negotiation over the next three hours Castro was to use the calculator himself to check details in the specifications – the performance of a very numerate manager, if ever I've met one. As we greeted each other he suggested I sit beside him on the cane sofa, but I refused, explaining that I had come to know the sofas well in my short stay in the house and this one had springs at that end of it which might well impale his guest. I took the chair to his right, and this proved a wise move too, because as the discussion developed I noted how energetically he sat

157

and how expansively he gestured. He obviously needed elbow-room, in fact every kind of room, leg-room, headroom, even room to rub his balls, which he did quite unselfconsciously from time to time. A curling beard and a mane of hair seemed to be vibrations of his large personality, but separately, his features were relatively smaller, the eyes quieter, the beard, as Arnold had said, wispier than the photos portrayed; and, as the gestures grew and the bones of his wrists and ankles began to show, I noticed that they were more delicate than the burly uniform implied.

The Cuban negotiating team joined us and seemed at ease with him and his vigorous questioning. Castro asked one of them, a Cuban sugar technologist who had graduated at the Massachusetts Institute of Technology, to act as interpreter. Having a good interpreter is a joy in my life: there is time to think between sentences. (There's a role for them between English speakers as far as I'm concerned, certainly between the British and the Americans and even between, say, a British manufacturer and a City man. I'd love one in the City.) Our MIT man did well until the moment, about three hours later, that found both him and me out. I was staring at Castro's face, listening to the interpreter and nodding gravely when Castro tapped me on the knee and spoke in English to say, 'No, no, this man is so tired he is repeating my Spanish to you.'

It was well past midnight, so there was a break. Quesada followed Castro back into the room and put a thumbs-up sign to me, shielding it from his colleagues with his other hand. We then spoke of other things: what did I think of what I had seen of Havana? I said the people seemed fit and fed but the shops I had seen were empty and the nightclubs shut. Were the Romans wrong with their formula of bread and circuses? Castrol thought a while and then laughed; he said that he thought he was a bit of a circus. I said it seemed to me that the US was being helpful by stationing their ships within sight of the shore: maybe they would realize that such provocation simply reinforced the will of his people? He chuckled, and really wondered if that had occurred to them. They acted even more helpfully when they sent spies. 'And when they land here,' he said, 'you can recognize them because they wear crash helmets and carry two radio sets.'

The talk was grand and we were to build the biggest sugar factory in the world. I flew out early two days later, in a small executive Russian jet, with a filmy blonde serving breakfast, and white rum offered with everything. Inexplicably we had permission to land at Nassau, but while my colleague and I were streamed into the normal passenger building the jet and its crew were isolated on the field: we could not even get a tiny thank-you bottle of perfume out to the stewardess. Nothing came of the grand talk of the sugar factory: the orders that came to us eventually were closer to the ground – extensive irrigation equipment.

I could have done with an interpreter when I got back to London for a fast-talking round of discussions opening up again with the Labour government. It was 1969 and my year's purdah was over, it seemed. Barbara's championing of my cause had not won the day for new salary structures in the public sector but it did win the year. Our *cause célèbre* had stimulated a House of Commons select committee inquiry into the question, and its report had echoed our original recommendation for pay levels on the boards of nationalized industries. I was called to meet the Secretary of State for Employment at the House of Commons – and there was Barbara. She had left Transport shortly after our battle – they really need a revolving door in that Ministry – and had been promoted to be Secretary of State for Employment. I was asked to see her at 2.40 p.m. precisely, so precisely that I made sure by being there five minutes early.

I hung about the corridor of ministerial offices, green-carpeted, with ominously amber lighting – was this to be my fate in limbo, forever amber? Tony Crosland, then running Trade, came along to his office and saw me, calling from a distance, 'What the hell are you doing here?'

Barbara emerged and swept me into her office, answering for me, 'He's seeing me, Tony.'

Tony followed me through the door and said, 'Well, I hope you're not going to offer him a job: I've something in mind.'

'Certainly not, Tony.' And as the door closed, 'Oh, I'm not but Wilson is. He wants me to ask you to be chairman of the Prices and Incomes Board. Aubrey Jones is about to announce his going any minute and we want to have a replacement at once. Will you do it?' Unhesitatingly I hesitated. I must be given time to consider. I did not like the sound of this: I had to be sure there was an Incomes Policy left to chair. 'But Peter, you can't keep refusing jobs.' I held on for a time but realized that the government needed somebody, and only personal reasons would excuse me from this duty. A few weeks later Barbara's diary records our meeting:

Friday, 29 August
Had Peter Parker in for coffee. He's been ill and I haven't heard from him. I told him that I didn't want to badger him about making up his mind over the PIB as there might be new developments, but he was all ready to give me his answer. It seemed to him that we would have difficulty in getting anyone to succeed Aubrey and yet keep up the momentum of incomes policy because most people would realize that the job might only last a few months. We could therefore either put in a caretaker chairman, which he thought would be disastrous, or find someone who was willing to be a fall guy for this government. 'I am willing to be your fall guy.' I told him about the possibility of a merger with the Monopolies Commission and he said that, whether or not there was a merger, his offer stood. Never in all my public life have I had such a disinterested suggestion made to me. I was quite overcome. This is the second evidence I have had of Peter's genuineness and I am more than ever ashamed that those conspirators at the Ministry of Transport influenced me against him.

Meanwhile, in parallel, Crosland had invited me to be the first chairman of the British Tourist Authority. This was an exciting job but a part-time chairmanship. I could not combine it fairly with my Bookers job, and I could not afford to leave Bookers for a part-time assignment. Again a refusal. And this time there was a shirty little note from Bill Rodgers, Tony's Minister of State, suggesting that I join the board at least, hoping that I could find a balance between my private interests and public duties. In the end – the best outcome there could have been – the remarkable Sir Alexander Glen took the chair, with outstanding panache. I happily served him on the board. No chairman I have ever known could exploit his non-executive board members more skilfully, exhaustingly, or amusingly. But Bill was right, annoyingly: I needed to find a better balance for myself and a widening range of responsibilities. By this time I was serving on Neddy and also on the Court of London University; I was chairman of Westfield College, chairman of my engineering trade association, and in 1969, chairman-designate of the British Institute of Management to follow after Lord Watkinson. And the pressure came on again from Barbara's department. She had it in mind to set up a Committee of Industrial Relations which would subsume PIB among other things. Would I talk about heading it up. I spoke with Sir David Barnes and Alex (now Sir Alex) Jarratt, her senior civil servants, who were explaining the proposition. I suggested that George Woodcock, the famous general secretary of her TUC was probably the right man for them if the job materialized. In fact Leonard (now Sir Leonard) Neal turned out to be the right man.

Then, in late 1969, came the offer I could not possibly refuse: the challenge to be the chairman of a new corporation which was to be created for the nationalization of ports. Fred (now Lord) Mulley was the Minister of Transport. Quietly and sensibly, at the very start, he told me that he did not believe Labour would win the next election. But before then, there should be plenty of time to pass the Bill for a national ports authority, and the Conservatives were probably of a mood to accept the good sense of the proposals for port co-ordination once they had been enacted. After all ninety-five per cent of the ports facilities were already owned by the State. I would chair a committee, on the lines of the Organizing Committee for Steel, to lay plans for the new corporation. The target date was about Easter or the mid-year, 1970. There was no problem over the pay scales for my appointment or for the top management: they were in line with those which Barbara and I had fought for and which now were adopted. I made the break with Bookers and I started at once. For the next eight months I worked as hard as I had ever worked, thoroughly enjoying myself.

All ports authorities which controlled more than 500,000 tons of cargo per annum over their quays were to be part of what I wanted to call the British Ports Corporation. Also, all but one, the Manchester Ship Canal Company, were wanting a co-ordinated strategy for ports. The container revolution had erupted in the mid-Sixties and was transforming port economics. The Lord Rochdale Report on the problems of British ports had been written in the early Sixties and I was handed it to study as a basic text. It had only a few lines about the use of containers, but in the few years since it had been written old operational methods, old working practices, old communities were suddenly ripped apart by containerization. Special ships were being designed to deliver boxes, stacked two, maybe three, high on quays; special cranes were developing to load them on to lorries or trains. Eight dockers were enough to do what eighty might have done before.

The existing boards of the port authorities were mostly dominated by the shipping lines and were big and ungainly, swollen with members representing special interests. The management of ports happened after lunch, it seemed to me. I toured them all. London and Liverpool, my first ports of call, impressed me as imminent disasters. They were overcapitalized in the wrong way for containers, overshadowed by big old trade unions, themselves overmuscled, blind Samsons, and just as blind to the future rushing at them. Their port boards were over-populated with local grandees and overawed by the big shipowners – doomsville, both of them, unless some rationalization took place swiftly.

The next port of call was Leith. After my London and Liverpool visits I had learned enough to ask particularly to meet some dockers on the spot, on the docks and not in some magnificent dining room. On the day of my visit, our shiny black convoy of three cars drew up unfortunately twenty minutes behind schedule on Pier No. 7: a press call had held me up. There was no sign of anybody waiting on the quay, just a small ship streaked with cement dust. At the very far end of the pier we noticed the silhouette of one man against the dazzle of the sea. I suggested that I might make contact on my own, not with the heavy mob of VIPs and uniformed police and port officials. The man was dressed for rough work and covered with dust, cap to booted toe, and he looked fed up. He told me I was late and that he had been left by his mates to tell me they had gone to have a bit of lunch. I explained the delay with the press, and I then invited him and his absent gang to come to dinner that night.

They did. It was a formal dinner with the board of the Port Authority. No sign of dust then, and seven of them mingled comfortably with the throng. After the few speeches, I talked bluntly to one of them who was close to me, at the angle of the table. 'You disappointed me today. I want to talk to dockers to learn their views on the new set-up, but you weren't interested enough to hang on when we were held up.'

He was just as blunt back.

'I'll tell you what happened. We were on a cement ship, and that was a bad start, wasn't it? We don't like cement ships. And then we were told Parker wanted to see us – and we thought Parker? Lord Parker, he's that fucking hanging judge, isn't he?'

162

I pressed on: 'But you're supposed to want this nationalization of the ports, aren't you?'

He became serious. He picked up a knife from the table, holding it by the tip of the blade and looking at me.

'You see this knife? When I was a lad, this knife was there then,' and he swung the handle high to one side. 'I saw what happened to my Dad, left on the stones when the knife was there. Now', swinging the handle to the other side, 'it's there, see, and you . . . ', bringing the handle to the centre and letting the knife dangle from the top of the blade, 'you can spend your life getting it here'.

The dockers and their communities were closed societies driven in on themselves by cruelly unimaginative management and organization, and that may be too kind a way of putting it. Their labour was permanently casual. There was no way for them to be loyal or decently involved in the ports' business. During the war, Ernest Bevin, the Minister of Labour, had devised the National Dock Labour Board to administer a scheme which aimed at combining the necessary flexibility with security for stevedoring: this kept the peace on the docks in war, and gave dignity to the dockers' hard life. It was 'fair do's' then; now, a generation later, this boon had become a barrier to progressive change.

I went to discuss the prospects for the Bill with the 'Emperor' Jack Jones, the general secretary of the Transport and General Workers' Union, who had been a Liverpool docker himself. The bust of Bevin was on the mantelpiece looking down on the 'Emperor' as he sat at his desk – signing, I recall, a letter to the Archbishop of Canterbury. Union power, which was to make the Seventies a decade of exasperation for industry and for the country, was embodied in this powerful, strong-willed, well-meaning leader fighting the wrong war. Thanks to Jack, I was given the unique opportunity to address a National Delegates Conference at Transport House. 'You'll have to talk to them yourself,' he had said and that was what happened. No speaker from the outside world had ever been allowed in before, said the Brother Chairman, as he introduced me to the packed, smoky hall. Brother Chairman ran that meeting. Jack sat beside me, occasionally whispering to me but never speaking aloud in two hectic hours. It is not always appreciated that the power of a general secretary of a union derives formally from the union membership by their constitution and no one is more constitutionally minded than a union member. Even the most forceful of personalities has still to toe that line as general secretary, or he will trip over it, as Scargill was to prove for himself, while breaking his union in two.

My ten-minute message to the conference began provocatively. I explained that most of the employers in the ports were co-operating in a new approach: would they? I wanted smaller boards, more professionally managed, and a national strategy for change. Containers were no longer things to come, they were here, so how would the unions participate in the strategy of modernization? I was convinced that we had got to turn our attention to the operational priorities in our competitive trade, to costs, to prices and profits – and to training and career structures. 'You never get or seem to want promotion,' I said. At one stage in the ensuing debate, a stout figure spoke from the back of the hall, holding both arms straight into the air as if the meeting were outdoors. The chamber was thick-aired by then, and noisy.

'I can't make out what he's saying,' I muttered to Jack.

Jack muttered back, 'Neither can I, but don't worry about what he's saying; what you need to know is he's from Liverpool.'

It was a most useful session for me and I was glad Jack had risked arranging it for me.

By the spring, the organizational plans were nearly ready. Our small headquarters team had found offices in Brook Street, borrowed from the National Ports Council: a compact old house with a handsome façade in bad need of a lick of paint outside and decoration inside. When we were formally constituted, I had plans for some three hundred people to move into another block, behind the National Gallery, near to Whitehall but not in it. Our proposed structure for the boards throughout the country was agreed by the Department, and most of the names of members for the parent board. The work had been 'six months hard', the hardest I had ever done. And I had thoroughly enjoyed myself because the mood of the industry was ready for some sort of change, for new ideas and enterprise. With ninety-five per cent of the port assets in public hands already, I was arguing that the Bill was for rationalization of the ports, not nationalization – and if the Bill had been properly named 'Rationalization' we would have avoided the total reflex reactions of the political opposition. Even as it was, at the outset the Conservatives were moving with the tide in and outside Parliament. Then came Selsdon; Edward Heath convened his opposition colleagues at Selsdon to prepare for the coming election and the political battlelines for 1970 were drawn up. Non-intervention became his battle-cry. The portfolio for delaying the ports legislation was given to Michael Heseltine. He was the right man for the job of filibustering. He thoroughly enjoyed himself. Everything began to slow up. Still, by the end of May the legislative work was formally concluded in the House with a Third Reading: I was told there was only left some final spit of sealing-wax in the House of Lords on Thursday.

The chairman of the Port of London Authority, Lord Simon, an old-world Conservative but still eager for change, invited me to tea at his office on the Thursday 'to celebrate', but by chance on the Monday evening I was at the PLA office, an Edwardian extravaganza of a building. My father, Tom, and I had been asked to drinks there before going on to the annual PLA boxing tournament at Bethnal Green. Tom loved boxing and the dockers have always been fine fighters; it was good of the organizers to bring him into the event. Over the drinks we heard the news that Wilson had called his surprise election. No time for that final seal in the Lords. Damn, is what we all said: more uncertainty for an industry in travail, leaving it with losses and confusion. The election took over the ports.

For two of the electioneering weeks Jill and I parked the children with Tom and Dorothy, and escaped to Cornwall. Jill tried to teach me how to walk, 'to go for proper walks', something I have never managed to do. I walk from A to B, or if it's exercise then surely the thing to do is to run. Robert Graves hit off this smallness of my mind perfectly: 'walking in no direction I never found easy . . . ' Better to toss a twig, and march off in the direction to which the sharp end points. Jill has always known better. There was nothing to do but relax. I sketched, feeling my life a doodle. One sketch was of Jill sitting at the top of a little hill, her dress-line flowing into the hillside. The point of it all, I thought to myself, really the shape of my ambitions.

Wilson lost the election, as the honest minister Fred Mulley had forecast when I had taken up the assignment all those months ago. News of the government's defeat came around noon. Our top team took me off to a good last lunch, and I was presented with a plaque that had been immediately unscrewed from our front door in Brook

Street. I gave my own toast: 'Warden of the Sunk Ports' and, symbolically, the port was moved from left to right round the table.

In the afternoon, I received a telephone call from the Ministry reminding me that the budget for my organization had been phased only for July: it would be cut off within three weeks. As I listened to this warning, strange waving wands criss-crossed my third-floor windows: the scaffolding was being raised so that the painting of our small headquarters could begin. I put down the phone, lifted the sash-window, and shouted to the gang below: 'Hold everything, I'm coming down.'

7

Trumpets and Drums

John Peyton, now the good Lord Peyton, became Transport Minister in the new Heath government of 1970, and he was my Minister for a day. It was my last as chairman-designate of the National Ports Authority. I received his genial call, 'This is my first day in this office,' he said, 'I hear it's your last. Perhaps we should meet. Somebody should say goodbye.' I appreciated the unexpected courtesy. John was a surprising man. He had been a prisoner of war, captured after the defeat at Dunkirk, and he always gave me the impression that he had decided in those years of confinement that nothing would fence him in again, ever, and that there was no more time to waste. He had a wry mastery of short speeches and a dangerous choice of words which made him one of the most pungent and entertaining of politicians. With so many phrases, polished and succinct, always at his command, his greeting to me was simple: 'Well, this is a bugger's muddle.'

Even that was a good deal more than my Labour ex-Minister, Fred Mulley, had time to tell me. For anyone serving as a government appointee, the abruptness of changing governments has to be experienced to be believed. On the exit of the Wilson government, Fred had disappeared without a word: it was a good thing I was not going to have to depend on a good reference from my previous employer. I saw nothing of him for three months, and that was when I invited him to my club, the Savile, for luncheon. It is one of political life's little, bitter ironies that Fred Mulley has registered most lastingly in the national consciousness as a dozy sort of chap, because of a famous and unfair photo of him nodding off at some parade when he was a Minister of Defence. Actually he was suffering the hangover of an exhausting all-night sitting: cameras may not lie, but they can be false witnesses. Fred was a sturdy-minded man, alert and shy. I was grateful to him for two things. One, for giving me the chance of the job and the other for taking the edge off its ultimate disappointment with his honesty: he had warned me at the very outset that in his view Labour would not be re-elected. At the luncheon, we reminisced. We dropped a tear or two into the excellent draught cider served at the Savile, as we brooded over the aborted new deal we had intended for the ports. It had been a damned near thing. There had been widespread support for my plans for the necessary revolution in management based on a strategy of rationalizing, not nationalizing. There had been an opportunity for a non-party, unifying act of managing change, an example of what could be done in this country if only our uniquely British, brainwashed habit of partisan economics had been set aside. It had very nearly happened – but no. Consensus interruptus. And the incoming Minister's brutally plain assessment seemed to me only too true ; indisputably the ports were in a muddle. Still, I believed the momentum for our new ideas of organization was unstoppable. Technology was transforming the industry. The container was a Trojan sea-horse crammed with the imperatives of technological and organizational change.

My farewell session with John Peyton was anything but funereal. He was as ready for change as I was. As I left his office, he asked me to send him a paper on how I saw progress in the organization of the ports 'without the Act'. Of course I agreed. After all I expected to have lots of time; the next few weeks, I thought, were going to be only too peaceful for me. That was a mistake. In a matter of hours I was back into ports again, this time not on a macro but on a micro scale of confusion.

I had just returned home that evening when I was contracted to take on a special assignment for a consortium of three merchant banks. The caller, John Pattisson, explained that his own merchant bank, Dawnay Day, along with two others, Flemings and Hambros, had invested in a small container terminal near Greenwich. It was not operating profitably. Would I be interested in advising on it? I pointed out that my knowledge of ports was very grand and very limited. I could do the Churchillian bit, I could despatch a note to Alexander instructing him to clear the enemy out of North Africa. 'But just how Alexander manages to clear the enemy out of Africa is something else again,' I said to John Pattisson.

John's reply was irresistible: 'Our problem in the City is that we're not even sure where Africa is. You know something we don't.'

I was hooked. I agreed to meet him the next morning.

In my work as chairman-designate for the ports, I had become impressed by the very challenges these merchant banks were wrestling with. There had seemed to me to be a need for a dock to take smaller container ships in the upper reach of the Thames. The big container ships gathered to load and unload at Tilbury, at the broad mouth of the river, and they took bulky precedence over lesser vessels, which were left jostling for attention. There would surely be a market for a dock closer to the centre of London to deal with the smaller ships, say up to 3,000-tonners. In that way, they would be sure of a berth and the shipper would save money by avoiding the long and costly lorry-ride into London from Tilbury.

I drove down to see for myself. It was 5.30 a.m., dawnlight across the misty Thames and into Greenwich. I had alerted no one and I had no right of entry, but there was a coffee-stall outside the gates of Victoria Deep Water Terminal, and a crowd warming up around it. I joined it to have a cup of coffee, and it was easy enough to chat with the dockers about how things were going. They were outspokenly aware of the lack of traffic at the terminal; its fate was their future and they had lots to say about it. Their analysis went to the heart of the problem. This venture, they had concluded, was cockeyed. Container traffic could only be handled successfully if there was a spacious hinterland to stack and manoeuvre the boxes. The four and a half acre site of Victoria Deep was a wholly inadequate strategic premise. As I've often found, the men on the spot had the answer. 'Ask the fellows who cut the hay,' as that wonderfully true writer of agricultural society George Ewart Evans said in the title of one of his books.

By the time I met John Pattisson in the City, later in the morning, I had found out enough for us to begin to sketch out a scheme for the essential expansion of the site. Over the next year we acquired the neighbouring sites, and Victoria Deep was able to develop successfully from a seventeen-acre base.

I became chairman of Victoria Deep and joined the Dawnay Day board. This was to mean more to me than becoming part of the City for the first time – although that was an important step in my management journey. A part-time but measurable responsibility at board level, provided the working model for my re-entry into the private sector and for a new start in life, post ports. When I had closed the door of my ports headquarters for the last time I had stepped out into Brook Street feeling like one of those Disney characters who is so busy running that he finds he has run over the cliff edge; for a moment, he is miraculously, ludicrously suspended, little legs thrashing about, scissoring the air – then he drops. In Disneyland there is usually a leafy tree to grab halfway down. In the deforested part of the jungle I was in in 1970, my downfall was uninterrupted. But at least the loud thud as I hit the market-place was as helpful as it was painful: my availability was made well known with a bang, and my conspicuous collapse made me wide open to offers. I was relieved, and also bewildered, by the pleasant rush of new possibilities. I sat in my improvised office at home, a cross between Walter Mitty and Little Jack Horner, sifting the suggestions that were piling up round me. Group managing director of an international company, of a famous toy manufacturer, of a management consultancy? Would I start a headhunting agency? Tinker, tailor, soldier, sailor? Rich man, poor man? Actually I was neither. I was not well off in that I had few capital assets. I had been a well-paid wage-earner, a manager, a full-time executive. This time I decided that I should take a new risk, or rather a set of risks. The *Financial Times* 'Men and Matters' column quizzed me on what I was doing. 'Going plural,' I said, and the word seems to have gone into managerial jargon since, describing a director who undertakes a variety of portfolios. I have found no previous reference to the phrase, which I had stumbled on during my first weekend, jobless, reading some Matthew Arnold to steady my mind. It seemed to fit the new pattern of work rapidly opening before me. My mother used to tell the family that when I was a little boy 'Peter wanted both the trumpet and the drum. Take him into the shop, ask him to decide on either, and he would say, "Both".' Going plural, I sought two objectives: to make capital so the family would be less vulnerable, and to be more independent so I would be able to take a stand on my own views about politics and industry. I saw no better way to independence than by increasing and spreading my risks and, inevitably, my commitments.

The model for my future had to meet definite specifications. Ideally I wanted to have two main bases, one in manufacturing and one in the City. Those established, I would be able to explore possibilities in international business and in high technology, both decisive in influencing the management of things to come. Because I was dedicated to the concept of industrial strategy in a mixed economy, there had to be room for service in the sector of public enterprise, and in the multifarious work of the National Economic Development Office.

Lastly, education continued to be an inevitable interest for me as a business manager, of course in terms of education and training for industry but equally in terms of achieving a more civilized balance between industry and academia. To my astonishment, this design for plurality was translated into action more swiftly than I had hoped in my wildest Mitty-Horner dreams. The pattern of the next few years tells the story.

Dawnay Day's project was fine for starters. It was a small merchant bank and its value lay in just that, its human proportion, its intimacy, and its team of excellent calibre. We knew each other's minds, we could move fast together, we hardly needed to finish our sentences. I found myself living out my belief in organizing an enterprise into the smallest groups possible. Our clients knew personally the man or woman they were dealing with, and that personal touch within small and medium-sized companies is a quality the bigger, named banks tend to find extremely difficult to sustain. That was true in the early Seventies and it is even more true at the end of the Eighties after the Big Bang, now deregulation has exploded the scale of financial services competing worldwide and sleeplessly. There was a market for the good, smaller service like Dawnay Day, itself a version of Victoria Deep, upstream and dealing with smaller craft.

Three years after joining Dawnay Day I became chairman. This happened in 1973, just as we moved into the turbulence of oil shocks and recession, economic storms which capsized a number of the secondary banks. Dawnay Day had the steadying ballast of the Prudential as a nineteen-per-cent shareholder and we survived without having to signal for help from the Bank of England's lifeboat. It was a wrench leaving it in 1976 to go on the rails, and it was a wrench to hear a few years later that Jacob Rothschild had bought it as one of his earliest shrewd decisions when he broke out of the fabulously well-feathered family nest to set up his own show. Dawnay Day is dead. Long live the high-paced, human-scaled, high-quality financial service.

That was one lesson Dawnay Day taught me. Another was that the City is too far from manufacturing industry, and that was why my plan was to encompass both. Too many of my generation of managers had chosen one and found themselves at odds with the other. This dichotomy is as old as our Industrial Revolution. Our society was the earliest to industrialize itself, and that process did not start in the

City. The great fortune-makers, the forgemasters, the steam and locomotive engineers, the owners of factories and railways in the North and Midlands, sent their money to London to be looked after, and there the City grew up, far from the source of the wealth it handled. Other nations set out to catch us up by running the two sides of their industrial development, finance and manufacturing, in a combined operation. We have suffered in Britain from our divided origins, the split of the island between the south and north of Watford. I wanted to see what I could do to bridge the Watford gap.

I touched my second base with the Rockware Group late in 1970 and became chairman in 1971. Rockware was, and still is, the biggest independent manufacturer of glass containers. In 1970 it employed some 7,000 people, with factories in Yorkshire, Lancashire, Scotland and South London. The process of glassmaking on this large scale is a wonder of technology, one of the most dramatic production processes I know, literally brilliant. Vast furnaces are blasting away all day and night, fed by computer-controlled silos of the raw materials, and from them pours molten glass, down through scissors which cut it into flying fists, bright red, dropping into the moulding machines below. Out of these appear the bottles, luminous red still, to go down the lines, cooling, annealing and being checked electronically and by the human eye for quality, to become one of life's most usual, most taken-for-granted technological miracles. Rockware was making about six million bottles a day. In other parts of the group, we produced rival products, plastic containers. My new head office was at our Greenford factory, west of London, and it took less than an hour to drive between that and my other base office in the City. For me, the geographical gap at least was not too wide.

In 1971 I also reinforced my City connection by joining the board of Shipping Industrial Holdings Ltd. With my two main bases, city and industry, secure, the other desirable parts of the design of plurality came into place: international business, high technology, public enterprise and education. Overlaps were considerable, convenient and useful. For example, my appointments in the public sector not only widened my experience of that sector but also took me into the international dimension. The Heath government made me a member of the board of its brand new British Airways in 1971; and already I was chairing the Marketing Committee of the British Tourist Authority where I served happily under Sir Alexander Glen. (It was he who introduced me into Shipping Industrial Holdings.)

On the educational front, I continued with the Foundation of Management Education, and became chairman of the Business Graduates Association. Also, I was invited to be deputy chairman of the Court of London University and, closer to the action – and there was plenty of student action around in those days – I was still chairman of Westfield College. Through the university I was asked to chair firstly the London University Computing Services (LUCS) – my learning curve in high technology rose alarmingly – and then Dillons in Bloomsbury, one of the great bookshops even then. It had been started by one of the most startling of starters, Una Dillon. Una looked like a beautiful version of Bertrand Russell, but in fact was like no one else, energetic and witty and wonderfully sharp commercially. She was one of three spinster sisters of genius. Theresa, the eldest, was a distinguished scientist; Carmen, the youngest, was a leading theatre and film designer who worked for years with Laurence Olivier, most famously on *Henry V*; and in the middle was Una, who in a few years grew her great store from a shop the size of a small room. About this time, through its acquisition by Dawnay Day, I also became chairman of Curtis Brown, the literary agents; so, suddenly and delightfully, I was into the book world, firmly supported by the book-ends of Dillons and Curtis Brown.

It is more difficult now, looking back, to make sense of these multifarious commitments than it seemed at the time. I felt the branches were growing naturally from the same tree, one tree, me. I felt no physical strain either. I used to run round the Round Pond in Kensington Gardens between 6.30 and 7.00 a.m. every morning, disturbing the sleepy ducks into the water. I admit that I evolved a law that let me off the exercise if I had gone to bed after midnight, but that was of course a slippery piece of reasoning leading to decadence: it simply built in the temptation to late-night parties. However, I was blessedly fit, I felt ready for anything. To me, all the variety made sense, was the delightful spice of life. For the next six years, I was to be making real money, and as I did so, was criss-crossing the frontiers of interests, economic, political and social. And all the time, in a mysterious way which I could neither explain to myself nor presume to define, I sensed that I was preparing for something else.

Meanwhile, in the thick of my self-interested life I must try to do the state some service. The familiar challenge to improve communications between government and industry became inescapable. Some years earlier, while I was at Bookers, I had had the seemingly boring experience of getting nowhere as chairman of the British Pump Manufacturers Association, discovering how ineffective our engineering trade associations were, and how, so far from stimulating progress, they inhibited fresh and fast thinking as world competition grew fiercer around what was then the UK's largest industry. By the early 1970s the British Mechanical Engineering Confederation, which a few of us had started a decade earlier, had been built up to the point when it represented a dozen significant groupings which together comprised over 8,000 companies; but still it could not pretend to speak for engineering as a whole. Throughout the various jobs I had had since Bookers I had stayed on the BRIMEC Council, and in 1971, as President, I set out to canvass other sectors. BRIMEC was a march of dimes: I needed a march of sovereigns. I went to see one, Lord Robens, who had left the Coal Board to become the chairman of Vickers, then one of the country's largest engineering concerns. Initially, he had his doubts: after all, the Confederation of British Industry existed to represent business as a whole. But that, I argued, was its strength and its weakness. The CBI had to be all things to all people; its membership included nationalized industries and consumers as well as manufacturers. Busy as he already was, Alf agreed to be Mr Engineering. And that tremendous man grabbed the issue by the throat, that is, at the top of the engineering industry, not the bottom where BRIMEC was getting stuck. He was able to convince the other chieftains of great companies, and in December 1975 the Engineering Industries Council was founded, with twenty-seven founder members, among whom I was included, although by then I had long left engineering as my main work. The *Engineer* magazine of January 1976 overgenerously described me as 'the brains behind EIC', and added 'It has taken Parker at least two years to get such known quantities as the captains of industry around our EIC table and then lob the idea at Lord Robens.' More like ten years, actually.

I had striven for the council as a vital step in the coherence of any industrial strategy. From the angle of the Eighties it might come under the general curse of corporatism, but a co-ordination of the efforts of enterprise seemed to be doing no harm to the reviving economies of Germany, France or Japan. An industrial strategy should not be regarded as synonymous with corporatism. There was, however a corporatist tide sweeping through the Seventies which seemed to be carrying along Left, Right and Centre. I was in the thick of that too and not enjoying it. I was a member and occasional attender on the Labour Party's Industrial Policy Committee, and I heard the talk of industrial regeneration. Judith Hart as chairman, with Stuart Holland as mentor, was busy knitting a complicated pattern of industrial plans, like a tricoteuse at the side of the guillotine of enterprise. Tony Benn succeeded Judith and on her foundation built the policies which were to become known as 'Bennery'. The Labour Party seemed to see the salvation of the economy in interlocking planning agreements between government and the public and private sectors of industry: overcooked plans and half-baked democracy were to be the orders of the new day. Trade unions were to be given more powers of intervention but not more responsibility for effective performance. The corporate plans of management were to be fully disclosed for consultation with the unions, but consultation carried with it no commitment from the unions in return. And in reality, how could it? If management called for a large-scale redundancy programme, was the trade union leadership likely to go along without a fight? Proposals that trade unionists should join a board as directors and corporately share such harsh decisions were naïve, or simply humbuggery between consenting adults. For years I had voted Labour for many reasons, but never because of its industrial policies; now I began to foresee a time when I would be voting against Labour because of its industrial policies.

Not that I was losing faith in the concept of some form of industrial strategy. I remained convinced of its importance, and in 1971 I was able to see the idea in action from the inside, when I was appointed chairman of the Clothing Economic Development Committee. No man has walked more naked into a conference room than I did into the clothing Neddy. I remember a headline quoted in the *New Yorker*: 'Nudist arrested for carrying concealed weapon.' If what was threatening about him was his dangerous innocence, I thoroughly understood. Appointments to little Neddies were a variation of the British passion for blood sports: the chairman had to have no vested interest in the sector concerned, and was therefore dangerously unencumbered with any experience of it.

The clothing industry employed over 300,000 workers and was in the throes of a battle for survival, facing revolutionary advances in technology and the competition of cheap labour overseas. It also had its special strengths. The employers had largely rationalized themselves and their trade associations; the unions were few, strongly self-disciplined and well led. There is bags of personality in the rag trade, in the big as well as in the small companies, but particularly in the small. The industry's little Neddy had pulled itself together, inspired by a maverick member of the NEDO bureaucracy, George Gater, bravely uninhibited and original, and I succeeded to a dynamic legacy from the previous chairman, Robert Appleby of Black and Decker. The committee thrived with self-critical research and with inter-firm comparisons; we organized visits of managers and unions to Europe and the US; we had user-maker meetings, difficult and fruitful as the mating of cheetahs must be; we continually reviewed the strategies of the industry; and eventually, in common cause, we created the Clothing Industry Productivity and Research Association in my last year in 1976. Subsequently, the clothing Neddy prospered under the expansive lead of Sir Basil Feldman. Despite the reduction in its role, and the gathering gloom around NEDO under the Lawson regime in the third Thatcher government, the clothing Neddy remains witness, in my experience, to the power of indicative planning and co-ordination of competitive enterprise. Both the failure of nerve in reflecting an industrial strategy and the contrasting overconfidence in planning should be left behind. I saw how the future could work in the clothing EDC.

Meanwhile, much closer to the bottom line of my life in the early Seventies, I was going through a totally new experience as a manager. I was being bought and sold. The early Seventies were a peak period for take-over deals; the mid-Eighties matched them but by then the rules, inadequate as they may be still, had improved. What was particularly depressing to me was that buyers and sellers of companies shared the same attitude as politicians and planners: they all roughly ignored management and the manager. Management was simply taken for granted. And management was doing far too little to make itself heard; it tended to become convenient. In speeches, I found myself adapting an old story at the time, about a scene of execution. The condemned men arrive and the executioner, as was the custom, asks each of them whether he wishes to face down or up. The first, a Conservative, says he wants to look down and down the blade drops – and it sticks just above the poor fellow's neck, so he's let off, as also was the custom. The same happens to the second, a Labour man: the blade falls but gets stuck, and he is reprieved. The third man, a manager, says he will look up, he likes to see what's happening. Just as the exasperated executioner is about to pull the lever, the manager cries out, 'Wait a second . . . I think I see what's wrong – I could fix that . . . ' The manager's natural tendency seemed to be to make life too easy for the wheelers and dealers. It was my good fortune to find myself in a whirlwind series of three bids and deals, each an opportunity to break that managerial reflex of convenience.

The first was with Associated British Maltsters, one of the biggest maltsters in the world at the start of the Seventies. I had been appointed chairman in 1971 and at my very first board meeting we were interrupted with the news that Grand Metropolitan had it in mind to make a bid for the company at the price of 115p. Our shares were standing in the market at a little over 100p. The board agreed that we should hold our fire; we should finish the board meeting, and I should meet Max Joseph, the Grand Metropolitan chairman, in the evening. Grand Metropolitan chairman sounds like some high priest and it gives exactly the wrong impression of Max, an unpompous, creative, venturesome man. I knew and liked Max but I had never traded with him. As I came through the door, he was startled: 'I didn't know you were chairman. We can do business then.' He was his usual, quiet smiling self; a soft handshake greeting me with that gentle way he had of taking control of so many companies. He used shyness as other corporate heroes use aggression; he spoke with the purr of a Rolls-Royce and a big cat. He had the opposite of what Sheridan described as 'a damned disinteresting countenance'; wavy, shiny hair, a lined face on which the lines pointed inwards, a face like the map of Europe. I have never known in this country a more private look in the expression of a tycoon. His office was of a piece with him, small, modest, but in an expensive corner of Mayfair between Davies and Brook Streets. That's what Max was, a top trader, a top-corner boy, the very best.

He placed himself behind his desk, and on the other side I faced him in a low-seated armchair (he avoided the usual tycoon's oasis, that spurious 'social area' of sofas and low tables in one half of the room). My memory of our brief encounter is eerily precise in parts:

'It's a buyer's market for malt these days, Max. You don't need us

177

to secure your sources of supply. And Max, much as we love you we don't need you.'

'Are you telling me my price is too low?'

'That's one thing.'

'But I've just bought Trumans and I was forced to climb a ladder with the bidding. That's not my way, and I certainly am not doing that again.'

'But why do you want the company, Max?'

'I've bought a brewer, and a maltster would make sense.'

'But we are the second biggest maltsters in the world – not just a little piece to fit your jigsaw. And have you considered how the politics of the Common Market might affect it?'

'Tell me about that.'

I did. He listened with what appeared to be genuine interest. Could it be I was really telling him something new?

'Fascinating.'

He nodded, hardly moving but setting off on a new track. 'Peter, why not join our board here. We could have fun together and there are other deals to do too.'

'I'd love to, Max, but surely one thing at a time. We are on opposite sides. I'm still learning about ABM but I do know already it's a fine sturdy business, it has a solid tweedy soul. In City terms it has hardly pushed itself into prominence, hardly sold itself; its public relations have been reserved to put it kindly. I reckon its shares are hopelessly underrated.'

'This is a deadlock.' Max walked round the desk, handed me a drink, smiling as ever, and saying, 'Tell you what I'll do. I'll break the deadlock. I'll go to 150p' – an uplift worth several millions to ABM shareholders.

I exaggerated shock: I half rose out of my chair, as if to look at his desk. 'Max, what on earth shifted? Is there something on your blotter that gives you a range of negotiating possibilities, or is there a corporate strategist chained to the floor under the desk whispering advice?'

Max laughed in that noiseless way he had – as if he were helpless to do otherwise but really not very keen about it – and said, 'No, honestly, I don't work that way at all. I don't go much for corporate planning. I can just about see three months ahead. And I've learnt something this evening. If you talk that way, you mean it all right.'

Then he made a circular gesture around his middle. 'I feel it here,

27   Peter Parker, Prince Philip and Sir Harold Hartley, the Secretary, President and Chairman respectively of the first Duke of Edinburgh's Study Conference, at Rhodes House, Oxford University, 1956

28   The Organising Committee for the Nationalisation of the Steel Industry visiting the Shotton steelworks in 1966. Lord Melchett, its new chairman *(second right)* is being greeted by steel baron Sir Richard Summers *(centre)*, watched by Peter Parker *(far right)* and Sir Monty Finniston *(third left)*, another future chairman of British Steel

29 Peter Parker, as chairman of Fletcher and Stewart Ltd, presents the Queen's Award for Export to the factory floor, Derby 1966

30 *Below left* Barbara Castle, Minister of Transport, in 1967

31 *Below right* Lord Campbell of Eskan, a portrait taken in 1987. Jock was chairman of the Booker Group 1952-66

32 Peter Parker's first day on the rails: the sign behind him reads 'Danger . . .'

33 The relationship between politics and the public sector: Bill Rodgers, Secretary of State for Transport, sells Sir Peter a ticket on their tour of the Great Northern Electric line

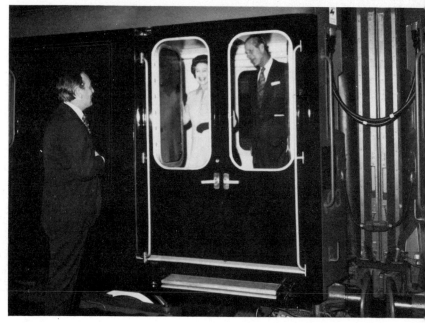

34   Delivering shining new royal coaches to the Queen and Prince Philip at Euston in May 1977, ready for her Silver Jubilee Tour of Britain

35   Accompanying Prince Charles to the official opening of the Gatwick-Heathrow helicopter link in 1978

36 Checking the tilt on the ill-fated Advanced Passenger Train at Derby

37 Talking to another Peter Parker, a porter with Amtrak, on a selling mission to Washington DC

38 and 39 *Left and below* Inspection of Firth of Forth bridge

45 *Above* Sketch of Peter Parker on tour by Sir Hugh Casson

44 *Left* Ceremonial kick-off on the inaugural voyage of Sealink

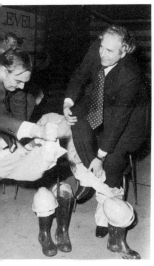

40 *Above* Visiting construction works on the underground Argyll line, with the Scotland Region General Manager

41 *Right* Close to the coalface and BR's biggest customer, the National Coal Board

43 *Below* At the Engineerium in Hove

42 Footplate training on the Cumbrian private line

46 Presenting Harold Macmillan with a model of the first 'living' locomotive, named after him, in 1979

47 *Below left* Sir Eduardo Paolozzi *(right)* showing Sir Peter a model of his sculpture, to be erected outside Rail House at Euston, in 1980

48 *Below right* Naming ceremony for Loco No. 86 229, the *Sir John Betjeman*, 1983

you know. That's how I do it.' It was the most specific example I had ever seen of an entrepreneur's gut feeling.

I said that the price was still not right: 'Now if you had said 160p, it would have made me nervous. At 150p we shall have to have a fight about it, and let the shareholders decide.'

We finished our drinks. And over the next six weeks we had an almighty public row about it.

I had never been in a public bid battle before and was the less inhibited for that. We met round the clock with our staunch supporters, the merchant bank of Charterhouse and Philip Darwin of Lawrence Prust, the brokers. Compared to the ugly take-over brawls of the Eighties, with their sophisticated dirty tricks and their nauseating orgies of self-praising advertisements, our punch-up with Gentleman Max was a Corinthian encounter in the history of the noble art of self-defence. The mobilization of our shareholders was my main aim, and (an innovation then) we convened big open meetings, taking on all comers in the debate over the bid, which we presented as too low and bad industrial logic. It was a clean straight fight. Max lost; he only attracted nine per cent of the company. It was the only bid he ever lost.

He and I spoke together a few days later: we bumped into each other on a street corner, as casually as that. 'What are you doing with the nine per cent?' I asked.

'I've already sold it, Peter. Good luck.'

But no good luck could save us. The nine per cent had gone to Jim Slater, the most famous of the wheeler-dealers, and we were, in the jargon, in play. So ABM, a profitable, confident and well-regarded company, was on the auction block. It was now only a matter of time while Slater built his stake and fixed his price, and that would have precious little to do with me or the performance of the company. The tricks of the take-over trade were simple and deadly, and they made many financiers millionaires. Often they made them media heroes too. The technique involved two basic moves. First, acquire shares in the target company, not under your own name but under the names of various nominees (people or companies) who would sell their holding to you when the time came. It was obligatory to announce a holding of ten per cent if it was in the hands of one beneficiary but the orchestration of a number of nominee holdings was not too difficult among friends. The second move was simply to arrange a 'concert party'. The first mergerer chatted to a second mergerer, and even a third or more, and, say, twenty-nine per cent of the shares might be 'orchestrated' in friendly 'unfriendly' hands. A holder of thirty per cent had to make an offer for the rest, but up to that amount the shares could be 'warehoused', ready for any acquisition dealer interested in buying the significant block – for a premium of course. And once a buyer was on the starting-block of the warehoused shares, the race for control was seldom in doubt; in a fifty-one-yard sprint the bidder would have a head start of twenty-nine yards.

I realized the race for ABM was starting when one of the well-known mergerers of the day visited me in my City office, arriving without an appointment. He was relatively young but looked out of condition to me; I noticed that his hand was clammy. He didn't make me feel good either. He spoke urgently, he wanted to buy ABM. Why? Because he had a spread of overseas trading interests and badly needed UK income for tax reasons. That seemed not a good enough reason to me. Could he claim that there was some industrial logic in his purpose? As chairman, I knew that, even in this mad, mad world of mergers, I still had to examine carefully any proposition that might be in the interests of the shareholders of a public company. I suggested that perhaps our two chief executives should meet at once to explore what mutuality there might be between our two groups. I warned him, 'If there is none, then we'll fight you.'

'But Peter, you'll lose.'

'Why?'

'I've got twenty-five per cent.'

'There's the phone, my friend. You'd better call the Take-over Panel at once.'

'Not twenty-five per cent in my hands. But I tell you, I can put my hands on twenty-five per cent whenever I want. I can get it off the shelf.'

Our two chief executives did meet but predictably they found no fig-leaf of industrial logic to cover the nakedness of the asset-stripper. I rang and reported this, and added, 'If you propose to me formally, you may be sure I'm not going to be married in white.'

That mergerer backed off a few days later. He rang up to say it was not timely, and sure enough the headlines were full of another of his whiz-kidding deals the following week. Two years later his bubble burst, but that was no satisfaction to me. By then ABM had fallen to Dalgety's. The deputy chairman of Dalgety's appeared in my Dawnay Day office one evening to declare the bid, and he had already acquired twenty-nine per cent. I learnt a great deal from that first blooding. Not least, I learnt the names of many of the nominee companies which were used to give cover to the warehousing operations. I traced many back to St Paul's Churchyard, the headquarters of Slater Walker – 'No. 1, St Paul's Graveyard', I called it.

This intelligence was immediately relevant in another bid battle that was beginning to flare up, this one at Rockware. I used to monitor share movements in as much detail as possible, and suddenly, sinisterly, I saw nominees familiar to me from the warehousing of ABM. I was determined that this time I could do something: there was no initial block of shares on the loose, as there had been in ABM with Max's nine per cent. I took a chance. I saw to it that nominee names were published in the press. In particular, the *Guardian*'s correspondents, Charles Raw and Lindsay Vincent, took a tigerish interest in hunting out more of the details. They tracked the names of nominee company directors and discovered that some of the names registered were quite innocent of their roles – some, it was said, dropped their shopping bags in shock when they were told that they were directors of a nominee board owning thousands of Rockware shares. With the help of Will Camp, a doyen of public relations, my campaign developed against 'Concert-going in False Beards'. The wide circulation of the nominee companies caused consternation; once alerted, chairmen of companies used to ring me to check out their own list of nominees. At last, the warehousing issue was well and truly exposed, and over the next few months I reported publicly and regularly the build-up of nominees' holdings in Rockware. Presumably, I asked deadpan, if these were related to one beneficiary then surely there would have been a declaration by now?

Tension rose. I knew I was in a fight but I did not know how it could finish. Nothing like this had happened before. There seemed no way to stop Rockware being sold off the shelf as ABM had been. Perhaps a funeral ovation by the chairman of the Take-over Panel at our burial in the Slater Walker graveyard was the most I could hope for. The take-over experts were making the most of the rules of the take-over game, which were as clear as they were loose. Nobody was breaking the law.

The cavalry came from the least expected quarter, from the Walker of Slater Walker. Peter Walker was promoted to be Secretary of State for Trade and Industry, and within days he was expressing a public interest in improving the Companies Act. Within a week there was a centre-page article in the *Financial Times* by Jim Slater himself, advocating new ideas for reform, including the proposal that there should be a declaration at the five per cent level of shareholding rather than ten per cent. The evening press rang me for my reactions to Jim's piece, and I was reported as being delighted to find the first fiddler of the orchestra now conducting it. Soon after, Jim and I met for luncheon at his place. And it was about time.

I was taken upstairs to his office, a large, square room, conventionally furnished, which oddly made him look all the lighter on his feet. He was quick-moving, nimble, blade-like. As we shook hands, he immediately turned me about and took me downstairs again. He was carrying his backgammon set under his arm, which seemed to me to be slightly overdoing the nonchalance, but he paused on the stairs to arrange with a colleague to play a session later. We entered what I took to be a basement boardroom and he sat at the head of a long board table, I on his right. I felt I was having a tête-à-tête in a bank vault. I also quickly felt a marvellous relief. This man was straight. I may not have liked his aim but it was straight. There was an arrowhead brightness of mind, a directness of manner, a wholesome absence of bullshit in what he said. None of these attributions, however, reconciled me to his style of doing business which seemed to amount to nothing more than trading in companies. He explained his general strategy quite openly. Where other investors spread their investments, he narrowed his; he was only into some 200 companies but was deeply into them. These positions he traded – 'I wake up lazy companies' – and he prided himself on spotting companies that could be helped to recover. He concentrated on the people in charge. I got the impression that, however thoroughly his analysts and researchers might vet prospective companies for him, he gambled on the jockey not the horse.

Specifically, he said that he had followed my movements, expecting some action in any situation I took up after Ports. He expressed regret that we had not met earlier, over ABM: we could have built up a major food group around it, he suggested. However, that was the past, and he now had a proposition to make of a different kind. He had decided to change tack, he wanted to stop being an in-and-out merchant. The row with Rockware was a complication and he wanted to come to terms with me. He was prepared to announce that his twenty-nine per cent position in Rockware was a long-term shareholding; this would deflate at once the speculation in our shares and stabilize the company.

'But what's long term?' I asked. 'Forty-eight hours for you is long term, I'm told.' To be convincing we would need at least a three-year deal, and 'by that time you should be able to disperse your block happily.' And, I added, it would be important to have a director on our board so that for the three years Jim would be on the inside, and so not able to deal.

There was no twisting and turning. He settled, there and then, and went off to his backgammon appointment. He had a gambler's gallantry about him, a verve which was appealing. Parker was the first one to call him, as he in his frank way once put it to a *Sunday Times* correspondent who then rang me, at Jim's suggestion: 'He said, you'd tell me how the Rockware formula works.' His arrangement with Rockware became his model for tidying up many of the trading positions he had taken in other companies.

One of these was in SIH, Shipping Industrial Holdings. His holding there was to be the trigger for what became, according to a former *Times* financial correspondent, Brian Basham, 'one of the longest and most fascinating take-over tussles in British commercial history'. This struggle over SIH began in 1972, when I took over the chair, and raged for a year, running furiously parallel with my defence of Rockware. The SIH story is well told by Brian Basham as a case-history chapter of a book called *Communication*, C. Northcote Parkinson's formula for business survival.

> The battle holds a special place in the memories of takeover aficionados because of the explosive emotions it aroused, the reputations it tarnished and the skill of the defensive in-fighting. The SIH board's defence against odds that eventually overwhelmed them at a price, was a classic, and their strategies and tactics, their organisation and liaison, the forces they marshalled and the audiences they communicated with are a worthy study for any manager who fears that his company may one day attract the attention of an unwelcome suitor.

Sir Alexander Glen had brought me onto the SIH Board in 1971, to chair part of the insurance side of this five-dimensional group. The other activities were ship-broking (they were probably the leading ship-brokers in the world), shipowning (of the second biggest fleet in Britain), freight distributors, and, to its misfortune, Clarkson Tours, the pioneer of the mass-packaged tour operators. It was the Tours that started the rot in the group and almost destroyed it. The travel company had made splendid profits until 1970, but its success exceeded the quality of the management. By 1972 it was crashing with losses of £4.8 million and was wrecking the group. The value of SIH shares also crashed to 168p from the 1971 peak of 368p. Despite being brimful of assets, the group's market value shrivelled to £28.5 million and perversely this made it a bargain, a dreamy, luscious object of desire in the eyes of the asset-strippers. I was asked to take on the chair of Clarkson Tours, and I did so on the condition that among my options was getting rid of it altogether.

At that moment, I was fortunate in finding Michael Pickard suddenly free to advise me. He was just the man, the coolest of cool professional managers in my generation, and he was only available because he had been overturned in a boardroom storm at Trust House. When the merger of Trust House Forte was created, Lord Crowther became chairman of the new group and made his young protégé, Michael Pickard, group MD. But the chemistry between Charles Forte and the young pro was that of boiling oil and iced water. Forte and Pickard could no more work together than, say, Parker and Weinstock, or Harvey-Jones and Lord King. (I'm guessing of course, but there's a fascinating party game: suggest the Best Impossible Partnerships.) Anyway, fairly quickly there came the inevitable boardroom coup; Crowther was up-ended by Charles Forte, and Michael resigned. I was the lucky one; I had Michael's expertise available at a critical moment. He was a colleague with me on the board of the British Tourist Authority and I asked his help.

One of my first principles of management is Wellingtonian: get as close as possible to the gunfire to see what's happening. Michael and I chartered a small jet from Luton to visit Clarkson Tours' troubled hotel chain in Spain and Mallorca, and it was not a pretty sight. Some hotels were superb value for the customer: these we were underpricing. Some others were new but mouldering, sometimes built, it transpired, with cement mixed with untreated sand straight from the beach: whatever we were charging was too much. We returned determined to dispose of the company, but it proved difficult to give it away, let alone sell it. Finally we had to pay to give it away – and that was a great deal cheaper than liquidating it, which I was ready to do as a last resort to save the rest of the SIH group. Liquidation would have cost the price of two large tankers, so in the end we gave Court Line £5.7 million to take Clarkson away. Court Line were keen to have it because they ran the chartered flights for Clarkson and had the first Airbus on order to add to their fleet. They were bursting with confidence, but sadly they eventually did just that: Court Line went into liquidation years later, in 1979, (though not because of the acquisition of Clarkson; it was their overextensive hotel projects in the West Indies that toppled them). For SIH's part that huge give-away was the most profitable deal I have ever done. Our shares moved upwards dramatically as the City revalued the group without the albatross of Clarkson.

I became deputy chairman of SIH at the end of 1972, the plan being that in the following spring I should take the chair from Jocelyn Hambro, who had been chairman of SIH and also chairman of Hambros (SIH's merchant bank) for many years. But the take-over storm was gathering, and by February 1973 it began to break, with a small rumble of thunder. A six per cent stake in SIH was discovered to have been accumulated by a £100 company, cockily calling itself Doddle Ltd. I recognized the cover name. Doddle is what we were damned sure we would not be. The old guard of SIH had decided on clearing the decks so I could go into action; we were racing against time and the take-over raiders. David Gault, a brilliant ship-broker whose gentlemanly strength easily misled people to think of him as merely gentle, became the new Group MD. Sandy Glen and Ian Morrow (knighted that same year), both deputy chairmen and begetters of the group's expansion, stepped off the board. Sandy to concentrate on his role as chairman of the British Tourist Authority, and Ian working closely with Hambros to take a leading part in the rescue of Rolls-Royce, among other plural responsibilities.

Throughout the hectic spring of 1973 my mind turned heavily to thoughts of Slater. Rumours were rife that he had seized 'large chunks of shares', in the words of the *Evening Standard*. What next? Not what anybody had expected. Slater offered his twelve per cent chunk to Hambros, who bought it – something of a shock to the board, to whom Hambros were advisers. It emerged also that Jimmy Goldsmith, once a Hambros client, had ten per cent of SIH and Hambros had asked the Panel's permission to buy that ten per cent without having to bid for the rest of the equity. I immediately visited the City Take-over Panel and warned the director John Hull that he must expect a hot summer.

On top of the tangle of Hambros interests, towering on top of them in fact, was a colossal enigma called Hilmar Reksten, one of Hambros' biggest clients and one of the world's greatest shipowners, a Norwegian giant of seventy-eight years, an outrageously piratical old sea-dog who barked opinions and orders and made the wide world his dog-house. I arrived home near midnight one day and found Jill waiting for me at the gate as I stepped out of my car, slightly the worse for the wear and tear of the day and night which had left me feeling like a gored bull. And that is what I probably looked like, gored and stunned, when Jill told me to turn around and drive straight back into town, to the Dorchester Hotel. Sandy Glen had rung her to say I must meet Reksten, whatever time it was when I got back. It was vital for me to connect with this man who had been a founder of SIH and held ten per cent of SIH's shares; he was demanding to meet me as the new chairman of the company.

I found the old man of the sea, sitting with Sandy in the Dorchester lobby, old but undoubtedly full of life, a business Viking of saga proportions. Born poor in the Oslo docklands never knowing his father, he had become twice over one of the world's richest ship-owners. The second time in 1956; he had been within hours of bankruptcy when the Suez crisis blocked the Canal and overnight his tanker fleet was precious again. In the war he and Sandy had met and fought on the same side, although that night they seemed to be fighting against each other – but with affection. He and Sandy shared a broad piratical streak in their nature: Hilmar had named his last two big tankers *Sir Alexander Glen* and *Sir Winston Churchill*. But that night this tall thin iceberg with shiny blue eyes definitely saw me as the *Titanic*.

'This is a disaster, you are not a shipowner. I am a shipowner. How can you be a chairman of Shipping Industrial and not a shipowner? Ridiculous. And how can you do it part-time?'

The three of us sat on a small huddle of high-backed chairs, a glaring triangle. His forefinger was wagging almost up against my nose. I found my own forefinger rising in response, my arm crossing his, my finger close to his sharp brow. Somewhat to my astonishment, I found myself asking him, 'Are you married?' Interlocked, both on guard in this absurd position, we were coiled like barbed wire. The conversation continued:

'Yes, more than once. Why.'

'How often d'you see your wife – the rate you're working round the clock and round the world?'

'Say twice, three times a month. Why?'

'Because I want to know something: are you wholly committed to her?'

'Course I am.'

'So you're part-time and wholly committed.'

'Yes.'

'Then it is possible, isn't it? Wholly committed to SIH but part-time?'

Our arm-guards dropped after that, and the night was a long and a merry one. Despite all the blazing hoops of controversy we had to leap through in the months ahead, Hilmar and I were able to keep contact, freely communicating curses and advice. He was consistent; he always said that he would have to go with Hambros at the end of the line. His transactions with them were incomparably greater than anything to do with SIH. And the end could not be far off. In SIH we knew that, but we were not going to go gently, or cheaply, into that good night.

By the AGM, the relationship between the company and its merchant bank, Hambros, was worn out. Obviously they were no longer backing us and we wanted to back off them. On the day itself, Jocelyn Hambro had a bad cold, so in his absence I took the chair at a crowded meeting. I decided to push all the manoeuvrings into the open by announcing that I could 'smell the brimstone of bidding in the air'. This raised the stakes; our shares started to move up.

The board of SIH made its dispositions swiftly and acted in whole-hearted unity. We appointed Kleinwort, Benson as our new merchant bank and Sir Charles Ball became our adviser; he was a doughty gladiator of many corporate defence battles and already my adviser at Rockware. This was a battle to be fought in the open arena of public interest and therefore we put a communication programme at the top of our priorities. Internally, a daily bulletin was issued for all levels of the community in the company. Externally, we met key journalists regularly, confidentially, frankly, and I was never let down by a leak or a news break. I have learnt that the only way to deal with trustworthy financial reporters is to assume their word is as good as your word. The facts of our split with Hambros were presented to the attention of Lord Shawcross, chairman of the City Take-over Panel, and of Gordon Richardson, the new governor of the Bank of England. Then, raising the stakes again, we commissioned the revaluation of our assets which, once it was made known, at once trebled the book values. Our shares moved up above 400p. One of our shareholders, European Ferries, had built up a speculative stake of nine per cent on the shaky strategy that perhaps some day their short-haul ferry operations might make a good fit with SIH's long-haul fleet. But Kenneth Wickens, the chairman of European Ferries, rang me to say that he had received an offer he could not refuse: 450p per share. The offer had come from a mysterious consortium, consisting half of Vlasov, a White Russian emigré shipowner based in Monte Carlo with a massive fleet worth some £100 million and half of Capitalfin, an amalgam of powerful Italian interests, including the Banco di Lavoro, Fiat and Monte Edison. The consortium, we discovered, had built up to a known fourteen and a half per cent of our shares.

The day came when a Dr Caiola called – out of the blue sky, you might say – identifying himself cheerfully as the director of Capitalfin, and saying to me, like someone in the movies, 'Today, I have you in my pocket.' He meant he had fifty-one per cent. The thirty-five per cent of shares controlled by Hambros had been bought at the price of 525p per share, and as far as the City commentators were concerned, to quote Basham, 'the fight was at last over. But not for Parker and his board.' As the consortium went on increasing its holding to sixty-one per cent, we steadfastly refused to accept that the Hambros deal had put a fair price on the company. We also claimed that the foreign purchase was a loss to Britain on two scores: the SIH fleet had been built up largely by the British taxpayers through government grants and allowances, and H. Clarkson, our ship-broking company, a world class specialist, was a unique British and City asset. Through the ex-ambassador on my board, Sir Patrick Reilly, we presented our case to the Italian ambassador: did these grand names of Italian business feel it right to come into such a messy situation? Questions were asked in Parliament about the City conflicts of interest and the warehousing of shares. Probably our most effective move was a visit to the newly formed Office of Fair Trading: ours was the first-ever application of its kind to attempt to stop a bid as a whole. This failed, but we did move the OFT to mediate, and the mediation proved of decisive importance. Vlasov and the Italians behaved magnanimously. Basham's record reads: 'Almost incredibly with sixty-one per cent of the equity, the consortium agreed to raise its bid by 35p a share and to guarantee to hive off the ship-brokers and insurance broking activities of the group into a separate company which would retain the H. Clarkson name.'

We had lost and we had won. Our shareholders had seen their shares more than treble in value over one year, and with the hiving-off of insurance and ship-broking we had achieved a delayed formula for a management buy-out, one of the earliest examples of the now fashionable formula. And we had quit at the moment that shipping markets were weakening under the oil crisis. The City reaction to the outcome was approving: the *Observer* even made me 'Businessman of the Year'. Basham said: 'Of itself, the SIH defence was a masterpiece carried out against overwhelming odds at a time when the company was at its most vulnerable.' But more important than the compliment was his conclusion that 'the defence owed its strength above all to the SIH management's determination first to preserve the autonomy of the ship-broking operations, and more generally not to be taken for granted.'

The victory of a determined management – now that was truly something to celebrate. Management had held together and fought back, and as usual, in my experience anyway, it became stronger as the battle got thicker. H. Clarkson did separate, and with the full co-operation of Capitalfin – viva! – the new company was set up, with myself in the chair and Carron Greig as chief executive. Twenty-five per cent of the shares were allocated to the management, with voting rights of twenty-nine per cent. Over a decade later, H. Clarkson plc was to re-enter the stock exchange as a public company, thriving and independent.

That decade later, business is now as it was in the Seventies, at the close of a roaring spate of mergerous years, and the questions which were relevant then are relevant still. Does our British economy gain from this shuffling of assets? What are the responsibilities of the giant international corporations straddling frontiers? What of the City's reputation in the middle of its cat's cradle of contradictory commitments? What price the management factor in all this financial manipulation? In the flaming light of my experience, I am convinced that our excessive interest in bids and deals has done little to stop the decline of our competitiveness nationally. Bids can, as Slater justified himself, shake lazy management; but these days, it is often the successful companies that are the magnetic attraction for the wheeler-dealer. And then, how are we to measure the effects of the distraction of management leadership, the short-termism that discourges research and development, the disruption of commitment of managers and of the whole working community of an enterprise?

This is obviously not a specifically British disease. It is the way the managerial world is running: diversification and acquisition are inseparable from the growth of large companies. In all the developed economies there has been a massive shift from the single or dominant business to the diversified conglomerate, but nowhere is the shift more dramatic than here in the UK. Between 1950 and 1970, a comparison between the US, West Germany, France and ourselves clearly shows our move from having the highest percentage of our industry in the single/dominant category (seventy-five per cent) to having the highest in the related diversified and conglomerate categories (sixty per cent). The same reasons for the trend, some excellent, prevail here as elsewhere, with the States most comparable to ourselves. Market share is seen to be crucial to profitability, and getting a slice of market share by acquisition is quicker than pushing and shoving for marginal advantages in the market-place. Also it makes sense to spread the risk, particularly for mature industries, as some indeed (like tobacco) are both old and shrinking.

Of course, this may be the trend of global business economics but the sheer humanity of the entrepreneur is also a factor. Many of those at the top have fought their way up, and the aggressive spirit brims over naturally into empire-building, or sometimes simply ego-building. It's more glamorous and more macho to be bigger and bigger, growing right out of the picture frame – like those portraits of the winners in the media, more and more enlarged so that less and less of the face can get in, until there seems only room for very-close-ups and only the eyes and eyebrows identify the hero. One justification put forward is that the bigger you become the harder you are to swallow. Maybe, but today nobody seems safe any more. The giants rise up from each industrial sector, their appetite 'so doubly seconded with will and power', and they drive themselves to seek markets and resources on a global scale. This is the way of the world. To a degree we should expect and welcome it, and the changes it brings which go well beyond business. But all that said, our merger and acquisition activity is higher, relative to the size of the economy, than in other countries. We are the most concentrated of advanced economies, and I believe that, whatever the reasons for what has happened so intensely in the UK, it has not done British industry that much good.

The experience of the British manufacturing industries is a gloomily convincing piece of evidence. Manufacturing is a declining part of the total economy in the UK. So it is in the US, West Germany, France and Japan, but as the most exposed part of any home market's business, it is still the most obvious measure of a nation's competitive effectiveness. From being the third largest manufacturer in the world in 1961, we are now a remote fifth and hardly deserve to be described as an advanced manufacturing nation in this pace-making group. There was a real decline of some twenty per cent in the output of manufactured goods in the UK between 1973 and 1983 and the calamitous years of 1979–81 account for the major fall. 1983 saw a deficit in trade in manufactured goods for the first time since the Industrial Revolution. The result is that the manufacturer is an endangered species in Britain, and whatever the main causes of this relative failure, the feverish British propensity to engage in mergers and acquisitions has certainly done little to correct it. In the wise judgement of Dr John Constable, who has been a most skilful analyst of this growth, 'indeed, it may have been a significant cause of the decline.' Of course, it would be absurd to argue that no acquisitive development has worked; but research into the results of take-overs supports Dr Constable in the general contention that 'there are more losers than gainers in the acquisition stakes. Too often, it is illusion of growth: if we are concerned with the country's economy the fact that the acquirer grows larger is not enough. The UK badly needs real growth in economic activity and not illusory growth.' Constable cuts deep into our national psyche: 'the British and American societies see making money out of money as a clever and more desirable activity than making money out of making goods sold in a competitive market-place. The former involves speculation, the latter requires investment.' One attitude is short-term: the other is what our main competitors believe in.

By the mid-Seventies the world recession had checked the take-over trend, as indeed the world stock exchange collapse checked it in the late Eighties. The crash in the Seventies did two things for me, one general, the other particular. It confirmed me in my prejudice: good management remains at the heart of hopes for recovery in Britain. The shocks of the slump thumped the message home: it created a new faith in humanity in management. From the rubble of fallen take-over idols, from the emptied colosseums of the corporate planning departments, from the crumbling Dead Sea scrolls of consultants' reports, from the Roman-like rigidities of (some) business schools, a new sanity started to rise – and not a moment too soon. The difference between managerial success and failure was seen once again to be to do with sticking close to the customer and seeing to the highest quality of service, and having to do with everybody in the enterprise taking pride in their job and mission as well as having the right external experts and advisers.

Much more particularly, the crash also brought to a head the unsettled problem of the Slater stake in Rockware. For a couple of years the relationship between Slater and Rockware had been as dangerous as any exposed power line would be but it had also been unexpectedly enjoyable. The Slater director who joined us on the board was an accountant, anxious and sharp, but still we felt the man inside trying to get out. He seemed to live with fearful stress because, like most accountants, I suspect he had reached the top by saying no very firmly and regularly – and living with Jim probably meant having to say yes. Tragically, still only in his forties, he went on a trip to Brussels, climbed the hill of the monument at Waterloo and died.

The same year, Jim Slater himself had his own Waterloo. It came at the onset of the banking crisis in late 1973. Just days before the crack of the property markets, and of his bank, I went with Jim Craigie, our fine Group MD at Rockware, to 'No. 1, St Paul's Graveyard'. We met over the small round table near the corner window of Slater's office and we suggested to him that the moment had come to market his shares by placing them among friendly institutions. Jim was agreeable but unusually unfocused. We went on to talk prices, and at this Jim automatically fell into one of his fast-thinking routines, one of his party tricks almost: he scribbled numbers on a small sheet of paper as we talked, and I was expecting him to come flashing back with alternative calculations. But there was a sudden distraction in his face, he pushed the bit of paper away from him, and abruptly agreed to our proposal. I glanced at the paper as we got up to go: the scribbles were simply strings of noughts. Two days later the news of his down-fall broke upon the financial world: while we were meeting, his mind must have been on bigger things, on the Jim-cracked empire crum-bling away to those zeros.

In the ensuing confusion of his crash, suddenly another Jim, Sir James Goldsmith, came into my life. The Bank of England had agreed that he assume responsibility for part of the Slater interests, including the industrial portfolio. Jimmy the Second assured me he would live up to the Rockware commitments made by the dethroned Jim the First. At once, I circulated a note to be put up on all our factory notice-boards, assuring the Rockware community that our long and hard-fought independence and stability was not going to be lost with the collapse of Slater.

That announcement mattered. Throughout the struggles for our independence, the whole of the Rockware community, from board to factory floor, had been kept in the stormy picture. Communications were crucial to any counter-attack we might have to make. Every year I, as chairman, with Jim Craigie, the Group MD, used to hold meet-ings with all levels of the organization at what we called Mini-AGMs. These were small open meetings in work-time, at which we presented to the total community exactly the same sort of facts we shared with shareholders at the formal AGMs. And when we asked for any questions, we usually got what we asked for: challenges from 'How much are you really paid?' to 'What are you going to do about Slater? We've invested our life in this plant. These quick-money merchants can do anything they like. What are you doing about it?' Held regularly over the years, these long encounters had built up a spirit of comrade-ship in Rockware which we all valued. That was at stake if we were to be rolled over by the wheeler-dealers. So being able to put up that notice around the organization mattered to the whole working community. There can be a numbing atmosphere of helplessness around in the target company at a take-over time. What the hell is really happening? Who's in charge? There spreads a gallows humour: if the boss calls, take his name. The mood is combustible. We reached Christmas 1974, and a mid-winter chill of rumour was blowing around the City that Rothschilds were putting the Slater block of shares in Rockware on to the market. Jim Goldsmith was abroad and ungetat-able. Something was amiss. The family set off for our country home at Minster Lovell for the few days' festivities.

On Christmas morning my father, Tommy, started to die. . . . Christmas morning. Another Christmas morning eight years before: the four children had assembled gleefully on the landing outside the bedroom of Dorothy and Tommy, tap-tapping on the door. Christmas morning had begun with the ritual of romping in to see their grandparents and compare surprises stuffed in the Christmas stockings. Dorothy and Tommy had stockings too, of course. Dorothy called 'come in', and as they did, she was sitting up in bed and smiling to welcome them. Just then she was struck by a massive coronary. In no time the ambulancemen were there – and Dorothy was gone. They took her down the stairs, not on a stretcher, but wrapped in a blanket in one of those canvas chair-things that are flexible around corners. One hand, that had been so firm, flopping. Our grief was an exact measure of the joy we had had of her. Christmas day was a mountain to climb, the family roped together. 'Under every grief and pine/Runs a joy with silken twine,' as Blake said, 'And when this we rightly know/Thro' the world we safely go' . . .

Tommy was late coming downstairs to join the rest of the family, who were rebelliously gathering in the hall for the Christmas morning service, rummaging for collection money, and tumbling about in the excitement of fun and games to come. There was loads of both to be had beside the log fire, and under the Christmas tree the merry-coloured parcels. I called up for Tom; then I went up to him. I found him in the bathroom, gripping the wash-basin, his trousers in disarray, in a real mess. '*Diable*', he could only whisper. I shouted down to say I would soon catch up with the party in church, and the big front door closed with a bang. Tom was quiet and perfectly calm as I washed him down and carried him to his bed. I brought a hot-water bottle and tea and sat with him. No words, no words. He dozed off. I joined the family at the service.

After Boxing Day, Jill decided that we should get Tom to London. We made for London on the Friday; the roads were bleakly clear, most people were taking the day off. On our way down, Sir Charles Ball, Rockware's merchant banker at Kleinwort, Benson, called me on the car-phone to say we must meet urgently. He had got wind of the possibility of some deal being done on this unguarded day, squeezed inconspicuously between the Christmas festivities and the weekend.

By the time I reached Charles he had had a call from Rothschilds, and a meeting with them was arranged. On the way there I had a call from Jimmy Goldsmith, in Switzerland, to say that he had heard of a deal which he thought would be excellent for Rockware: 'You'll be pleased.' I doubted it. He was sorry not to be with me but he had the 'flu. When I met Charles, I was told that Pilkington had bought twenty-nine per cent of Rockware, and I was anything but pleased.

What about the agreement not to sell without our agreement? Sir Alastair Pilkington, the chairman, rang through, sensible as ever, amicable and welcoming. I told him that I presumed he could not have been aware of the prior understandings, and much as I admired him and his great group, we had no wish to be dominated by a big glass brother with twenty-nine per cent. Anyway why would he want as much as twenty-nine per cent unless it was to position himself to take control at some point? Alastair sounded genuinely surprised and upset; he asked if I wanted him to come down to London for dinner. Inexcusably, I lost my temper. I said he must decide that for himself: after all, he'd decided to buy these shares without consultation. But Alastair kept his temper; he came down to town, and at dinner together at the Connaught I pressed into his hands the letters that had passed between me and Goldsmith, and Slater before him. It emerged that Alastair had not been aware of the history: communications had broken down somewhere and he was as sore as I had been in the morning. The dilemma was that he had committed himself to the purchase of the shares and arrangements were ready to move into the market next morning when the stock exchange opened. I spoke to Lord Rothschild at breakfast-time to be sure he was aware of the full story, and the tangled skein began to unravel swiftly and honourably. A compromise was agreed. Alastair floated off nine per cent of the shares and brought the Pilkington interest down to about twenty per cent. Rockware's independence was secure once again and, more than that, the Pilkington alliance would reinforce it.

During the short siege of Rockware, Tom's decline had steepened. After a few days at home, he had to be moved to St Bartholomew's Hospital, in the care of John Griffiths, a great surgeon and a great friend, and of Mary, another friend, who was his incomparable ward sister. Tom knew nothing of hospitals. He had spent only one night of his life in one, three years before. He had been on one of his long London walks with Busta, our Yorkshire terrier (Busta – short for

Bustamante, the Jamaican Prime Minister, to whom he bore a colourful likeness). Tom had been a limitless wanderer; nowhere seemed
far to him. Once he had strolled from Notting Hill Gate to Greenwich
to see the Cutty Sark. But on one of these patrols, on a stifling hot
day, he had dropped in a faint in Park Lane. A police car had whizzed
him to Paddington Hospital where he came round bewildered to find
himself in bed, in one of those casual, disheartening hospital shifts.
Jill, from her surgery, and I, from the City, rushed to him. Checking
with the matron I saw the police form clipped to her check-board.
His age had been guessed as 'early sixties': he was eighty-five then.
I told him this and it cheered him. We left him for the night, defiant,
sitting dangling his legs from the high bed in the corner of a busy
ward.

Once in Barts he was on a saline drip, but he faded fast. Two last
things he whispered. One I could hardly follow, but the gist was that
'when it comes to it' he had always wanted to 'take a pier-head jump'.
This was the sailor's expression for boarding ship at the very last
minute, after staying ashore as long as possible, and that was what
Tom did: on earth for eighty-eight years, then off with a bound and
away. The last words came in a conversation about what was happening around him. He was very impressed, thumbs up, with the welcome
and care that Mary had given him, and with the crisp efficiency that
went with the bustle. And, drowsily, he muttered about the way Jill
had fixed all this. 'She's a blooming marvel.' His eyes were closing,
but he pulled at my hand so I leant close. 'A blooming marvel,' is
what he was still whispering. That seemed to cover most things:
certainly Jill, and also certainly, an amazing life and times, a merry,
gallant man, a forgiving, always surprising father.

He lived on another day, asleep. The next evening, I watched him
sleep, put alone in a small white room, everything baby-clean. Those
short strong fingers suddenly soft. I wished he had not lost the last
ring he had designed, the one with the star sapphire set in white gold.
We had been holidaying in Sri Lanka, the whole family, and Tom,
always roving, had gone off with the youngest boy Nathaniel – remarkable how in a family the oldest is often closest to the youngest. They
had found a jeweller's shop near our hotel at Ben Tota and Tom had
designed himself a ring. We had known nothing of this, and naturally
Nat was sworn to secrecy so as to make the finished product a
spectacular surprise for us all. It was. We only discovered what was

happening on the penultimate day when a stranger, the jeweller, came to the poolside and waved to Nat, who waved to Tom, and they all three disappeared. Nat was back in five minutes, just a bit flustered, to explain that Tom needed cash. Understandably the village jeweller was having trouble verifying Tom's Barclay cheque on his Bedford account. Back went Nat with the wherewithal, and Tom returned in triumph with his dashing design: a thick band of white gold which swelled up like a glittering wave round a handsome star sapphire. When we arrived home from Sri Lanka to Heathrow, at four-thirty in the morning, I presented a list of the family purchases to the Customs man, and at the top of the list was the only extravagance in the family: that star sapphire set in white gold. All the rest was trivial.

'I'd better see that,' the officer said, naturally looking at Jill standing beside me, the family sitting dazed behind us on the luggage. I explained that the ring was not Jill's but my father's, and I called back to Tom.

'He wants to look at the ring.'

Tom roused himself and sprang forward holding his hand out to catch the dim light.

'Isn't it fine?' he said to the customs man, 'I only wish I'd done the same with a good ruby, they've excellent rubies in Ceylon.'

The customs officer looked at me and Jill, and said to Tom, 'I pass. Good luck to you, sir.'

Tom lost the ring a year later playing with the boys in the park.

I last saw Tom laid out in the Bart's chapel. Icy as it was in there, Tom was colder. I kissed his brow and was startled by the stone-coldness. Madame de Stael said 'La mort ne nous sépare pas: elle ne fait que nous rendre invisible.' Still, like every son, I wished and wished. And one thing I wished was that Tom had lived to enjoy the new home and happiness that we were just coming to at last, at Minster Lovell; not a family retreat but a family advance.

Jill had visited Oxfordshire and had had a vision. She saw a collection of very old farm buildings clustered beside the elegant gaunt ruin of Minster Lovell Hall and somehow she saw our future there. Lady Reilly (Rachel), who was president of the Oxfordshire Council for the Preservation of Rural England, had driven Jill there to look at it on a grey day. Rachel had a serious purpose, she always did. She was the wife of Sir Patrick Reilly, the former ambassador to Moscow and Paris, and she had that formidable ambassadress's sense of command,

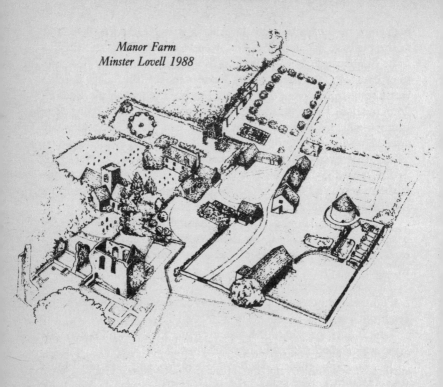

Manor Farm
Minster Lovell 1988

which simply gets things done, and no nonsense. On that day with Jill, the ambassadress was determined to stop the fragmentation of this medieval complex of a farm into several bijoux weekend places. She was against the conversion of the Cotswolds into Sloane Square with grass. University College, the owners of the farm, had some 350 acres of the farmland a year or so before at what later seemed relatively low prices, at some £300 per acre as against the £1,000 per acre prices that were prevailing in 1973. To recoup, the college had gained permission to sell the farmhouse and its buildings for a series of small separate developments. But the ambassadress, Rachel of Rural

England, was determined to roll back those permissions and to see that the farm was sold as a whole.

And of course, so it came to pass – eventually. A year later, the whole farm was put up for auction in the afternoon at the Randolph Hotel in Oxford. I did not bid. Instead, Jill went to the auction accompanied by our dear and wise friend, Rayne Kruger, an experienced bidder who had been richly successful in property and was prepared to bid for me. I had only once bid for a house, and that was at an auction in the stately Old Swan Inn beside the Ouse in Bedford, when I bought No. 25, St Augustine's Road for Dorothy and Tommy, the house they had rented for twenty years. I recalled now the explosion of excitement and delight. Twenty years on, here I was hoping to buy the Manor Farm at a price which would have bought more than twenty-five 'No. 25s' – so I reckoned to put my trust in Rayne. Before the sale, he and Jill had luncheon in a room at the Randolph, 'made sinister', as Jill said, 'with jolly, confident competition, people in hefty tweed suits which have those bottomless pockets'. Reassuringly Rayne ordered a bottle of superb claret, which Jill impounded for herself, insisting that she needed it while he surely needed to keep a clear head. Jill had never been to a sale before and was amazed by the muted proceedings. Hummed bids, casual looks, small gestures, and in no time, 'going, going, gone'. Gone! Gone? Where's it gone? Jill clutched at Rayne. 'To you,' he said. With characteristically perfect judgement, Rayne had joined the bidding late, blithely went well over the negotiating limit I had set myself, and won.

And made all the difference to our lives. It is the only property deal I know in which everybody ended smiling. University College smiled with relief; Rachel with a sense of justice; all the Parkers simply with pioneering joy; and Jill with 'The Purest of Pleasures' – a few years later, this, a quote from Francis Bacon, was what she called her book about her making of a romantic garden at Minster. For me, the next seven years were to prove the home at Minster Lovell more than the purest of pleasures: it was a sheer necessity, a private siding in my life with British Rail.

8

'The Problem with the Railways'

Suddenly, in spring 1976, it was all change. I was appointed chairman of British Rail. Friendly letters poured in wishing me equally congratulations and commiseration. But to hell with commiseration, how could I be anything but chuffed? Here was noble work to do. I should have tackled it about a decade before, and after years of plurality the prospect of the magnificent obsession was pleasing. Anyway, I had fifty-five million people to help me: everybody seemed to be an expert on railways and ready with instant advice.

True to form, the process of appointment to the public sector was full of surprises. Indeed at first it was the chairmanship of Steel that I thought I was being asked to consider. Tony Crosland, the Secretary of State for the Environment (which then included Transport), invited me to take over the chair of the railways; but about a week before, quite separately, another Cabinet Minister had approached me with the proposition that I should follow Sir Monty Finniston as chairman of the British Steel Corporation. I knew and respected this other minister: I had no doubt, in the two discussions that I had with him, that he was genuine and that he spoke with authority, but whose authority? There was an ambiguity, serious and curious, in his approach because he was not the minister directly responsible for Steel. Eric Varley was: why was Eric not in touch? The other Minister assured me there was a good reason, and all would be made clear in due course. Meanwhile, he persisted, where did I stand? During the week of this mysterious approach there was much talk in the press of a new chairman being recruited for BR, and a few friendly journalists, usually well informed, rang to sound me out. My name, they said, was one of the 'probables' circulating around the corridors of White-hall. So little escapes them: I myself knew nothing at that stage, but they were proved right. Sure enough, soon I was in the waiting-room outside the office of Tony Crosland. Even there, sitting in one of those awful, skiddy, plastic-covered, so-called easy chairs, I received a coded message from the other Minister who had got wind of my meeting with Tony and urged that I should avoid committing myself to anything until he had spoken again. Too late: within minutes Tony was asking would I take on the railways and I was saying, 'Of course.' I'd wanted to do it ten years ago.

That settled, I had two questions. Was I the first to be asked? And, if I was to break off my career in the private sector for public service, where, in his opinion, could I be most useful? I mentioned the rumours of the Steel appointment and reminded him that I had six years with the British Steel Corporation: I knew something about that industry, and zilch about railways. Tony was truly taken aback. 'But there's really no question of you doing Steel, Peter. I'll show you.' He produced a paper dated months earlier and agreed by key ministers including himself and Varley – but not the 'other' Minister. The paper listed columns of names, one headed BR and the other BSC, and no names were in both. These were the candidates for new appointments to the two chairmanships, and the order in which they were to be approached. I was the first for railways: I was not on the Steel list. (Incidentally, Ian MacGregor's name was on that list even then, in the Labour days.) This evidence was incontrovertible. I said no more about Steel, and I never mentioned to Tony the indirect move to rustle me from the Crosland corral.

We both relaxed over a short scotch. I noticed how tired Tony looked; he had his explosive look of being formidably on the top of everything and ready to go over the top if contradicted. What an extraordinary capacity for putting people out or at ease that man had, a powerful charmer, serious and fun, a Cavalier among the Roundheads. I admired and enjoyed him, and adored his wife, Susan. 'I'd love to do the BR job myself,' he sighed, 'just to be able to stay occasionally in those lovely, comfortable hotels all over the place.'

Sadly, next day, where I was going to stay, indeed to live, became an ugly, spoiling little problem between us, as our two private offices went into the slow-motion ritual about my detailed conditions of service. It seems ever so with the transfer of employment from private to public enterprise, and incidentally it is most often pensions that particularly make for trouble: I was four years with BR before I received a tight-lipped note to say my pension arrangements had been finally agreed. But in April 1976 the immediate issue was my housing problem in London. I knew, and so did Jill and the family, that going to work on the railways meant we would have to sell our home in London. My annual cash flow was going to be cut to a third and loan structures would be insupportable once we had to live on the going rate for a public enterprise chairman. I had to pull in my financial horns. That was all right, it was my business, no regrets, a straight-forward decision, my choice – our choice. But I enquired whether there was any traditional mechanisms to sustain us, a tied flat or something that might go with the job. Tony and I met too late the next night and we rowed about it. Tony loathed the squalid details, saw them as piddling irrelevancies to a great mission. And of course they were. Anyway, there was really no time left for personal consider-ations. Dick Marsh, then chairman of BR, made public his intention to go, and for good order we had to release at once the announcement of myself as the new man.

Later that year I had to sell 35 Brunswick Gardens. On the basis that my contract with the government was on the usual five-year term, we took a short lease on a modern brick box in Chelsea, reasonably close to Jill's surgery and my headquarters in Marylebone. It was the first real railway thing I did, move house; railway families do it all the time. Of course it was a bad time to put a house on the market (it always is) but it was a wonderful time to come on to the rails. Every-body wanted change at BR. Railway fortunes were at an achingly low ebb. When Dick Marsh had been appointed five years before, the Conservative government had given him a rosy prospectus for BR, with a glorious long-range strategy and commitments for investment to match. The strategy had lasted no time; it crashed into the buffers of a financial crisis in the country and blew up in the flaming inflation of the next few years. A very fair BBC 'Panorama' programme about my introduction to BR in 1976 described the industry as 'demoralized, embattled and £500 million in the red'.

The prospectus Tony handed to me at the start was the opposite of a glorious vision; it was a limp proof copy of a Green Paper on Integrated Transport about to be launched on a sceptical world. I studied it overnight and saw no help in it for BR. Tony had applied his brilliance to trying to answer the old riddle of reconciling competi-tive modes of transport into a co-ordinated policy. It read well enough, in some parts even beautifully. There were detectable touches of

Tony: the bold scale of conception was his and so were the elegant flashes in the drafting (there was even a quotation from Proust). It was also the last serious review by a government of transport policy overall; no one since has had the nerve to attempt it. But the tone of the document had a dying fall, there was a defeatist courage about it. I had no objection to integrated transport: some degree of it is a sheer necessity in any civilized society. What was depressing in Tony's document was that it implied a reduced railway. What he really believed came through in a remark in his early briefing: 'Peter, I see a future for BR as a smaller, sensible little railway.' Instinctively I could not agree: surely we would test the market by having a really determined policy to sell the services of railways. That Green Paper was a depressing, sophisticated muddle, eventually published in orange covers and something of an embarrassment all round.

By the time it appeared, Tony had been promoted to Foreign Secretary. Peter Shore came in as Secretary of State for a couple of months, time only to give transport policy a civilized glance. Then Callaghan's new government was formed and Transport was split off from Environment and given Cabinet status with Bill Rodgers as Minister. Excellent news: a new ministry, and a new minister, in new partnership with a new Permanent Secretary, Peter Baldwin (later Sir Peter). Bill, Peter and myself were all coming new to the old challenge of railways. If Tony could quote Proust, I could quote Philip Larkin, that last line from 'Trees': 'Begin afresh, afresh, afresh.' Bill, who was to prove a firm, shrewd Minister for two years, gave the Green-Orange Paper a decent, tactfully quiet burial and began afresh on his own White Paper. He seemed more positive about railways and readier to listen to a positive BR.

My line, from the start, was that it was up to us in BR to make the running of the railway. We should not look to government for too many answers until we had put together our own business-like propositions. It was little use asking them what they wanted of us until we knew what we were capable of. Could we have a popular, well-loaded railway? We had to take stock of our competitiveness and above all recapture the interest of the nation in their public service. After thirty years of nationalization Britain was baffled by BR, and more than a little bored. 'The problem with the railways' was the way too many politicians, civil servants and customers used to begin their sentences when they met me. We had to start them talking instead – or if not instead, at least as well – about the opportunities for railways. That I saw, from the outset, as a basic political and marketing 'problem with the railways'.

When I began with BR I had been given a farewell present from my merchant bank, a Victorian anthology of Punch cartoons on the railways. The introduction, written a hundred years ago, read like a typical chastising editorial in today's *Evening Standard*, that champion of the commuters. The jokes were the good old jokes, all there, part of the folklore that surrounded the familiar British love-hate tradition with trains, a family joke. I sent the book to an evening paper, offering prizes for up-dated versions of the captions to the drawings. It seemed to me that anything that would help to recover the Victorian values of a good-humoured, ragging relationship was an advance on the sour blight that seemed to prevail over BR. Good humour took its place among the objectives of the corporation. A few years on, Prue Leith, the famous chef and entrepreneur, was to join our board, the first woman to do so. I was asked, on a television programme, what she was supposed to do. 'Among many things,' I said, 'uncurl the sandwiches.' And with her usual dazzling attack and with the enthusiastic support of Travellers Fare, she did just that. The line was well taken by the public. I was relieved; this was some measure of progress, we could take a joke again.

But at the beginning, in 1976, the public mood was bleak. Over the years people had become grimly accustomed to railways being connected with rising payments from the taxpayer, and the scale of the massive subsidies was taken as proof that the railways were massively inefficient. Railways had access to the public purse but apparently not the public mind or confidence. Always something of a music-hall joke, even in the good old days, they were now simply beyond a joke, clapped-out, unreliable, expensive and nationalized. The railways were no fun any more, the country had had enough.

That exasperation was more than a mood, it reflected a technical reality. The country had had, in fact, too much railway for too long. Railways had run into the twentieth century with gross overcapacity. In the nineteenth century the barbaric triumphs of the steam engine, supercharged with Victorian optimism, had led to a rampaging railway mania and the creation of more track than made sense. After the First World War, the Railways Act of 1921 grouped some 120 companies into the big four, the London and North Eastern Railway, the London,

*Comic strip framed and given to Peter Parker by the Rockware staff
on his joining the railways*

Midland and Scottish Railway, the Great Western Railway and the
Southern Railway, but these four lacked competitive freedom because
they were linked by a common carrier obligation and the regulation
of the Railway Tribunal. They had no flexibility to match the advent
of the motor vehicle. By the Second World War they were in gross
financial difficulties, and six years of war took a terrific toll: they had
to work their track and rolling-stock to the limit, with minimum
maintenance and replacement. Then on 1 January 1948, nationalization day, the country bought it: a huge, run-down system saddled
with a capital debt of almost £100 million – and pounds were pounds
then.

Initially, because road transport facilities were linked, railways produced an operating surplus, but they could never generate the cash
flows to sustain the capital programme of the enterprise. By 1955
even the operating surplus had dwindled to nothing, and from then
on operation losses mounted inexorably. By 1962 the deficit had
reached £100 million and government had to act. In 1963 Beeching

was brought in and his administration was the first and final effort to make the whole railway commercial. The whole system was to be examined leaving the social costs out of the calculations and approaching it from the acute angle of sheer financial efficiency, using rigorous accounting and coherent corporate planning. A new, glittering toolkit of management techniques was deployed to reshape the network according to Beeching's Plan: capital debt was written off, and so too, on a wide scale, were lines, stations, depots and services. The Plan reads now like Overconfidence on a Monument sighing at the grief-stricken, misspent old age of the Railways. Its final sentences would fit an anthology of famous last words: it concluded that much of the railways' deficit would be eliminated by 1970.

The concentration on obvious loss-makers, on pruning the dead wood, was meant to leave a healthier, more fruitful tree, but that was not what happened. Beeching left in 1966. By 1968 the figures had scarcely improved and the deficit was again £78 million. Perhaps a more accurate analogy than tree pruning might have been that of cutting off tributaries and drying up the main flow of the river, though that is not quite right either, nor is it fair. I want to do justice to the Beeching years. He was a managerial colossus and his achievement was colossal. Without his cuts, the poor results that followed would certainly have been worse than they were. When it came to my turn to struggle with the Leviathan, I could not have even dreamt of success without Beeching having done what he did more than a decade before me. His was life-saving, hero's surgery. He made the railway manageable.

But that was not his main objective, not what he set out to do. He had meant to make it totally commercial, and that, to my mind, was Mission Impossible. For there was no core to the concept of a totally commercial railway. The logic of the remit given to and accepted by Beeching could only lead to the fragmentation of the national system into smaller and smaller smithereens, some commercial, some not. Railways are not just a business problem. Governments of varied hue, shades of red or blue to begin with, have ended up bruise-coloured from the struggle of trying to deal with railways on that limited basis. In the end they have all had to admit, through gritted teeth, that there is a need for a national policy and that certain services must be operated for social rather than economic reasons.

So, after all Beeching's executions, the Labour government still had to write a new testament White Paper on Transport Policy in 1966, enacted as the 1968 Railway Act, in which the idea was that lines that were run as a social service were to be dissected from the commercial system and paid for by government 'grant aid'. This turned out to be only another mouthwatering mirage. The idea was to allocate results on a service-by-service basis, that is to say by deciding which particular lines were 'social' and which should be 'commercial'. Unfortunately the accounting systems simply could not cope with the confusion of joint costs: after all 'social' trains ran over the same track as the others and were dependent on the same vigilant signalmen, the same crews at stations and depots. It was an accountant's hell – or heaven; it would take an accountant to tell the difference.

By 1974, the deficit was back to the £100 million mark of just over a decade before. Once again, a fresh initiative was called for, and this one was launched by the Conservative government and enacted by Labour in the 1974 Railway Act. It was a realistic advance, flat-footed, unfancy and just about workable. It abolished as too elaborate the concept of precise individual service-by-service criteria, and recognized the element of infrastructure (mainly tracks and signalling) in arriving at the true 'social cost' of operating unremunerative lines.

Fascinatingly, it was the new world of the EEC that was being called in to help redress the balances of the oldest railway in the world. EEC regulation 1191/69 (hallowed be its Section One) defined a Public Service Obligation, the 'PSO', which was global, unallocated and paid as compensation to transport undertakings obliged to maintain 'the provision of adequate transport services'. The 1974 Act adopted the PSO formula. British Rail was required to 'operate their railway passenger system so as to provide a public service' which was to be 'comparable generally with that provided by the board at present'. In other words, as far as the size of the network was concerned, it was 'Carry on, BR.' Of course that could only be half the equation of a decent policy: the necessary funding had to be thought through sensibly as well, and that is where that initiative ran into trouble. The politicians had much more difficulty with the financial decisions than with their generalized directive to carry on. Sustaining the scale of the system was likely to keep most constituents happy: stumping up the cash to make it happen was something else again – and again, and again, as the years ahead proved. For railways the signal had got stuck on an amber, or in the railway jargon, a yellow, which in all the political circumstances was more appropriate.

In 1975, a time of general economic crisis, the Labour government had introduced cash disciplines to control all the public sector borrowing requirements: they were a blunt instrument but necessary and bitingly successful in the years of inflation ahead. Their effect on railways was to fix the PSO for 1976 at the 1975 level in real terms and to keep it there 'in subsequent years'. In short, BR was being directed to run the business 'with due regard . . . to efficiency, economy and safety' but on a fixed sum. In the short term there was much to be said for this intense pressure on productivity in public enterprise: productivity there needed a kick in the pants. Here was a bracing challenge, and in my view not a moment too soon. But it could only be a short-term formula. Investment needs were piling up and the danger was that the brace would turn into a strait-jacket for the business of BR in the long run. In my first public report in 1976 I declared that productivity was the rock on which we had to build the future BR. Undoubtedly efficiencies should be stepped up and manpower reduced. However, productivity means more than the reduction of manpower, important as that is in an industry which has more than sixty per cent of its costs in people. Investment also had a part to play in improving performance. Only about a tenth of the old number of signalmen would be needed in a modern signalling system, but introducing it called for massive investment. A failure to synchronize investment with cuts in manpower would be a lost opportunity to accelerate change. Which was very nearly the story of what happened in my time.

In that first annual report, I confirmed my commitment to a 40,000 reduction in manpower, but I also exposed the growing contradiction of policy. 'It is plain that the balance will be increasingly hard to strike beyond the immediate short term. To avoid damaging the long term, there is now an urgent need for coherence in transport policy towards the railways.' For a fixed sum I could run a railway for a long time, but what kind of railway? A declining railway. There could be no permanent way of living within a fixed cash limit if we were to keep up standards on an 11,000-route service. Something would have to give, first quality, then the size of the service. Cash constraints could not be the total objectives of this or any business. It was as if the politicians were to ask Covent Garden Opera to go on playing after midnight, not caring what they were supposed to play.

So what next? Shrink the size of the system? But strong MPs of all political complexions went pale at the thought of cutting out the wretchedly inadequate rural services. Be more efficient? Yes, of course, but in no way would phased savings add up to the necessary investment to prevent deteriorating track conditions, poorer and slower services, and a slowing down of the introduction of our flagship, the High Speed Train. In no way could there be a sensible future for the railways without more investment, without electrification, without a determined strategy for the development of rail as part of a common-wealth of other modes of transport. Improving the service to the customer meant improving the technology of the system, and that would make it safer than ever, more efficient, more popular, better loaded, more economic. Even so, none of the sums would add up if there was no vision of a prosperous public railway. The question was, did the country want a modern railway or not? BR badly needed an answer, yes or no. 'Er' was not good enough, and we seemed stuck in an 'er' period.

I was given a temporary office while I began part-time in the spring of 1976. It was a room with no pictures, at the end of a tunnel-like corridor in the Rail Headquarters, 222 Marylebone Road. Once the Grand Central Station Hotel, this huge block had been built extravagantly at the start of the century, but the company had collapsed, probably under the costs of its own splendid flourishes of space and staircases inside, and of elaborate brick and ironwork outside, handsome and exuberant, if battered, to this day. In both great wars the building had been used as a transit camp and hospital: I was not the only one to sense a lingering atmosphere of the casualty ward about the old place.

The lack of pictures about the corridors and in my room did nothing to dispel a vague bereftness in the air. It was explained to me that pictures had been removed in the early Sixties, a different sort of Beeching cut. I could appreciate the dramatic reasoning that might have prevailed then – clear the past from our sight and concentrate on finding a future – but in my time I felt a different urgency altogether. I had to get the act together. Above all we needed to draw inspiration from the entrepreneurial past, from our great days, and this could help us to correct an imperfect present, and make the most of a future that was there for the grasping were we bold enough to make the change. Most of the pictures had gone (properly) to the York Museum, but a few had been left, probably in the basement. I went down there with James Cousins, the irrepressible (thank goodness!) director of industrial design, and, after rummaging, we together brought up a few fine leftovers, including a most unusual Cuneo, a small rural scene, one of the few I have seen by this master of railway oil-paintings in our generation. We nailed our pictures on the wall at once. It may seem a trivial enough moment to remember but I enjoyed it; it meant much to me. Pictures in an office may be the subjective choice of the occupier, but they are part of a mosaic, the style of any organization, the character of any enterprise. Design of the product and the environment makes a decisive statement about a management, good or bad, conscious or unconscious. What managers relate to, what they value, stand for, even what they think of one another at work – these show through in details of design. Your letterhead as well as what you write speaks for you. What you wear is your state-ment. What you live with on your wall says something. BR already had a pre-eminence among the railways of the world for its corporate design; I knew that, and became resolved to reinforce and develop that priority in BR with all my might. The look of railways, the stations, the rolling-stock, the uniforms, the environment in and around the stations – these must state our mission as a clean, safe, high-quality service.

I was standing, only a few days later, on the staircase in Paddington having my picture taken for *Fortune* magazine. Those photo-calls always take longer than you think, and resignedly, idly, as I waited for the clicking to stop, I was watching an old ticket inspector standing by his gate on the level above me. He wore a corrugated woollen uniform with epaulettes of dandruff, and I was mentally writing him off, an 'er' man in an 'er' period. He caught my eye, came down the steps, lively as a tour guide. 'You know that very step you stand on is where Frith, the Victorian painter, stood to do his famous picture of our station.' I had been wrong and, worse, I had made the cruellest of mistakes in management: I had underestimated his pride in the job. He was lovingly deep in the detail of what he did and where he did it. How could I set up an objective, a vision for BR enlivening and personal enough to make him feel that his part in it, his own design, his individual performance mattered? That it mattered he be smart and do his buttons up?

Gradually, in that limbo phase of early explorations before taking the chair, I was helped to see a vision of what might be for BR. The truth is that, with all the professionalism in the management world, nothing works in any enterprise without the vision. In some businesses, the vision is given; what you are working for is already established, like the picture on the top of the jigsaw box. For someone joining some corporate giants, say ICI or Unilever or Shell or IBM, the broad design is there, on the box-top, to help anyone starting at any level. In 1976, in BR, there seemed to me to be no picture on top, and too many bits to the jigsaw. Fortunately, between my coming aboard part-time on 9 April and taking the chair on 12 September, there were five spacious months of reconnaissance, picking up clues and piecing them together. This time crossing the frontier gave me the chance both to disentangle myself from my private enterprises in decent order, and to prepare for the shocks of full-time work in a nationalized industry, management in a cold climate.

Not that I had any right to be shocked. As a part-time member I had served on the boards of Steel, the Airways, the British Tourist Authority, and the Ports – experience on land, sea and air, if not on rail. I knew well enough that management in the public domain of business was significantly different, but in BR the shocks had the jolting intensity of a live rail. Take the first shock of all, public relations. I was used to the deadening way any national industry was perceived by the public but the glare of publicity on railways is constant. And as a marketeer, I say, a good thing too; the fact that the British people care about railways makes a very good start if you are trying to sell tickets. Trains run deep in our national psyche, and transport is an emotional business in any language. I received a postcard of congratulation on my appointment which had on it 'Time Transfixed' by the Belgian surrealist painter, Magritte: the picture shows a solid bourgeois mantelpiece in a plain wall, and whanging through the fireplace is a fine, black locomotive, unstoppable, puffing passionately. Magritte's subconscious special on track is a mysterious business, but there is no need for surrealist subtleties to picture the symbolism in the mind of the commuter. The train taking you to work is not always a transport of delight if work is a bore or going badly; and coming back from a hard day at the office or factory, the crowded staleness of a station is not always a completely satisfactory point of departure.

Just how emotional a business I had got myself into became obvious to me at every party I went to that summer, as it has been ever since. I found it a rule of nature that everybody I met had one or more relatives involved with the railways. It seemed suddenly the whole nation was a railway family, and everybody had news to tell me, mostly bad. Now, for years before this, at parties I used to glance across the crowded room to see if Jill was looking cornered, and if she was I knew at once that she was being subjected to a medical 'bomb' story, or more often was being asked to give her doctor's opinion. (The only way to check that sort of thing, according to a lawyer consulted by one of Jill's medical colleagues over their drinks, was to send a bill next day. And that's exactly what the lawyer did to the doctor.) On the way home, I would usually not make matters any better for Jill by coming out with some dread, patronizing remark such as 'Well, you know what people are like Jill, it's only natural.' Now I was in BR, the boot was on the other foot with a vengeance. Friends of years' standing started to buttonhole me at parties, blazing-eyed with their 'bomb' stories; their late train that morning, blocked lavatories on the Biggleswade express, curly sandwiches. Only at a farewell party, at the end of my railway career, did I develop a technique to cope with these friendly onslaughts. It worked perfectly. As a best friend was in mid-tirade I started searching my pockets, and instinctively my friend pulled out a pen and handed it to me, without a pause in the complaining. Then, as he continued, I tapped round my pockets again, both front and back this time, and sure enough, my friend, still belting away, searched his pockets and pulled out a piece of paper. It was then only a matter of my saying crisply, 'Let's have the detail again, time exactly, what exactly.' And once the note was made, I handed back the pen with thanks, then the paper as well, and solemnly, magically, normal friendship was able to resume.

There was no getting away from it, public interest was intense. We had better make the most of it, I thought. If newspapers seemed to find regular space for railway news, we had better fill it rather than let it fill up anyhow. A policy for public affairs and communications needed to be designed to keep the initiative. After all, BR has an open day every day. Running some 20,000 trains every twenty-four hours, serving two million customers, meant that, even at a complaint

You're never alone when you are stranded

rate of .01 per cent, I was going to be wading ankle-deep every morning through letters from 'Disgusted, Platform Nine'. This was not life in a goldfish bowl: we were in a bowl of piranhas.

Being in the public arena meant that we were in a political arena too, and that was the second shock. The inevitability of the sheer politics involved in the management of any public enterprise is old hat, and mostly I enjoyed that, probably more than I should have done. Politics are as inseparable from the business of the public sector as a shadow, and like a shadow point away from the sun. Throughout my work in that sector I had grown familiar with the distortion that politics could cause in the ordering of board priorities. So often I had seen nationalized boards struggling with the wrong problems, being forced closer to the politicians than to the customers by the political

213

implications of their business. I would suggest that public boards offer only the most extreme example of a fundamental weakness of Britain's overall management of the economy, which has afflicted our competitive performance in the private sector as well as the public: that is, the cursed intrusion of adversarial politics into business issues far beyond the capacity of ideologies to resolve.

Nothing new there, but in BR what came through to me with stark clarity were two special repercussions of the political process. First, the mobility of ministers. Early on, I visited the Western Region, the old beloved GWR, God's Wonderful Railway (only its few, lonely, pitiful enemies called it Grub, Water and Rations). At dinner with my new colleagues, we calculated there had been fourteen Ministers of Transport in twenty-five years; the engineer among us that night was only the fourteenth chief engineer of the GWR since the young Brunel in 1836. During my five months, I had had three ministers: Crosland, Shore and Rodgers. My predecessor had had five in five years. This mind-boggling, soul-boggling mobility of ministers goes on and on. I was to work with six ministers altogether in my seven years, and I missed my seventh only by a couple of weeks. Of course, I loved every one of them, but such enforced fickleness does make the essential connections between political and railway timetables that much more risky in terms of any corporate planning. Some mobility, like original sin, is to be expected, but in the word of Queen Victoria's original complaint about the speed of trains, we suffered an excess of mobility.

There is a double danger in this. A change of ministers not only disrupts the relationship between the Department and the industry; it also – less obviously – renders both the Department and the industry less able to hold their own in the infighting of power politics in Whitehall. As any chairman of a public enterprise will recognize, that is not good news. From the industry's viewpoint, too many departments, not only Transport, can seem diaphanous, and through them – only too clearly visible to the chairman's naked eye – is Whitehall's mandarin version of Thug's Law, the Treasury.

The second symptom of the process of politics that showed more vividly in BR than in anything I had known before was the sheer constancy of political interest, the non-stop breast-baring that went on. At my inaugural press conference I described the railways as the citizens' business. I didn't know the half of it. I had meant what I still utterly believe: that transport was an enterprise at the heart of the quality of life in any society, and that a sense of service to each individual among those two million daily passengers was what made the job as exhilarating to me as it was exhausting. But at the outset I was innocent of the political implications of what I said. I quickly learnt that being a citizens' business also meant being subjected to report after report after report. This monitoring stretched well beyond the reach of the department sponsoring us. Apart from the range of Parliamentary Select Committees, there were the Office of Fair Trading, the Monopolies Commission, Consumer Councils, ad hoc inquiries, and numerous widespread independent institutions such as the Political Studies Institute and transport agencies in the UK and in Europe. Apparently BR had to steer its course by a swirling constellation of Star Chambers. In the Seventies, I reckoned that there was a major investigation of our efficiency for almost every year of the decade. The costs of coping with them were awesome, and the strain of responding regularly, and with grace, was a discipline for the soul.

Conversely, these inquisitions were always an opportunity to put the railway's case with a recurring, mounting conviction, and there were some hilarious redeeming moments. Once the Minister of Community Affairs, Mrs Sally Oppenheimer, decided to call in the Monopolies Commission to see whether we were giving value for money in our commuter service. This, it was said, was somewhat to the surprise of our own Minister of Transport of the moment, Norman Fowler, but anyway the commission got down to its work with the courtesy and thoroughness I had expected of it. It hired American experts to advise and check our evidence. Coincidentally, Transmark, BR's own company of international consultants on transport, which was operating in over thirty countries around the world, had just won a lucrative contract to advise the Office of Transport in Washington on the handling of Amtrak. The two consultant groups must often have crossed mid-air in mid-Atlantic; it was difficult not to feel a pang of sympathy for those well-paid prophets reciprocally not being honoured in their own countries, even if they were making profits abroad.

Then there was the clerk of one House of Commons select committee who, after the session, pursued our team down the corridor to apologize because 'the committee was not on top form today'. That had been true. 'I can only apologize,' he said, 'but the questions were all clearly written out, it's just that some of the members didn't read them very well.' Actually this was not typical of all the select committees. I learnt to value their independent scope and intent, and their courage. The Department generally seemed far less sympathetic to their probing and I could see why: the select committees were independent, they were always ready to listen to our unpopular priorities of better planned investment and longer-term strategies. They supported our initiatives for the Channel Tunnel, for instance, long before the Tunnel was a popular cause. I came to regard the open sessions before select committees as an opportunity to widen the hearing of the Railway's case. From the start, I saw the meetings as a form of Extraordinary General Meeting of the company at which our team of executive directors could appear before the shareholders to speak for railways and to show off the mettle of our management. During that spacious summer, I studied the voluminous reviews of our business; in those months, I was not so much brainwashed as dry-cleaned and pressed by stacks of studies. It was hard to think of any industry more reported on: it was a wonder to me that BR management had not died of overexposure. So, I concluded, we had better simplify the questions that were bound to be put to us, and be clear what we wanted. Let 'em all come; each was an opportunity to explain and to ask questions of our own.

Trade unionism might properly be taken as yet another part of the inevitability of politics in public enterprise. After all, the trade unions are written into the nationalizing statutes as part of the consultative process. But the attitude of the unions in public enterprise is a discrete phenomenon and deserves to be taken as such – a quite separate shock. Nationalization was the process that was to give them, as they saw it, a new role in the governing of the country, let alone the industry. There were three main railway unions, the National Union of Railwaymen (NUR), the Associated Society of Locomotive Engineers and Firemen (ASLEF) and the Transport Salaried Staffs' Association (TSSA). These unions had a long, proud history and generations of commitment, and they had about them an independence that sometimes seemed to keep them from being a part of anything or of anybody. Even of BR, even of the future. Even of each other in the brotherhoods. Sometimes, as in the National Union of Mineworkers (rail and coal grew up together in the nineteenth century, grew strong together), the trade unions behaved as if they were an alternative government, a law unto themselves. Yet with all their differences and differentials, they were still aware of the community of railways. I discovered complexities in the union attitude – a glimpse of the future, too, as it turned out. I went to a dance with ASLEF.

Ray Buckton, ASLEF's General Secretary, invited Jill and me to come to a regional Social in Portsmouth. It was a memorable event. I had known Ray on and off for some years: he was a bushy-tailed, good-humoured, wide-ranging personality in those early days. 'It would give you the chance to meet a driver, Peter, on his homeground – in fact, hundreds of them.' Sure enough, there were over three hundred of all ages, crammed in a low-ceilinged dancehall which throbbed with hefty rhythms and quivered with coloured lights. This was a well-organized annual outing for pensioners who were there in force – the Union paid for them and cherished them generously. This was all explained to us by a convivial, bay-fronted driver, who was chairman of the evening, while putting Jill and me to the right and left of him at the top table. Behind us, a long window, the evening bright blue, the view of seamless sea and sky. In front of us, copious wine glasses, and beside them the alternative of three small bottles of beer each. We said we'd stick to wine, but our host still whipped the tops off the bottles and said, 'Driving can be a thirsty business.'

Jill soon found herself dancing in a circle of widows who were bouncing around in one corner of the crowded floor, holding hands, laughing but not hearing each other's jokes over the cheerful din. One of them, very short and smiley, said something to Jill, who, relatively tall, strained to hear but couldn't quite. The bouncing went on happily and Jill caught a few words on each bounce: 'Isn't it . . . a lovely . . . do'.

It was that, and impressive and moving.

My own conversation on the dance-floor was less heartwarming. The regional organizer, Derrick Fullick – a name to conjure with in later years – was formally the host, and therefore Mrs Fullick was my first partner on the dance-floor. But before that there had to be the speeches, which were not without the odd moment of drama. The local MP opened, politely encouraging a welcome for me. I answered carefully, and lightly, a learner wobbling a bit as I made my way down a tightrope of tact. So far nothing to spoil the party. Then Ray rose, with thunderous confidence. He always made speeches in a burly preacher-like tone: I wondered if he had ever heard of the Scottish minister who intoned 'O Lord, we pray we may be right because we are verra, verra determined.' He was certainly in powerful voice that night. He began rivetingly. 'What is it we have always wanted?' he cried out, 'What is it? I'll tell you – we've always wanted a railwayman to run the railways.' The hall hushed, a bit embarrassed I guess, but Ray knew what he was doing and had good nerve. He knew the orator's trick of the repeated question, and hammered on, 'Isn't that what we all wanted?' He was not to be denied, looking around, punching the air, and sure enough at the third time of asking, there was consenting applause. 'Right – that's what everybody here wanted. And out there too, that's what they wanted.' Ray threw an arm backwards to point through the window, 'out there', where there was nothing I could see but that dreamy blank of blue. More applause. I peered round the Falstaffian front of the Chairman to check on Jill: she gave me the luminous impression of somebody pretty resigned in a stained-glass window. Ray having given me the hard word that no doubt kept him onside with his militant friends, now rounded cunningly back to the rescue of the occasion. 'But when Tony Crosland rang up to say that chairman would be Peter Parker – I said, "Then that'll do".' There was a splatter of relieved applause to make us welcome at last.

But it was not universal, as I discovered when I tried to lead Mrs Fullick on to the floor. She was a thin fury, dressed in red nylon, that brushed nylon which looks as if it will give a man a shock if he touches it. It did. She was speaking to me but I had the same trouble hearing above the merry hubbub that Jill had had. As we clutched each other, I caught sight of Jill, far off, at the top table with the other wives going up to talk to her. Later, she told me they were saying, 'We're not like that.' It seemed they knew what I was in for. I jigged, doggedly but hopelessly at odds with the battering rhythms. My partner was looking up wide eyed and her lips were moving. I leant down towards the passionate face to hear the words; I still have the image of the small scarlet straps of her dress rounded over sharp angles of shiny shoulder bones. To my astonishment I found I was being asked how I could serve such a disgusting government. She was talking of the Labour government – and she was certainly no Tory. I am sure there is a rich seam of research to be worked on the influence of The Wife in the history of trade union leadership. Her husband was about fifty and had thick, straight white hair. He was known as the Silver Fox by his friends and the White Rat by others.

At two in the morning, black coffee and white-bread bacon sandwiches were brought to a corner table to revive us. Fullick was handing me a plate when he asked me, 'What d'you make of it all?'

'I've thoroughly enjoyed it, thanks. It's certainly a family business, isn't it?'

Still holding the plate of deathly white sandwiches, the Silver Fox/White Rat said, 'It is, and that's why you'll never beat us. You'll see.'

'But it's not you I'm here to beat – it's the competition.'

'You'll see.'

And years later I did see. A clash with the leadership of ASLEF was always a possibility, any time from the beginning, but fortunately the president of ASLEF in 1976 was Bill Ronksley, a card-carrying Communist but as straight as a die-hard, old-fashioned Communist could be. It was said he was a railwayman first, a Communist after that. In the year of troubles and strikes, in 1981 and 1982, his successor was to be Mr Fullick, who carried a Labour Party ticket but gave the impression of being the other way round to old Bill. I was determined not to follow the Fullick formula of reflex confrontation. Confrontation there might well have to be, but not at once. BR had to be stronger to be ready for it. Building up the business, regaining public confidence and making our board and management strong and confident – these were the priorities of the first order. What I needed was a unified board with coherent polices, and success in the market as proof that the railways were not in decline but well worth backing. Which brings me to the next shock for the entrepreneur in public business.

In a public enterprise, board appointments are made statutorily, made by the Minister, who is also responsible for negotiating pay and conditions and deciding the increases after that. This means that the chairman's powers to balance the board's composition and inspire his top management financially are feeble in comparison to those of a business leader in the private sector. There, the chairman normally carries a special responsibility for the composition and conduct of the board, and he is also responsible for the pay structure at the top, especially if his office is combined with that of the Chief Executive (understandable in my view). That pay structure should match the market rates and have some kick of incentive in it. In the public sector, the Minister is literally in the Act and, as the Act puts it, he makes the decisions on appointments 'in consultation with the chairman'. Between the Jamesian commas in the legislation lies the subtle possibility that consultation will mean the understanding and agreement of the chairman, and it proved so in all my time at BR. If the Minister and chairman – and the Permanent Secretary – are in harmony, generally speaking the scheme will work. A wise chairman will consult closely with his own board about its requirements, and a wise minister will encourage the chairman to take the initiative and put up names. While I was at BR only one appointment was not my original recommendation and, after a testy start, he turned out to be an invaluable support to the board.

Moving up to the September starting post I vowed to prepare a convincing case for a new board structure. The board I joined had distinct strengths. It was compact; eight members only. It was strategic; it contained the headquarters' executive corporate team of functional heads covering the four areas of planning, finance, personnel, and the large subsidiaries of property, shipping and hotels. This team was balanced by a small, powerful group of three non-executives. There was Sir David Serpell, an ex-civil servant whose wide experience included both Treasury and Transport, where he had been Permanent Secretary. He was an outstanding friend of railways who combined, most quietly and fearlessly, brilliance, wit and a sufficient knowledge of railways (he knew enough to frighten transport professionals). Then there was Lord Taylor of Gryfe, on the International Advisory Council of Morgan Grenfell, a Labour Peer (waiting, I suspect, for the SDP to be born), a former chairman of the Forestry Commission and once leader of the Co-operative Wholesale Society: an independent mind, canny and open, articulate, tireless, discerning and demanding.

Finally there was Sir Alan Walker, deputy chairman of the Midland Bank, chairman of Thomas Cook, former chairman of Bass, an establishment top industrialist but with a piratical gleam in his eye which I always found comforting. A competent and strategically balanced board, then, but as all the board non-executives, and some of the executives, told me as soon as I arrived at BR, still lacking the thorough mix of railways experience that was essential to give the board credibility inside and outside the organization.

My first attendance at the board in May as a non-executive made

Michael Bosworth

an indelible impression on me. I sat next to Michael Bosworth, the executive deputy chairman. I was simply listening and watching and passing scribbled questions to Michael. I was revelling in that moment of ephemeral delight in a manager's life, the blissful dawn at the beginning of a new job when you can ask any damned fool question because no one expects you to know any answers, and you'd be even more of a fool if you thought you did. The more experienced the manager the more valuable and thoroughly enjoyable is that brief renewal of professional innocence as a starter.

I was intrigued by the boardroom itself, the only haunted boardroom I had ever been in. It was a great chamber, with a long platform running almost the length of the back wall, on which were three solemn ranks of high-backed chairs, about eighty of them, ready for

Banquos galore – the ghosts of the staff officers who had sat there in the days of General Sir Brian Robertson, chairman of the British Transport Commission. The great man would summon individuals down to give evidence to the board sitting in square formation in the body of the hall. Time had marched on a bit since then, but at my first board I watched a steady stream of executives brought in from a large waiting-room and they had a route march to join us. I scribbled a little note to myself there and then:

(1) Use the waiting-room as the boardroom.
(2) Bring railway executives on to the board.

Not one full-time railwayman was on the board at that time. The chief executive, David Bowick, attended the board, but by his own request was not on it. Roughly his view was that the board seemed to have its hands full with the politics of the business, so let them get on with that while he and his mates ran the railway.

During this period of reconnaissance I spent as much time as I could with David Bowick and his mates. I found them to be managers of rare quality, generally much better than the belittling gossip of the media, Westminster and Whitehall allowed. In industry generally, the reputation of railway managements stood taller than it did in political circles; anyone who had to negotiate commercially with railwaymen, buying or selling, was the least likely to run them down. It was particularly the press and the politicians who had a poor opinion of them, and also the intellectuals of the civil service, whose long if baffled familiarity with railway operations had bred not so much contempt as a low expectation of any final solution.

My assessment of the managers was quite the opposite. I soon reckoned that the railways bred general managers with an enviable range of business experience, and for one reason among many others. From the start, young managers are brought up close to what the customer wants. In the urgent and demanding world of a passenger station or a depot there is no dodging responsibility for a wide range of the functions that are the making of a manager: pricing, man-managing, operational, customer and community relations. There is a frequent need for quick decisions. Commercial leadership is inculcated early on and at every stage. Railways have to be shaped as a horizontal business, big and flat, and responsibilities have to be spread – and so they can be seized by those with an appetite for them.

David Bowick

Of course not everybody in BR management enjoyed that good appetite, and in assessing the quality of management there was a negative to put up against my positive view. The breadth of the railway manager's development was undeniable but it was limited to the inside of the system – almost as if he were in an Army career. Indeed in the mid-nineteenth century the railways were originally organized on military lines. The building of the London and Birmingham Railway was a marvel of mobilized will and power and a great deal of managerial credit for its completion within three years must go to former military commanders. In those days the Army and the Navy provided the only managers trained to cope with thousands of men, with discipline and timetables, safety routines and logistics, who were also trained to give the leadership that makes things happen through people. The military traditions I had noticed in the great chamber of the boardroom were resonant in other ways: canteens and dining-rooms were called 'messes' and managers themsevles were often called 'officers'. And prevalently, there were the hierarchical habits and stiffness that go with a military posture. At its very best it showed in a managerial attack which had about it the discipline and élan of the Grenadier Guards. But as soldiers, I used to say sometimes, they were too good, too hardened, too tough, too ready to take the flak, the constant barrage of critics, the surprise cavalry charges of consult-ants, the sapping and mining of politicians – and the garbled messages from headquarters. At its worst this stoicism could lead to the attitude of the old soldier who simply carries on, just getting away with it.

With the bunker mentality goes the danger of management develop-ment becoming a kind of cloning. The temptation of top management is to make young managers in their own image and call the result tradition. The inbreeding of management is an occupational hazard in any large corporation and it was particularly so for rail under siege. I took that seriously. By the time I left the railways, the British Transport Staff College at Woking was moved out of its magnificent house and gardens to become part of the Ashridge Management College, and transport courses for senior management have continued successfully, in the open air as it were, in the context of Ashridge's excellent business studies as a whole.

In the summer of 1976 I heard the case against railway management often enough – but cheerfulness kept breaking in. The management I was meeting had all the makings of a winning team which could be put in place on the board, recruiting from the inside, not, as with Beeching, from the outside.

I approached the build-up of my board with no preconceptions. I am not in love with formula-management at any level. I have flirted with it a little, in speeches and conference, articles and books, but nothing serious, and certainly never in the boardroom. The manage-ment of a board is not to be trifled with. For me it is an art form, defying formula. No board is ever perfect, and the best is one that can change itself, adapting its structure to its purposes, its market and circumstances. The shape of it should be as functional and natural as any good locomotive has been since the Rocket. Locomotive design has altered in response to the demands of accelerating speeds, of technological evolution (say from steam to diesel), of markets and of the latest materials available. So should the design of a board be responsive. But while the chairman might like to think of himself as a driver, it is practical wisdom to remember that success in that job is as much dependent on others as is a conductor's performance on the orchestra.

No enterprise I have ever encountered has been in an ideal state. Ideal boards are made in heaven. They are probably small, non-executive except for the managing director, and eternally, blissfully above the hurly-burly of the day-to-day. But I am guessing; non-ideal boards are the only boards I have known, they are earthy, of the earth, or rather of the market-place. In the market-place, boards have to be adaptable in size and attitude, close enough to the executive to see that their policies are earthed into the realities of action. Many other countries seem to prefer their boards on the celestial model, supervisory and strategic, part-time, sitting on high in judgement with management in the dock, and only the chief executive able to approach as equal. I totally accept the theory: the board is there to set the direction of the enterprise, not to run things. But I am suspicious of the theoretical layering of strategic and tactical decisions, of long term and short term. These are convenient terms of analysis, but they are not the flesh and blood of board life that I recognize. I have found the reality and credibility of a board are derived from the mix of non-executive and executive. It is an awkward mix but also constructive and creative and real; the long-term and short-term in enterprise connect, they are the dramatic extremes of one managerial continuum. To stress exclusively that the board is strategic and separate from the executive is to make one good point at the expense of a better one: that is, that the board must be close enough to the executive management to be believable to those who have to do what it says. I go with Gonzalo in *The Tempest*:

> I' the commonwealth I would by contraries
> Execute all things.

I became clear about what I wanted. I wanted it both ways, and quickly; a board that could sort out the strategic policies but do so in the presence of the top executive. This way we could do without a layer of executive directors at the top of the railways but just below board level. Executive directors would be in the boardroom, and board decisions and communications would be more direct down the line.

225

I knew I was taking two unavoidable risks. The board would in theory be too big, and I was bringing through the board too many lines of reporting to myself as chairman and chief executive. But in the crisis we were in these were secondary problems. The creation of a unifying, balanced board was primary, and that meant bringing leading executive railwaymen on to the excellent but limited board already there. I had to seek out career railwaymen who had the stretch to combine their operational experience with the larger responsibilities of board membership.

Obviously, the chief executive of the railways, David Bowick, had to be there. He was a wonderfully stretchy character, a shrewd and generous Scot with charm and a superb planner's mind. Once he had been very stout, then he had slimmed drastically into an Edward G. Robinson chunkiness, but with the economic instinct of his ancestral tribe he went on wearing out the baggy suits of his rumbustious past, which flapped around him like a badly tethered tent. As a manager, David had everything but brakes to stop himself overworking.

His deputy was another Scot, Ian Campbell, a fourth-generation railwayman, proud to point out the bridges his father had built; he himself was just about to be the president of the Institution of Civil Engineers. He had gusto, a fine presence and a singing voice, and loved what he did. There were also two other Scots, part of this MacMafia of the railways, also both career railwaymen, and very different. Bob Reid was an Oxford man, an ex-prisoner of war in Italy, quiet and fierce with a firm smack of command, son of a governor of Bengal, and in one of the hottest seats at BR: he was general manager of the Southern Region, based in Waterloo. By the time I met him he was bald, but I had been warned that he had had red hair once and the temper to match had not disappeared with it. Jim Urquhart, general manager of the London Midland Region, was educated in the railways but ready for anything, a resilient, powerful negotiator, competitive and determined in meticulous detail about all he did. Hard and kind, he was a fighting believer in BR, but he had a countryman's relaxed solidity. He looked as if he had just come back from a fishing holiday where very little had got away.

Then there was Cliff Rose in Personnel and Industrial Relations, the youngest of them. He had begun as a booking-clerk at Princes Risborough. Strong-shouldered, athletic, assiduous, he had a way of simplifying and driving issues to conclusions. Sometimes he would

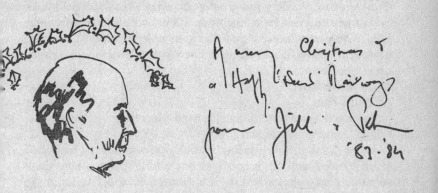

talk of the railways as Hindus talk of the Ganges, divine and fertilizing
– he'd actually say 'Mother Railway'. If people didn't like Cliff Rose
there was something the matter with them, not Cliff. He was a dove
who was to become a hawk.

Closest to my office – and to all my affairs and in friendship over
the years – was the Chief Secretary of the Board, Gerry Burt. A
Board can only succeed if the Chairman and the Secretary are really
close. At our first encounter Gerry brought eighteen points on his
agenda for action, and day after day it seemed to go on like that; he
never seemed to have less than eighteen points. He had the thoroughness of a real railman; he was quiet, deft, utterly determined and
probably enjoyed his Rasputin reputation at the centre of things. His
whole working life had been on the rails, yet he was to prove a
surprising ally for change – he was the sort of administrator who gives
bureacracy a good name.

These men, all self-starters, began to teach me their trade. My
hope was rising.

The first week in September 1976, the last week of reconnaissance:
I was heading on a mid-morning train to Charlbury, alone in the
carriage, watching the September landscape slip away, that end-of-
summer, solemn, darker green. My mind thoughtless, the wheels
muttering their mantra, I was trying to stay loose as a boxer should
before he steps into the ring. When the grizzled guard came in to see
my ticket, I held out the gold medallion that entitled me to free travel
anywhere on the railways – it was its first outing. I kept looking out

of the window, avoiding conversation, enjoying what I reckoned to be my last peaceful ride for a long while. I felt the medal taken from my palm. I turned to see the guard examining it thoroughly, even the unattractive plastic label ('Made in Hong Kong') tagged to it with my name typed on.

'So you're Parker.'

'That's right.'

He moved a step towards me, his hand outstretched to shake mine, saying, 'And the best of luck.'

As we shook hands, glancing at each other, something happened which I have found can happen greeting a total stranger. Something seems to click noiselessly, there's a connection, and sometimes the stranger's other hand comes over and forms a clasp to reinforce it.

Unfortunately, at that juncture, the stranger goes on to say, as the guard did, 'And I'll tell you what's wrong. The problem with British Rail is . . . '

I laughed to interrupt him and protested that I had a few days still clear before the awful truths dawned, or more probably crashed about my head. 'My only problem at this stage is not losing this gold medallion.'

We discussed a number of frivolous suggestions before deciding that the safest thing to do was to hang the medal around my private parts.

Chuckling, he slid the door closed; then, face straight, he re-opened it. 'Of course, in this job, you could lose them too.'

9

The Recovery of Belief

(British Rail 1976–9)

There was no difficulty in deciding where to start. At nine o'clock on 13 September, 1976, my first morning, I met the management, two hundred of them, at BR headquarters. I had written no text: the last thing railway managers needed was more lectures. It was confidence in one another and what we were to do together that mattered. What I did have was a set of five headings, 'a fistful of priorities':

First, catch a national policy for BR: everything that follows swings from this.

Next, look at the size and shape of the organization. It should be based on the smallest groups possible and be as close as possible to commercial realities.

The aim: a competitive railway, with productivity as the priority that will never go away.

Trade Unions and Change: the shotgun marriage?

'Sparks to cross gaps': communications policy within BR and with our many publics outside – our individual and corporate customers, suppliers, politicians (local and national) of all the parties, export markets – and also the voters, who'll have the last word. BR is a citizens' business, and if we have a case for the future then the voters should hear us.

The question to the assembly: was I on the right lines? The direct approach of that morning's meeting was to set the pattern for my meetings throughout BR, and in public, over the next two years. It was the first step in the advance towards a recovery of belief in the future of railways, and in ourselves as managers of it. My fistful, the five interdependent priorities, were my agenda for the rest of the Seventies. I repeated them with a ruthless lack of variation – propaganda is repetition.

'First, catch a national policy...' The roomful of management experience responded, and ideas grew between us all. National policy for BR meant a bipartisan understanding in Parliament which then had some chance of being believable in the country as a whole. It definitely did not mean simply asking the government what to do all the time. There was little point in pressing politicians with questions they could not answer. We had all had enough of that: it was the old game, a maddening sort of political snakes and railways that had spread confusion and disappointment pretty evenly over three decades. Railways knew only too well that railways and politics ran together on the same track but on separate timetables. Five years was short term for us, eternity for MPs. BR must try something new.

It was up to the professionals to recommend the strategies and tactics for the business. We had to define what we could offer both as a public service and as a competitive mode of transport. BR had just published a fierce challenge to itself, a booklet called *The Opportunity for Change*, and for me this defined our problems and prospects with the beautiful distinction of thunderclouds. How to earth the lightning? Straight down our managerial backbone. I began with one prejudice, that we should build up a new management structure from within, recruiting outside only for special expertise. We had, after all, some ten thousand people classified as managers, a sizeable list of candidates. There had to be the skill, drive and judgement within the rail community to put its own act together.

The challenge we were putting to ourselves was plain: had we a service to offer the country that was value for money? That was the question being asked by everybody, the individual customer as well as the banker and shareholder. The days had long gone when we were virtually the sole existing carriers. BR had no monopoly over the provision of public transport, and increasingly faced competition from private transport. The bus, car, lorry, aircraft, ship, even the bicycle, these were all competitors. What made things still more complicated was that different modes of transport were (and still are) financed differently and with different degrees of official benevolence. There is, for example, a tax system that ensures that half the cars on the road are not owned, and so not paid for, by their drivers. But whatever the complications in our competitive life, the question remained stark, simple and loud: had we a viable and attractive product to offer? If so, then BR could make some sort of a deal with the public which the public could understand. We should settle a contract and cool the issue of our future.

I believed in the case for the railways and that roomful of management believed in it too, with much more justification than I could muster. My case was argued with all the passion of a convert. The railways existed: they were a national asset of immense value, part of the wealth-creating process of the nation, part of its production line. They were basic to Britain's essential industries such as coal and steel, basic to the civilized life of its great cities, and basic to the quality of life of our society. Compared to our competition in the air and on the road we made far less noise pollution, caused far less environmental stress, consumed far less energy and created far less mayhem in terms of fatalities and serious injuries. Also, looking ahead, BR lent itself to the application of high technology and a measure of automation more readily than any other system of surface transport.

But were we value for money? That was the £358 million question in 1976, because that was what the government paid for the provision of rail passenger services. International comparisons were in our favour. No passenger rail service of any size anywhere in the world was producing conventional, commercial returns, and the British government's payment, as a percentage of the GDP, was running at only a little over half that of the average of main European railways. But 'abroad is abroad' and international yardsticks were treated sceptically: the reality was a general presumption that BR was not giving value for money, and we knew we could and should do better. The economic crisis of the mid-Seventies was forcing the pace of change throughout the country. BR had to become much more convincing in its claim that it was doing all it could for itself. It had to generate much more cash for its own needs, and to do so it had to shed surplus manpower and out-of-date working practices in management and unions. This was the only way to win back national confidence and a national policy for a future railway. It might take years to get there. Other than by a cataclysm, nothing big changes quickly in human organizations. But making change happen on a big scale was the only way BR would clinch a durable deal with government. As I saw it, that was my mission. My hope was to complete it in five years. Actually it took seven – to the week.

Before that session finally ended, I was unexpectedly nailed to a definition. I had emphasized the role of management: what did I mean by management? My answer was that I had always seen it the same way, as three-dimensional leadership, economic, entrepreneurial and

231

social. The economic dimension is instantly recognized: it includes the professional process of combining commerce, administration and technical skills towards profitable objectives. The entrepreneurial side is far more difficult to measure, but what is measurable in management is seldom all there is to measure, and it is not always the most important. Around 1800 the French economist, J. B. Say, had to invent the word 'entrepreneur' to describe the man at the interface between assets and customers. This is an area of imagination and energy, of risk-taking and risk-making, of seizing chances that others do not seize, of seeing ahead and somehow letting the future have your way. Ill-defined, all that, but well established: I reckon one entrepreneur can recognize another at three hundred yards on a misty day.

In the social dimension we are far less at home. I am thinking of our emerging role as business managers in co-ordinating two cultures, that of the enterprise and that of the community – and these two forces do not necessarily thrust in the same direction. It is this social dimension of management that we must try to explore more thoroughly. I believe it will be the decisive dimension. We shall have to prove more capable of interpreting our business objectives in ways that make more sense in social terms. I believe the board agendas of any sizeable company in the 1990s will not be able to leave social policy hopefully under 'any other business'. The concept of the economic company may well seem as dead and skeletal to the next generation as the economic man in our own. Management will continually try to manage this reconciliation of its methods and its purposes with those of the community within which it works.

A manager's success in fusing all three dimensions depends on his or her capacity to lead. People prefer being led to being managed. I suppose that is because the process of good leadership makes a leader understand how much depends on others. He has to listen to them, and that means being accessible.

As a new man I felt I had better be out and about in the railway community. I spoke to David Bowick, the man who did more than anyone to start to make a proper railwayman of me. He began by handling me with the practised care of a railwayman who had dealt with more than a few incoming chairmen before. 'I can lay on the usual chairman's tours. They take about two days a month.'

'Fine. How long will it take me to get round the system?' David had a trick of suddenly going poker-faced, but this time his mask in no way obscured the merriment in his eyes.

'Ah, about three and a half years, to see the whole system. It's a big thing.'

'Isn't that the average length of a chairman's term?' And we both laughed.

He was right, of course, it was a big thing. BR at that time employed overall about 243,000 people and operated 18,000 passenger trains, 3,000 freight trains, over 2,000 stations, fifty-five ships at sea, 12,000 yards of quays operating in twelve harbours, twenty-nine hotels and 181 restaurants and catering units on stations. It was much too big.

David and I fixed a programme of chairman's tours which had me out in the system for two days a week on average. I had meetings of management and meetings with unions; sometimes a dozen people were there, sometimes two hundred, and in between these there were more meetings with local press, politics and business. These meetings made all the difference to my life, they were a strain and a delight. And my fistful of priorities stood me in excellent stead as an informal agenda for the hundreds of sessions which taught me so much. Face to face meetings were my chance to learn the trade in the best way, through its people, people who operated the railways and people who used them. To this day I can unroll a personal map of memories and on it I can flag encounters up and down the line where I learned something, from top to bottom of the network, from Scotland to the South.

For instance, I had been briefed carefully about the special interests of the railways in Scotland, the Tartan Track: be ready for the regular complaint that Scotland never received its fair share of BR investment in track, signalling and rolling-stock. At my first morning meeting I spotted a guard in the front row, smartly turned out, trim grey hair and a bright blue gaze; but as I spoke he kept averting his eyes downwards to concentrate on rubbing the knees of his well-creased trousers. He had a question for sure, I thought. You can usually spot questioners with the well-rehearsed question: they are trying to concentrate on it, avoiding any distraction like listening to the speech itself, and the sign is that they rub their knees, going over the question again and again in readiness for the moment. The guard was on his feet the second I sat down.

'You've got it all wrong,' he said, 'all wrong. You don't know the detail, you see. We've got to have the locos to get up the hill to us here. We've got to have a bigger slice of investment . . . '

I had been primed for this, and I let fly with rehearsed responses of Scottish and English and Welsh capital expenditures, but my recitation slowed up as the guard, on his feet the whole time, shook his head slowly and sadly.

'No, no,' he was saying, 'Wrong again. You've a lot to learn. It's not at all a question of those other countries doing better than Scotland, it's those buggers in Glasgow who hog the best locos for themselves.'

Next morning, leaving Inverness on an early snowy morning in the observation coach, I noticed headlines in the local papers about the snowfalls blocking all traffic but the trains: the trains had got through and were still criticized for being late. We headed off through the white mountains engraved with the dark green and brown forests, and from my vantage point in the observation coach I noticed something else, footsteps along our track. A railwayman had been out in the freezing wee hours, unpicking ice from the points along our way for miles and miles. Railways can be a tough, rough job – and dangerous. I recall that year; we were responsible for 700 million passenger journeys. Not a single passenger was killed, but more railwaymen were killed in action than miners in the coal industry.

Quite different from my Scottish education in the dedication and the rootedness of the railwayman's commitment was my abrasive introduction to the Southern Region. My tour ended in a tense hour with the unions at Waterloo, a crowded, factious session. The last question was memorable: 'How long are you going to be in the chair? Are you going to be with us as long as it takes you to get a knighthood, then go?' I replied that my contract was for five years, the normal term for a chairman in the public sector. But if I was being asked how long I thought it would take me to do the job, then I could not be sure.

'Consider this,' I said. 'An outsider has been brought into railways. Why? It's usually because there's been a breakdown in the trust between the nationalized industry and its shareholders, represented by the government of the day. There's a born-again-start-again hope in making an appointment from outside. The appointment of a chairman from the inside of a public enterprise is a sure sign that shareholders and business are getting along well. So one way to describe my mission is this: it's to make an internal appointment possible some day. My idea of success in this job is to be succeeded by a railwayman.'

At the time, I was not aware of the full significance of this exchange of question and answer. Neither was Bob Reid, the general manager of the Southern Region, who was chairing the edgy session. He was to become Sir Robert, and chairman of BR, my successor.

Of course, chairmen come and go. That lesson was illustrated for me by my visit to Cardiff on the famous day when we carried out our first experiment in having a Senior Citizens' Day: anyone with a Senior Citizen card could go anywhere for one pound. We were overwhelmed by the energetic and ecstatic readiness of senior citizens to do just that. Some turned up, for instance, at Carlisle asking to go to London. ''Fraid you've just missed it,' they were told. 'Well, give us something for Edinburgh or Glasgow then.' It was a great day for railways, for the warmth of goodwill that it generated, and for the profit; we added 100,000 more Senior Citizen cardholders that day alone, worth annually £750,000 to BR. When I arrived at Cardiff on a tour of inspection, the platform was a sea of white hair. My posse tried to make a parting through it, but I found myself stopped by a determined, excited old man, in a shaggy raincoat, who grabbed my hand and pumped it hard.

'You've done us proud, very proud,' he was saying. 'You're doing well, a great job, a great job.' My colleagues circled around uneasily, unused to this, but naturally I clung to him, feeling that this didn't happen often enough and I'd better make the most of it. But then, still holding me, he urged, 'Keep it up, Sir Richard.' More than a shade disillusioned, I heard one of my party whisper to him, 'This isn't Marsh, it's Parker.' The old man caught on at once. 'Right,' he said, 'Keep at it, Sir Richard Parker.' And fair enough. The job was bigger than any one man, and railways have a long history. Passing chairmen fade into their due proportion in the vast perspective of what Brunel called 'the noblest work in England'.

There was no doubt that an outsider had been invited to take the chair because the relationship between BR and the government had deteriorated badly, and for many reasons. Dick Marsh, my predecessor, suffered from double vision: he had seen the problem of nationalized industry first as a Minister and then as chairman. As Minister of Transport ('of no delight', to adopt his words) he had long known that the heart of the matter lay 'in the total lack of clear objectives'. Five years as chairman of BR had confirmed his experienced and jaundiced view.

He had been brought into office by John Peyton and Peter Walker in the time of the Conservative government. When Fred Mulley took over as Minister under Labour in 1974 the process of predictable disenchantment accelerated. Marsh and Mulley did not mix at all well. The last year of his contract was one of tragedy and farce. His second wife was killed in a road accident, a sadness he bore with great gallantry. Then finally, in the spring of 1976, leaks burst out in the press that he was to be replaced, and he decided that 'the nonsense could not go on.' His last correspondence with the Ministry left him helpless with laughter and frustration. He was asked to carry out an inquiry into the financial results of a British Rail decision to refuse to carry pigeons who had lost their way racing. He answered that he would pass the matter to his successor: 'In doing so, I would not wish it to be thought that I view the matter lightly. In many ways it has a direct relevance to the present plight of the nation.'

The National Economic Development Office made the same point rather more solemnly. In a report made just as I was about to move into the chair, it criticized the historical relationship of BR and the government as 'overlapping and confused, what each expects of the other is ambiguous or unrealistic.' So I arrived at a very good moment: surely things could only get better. In fact, my luck was in. Bill Rodgers, as the new Secretary of State of the newly formed Transport Department, was immediately helpful and his declaration that he would publish a White Paper on Transport Policy as soon as possible gave new hope. This was likely to take a year or more, but at least the prospect of it eclipsed the dreary consultation paper, the Green Paper in orange covers, which had tried to point BR into a genteel, irreversible decline, and which had threatened to ambush me on arrival. We now had time to make our reorganizational moves in BR and to present the case for railways afresh.

By Christmas 1976 the major reconstruction of the board had been accepted and implemented. My aim had been to add four new executive members to bring railways experience into the board, so as to tighten the lines of communication and to strip out one level of executive directors below the board. Also I was able to give a public emphasis to certain new functions brought into the board for the first time and specified as part of the portfolios of new executive members, such as Innovations, Productivity, Exports and Marketing. The result was a board too big but well balanced. It numbered fourteen: four new rail executive members, four executive corporate members at Headquarters, five non-executive members, plus the chairman. To keep the pressures reasonable on myself, I set up my 'dams' in the organization, a deputy chairman and two vice-chairmen.

By early 1978, when the White Paper was due, the reorganization had settled down and the new BR was stirring. There were unmistakable signs of Spring, blossom by blossom breaking out all over the place, and some of them in pretty unlikely places. In particular, Hornsey depot. We had laid on a special tour for the Secretary of State and his entourage of very civil servants, and its climax was not where you might expect a climax to be, but in the Hornsey control room. For us it was the happiest occasion. We were celebrating the Great Northern Suburban Electrification, and the Minister was inaugurating the line. The tour had begun impressively with a view of the King's Cross power station. I only wish that, for security reasons, these power stations of BR were not set apart: they would be a fine sight for the traveller. It is wondrous comfort to behold the sophistication of the high technology that goes into having a good trip, impossible not to be impressed by the quietness, the calm, the competence in the high-tech control room, a glimmering universe of signal panels flickering with lights like shooting stars tracking ahead of the trains.

At Hornsey, we had the opportunity of dramatizing the message of the day: electrification was the way to translate the old railways into a future industry. And what was being baptized on the Great Northern by the ceremony was only a beginning: we wanted to impress the Minister particularly with what was not there. There were large blank panels besides those just installed and working, and on them we had put cardboard signs, ready for the electrification of the Midland and East Coast Main Lines: 'Just in case anything like that eventually happened,' I explained to the Secretary of State. From Newark, where electrification stopped, arrows pointed to Edinburgh; from Shepreth Junction to Cambridge; on the Midland diagram arrows aimed at Derby and Sheffield. The media reported the Hornsey control room as 'a powerful declaration of intent'. Exactly: electrification was firmly on the cards.

At the banquet at the Great Eastern Hotel the atmosphere was

spirited and confident enough to make even those exuberant Edwardian wall and ceiling paintings seem at home. Bill put away his formal
speech and spoke as he felt. The authoritative journal, *Modern Railways*, wrote later, 'it matters little whether or not this was inevitably
a practical politician's disarming ploy because what followed was as
glowing a tribute to the railways from the ministerial overlord as we
can remember. Mr Rodgers "felt in his bones" a peculiar confidence,
which regretfully, had not characterized the railways in recent years.'

Bill had been lobbied powerfully by what he called 'the experience
of the railway and the experience of regeneration'. He went on to say,
'British Rail is not a lame duck, but a very successful business enterprise whose object is meeting people's needs and which will also have
some obligations for which the government is prepared to pay under
the terms of what you, chairman, have chosen to call the contract.'

I was glad to hear the term contract beginning to come through. It
was crucial in our campaign for the recovery of belief in the railways.
We had to clean up the language that was used to describe the
accounting by the government for its 'required services'. At my early
BR board meetings I had come across a tangled string of words
symptomatic of muddle. Subsidy? But these were monies to compen-
sate for complying with government requirements. 'PSO, the Public
Service Obligation', was gobbledegook for what the government
wanted. Support price? Grant? Government payment? Compensation?
All these terms were trotted out lamely in our reports and reports
about us. The presentation of BR results to the public was a regular
misery. I remember the headlines about the losses of over £500 million
in 1976 when I was starting: this was the deficit before the government
paid its bill for services rendered. Annually BR was left dejected, in
deficit and defeat, trailing its colours in the dust. No wonder buttons
were not being done up. What good trying? Under such a rotten deal
nothing the individual railwayman might do seemed to be able to stop
BR looking like permanent losers. We were trying to run a railway
for ever through the valley of the shadow of deficit financing. The
only answer was to have a contract, to make the deal between the
railways and government better understood by politicians, railwaymen
and the public.

This difficulty was not peculiarly British. I met many of the heads
of railways all over the world, and all of them without exception agreed
that this was the curse of their public relations. The story was the

same the world over. Railways had become inevitably associated with financial failure, with high levels of subsidies, and therefore with inefficiency. Who was really responsible? The accounting for railways as both a commercial and social service is notoriously difficult, and to politicians it is embarrassing and painful. Who is really responsible for the closure of, say, a poor little rural service? Is it the bad manager of the railways or the unimaginative, mean-minded politician? The constitutional formula is that the day-to-day responsibility for managing the system is with BR, but real life tangles the clear lines of the statutes. For one thing, by another statute, the Permanent Secretary is responsible to the Public Accounts Committee of Parliament for the monies voted to his department. And for another, the economic management of the country bears on the management of the railway: there is a clear connection between a national policy of financial constraints and the crumbling edge of quality, reliability, comfort, even safety, of the railway. To an extent muddle suits the politician as it suits the complacent manager. Social decisions about transport are as sensitive as a sore tooth, and when it comes to closing one line or putting more investment in another, biting the bullet is agonizing. I decided that there had to be a better way to explain to the country and the customer what was expected of BR and of government, national and local. That is why, to be fair on all sides, I began to talk of a contract.

Ten years before, in Command Paper 3057, a White Paper had stated that 'the touchstone of a sound railway policy is the extent to which it meets the country's overall transport needs. Commercial viability is important, but secondary.' Almost a decade of doubt and sorrow on the rails was expended in trying to account the cost of the socially necessary services too exactly, but finally there came an acceptance of the EEC formula: the 1974 Railway Act made the Secretary of State the competent authority of Great Britain, empowered to impose general obligations over the board for services which the government thought were desirable for social or economic reasons.

I used that as the basis of my contract. The government was buying rail services from BR much as the Passenger Transport Executives of the Metropolitan Authorities were doing at that time. It was well known to be our single shareholder and our banker, but not our biggest customer. It was the wish of the customer that there be a social railway; so let there be a price paid, annually agreed ahead of time, and this could justifiably be taken into our normal BR income. The government was a paying customer to be accounted for with our other two million customers. This I termed the Contract. In my first Annual Report in 1976 I reported an operating surplus, and wrote: 'Despite inflation and the continuing recession, BR beat the contract price targets set in advance by the government for providing rail services in both passenger and freight sectors by a total of £64 million'. The headlines were able to speak well of BR at last, and did.

We knew the contract idea could only be a ready reckoner until our accounting systems were more refined. To a degree, the word was cosmetic – but I had nothing against cosmetics for an industry of a certain age. It gave us a clarity and an open commitment to more business-like objectives while, with the inspiration of Derek Fowler, the board member responsible for finance, we developed the accounting accuracy to make more specific contracts for each sector of the business. These sectors were defined as Inter-City, the Commuter Network and Provincial Services, and they were to transform the old geography-based structure of the railways. I held to the contractual position explicitly, with the public and with Parliament in the select committees. I did not want a subsidy for BR, I wanted a contract. There was no denying that subsidy was involved in transport policy, of course, but the subsidy went to the passengers, not to the railways. We should be treated as railway professionals and on contract. Subsidies are sickening to enterprise, contracts are quickening. Against a contract we could be judged. If we could not be properly judged, there was only the slimmest hope that we would ever be judged fairly. With a contract, government and railway communities would be able to take pride in the performance of BR. Without a contract, the outlook was the familiar old misery of misunderstandings, with BR back on the defensive, being patronized, patted on the head annually by politicians and given a subsidy to make up for our shortcomings. We had to strive towards a new deal based on this reality: what a government paid us for passenger services was what the government had ordered and what it owed.

The idea eased the tensions around us. By 1978 the House of Commons debate on railways glowed with a bipartisan belief in their future. All sides of the House seemed to be reacting favourably. Norman Fowler, as shadow Minister, declared that 'The concept of the government entering into a contract with British Rail to provide a service which cannot be totally financed through the fares is a concept that Peter Parker, the chairman of British Rail, is anxious to have accepted. In broad terms, it is acceptable to both sides of the House, but it is acceptable provided the contract is as specific as it can be made.' And the Secretary of State answered by saying 'Like the honourable Member for Sutton Coldfield, I think the idea of a contract is a good one.' Then, in a political language long dead, he went on to say, 'We are travelling this morning in a warm capsule of consensus.' In our results of the next few years we were able to declare a surplus after the contract payment; and ever since, BR's results have been announced on that basis. Trains were no longer drains. That meant a great deal to us in BR, and to our credibility nationally – and internationally.

I saw the international scene as a vital stimulus to the reawakening of the public's interest, and still more, of its belief in our potential. I believed and campaigned on the slogan that it was the age of the train. My evidence was what was happening elsewhere: there was a renaissance of railways the world over. This we knew from the profitability of our own international consultancy, Transmark, which was working on over seventy-nine projects in six continents and twenty-nine countries. I was delighted when I received a letter congratulating BR on its Transmark service, signed by 'The chairman of the real BR – Bangladesh Railway'. Exporting BR skills was another way of registering the quality of the home team. A prime target became the United States.

When Pen-Central Corporation crashed, to this point the biggest corporate failure of the twentieth century, the US government found itself having to own and run its railways. Wisely it looked around the world for advice. To win the three-year contract in strong contention with the Japanese and European competition was a victory devoutly to be wished by our Transmark. I joined the team in Washington to help make the pitch. The selling trip was just one more step in the hard-fought negotiation by our consultants, but it proved more than that for me. It was a test of our standing in the world. Also, as so often happens on business trips, those travelling learn a lot more about one another. In this case, I was accompanied by Bob Reid, whom I'd promoted to the board as its Member for Marketing.

At 10 a.m. on a crisp September morning in 1978 Bob and I, with the Transmark team, paraded before the US Congressional

Committee on Transportation and Commerce, which was investigating our bid to be appointed Consultants to the Federal Railroad Administration. The committee looked down on us dauntingly from mahogany heights. The chairman was charming until the television lights switched on and that changed everything. In a blaze of glory it seemed a new sun shone for him and his colleagues; it was a different day, the earth moved, cameras swooped into action, and suddenly the chairman was looking remarkably like that Eagle Muppet, glaring at me. 'Sir Peter Parker, I'd like to put this question to you right now: are you here to peddle nationalization?' That no doubt was what his constituents would have wanted him to say, but actually he was helping me because by sheer fluke I had an answer ready. The day before, we had come into Washington by train from New York, and there was a welcoming party to meet us. Watching was a young black porter who pushed through it towards me to ask if I was really Peter Parker? I confessed. 'But that's my name,' he said, brandishing the identity badge he wore on his shining blue overalls. The coincidence was hyped with photographs and fun, of course. 'My ma ain't going to believe this,' Peter Parker said to me. 'No-oh way.' The fun of the coincidence had triggered in my memory another historical connection between my name and the invasion of the States in 1812. I had come across it by chance during a visit to Baltimore some thirty years before, and I remembered dimly an uncharacteristically damp poem by Byron in memory of the British naval officer, Sir Peter Parker, who had been killed landing on the coast of Maryland in the American War. So, to my own amazement, my subconscious was ready to answer the Eagle Muppet on Capitol Hill. I told him that the last man with my name and designation who had come to his country with a radical idea had been plugged between the eyes as he stepped ashore. I explained a bit, and Eagle Muppet thoroughly enjoyed the reference – even when I was able to go on, with a gesture towards Bob Reid and our Transmark colleagues, 'But of course, didn't the rest of them get through to burn the White House?'

The business of the Congressional Committee developed more easily and seriously from there. We were invited to describe BR's experiences, warts and all, in the always-tense relationship with government as banker, shareholder, customer. We argued that a strong board, independently minded, sometimes awkwardly strong, was a boon to government; that railways were a political business but not necessarily party political. Corroboration of our evidence came directly from that 1978 Hansard debate which revealed a bipartisan commitment to a future for BR. At one point Eagle Muppet was so impressed with Bob Reid's testimony that he invited Bob to make a take-over bid for Amtrak and Conrail. Bob had no trouble in resisting the offer, but Transmark did win the contract with the Federal Rail Administration. That year it also won the Queen's Award for Export. When the announcement was made, I scrambled on to the slippery wet roof of our Marylebone headquarters along with Sir Robert Lawrence, the chairman of Transmark, and Ken Smith, the founding MD, and hauled up the Queen's Award flag – a victory for the permanent way to flutter high over the permanent traffic jams beneath in the Marylebone Road.

The international perspective went on being invaluable to BR in the support of the two major projects which I relied on to transform our fortunes long beyond the immèdiate crises that conditioned our lives: electrification and the Channel Tunnel. Electrification was the first of the mega-schemes to take shape. I had been convinced quickly that the future railway would be electrified. For our mainline customers, electrification offered the most reliable, the cleanest and, once done, the cheapest railway. For the railway supply industry, it offered scope for development of better products, more jobs, and the prospect of exports based on experience in a steady home market. For BR, it offered improved efficiency, with lower operating and maintenance costs. It was inconceivable that we would be spending money to sustain our services over the next two decades and not electrify. International studies enabled us to make startling comparisons. We lay a lowly seventeenth in the league table of electrified railways in the world; only Poland, Czechoslovakia and Portugal had less electrification than our twenty-one per cent. A joint BR/Department of Transport Review of Main Line Electrification was agreed in Bill Rodgers' time. By 1979 it issued an interim report with a convincing case; by 1980 the final report made the case conclusive. It argued an eleven per cent return above inflation for the largest and fastest programme bringing the proportion of electrified network up from twenty-one per cent to fifty-two per cent. Over a twenty-year period, electrification would extend from London to Edinburgh and Aberdeen, and from Edinburgh to Glasgow and Carstairs; to Sheffield; across the Pennines from Liverpool to York; from York to Birmingham; to Bristol and Reading; to Holyhead; and on to the West as far as Swansea and Penzance. The cost would be £775 million above what we would have to spend anyway on the services over the twenty years, an extra investment of £30 million a year, rising to £60 million at the peak of the programme. Slumps and strikes were to eclipse that total approach, and the case to government had to be re-made, excruciatingly slowly, line by line. But eventually it was on, and today the new advance of electrification is moving ahead swiftly and irresistibly. One of the last ceremonies I attended as chairman in 1983 was the dawn of the new advance: I dug the hole for the first electrification post in Ayrshire. The stainless steel spade that I used was sent to me months later, when I was out of BR; it is still well used in my garden at Minster Lovell, a peaceful and glittering memento from a hard-fought battlefield.

Of course, the other mega-scheme beyond the current crisis was the restart of the old dream of the Channel Tunnel. The 1974 Labour government had come to power to find a colossal public sector borrowing requirement on its hands and three vast schemes in various stages of development: the Concorde, the brave Maplin plan for another London airport at the mouth of the Thames, and the Channel Tunnel. The government felt it could afford only one prestige project, if that, and Concorde was it. The Tunnel was condemned as too grandiose a set of calculated risks, and particularly the railway component was extravagantly budgeted. In fact BR, drawn into the planning at too late a stage, had escalated costs prohibitively by proposing a new Southern railway line to serve the new traffic. When I came to BR in 1976, the project was pronounced dead. Bill Rodgers' own position began passively, and it was still so in 1978 when he could only go as far as saying 'it would be ungenerous not to consider propositions coming from the European Community even though such a scheme did not feature in Britain's present priorities.' But by then BR had reopened the files, and we were planning in a way that was going to make it difficult to close them ever again.

I had only been chairman a few weeks when I received a note from Sir Arthur Kirby. I had met Arthur in 1969 when he was chairman of the National Ports Council, which was about to be subsumed into the National Ports Authority I was to set up. Before that he had been a renowned chairman of the East Africa Railways, and he was permanently in love with the 'bright ribbons of steel' as he called them. He had retired in 1976 but was still active, still a starter. His note urged me to meet an old friend of his, Sir James Farquharson, the chairman of the Scottish Transport Group. Arthur recognized that I was being inundated with advice, but if there was still a chance that I had a moment to think a little for myself, I should listen to Sir James. I arranged a breakfast meeting at the Paddington Hotel at once. David Bowick and I went there, curious but frankly expecting not much more than a seasoned homily on the lessons of experience. No such boring thing: this brisk old man had the future in him.

'How much do you know about the Channel Tunnel?' he asked me, snap, crackle, pop, with the cornflakes.

'No details at all,' I answered. 'All I've picked up so far is that it's not on anybody's agenda any more. Stone-dead, is what a Minister called it in a briefing session.' Stones were about to speak.

'Well,' he said, 'in Scotland we need a Channel Tunnel: our containers ought to be reliably in Milan well within twenty-four hours some day.'

And that's how the project started up in my mind. His spark was eventually to give life to those shrouded engines stalled in the aborted Folkstone tunnel. Over that breakfast Sir James reminded me of the post-mortem report which had been written by Sir Alec Cairncross when the project had been finally abandoned in 1975. Enthralled, I read it the following Sunday, in the orchard at Minster Lovell. It demolished any prospect of the scheme proposed, but there was one ray of hope for the future: it recommended that the possibility of a single, six-metre, railway-only tunnel should be explored. Here was a new beginning. The BR Board backed a £500,000 study to be made with SNCF, the French Railways, on that modest possibility. We took the decision with no encouragement whatsoever from the Department – even less than that really – and drew up our own terms of reference based on four key points. The project for a tunnel should be commercially viable; it had to be able to stand on its own. It should be environmentally acceptable; we did not want to have the green-sandalled army on the march in Kent and the South as it had been before. It should be based on market forecasts which allowed for the prosperity of the existing ferry services – remembering we owned Sealink in those days. It should be based on our existing Southern Railway network, not on the unrealistic assumption that we would have the funds to construct a new line. (Only the French would think of something like that, as indeed, years on, they have.) Ten years on, with the plans for the Euro-Tunnel well advanced, there are fierce debates about the route of the new line to be built to the coast – but the now-forgotten fact is that the entire project would probably never have started if we had not begun it in the most modest way, making use of what we had. Our hopes would have been scorned as extravagant and fanciful.

SNCF and BR worked together for over a year and a half with all the secrecy and comradely fighting spirit appropriate to an underground movement. In the early Seventies, the energy, excitement, almost astonishment of finding a way to bring the Tunnel to life again had been absolutely mutual, but then, in 1975, perfidious Albion had unilaterally pulled out when half a mile of hole had already been dug. But the French fury with us seemed not to detract from their passion for the old Napoleonic dream of a Tunnel. Giscard d'Estaing, President at the time, was said to be personally unenthusiastic about the scheme, but the French railwaymen had no doubt. Our *entente mutuelle* made a nonsense of the old British tradition that the French make awkward partners. The railways on both sides of the water revelled in taking the initiative, in not being taken for granted and dragged in at the end of all the scheming, as they were the last time round.

I was impressed by SNCF in three particulars. In France, despite a kaleidoscope of governments since the war, railways were not a gnawed bone of political contention. Secondly, they seemed unafraid of big decisions. With Gaullist thoroughness, the transport of Paris had been transformed over a decade to keep car congestion down; the Paris commuter was encouraged onto the rails. Once their high speed train (*Train de Grande Vitesse*) was decided, it was backed to the hilt, with new track and new stations. When one of their most senior researchers visited us, as we toiled through the myriad complexities of our detailed analysis, I asked him how he thought the calculations were stacking up. He smiled and replied that he was fairly relaxed about them; the situation that he was really trying to assess about the Tunnel's prospect was simply, have the British the will to do it this time? That mattered more than anything, didn't it?

Thirdly, characteristic of the French, the railways gave a central, honoured status to their engineers. I have noticed over the years rules of nature that give some reliability in an uncertain world. For instance a lady with a mink coat will tell you about it even as you meet sunbathing on a beach: 'Too hot for my mink today.' Or an Etonian on dry land will wear his tie. Crossing the Atlantic from New York on the Queen Mary many years ago, Jill and I shared a table with a young British couple. First night out, it was permissible to wear lounge suits for dinner. The husband wore his Etonian tie, and it disappeared for the rest of the voyage. One morning I came down to breakfast to find him in the tie again. I went straight to a porthole and, of course, we were in sight of dry land, Cherbourg. Another rule I added after working intimately with SNCF: a reliable reflex of French nature is that a Frenchman who has been clever and lucky enough to go to the Ecole Polytechnique will tell you of this blessing, and pretty well at once. The significance of this in dealing with SNCF was that their leadership was from that stable: seventeen of their top management were Ecole Polytechnique engineers. Only too characteristic of British industry, there were no engineers on the board of BR when I arrived and, damn it, only three when I left.

Both the SNCF and BR boards adopted the recommendations of the joint study group and simultaneously we made them public. I announced the proposal in a speech at the Anglo-American Chamber of Commerce. Here was a scheme for a rail link less expensive than any previous plan, and SNCF and BR, both traders in transport, saw the six-metre tunnel as a commercial proposition. 'It is a project which will open new markets for Britain, and will have an impact on transport throughout Europe, making concrete the European idea.' We recognized from the start that this was a bargain basement proposition, £50 million annually from each country for seven years. But even so we recognized that it was likely to be attacked as grandiose lunacy – and it was. What we wanted to do was to re-open and widen the debate. I took great care to make clear that our limited approach was devised to be enlarged: it did not exclude grander designs, if the resources and the will existed to find another way. Our 'mousehole' was for starters. After over a century of false starts (which had much more to do with our offshore islanders' distrust of a physical link with the continent than with technical or even commercial complications) two determined railways were presenting what could be done profitably if railways were forced to do it alone. But the chances for that were remote. What we true believers took to be self-evident was that the day of the Tunnel would come and that whatever the final form agreed for funding and organizing, it would include a rail link.

Of course, competitive schemes were rapidly proposed, all on a more lavish scale than ours: motorways via a bridge, bridge and tunnel together, twin tunnels for rail and rail freight. There was a common denominator, each had a track for trains. Ian MacGregor, then of Steel (and later Sir), was pushing his steel bridge with might and main, using all the force of his intimate position in Thatcherite court circles. I always felt his to be the least likely proposition, romantic and untypical of Ian. The Channel is the busiest seaway in the world and complicating it with a bridge was yet an extra hazard. But even Ian had a railway in there. 'I offer you a railway free,' he used to say to me, 'and you refuse.'

Gradually the Tunnel was being taken seriously again. A select committee of the House of Commons pronounced in favour. In the 1979 party election, to my surprise, I saw that Bill Rodgers was coming out in favour as well. When Norman Fowler took over he at once set up a study group to advise him. By that time, too, the French had Mitterand as President, whose father had been a station master at Angoulême, and the new Prime Minister, Pierre Mauroy, had long believed the Tunnel would bring jobs and money to his power base around the Pas de Calais. BR would have to be patient; there were sure to be years of dispiriting doubts and delays, but just as surely in the end there would be a Tunnel with trains.

For BR the Seventies were closing with a promise that the Eighties would be a decade of development. Electrification and the Tunnel were in our sights. Our 1979 results made good reading. In a year racked with industrial disruptions, and ending with inflation in the winter of discontent, we came through with a surplus after interest and service charges, and for the fourth year in succession we lived within the contract. The railways were costing the taxpayer seventeen per cent less in real terms than five years before. 'A Comparative Study of European Rail Performance', which we had commissioned through Leeds University, showed that of the ten main European systems, BR was the most cost-effective, the best value for money. Passenger mileage was the highest recorded since 1961, when the rail network was thirty per cent bigger and there were half the number of cars on the road. Over thirty-five per cent of the passenger revenues were coming in from the reduced fares and special promotions: rail-cards for families, students, senior citizens, were reaping a £79 million harvest, with the disabled person's railcard imminent. We were moving to a popular and well-loaded system. That was the good news. Above all, management believed in itself.

And just as well. The 1979 results and international comparisons had bad as well as good news. They recorded the painfully familiar priorities: that the national recession was deepening, that we were running the railway very hard just to stand still, that we were replacing our assets at a slower rate than any other European system. Only sixteen locomotives were built in 1979 out of a total fleet of 2,000 which needed replacement. In the late Fifties and early Sixties there had been peak spending on new rolling-stock and track, much of which had, by the early Seventies, begun to wear out. Replacing it created a bow wave of investment which was still building ahead of us. I knew that unless our investment levels were lifted by thirty per cent just to replace worn-out assets, the consequences would be lower quality in terms of the speed, frequency, comfort and reliability of service. There were productivity gains to be made, but not enough in themselves to pay the high price for having had to adopt the low-cost solution to the investment problem of railways throughout the Seventies.

Yet we could do more for ourselves. Even if productivity was not enough in itself it was still the rock on which to build the future BR. Only by showing that we could use what we had would we win the extra resources we must have to fulfil the promise the management felt full of. We published *A Challenge of the Eighties*, signed by every member of the board, which identified fundamental changes in working practice that were vitally urgent. But progress was frustratingly slow in negotiating change. Our concentration had focused on establishing a clearer national policy, on recovering the public's confidence in our future, on proving ourselves in the market-place. Now we were strong enough to prove ourselves in dealing with inefficiencies obvious to us and to our customers.

This was the BR mood as the new Conservative government came in. Some friends had called into my office to have a drink on the news of Conservative victory at the polls. Norman Fowler, Shadow Minister of Transport for the previous two years, leaning on the doorway, told me he was doubtful that he would be in the Administration. All my soundings in the Conservative Party well before the election had suggested to me strongly that he was a favoured candidate, and I hoped I was right. At that moment, however, the party politics of the railway were no longer our primary concern. Generally there was a down-to-earth recognition of the balance sheet of change. Improvements in productivity generated within the railway would generate enough confidence for any government of the day to respond with more flexibility and more investment. That was it.

Or was it? We had already come some way, but there were radical changes still to be made that struck directly at conventional working practices. We had to push ahead with our drive towards productivity and lower manning levels. It was becoming starkly clear to me that while we might hope to win the battle we could not hope to avoid it.

In the next few days I visited Peter Baldwin, my Permanent Secretary at the Department. The election and the aftermath of Cabinet-building created a short lull for them there. Furniture was piled in the corridors, and stepping into a big, empty office I asked if they were doing a spot of redecoration. 'Oh no,' said one of the senior figures, 'just making room to practise a few U-turns.'

10

Anatomy of a Strike

(British Rail 1980–2)

Two o'clock in the morning, a beautiful July night in 1982 and, I thought, the makings of a good party.

Our small negotiating team was gathering in the secrecy of Marsham Street, utterly empty at that hour, and well away from the media and the ACAS building where we were due soon to meet the TUC's cabinet, its Finance and General Purposes Committee. Marsham Street is the home of the Department of Transport – an ugly building, one of those squeezed out of a cement tube all over London in the Sixties – but, tonight, I thought, how sweet the moonlight sleeps even on the Department of Transport.

We said little to each other. There was no need for much briefing as we moved to the climax. We would hold to the same line of negotiation that we had held for the hard strike-ridden year past. I was sitting waiting on a parapet, high off the pavement, the stone chilly on the bottom, but no matter, not tonight. I and all my colleagues there, Bob Reid, Jim Urquhart, Dick Wilcox, Sydney Hoggart, were warmed through with certainty. And, I thought, it had not been one year but three hard years . . .

It started in 1980 when I had been invited by the new Conservative government to serve as chairman of BR for another five years. Through the tall windows to the south of my sixth-floor office at Rail House the long view was tempting, buds glistening on the tiptop of the trees just below, and blue, blue skies beyond. The long-term future looked fine for BR. I had become a passionate railwayman, with the special zeal of a true convert. I was enjoying the years of comradeship in BR. I had never felt alone. 'The railway community' was a vision that I found compelling; its current travail and its transformation were formidably real to me. I believed in what I was doing and I loved doing it. The long view was certainly tempting, but there were other views, other voices, shorter views, gloomier voices.

251

Go when the going is good, was the quiet advice of some friends, not in BR. The public mood of those years was on a relative high over railways: *The Economist* (20 June 1981) reported, 'Sir Peter Parker, the chairman of British Rail, has won a victory . . . four years of tight bookkeeping under Sir Peter Parker has brought BR success undreamt of a decade ago.' And weren't electrification and the Channel Tunnel now clearly on the cards for the Eighties? Not a bad time for farewells. The family, as ever, was ready for anything. We were used by now to the glare of the television cameras, the media on the doorsteps, the telephones and late messengers, briefcases on the bed, the relentless unreliability of my diary which was a kind of skidpatch in all family arrangements; although one wise child did ask me, is there a life after railways?

But the fact was that I knew I had not finished, simply that: I had not finished the job I had set out to do. Nothing that was promising for BR would be fulfilled until the nettle of productivity had been grasped. The so-called victory for electrification was unconvincing at that stage; it could only be justified if 38,000 jobs were shed from the system. Who would trust the Tunnel project for the twenty-first century if the trains through it were driven with working practices defined in 1919? Our freight business had clambered out of its £66 million loss in 1976 to reach break-even, but how could it ever make proper profits and be competitive if BR's use of crew members per million train miles were twice the average in Europe? Independent research, which we had commissioned to compare the performance of the ten leading railways in the world, pinpointed the good news that we generated more investment for ourselves through revenue than the other main railways, but the bad news was the undeniably poor productivity of our drivers. We were still not giving the taxpayer value for money at a time when the pressures on the national economy were intensifying.

1980 was a grim, demanding year of recession for industry in the UK, and also for BR, the conveyorbelt for the wealth-creating process. I have always argued that bad times are good times for managing change: in 1980 there was an opportunity to innovate and we had to seize it. We had to achieve fundamental changes in productivity – the rock, as I had insisted from the start, on which to build BR's future. Over those high, reassuring poplar buds there might be a dazzle on the horizon. At the level of gnarled, tangled old roots there was still much sorting out to be done.

So I negotiated a contract for a second term with Norman Fowler, who despite his own doubts had indeed become Secretary of State for Transport, and with Peter Baldwin, the Permanent Secretary. We came through the negotiations still friends! I agreed to continue but I refused the offer of five years; so, with Number Ten's backing, a proposal was made that I should take a three-year contract. We settled for two, which in fact from the time we were negotiating, with a year left to run on my original contract, was three years. 'By then we should be in the clear, don't you think?' I remember saying to Peter, who had been the essential, good-tempered go-between, and he agreed. We both knew what lay ahead: the probability that BR was about to hit the buffers of the unions with the worst bang in the history of modern railways.

At that time, the understanding between the board and the Department, between Peter, Norman and myself, was realistic and remarkable, completely uncomplicated even in our differences. We were all taking risks, including Norman, who showed a daring which belied his Spitting Image, with its conventional manner and Austin Reedy voice. Norman had the courage to be accessible when I needed his help. For instance, in 1980 the board of BR hit one of those explosive moments of exasperation with government and the slowness of its investment decisions. Board members reached an end-of-tether mood: if the politicians and civil servants think they can run it, let them bloody well get on with it, what are we here for anyway? Norman agreed to meet the full board at the Department and accepted our request for an independent review of BR's future funding. That was the origin of the so-called Serpell Report which was to surface so controversially in my last year, and which did good despite itself. But it was Norman's willingness to meet the Rail Council that was the most adventuresome: he was honour bound to meet my board in full cry, but meeting the Rail Council with the union leadership on it was a much riskier step to take in those early days of confrontation.

I had created the Rail Council in 1979 to be the industry's top forum, at which the executive members of the BR board could meet the unions, and explain our policies, problems and prospects. I had never accepted the logic, recommended in the Bullock report on industrial democracy, of 'worker representations on the board'. How could management ever manage if its plans were to be based always on a compromise policy that would get the consent of the union members of the board? How could the union members agree to co-operate in plans which reduced the membership of their constituency? Just before coming into the chair in 1976 I had arranged a private dinner with the leaders of the Transport Salaried Staffs' Association (TSSA), NUR and ASLEF. We met in the small, colourful room at the top of The Gay Hussar in Soho, which seems to have been able to combine charmingly for years a radical easy-going clientele with the ambience of the collapsing Austro-Hungarian Empire. I put the question to my union guests: was a position on the BR board one of their objectives? And the three of them, uniquely of one accord, each said no, and never say that to us again, Peter. Quite rightly they saw their job as negotiating, not managing. My views exactly: management must act and the unions must have the chance to react. To ask the unions to pretend to manage is impractical, unfair and phoney. That said, my stand was that modern managers should dare to share their problems and modern unions dare to listen; then, after consultation, the managers must decide. The Rail Council was conceived in that light.

Its formation was greeted by Sid Weighell, the general secretary of the NUR, as open and democratic, and 'a very good idea'. Sometimes it did not feel so, only stale, flat and unprofitable. Trade-union-speak can be almost unspeakable, but alas not altogether. Sitting through recitations of prepared trade union committee rhetoric, I found myself developing a whole new set of tummy muscles. And it must be said, the existence of the council did not prevent the plague of ASLEF disruptions that brought near-disaster to BR. Ultimately, however, I believe its existence was a decisive contribution to our successful strategy for change. Without that forum, and its genuine effort to foster a community of interest, we would have had little chance of keeping close to TSSA and NUR or, together with them, keeping faith with the vision of a future railway through the divided times ahead. The isolation of the ASLEF executive and its militant stupidity was going to be crucial to my strategy.

The council began as an uneasy experiment. ASLEF did not for-mally join; its executive only agreed to attend, and this was a tiny, dispiriting omen. After twenty minutes of its first meeting, Sid Weigh-ell interrupted the proceedings with one of his outbursts of impatience which I came to rely on to give some human proportion to the proceedings. 'Chairman, I thought these talks were to be different. In fact here we go again chasing each other round with the usual stuff, criticizing this and that.' I was relieved. To my ears those first twenty minutes had made a dull, low sound like 'plonk', with the opening items of the agenda running immediately into the old ruts of detailed grievances and current negotiations – just the argy-bargy I wanted the council to rise above. 'I know very well what you want of us,' Sid said, 'and I know you know very well what we want of you. But at this rate we'll neither of us ever be satisfied. I am starting from this point: that the NUR is seeking a new deal, and is ready to confront the problems of the industry.' I could do business with such a man: the council soon established itself as a crucial force of communication and consultation.

There is no doubt that Sidney Weighell was an exceptional leader. He was awkward, arrogant, unclubbable, and he was decisive, visionary and convincing. The spirit of the man was clear in his sharp, straight features and in equally sharp, straight talk. His railwayman father had told him that if you can't say what you want to say in ten minutes, you must be telling lies. And his father had probably learnt that from his railwayman father: the Weighell passion for the railways was three generations long. His oratory from a platform, almost always on the attack, could sweep a hall off its feet, like a fiery new broom. Possibly the best Labour speech of a decade was his 1978 address at Blackpool in support of an incomes policy, an onslaught against those who talked about public ownership, a planned economy and a free-for-all on wages. 'If you want the call to go out at this conference that the new philosophy in the Labour Party you believe in is the pig trough – those with the biggest snouts get the biggest share – I reject it. My union rejects it. And if I am the only one standing here saying it, I will reject it until I drop down dead.'

Yorkshire sturdiness showed in accent and stature, a compact, trim style that people, and the television camera, certainly liked. Born into railways and trained as a driver, he had been a professional football player on the side (he played for Sunderland just after the war, and well enough to run a second-hand MG sports car). But by the time we met he was physically frailer than he appeared. Twenty years before, his car, crammed with his family and their Christmas presents, was in a head-on crash while crossing the railway bridge at Newark.

255

His wife and four-year-old daughter were killed; he and his son survived but were seriously injured. For months he walked the moors and fished for trout and thought of quitting the union. Slowly he started to piece life together around his son. Then happily he met Joan, a market researcher from Birmingham; he remarried, and she brought a new proportion to his life, saw that it was less tyrannously dominated by union affairs. To some extent this made him less one of the boys, less clubbable. Always I felt him a private, sad man, with a grim humour. My smiling puzzled him. At a very tough moment he once said to me, 'I think you smile because you are too old to cry.' I told him that as a boxer I had been taught not to show your opponent that he can hurt you – and anyway with teeth like mine it stands to reason not to close your lips if there's a chance someone's going to belt you one. Later Sid wrote about us in his memoirs. *A Hundred Years of Railway Weighells*: 'We had a good working relationship from day one . . . I often used to think what a team we would have made if he and I had been able to work together with only one union in the industry.'

The ideal of the one big union never struck me as anything but an ambiguous blessing: fine, if it were to be led by a Sid Weighell, but what if a Scargill grabbed control? It was a will o' the wisp of union debate. The TSSA, the white-collar union, shared the sensible stance of the NUR leader on collaboration between rail trade unions, and Tom Jenkins, its general secretary, was a steady mind, moderate in all things, courteous, meticulously mannered, soft-voiced, sure-footed, with none of the jazzy aggression which had made his brother, Clive, more famous. Unity, however, seemed not to figure in the forefront of ASLEF's mind. The closer it got to any crunch of real change, the closer the ASLEF executive clung to its past. Ray Buckton, its general secretary, was another Yorkshireman, born only a few miles from Sid Weighell, but the rivalry and animosity between them was as obvious as a kick in the teeth.

It is tempting to simplify the chaotic dramas of 1981–2, just about to unfold, by pointing to the lack of unity in the unions and the personality clashes between the leaders of NUR and ASLEF. That would be far too facile. Ray was a symptom, not a cause, of the chaos in the policy of ASLEF. He was an example of how far a decent enough fellow can allow himself to be driven in directions he has no liking for. It is difficult now to remember Ray as he was before he got into the wretched hole that he and his executive dug for themselves in one of the bitterest of battles of modern industrial relations. Before the ASLEF strikes, however, he had been in 'a better 'ole'. He was well known in industry generally for working hard and genially in several good causes of safety and welfare, well beyond the call of his duty as the general secretary of a small, if once distinguished, union. There was a regular rumour that Ray had sought a large role on the international side of the trade union world, and that might once have suited him well. In fact, very early in my job and not entirely in jest, I suggested to Bill Rodgers, my Secretary of State during the Labour government, that if J. B. Priestley had been writing the script for the next few years he would have had Ray typecast as an old-style trade union leader who is removed out of the path of progress by being elevated to the peerage, to become the governor of a far-off, tiny colonial island, at the edge of the empire. Ray might have been fine there, feather-hatted and bonhomous, improbably booming messages from the Queen to an awed multitude of 'the lads'.

But perhaps Ray had become too comfortable to move. The head-quarters of ASLEF were in a gorgeous Edwardian house in Arkwright Road, Hampstead, once the home of Sir Thomas Beecham. In a panelled office, with comfortable easy chairs in shiny red-buttoned leather, too often filled with Labour attachés from Iron Curtain countries, Ray flourished cheerfully and cleverly. He was nimble, a quick wit, with an eye for the detail that could matter in a bargain. Jill and I once took him and his delightful wife, Barbara, to see Shaw's *Saint Joan* at the Old Vic, and on the drive home Ray waxed enthusiastic: 'What makes Shaw so good? No action really, but still so good?' I suggested that Shaw always gave the Devil – the Inquisitor in *Saint Joan* – the best arguments in his plays and then beat him: that was the excitement. 'Thank God, Peter, he isn't in our negotiation.' Barbara, dark eyed and pleasant and sensible, was the daughter of the engine-driver for whom Ray had been the fireman when he was making his way up the career ladder in the days of steam. I complimented him on marrying the boss's daughter. Nowadays, of course, there are no firemen to shovel coal: the 'F' of ASLEF is, as so many ASLEF members became with the advent of the diesel, redundant. The technological revolution decimated the union membership and a proud union went into retreat. In the bitterness of losing members and status, not too surprisingly, the militants began to win control of the executive. Ray Buckton, as general secretary, went with the Militant Tendency, although I still doubt whether he was one of them. He did not sit or have a vote on the executive of the union. Once during a small, early crisis, I decided to invite the general secretaries to meet with me together in private session. Sid Weighell and Tom Jenkins came alone. Ray rang to say he was not able to come alone and set off with his minder, despite my telling him that this would wreck the meeting. He arrived in my outer office with his president, and that infuriated the other two. They could not stay if Ray had brought his president when they had not brought theirs. Ray pleaded with us. His president sat outside, and there was wretched Ray in the doorway of my office, torn between his common sense and his president's Big Brotherly attitude. We had the meeting without him and that particular crisis was resolved, but Ray could not slip the executive leash – or at least never effectively tried to do so.

The splits between the vivid personalities of Sid and Ray at the top of the unions made good copy, but their clash only dramatized the historical tensions between craft and industrial unionism. Between 1919 and my time NUR and ASLEF had eighteen fruitless debates over the idea of a single rail union. Unionism, ironically, is where class warfare is waged in an organized way, where differences and differentials are defined with Byzantine sophistication. The drivers felt a cut above the rest. 'A woman could do that job,' one driver explained to me on one of my early footplate rides, when we were talking about NUR guards, 'and in the war, you know, some women did.' Once ASLEF had been a member of an elite among unions, now it sat at the table of the great Trade Union Council only because Emperor Jack Jones of the Transport and General Workers' Union had seen to it (if ASLEF wanted to avoid an alliance with the NUR, the TGWU was ready to welcome it in). The driver grieved over past glories. Once an engine-driver was what most boys wanted to be; now nobody bothered to stop and have a word with him about the journey, good or bad. Once the King of the Road, rising from cleaner, through fireman, to the throne on the footplate; now he was in unglamorous exile. Once he was inseparable from his locomotive, his castle and his home, cherishing it and its reputation for meeting the timetable, frying breakfast on the shovel; now he and it were computer-programmed through the depot. Once sure of his place, superior, knowing the shedmaster; now he was adrift in the impersonal professional world of area managers and operating managers. The key question during the making of any driver was the instructor's 'Have you hold?' Gradually the driver's grip on things was in truth slipping. It was as if esteem was lost with the loss of steam, self-esteem and other people's. And as I was bringing the chips down for change at the beginning of the Eighties, just when the union most required a prophetic, restoring vision, the executive was in the hands of class warriors battling in the trenches of 1919 agreements which had enshrined the sanctity of the eight-hour day.

'There is a phase of ancient history which ought never to be forgotten by those who wish to understand their fellow men,' wrote Rebecca West in the prologue of that marvel of a book, full of radiant darkness and lightning, *Black Lamb and Grey Falcon*. She described the Donatists, a fourth-century body of Christian schismatics of the Church of Africa, who were wreckers of the Church. 'They raved . . . But though those people raved, they were not mad. They were making the only noises they knew to express the misery inflicted on them by the collapse of the Western Roman Empire.' The Marxist militant sounded something like that. 'They had to use the vocabulary given them by the Church; and they screamed nonsense about the sacraments because they very sensibly recognized that the Western Roman Empire was going to die, and so were they.' And so it came to pass with the ASLEF executive and its reactions to the age of change. Bound by its prides and prejudices, the executive seemed set on wrecking any hope of coherence in the trade unions' responses to BR's careful programme for improved productivity. Even the ardent advocacy and sheer cunning of Len Murray, general secretary of the TUC, could not deliver unity among the unions. By 1981 Len seemed ready to settle for a lesser dream than the big union: he came up with the proposal for a Railway Trade Union Federation, which was finally embodied in a stately sounding agreement and duly signed. An executive committee for the federation was nominated and the first annual conference fixed to be at ASLEF's headquarters in Arkwright Road, as a signal of solidarity. But this was doomed. ASLEF, with its new president, Derrick Fullick, an arch-Donatist, proved not to be in any mood to take too seriously its own signature on this or any other agreements, either with the other unions or with BR. In the last two months of 1981 bad faith had begun to infect the thin air of confidence which the summer negotiations had generated.

1981 was the Year of the Tiger for BR: throughout it there were bright bands of hope alternating with deepest black. The hope mostly shone fitfully through the Rail Council, where I saw signs that we were building an understanding of the changes we needed to establish as the premise for BR's operation in the Eighties. We discussed frankly the reality that modernization of the railway meant more than money for maintenance, new trains and electrification; it meant providing evidence that we were modernizing working attitudes as well. A special meeting of the council had been convened at BR's Training Centre in Watford as early as 1979, and there 'Parker spelt out the gravity of the situation,' as Sid Weighell records it. 'He told us that the industry could not go to government with a begging bowl. We must show what we can do for ourselves. He saw the alternatives as either tackling British Rail's troubles constructively, or slogging it out in trench warfare. The slump was now biting both the passenger and freight side of the business, and the board's financial position was deteriorating rapidly. Parker told us that the option of doing nothing was not open to the board.'

At Watford the meeting began, of course, by hammering one another, but then, having survived that obvious ceremony of ritual suspicions, both sides hammered out together a detailed statement of what we in the industry could do for ourselves and, on that basis, what it was fair and realistic to expect the government to do, even in hard times. By the end of the conference there it was, handwritten in accounts style on a blackboard, the Council's balance sheet of change, what we must do and what the government might do. Twinning the aims of productivity and investment was the best, slim hope I had of change without the blood, sweat and costs of confrontation.

The balance sheet seemed to strike a chord among all the parties present and also with the government, at least to start with. It was on that common ground that Norman Fowler, as Secretary of State, had that first meeting with the council in January 1981. At it, he told us that the balance sheet was useful and important and helpful to him in discussing railway affairs in the Cabinet – clearly not a favourite topic, we were given to understand. 'There was need for a sensible bipartisan programme,' was the Secretary of State's non-confrontational comment. We were still in the days when a Minister was not afraid to be caught alone in a meeting-room with a consensus. Norman met the council again in June, and again there was some reasonably firm common ground. His news was positive: he was putting up our borrowing limits and he was able to show good intentions for the future of the railways by conditional agreement to the ten-year programme for electrification.

Alongside these brightening prospects were darker signs. The 1981 wage claim from the unions was in progress – although that was hardly the word. BR had launched its own spring offensive by linking pay to productivity, as our council meeting with the Minister linked investment to productivity. This was made unequivocally plain by Norman Fowler and myself. We stood by the board's 1981–5 Corporate Plan with its commitment to a cut of 38,000 in the workforce. Also, the electrification scheme for East Anglia which had been put to the Department for approval could not be advanced without a convincing conclusion to those raucous pay and productivity negotiations which made an unpromising contrast to the Rail Council's agenda. There was no way, I insisted, that the board would call for more money unless we could see it spent efficiently.

The balance was on a knife-edge for months, but by the time the council next met, in December 1981, there had been a widely acclaimed pay and productivity settlement. There had also been a change of minister; David Howell from Energy took over from Norman Fowler, who went to the DHSS. David, roughed-and-tumbled as he had been in Cabinet controversies over North Sea gaspipes and pricing, did well to pick up the wavelength of the railways. At the council meeting he spoke fairly about the progress in productivity and our management of change. Therefore, on his side of the balance sheet he had decided both to raise our borrowing powers again and to give the go-ahead for the East Anglia electrification scheme. Better and better. The East Anglia decision was announced just before Christmas, coinciding with the NUR's signature on their agreement with BR on flexible rostering – a phrase of which the wide world outside was blessedly ignorant for at least a few days longer. A Merry Christmas.

I always enjoy Christmas cards exchanged in corporate life. Tycoons often seem to find the season of goodwill – to themselves – irresistible. I remember one who kept sending annually a full-length portrait of his enormous, oblong swimming-pool. Then there was a large and memorable card from Robert Maxwell: a garden, a gigantic Christmas tree, spangled with lights, dark shapes of people having a good time.

Inside the card it was explained that the photograph had been taken at Maxwell's home, to celebrate the birth of our Robert . . . In BR the messages tended to be more ironic. I had one from Sid, with his name, a charming personal message and a rubber-stamped signature; one from one of my Ministers, his wishes of comfort and joy for a chairman in the public sector illustrated by a pale watercolour of the Tower of London, 'a river view of Traitor's Gate'; one from ASLEF, 'Peace on Earth,' it said, with a nervous white dove in a bell-tower, anxiously waiting for its cue. But as for a merry Christmas in 1981, that hope was to end blackly. Without any warning to the other members of the brand-new Rail Federation, ASLEF decided on a national stoppage on 13 and 14 January, and a ban on overtime and rest-day working from 1 January. Unhappy New Year.

By now, with luck, the detailed story of the 1982 ASLEF strikes can only just be remembered by most people. I hope so. They spread sporadically over two weeks of January and February, and flat out for two weeks in July; but the contagion of threats and the strain of uncertainty spread over six months, hellish nights and days for the nation and its economy, for train travellers and freight customers in industry. The labyrinthine processes of negotiating procedures, the grotesque fixation on flexible rostering, the way that there seemed no end to the nonsense simply infuriated people. In time the struggle and the ASLEF defeat has dimmed into a longer perspective, and the railways were certainly the better for it. Look around you. It was a necessary journey through hell.

Often I hear this breakthrough by BR described as one of the early milestones in the Thatcherite march against the forces of trade unionism; BR was a starter in the saga of how the over-mighty barons of the TUC were to be humbled by economic realism and the new legislation. But that is not how it felt at the time in BR, nor, most railwaymen would say, how it actually happened. For one thing, the conflicts with ASLEF (and, it should not be forgotten, with the NUR) were before the laws on balloting for strike action. The conduct of BR in handling the strikes were our business, and the Thatcher government's part in the struggles were essentially two-fold: it kept out of the board's way in the fight, and it stood firm throughout. It was much more solid in support of the board and myself in the worst of it than were some Conservative backbenchers and some of the press. At no time was I nervous of my back, although my front was more than a touch bruised and dented. The Secretary of State, and the Prime Minister, did us the compliment of knowing that this was our fight for efficiency. We had worked for three years on our strategy for change. We in the BR board and management knew it was our business: the making and breaking of the 1982 strikes happened mainly on the rails.

This is what happened. Through the last years of the Seventies we had developed our strategy for changes in organizational and working patterns; our declaration of intent was made public and plain in our document, *Challenge of the Eighties*. We wanted to win commitment from the whole railway community but the possibility of major conflict with one or more unions was always there, from the 1980 negotiations onwards. Tension mounted from the turn of 1981 when the unions submitted a claim for a thirteen per cent increase. It was an inauspicious number anyway but particularly eerie in the middle of a slump, when freight and passenger services were losing ten to twelve per cent of their business, about par for the declining course of British industry in the bleak year of recession. We countered with seven per cent in April, and insisted that productivity improvements be linked with more pay. The unions had the right under the negotiating procedures, their holy sacraments, to go to the Tribunal, and of course they did. The Tribunal, under Lord McCarthy, awarded a backdated eight per cent and a further increase of three per cent to be paid in August. I was already heading for a half-year loss of nearly £40 million, and this award would cost another £50 million.

'Parker dug in his heels,' was what Sid Weighell said. I said that we would only pay the three per cent if we were satisfied with agreements on productivity. There were six specifics: first, fewer men in the cabs of freight trains; second, fewer men in passenger-train cabs; third, 'open stations', where tickets would not be collected at the barriers; fourth, the 'train man', a new grade to open up career prospects with the option of becoming a driver or conductor (this radical innovation would enforce a degree of collaboration between ASLEF and NUR); fifth, one-man operation of certain trains; and sixth, flexible rostering. 'Talks almost broke down when Parker demanded a much more precise form of words to cover each of the six productivity agreements.'

Much the fiercest fight at this stage was with the NUR, about the manning of freight trains and about running the Bedford–St Pancras electrified line with one-man operation; flexible rostering still attracted only the barest of mentions. The marathon of negotiation went on and on, and according to the NUR leader was the hardest in his life. It was not the hardest for me (that was to come) but it was certainly the most dangerous, because I had all three unions together at the barricade, fighting the changes. Two of them, the NUR and ASLEF, announced that there would be an all-out stoppage on 31 August. Press headlines were lashing both sides and lecturing us all on the need for common sense. But a week before the strike day, at the Advisory Conciliation and Arbitration Service (ACAS), a deal was done. At the settlement Sid Weighell spoke for the three unions: they would honour to the letter the understanding on pay and productivity. Dick Wilcox, our skilled and wise director of industrial relations asked the ASLEF representatives, the president, Bill Ronksley, and the general secretary, Ray Buckton, 'You understand what you are doing?' They said they did and they signed. As Sid Weighell said, 'There was no fudge there.'

ASLEF were agreeing to this statement: 'Negotiations shall take place to establish variations to the rostering agreements, with a view to introducing some flexibility around the eight-hour day, but without producing unreasonable variation in the length of each working day or week. These discussions shall be concluded by 31 October 1981.' This was the commitment to flexible rostering, this was the lit fuse.

Flexible rostering was common practice among the best rail systems in Europe. The international comparison we had commissioned through an independent survey showed that while we were above average in labour productivity per man among the ten most advanced railways in Europe, our freight-train crew productivity was very low. The fact was that fitting a driver's day rigidly into eight hours was surprisingly wasteful. Time had to be set aside for briefing and for rest periods, and still more importantly there was an agreement that a driver should always be able to sleep at home. This often meant that the second half of his day was spent travelling back to his depot on a train driven by someone else. The result was that, out of his eight hours, a driver spent on average a mere three hours and twenty minutes actually driving a train.

There was no way BR was prepared to accept that waste and argue for more investment. Why should the nation pay more if we did not help ourselves? What made the resistance to flexible rostering doubly futile was that its effect on the drivers would not be to make their lives harder. The economies it offered would instead make it possible to offer them better rewards and better working conditions, with a shorter working week, fewer unsocial hours and more rest days.

The summer storms of negotiations ended with resounding sighs of relief, and outright applause from the press. I even heard that Number Ten had a party to celebrate. But at our press conference at BR's Rail House one journalist came late into the packed room. He explained that he had been to the ASLEF press conference, and 'I have to tell you,' he said ominously, 'they sounded vaguer about their commitments than you sound here.' Sure enough, almost at once there were scuffling noises of retraction coming out of the ASLEF executive as Bill Ronksley and Ray Buckton started to wriggle under the weight of the new and historic commitment. By the autumn Ronksley was replaced as president by Derrick Fullick and the scuffling and wriggling behind the scenes became more sinister.

Still, for a while there was a momentum of hope. That autumn glowed with public approval of BR, beguiling us with its unaccustomed warmth, encouraging us and defrosting the host of rail projects which the months and months of negotiating had numbed. We were able to concentrate again on electrification, on a fresh deal for the commuter in London and the South East, on the cross-London link and on the ill-starred Advanced Passenger Train, the APT.

To my special delight, our campaign for the Chunnel was brought into the news again by President Mitterand's first visit to Mrs Thatcher in London. At the end of their discussions, there was a dinner for Mitterand in Downing Street. I was particularly glad to be there because I had been warned that the Tunnel, never a favourite item with the Treasury, was not likely to feature on their main agenda. In fact, the Tunnel had emerged as a major talking point between the two leaders of political opposites. Each naturally was looking for something neutral between the two countries and, naturally, that turned out to be the Chunnel.

I recall the evening as a glimmering oasis in the desert of nitty-gritty priorities of that time. Ministers and guests sat at five or six round tables in the grand dining-room which was full of fine old pictures – one of them, I noticed, of a brave British admiral, very young looking and with sword poised cockily against a becoming background of French fleets burning and smoking. Mitterand proved

BR Chairman deals with burning issues: signing a petition to preserve
the coal fire at his local station

a debonair star. I sat at Geoffrey Howe's table, with David Howell, the Secretary for Energy, beside me, neither he nor I having any notion that within days we were meant for each other (he was about to be moved to Transport). The Prime Minister read her speech carefully, allowing herself only one light touch: she thought the idea of a seven-year term of office on the French model had its attractions (only limited attractions, however, in view of her unprecedented electoral record since then). The formality of Mitterand's reply in French did not inhibit the direct and urbane toughness of his style; it was a golden crust of experience covering the usual rich stew of diplomatic things that have to be said. People liked him, our response was genuine; he felt that, and smiled genuinely at us. Still smiling and sitting, he said conversationally that the British were not always easy to understand, and he wanted to tell a train story. Geoffrey nodded to me as if to say bad luck, it was bound to happen to you. But no need for sympathy: Mitterand then told what is now one of my favourite tales of trains. In the war, he was a captain in the Maquis, the French underground, and in 1943 he had come to England for secret talks. For his return trip to France he was told to catch a train to Dover and from there he would be smuggled across the Channel by boat. Slightly dazed by the ordinariness of the arrangement, he was relieved to hear that he would be disguised for the train journey so that this route for returning Frenchmen was not observed. The disguise was simply that he sit in the corner of his carriage reading *The Times*; whenever anybody looked his way, he should raise the opened paper in front of his face. The strategem worked perfectly. Nobody even entered the carriage. Passengers appeared at the door, peered into the carriage, and passed on. Brilliant, the British. He folded his *Times* when he reached Dover, and as he opened the carriage door into the corridor he noticed that a patch of paper, blank to him from the inside, had been stuck on the glass. It said 'Reserved: One French Officer'.

During the drinks afterwards, the Prime Minister told me how pleased she had been with the final outcome of BR's summer negotiations. Although she has always known well enough that I am, politically speaking, a non-communicant, we seem never to have had difficulty in communicating in other ways. The clue to dealing with her seems to me to be that you have to be on your toes, like a boxer, all the time. She has a quality startlingly unusual in a woman: she is a bruiser, a tough, a thug even, and she enjoys a fight, confident she can punch more than her weight. This is not a matter of goodness or badness; it is simply a reality, and even in small talk you had better be ready for the swing to the point of the jaw. We were not to speak again for more than a year, much of it spent in a struggle with the unions in which, ironically, I was to be branded by ASLEF as Thatcherite.

By Christmas 1981 it was depressingly obvious that ASLEF was, as Cliff Rose put it, 'simply messing us about'. They refused to admit any commitment to flexible rostering, and flatly denied the essential connection between the summer pay deal and productivity. The only way for us to force that reality into the open again was to withdraw our own commitment to pay the three per cent, due at the end of the year, until the link was restored. There had to be a showdown which in all probability would end back at ACAS where the agreement on our six-point plan had been established originally. There the links between pay and productivity would be reforged and ASLEF brought back to order, through the industry's tribunal machinery if necessary. I had confidence that our case would survive the gruelling process of procedures, and it was vital to show the whole railway community that we were behaving justly, otherwise we would unite the unions against us. As it was, we had nine-tenths of the railwaymen with us. Trade unions are talmudic in their devotion to their constitutions and to their rituals of negotiation by the rule book, often infuriatingly irrelevant to enterprise in an economy struggling to hold its own in world markets, but I knew that we had to keep our nerve and survive the achingly long procedures if we were to keep TSSA and NUR on our side – and ASLEF isolated. That was fundamental. It was also going to prove very wearing and confusing to the customer and the country.

The next move was ASLEF's announcement of its New Year campaign of cancelled overtime with all-out strikes on certain days. This disruptive tactic suited ASLEF, a relatively poor union, and it totally discomfited the country. Calling these 'days of action' always impressed me as monumental cheek: days of inaction is what they were. The travellers' reaction was epic. Commuters responded heroic-ally, sharing transport, sleeping on camp-beds in offices, setting up their own flexible rosters for work. Their sustained support was cru-cial. I had always been told, three days of strikes and the commuter world will have your guts for garters. Quite the reverse: the commuters were determined to hold out. It was their finest hour. There was almost a wartime spirit on the rails in that siege of a winter with its heavy snowfalls. I have to say I felt no fatigue, no wobble of the spirit: there was a sense of certainty and comradeship. Only once I caught myself juddering. One night, returning very late to Minster from London, I found the telephone lines had broken down and I had no way to reach Jill. A car from Oxford could do no more than drop me at the bottom of the village's small hill, shining in the moony dark. With a bulky briefcase under each arm, I waded waist deep in the soft snow to our house to find that Jill had set off to find me an hour before. It took twenty minutes to reach the dark house. I had no key. In all those months of crises, I was seldom alone for more than a moment: now I was shaken to find how bleak I felt, how lost.

Blake wrote:

> If the Sun and Moon should doubt,
> They'd immediately go out.

There was no doubt in the BR Board and management. We had to stick it out. Still, we began to recognize that as public passions rode higher and higher, our case became blurred. Doubters in the media emerged: had we been guilty of fudging the 1981 agreements in the first place? Buckton, given equal time on television, insisted that pay and productivity were separate deals. In a three-cornered 'Panorama' interview, presided over by a reasonable and miserable Robert Kee, I had Sid Weighell raging quietly to me about Buckton on one side and Buckton enraging me on the other. The confusion grew over the weeks. There was understandably a run on public patience. Violent editorials urged me to close the system and have done with the union. But slamming the railways shut at that time would have been playing into ASLEF's hands by uniting all the railway unions and the whole TUC against BR. It would also have caught the government at an awkward moment of crisis. The fight had to be brought back into the proper machinery first, back to ACAS, back to the Tribunal, back to the agreement of 1981 and to productivity. Eventually, excruciatingly, it worked out just so.

By February we were back to ACAS, who promptly, as we wanted, referred the definition of ASLEF's commitment to the Railway Tribunal. They also, as we expected, said that we must pay the three per cent. Pat Lowry, the head of ACAS, met Cliff and myself before the news release: 'You'll have a bad time for a few weeks, people won't understand.' He was right. Buckton crowed over the three per cent: the drivers had their money and was that not victory? We had used the retention of the three per cent to bring ASLEF back to judgement but our return to ACAS was taken as a defeat. The public was cruelly disappointed in BR. Travellers had rallied to the battle-cry of nothing for nothing, and wasn't I paying three per cent for nothing? Industry too was thoroughly confused: what the hell was going on? Employers had been as stoic and warlike as anybody, but from their viewpoint all that had been achieved was that BR was trapped into the humiliation of a time-consuming, compromising tribunal. And wasn't it chaired by Lord McCarthy, and wasn't he 'on their side' anyway? True, Bill McCarthy was a Labour peer, but it was unfair to suggest that there was a crude bias in his conduct of the Tribunal: in any case there were two other members of it, one nominated by BR, the other by the union, and both were men of experience and calibre. McCarthy was a learned man, a scholar and a reformer with an eager mind and a shyness which sometimes spurted aggressively; he was also a lover of theatre and up to Mastermind-standard of erudition on the subject of Henry Irving in particular. A complex character, easier to like than to know. There was enough wrong with the negotiating machinery of the railways but it had little to do with Bill as chairman. I criticized it for being an excuse for delay; it was too easy for both unions and management to pass to others the hard decisions of economic efficiency. However, over the years the tribunal had been a general agent of change in the right direction, and while Bill may sometimes have been overgenerous in his awards, he was not over-tilted to one side or the other.

In those testing months of early 1982 I was unswervingly sure that, when our case was put again to the tribunal, it would see that ASLEF had failed to deliver their promises on productivity and must now do so. The trouble was that the tribunal took far too long about its deliberations. Weeks passed before it came to its judgement, finally justifying our charge against ASLEF. Perhaps Bill McCarthy felt a cooling-off spell would do no harm to the industry, but in fact the long delay damaged BR's reputation badly. We were left on the bare mountain of national disapproval and doubts for too many nights and days, and we were put through the wringer by the press, force-fed on a daily diet of damnation: we were knock-kneed, pusillanimous, gutless, incompetent. Ironically we were even damned with faint praise for being 'only any good really in the field of public relations' – which was exactly where we seemed to be fast losing ground.

One weekend, in the cruellest of months, April, I was roasted in a Sunday centre-page article by a Conservative MP; and while I was sizzling on his spit of scorn, there was a jolly cartoon above. In it, a soft, nude bundle – me – was being prodded into walking the plank by my tormentor, Buckton. However, no public service could expect any quarter from the right-wing press, and I took ample comfort from Dorothy Parker's reaction to criticism from an enemy: 'If you are wearing a crown of thorns, why should you worry about a little prick like him?' That afternoon I was surprised by a call from Norman Fowler, who was then no longer Secretary of State. He explained that he had just been lunching with the Prime Minister at Chequers. She had read this latest blast at BR and myself and had asked Norman to get the message to me that I was not to be worried by it: she knew what my line of policy was, knew where we were along the line, and supported it. I thought this an imaginative and generous gesture to make across all a prime minister's priorities, across departmental lines, and across political lines as well.

To make things worse, the NUR was stalling on some other points, particularly on the timing of our programme for taking guards off freight trains and some passenger trains. On both these issues NUR was being as tenaciously obstructive as ASLEF on flexible rostering. The trains built for the new Bedford–St Pancras line, where we had spent £150 million on electrification, were designed specifically for driver-only operation. The sliding doors could be opened by the passengers, there were closed-circuit television stations and a radio link between driver's cab and signal-box. At first we put guards on these trains, and so far from being worse off under flexible rostering they benefited by a shorter working week, more rest days and less clocking on during the deep night hours. In moving over to single manning, the board were offering to find other work for all the existing guards employed on the route. There was no way BR was going to advance further electrification schemes if the investment was not being efficiently worked.

The manning of freight trains was the other issue, and its importance to the NUR was as much symbolic as it was economic. The modern freight car was fully fitted with automatic brakes and a driver's safety device which could not be vandalized: over a period of three to five years, these technological advances offered potential savings of more than 2000 guards from freight trains and other trains not carrying passengers. The NUR had responded positively over the years to the new technology that had modernized railway signalling and track maintenance and renewal work, and manpower levels in BR had gone down by about 15,000 in less than the last two years. Now we needed to improve the productivity of train crews, and the board had always been willing to share some of the savings with the crews.

The spring of 1982 brought a very phoney peace. The tribunal

could not be hurried; it took its time and Whitehall watched sceptically, lobbing the odd-ball question like 'How long does it take to
train a new force of drivers?' We could hear the beat of militant tom-
toms in ASLEF and the NUR. The NUR had accepted flexible
rostering peaceably, but were not progressing towards the deadline
with our plans to take guards off freight trains, or accepting one-man
operations on the Bedford–St Pancras run. We stepped up the pressure by making a minimal offer as the basis of the annual wage
bargaining: we had already lost about £80 million through ASLEF's
seventeen days of selective strikes and we held to the principle that
BR could afford nothing that was not tied to productivity. BR was
owed productivity from previous years' agreements. The reality of the
value-for-money railway had to be rammed home. In the words of a
Guardian editorial: 'Sir Peter has given a clear and specific ultimatum.
Accept by 30 July and you gain five per cent increase. If you do not
accept, we will enforce flexible rostering, and discipline drivers who
refuse to work the new timetables. If strikes result, we will not leave
the five per cent on the table while we fight things out.'

It was not only ASLEF delaying my six-point plan. The NUR
militants were gaining ground and Sid, for all his vision and charisma,
was still not delivering on a crucial issue. Under no circumstances,
he wrote to us in June, was he able to discuss one-man operation of
trains. Nothing for nothing was my answer to that: and I would not
budge on the five per cent offer.

Then at last came the tribunal findings: unequivocally, ASLEF
were committed to the productivity agreements made in the summer
of 1981. ASLEF had been arraigned at the bar of the tribunal, and
the whole railway community had to agree that ASLEF had not a leg
to stand on. There was no longer a question of whether there would
be flexible rostering and abandoning the eight-hour day, but simply
how. McCarthy had repainted the goalposts, and people could now
see they had never moved. BR were now ready to move at once into
action by starting to put up flexible rosters at certain depots.

Almost simultaneously, NUR became the threat. Our stand on pay
had given the militants on the NUR executive a stick with which to
beat Sid. In recent years the balance of power had gradually moved
to the militants, who attacked Sid for being too close an ally of change,
too much of a collaborator with me and the board. In May, the
executive called for an all-out strike. Sid had advised against it; he

recommended instead a selective set of strikes, bringing out key groups such as signalmen. This would have been a nasty mess to contend with, but the extremists, perhaps overexcited by the climate of battles in the Falklands, wanted their national drama of a total stoppage. So the prospect of a war on the two fronts of ASLEF and NUR loomed before us.

My team was called urgently and regularly to the Department to explain our campaign. Were we not now faced with what we wanted least, an all-out battle against united unions? David Howell, the Secretary of State, kept a steady nerve in the midst of the uncertainties and held on to our assurance that while we were close to the edge of the abyss we were also close to a breakthrough. The militants were grossly overplaying their hand and underestimating our strength. This was the time when, understandably, the pressure of doubts about BR's competence showed most stressfully, not so much from the Department as through the Department from other and higher parts of the government. The stakes were high, if different, for all of us. As often in war, those closest to the action are most confident, probably for no good reason, because there is no practical alternative. After our sessions at the ministry, Bob Reid, Jim Urquhart, Cliff Rose and I would walk round to the nearest corner pub, the Barley Mow, for a quiet word and a quiet pint. In the worst of times, those were the best of times: I suppose our Barley Mow Club only met about three times but I can remember the fellowship of the four of us in that crisis as something of a joy in action. I have never thought that management is necessarily weakened by friendship and certainly the Barley Mow Club stayed in surprisingly good form. Others outside could see that the worst might happen, a war with the united nations; inside we were beginning to see that there was a way to win, and swiftly too.

We were sure the NUR strike would fall apart. The extraordinary thing was that Sid himself thought the same. A few days before the strike was to begin officially, he came to see us at Rail House one evening accompanied by his staunch president, Tommy Ham, and his closest trusty, Charles Turnock. They were all heavyhearted. The NUR militants, thrilled by ASLEF's ravings about a victory over the three per cent, were running wild, pushing their luck and even physically pushing Sid. There had been an incident when Sid had been shoved by 'one wild man', as he put it, who leapt over his desk to crash him to the floor. Charlie Turnock, an ex-commando sergeant-major, had sorted that out smartish. These three were reasonable trade union leaders, railwaymen who entertained no absurd hopes of breaking BR or derailing the Tories. I am sure they agreed with me that the militants were more interested in politics than the railways. Sid put it fairly and squarely: could we not offer something to his leadership to help keep the initiative against the wild men? I had to say 'nothing'. Sid was bitterly, bitterly disappointed.

'If you strike, you'll lose,' I said, 'and there's my evidence for saying so.' I pushed a file towards him. BR had developed a sophisticated intelligence network, with field surveys and independent opinion polls. 'We reckon you'll last three days at most, Sid.'

Sid did not touch the file. 'I don't need any of that,' he replied, 'I've already told them they're daft. And that they're going about their daft purposes in a daft way. But they're not listening.' I knew he felt utterly isolated in his executive, and now felt that I was letting him down. Hadn't we agreed from the start there was a mighty mountain to climb to get the railways right, that we were roped together for the ascent? When we escorted the NUR leaders out of the building and into the dim evening, Sid said, 'I'll never set foot in this building again.' He did, but not as general secretary, and only to say goodbye to me a year later when I was about to go.

We had to confront the NUR and win quickly. On 16 June I sent out a letter to the 225,000 members of the BR community – 170,000 railwaymen and women, and 55,000 employees in subsidiary companies. The letters were sent to home addresses, an unprecedented move in industrial relations. 'Make no mistake – if there is a strike, there will be no pay increase, no job to come back to for many, no prospect of investment in electrification.' A week later, on 23 June, I wrote to all employees again, at their homes. I headed the letter, 'You, your family and your job'. This was followed up with another: 'Dear Member of Staff, it is now one minute to midnight ... I am asking you to follow your own interests. I am asking you not to strike.' And then in emphatic blacker print: 'If you decide not to strike, the board will not accept loss of trade union membership as a cause for dismissal.' Battlelines were not clearly drawn. BR was breaking the principle of the closed shop, approaching the employee and the family directly and at home. The significance of the personal approach was described by the *Daily Express*: 'The Parker letter is potentially of

49   The Railway Board of 1979: *(left to right)* Jim Urquhart, Bob Barron, Bobbie Lawrence, Mike Bosworth, Sir Peter, G. Burt, David Bowick, Simon Jenkins, Cliff Rose, M. Posner, Ian Campbell, Sir David Serpell, Bob Reid, Viscount Caldecote, Derek Fowler, Lord Taylor of Gryfe

50   With Sid Weighell *(left)*, NUR General Secretary, at Frant, the union's training centre, in 1980

51 Certificate given to Sir Peter at the NUR Annual Congress in 1981 – the next year he was booed

52 Rail strike off! Tom Jenkins, Sid Weighell and Ray Buckton announcing the rail unions' acceptance of the ACAS peace formula, 21 August 1981

53 Light at the end of the tunnel: a Brunel drawing for the construction of the Great Western Railway (or God's Wonderful Railway) which hung over Sir Peter's desk at Rail House

54 Sir Peter welcoming the Prime Minister and Denis Thatcher to Euston in 1983 for the naming of Loco No. 86 311, the *Airey Neave*. Lady Airey is looking on

55 A BR Region farewell dinner in 1983 with Lady Parker and the London Midland General Manager presenting Sir Peter with *Essick's Catalogue of the Separate Plates of William Blake*

56 An engraving sent to Sir Peter by the Poet Laureate in 1983 for the farewell dinner held by the BR Board

57 Six BR chairmen on a London outing in a vintage carriage in 1984: *(left to right)* Lord Marsh, Sir Stanley Raymond, their host Lord McAlpine, Sir Peter, Lord Beeching, Sir Robert Reid, William McAlpine, host and chairman of Railway Heritage, *(sitting)* Sir Henry (Bill) Johnson and Sir John Elliott, chairman of London Transport

I have shared with Peter Parker his love of Railways. As he moves from the sto waters of office, I wish him tranquillity and prosperity — John Betjeman

STEAMTOWN CARNFORTH

58   Dinner at Lincoln College, Oxford, in 1983 to mark Lord Murray's 80th birthday and the launch of the Keith Murray Award. With Sir Peter *(centre)* are four Rectors of the college: Lord Murray *(fifth left)*, the Rev. Vivian Green *(fourth left)*, Lord Trend *(fifth right)* and Sir William Oakshott *(fourth right)*

59   *Below left* Back to Rockware and the promotion of bottle banks

60   *Below right* Sir Peter performing the topping-out ceremony of the LSE's new student residence in 1988

61 Katayama-san, chairman of Mitsubishi Electric (Japan), and Sir Peter break into a barrel of *sake*, the *taru-zake*, at the *kai-sho-shiki*, the opening ceremony of the Mitsubishi Electric (UK) factory at Livingstone in 1984

62 Tominaga-san, MD of Mitsubishi Electric (UK) sent Sir Peter this calm view as his farewell card

When you drive the hardest bargain with an American, he may cry, "You're killing me!" An Englishman may say quietly, "I'm cutting my own throat, you realise." We Japanese stay silent, but our minds go back to Kiyomizu Temple. There, in a place of traditional peace and tranquility, one can look over the balcony and see . . . nothing but a sheer drop to certain death on the rocks below. And we think, "With what I've just agreed to, I might as well have jumped!"

63   The Parker family: *(left to right)* Alan, Nat, Jill, Lucy, Oliver and Sir Peter

64   In the garden at Minster Lovell with his weekend briefcase of 'business and desire'

65 *Hone-shiba no*
    Karare nagara mo
    Ki-no-me kana

The brushwood,
Though cut for fuel,
Is beginning to bud.

revolutionary import. The head of a nationalized industry is telling his workers that if they defy their unions by refusing to strike, and if they lose their union membership in consequence, they will keep their jobs.'

Sid Weighell sent his counter letter to his members on 24 June: 'Dear Brother . . . Sir Peter knows that unless he breaks the NUR he cannot do the Tory government's dirty work.' And just to add to the garishness of the scene that day, I saw a newsflash reporting, of all people, Mr Fullick, president of ASLEF, pompously saying he felt there was still hope of a settlement of the dispute: 'We have a joint meeting of the Federation, chaired by Len Murray.' Mr Fullick, it was not reported, felt that Sir Peter Parker, chairman of British Rail, 'had not encouraged the union leadership to pull back.'

Pull back? Only a month before this cool effrontery, ASLEF had sent me the following letter which I have treasured ever after as a monument to irresponsibility:

Dear Peter,

I have received your letter of 19 May in which you advise me that you have convened a special meeting of the British Rail Council on Tuesday 1 June 1982. However, as our people will be taking a holiday on this date and our office will be closed, I am afraid we will not be able to attend.

Yours sincerely,
Ray Buckton.

Pull back! Backwards was certainly not the way we had to pull.

The NUR strike began on 28 June, the day that their annual conference was convening in Plymouth. This was a blessed coincidence which fatally weakened the grip of the militants on the executive. By the NUR constitution, while their conference of seventy-seven delegates is in session, the executive is dissolved and its powers of decision rest with the assembly. Sid, furious as he was with us, nevertheless seized his chance to mobilize the moderate majority against what he called a daft disruption. By a vote of forty-seven to thirty the action was called off. Within forty-eight hours, the strike had collapsed.

There was no time for celebration. Only hours after the NUR were due back to work, the ASLEF executive made a decision which was as stupid as it was deadly to their cause: there was to be an all-out strike of drivers to begin on 4 July.

For the past two months ASLEF had been stubbornly resisting the tribunal's decision on flexible rostering as totally unacceptable. The new rosters were already proving both workable and welcome to the NUR drivers, and we were ready to introduce them to the ASLEF drivers through a series of experiments on different services. A month was spent on the combustible discussion of just how this should be done, but it was time wasted. ASLEF had no intention of agreeing to any realistic experiments. What made this time particularly dangerous was that the separate negotiations with ASLEF and NUR were racing in parallel and it was absolutely essential they be kept apart: a combined attack by both unions would have been hard, if not impossible, to resist. And that was the same month when NUR was coming under pressure to resolve what Sid Weighell called 'the single biggest headache for the NUR', the manning of the Bedford–London Line's new electrified service, due to operate at the end of that May. A damn close-run thing. Throughout May those militant tom-toms banged away more loudly and more confidently than ever. The signals between the wild men in both union executives were not difficult to interpret: the militants' war with BR had escalated into the politics of trade unionism versus the Thatcherite government. Nicholas Jones, the BBC's industrial correspondent, wrote later, when the strikes were history: 'For management, the split between the rail unions had provided a classic example of how to succeed by a policy of divide and rule.' I had had nine-tenths of union membership with me on the strategy for change until ASLEF's refusal to fulfil the commitments of 1981. I had spent years of open management, consultation and communication to build up that support. I was damned if we were going to let the hard left rubbish that by their militant alliance between ASLEF and NUR.

On 28 May the board declared that flexible rostering would be imposed from 5 July unless, by 30 June, ASLEF had agreed on the experiments that were to introduce it. This risky timetable was based on a conviction that we could dispose of the NUR disruption swiftly, and the decision at their conference proved us right. While the militants in NUR were making the running, ASLEF had kept itself below the parapet as long as possible, but the suddenness of the collapse of NUR's strike seemed to panic the ASLEF executive. It lost its cunning and lashed out crudely at us, hopelessly misjudging our strategy and the swiftness of our waiting counter-attack. When Cliff Rose came into my room with the astonishing news of ASLEF's all-out strike, I remember him saying, 'They have come hard on to the punch.' I agreed and pointed to a Brunel drawing I had on my wall. 'I see the light now, don't you?'

Brunel's picture of a tunnel fascinated me. It was just one of the many drawings he made in the early 1830s for the design and development of the Great Western Railway. He was then only in his twenties. There had been no engineering endeavour in history on such an epic scale. He surveyed every inch of the immense adventure with his own eye. The hero was up at 5 a.m. for what was often a twenty-hour day, cloaked and on horseback through the morning mists, searching for what he was determined would be the best if not the cheapest route between London and Bristol. And we still use it today for the High Speed Train. Tunnels were tricky propositions in those days, not so much a problem for his engineering skills as a problem to sell. The politicians who had to agree the bills for railway development, and the investors who had to agree the money, were all nervous of tunnels, unfamiliar, unnatural, new-fangled, frightening things. The proposed tunnel through Box Hill was condemned in a Lord's Committee hearing as 'monstrous and extraordinary, most dangerous and impractical'. A witness imagined two trains passing in the tunnel: the noise 'would shake the nerve of the assembly'. Another said, 'I do not know such a noise . . . No passenger would be induced to go twice.' My picture showed a tunnel of delights, the lines thin, firm and bold as young Brunel himself, but the whole scene was softened and enchanted by a wash of stone colour for the arch-work and pale green for the trees and bushes on the top and the side. The daring innovation was made pretty as a picture: the tunnel straight, airy, with a round 'O' of pleasure at the end. And there is an extra master touch of marketing bravado, which gives the prospect a spacey, Chirico-like surrealism: the railway lines are not drawn in and you notice that long after the overall impression of a lovely clear view of a tunnel with bright light at the end of it. I had had the picture over my desk from 1980 onwards.

The ASLEF all-out strike began at midnight on 4 July. This was another national crisis caused by railways and the country was simply furious with ASLEF. Mrs Thatcher, in a speech at Cheltenham, invoked what she called the Falklands spirit. Even Ray, rhinoceros-skinned as he had become from the previous exposure, seemed stunned by the fury ASLEF aroused. He stayed in his bunker at Arkwright Road in the early stages of our communications battle and he took none of the initiatives of misinformation which he had launched to make the most of his surprise attack in January and February. We in BR had learnt from those wretched months of misunderstanding. We had improved our techniques of exposition to the nation at large, to industry and to the individual customer. The advertisements putting our case in the press were simpler and sharper; our sentences were shorter on television. And this time our intelligence was impeccable: we were able to monitor the shift of opinion within the union from the outset. Although only ten per cent of ASLEF drivers broke the union line to come to work we were able to interpret the considerable significance of this fact. This small fissure was a dramatic break in the record of proud discipline in the old tribe called ASLEF. Nothing like this had ever happened before, and our steady-eyed regular opinion surveys showed a real unhappiness among the rank and file. One outstandingly new tactic was a telephone information service by which any driver could call free of charge into BR to ask what flexible rostering meant for the individual on the job. While the war of words went on, we put up the rosters.

In those dread weeks of January and February the issues had been nothing like as clear-cut to the outside observers, or rather sufferers. This time ASLEF's reckless belligerence and their raving about derailing the Tories were patently offensive nonsense to any citizen: like the thirteenth strike of a clock it shook everybody's confidence in anything they had stood for earlier. The board was solid in its unity: you can do little that is great without a united board. David Howell, too, was a stout heart in it all, and Peter Baldwin as staunch as ever. But the crisis involved much more than the Department and the railways: all government was concerned. Inevitably and day after day our corridors were kept humming and buzzing with queries and theories and my room kept filling up with representatives of key parts of the government, including some of the advisers at Number Ten. What were the legal implications of suspending the guaranteed week? Would we be wrong-footed by injunctions? Would our challenge to the closed shop exasperate the other unions and force them into unity with ASLEF who were desperately keen to make this a fight for the survival of unionism? Buckton had issued circulars referring to my determination to destroy ASLEF: could we not train a whole new lot of train drivers? Sensible challenges, but sometimes, behind the probings, we knew well enough there were parts of the government who disliked railways, disliked me as 'not one of them' and doubted the competence of our management.

I cannot say that any of all this distracted us much, and only a very few times did I have to check my visitors with the obvious question: 'Who's running this strike anyway?' The hectic dangerous uncertainty from one day to another was some defence against interference: no one was going to take over the board's responsibility, at least not while the train was in the tunnel. Confident as the government was feeling after the triumph of the Falklands, there was really no serious shove from that direction, nor need for any. This was the board's battle, and we wanted to be able to win it with our authority reinforced within the organization, not weakened by any evidence of having been manipulated. At a meeting of the National Economic Development Council, in the middle of the ASLEF conflict, I scribbled a note to Norman Tebbit, then in Employment, apologizing for having had to cancel a meeting with him on training. I ended with 'See you soon then.' His note on the back of mine said, 'Yes – though if the press had become aware that you had visited me they would never have believed that we were talking about YTS (the Youth Training Scheme) or that I had not given you marching orders for your campaign! Norman.'

From the Labour side, the political messages were necessarily as divided as the politics of the unions. I had visited the TUC headquarters just as the storm clouds were gathering, on 7 June, to meet the Shadow Minister of Transport, Albert Booth, with a few Labour MPs and the union leadership. The discussion had given me the chance to stress that the board would seek no investment to modernize the railways until we had the prompt delivery of two years' worth of promises. Labour had still not tumbled to the hollowness of ASLEF's case. I could appreciate their confusion. The TUC had backed ASLEF in the January and February strikes, but then Len Murray had been a signatory to the ACAS agreement in February recommitting ASLEF to change. A new layer of confusion came when Michael Foot's speech at the Durham Miners' Gala was circulated: the text released to the press included something he did not in fact say when he came to deliver the speech, a passage accusing the board of 'an extraordinary desire to pick a fight with the rail unions'. This struck me as a black joke of the Left, pretty rich after months of toe-curling contempt poured on to me from the right-wing tabloids about our fear of a fight. Michael Foot and Albert Booth had been led into the trap which ASLEF had opened up for them: they were cast into the role of 'the strikers' friend'. Labour was caught supporting ASLEF defiance of a commitment to working practices which NUR was working. If ASLEF were right, then the NUR were fools, but in fact the NUR drivers were discovering that the new rosters really did give them the better working conditions and better rewards we had predicted.

The first week ended with a slow trickle back to work, remarkable in the context of ASLEF's record of union discipline, but still too gradual. Each day was costing BR and the taxpayer millions of pounds. We were improving our skeletal service marginally day by day but picketing and intimidation were intensifying. We kept up our equally intense campaign of communications, trying to reach the media, our passengers, our customers in industry and, above all, the strikers themselves through letters posted to them at home. According to our intelligence, we were making sense. What was the next step? Suspension of the guaranteed working week? Dismissal of the workers? The legal complications were horrendous, and anyway such measures would also close the ranks of ASLEF with the other unions. Therefore, in the second week, we decided to do the unthinkable: we made it known that we were about to close the whole system. The next day there was a turmoil of meetings between the Labour Party and the unions. From these, Michael Foot and Albert Booth came to my office minutes before the announcement of our decision to bring the shutters down. They proposed that we withdraw the flexible rosters put up at seventy-one depots because they were sure 'ASLEF was now ready to face up to their responsibilities', but their well-meaning formula meant nothing. It only echoed the ASLEF promises of a year ago. Michael rightly discerned that mistrust was the root of the problem – those gnarled, tangled roots . . . Their concern came too late. Albert said that ASLEF told him they did not believe the rosters we had put up were genuine rosters, and that really finished the interview. Those rosters were real enough. So was the decision to close the railway.

Len Murray at last started to move into action. His inaction to date had baffled me. I knew well enough that this sophisticated negotiator had been following each twist and turn of the ASLEF story from the bad moment he had too quickly been drawn into it to give the union his public backing in January. At the end of January we had a private meeting of minds reviewing the damage. Both of us were ready to resign if ASLEF's commitment were not made to stick: I because I had taken my stand on the rock of productivity, Len because he believed in the justness of trade union procedures. Therefore it was a matter of working the dispute back to those procedures – which indeed is what happened. Len and I had met and worked a little together over the years, and I admired him as a man and as a supremely subtle dealer. He was an artist of commas and colons, never allowing himself the luxury of a full stop, always trailing, like a tentacle, a thin possibility curling to catch the slightest chance of a trade-off – or on. The job of general secretary of the TUC is pretty well a conjuring trick, the nearest thing to the Indian rope-trick I have come across. It is tied to simply nothing up there. But Len's goodwill, tirelessness, selflessness and sheer decency were blessings that the nation hardly ever bothered to count.

I had valued some of those qualities during the lorry drivers' strike of 1979, when the NUR and ASLEF militants were stirring some troubles in BR. I had tried to make contact with the TUC but Len had been subsumed in the negotiations. At one in the morning I had a call from him at home and a detailed talk. He was to see the rail unions next day: 'I can get them over the first two hurdles you've described,' he said to me, 'you'll have to manage the third.' There was this man in the small hours dealing with what were relatively small priorities for him but vital for me, and in the upshot BR had relatively little trouble in that tumultuous time. Len could get no public thanks for his help, but his intervention, the generosity of his time, was typical of him. He was one of industry's gentlemen.

Perhaps too much so, I thought, when we reached the big emergency, the May days of 1982. Once the tribunal had ruled in our favour Cliff and I had sought a meeting with Len to make it plain to him that BR was determined to implement flexible rostering. We urged that he influence ASLEF to co-operate before worse befell the railways, the country, ASLEF itself and the TUC. Len was frank and aware as ever but, he admitted, helpless. He described ASLEF as unbiddable.

'But Len, you can blow the whistle on them. They misled you once. And if you did, the trade union movement would stand a damn sight taller in the country's estimation.' Len's reply was that 'They'll have to get deeper into the mess before I can do any good.' He may have had what was called in the old-fashioned phrase a first-class mind; the pity was that he had to use it in the old-fashioned context of the TUC. He could not intervene until the TUC reacted as a whole, and as he foresaw, so it happened: it was a real mess.

Setting the date for the closure of the system, like the sentence of death, concentrated minds wonderfully. Over the next few days, Len was not in touch with us but we sensed him moving behind the scenes. Two senior members of the TUC, David (later Lord) Basnett and Moss Evans, asked to meet me in an off-the-record session in my office. They arrived like medieval potentates. Cliff and I, keen on telling all, dived into details, but these were waved aside, rather grandly we thought. It was the broad scene they wanted, they said. David spoke in quiet tones and with a slow upward gesture of the right arm, lofty even. I had a sudden vision of medieval robes and the carefully raised fur-edged wide sleeves: these were barons indeed. But for all the calm mien and the ponderosity, it was plain that they both were alert to the peril to unionism and the nation. Something had to be done. They never said it in so many words, but we knew they sensed that the continuation of the ASLEF strike pointed to disaster for that union and for unionism.

During the second week a special meeting of the Finance and General Purposes Committee, the inner cabinet of the TUC, was being convened. By then ASLEF's resistance was cracking all round the country. On Friday morning, 16 July, our team, the war-party, was round in Marsham Street to keep the Minister abreast of the moving scene, and light was blazing at the end of the tunnel. As the day progressed, ASLEF was falling into increasing disarray. Cliff Rose was at the corner of our conference table, but his eyes seemed blurred and strangely discoloured, his face yellow. When he left the room, Bob Reid said to me that those signs, and the way Cliff had scratched at his forearms, reminded him of the jaundice he had caught fighting in the Western Desert in the war. The doctors confirmed

Bob's fears, and Cliff had to leave at the moment of climax, stepping out of the ring in which he had fought so bravely.

The Finance and General Purposes Committee of the TUC summoned all the railway union leaders to its Congress House. The day began as a farce, with Sid being ambushed by a mob of militants on the way in and needing police protection on the way out. Ray Buckton was cheered on his arrival, and that year's chairman of the TUC, Alan Sapper, General Secretary of the Association of Cinematograph, Television and Allied Technicians (ACTT), roundly restated his undying support of ASLEF. But for ASLEF the next twenty-four hours were to have the action, unity and doom of a Greek tragedy.

Each rail union in turn gave the committee its interpretation of the disastrous scene. Then the committee struggled for a compromise but finally had to make its way to the home of face-saving formulas in industrial relations, ACAS. From there, a feeler came through to me to see whether I would be prepared to join discussions. I answered that I was glad to appear but not to negotiate. I would come to explain, once again, not simply where we stood but where we were going: more flexible rosters and the fulfilment of the full 1981 agreement. And then we waited. And waited, for hours and hours.

It became a still, warm evening. With time heavy on our hands, we talked and thought of Cliff. For dinner, the war-party set out for a private room in the Charing Cross Hotel; it would be easy to get to ACAS in Lambeth from there. The press were thickening around the door of ACAS and also at the door of Rail House: our car left the garage by an exit out of sight of our entrance. Signals were waiting for us at the hotel, saying that it looked like 'a late one'.

After a bite, I slipped into a bedroom to have a nap. I am lucky the way sleep comes quickly, at the drop of a hat, in any free moments of the day. Like a filing cabinet, shutting drawer by drawer, so I shut up, sometimes even in mid-sentence, Jill tells me. That night I flopped down fully dressed, and the drawers shut easily. I had only been asleep half an hour and then – alarm bells, thrilling shouts, sounds of running. An outbreak of fire had been detected and in a few minutes the hotel was turned inside out. Our war-party mingled in the large crowd outside in the courtyard around the Cross. More hanging about. I learnt something: Charing Cross derived its name from Edward I's beloved wife, '*chère reine*'. And Nelson's column is the height of the Victory in full rig . . .

Fire engines roared to the rescue and soon, through the lit windows, firemen could be seen trotting calmly through the rooms, floor after floor – in short-sleeved white shirts, I noticed: could it be summer drill for firemen to keep cool in case of fire? Something odd there. And odd too that we had come to the hotel to keep out of the limelight, yet here we were lit up in a sort of Breughel carnival. We made off to the nearest hostelry which, totally inappropriately, turned out to be the Savoy. We dispersed as inconspicuously as possible in the sumptuous hall, and made camp. Jim and Dick, acting as our scouts, kept contact with BR headquarters and ACAS and reported our unlikely new base. It seemed an odd place to be fighting a battle to keep costs down. We hung about the lobby for about two hours while the TUC's committee were locked in their marathon session. We reckoned it was unlikely there could be a conclusion that night; better to take turns of rest in readiness for more tomorrow. Bob and I made our separate ways home and about 1.45 a.m. I tumbled into a bed that Jill had just returned to from a patient – she was on night call for the practice. Flexible rostering, my life, her life!

In moments, I was roused by a bell for the second time that night. Jim Urquhart was on the phone to say he thought we must reconvene at once. He had already alerted Bob. There had been a call from Pat Lowry's office at ACAS; nothing was certain but there might be an opportunity to set up conclusive talks between the TUC committee and the board. Right, of course, I should be there. When a strike is costing £5 million per day and it can be shortened by hours or even by minutes, it is worthwhile. We agreed to rendezvous at Marsham Street, outside the Department, parking our cars where we had parked about twenty hours before to brief the Minister. It seemed ages ago. Cliff had been with us then. My journey was shorter than Bob's, so we waited a few minutes, silently. I sat on the high stone wall running along the pavement, literally kicking my heels. There were no tactics to consider, no subtleties left, no angles, no more messing as Cliff would say . . . Two o'clock in the morning, a beautiful July night in 1982 and, I thought, the makings of a good party.

Bob arrived and we set off immediately for ACAS. Our session with the full TUC committee was brief. A large room, three sides of it lined by the rumpled shapes of the committee members. Some might say that trade union leaders don't often look like people but these did, tired, untidy, ordinary people. We made up the fourth side, probably looking like them, facing the chairman, Alan Sapper of ACTT, and Len Murray. Len did most of the talking for their side, and he was obviously looking for a fig-leaf to cover the ASLEF misery. Would we pull down the provocative rosters and start with a clean sheet? ASLEF was now quite ready to experiment. The room was full of many people I knew, sitting exhausted, grim, aching for an end to it all. They knew well enough that I would refuse to lower those rosters. There was no way that BR would reopen the railway without cast-iron commitments, and that meant their assurance that ASLEF would call off the strike immediately and cease the lamentable, lying propaganda about the 1981 agreements. They knew well enough, too, that I personally had fought hard for the reputation of public enterprise against the grain of Thatcher's government and that I believed in the future of the railways – that I wanted a modern railway with new investment but I wanted working attitudes to match. And that is what I said.

The war-party returned to an over large waiting-room – and more waiting. Len and the chairman came in again to clarify the practical steps we wanted to settle the terms. Then more waiting. Then a real dawn, through high windows, with the sound of mild thunder, growing louder. That turned out to be the committee on the march down the corridors, returning to Congress House. Hurriedly the parties agreed that there would be no public statements until the exact terms could be pronounced later in the morning.

Our war party left the building together, through an avenue of press.

'No statements yet.'

'But what's happening?'

'Breakfast,' I said, 'eggs sunny side up.'

That should have been Cliff's day. Cliff loved the railways – 'Mother Railway', as he called it in relaxed defiance of the professional managers in the corporation and the government who shirked the sentiment. He had hated the stupidity of the strike and the break in the railway community, loathed the breaking of faith which he felt had been ASLEF's curse on their great achievement of the 1981 agreement. He had fought magnificently, in good temper (far better than mine) and with unfaltering judgement. During that black and white Christmas of 1981 he had forecast the length of the struggle we would have, and he was right almost to the day. A manager of

Charlbury

```
15.00 dep. Paddington  arr. 16.22
15.31         "             17.52
17.00         "             18.20
```

Oxford

```
13.50 dep. Paddington  arr. 14.50
14.45         "             15.51 (change at Didcot)
15.00         "             16.03
15.50         "             16.50
xxxxxxx       "             xxxxxx
16.27         "             17.30
17.00         "             18.01
```

Cliff Rose

peace, he had been unshakable in action: our dove turned not into a hawk but an eagle. But alas, he was not there on the day the railways finally came through, to the triumph he fought hardest for. How much BR owed that man, then and now.

By lunchtime it was all over. I had headed out to Minster Lovell. Len called me there to say that ASLEF had accepted all our terms and preferred that he tell me of the capitulation. We spoke a while, and the last thing he said was, 'OK, Peter, that's it then. Don't shoot any prisoners.'

Cliff Rose died a year later. It was cancer.

11

No Music at Midnight

(British Rail 1982–3)

Starting to stop was the hardest thing I ever had to do in BR. The strain of stopping must be the same for everybody who loves what he does.

Discreet soundings were taken of me in the autumn of 1982: was I really set on leaving in September 1983? I had no doubts. By that time I would have 'done' seven years, and surely that is usually quite long enough for any large organization to have the same leadership. There are many reasons, some of which the leader would probably be the last to acknowledge. The main reason is simple enough: to give others room at the top. But then less obviously, creeping up the back of the leader's mind, there comes complacency, that soft-footed thief of time, a master of disguises of course, now looking like a lifetime of experience, now like gravity, or stability or unflappability. You find yourself losing time in defensive talk over past decisions, especially the wrong ones. You lose impetus as a starter, you look over your shoulder too often, reflecting and not renewing, repeating and not redefining, stroking and not spurring on, purring and not prodding yourself. So without noticing, you find the little fat thief is padding about your life and settling in like a comfortable friend.

We all know Napoleon's question about any candidate for the appointment of general: has he got luck? Less familiar is his answer when asked how long the luck of a general could last: six years, he said. Actually, I saw my seventh year ahead bringing me more of that precious stuff: it was not an ebb but an incoming tide of better times for BR in the Eighties. Still, there was no doubt in my heart that I should go; any temptation to stay was self-indulgent. It was not that I was fooling myself with a consciousness of duty performed, which according to George Herbert 'gives us music at midnight'. I knew something of my sins of omission and commission, and whatever history would make of my term of office, I hardly expected it to make a musical. The fact was that I felt incapable of adding anything new to the great party of the railways. The next phase of development and implementation in BR would be best in the hands of a railwayman and I knew just the man for it.

But there were two hurdles to clear before my exit. One was to get the long-term policy for BR set out clearly, quantifiably and publicly, to ensure it was defined with vision and pursued with stamina. Such a settlement with government had been my original objective in 1976. The other, equally ambitious, was a smooth change of gear on my succession. The last test of a leader is choosing someone to take over from him or her. For starters, nothing succeeds like a successor. These were my two high jumps in the final phase, and I nearly fell at both.

I had hoped that the years of hunting for a long-term policy for BR were going to end with the findings of the independent inquiry into our future set up in 1982, the Serpell Report. Certainly the report made an end, but not at all as either I (or, I believed, Sir David Serpell) had expected or wished. Instead of providing a calming exposition on what the role of an efficient railway might be and how to match that with investment, it provoked a first-class row, ending in a conclusive but second-class victory for BR.

The logic of events that reached their climax with the Serpell committee's appointment in 1982, and the strong debates over its results in 1983, was begun long before then; this was the real story of BR's psychological war to win back the hearts and minds of the public.

I had said from my start in 1976 that BR was the citizen's business. The backing of the public was the earliest step in the critical path to change. Modernizing the running of the railway meant changing attitudes in management and workforce and that could not be done without the co-operation of the unions. To win that, as the 1982 strikes were to prove, we needed to have the weight of public opinion with us. Also, modernizing the railway meant modernizing its assets – new trains and a new signalling system – and that meant a strategy for investment with a ten- to twenty-year horizon, which was just what no government over the previous ten to twenty years had been able to stomach. Post-war rail policy had only ever had the puff to run the gamut of strategic options from A to B. A was for *per ardua ad hoc*: it would be dangerously embarrassing in parts of the country, in rural areas particularly, to let railways die – so keep them alive, just, but certainly not kicking. B was Beeching.

BR had to break out from this narrowing view of its fate. We had to recreate the public's confidence and goodwill towards rail. This would be good for sales and would also better our political chances when inevitably the big investment decisions were brought before any government to be judged. After all, a popular, well-loaded train is full of voting citizens. So BR had to set out to revive the faith and pride of as many citizens as possible in their superb and miserably underrated asset. We had to make it plain that BR itself was a citizen active in the affairs of the public, vital to its future. That was the idea behind my creation of a BR department of public affairs. I had inherited a sophisticated public relations set-up, effectively run by Eric Merrill, but a policy was needed to expand that, to risk more money and people in a campaigning effort to connect with our many publics; Parliament and local government, Whitehall, employers, institutions, the trade unions and the TUC, environmentalists, people in education and the media – and the citizen. We were going to need the support of every available friend when the moment of truth came in the talks with our banker and shareholder, the government.

The conversion of the platitudes of good intent into practical plans and day-to-day programmes was a job for the experts. We developed some of these programmes inside BR and others with the help of professionals, in particular Will Camp, an old friend and the doyen of public relations in the public sector. At last the time of the professional communicators in industry seems to have come: they have arrived with the gliding rush of sequinned champions coruscating on thin ice to take a bow. Of course there are still uneven standards in the new function, but I believe a manager who has not taken the trouble to get the feel of it is ill-advised and, if he or she is to rise to the top, ill-equipped for the promotion. The public itself is rightly wary. It is coming to expect good packaging of products and politicians but remains more interested in finding out what is inside – I hope. A policy in public affairs can only be a thorough success if there is a genuine article of faith embodied in the message. Without it, all the expert plans and programmes will wither. In BR we had well-wrought statements and highly professional campaigners in the psychological warfare of enterprise, but we still had to achieve a genuine attitude towards change in our own railway community – once we had that, it would show through in a myriad natural ways as we went about our business.

Quite simply I believed that to capture the public interest we had to be a damn sight more interesting – the look of railways, for instance. New uniforms are hardly the stuff of history, but designing out the stiff lines of the early Sixties issue was an outward and visible sign of a change of spirit. Conventional wisdom told me that it would take four or five years to make the switch from that somewhat teutonic old-fashioned cut to a blouson style. Management did it in two. Also we saw to it that the issue of new gear to recruits was no longer in lumpy brown parcels, Pentonville-fashion, but on hangers.

If the cut of our job was worth attention, so were our manners. Trains may have their own mysterious charm, but our service could be downright charmless: there are definitely days on the rails when you have to be reminded to smile. We developed a wide range of training in various aspects of customer care and I bored on and on about making our travellers feel welcome. Smile: BR can do anything if it tries.

Brightening uniforms and service could only be part of the new look of things generally: we had to do something about the stations and the travelling environment. BR's expenditure naturally had to be aimed first at getting the passengers or the freight safely to their destination, and there was too little money left to do all that we wanted in order to clean and restore the stations. However we had to show willing. A new post was established, a director for environment, unheard of in those days of the late Seventies. Bernard Kaukas, a former chief architect in BR, had the nerve to become a one-man commando, and he more than anyone forced the environmental idea on to BR's agenda, where it has flourished since with resources far beyond any he was able to deploy. In war, to attack across barbed wire, sometimes one man throws himself on it so the others can clamber over him, and Bernard did that for our railway heritage. He was a starter in hard times when to advocate environmental standards was considered by some to be peripheral and pretty frivolous. He persisted bravely and inventively; extra funds were conjured from well over one hundred local governments by BR going into partnership with them, and matching pound for pound their investment in rehabilitating stations which once more could become centres of civic pride. He pioneered youth employment schemes to improve the landscape of stations, and promoted the use of some that had become disused (the Brunel Museum of Bristol is witness to that type of initiative). He also encouraged the upkeep of station gardens by the local community: I saw a note in the ticket office in Larbert, Scotland: 'Thanks for all the flowers. Please no more roses, we have enough.'

Even our new headquarters building had the odd touch of Kaukas in the night of economic constraints. Two pictures by John Piper were painted, one of the Brunel bridge and the other an astonishing view of the Firth of Forth bridge, painted at sunset and delicate as a cat's cradle of soft pink wool. Then he and David McKenna, chairman of the design and environment panels, invited Sir Eduardo Paolozzi to accept a commission for his first outdoor sculpture in England. We had decided that something was lacking in the appearance of our headquarters: we needed a contrast to relieve the strict Seifert architecture of the buildings – a cavalier gesture in the midst of all that functional dark glass. Paolozzi erected a massive silvery shape, magnificent, hypnotizing from all angles, to me, to the people in the offices around and above it, to the train travellers crossing towards the station, and to the man on the top of the Euston bus, although only when the view was leafless. 'Piscator' he called it, and he hinted that he was as intrigued and mystified by the name as I was. For me the shape was in two inseparable halves, the halves of our industrial society, the human and the mechanical, imagination and management, the individual and the organization, huge, rounded bones of shoulders topped by a tilting, precarious load of technological patterns and battlements. We see what we are, I suppose. There is a slight hollowing on one side, vulnerable as a collar-bone; it makes a shelter, a camp for the night on the bare mountain. Some dawn Charlie Chaplin might be discovered snuggled there, as he was in that famous movie, asleep on the statue in *Modern Times*. Or more probably, one might find Sir John Betjeman perched there, laughing helplessly.

Now there was a man: Sir John Betjeman, worth his weight in gold passes in the battle for the hearts and minds of railways. For me, John was a hovering presence over the railway scene, a friend, an inspiration, a sheer joy, and he became our 'third living loco': the first was named Harold Macmillan, the second, Lord Olivier, then came the good John. I called him the Poet Laureate of the Railways; he seemed to use them as a metaphor of life.

291

> The old Great Western Railway shakes
> The old Great Western spins
> The old Great Western Railway makes
> Me sorry for my sins.

One night, late, I went to join Jill at a dinner party and John was there. Late as it was, it was luckily still coffee-time. Guests were moving into another part of the room but John waved me to join him at the table because his legs were beginning to bother him. 'I walk like a crab.' I sat with him while he told me what a lovely job I had working with those lovely railway people, the best sorts in the world.

'You know, I carry a book by a railwayman around with me most days.' He pulled out a small book from his back pocket; it had a softish black cover. 'It was privately printed, *Prayers and Thoughts* by Walter Sinkinson, very Blakean stuff.'

Next day, I found out that this Walter Sinkinson was a retired signalman in the Midlands. I wrote to him at once that the Poet Laureate admired his work and carried it about daily; I'd seen the black cover curved to the pear-drop shape of the Betjeman hip. Coincidences piled on coincidences. Astonishingly, next morning, I received a letter from Walter Sinkinson, crossing mine. He wrote in an elegant copperplate script, telling me that he had heard me being interviewed about the railways and I had mentioned William Blake: would I be at all interested in poems and prayers which he tried to write in the Blakean spirit? Some were enclosed. They were truly Blakean, full of Mental Fight which is the delight of Eternity, the mystic dilemma of seeing a world perfect to the Vision and feeling a need to change it, descending from Eternity to Time. The ideas were firm and delicately stated, and on their foundation our friendship by correspondence developed, and came to include Bernard Kaukas who visited Walter, encouraged him, and arranged a small exhibition in Marylebone of the exercise books which Walter had filled with his crayon drawings. Then came the day Walter met John, another small mystery.

John had allowed us to use his name to re-christen the Restaurant at Charing Cross. It had been one of his haunts as a young man, a place where his group of friends would gather. It overlooked the platforms, a comfortable bar with a leather-bound series of books, the works of Ben Jonson; 'and there,' as John said, 'one used to have a drink and look out on to all the people going down to their trains, poor dears.' To make the most of the christening, we laid on an evening trip by special train, an observation coach, circling London, setting out from Victoria and arriving at Charing Cross for the ceremony. This weaving through the rushhour without once disrupting the normal service of the busiest network in the world was a bravura performance of traffic management, a pyrotechnical display of operational brilliance, which sent John into raptures of admiration at the skill and the daring of it all. He wrote to me afterwards of his delight with the tour, 'First the moon was on my left, then on my right.' But he also impressed the professional railwaymen with him as guides in the coach. 'He knew the network, the buildings along the line, everything,' one of them, an architect, told me, 'He even knew my father.' In his speech at the re-christening ceremony John was in full flight, when I spotted Bernard Kaukas with Walter Sinkinson and his wife in a corner at the back. We had invited them down to meet John although we had not given John any hint of the surprise. But, inexplicably, there was no surprise at all. Bernard brought Walter through the crowd, and before he could introduce him, in the midst of all that chatter and excitement, John stared a moment and said quietly, 'You must be Walter Sinkinson.'

How comes such a tiny moment in the hurly-burly world of BR? What is such a moment of hush doing in the middle of talk about public affairs? Giving proportion, sanity, joy, all the ingredients I wish in the middle of any busy manager's world. John loved the railways. His love was constant and, as with all his loves, in detail. He appreciated the railways by knowing intimately the work that went into them and the people involved in the work, just as his love of architecture was not for architecture pure and simple but for the way lives were lived in it, by it, for it. What he could express was what I felt, and what I thought the railway community felt, about the work they did. I have never known an industry in which more workers (and that includes the managers) loved what they did. In such a climate the growth of a successful policy for public affairs gave me a head start.

I set out to simplify and to programme the messages BR had to communicate in the late Seventies, and to do this I moved towards an integrated advertising campaign. Before 1979 BR used at least three main agencies. We decided to concentrate on one, and we appointed ABM (Allan, Brady and Marsh) after one of those agonizing 'beauty parades' of competitive presentations by a variety of excellent candidates – agonizing because so often those presentations are self-consciously over-rehearsed, phoney and artificial just when the client is seeking a real-life support system of wit and frankness. ABM was fresh and growing at that time, independent and with an appetite for the pioneering work we needed. Through ABM our commercial and our corporate programmes were each separately devised.

Commercially, the impact came from the unexpected slogan 'The Age of the Train'. We believed it. This may be the age of space and of robots, of microelectronics and of macroeconomics: it is also the Age of the Train. From the first it was proposed that Jimmy Saville should 'front' the campaign, and I was taken aback. I asked to have the market research repeated. It was, most persuasively, and I was proved completely wrong. Of the many television personalities 'tested' on the questionnaires, Jimmy came up trumps because of people's perception that he would only do what he believed in, whatever the money. Some television celebrities might do an advertisement for a fortune, or even a laugh, but Jimmy would be genuine. That was what our analysis revealed, and the years proved it to be so. Jimmy served BR with the unique fervour which he radiated on behalf of all his good causes. T. S. Eliot once wrote an essay in praise of Marie Lloyd, so fascinated was he by her authenticity, and there is that rare quality in Jimmy Savile. His character is an astonishing and shrewd mix of innocence and experience, something of a Shakespearian fool, God's fool, the responsible clown who fixes all your dreams, who is generously mad and who owns a pale, heavenly-blue Rolls-Royce and will give anybody a lift. And who loves trains. He fixed us cheerfully and firmly among the personal passions he devoted to hospitals and mental homes.

This was particularly so when we launched our programme to improve travel for the disabled. Our initiative was led by Bill Buchanan, a former Canadian Railways director in London who fell out of a tree in his garden and wrecked his back. I wrote to him with BR's best wishes, and asked him when he could be free and able to join BR to give us the benefit of his new-found skills. Bill came in his wheelchair, saw our problems in ensuring travel without handicap, and conquered them. From his chariot he led a charge of reform across the network, and nowadays BR is recognized the world over for its enlightened approach to disabled travel. I recall that at one of the points of breakthrough a ceremony was arranged to launch a discount ticket for the disabled. Jim came to it to wheel a disabled lady aboard, but her chair jammed in the entrance to the carriage. Hers was a normal wheelchair – that fact had been checked with her before the photo event – but she had had it for eight months and the frame had spread fractionally. After the obvious hitch, we squeezed through, but some of the press were ready to make a spoiling story of the embarrassment. Jim showed his temper with them, quietly and effectively. There was nothing but good news of the launch in the papers next day.

I invited Jimmy to my office one evening to meet some executive members of the board, and we surprised him by giving him a gold pass for the year. He had done well and been paid well for success, but I wanted to mark the extra dimension that he had added to his assignment, a quality of dedication we had not expected nor even guessed at. He refused the pass, or rather postponed it, asking if he could have it for the next year. For one thing he was too busy to enjoy it at the moment and for another he had just received an honour from the Pope. That was enough for the year; he'd prefer to save up the pass for later.

Parallel with the marketing of our services we launched a campaign of corporate advertising. This was a different, more dangerous venture altogether. We aimed to draw attention nationally to BR's achievements and its needs for investment if we were to do better. Nothing on these lines had been attempted before by any enterprise in the public sector. Our target was the opinion-formers, which we specified as politicians (especially Tory MPs), local authority leaders, heads of industry, senior civil servants, the media, and the travelling public, particularly the commuter. We budgeted a relatively small figure, half a million out of a total promotional budget of £19 million, for a twelve-month programme of advertisements in the press and on television. Our aim was to illuminate the fundamental issue of financing a modern railway.

Our first appointment as director of Public Affairs (and he is still there) was Grant Woodruff, a mathematician as well as a gifted communicator. On his wall he kept a map of commuter-land – the special target of London and the South-East – and on it, picked out in appropriately bright blue, were the Tory constituencies. Exerting pressure without alienating those in power was the political risk I took, and I took it as a personal responsibility: I have the scars to prove it. I vetted every word of advertising copy and even the format. My personal test of an advertisement, for any manager selling anything, has always been that it could be shown to friends in the living-room without disbelief, dismay or howls of derision. By that standard our advertisements probably passed muster and, according to independent research, gradually BR made progress. But there was proof, too, that I was not making the life of our own Secretary of State, Norman Fowler, any easier. I was told of one of our advertisements in the Cabinet room lying grimly beside the PM's blotter. I was sorry about that; I regarded Norman as an ally, but frankly that was the political risk. Our corporate publicity had never been likely to win many friends among the policy-makers whose investment policies we were putting in question. The objective was to create a new and warmer climate of general knowledge about BR so that when the day came when policy changed towards us – as it would and did – the support of railways would be welcomed by the citizen as good sense.

So we persisted. Each advertisement included a paragraph explaining our purpose and justification: 'An industry as much in the limelight as ours has a duty to address itself to a wider audience which needs to be well informed if it is to play its part in helping to form public opinion.' Our first effort in the quality papers was headlined 'How long can we go on running the most cost-effective major railway in Europe?' and the copy was serious reading. We quoted independent research to make the case that there was nothing freakish about BR's dependence on public payment for the social railway element of the business. What might be considered to be very odd, we suggested, was that on average the eight biggest European railways received twice as much in relation to their countries' gross national product as BR did. Furthermore, in Germany and France, government paid normally between thirty-five and forty-five per cent of total costs, in Italy nearly seventy per cent. Our twenty-seven per cent of turnover looked skinny, even 'mean' in the words of the *Financial Times*. Government's reaction to this initiative in public communication was predictably not marked with the slightest enthusiasm. However, we were delighted to find that its expressions of irritation were mingled with remarks of pride in genuine national achievement when our affairs next came to be debated in the Houses of Parliament.

Our next advertising shot was to promote electrification as the way to ensure the cheapest, most reliable railway of the future, 'the best hedge against any future energy shortage'. The third provocatively exploded in the no man's land of road and rail costs. We argued that the then average cost per mile of the sections of the new M25 (allowing for overheads) was £8.4 million, enough to buy four HSTs or electrify twenty-eight miles of route. This stirred up both the formidable road lobby and the Advertising Standards Authority who on the one hand upheld the complaint against us that our comparison might have misled people while, on the other, it rejected the challenge to our figures. I was rebuked, but still I was glad to have the evidence of a widening interest in us and in public transport: through it the country might be presented with more coherent quantification of road and rail projects. It was not a question of either/or; the fact was that the country needed more investment in both types of infrastructure. And while we were on the subject I had the opportunity of pointing out that a Mr Railway was available to answer for his sins, but who was Mr Road? Nobody. Roads were a large contingent in the Department of Transport, faceless and without a bottom to kick either. We went on with five more advertisements, and then began to alter tack after the government's announcement of its conditional commitment to a ten-year programme for rail electrification.

The standing of railways, according to the Opinion Research Centre, showed the strong impact of the campaign. There was a vast increase of questions on BR in the Commons, thirty-two in one day in January 1981, and half of them were to do with the lack of investment, our central message. Talks and speeches and press coverage showed that the facts and even the words of our advertising copy had permeated into the public awareness. The Secretary of State himself said, on Scottish television, 'In terms of cost-effectiveness, British Rail, I think, stands comparison with any other railway system in Western Europe.' BR itself was able to discern through the cuttings that Fleet Street was treating railways as a serious and deserving candidate for much higher levels of investment. The *Financial Times*, on 5 March 1981, published the analysis: 'In just eight months British Rail's corporate advertising campaign has created the desired impression in high places,' and 'The BR campaign is almost certainly the boldest, most vigorous and most skilled use of corporate advertising by a nationalized concern seen in Britain to date.' Since those days, corporate campaigning in the public sector has become as customary and sophisticated as it is in the private, and the government itself has become a heavy-spending exponent of the technique.

We did our best to reinforce the public interest that was aroused through a series of booklets on key themes for the future: on electrification; on improving the commuters' lot with a Commuter's Charter; on a new deal for London and the South-East; and on a Cross-London Link, reopening old tunnels beneath the metropolis. We also launched our booklets on the Channel Tunnel – the first signs of resurrection after the project had been 'killed off' by the Labour government in 1974. All these developmental strands were woven into one comprehensive document called *Rail Policy* which emerged in the tense spring of 1981 when swallows and strikes were in the air. The title was somewhat in the humorous vein of Gandhi's answer when asked what he thought of western civilization: he said he thought it would be a good idea. This was the BR Board's own declaration of possibilities for rail in the Eighties, a declaration of faith. We foresaw by the end of the decade electrification well into its stride; new electric rolling-stock ordered for commuter services; refurbishment of stations; specially designed trains on the line to Gatwick – and among other splendours it was hoped that by 1990 the Channel Tunnel would be imminent. BR, under Bob Reid, has since scored most of those winning goals: the future of rail in the Nineties is more promising than it has been for a century.

The one spectacular miss-hit was the Advanced Passenger Train. One of three prototype APTs stalled in the snowy December of 1982 on its maiden public debut. *Private Eye*'s cover announced: The APT arriving at Platform 4 is fifteen years late.'

In the late Sixties this breathtakingly original vehicle had been conceived in the highest hopes. It was to be the British solution to a need recognized worldwide for a second generation of fast trains to succeed the high-powered diesel and to compete with the airways. In 1968 Lord Marsh, then Minister of Transport, agreed two major research projects for BR. One grew up quickly, the very successful High Speed Train capable of 125 m.p.h. It was introduced into service in 1976 and was hailed as the climax of conventional suspension and diesel technology. The other, the APT, was in fact inspired by the experience of its competition, aeronautical technology, and was designed to travel at 155 m.p.h. Its attraction was not only its speed: it was meant to cope with BR's natural disadvantage, its curvaceous track, roughly fifty per cent of it on a bend. This was to be achieved through a revolutionary gyroscopic control that would allow the train to tilt to take the curves at speed. Japanese and European railways were able to invest in straightening and strengthening their tracks: BR could not go for that expensive option. It had to use the existing infrastructure, so it designed a train that could negotiate corners at a speed a third higher than the normal vehicles without more money being put into the lines.

This, as my predecessor described it, was a massive breakthrough, and throughout the Seventies its development was one of the wonders of the railway world. According to Marsh, Britain was probably eight years ahead of any other railway with this sophisticated equipment. But its development was harassed and inhibited by 'all the changes in investment policies'. I suspect also there was a clash of managerial wills, between those who felt safer with the older technologies and those who came to BR's Derby Research from outside the industry, with what the old guard regarded as new-fangled theories and airy aeronautical ideas. Whatever the reasons, events proved that BR, under economic pressures, had not been able to work out the essential managerial equations basic to any macroeconomic project of innovations: if you want to go to the moon, you have to see that the quality and quantity of resources are calculated to match the high endeavour (as, in fact, the Americans did). There is no point in wishing for the moon and not willing the resources, and the British tend to do just that. That is why so often we have failed to exploit commercially the originality of the British invention. The total investment costs of the APT were £37 million: if it had received a fraction of the funds that went into Concorde the saga would surely have ended differently.

My board, led by Ian Campbell, vice-chairman and executive member for Engineering and Research, concentrated meagre resources to bring the prototype designs to completion. Secret test runs during 1982 went encouragingly. There was even a trial which rehearsed a royal journey and Ian went off one day 'to be the Queen'. That afternoon he rang me to say that the Queen had come off the tracks, skidding parallel to the line for some hundreds of yards. No harm done; very stable and stately the whole mishap, but that was little comfort. The critical difficulties of braking and tilting still bedevilled the venture. Gradually they were overcome, confidence grew again and the day came for a trial public run. It was scheduled for early December 1982, before snows were usually to be expected, so the experts told us. The gleaming express, packed with officials and media and the first fare-paying passengers, pulled out (before sunrise) from Glasgow Central Station on 7 December. It completed the four-hundred-mile trip to London in four hours, thirteen minutes and fifty-nine seconds, arriving one precious minute ahead of schedule. It had driven into the record books – almost an hour and a half quicker than the regular inter-city service – and had set a new speed record of 137 m.p.h. for a train with paying customers aboard. The passengers' own reactions were anything but unanimous, varying from 'wonderful' to 'queasy-making'. The swinging tilt had startled everybody: 'We must get used to having our breakfast seeing the ground out of one window and the sky out of the other.' The *Guardian* reported a stoical stewardess who, when asked how she coped with it all, announced 'I just stand there with my legs open.' But on the whole the press of 8 December was exhilarated and pleased. The trip from Scotland had been a triumph.

The trip back was doomy, and the press on 9 December reported every grim detail of the struggle through the Arctic conditions of a surprise blizzard, the worst in fourteen years and completely unforeseen by the Meteorological Office. The APT could only limp home, well off its schedule, although still faster than the regular trains. But much worse, the tilting mechanism had worked irregularly and this was a *coup de grâce*.

Private Eye's awful, accurate cover stays with me still:

'Welcome aboard the APT, stopping for repairs at Penrith, Crewe, Glasgow, Penrith, Crewe . . . '

'Waiter, have you seen my sausage roll?'

'Yes, sir, it's the tilt mechanism.'

We could not protract the development any longer. We had to go firm on our fleet strategy for the late Eighties. There had to be something ready to take over as the HST aged and our electrification programme was widely introduced over more of the network. The APT has been too long in gestation, too ambitious in a thousand innovations, and steadily under-resourced. The technical lessons of advanced design were no doubt valuable to the work on the next generation of inter-city trains but this was a defeat, all the more bitter because I had overexposed the promise of the APT. Its failure winded BR at the wrong time, just as we were rebuilding our fortunes.

All in all, however, because so much has been achieved, *Rail Policy* reads pretty well now, far better at the end of the Eighties than it did at the beginning when we offended Whitehall by daring to publish it. At the time, it seemed to many strident and over-optimistic, and it fell flat with the government, who never replied directly to the document. But the board was not to be deterred and insisted on pressing the long-term issues at every opportunity. Eventually, in the early summer of 1981, there was an unprecedented encounter between the full board and the Minister in the department. Unprecedented and uncomfortable, but fruitful, because as a result of it the Minister agreed that there should be an independent look at future funding. Months passed and then the Minister himself passed on. There was, however, no lack of short-term excitements to fill the lull in our battle for the long term. This was the time when the industrial relations field was turning into a killing ground of hopes for a peaceful outcome to our negotiation for change. Despite the current dramas, the board persisted with its stand that strategy should not go into eclipse, and about a year later, in 1982, we had another encounter between the Minister (now David Howell) and the full board. The aim was to refocus on the need for an independent enquiry, and after that outspoken session a chairman was appointed within days: Sir David Serpell.

Everybody but David Serpell himself felt this was an ideal selection, and it came from that steady fountain of ideals, Sir Peter Baldwin, the Permanent Secretary. The signs seemed auspicious. David Serpell was on the BR Board and had been for many years. Before that he had been Permanent Secretary at the Department of Transport. His acute judgement on the board was respected; he was tireless, fair, gently ruthless if necessary, and deeply committed to BR's battle for the future. Throughout his years as a member he would send communiqués to his colleagues on exceedingly old but relevant sepia postcards, and what was on them was always witty, funny and fresh as war paint. He was anything but eager to take on the burden of the enquiry. He complained that he was beginning to creak like the stairs in his home in Devon, where anyway he should be spending more time with his wife. Also he would have to establish his independence as chairman by leaving the board, and he truly enjoyed the board as much as we valued him. So David Howell, Peter Baldwin and I met him in the Minister's office in the House, and we pushed. This paragon of public service said yes, an act of sacrificial generosity.

David and I stood together, just the two of us, outside the Commons, and the evening air was spring-like, the light the colour of pale dry sherry. David beat me to the thought by inviting me to his club, the Oxford and Cambridge, where, even better than sherry, we had a glass of champagne. We were heading from the club lounge and down the stairs to collect another glass when we met Peter Baldwin on his way up, smiling. 'I was looking for you both, and thought I might find you here. May I join you?' That was the mood, promise-crammed: we were all delighted at the prospect of the review.

But through the rest of 1982 the plot thickened and curdled horribly. Two other committee members were appointed, to make up the Serpell Committee, and one of them put in his own minority report at the very last moment. The final outcome was not what BR, the Department or Sir David Serpell himself had wanted, and its publication at the start of 1983 provoked a furore. Instead of firm recommendations on the future railway and its funding, it had become embroiled in the too familiar urgencies. Its findings, weakened by the minority report, were not conclusions or recommendations but options, and some of these made scary reading for politicians who were just beginning to groom themselves for the General Election. David Howell did his best to defuse the debate by eliminating the wilder possibilities of a skeletal BR running on high fares, but too late, the options were in the open fire. The media were full of them.

We had to counter-attack promptly, challenging the methodology and especially the limitations of the report. It gave no consideration to the quality of services, only to economics. It made no adequate reference to the study of international comparisons. It failed to acknowledge the pace of changes already in hand: we had been shedding jobs at the rate of 1,000 per month for two years and already 24,000 jobs had gone, out of our 1985 target of 35,000. And the report was no help at all over a most critical component of BR's future, electrification. At the same time, we affirmed its positive elements, of which there were many in danger of being submerged by the immediate headlines about optional cuts. Inevitably and fatally, the authority of the report had been weakened by its minority submission, by its awkward offer of options to politicians thinking about other things before the General Election, and by the outburst of public opinion:

the citizen was not happy that the railways should be doctored yet again.

Still, the sound and fury around the Serpell Report signified something. When the controversy subsided BR stood the stronger for it, its strategy and its network intact and even endorsed by its fierce rejection of confusing alternatives. Agonizing reappraisals had been made, a series of hostile alternatives to BR's policies had been exposed and tested to destruction in an intense national debate. The result did BR a power of good. I was able to write into my final corporate plan for 1983–8 the major assumption that there would be no 'fundamental changes in transport policy' and BR could now get on with it. 'The aim of the Plan is to take the business out of recession through increased volume and improved labour and other productivity, leading to a reduction in real terms of the cost to the taxpayer. It indicates that rather an attractive prospectus is achievable.' Serpell had cleared the air after all.

All the same, there had been some nasty moments in the process. For the second year running, in the heat of the kitchen, there had been a meltdown of my reputation in the right-wing press. On 27 January 1983 the *Daily Mail* had a banner headline, 'Angry Howell Pushes Parker Into Sidings', with the industrial editor revealing all:

> British Rail chairman Sir Peter Parker is expected to be shunted out of his £60,000 a year job later this year. Sir Peter, who had helped to lead the railways into a bright new future, infuriated Transport Minister David Howell with his savage denunciation of the recent Serpell Report . . . In what appears to be a face-saving exercise, Sir Peter hinted on Tuesday that he may not serve another term. But a senior rail official told me, 'It has all the marks of a political assassination.'

The word that came to my mind was 'sic'.

The truth was that throughout that period of rumpus I had been working with the Department's appointed headhunter to find my successor, according to our agreed plan of three years before. As the search widened, I must have been rung at least a dozen times over as many weekends by friends asking the impossible. 'Sounds like another of the heavy breathers on the line, Dad,' was the way my boys would call me to the phone. Then would come the impossible question: 'Off the record, Peter, I've had this approach, and I thought

I'd ring and have a quiet word. Can you tell me about the job, what's it really like?'

In fact, the telephone went on humming and ha-ing alarmingly for far too long. I did not like the sound of it at all. Good friends, all, but none of them my choice for the job. My hope was Bob Reid. He was the only candidate from inside the railways with a chance, and this would be his only chance – that had become part of my reason for going. Bob was older than me but had years of steam, or rather electricity, in him yet. If the railwayman was passed over this time round, it could be many years before there would be another opening for a rail chairman from the industry.

I was well aware that there was prejudice in high places against any candidate from within the railways. After all some of the closest advisers to the Prime Minister were well-known knockers of rail. Sir Alfred Sherman, the severest of critics, who even wrote the odd leading article for the *Daily Telegraph* on railways (indeed some of the oddest), was obsessed by the idea of concreting over our tracks to make roads. The only and final answer to Alfred proved to be to take him seriously. I solemnly issued a challenge: we would commission independent research into any project of his choice for concrete conversion on condition that he accept the findings. Alfred agreed the terms and the study came out favourably for us. Alfred honourably shut up. Has anybody heard any more on the subject which had been rattling along for years? No.

Of course, in the last analysis, the appointment of chairman would have to have the approval of Number Ten, and the question that was always asked was, what was Mrs Thatcher's attitude to railways? Years before, she had come to luncheon with us at BR as Leader of the Opposition, accompanied by Norman Fowler, then the Shadowiest of Transport Ministers. She had talked to us about nationalization with a hearty, dismaying adamancy: to be nationalized, she explained, was an industry's admission of failure. She did not spell out the implication, that – well chaps, it must follow surely – only failures would work in the public sector. However, these general views of hers were well enough known, and were not specifically directed against railways. In the event, as the Conservative manifesto of 1979 revealed, there was almost a bipartisan policy for BR at the time. She had made one brief personal criticism about travel by rail at that luncheon, about her dislike of open carriages and their lack of privacy, but I explained that market research had positively confirmed that the public, on balance, preferred the spaciousness of the coaches, that families with children felt freer and women travelling alone felt more secure. The matter was discussed without much emphasis and our curiosity about her personal feelings for our particular mode of transport was not aroused.

However, as Prime Minister her attitude became curiouser. Mr Ashton, MP for Bassetlaw, asked a question in the House on 20 July 1982: when had the Prime Minister last travelled by train in the course of her official duties? Hansard records: 'The Prime Minister: Since taking office I have not travelled by train.' There were many interpretations of the mystery. One, I found, was part of the folklore in the railway community. When she herself had been Shadow Minister for Transport for less than a year in the late Sixties, she had been invited to address a course of BR senior management at our British Transport Staff College. She sailed into the lecture room just as Mrs Spottisworth had come sailing into the room according to P. G. Wodehouse in *Ring for Jeeves*, 'with the confident air of a woman who knows that her hat is right, her dress is right, her shoes are right and her stockings are right.' While Mrs Spottisworth had the additional confidence of 'a matter of forty-two million dollars tucked away in sound securities' Mrs Thatcher had easily the equivalent in knowing she was right and the railway managers were wrong. The result was that the session became a row which blew up to the top where Sir Henry Johnson was then sitting as chairman of BR; he eventually extracted an apology through Ted Heath. Maybe that never happened; there was a discretion that shaped the end of any evidence about it, yet even as fiction it shows how hard imagination in the railway community was at work to explain Mrs Thatcher's legendary antipathy to trains. Naturally, I regretted her habit of not catching trains: bad luck on BR, but with the complexities abounding in the life of a Prime Minister, it seemed fair enough to me that her taste in travel should be thoroughly indulged if that made the burden of her extraordinary schedule more tolerable. Furthermore, whatever fun the media made of all this, it would have been bizarre to think she would allow personal factors to weigh in the matter of high policy and public transport. And anyway, in other ways, the Thatchers had good railway connections.

I came to meet Denis Thatcher a few times, and it was easy and enjoyable to talk business and rugby with him. Business, because he was the chairman of Chipman's of Horsham, a Burmah Oil subsidiary manufacturing chemical sprays which BR bought to keep down the weeds on railway banks. BR must have been one of his company's biggest customers, and when I visited the Chipman plant I inspected the spray-wagon that was used on our tracks. And rugby because he had been a first-class referee of the game: he adored the sport and for many years must have given up his weekends to it. We discovered games we had in common, games he had refereed and in which I had played at Goldington Road for Bedford and the East Midlands. It struck me that there was a certain poignancy in my relationship to both Thatchers as whistle-blowers, one after the other, in my career.

It was only in the last year that the PM's separateness from trains really began to tell on me. It dawned on me that her approval of a railwayman as chairman of BR was increasingly unlikely unless she had met one. I had to find a natural break for that to happen, and BR owes a great deal to a railway enthusiast, Mr Richard Clayton of Farnborough, for the break we so badly needed.

Mr Clayton had read Airey Neave's book about his escape as a prisoner of war from Colditz, *They Have Their Exits*, and he wrote to the Prime Minister to suggest to her that a train be named after him. The letter was passed on to me. In fact, Airey Neave was already on our list of 'possibles' for a naming. We had a number of categories for commemoration: his was in the category of courage. Trains had furnished his escape route across Europe and on his return he had been debriefed on the second floor of our railway centre of operations, No. 222, Marylebone Road. We chose a loco', Class '86/3, destined for the London to Norwich route which was being electrified. It was a line which Airey Neave knew well as the route to his family home at Ingatestone in Essex. I wrote to invite Mrs Thatcher to speak at the ceremony and, together with Lady Airey, to name the loco' at Euston on the very day of the year he had reached the station at the end of his epic escape, forty-one years before. She agreed at once. But then, just a few days before that date, she announced an even more important one, the date for the 1983 spring election, and we heard that her own campaign was to begin on the day of the unveiling. As I expected, I was then told that she had to pull out of the luncheon the board was giving to the Airey Neave family – and at which she would have met Bob Reid – though she could fulfil her part in the ceremony in the half hour available.

Railways handle state occasions with the awe-inspiring aplomb of a long tradition which is splendid, imaginative and very careful. The siding at Euston was bedecked in high old style, blue hydrangeas along the platform, and a blue, not red, carpet. Intense secrecy surrounded the arrangements, and security ringed the crowds that had arrived for the event, which after all was horribly linked with the IRA and their murder of the man we were to celebrate. Outside in the street there were demonstrators yelling. Inside the station the ceremony was quiet and touching. I noticed, standing behind her, that the PM had handwritten her speech notes as I had mine. Both the PM and Lady Airey were most moved as, for the first time ever, two people shared the unveiling, each taking a cord either side and drawing open the curtain to show the steel plaque and the handsome lettering on the loco'. We tried to relax a moment after that. Then I said that it was the custom to have a word with the driver, and her shoulders hunched. 'It's all right,' I continued, 'I think we've chosen a driver who votes for you.' She climbed into the cab cheerfully, and was sitting in the driver's seat and chatting with him by the time I brought up the rear of our small posse.

The driver was very much at his ease, standing at the back of the cab while the PM at the controls responded to photo calls. He said suddenly, 'But you don't like railways, do you, Prime Minister? That's what they say, you know.'

'Ah, I've told your chairman about that – the open carriages don't suit me.'

That took me years aback. I joined in. 'You'd find we see that Prime Ministers aren't disturbed and are given the privacy they need.'

'A good thing,' and she clambered down from the footplate, handshaking and waving. We stood together for a moment in a small huddle to keep away the long microphones poking their pockmarked noses into the conversation. Sir Robert Lawrence, my BR deputy chairman, was acting superbly as usual as the Earl Marshal of the programme, and he was signalling to me that the PM's half-hour was up.

'What are you planning to do now?' Mrs Thatcher asked me.

I explained that when she departed there was to be a luncheon at Rail House for the Airey Neave family, and a 'celebratory glass of champagne before that'.

'Well,' the Prime Minister said, 'I could do with a drink myself.'

For me, that was the most delightful surprise in a last year full of them. It meant that after all there was going to be a natural opportunity to introduce a few railwaymen and one in particular. The only problem was to get to Rail House ahead of her; we had no special security laid on there for a Prime Minister's presence. She stepped into her car and glided away. Seconds mattered. Bobbie Lawrence came to the rescue; he used the intercom to contact the escort vehicles ahead of her and efficiently slowed up the progress of her caravanserai. My own car was some distance away. Then I noticed Jill talking to Denis Thatcher who had characteristically turned up to the party self-propelled, or to be precise, in an experienced-looking station wagon loaded with his golf kit. 'He'll take us,' Jill called to me, and I saw her helping to make room by swinging a suitcase off the back seat which was covered in not-very-new tufted yellow nylon. Denis, with his detective beside him, sped through the formal checkpoints and manoeuvred nimbly through the string of black limos which had been slowed to the pace of dignified hippos. He rounded the awkward driveway in front of Rail House, ahead of the PM. 'Told you I'd do it for you,' he said to me, tossing the keys at an amazed commissionaire, and so he had. He had given us a few seconds of crucial lead time.

The surprise party stretched to forty-five minutes. The PM relaxed, chatting to people around the room, and met Bob Reid. I often wonder if an elaborate system for management succession can possibly survive any engagement with the reality of sheer luck in business. Certainly Mr Clayton was a piece of the sheerest luck, and just in time. All that was in May 1983. Time was running out. I was leaving in early September and there was still no announcement about my successor.

In the ministerial reshuffle after the election there was yet another change of Secretary of State. David Howell was out and Tom King came in, with a very direct, executive-minded, no-nonsense, studied let's-get-on-with-it look about him, forearms flat on the desk. 'What can I do to help?' he asked.

'One thing above all. Settle the succession,' I answered and I repeated my recommendation of Bob. Bob was the natural. He had been in the thick of the radical reform over the years. Widowed, dedicated, proven, his age had only sharpened his appetite for changes, and two fundamental advances owed much to him. It was Bob who had established the marketing function for me at board level, and it was Bob who as much as anybody had contributed to the fulfilment of the principle of smaller groups in BR by the creation of the business sectors of Inter-city, Network South-East, Provincial, Freight and Parcels. Different as we were in style as managers, our partnership had worked well and most friendlily, and it was the difference between us that convinced me that Bob was the right next-man-in. Railways could do with a quieter time, a quieter man. The corporate plan of the board for 1983–8 was set, and in the plan was the firm basis of the contract I had sought from the start between government and railways. Bob would deliver its promise, I was sure of that. And if all that was not enough, he was not 'political' as I was: he was 'one of them'.

I waited for the decision on the chairmanship with more anxiety than I had known in my seven years. I had argued publicly for continuity of BR policies, but I can see now, ex-post, that I was probably as selfishly anxious about myself as I was about my successor. If an outsider had taken over I would have had to admit to a failure. I had myself declared that the appointment of an outsider to a public sector job could be interpreted often as a declaration of doubt in the top policy and people. I had become inordinately proud of the BR management and board and I was seeking a confirmation of confidence in them from the shareholders. July was a murmuring month, and gossip flowered exotically through the summer. A senior Tory backbencher was strongly tipped but a counter-rumour suggested that this was unlikely after all. The uncertainties caused by a by-election would be a bit embarrassing. I was into the last month. Tom King and I found ourselves engaged in vague talk about me 'carrying on for month or so'. Bob went off on his annual holiday, a pilgrimage to a remote spot in the hills of northern Italy which he had known in the war. Special arrangements for contacting him by messenger from the nearest village were laid on in hope. In my last couple of weeks, our hope was fulfilled. Bob Reid was appointed.

In the formal if funereal words of BR's Annual Report of 1983 I 'ceased to be chairman from the 11 September 1983'. Naturally I read the report, published six months after my demise, with the avidity of a ghost reading his own obituary. The cover had a dazzling picture of exactly where I want to be buried: the white terrazzo floor of the concourse at Waterloo Station. Waterloo had responded quickly and handsomely to our clean-up campaign. The stone came through a rich whitey cream; the brick work recovered its warm deep blush, an afterthought pink I called it; the information panels, the lettering, the shop-fronts all pulled themselves into line with brightened fascias. But the old dark floor of the concourse still deadened everything. Why not white terrazzo? Because, we were told, people will slip and break their ankles, their legs, perhaps their hearts. Especially in wet weather. And anyway it would be too expensive. Reluctance has a thousand reasons. Despite them all, we experimented with a patch of terrazzo outside our fast-food shop, Casey Jones. People survived and the economics proved not daunting after all. We had started something. That small white circle, which marks my spot, spread in time to lighten all the main stations with shining terrazzo. So, for me, the choice of the report's cover photograph was well judged, and under it my mission was laid to rest in the contents.

Bob Reid's first statement made a ghost a very happy man. The operating result for that last year was the best ever in the twenty-one year history of the Railways Board. The number of total staff employed had fallen by nearly 39,000 in the last three years alone. Passenger receipts had risen by eleven per cent in 1981 and twenty-three per cent in 1982. 'My appointment as chairman,' Bob Reid wrote, 'was a signal that government was prepared to back the strategy set out in our 1983 Plan. That strategy keeps the railway largely at its present size. It reduces the call on the taxpayer by achieving lower costs and higher volumes. It begins to provide the investment for our long-term future.' Best of all he continued, 'This was the basis for the government's detailed objectives for running British Rail which are set out opposite.' At last BR had the 'contract' supplementing the statutory and financial duties of the board. With the electrification programme on the way, and authority given for replacing the ageing diesel multiple-unit trains, massive assurances were there at last for a quality service on the rails into the next century. And soon, the Euro-Tunnel, the longest macroeconomic shaggy-dog story in history, was to be given the go-ahead, as if after all it were the most natural thing in the world to do. The BR connection with the rail networks of Europe and beyond seemed assured, and thereby a new prosperity.

Around the time I 'ceased' I was often asked to write about BR and hard times. My answer was that I did not want to produce a grunting book about railways; I might have been a bit tired as I stepped out of the ring and there was a danger that I might be in a bruise-pressing mood. Now, when I think of railways, I find myself only full of hope for its future – this is the Age of the Train – and full of memories of the good times.

One such good time came in my first year out of BR. The clan of the McAlpines have a family tradition of closeness with railways; their company built the West Highland line in the last century and they are active contractors to BR today under Lord Edwin McAlpine. Bill McAlpine, his son, is arguably The Enthusiast of all railway enthusiasts: he has a private station of his own and workshops at Carnforth where among other national treasures of old locos and coaches is housed *The Flying Scotsman*. Edwin and Bill had the happy idea of inviting all past BR chairmen and the present one to lunch in one of their old saloons. We assembled, Lord Beeching, Sir Stanley Raymond, Sir Henry Johnson, Lord Marsh, myself, Sir Robert Reid and, as an honorary member of the party, Sir John Elliot, who had been a wise and witty chairman of London Transport. I have no idea what the collective noun is for the ex-chairmen of BR – a siding? Whatever it is, we provided a parade of proof that in management there must be more than one way of doing anything. Our tempers, our styles, our prides and prejudices, our disciplines and careers, our capacities for happiness and unhappiness, our politics, were all so different – the same bed of nails but very different dreams. Only when our talk touched on the exposed nerve of the government–industry relationship did I sense unison. No one could get that right for long. Down our different spokes we came to the same hub of experience, the common denominator of our lives, the railway connection with politics. We would have had to have the McAlpines add a couple more of their coaches to cope with the twenty-five or so Ministers that the five ex-chairmen had served; Bob Reid has had four since he started at the end of 1983. So it goes on. The pendulum is swinging hard now towards privatization in the public sector, but in my view railways, in whatever ownership, will always enjoy or endure a semi-detached life with government.

Some time before, Jill and I had dinner at Windsor Castle and after it the Queen and Prince Philip showed us some special items in the Royal Library which had a bearing on railways: royal diary entries, beautifully illustrated books of early trains – and a handwritten letter from Lord Aberdeen, the Prime Minister, to Queen Victoria in the 1850s, reporting a Cabinet meeting:

Lord Aberdeen presents his humble duty to your Majesty and begs to inform you that the discussions of the Cabinet yesterday were of considerable importance. A very important suggestion was made by Mr Gladstone, having for its object to bring the whole Rail Ways of the Country more immediately under the control of Government. This would be effected by a sort of joint ownership; but as the project is only in its infancy, it will require more communication with the Board of Trade, as well as the Directors of the leading companies, before any decided opinion can be formed.

Over more than a century since there have been many decided opinions, particularly about the 'sort of joint ownership'. In our individual ways, we chairmen had all tried to move down the track towards 'more communication' between the government and the vested interests and the citizen, and from the evidence of that luncheon not all of us had enjoyed the journey. I cannot vouch for any conclusion we came to: the day was a merry one, imperfect only in its brevity, a memory-tour with one stop only, at a platform out of sight of most of the rest of Clapham Junction, and there we lunched only too well. The wine I do remember; with that McAlpine touch of style and accuracy it was a 1963 vintage, from the first year of Dick Beeching's chairmanship, the first starter among us. The Reverend Sidney Smith described his idea of heaven as eating pâté de foie gras to the sound of trumpets. For me that merry lunch up the Junction, drinking Cheval Blanc '63, comes pretty close.

That was a party of recollections in tranquillity, quite unlike the farewell parties which strung across my last months in BR in 1983. These were more hectic affairs, swinging like strings of coloured bulbs and buntings at those summer evening fetes where the weather has turned out to be a bit uncertain but nothing must be allowed to spoil things. August was tense. The succession was still unsettled, the Serpell hangover ached, and the Corporate Plan was about to be presented; but Jill and I, in all regions and in all the businesses, enjoyed a series of memorable parties which made it seem roses, roses, all the way out. Even at the Rail Council with the unions there was a last luncheon – sans ASLEF, but still I was able to tell of my experience with a very durable driver during the Strike Age of the trains. He was the mayor of Warrington at the time we opened the brand-new station there; a shiny day, a buoyant crowd, the sun bouncing off the brass in the school band, and the Mayor resplendent in glittering regalia. Then I noted the odd diadem of sweat braiding his strong white hair. His eyes were troubled too, and as we shook hands on the platform, the tension was tangible. To break the strain I put my hand over the mike and asked what the motto on his badge of office said. He snapped into confidence, eyes clearing in a flash:

'Deus dat incrementum,' he replied.

'What does that mean exactly?'

'It means,' he said chuckling, 'For God's sake give 'em the increase.' His advice may not have been relevant at the time, but that humour would always be useful in running a railway, in his job or mine.

Over the last months, the string of parties was the lifeline Jill and I needed. It was hard stopping, and the friendship and fun of the railway community at these celebrations eased our hearts. I had to admit regularly to being 'schizophrenious', to quote Ogden Nash's poem 'A Solution' – which I did at the drop of a hint:

The world contains so many beautiful things to gaze at
That gazing is an occupation that you could spent days at,
And these beautiful things are of so many different kinds, or
    shall we say heterogeneous,
Such as the sun and moon etc. and butterflies and mermaids etc.
    that to list them all you would have to be an etcetera genius.
So I shall hasten to a landing
And mention two beautiful things that are to my mind
    outstanding,
And one of them is to be on a train,
And see what we see when we flatten our noses against the pane,
And the other is wistful enough to make anybody feel cosmic
    and pious,
Which is to stand beside the track and wave at the passengers
    as they rocket by us,
So that is why rather than be an etcetera or any other kind of
    genius
I would rather be schizophrenious,
Because I should regard it as the most satisfactory of stunts
To be able to split my personality and be in two places at once,
For who could be so happy as I

Sitting with my nose against a train window watching me wave
   to me as I go rocketing by?

At last, the last night, the last party, the last chord of farewell. It
happened to be the turn of the (Great) Western Region. Jill and I
were invited to Paddington; always a pleasure, of course, but we did
wonder what next. Straight-faced, our hosts said that we were going
by HST to Didcot. Didcot – God Wot? A surprise party. There
waiting for us at the station was a locomotive with its steam up, and
I was put aboard the footplate which was crowded with friends. We
were to drive to a great dinner organized by BR in the Great Western
Society's siding alongside the main track very close by. That was a
delightful thought in itself: I had striven to do what I could in my
time to see that the voluntary railway organizations devoted to steam
should be encouraged by BR, not discouraged as apparently they had
had to be in the Sixties. As I saw it, steam warmed the market for

railways generally, and I had no truck with the argument that the fascination with steam engines is mere nostalgia. BR should be well past that idea of the past. Those old engines are victories of adventure and imagination and inspire a lasting respect for those most desirable of qualities. Works of art come through time and a steam loco' is for many a work of art. That night I was done the honour of being allowed to take the controls. Despite the chorus of advice I was given from friends all round, I still managed to make a nonsense of this ultimate responsibility on the rails. I put the old beauty into reverse. That was my final official ride – going backwards, steam blindfolding me, billowing around like history, whoops of good cheer and derision in my ears, the engine puffing enough, enough, enough. And about eight men on the footplate. Certainly time to go.

12

Business and Desire

In my first weekend off the rails, September 1983, I was prowling my garden beside the elegant ruins of Minster Lovell Hall quoting the Bastard in *King John* to a television camera: 'Mad world! mad kings! mad composition!'

The BBC was completing its canon of Shakespeare plays and I stepped out of railways just in time to do the commentary, 'Shakespeare in Perspective', for *King John*, their last production. It was the perfect break.

Shakespeare's hand of glory converts these thirteenth-century star wars of crooked kings and queens into recognizable men and women, and delves into the mysteries of leadership and duty and community – the issues which had fascinated me throughout my working life. I had no trouble translating the themes into the flatter language of my managerial world. How does government lead an advanced industrial democracy, with its share of real bastards and barons roaming around? How does the national interest balance with the internationalization of business? 'London hath received, like a kind host, the Dauphin and his power.' Today we have 'received' not only Europe but the Americans and the Japanese. How does the manager weld order and unity, reconciling economic and social responsibilities, or less pompously, efficiency and happiness? King John was a most competent manager; learned too, with his magnificent library, and he had the gene-coded energy of his Plantagenet parents. But there was a real snag: John was a crook. How does the manager sustain ethical and human values on the job and in the community? These questions had fascinated me at work all my life, and were to do so for the next five years.

Oddly, immediately I was clear of BR, a number of media proposals were put to me. They ranged from a weekly 'business hour', thirty-six times a year, to a six-part programme on industrialization (the length seemed cunningly calculated to be half of 'Civilization' according to Lord Clark). I would have to stop the business world and get off to do any of these things – the most manageable proposition would have been to stand in for Jimmy Young during a short holiday. But all vanity, sheer vanity to contemplate. I had my own scheme. BR had been a magnificent obsession for seven years; now at fifty-nine I sought three things. I wanted the freedom of plurality again, to force me to learn about new opportunities and relationships in business. 'What's new hereabouts?' I love to think of the grand old man of railways, Robert Stephenson, walking around his village, hitting the ground with his stick, asking that terrific question. Also, I sought the scope to speak my mind freely again over a range of social and political issues. British politics were being transformed by the Thatcher regime; party lines were in confusion and crumbling: where did I stand as a manager and citizen? Finally, I sensed management to be in a new stage of evolution, in two areas particularly, the role of the multinational corporation and the evolution of social responsibility. I wanted to be part of that.

Plurality restarted exactly where I left it to join BR in 1976, in the chair of the Rockware Group, manufacturers of glass and plastic containers. When I had signed for my second term at BR, I had promised to return as part-time chairman to Rockware at the end of my duties, and the prospect had seemed pleasing enough then. Rockware was finishing the Seventies in a mood of rollicking prosperity, but the slump of the early Eighties shattered the glass container industry: in 1983 its £400 million sector of Britain was making a £40 million loss instead of a £40 million profit. Rockware was taking its full and fearful share of the disinflationary punishment.

The day after I left BR I was back on BR premises at the Great Eastern Hotel where Rockware had hired a spacious chamber for an extraordinary meeting of the troubled shareholders. Ironically it was the room in which I had toasted Bill Rodgers as Secretary of State for the celebration of the Great Northern Line electrification. There was not a nostalgic second to waste. Nothing so concentrates the mind of a businessman as a possible sentence of liquidation. Rockware had to raise £10 million to rescue itself by restructuring its balance sheet. I had come off the train to get on my bike, setting off at once on a round of City institutions. We watched the smiles of bankers who once had competed to lend us money tighten into thin-lipped scepticism over our chances of survival (the honourable exceptions were mostly in Scotland) and we began to enjoy the riddle going the rounds of manufacturing industry in those bleak days:

'What's brown and white and spotted and looks good on a banker?'

'A Dobermann pinscher.'

In the end we succeeded on the basis of a three-year plan of recovery, but the scheme put us in thrall to a consortium of seven bankers.

Good management in perilous circumstances is often the accentuation of the obvious; to the professional it is almost like carrying out oft-repeated lifeboat drill. I had had the luck to recruit Frank Davies, in his middle fifties, from a major international, and the executive team made all the right moves for the rescue operation: it managed for cash, decentralized into the smallest groups for action, reduced the workforce and raised productivity, and opened wide the lines of communication throughout the Rockware community, up, down and around. But more than all these professionally proper things done, what mattered was the fun and camaraderie that perversely flowered from the stony ground of the crisis. By the third year we were able to heave the banks off our backs by a well-supported rights issue, and by the fourth year the risk-takers, the convertible preference holders, had quadrupled their money. Our shares which had been as low as 12p reached 130p just before the froth was blown off them by the gale-force winds of Black Monday on the Stock Exchanges in October 1987. More significant than the gyrations of equity prices, Rockware was producing as much glass as it had been ten years before with half the number of employees, and almost half those employees chose to become shareholders in the company.

Of course survival is only a start. Once the boat is clear of the rocks there is the more subtle decision to face of setting a new course. Our policy was to be stronger in glass but less dependent on it, so in 1987 we began to grow by acquisition, always organically and on the basis of willing buyer, willing seller, but as we expanded we ourselves became a target for bigger groups on the same crowded, jostling take-over trail. The mid-Eighties were years of record activity in bids and deals. I was back breathing the steamy air of a familiar jungle.

And plural days were here again. During the recovery of Rockware my portfolio had filled brimmingly with other business commitments. The links grew naturally enough. My way back into the City came through a return to H. Clarkson plc, the ship and insurance brokers which I had chaired before BR. Soon after, I was invited into the chair of Target, the insurance group which had enlarged and prospered mightily since the days I had first known it as a promising little subsidiary of Dawnay Day, the merchant bank I had headed in the early Seventies. Then two new sectors of the City opened to me. In the first, I took the chair of a modest capital venture fund which staked a nerve-racking variety of companies, from natural health foods to sophisticated ground-to-air signalling systems. What these companies had in common were the growing pains of the second stage of development: they were supposed to have come through the start-up phase, had learnt to walk but were not running confidently. Our capital venture, unlike many which provided purely financial investment, had the management resource to support the businesses in their time of trouble. For success and growth usually mean trouble: the starter of a business who can manage its success by building a team is as rare a bird as the trade unionist who becomes general secretary by winning a reputation as a battling protester, and then manages to make peace with the realities of competition and efficiency. The other new challenge for me was to chair a public company in the business of property and leisure. This was a challenge with a difference: it brought me into a top team of managers, all of whom were under forty. City analysts and market makers rightly worship youth; age wearies most of us but particularly them. Luckily this board is combining the old with the new, and the energetic marriage of youth's perennial wisdom to the lovely insecurity of long experience makes a very happy couple.

Meanwhile, outside the City, various things were stirring. By a happy irony, after being the object of attention, for better or for worse, of various headhunters, I became chairman of a successful company in that field, Whitehead Mann, giving me the chance to help refute Barbara Castle's understandable but sweeping condemnation of these agencies. Two elements essential to the pattern of my portfolio fell into place: high technology and international operations. I joined the UK Advisory Council of the American electronics group, Honeywell; and then – the riskiest move of them all – I took the chair of a Japanese company, Mitsubishi Electric (UK).

It has been a delight to find that my activities in the public domain have provided a sane balancing load to business in the private sector. In the field of education, I was still deputy chairman of the Court of London University, and in 1988 I became chairman of the London

School of Economics. In the management world, I still chaired the Advisory Council of the Business Graduates Association (which had grown from 182 members, when I took over about twenty years ago, to 3,750). Then I was elected chairman of the British Institute of Management for the term of 1984–6, and at the same time was drawn into the presidency of the Design and Industry Association, a forum in which experts and laymen have been able to keep in touch and in good temper since 1915.

This was a period when at last management was awakening to the priority of design. It is an integrating force in any enterprise but lamentably management education had simply omitted it from its programmes. I raised funds and approached the London Business School to start the Design Management Unit there. This, to our amazement, turned out to be the first such department at a business school anywhere in the world, a pioneering status we discovered only after we had started it. Under Peter Gorb's leadership it prospered swiftly and has since become a model for many distinguished imitators among business schools, here and abroad. On another part of the advancing front of design, as a trustee of the Conran Foundation, I took on the appeal for the Design Museum on the South Bank of the Thames. Sir Terence Conran's vision in retail and design has changed the way a generation of Britons has felt at home, and now his generosity has been the foundation for the inspired conversion of a warehouse on Butler's Wharf in Dockland. Now the Design Museum on the banks of the Thames, in its bright, white cladding, is a shining champion of quality throughout the mass-production world. Further upstream on the same South Bank, I was put to work for the public sector again; the Minister of Arts appointed me to the board of the Royal National Theatre where I became responsible for its Development Council.

Maybe I'll die of sprawling. Certainly I live that way, but when people tell me I am doing too much they usually mean I am not doing enough of what they want me to do. Maybe I could not do the little I do if I did not do other things. And I can do more because I don't play golf. Dr Johnson defined wit as the unexpected copulation of ideas. Perhaps in this light my diary looks like a laughing matter; but the interests do not conflict, they reinforce each other, help me keep my acts together. I feel I am in one play, not vaudeville. They connect with ideas that have driven me in the political, educational and managerial arenas. And I am discovering that even plurality itself is an idea with a future for starters. In this glorious spread of things to do, as much by luck as policy, I find myself bearing witness to a new gospel of work.

The 1980s have been making plain a new design for working. There has been a series of unmistakable trends: the shift from industry to services, from labour to manual abilities to 'knowledge' skills, from one on-going career to job-mobility, from stiff organizational structures to networks and teams and task-forces, from sexual clichés about who can do what to an openness to talent, from the full-employment society to the part-employment society, from the idea of a job and retirement to that of the third age of life. As Professor Charles Handy, the outstanding prophet of the new world of work, put it in his book *The Future of Work*: 'The signs are that we are already being forced into a world where the job is a necessary part of life, but only part of it. Jobs for all, yes, but no longer jobs for always.'

I can see that by the start of the next century the institution of the individual, which we call a career, will have to be much more flexible and in the process will become more attractive. Dual or multiple employment might become quite ordinary, not necessarily just to make extra money but as part of a way of life, more satisfying and thus more efficient than following the routine of one function and one employer. Given that the work is there to be done, it might be taken in smaller, sweeter lumps. I find plurality has surprising advantages. So might others. People would appreciate better how others make their living, and would perhaps be less prone to make those easy generalizations about others that they so resent about themselves. Employers – and unions too – would be less dominated by the notion of a single work group, and also less dependent on it. Most people have probably never thought in these terms, and certainly the tradition of managers is against the trend – 'temps' and 'casuals' are treated casually – but part-timing and flexibility and variety are becoming serious business. Obviously change is not popular, otherwise more people would choose it for themselves, but attitudes are changing, cracking under the pressure of high technology and global competitiveness. Many married women have been managing their lives wonderfully well along these lines for years, and other people, less respectably, have been romping about in the black economy, having a high old part-time dually employed.

The enlarging minority who live in this more flexible way seem to enjoy it. So long as one can endure the relative lack of security, it can be quite rejuvenating, as I have noticed among the early retired. There may be more bits and pieces in the plural life, but it makes a larger whole. Leisure becomes less a simple contrast to work. Those old words need watching: they can somersault. Leisure in Greek is *skole* and in Latin *scola*; 'school' does not mean drudgery but leisure. Our definition of work as employment, with its contrasts of unemployment and retirement, is in need of a good shaking.

Charles Handy, in his latest book, called *Age of Unreason*, describes an upside-down world of fundamental change that lies ahead of us. More often than not change means merely more of the same, perhaps happening more rapidly, but now change itself has changed. What faces us is radical discontinuity. For instance, changes in information technology and biotechnology are already turning our world over, and plurality will be one way of working and learning and living with that revolution.

For some, and I am one of them, the work revolution is fun and rewarding, a life of choice and enhancing wholeness. For others it is, sadly, hard going. It means the misery of lacking work and lacking education. To advocate variety of work to people who have not been educated and trained in adaptable skills is crass or cruelly cynical. There is a bleak and desperate transition between the old world and the new one waiting to be born. Just as there is more to work than making a living, there is more to being unemployed than a reduced income. There is the shock of loss of habit, of fellowship, of self-esteem, of purpose in life. Normally what we do is among the first three or four points of any general description: John Smith, age thirty-five, married, fitter's mate of Skid Row, Wit's End. Freud described work as man's strongest tie with reality. The wrenching decade of the Eighties has cast loose too many for too long, leaving them out of work and out of step with an increasingly more fortunate and uncaring society. For them, unemployment is a shame and a hell; for the rest of us it is a shame on us and a waste, and in the longer run it could be devilishly dangerous. The Bastard said:

> Now by my life, this day grows hot.
> Some airy devil hovers in the sky
> And pours down mischief.

The waste of people is the mischief. For instance, forty per cent of school-leavers are have-nots; they are entering the world of work *sans* credits, *sans* literacy, *sans* numeracy, *sans* skill and *sans* much hope. Demographic trends point to a third fewer eighteen-year-olds in 1995: youth then will be in a sellers' market, but only if the young have something to sell. Skills will still be in enragingly short supply, but those without skills will be as helpless as they are today. Britain educates only fifteen per cent of its youth beyond the age of eighteen, a far lower ratio than those of our serious competitors. Shortage of skills at every level up to that of graduate engineers and managers is the chronic business problem now, as it has been for my generation. Essentially these issues are the well-worn stuff of politics, but emerging from my immersion in the public sector, I rediscovered them set in a radically altered perspective. Something has happened, of course. Thatcher has happened, discontinuity incarnate. Bomb-like, Thatcherism has landed, for good and ill, and blasted away the haggard self-delusion of the three parties. Politics have become interesting again.

As an industrialist my first concerns with any government must be with its policies on education, industry and the management of the economy. For decades, industry's dissatisfaction with the educational system has been consistent and ineffective. School-leavers arrive ill-educated and ill-qualified for work, its disciplines and its team spirit. Products of higher education make no better job of it, for opposite reasons: they are overqualified in some ways but in others unfit for enterprise, with its risk-taking and risk-making. The academic system has been incestuously dedicated to pleasing itself; its pinnacle of achievement has been academic success. The 'better' the school, the more likely it was to be taking industry for granted; industry was where others went because no other choices were available to the poor little blighters. Then throughout the first Thatcherite decade the arguments mounted, with industry beginning to become less smug as the problem became more urgent. It also became aware that it had to be clearer about its needs, about its commitment to the communities in which it operated, about its own unattractive image which put off the very talents it needed to attract. Schemes of collaboration with schools began to proliferate. Local industry linked with every secondary school, and with as many primary schools as possible. Managers were seconded to help teach, and teachers were given direct experience of local companies. Such collaborative moves were all sensible, small signs of the reforming times.

The climax has come in the grand slam of a new Education Act which surely gives industry all it desired in its emphasis on entrepreneurial culture. But as in so much of Thatcherite reform there is an uneasy feeling of overkill. The pig has been cooked by burning the house down. There is the delicious smell of crackling but where is the party? Industry's strong case for a change has finally been heard and acted on – but at a price. The *Financial Times* summed up in a leader in February 1989: 'After a decade of austerity, university teachers are an ageing, poorly paid, fractious and frequently demoralized profession.' In most schools the crisis in morale is no less. In business, the morale of the manager makes all the difference and what I know of education suggests the same. With the right teacher most obstacles are overcome; without, nothing constructive can happen. Respect for the teacher must surely be central to the new design of education – 'one of the greatest and noblest designs that can be thought on and for want of it thereof the nation perishes', wrote Milton.

The strong case that industry can make for participation – and I have argued it for myself – has its limits. Education is too important to be left to us businessmen. Sir Keith Joseph, as Secretary of State for Education in the early years of Thatcherism, warned of vocationalism as excessive concern with the immediately useful to the neglect of cultural values. We are properly obsessed with the useful, the profitable, the competitive. But watch out, lest we get all that we ask for, products of education that fit our purposes like a glove. That would be most inefficient. Any design 'fix' by industry today, tomorrow's world will alter. We need a rising generation that will criticize and improve our performance, that will last, founded in anger. Starters are not robots. What is education for? Not to groom a managerial elite, not to be like Dickens's Mr Choakum, pouring doses of heartbreaking questions into his class, 'that inclined plane of little vessels arranged in order, ready to have imperial gallons of facts poured into them until they were full to the brim'. Education surely should be the endeavour to sustain the ability and desire to learn, from the earliest age through the rest of our active lives. And the earliest age is when it should start. Provision for nursery education has long been honoured in the breach rather than the observance, and ever since the

Fisher Act of 1918 we have promised and compromised about our nursery schools.

This is a perspective that most business literally has too little time for. High-tech future industry insists on long views but paradoxically most of corporate life has a Hobbesian tendency to be nasty, brutish and short. Sharp-angled views from the bottom line do not always reach the horizons of the twenty-first century.

Beyond our industrial needs, we managers will have to learn new flexibilities in our attitude to work and leisure. Education will have to go on being true to itself, to be about learning how to learn, and to want to go on learning. Education is essentially a risk business. Business should understand and settle for that.

I discover at the London School of Economics a historical parable, a true one. It concerns the foundation of the school. In the 1890s a rather eccentric and well-off Fabian blew his brains out, leaving £100 to his wife and £10,000 to his Fabian friends, for which Sidney Webb became responsible. George Bernard Shaw pressed Webb as a good friend and a good collectivist to set up a school of propaganda: 'The Collectivist Flag must be waved and the Marseillaise played if necessary in order to attract further bequests.' Webb however, held to his own vision of a school with the dual mission of practical education and fundamental research, not simple propaganda. In 1885 it opened with a non-Fabian director and lectures covering a wide spectrum of political colours. Since then the school has flourished, and at the last count there were seventeen LSE graduates on the Conservative side of the House of Commons and nineteen on the Left. It is a parable worth the contemplation of a business-like government: a Senior Common Room at a university can never be turned into a Chamber of Commerce.

That is, of course, an outrageous notion and in nobody's mind. The business-like approach toward cut-backs in funding universities, as I have seen it applied to London University, is simply intended to produce more efficiencies and more market-orientated management. Nowadays so much is ossified in universities that a shock to the system is no bad thing. Tenure and budgets, for instance, are matters to be reassessed. Yet gradually government and academia work themselves up into adversarial roles. The University Grants Committee, once an interpretative and independently trusted mechanism, becomes the University Funding Committee, with a majority of businessmen aboard. The federal system of London University comes under challenge in the name of freedom for the colleges and institutions; and rightly or wrongly, if the federal system and its Court are disintegrated, the lines of responsibility will run straight through to central authority, the UFC and the Department of Education and Science. Not for the first time – local government reform is another example – the New Right finds itself pulled in contrary ways. In their heyday, the Labour governments centralized economic matters and promoted freedom in most other things. Thatcher governments have found themselves centralizing more political power than any other modern government in peacetime and promoting freedom in economics.

The freedom of economics is not without paradox either. Industrial policy: we have and we haven't one. In the Nietzschean rhetoric of the New Right, industrial policy is taboo: true success in enterprise is not the child of planning but of the market's natural selection. The dominant ideology of the day is that market forces rule and it is not OK to hint at anything to do with interventionism. I have quoted Michael Heseltine's remark from his article in *First* magazine, April 1987: 'It is no longer possible to sustain the argument that Britain does not need an industrial strategy . . . and even less credible to argue that we have one.' I agree with half of what he says. There is certainly a need; but the fact is that we do have one. Governments have an industrial policy willy-nilly; they can no more decide to be quit of it than, say, rid themselves of foreign policy. What we lack is a policy that is discussable.

I do not believe that any industrialists and politicians seriously addressing the agenda of the future are attracted one little bit by yesterday's solutions of massive interventionism. Nor do they deny that the agenda must begin with a square-facing of the market forces which are shaping the global economy. The rest of their agenda, however, still calls for a definition of public policy covering investment in the country's infrastructure, in public services, in research and development and, parallel with economic priorities, a social policy for education and training, the environment, and the consequences of change for the community. These priorities condition one another, and now are set in the larger perspective of an integrating Europe, where talk of industrial policy is less inhibited. We need to talk about it too, openly, coherently and as a whole.

I gave the Dimbleby Lecture for the BBC in 1983 on this need for coherence. My premise was that the active influence of government at every level of industry in a modern economy was inevitable but nowadays ineffectively debated and constrained. There are challenges to democracy in this. The sovereign power of Parliament and its traditional procedures struggle to cope convincingly with the pace and force of business and technology; we along with other advanced industrial societies have become more corporate in too many ways. 'Elective dictatorship' (and I do not aim the phrase against this government alone: it was after all invented by Lord Hailsham when he was opposing a Labour administration) is drawn to make deals with corporate business and unions. I proposed in my lecture the opening-up of the processes of economic policy-making through a Council of Industry, constitutionally created, advisory but with rights of debate and consultation, and with an independent chairman. Its membership would span the main sectors of business – manufacturing, finance, agriculture, commerce – and would also include customer interests and independents.

None of this was any more fashionable then than it is now. My ideas for more open government were seen quite correctly as a move toward sharing power. Was this proposal not building up something like a third house of Parliament? Were there not echoes of Fabian, Churchillian, Gaullist thinking? And what about corporatism? Thatcherism may be centralist and absolutist, but it is also splendidly anti-corporatist, at least in intent. Was I not adding to the risks of corporatism? No to that: my intent was totally opposed to it. I intended to limit the corporate powers that be by regular exposure and debate over our economic and social purposes and policies. I wanted, above all and obviously, to make the connections between those purposes and policies, and I saw the Council being a support to Parliament by offering to it the business experience and advice which is not abundantly in evidence among the members of either House. Unfortunately, while a great deal of reform is meat and drink to the New Right, there is little stomach for any constitutional changes. Meanwhile, I notice, a new version of corporatism thrives. The corporate powers of the unions may be moribund but long live the kings of private enterprise, laurelled with wreaths of new responsibilities for the sponsorship of education, arts, health and welfare.

Meanwhile the deadpan complacency both of the ruling party and of Labour towards the growing interest in constitutional reform may become harder to sustain. The big idea is getting around. I joined the Social Democratic Party when it was founded to break the mould, but the truth is that Thatcherism has broken the mould, and even as a devout non-believer in the absolutism of the New Right I am grateful for that. It has certainly shaken up my constitutional ideas. Voting for the Alliance in 1983 taught me a lesson, shamefully late in my day; it was a crash course in electoral education. In that election it took only 32,777 votes to elect a Conservative MP, 40,482 to elect a Labour MP, and a massive 338,080 to elect an Alliance MP. Representation around the country was ludicrously one sided: all fifteen seats in Hampshire were Conservative, and in Liverpool and Glasgow the Conservatives had no MPs at all – this at a time when more and more splits were becoming obvious in our society between North and South, job holders and job losers, and racial minorities. The lack of logic or justice in this crazed system of swings and roundabouts should have been obvious to me before. When I had stood as a Parliamentary candidate for Labour in 1951 the Party had polled over forty per cent and lost narrowly, and in 1974 it polled twenty-eight per cent and won narrowly. The latest nonsense in 1987 provided the Alliance with only 3.7 per cent of the seats in return for 24.7 per cent of the votes relatively evenly spread about the country. If the principle of proportional representation had applied in 1987 the allocation of seats would have been 274 Conservatives, 200 Labour, 146 Alliance.

There is much more to this than a loser's lament, whining about not winning: the gravity of the reformer's case crosses party boundaries. I have seen that for myself as Treasurer of the all-party Constitutional Reform Centre, and as vice-chairman of the Campaign for Fair Votes started in 1984. That was an all-party crusade for a national referendum on PR. During it Charles Morrison, a Conservative MP and chairman of the National Committee for Electoral Reform, issued this statement: 'Every opinion poll which has been conducted in this country shows the majority of people wish to have a fairer electoral system. Proportional representation would ensure a Parliament much more in touch with the fundamental good sense of the British people.' Of course the government of the day is not willingly going to make a move. Politicians in power are only human; they cannot be expected to change the rules of a game they are winning. Yet it does not seem to me that the players alone should decide how the game is played: a referendum should help to do that. Our campaign was buoyed by polls that showed a mounting of public interest despite the duet of denunciation and scorn from the two main parties.

The art of governing over our form of democracy is to act like a majority when you are only the biggest minority. The art of leadership is to act as a representative of a much larger constituency than those who voted for you. The art of being governed is to be sure that you as a citizen are not so taken in by the show that you forget your citizenship. You need to act out your part in the play to the full – even a bit part – speaking out clearly for what you want.

You as manager too, perhaps. In 1978 the CBI passed a resolution urging 'improvements in our constitutional system' and in 1981 a leaflet was published by a group of industrial leaders entitled, *Industry Needs Electoral Reform Now*. In 1987 I signed the Constitutional Reform Centre's document called *Good Government: Better Business* and sent it to five thousand managers. The day of the press release I was in touch with each of the directors of the CBI, the BIM and the Institute of Directors. All were supportive (one even said so publicly). It was good to know that I was building on a degree of awareness in industry of the need for change in the working methods in Parliament, Cabinet government and Whitehall, an awareness that the operational structure of government was out of joint with the technological and market forces crucial to the success of enterprise.

Good Government: Better Business went wider than the issue of PR by questioning the management of Parliament, Cabinet and Whitehall. The broad front of the reformers stretches wider still, to cover the range of constitutional concerns coming into the national debate: the weakening of countervailing powers such as an independent judiciary or a fully legitimate, revising Second Chamber; the absolute rights and freedoms of the citizen and the related issues of a Freedom of Information Act and a Bill of Rights; the intrinsic legitimacy of local government powers which can be thwarted by the sovereign Parliament; the relationship of all these questions to the European Community. The checks and balances in our democracy are in need of adjustment. A political party with a minority of votes at a general election can capture a majority of seats in the House of Commons. It can then exert the power of the Crown in Parliament and legislative powers without limit. The sovereign body is the House of Commons and an arrogant executive can whip that into three-line order at will. That is the challenge for reform which is now emerging.

The opportunity for a national debate on constitutional reform crashed under the landslide of the 1987 election, when the Prime Minister was returned, a goddess triple crowned. Her third government was yet another minority, this time with forty per cent of the votes cast, but no matter, there was a thundering majority of Conservative seats. But so what? No government in power is going to listen to the case for proportional representation, least of all this one. A bold and successful woman seems to have established permanent residence at Number Ten. The Bastard again:

> St George, that swinged the dragon and e'er since
> Sits on his horse back at mine hostess' door.

History will probably credit the hostess at Number Ten with a higher score than one dragon. Did she not swing the dragon of rip-snorting inflation, slay dinosauric unionism and at least scotch, if not kill, the snake of defeatism in enterprise? These are brave achievements, real however much her propaganda machine makes them unstomachable for some of us (who are not 'one of us') by over-egging the cult of personality. Thatcherite propaganda has a Tudor style about it: it ruthlessly eliminates any successes of the past and dramatizes any failures, as Shakespeare did. She has ruled with a Tudor toughness and contrariness: adamant and expedient, dictatorial and ruthless and charming, vain and courageous.

I take comfort from my belief that the democratic principles at stake are more durable than personalities or parties. After a century of reforms that gave the vote to everyone, people are beginning to see the sense of moves to make each citizen's vote equally valuable. Critical interest is spreading into the unions and into the Labour Party itself, though critical interest is not near critical mass yet. Mobility in British politics is likely to be a convergence of events. When he was at his peak as Prime Minister Harold Macmillan was said to have been asked what, if anything, worried him. He answered, 'Events, my dear, events.'

Firstly, there are economic events. It is true that inflation is curbed, if not eliminated, taxes are reduced, market forces are revived and the world lauds a restoration of British pride and stability. Undoubtedly management has been given every chance to pull itself together, and as a manager I am conscious of a lack of grace in pointing out a darker side to this so-called supply-side miracle. After a decade endowed by £78 billion of North Sea oil revenues, Britain has a record deficit on trade, and has reduced its manufacturing base, on which exports have depended, by twenty per cent. We have rates of inflation and of interest higher than other advanced industrial countries. Investment in research and development, in education and training, is dragging below that of our competitors. And unemployment levels, after twenty-four adjustments in the way they are calculated, still hover round about two million. The transformation of the economy is still work in progress.

Secondly, politics – the very supremacy of the Prime Minister's personality has rearranged political parties, including her own. She has the style of the Victorian actor-manager who did not bother to rehearse very much with the rest of the cast: 'Just tell them all to keep six feet away from me.' This glorious isolation leaves room for manoeuvrings on the rest of her stage, and new groupings are emerging from the pieces of her broken opposition. The New Right has no monopoly over radicalism: the radicalism that was unsettling the Keynesian-Butskellite commitment to welfare and the mixed economy existed before Thatcherism and will do so after. The old Labour Party which Thatcherism has sunk was already sinking fast, and the breakaway of the Social Democrats proved that the rival forms of radicalism were real and coherent.

In the mid-Seventies international markets and the International Monetary Fund turned Denis Healey's car around at the airport, and Labour Party politics were turned around with it. The days of collectivist solutions were numbered, passing away in a final agony of strikes and a nightmare of inflation in 1979. For all that, the current ideology of unbridled individualism in an open market is not the only alternative to collectivist muddle and decline. Mrs Thatcher, as a populist leader, senses that already and she is reaching out towards some of the other forms of radicalism to make them her own. Environment is a most startling example. Suddenly I feel respectable. I have been a Friend of the Earth for some time, and recently deputy chairman of the Trust, and I know something of the loneliness of the long-committed runners of such environmentalist organizations. Now we have respectability thrust upon us by the Prime Minister's public conversion to the cause. There are other radical causes which she might find less digestible. Industrial policy on a European scale for instance, regional dispersal of power, investment in public service, or that lit fuse, constitutional reform. And these are some of the potent elements that will be adopted by new political alignments, either into a new party such as the Democrats (of which I am a member, and chairman of its Trustees) or into the links forged between a renewed Labour Party, or parts of it, and even parts of the traditional Conservatives at bay. Thatcherism triumphant may well be uniting the scattered hosts of her opposition. From their thwarted turbulence, events, my dear, are always possible.

Thirdly, events in Europe are bound to be unsettling. Some are meant to be, like the creation of the single market by 1992. Others are less planned and more unpredictable. One example of the unexpected might be the Gorbachev effect: a thaw on the European Community's Eastern frontier could encourage aspirations to some form of unification of East and West Germany, and an easing of understandings between the Eastern European countries and Europe as a whole. The nature of the Community might well then be something quite different from the dream of the federalist founding fathers.

None of this is bound to happen, but what is happening already is forcing us out of the even tenor of our British ways, legally, politically and economically. Legally, through the European Convention of Human Rights; politically under our treaty obligations to the EC; economically, as the Single Market develops. The sovereignty of Parliament is not what it was, nor can our rival political parties pretend to enjoy the same scope for their competing economic visions. Just as the acceptance of market forces has become the test of credibility for any party programme in Britain today, so the European Community will be the basis of our future politics. And under these conditions it seems to me highly probable that issues of social policy will gain a new prominence, such as health and housing, even the arts, and certainly the liberty of the citizen and the way we run the country – a country adjusting uncomfortably to the loss of some of its independence.

The politicians will rightly fuss about modified sovereignty but I suspect international managers will be readier to acknowledge the process of interdependence which extends already well beyond Europe. 1992 symbolizes a regional market within the global economy that we have had to live in for some time. Computers are girdling the world, like Ariel, 'in a twink' and capital flows round the world and back 'ere your pulse beat twice.' Any attempt to hedge our sovereignty behind the exchange controls again is unthinkable; we are already subject to the instantaneous demands of international money markets. Our economy is fatefully tangled in those vast problems that worry the rest of the world: the constant imbalance between the physical and financial economy world-wide, a tenfold discrepancy with too much money flying too fast around the global village market-place; the imbalance between the advanced industrial states, with the US, once the biggest creditor, becoming the biggest debtor; and overhanging the scene – for all the write-offs by the big banks – the shadow of Third World debts. These are the formidable issues which overarch everything.

Nowhere is the force of these earthquaking problems more subtly gauged than in the City of London. Nowhere is the force of international business in our time more startlingly revealed than in Japan. Since railways, I have managed to work in both areas.

The City I returned to in September 1983 was Big-Banging itself out of recognition – almost. The high style and salaries, the aura of implacable self-confidence were all as recognizable as ever, but the excitements of deregulation and the internationalization of the Square Mile were transforming the scene. Even the self-confidence was not quite what it was. The scale of the sleaziness in the Eighties had spoilt the atmosphere. In the past, the odd case of corruption had been the exception to the rule of trust: any self-doubt pierced the self-confidence as briefly and harmlessly as the sword that the magician plunges into the box with the lady inside; the lady steps out smiling, alive and well and living in Threadneedle Street, not looking her age at all. But Lloyd's scandals, the insider dealings, and a new, raucous loads-of-money attitude have made the Square Mile look less square than it did. (It is surely no coincidence that an Institute of Business Ethics has been founded recently, or that some business schools are extending their studies and introducing ethics to their programmes.) I have no doubt the City will survive this dismaying phase of publicity. It is a brilliant, talented place as strong in its traditions of trust and integrity as it is in its world-class skills and imagination; but it is already moving from its old ways, from the implicit to the explicit, from the self-regulatory to the regulatory mode.

Nationally, the enlarging community of new shareholders means there are many more citizens of the City, and at last popular capitalism is forcing the pace of communications. You can no longer be 'something in the City', that old phrase of glamorous anonymity: you had better be ready to explain yourself. The City's contribution to our democracy's prosperity is simply enormous, but it is still far too much of a mystery. I have lived with this urgent need for improving communication by the City all my working life, and there has been measurable progress – but not enough.

One reason for urgency is the worldwide intensity of mergers and acquisitions. From where I am in industry and in the City I grow more acutely aware of the two different cultures. The short-termism of the City is accentuated by the wheeling and dealing. Pressure is constantly on companies to keep producing greater earnings per share whatever the cost to sound strategy and to research and development. But there is more to the strain than timetables: there is the cultural contrast of values and loyalties. Mergers and acquisitions, 'Ms' and 'As' in the jargon, symbolize the clash. The management and staff in manufacturing industry often feel like the poor bloody infantry, slogging on at the mercy of the cold-eyed generals back at base who seem obsessed with their dawn raids and take-over battles.

It is fascinating to speculate on the impact that the promotion of a wide shareholding democracy might have on the freebooting of Ms and As. It is devoutly to be wished, of course, that the spread of shares will spread an understanding of the realities of competition and commitment. It will also speed the challenge to the City to explain what happens in the bids and deals. The new citizens of the City, worker-shareholders, are bound to notice that while shareholding is spreading, the control of shares and of their values is narrowing. The idea of a shareholding democracy is excellent, but the reality is that institutional investors control about eighty per cent of the shares in Britain, and when it comes to a take-over battle it is usually the shareholding plutocracy of pension fund managers that decides the issue, and therefore the fate of the working community. There is going to have to be some very hard thinking on a code of higher standards of communication, between companies and shareholders generally, and between companies and their worker-shareholders in particular.

Overlaying the frantic activity of Ms and As has been the bonanza of privatization. The bulls of the City have revelled in this rich new pasture. I have no quarrel with bringing some of these national businesses back to the market: the managers involved must be glad of the bracing fresh air. I say some, because the case for making public utilities such as electricity, nuclear power and water into monopolies in the private sector seems wretchedly ill-conceived, the dogmatic indulgence of a headstrong government, and privatization is likely to prove as much an oversimplification as nationalization.

Railways are the latest candidate for glory. At one extreme of the coming debate over how BR should be privatized it is easy to argue about peripheral prospects: for example, your aunt's savings would probably be safe in the Gatwick to Heathrow 'dedicated' passenger service. At the other extreme, more complex and sophisticated, there is the argument for an integrated network, balancing the trade-offs between the variety of business sectors in the transport group. I suspect that a patchy political compromise will be the outcome. BR will probably become a licensing track authority of some sort and there will be an attempt to float off some sectors – freight, parcels, even Inter-City. The public interest, however, will continue to be stuck with the politically sensitive rural lines and the expensive commuting services crucial to the life of our great cities. Roughly, it will be a re-run of the young Gladstone's formula of over a century ago.

My own instinct is first to argue for change in terms of the customer's interest. The passenger will be seeking more comfort, safety and simplicity in the service offered; industry will want to exploit the national network and its extensions cross-London, cross-Channel and linking with the developing high-speed rail network in Europe. What will secure those improvements? A management geared to give a high quality service by the updating of the technology and attitudes of each of its national-scale businesses. That is how BR has been revived. That is how investment strategies have been developed for the Tunnel and, with the fourteen railway administrations in Europe, for further development into the next century. That is how rail solutions are being devised for coping with the congestion of London and with the fifteen to twenty per cent rise in travel on rail by the year 2000. My instinct is, therefore, to sustain the integrity of management of policy in this new age of the train, and that means settling rail policy within the perspective of a transport policy for the country. No government can avoid its responsibility for keeping a coherent view of transport as a whole. Privatization will do little to lessen the role of any government in coping with congested airways and roadways as the lava of traffic pours over cities and countryside. It would be sad if the debate about the ownership of railways gravitated to political extremes again. Railways continue to rouse passion and in a way I am glad, but this time I hope it will be passion without politics. If rail is inevitable, let us lie back and enjoy it a bit.

And if privatization does befall BR, then the City once again will be brought into action to market a national asset – but the City that does this will have changed rapidly in one overwhelmingly important way. For the City's role nationally is only half its story these days; in the Eighties it has become ever more internationalized. It can claim to be one of the three capitals of capital in the global economy, and working in it puts one at the sharp end of some awkward questions. How relevant is business patriotism or industrial sovereignty? It may not matter too much if Nestlé take over Rowntrees, but there is more to this wheeling and dealing across frontiers than the Swiss swallowing our sweeties. The British motor and electronics industries, for instance, have been subject to deals, not necessarily aggressive bids, often in stages of collaboration. Ours is one of the most open markets in the world, but does this mean that our corporate assets are up for auction to the highest bidder anywhere? Who owns what matters far less than what is good or best for the customer. Obviously we are sensitive to ownership up to a point – the Kuwaitis have had to control their enthusiasm for BP – but what is the point exactly? Reciprocity between countries is the neat answer, but not easy to establish.

As I see it, individual patriotism will never die, but it is fading away. The emergence of the European Community is one measure of it. The power of the international corporations is another. The logic of the global economy is that there will be global corporations, but the reconciliation of national pride to this reality of world capitalism is not to be taken for granted. At the operational level, the international manager has to go native. He or she must see to the promotion of local nationals, must invest in research and development on the spot, and integrate the company into the life of the community. And beyond all that there is also another level of understanding to be achieved: the fit of the international corporation into the broad scheme of economic things in the host country.

I accept the growing habit among economists of using capitalism to mean big business. This is the thesis of Francis Braudel: 'Increasingly Capitalism is being used as a *superlative*.' If we follow Braudel, we can make the vital distinction between capitalism and the market economy, between monopolist prices and market prices, between the two tiers of the capitalist system – the international forces of big business and monopolists at the top and the small and medium concerns who live in the truer market economy. Braudel instances the little firms of the '49s' in France, carefully keeping below fifty employees to avoid the regulations that control large enterprises; the thousand businesses once bustling in the old city of New York and now driven out by the big suppliers from out of town; the textile companies that thrive in Prato near Florence. Braudel says that these cannot be defined as examples of true capitalism – that would be completely wrong both socially and in terms of economic organization. Below these two tiers there is the basement filled with economic activities outside any formal market controls – moonlighting, fraud, housework, the economic *puria* of St Thomas Aquinas.

Welcome, then, to the international concept of capitalist technology and management. Welcome to the mix with the market economy where the medium and smaller enterprises flourish and where imagination and innovation spring. Welcome to a distinction between the market economy, which reconciles the international corporation with the creativeness of the host country, and big-business capitalism. By making this distinction we can avoid what Braudel calls 'that "all or nothing" which politicians are constantly putting to us, as if it were impossible to retain the market economy without giving the monopolies a free hand, or impossible to get rid of monopolies without nationalizing everything in sight.'

From the theoretical to the practical; one of my ambitions post-railways was to reconnect with international business, and the opportunity to do so in the most venturesome way had me winging across the world.

Taking the chair of Mitsubishi Electric (UK) in 1984 was a surprise all round: to the Japanese who had never tried the experiment of a *gaijin*, a foreigner, as chairman in any part of their affairs; to me, who had lost touch with Japan and the Japanese since 1946; and to many friends with whom I discussed the move. Some, straight out, condemned me as a turncoat. I was switching sides: I was not so much a Trojan horse as a Trojan ass, letting the Japanese in to British and continental markets. Some friends who had been through terrible times in Japanese prison camps were puzzled, even disgusted that I

337

should treat with the enemy. Others said there was an urgent job of bridge-building to be done. I flew to Tokyo to decide.

I brooded over breakfast at the Imperial Hotel. I was alone and doodling in my sketch-book the view from my window of the Imperial Castle wall. Its huge, rugged blocks of grey granite looked immovable, but reflected in the green moat below they danced with the lights of the sequinned sun. The dark water was patched with white autumnal mist. Part of the mist suddenly became a white swan and floated my way. A *haiku* would have fitted the moment like a glove, but my Japanese was too poor now and I had business to attend to. I spent the day in discussions, discovering what Mitsubishi Electric did – everything from satellites and earth stations and powerhouses to semi-conductors and a vast range of the most advanced electronic equipment – all adding up to about $15 billion in annual turnover world-wide.

The head of its international activities was Yufu-san. Blake says Energy is Delight: Yufu-san is a delightful businessman with a vision and ceaseless drive and charm. He is short, thin, and his dart-like shape shoots accurately at export orders all over the world – if God had meant people to fly he would have made them all like Yufu-san. His capacity for making his colleagues feel braver than they really are and less sleepy than they really feel, has won contracts all over the global markets. And he understood my brooding over my decision – despite my poorly remembered, broken Japanese which lay like rubble in my memory.

That night Yufu-san and I dined together at a traditional inn by the harbour with Takagi-san, a wise friend and the former chairman of the Japanese National Railways, who shared with me at that time the record for the longest term as head of a major railway system. We talked late and reached that relaxed stage when, in customary style, a pad, ink-block and *fude* (brush pen) were brought to the table and we each tried to put something on paper. I remembered the white swan and the castle wall dismantled in its reflection in the moat, not so much a thought as a feeling still not formulated; that is how *haiku* are made. Pretty pusillanimous not to try, I thought. I wrote in seventeen English syllables about the castle wall dancing with flakes of light, the mist and that swan born of it. Next morning a messenger came early to my hotel room to tell me that Yufu-san had been thinking about the *haiku*: surely it meant that I had decided. He was right, I had. And I have lived on the busy frontier of East-West trade happily ever after.

I had three aims in taking the job: to establish more high-tech investment and more jobs in Britain; to encourage more collaborations in joint ventures, in research and exports; and to close the cultural gap between our two peoples. There are superficial similiarities between the British and the Japanese, of which not too much should be made. We both suffer an unreliable climate, both enjoy a taste for tea, both celebrate royalty still, both are islanders and have a separateness which receives a mild shock when we drive on continental roads running into other countries – ours all lead to the sea. But still there is the gap of ten thousand miles of clouds and waves between us which the Shogun wrote about in the first letter between the two islands, to James I, almost four hundred years ago. And something more than the elements makes us keep our distance. The British memories of war, the baffling obscurity of the Japanese language, and now their phenomenal, frightening rise to economic power and their sheer ubiquity – these make an explosive mix, just under the British skin, ready to erupt when some politician blows his or her top over a trade issue of maddening but temporary relevance. Or the Emperor dies. To shed our stereotypes of one another is going to take time and imagination, political statesmanship and, too often forgotten, good management in our international corporations that trade each way.

For a start, I have begun to relearn my Japanese, or at least try. The advantage of speaking a foreign language in trade has been traditionally and cheerfully underrated by British management. This was brought home to me when I was charged by the University Grants Committee in 1985 to make recommendations on the future requirements of diplomacy and commerce for African, Asian and Arabic languages. There had been national spasms of concern over the language priority in Britain twice before in the post-war period which were expressed by the Earl of Scarborough's Commission in the late Forties and Lord Hayter's in the early Sixties. After that more than twenty years elapsed before it was proposed that another commission should be set up, and then, according to a top level source in government, 'Madam put her little foot down: she wasn't going to have a lot of grey men telling her what to do.' Eventually, however, it was agreed that not a commission but an individual should be asked to tackle the priority, solo. I admit that more than once in the course of my investigation the unworthy thought did occur to me that wily Whitehall had devised a mission impossible. But I was saved by a safety network of friends from academia, industry and – surprise, surprise – Whitehall.

My report, *Speaking for the Future*, showed that our country's traditional capability to teach these hard languages at university level had been eroded to a point of peril to the nation. Unexpectedly I found that the government departments, above all, the Foreign Office, had measured the need and the urgency most efficiently. Industry's attitude, on the other hand, was robust, short-term and short-sighted: wasn't English the *lingua franca* of world business? Surely a quick fix on a language course was always available in an emergency? Only slowly are British managers realizing that their main competitors are speaking English too, as well as the language of the customer. I recommended that the funding of the faculties at universities be restored at least to 1979 levels, and to general amazement, that is precisely what happened. The government accepted the report and forty-five new university posts were created. Gratifying maybe, but this is only a start. At the time of my investigations, only fifty graduates a year were qualifying in Japanese, and these, naturally, were not necessarily business-minded students. The doubling of that output, as my report recommended, was accepted, but that target is miserably limited. So much more could be done at university and polytechnic level where learning Japanese, or any other language, alongside a main degree (engineering, economics, or whatever) would break the spell of strangeness in the minds of young people. To become an international manager must mean managing at least one other language, so the earlier the start the better.

Mitsubishi Electric (UK) (MEUK) has more than a thousand people employed in the United Kingdom. In the two factories in Scotland making televisions and video recorders the productivity is equal to that in Japan and our plants have prospered. I see there the vivid proof of two realities for British management: the perfection of the production technology and the evidence that it is perfectly transferable. Japanese technology has come across and so has an attitude. There was a factory party for the formal opening at Livingstone. Katayama-san, the chairman of Mitsubishi Electric, and I cracked a large keg of *sake* with a wooden hammer. I hit too hard and drenched both of us, but there was more than enough *sake* left to go around and around. 'It's smashing working here – you should see if you can get a job,' my wife was told by a slightly tipsy young girl.

Of the 250-strong workforce equipped with highly sophisticated machinery, the average age was 17.4 years and that included only four Japanese managers. There is a directness and accessibility in the management which is obvious: managers are visible on the factory floor, ready to step into the assembly line, eating in the canteen – get-at-able. Quality circles are not just talk, they happen, many calling themselves after pop groups and working on immediate issues of, say, quality and cleanliness. I have noticed that often in British factories managers' offices are clean and the shop floor cluttered: in Japanese operations it is the other way round. Hundred per cent quality is what the working community expects of one another: zero defect is a normal ambition. There is a tale told of a British company ordering 1,000 units, and stipulating a three per cent defect rate. Sure enough the Japanese supplier sent the 1,000 units and, separately packaged, the three per cent defects.

The immensely successful Japanese corporations operating world-wide have yet to evolve their own version of international management. On this score they are learning fast and from the West again. It is easy to forget how recently Japan has risen to be the richest nation in the world – and it must still be bewildering news to the peasant sweating in the fields of Hokkaido or the commuter sardined into his train, or to the young executive and his family in their tiny flat. As a nation they are learning about the new responsibilities of being a world power, about defence strategies, aid programmes, the opening of their own markets and the adjustment of their colossal surpluses by spending more on themselves.

The evolution of their international companies tells the same story of rapid adaptation. Japanese factories have been planted mostly in clusters in Scotland and Wales: as strangers, they obviously feel cosier and safer together. Their excellent factories are welcome and encouraged but they are a form of production colony, far from the common-wealth style of long-established internationals. They have still to dig into a deeper relationship with the host country, in research and development, in the localization of top management, in commercial collaborations, and in the broad span of community relations which gradually 'nationalize' an international company.

Take IBM. It is a supreme example of a nationalized international, and its chairman in the UK, Sir Edwin Nixon, was an obvious choice as a member of the British team when the UK–Japan Group 2000 was founded in 1985. This is a small forum, an informal summit of industrialists, diplomats, bankers, economists and so on, about fifteen a side, which meets once a year to consider the long-term developments in our two countries; we are briefed and we report to our respective Prime Ministers. IBM's chairman has fitted in completely. Wherever IBM operates, its corporate sovereignty is never in doubt, but its social policy is such that it seems at home everywhere. The Japanese are well aware that the next phase of evolution must be towards the commonwealth style, this international subtlety, I call it. Sony has been probably the quickest off the mark, maybe because it is new (it originated post-war) and has fewer traditions to untangle than the older, great trading conglomerates, the *Zaibatsu*, such as Mitsubishi. But now, young and old, all of them are on the move. *Yendaka*, the high Yen, being the almighty currency, has given Japan the power and scope for a new approach to investment overseas. I am sure that there will be a new wave of expansion in the 1990s; it has already begun. It is fascinating to me as a committed 'Tunneller' that while British capital hesitated to invest in the early days of launching the Euro-Tunnel, forty per cent of the initial funding came from the Japanese.

There will be more acquisitions and partnerships as well as green-field developments, but these will be meticulously quiet and careful, in contrast to, say, the Nestlé and Rowntree battle. I am impressed that the Japanese internationals are investing more than their money; they risk their best people too. I have had two managing directors of MEUK, one a physicist, the other an electronics engineer, and each spent seven or eight years in the UK, learning the language and culture here. When British enterprise can provide more top quality young managers ready to spend time in the Japanese markets, learning their language and culture, I shall be more convinced that we mean to do business there. There are some British companies doing just that already, but it's the old British story, there are some good 'uns but too few.

The Japanese also know well that they are at an early stage of international management and that there is more to it than exporting good managers. The risk has to be taken, sooner rather than later, to trust the best managers to be found locally in the host country. There is a need to promote and exchange managers, and at the top levels. On our side ICI and Amersham have a Japanese member on their boards in the UK, but this exception proves an unimaginative rule.

British managers who work with Japanese are at a new frontier. In the give and take of cultures they have to learn to give and take time. I have learnt patience from Japan, sitting through the process of *nemawashi*, the careful root-binding of ideas to make it possible to move them. No macho Western manager wants to believe it, but the Japanese win by commitment and consensus. Their enterprise is management by committee, the country is a committee, and their management moves on the lines of a sumo wrestler. Ideas develop slowly, ponderously; action strikes like lightning. Also I have learnt that, contrary to managerial mythology in the West, the Japanese are not beautifully trained robots; they take risks with people. I spoke with Tomi, then MD of MEUK, about job specifications, and he admitted that he was not in favour of them. 'If I say exactly what to do, maybe that's all he'll do,' said Tomi. Their attitude is complex, full of contraries. Their management is highly detailed, yet it is readier to live with unpredictability, ambiguity and uncertainty than we in the West are. It may be stiffly respectful and hierarchical, about age particularly, but it is scrupulous about listening to views and news from every level, from the very bottom of the organization upwards; courteous and evasive about ever saying 'no' directly, but quietly certain about what its objectives are; technically based in its professionalism of management, but wonderfully realistic in admitting that the best management is an art; relentlessly competitive as between companies, both in Japan and overseas, yet ultimately responsive to the fact that there is a commitment beyond their corporate sovereignty. Where there is a national will, that is the way, and it was the national will that recreated Japan post-war. Nothing was written in the stars to say they would ever rise again as they did. The nation decided and worked with a unity which is not to be as easily copied as their production technology can be copied and as ours was once copied by them.

We cannot copy their industrial policy because we cannot adopt the social structures which make it work. Nor should we necessarily want to. Britain, for instance, is still managed by the politicians of a vying two-party-ocracy; Japan is a consensual technocracy which is relatively classless, with their top-managing old boy networks in public service, law, banks, medicine, civil service and business corporations drawn from the high-achieving universities where recruitment is by merit. Regard for the politicians is ambivalent. Their broking skills may have propelled them to office but these are not the qualities of the elite who have earned their position in the exam hell of the educational arena. All the same, their networks work closely (sometimes far too closely, as recent scandals have indicated) and the consensual management of the country is reinforced by a common respect for facts. The Ministry of International Trade and Industry (MITI) publishes its 'Visions' of world trends and how they affect Japan, and these are legitimized by an Industrial Structure Council, big and clumsy maybe, but broadly representative. (Interestingly, unions and women's groups have about the same membership.) This 'appreciation of the national situation' is taken seriously and so is the annual Economic White Paper published by the Economic Planning Agency.

All this marks a fundamental difference between us. The Japanese have a consensus based on shared and respected facts, assumptions and values. The British purpose-built agency for growth and change, the National Economic Development Council, has never had a common ground to build on. For the British, industrial policy has often reduced itself to a dogfight about who can pick winners and losers in industry. For the Japanese, it has been a transparent process of discussing and defining reasoned expectations about the future which are widely known and accepted. This has given them the nerve to take courageous long-term decisions, and then advance step by step along the selected path of this or that sector of development: motor cars and cycles, electronics, ships, and now financial services. It has meant co-ordination of investment and retrenchments, promotion of research between government and individual firms, with, say, new materials, with biotechnology, with vital innovations which are risky and whose possible rewards lie beyond the immediate horizon of profitability. It has meant strong trade associations working closely with government departments – how else would they have moved so swiftly and drastically to cut back on their shipbuilding capacity when the markets fell away? It has meant the open demonstration of the need for changes and, with that, a concern for the feelings of people affected by them. That combined economic and social attitude, both in the management of their economy and in the management of their enterprise, is what lies behind the record of Japan's post-war resurgence.

Takeo Fujisawa, co-founder of Honda, was asked to compare Japanese and Western management. He was as polite as he could be: it was ninety-five per cent the same, and different in all important respects. Five per cent may be a tiny figure, but revolutions are led by minorities. In 1985 I wrote the introduction to a sort of revolutionary handbook, one of the Penguin classics in management, *The Art of Japanese Management* by two Americans, Pascale and Athos. Their analysis of the components of success in any enterprise anywhere is arranged into the inevitable checklist (if Moses were to come down the mountain today, I am sure he would be presenting us with a checklist) and they reduce their careful and exhilarating research into seven 'S's. The first three 'S's are strategy, structure, systems. They call these the 'hard' 'S's and any manager worth his salt would agree; there can be no substitute for them. The next 'S's are style, staff, skills and super-ordinate goals: these are the 'soft' 'S's, and they are vaguer qualities that the professional literature often rates as optional, decorative not decisive, mere froth. But that froth, the authors argue, has the force of the Pacific – and in my opinion the Atlantic as well. It may well be that in the world we are entering these subtler qualities will have the power to make or break not just companies but whole economies.

This analysis confirms two messages that are implicit, I hope, throughout this book. First, whatever it is that has made the great Japanese corporations so successful is evident equally in great corporations all over the Western world. To celebrate them is to celebrate the significance of excellent management everywhere. The message is not that Japanese management is supreme; it is that success in any enterprise depends above all on the quality of management. What matters is not whether the management is Japanese, American, British or Ruritanian, but that it is excellent.

The second message is that there is more to management and the relationship of society and industry than we have dreamt of in our philosophy of management in the West, or at least dreamt of for a very long time. Almost five centuries ago the departmentalizing of society in the West began. The pattern of disintegration is traceable to the division of the powers of Church and State during the Reformation; institutionalizing separately men's spiritual and working lives made the break-up of the latter that much easier, and economic developments followed the logic of fragmentation into the division of labour. People took their place in the new industrial world, and this place turned out to be along with the other factors of production, labour, land and capital, all meshed into the production system. In this country that system has become increasingly dominated by managers who, as trustees, not owners, are the professionals of the economic department of Western culture. So the mission of managers has narrowed in a way that limits our achievement and potential – and ultimately our vision. We find it hard to make the natural connection between the 'S's. Our management is quick on the draw with the hard 'S's but fumbles the soft ones. That is how the West was won but it is not how the East is winning.

There could not be a better time for British management to bring its act together, and there are encouraging signs that this is happening. The Eighties are ending with a remarkable new strategy for management education in Britain, headed by the Bob Reid who is chairman of Shell. It was at my meeting at the British Institute of Management in 1985 with Sir Keith Joseph and the CBI that the BIM's then Director-General, John Constable, was asked to head an investigation. The Constable report, together with the Handy report which NEDO sponsored, highlighted the country's need for a quantum leap in making management education available to the many. Against this analysis, a nationally co-ordinated initiative is taking place in the UK to prepare management for the twenty-first century. This is the start of a second crusade. The first crusade of the Fifties and Sixties provided a gallant push for the business schools and their high-flyers but it fell far short of Jerusalem. This second attempt is wider-scale, flexible, business-led and market-orientated; it will deploy to the full a new technology of teaching, such as the Open University and the Open College of the Air offer; it will emphasize self-development in contrast with organizational support. The grand design must aim at more than improving professionalism in British management: it must make it normal. And I would hope this provides the opportunity to define the role of the manager more ambitiously, by which I mean more humanly and more socially.

More humanly because management as a professional discipline is quite grown up now, and as a sign of maturity it must admit that it is a human process. Of course managers stereotype to make things simpler for ourselves. At one extreme is the macho-manager, Citizen Kane, at the other the A-team, cartoon musketeers, one for all and all for one. If either stereotype did its own thing exclusively, the wrecking of any organization would be guaranteed. We have to grow out of simplicities and relish *Thriving on Chaos*, the title of Tom Peters' latest book which, thank goodness, is a bestseller. I welcome with all my heart the rise of humanity in management thinking. Because, with all its necessary disciplines, management at its best remains very much an affair not just of the head but also of the heart, where ideals come from. That is what makes management such a rum business these days, both more professional and more mysterious.

Then, our second point, the manager's role must be defined more socially. The future manager will be running flat out to keep up with the enlarging agenda of social policy set up by UK and EC legislation, by community expectations, and I would expect, the manager's own. None of these items can be relegated to Any Other Business. Some are internal to the community life of any organization: equality of opportunity at work, eliminating sexism and racism; the encouragement of wide shareholding among employees; these demand participation in the enterprise through decentralization, consultation and at the least two-way communication. External relations are no less demanding. Consider the environmental imperatives: we must halt the horrible habits we have grown into, infecting land, sea and air, scything forests, raining acid on ourselves, drilling holes in the sky; we must recycle resources, enhance through design our landscapes and cityscapes. Consider the items, see how they grow: commitment to the educational system; combating unemployment through co-operation with local initiatives and voluntary activities; sponsoring the arts; relating to the social policies of the EC. And if you are an international manager, there is still more to do, establishing accountability and acceptance, and 'nationalization' in the host country. Many of these responsibilities of the future manager are not reflected in our inadequate company law, but that inadequacy will be one more item on the plate-load of social challenges before management today and tomorrow.

All this is not an agenda of add-ons and options. These together are the conditions of success and prosperity for management in any advanced industrial society. More than that, they give a wholeness and a status to the citizen-manager's role, integrating economic and social purposes, and refreshing both. I want managers to claim full citizenship, to renounce the stereotypes, to enjoy the natural stretch of being normal. There is no need to be half a man, or woman, to be a manager. As Hamlet said to Horatio, 'every man hath business and desire.' We can keep things in the right proportion. Enterprise is there to serve society; the other way round would be grotesque – although be wary, it is always a possibility.

So the manager's star rises. I see it as five-pointed. The manager is a risk-taking professional accredited by degree or tested experience; an educator in or outside the organization; an internationalist in the world market, shrunk as it is by high technology and the interdependence of trade; a politician, however reluctant, interested in the efficiency of government as any efficient government is interested in business; and finally a citizen dealing with other citizens in a community of work, because democracy continually advances, cannot be unlearned, and is very unlikely to go away. Only a paragon could keep all these roles reconciled: I have never met this ideal manager but I have met managers with ideals as well as success. One quality these starters all seem to share is sheer humanity. Another, though not universally, is some amusement at the human predicament of doing things for people through people – the manager's job.

What was it a great starter had said? I was watching his son marching alone up the aisle of Westminster Abbey, carrying his father's medals glittering on a dark cushion. Sir Peter Medawar's friends and admirers were packed in the vast church to attend his memorial service. We were celebrating one of this age's noblest minds, an eminent scientist and manager of research, a Nobel Prize winner for his original work on immunology, a hero throughout his long ill-health, a generous, lucid, funny man. One of his books, *Advice to a Young Scientist*, would feature in my list of essential reading for young and old managers: 'Although it is thought to be true (I quote Stella Gibbon's mock Lawrence from *Cold Comfort Farm*) that there must always be a deep dark bitter belly-tension between scientists and administrators, one of the benefits of increasing age and experience is the realization that everyone gets on better if a generally matey atmosphere prevails.'

One of the benefits of increasing age and experience, for me, has been to learn to value the Medawar tone of voice. It is the still, small voice that reminds us what we are and who we are. It is a cure for jargon and pomposity. It is a ground for optimism. It is individual. It makes me hopeful that the high-tech information society will not tempt us into the evil of dehumanizing work and centralizing control but lead us into smaller, flatter organizations of the sort that are arising in sunrise valleys. It translates easily all over the shrinking world. It is the sound of the confident professional, the wavelength of sanity and civility, good humour and community. It has me thinking about the simplest rules which I have always used to underpin whatever professionalism I have. In no special order:

Eat and drink less, and laugh more: don't think you have to be unpleasant to be strong.

Somehow find a way of sleeping twice a day.

Do all your sums, look hard, but don't forget you still have to leap.

Hire people cleverer than you are and delegate more than you think is good for you, and take the blame.

Learn one other language at least; appreciating another culture will help you understand your own, and it's never too late.

Find things to praise in people but don't too easily trust yourself about yourself – you're such a flatterer.

If you're in a hanging mood, hang people like pictures, in the best light, and when you do find yourself particularly unkind and unconstructive, are you sure that you are being uncharacteristic?

(That said, keep William Blake in mind: Damn braces, bless relaxes.)

One minute of your time could be somebody else's day, good or bad, courtesy or curse.

Round tables for meetings do make a real difference, I promise you.

And take your problems home – the family has shrewdly sized them up in general terms anyway, but without the detail it is even more worrying for them.

Our four children have left home now but by a minor miracle of family planning we are five minutes walk from each other in North Kensington. We have each other's front-door keys which means that it is not easy to lose the threads of the narrative of Parker Place. Jill is in general practice at Notting Hill Gate, Lucy directs on television and stage, Alan has his own business in the City in financial public relations, Oliver and Nathaniel both act. I think of the Manor Farm at Minster Lovell as home now. I have started to garden, learning from Jill. Perhaps, at last, I shall learn patience – not today, of course, tomorrow. I plant a bulb and still am secretly disappointed that I do not have to snatch my head back as it shoots up. Slowly, though, I am learning. Nature seems to abhor extinction, all it knows is transformation. The sheer continuity of things sustains me. I think of the starts that seem stopped, but I cannot be pessimistic, I have no right to. I have never been busier in my plural portfolio nor more seized with desirable commitments. So I count my blessings as I was taught as a child. I have had a fine time so far.

'Two things fill the mind with ever new and increasing wonder and awe, . . . the starry heaven above me and the moral law within me,' Kant wrote. Under the starry skies, I have been gathering logs from the barn at Minster Lovell: the fireplace is large and burns big ones. My thin torchlight shows green sprigs on the pile of them, seasoning over winter. Centuries ago, a Japanese poet made this *haiku*, it seems for me:

Hone-shiba no	The brushwood,
Karare nagara mo	Though cut for fuel,
Ki-no-me kana	Is beginning to bud.

I am looking back over today's diary, filled with business and desire. The dawn entry reads: 'Must finish this book – *For Starters*.'

EPILOGUE

Once upon a time there was this man who started to tell his own story. After writing 1,000 words of autobiography he gave up because he found he wasn't in it. The events surrounding his life always seemed of far greater significance than he dared claim for himself. . .

That, of course, must be fiction. In fact, the ego turns out to be a tough old thing, a survivor, self-justifying to the last gasped paragraph. But I found real hazards to be faced in making the journey into the here-be-narcissism country of memoirs. I set off blithely to seek the truth, but when I cornered my quarry it sometimes turned out to be far less attractive and flattering than I had hoped. But facing realities, right- or wrong-footing me, is what this experiment is about. This is not a management text, not a how-to-management book, it is more a see-through-management to life-as-a-whole-book. The first edition I subtitled the Business of Life, not the Life of business. There are several reasons for the title *For Starters*, one of them being that I am still in action: when I have stopped, with luck there will be *For Afters*.

There is another hazard of memoirs: the temptation to try to tidy up one's life, round it off at the end. After the book was out and about I saw that I had fallen into this trap, but I am happy to confirm that much as I suspected, life laughs at tidy-uppers. In the light of all that has happened since its first publication, my last chapter reads more like a preface than an epilogue. It set out my rough agenda of new starts, five long-term priorities which would be facing the future manager of any enterprise, public or private, large or small. In no special order: environment, the new Europe, the continuing economic failure of party politics in Britain, the phenomenon of Japanese competition – and the growing-up of management. These issues loomed only too obviously. What I did not foresee was the rapidity of their development, nor the way they have interlinked. They are all variations on the theme of internationalization: willy-nilly, we are becoming citizens of the one world.

I begin with the Big E – the environment is a borderless priority for the world. Not so very long ago, to care about the limits of our planet was an optional extra in business circles. At the start of the Eighties a few Annual Reports featured environmental policies, but remarkably by the end of the decade the greening of companies' commitments had become conventional wisdom. There is now a 360° urgency around the globe; the pollution of oceans, rivers and ground water levels, the thinning of the ozone, acid rain – these horrors are no respecters of sovereignty. 'One touch of nature makes the whole world kin', Ulysses said. Plainly, national governments can overcome environmental challenges only by sharing power in some form of supernational co-ordination. In this context, the nation state is an idea whose time has come and is going.

In other contexts too the obsolescence of that notion becomes evident, particularly in the framework of the European Community. The continent is no longer isolated. The remnants of British ambivalence towards membership of the European Community look increasingly quaint and quarrelsome. For a long time yet, there will be arguments and negotiations over just how we fit with other member-states. Culturally, there will always be an England, and a Scotland, a Wales and an Ireland, but co-existing in the Community. The awareness of a European destiny is shaping our end as islanders. And already, beyond that reality, there is talk of how the Community will relate with a new wider Europe, even to the Urals.

It is this decisive tilt towards our continental future which unbalanced Mrs Thatcher and brought her down. When I was writing this book, I characterized Mrs Thatcher's style as that of the overconfident Victorian actor-manager who never bothered to rehearse with the rest of the cast. 'Just tell them to keep six feet away from me.' Her self-glorifying isolation left more and more room for the manoeuvrings of the bit-players on the rest of the stage. So she who had lived by the sword as swashbucklingly as any democratic leader this century, died by the sword. At her overthrow, her own rather old-soldierly comment was that it was a funny old world. Historically, I believe the reaction will be that it was a funny old electoral system that let Thatcherism happen.

Our first-past-the-post voting system means there is always the risk of an elective dictatorship. The supremacy of Thatcherism was based on a party supported by little more than two-fifths of the voters and

Epilogue

less than one-third of the total electorate. We have a system in which everybody has a vote but votes are not equally valued. Encouragingly, despite the heavy-breathing opposition of the older political parties, public interest is building up to a critical mass: opinion polls over a decade show a 2:1 or more majority for reform. The case for some form of proportional representation is political and part of the larger argument for at long last modernizing the constitution. Business must be ready to join this reforming debate. Pre-Thatcher it was. The Confederation of British Industry at Conference in 1978 voted to 'press forthwith for early reform'. The way we run our ramshackle of democracy has a great deal to do with the way British business keeps running into trouble. We have been outpaced in Europe since the end of the Second World War by France and Germany, and recently Italy. None of these countries vote as we do. Is there no connection?

Ironically, the most successful economy in the world at this moment, the Japanese, hardly seems to bother about its politicians. However, they do bother most meticulously about the relationship of business and government, that is, the professionals in the government machine; the Ministry of International Trade and Industry for example. That partnership has astonished the whole Western world by beating us at our own business game. 'Catch up with the West' has been the Japanese motto since the Meiji Revolution – perhaps the most success-ful revolution over a hundred years. Now, even the best of Western enterprises know there is much to learn from Japan.

The lessons are more complicated than trying to transplant their brilliant production technology. They involve ideas of consultation and participation, interdependence and teamwork, quality and service. Also, spiritual ideas. Recently, at the headquarters of a famous Japanese high-tech corporation I was challenged after my talk on transnational management. I had argued that Japanese 'internationals' are coming out of a stage of investing abroad through establishing what I term 'production colonies', and moving into a commonwealth stage familiar to many British corporations. They are developing multi-national management and policies of corporate citizenship in the host countries of Europe. I was asked whether I thought that some prob-lems of collaboration between Japanese and Western managements might be traced to the different philosophies and religious beliefs. 'After all, Confucianism is fundamentally optimistic', he said, 'while Christianity is pessimistic about human nature'. I agreed – learning

353

about Japanese management without learning the rudiments of Confucianism was dangerously simplistic. And silently I started asking myself questions. International management will be a pacemaker among world institutions, but are we not taking for granted its growth will be an extension of Western experience. Japan's version of capitalism is not that of the West. So what will emerge after the twain meet? Also, I wondered, could I imagine such a question being raised in the homelife of our good British boardrooms?

Not that I am suggesting that all Japanese management is the model of excellence. There are examples of excellent management in Japan, but so there are all over the world. The significance of the Japanese achievement which has literally staggered Western competition is that it had depended, above all, on the quality of its socially minded management in partnership with government – I repeat, not so much with politicians. Anatomize their best management and it reveals the three-dimensional qualities of best management anywhere.

Which brings me to the plot of these memoirs and to my ruling passion – the evolution of the concepts of management in my time. I have been witness to the growth through its three dimensions. The first is professionalism, the necessary mastery of functional disciplines. But professionalism, like patriotism, is not enough. There is a second dimension, entrepreneurship, which for me includes leadership; far less easy to measure, but then what is most measurable in management is not always the most decisive. No formulas work convincingly here. We cannot programme for spontaneity, for resilience, for that spirit which recognizes that after all the most careful managerial calculations, you still have to leap. Third is the social dimension where management makes an effort to reconcile business and social purposes. In fact, it seems relatively effortless for the Japanese. Their enterprise seems to have grown up naturally in this third dimension, with business and community working if not in harmony then in unison. Western enterprise has only gradually and recently grown into it.

However, nowadays the concept of corporate citizenship, even the manager as citizen, is one that begins to prevail over advanced industrial societies. Management has the responsibility of keeping the balance of interests between shareholders, customers, community and workers. And it is not a bit easy. Company law is not particularly helpful: in no way does it reflect the cat's cradle of commitments, potentially contradictory but each one of them real. There are hard questions ahead for modern enterprise in defining its role.

Ultimately the answers will be up to the individual manager, and this leads me into the fourth dimension. It is relatively unexplored in managerial literature, no doubt because it is not easy to be professional about: the inner life of the manager. I put this at its mildest. As a professional myself I have to watch my language. Soul is probably the right word because it tries to express the individual consciousness of some absolutes in the invisible world. I mean no dogma. I mean absolutes in the sense that for a scientist a set of equations represent an eternal truth; for an artist, beauty; for the poet, imagination – they are all seeking the truth and a good life, but what are we to say absolutes mean for a manager?

Perhaps this theme seems too much an embarrassing invasion of privacy, an intrusion into the secret garden. I think of it as more of an allotment, not far from the works, when I can plant and grow what I need to feed the inner manager. The future will call heavily on the creativity of a manager, as much as a capacity for command and control, and the creativity of a manager is rooted in his or her own set of beliefs. Self confidence and courage, openness, the ability to listen, to decide and lead – these spring from there and cultivate a sense of joy in responding to risk and the unforeseen, fair or foul; and the sense of duty to deal honourably with profits and people. Success in managing this way is not 'up to' the government or the unions, it is mostly down to one's own account. A manager has to audit these inner values which are unseen on the balance sheet. The happy manager is the one who manages the reconciliation of both accounts.

I have written my accounts in the form of a manager's tale. Chaucer's Canterbury Tales revealed 'characters which compose all ages and nations', and as William Blake commented, 'Every Age is a Canterbury pilgrimage'. But there is no manager among them. There is the Merchant, expert in deals, slick on the foreign exchanges, rather flashily dressed on a high horse, impressive but pompous. Frankly he bored Chaucer who said, 'He was a really estimable man, but the fact is I never learnt his name'. If a Manager had turned up to be the thirtieth member of the pilgrim company that spring evening at the Tabard Hotel in Southwark, I hope Chaucer might have seen more in this character of action that he did in the money-maker. Perhaps

the host ('who spoke of pleasure among other things') would have let
the Manager draw the short straw and tell a tale. After all Chaucer
urged,

> 'It makes no sense, and really is no fun
> To ride along the road as dumb as a stone.'

A manager is a pilgrim, or at least a starter: 'You're off to Canterbury
– so Godspeed.'

INDEX

structure 220–7, 236–7; Channel
Tunnel 216, 243, 244–8, 252, 298,
310, 335, 342; commuter
services 215, 240, 295, 298, 335;
Derby research centre 96;
electrification 237, 243–4, 252, 261,
264, 265, 271, 274, 276, 296–7, 298,
300, 302, 306, 310, 317; and
environment 289, 290–1; financial
planning 204, 205–9, 230–1, 238–41,
248, 252, 295–7, 302, 310; flexible
rostering 261, 262, 263, 264–5, 267,
276, 278, 280, 281, 284: and
government 205, 207, 213–6, 238–41,
289, 311; High Speed Train
(HST) 297, 298, 300; manpower 208,
263–4, 271, 272; pay and
productivity 208, 249, 250, 252, 259,
260, 261, 263, 264, 272, 281;
privatization 335–6; public
relations 204, 211–13, 288–98,
302–3; Rail Council 253–4, 260–1,
312; Railcards 235, 248–9, 294–5;
Scotland 233–4, 300; steam 314–5;
trade unions 216–9, 253–86, 288,
289, 312; Transmark 215, 241–3;
Travellers Fare 87–8, 204
British Steel Corporation 142, 143, 200,
201, 211, 248
British Tourist Authority 160, 172–3,
184, 185, 211
British Transport Commission 135–6,
222
Brittain, Vera 58
Brodsky, Joseph 14–15
Brooks, Sir Ray 141, 143
Brown, George (later Lord George-
Brown) 152
Brown, Martha (maternal
grandmother) 3
Brunel, Isambard Kingdom 277
Buchanan, Bill 294–5
Buckton, Ray 217–18, 256–8, 264, 265,
269, 278, 279, 283
Bullock Report 253–4
Burma, war in 20, 23, 27–32
Business Graduates Association 127,
173, 320
Butler, Lord R. A. 54, 134

Butskell (Butler-Gaitskell) 134, 331
Byron, Lord 242

Cairncross, Sir Alex 145
Callaghan, James: as Chancellor 141,
149, 152; as Prime Minister 134, 203
Cambridge University 127, 128
Camp, Will 289
Campbell, Ian 226, 299
Campbell, Sir Jock (Lord Campbell of
Eskan) 103, 104, 106–7, 108–9,
117–21
Capitalfin 188–9
capitalism 38, 40, 80, 139, 333, 336–7
Caribbean 107, 108
Carpenter, Humphrey 61
Casson, Sir Hugh 99
Castle, Barbara 56–7, 144–54, 159, 319
Castro, Fidel 114, 155–9
Catlin, Shirley (later Williams) 58–60
Catlin, Sir George 58
CBI see Confederation of British Industry
Central Intelligence Group (later
CIA) 39
Ceylon (Sri Lanka) 196–7
Channel Tunnel 216, 243, 244–8, 252,
298, 310, 335, 342
Chiang Kai-Shek 10
China 1, 35, 156; childhood in 5–13
Chipman's 306
Churchill, Sir Winston 40, 51, 54,
136–7, 327
City, The 168–72, 317–19, 333–6, 350
Clark, G. N. 46
Clarkson, H., PLC 318–19
Clarkson Tours 184–5, 188–9
Clay, Henry 75
Clayton, Richard 306, 308
clothing industry 175–6
Cold War 40, 53, 155
Colyer-Fergusson, Sir James 245
Common Market see European
Community
Commonwealth countries 120, 188
Commonwealth Fund Fellowship 70–1,
74, 96, 98
Commonwealth Study
Conferences 92–101, 104, 127
Communism 21, 22, 40, 53, 54, 219

Index

INDEX

Index

Index

INDEX

Index

All Pan books are available at your local bookshop or newsagent, or can be ordered direct from the publisher. Indicate the number of copies required and fill in the form below.

Send to: **CS Department, Pan Books Ltd., P.O. Box 40,**
                   Basingstoke, Hants. RG21 2YT.

or phone: 0256 469551 (Ansaphone), quoting title, author
               and Credit Card number.

Please enclose a remittance* to the value of the cover price plus: 60p for the first book plus 30p per copy for each additional book ordered to a maximum charge of £2.40 to cover postage and packing.

*Payment may be made in sterling by UK personal cheque, postal order, sterling draft or international money order, made payable to Pan Books Ltd.

Alternatively by Barclaycard/Access:

Card No.   ☐☐☐☐☐☐☐☐☐☐☐☐☐☐☐☐

Signature:

Applicable only in the UK and Republic of Ireland.

While every effort is made to keep prices low, it is sometimes necessary to increase prices at short notice. Pan Books reserve the right to show on covers and charge new retail prices which may differ from those advertised in the text or elsewhere.

NAME AND ADDRESS IN BLOCK LETTERS PLEASE:

....

Name————————————————————————————

Address—————————————————————————————

————————————————————————————————

————————————————————————————————

————————————————————————————————

3/87

The
Mother
Load

KATY COX

CORVUS

First published in hardback in Great Britain in 2023 by Corvus, an imprint of Atlantic Books Ltd

This paperback edition published in 2024 by Corvus

10 9 8 7 6 5 4 3 2 1

A CIP catalogue record for this book is available from the British Library.

Paperback ISBN: 978 1 83895 320 1
E-book ISBN: 978 1 83895 319 5

Printed and bound by CPI Group (UK) Ltd, Croydon CR0 4YY

Corvus
An imprint of Atlantic Books Ltd
Ormond House
26–27 Boswell Street
London
WC1N 3JZ

www.atlantic-books.co.uk

1

The Final Countdown

It's 6.48 a.m. I'm lying in a child's bed, with cuddly toys wedged under my arms and legs and something sharp digging into my lower back. I reach down to remove the offending item, wincing as I peel it off my flesh. It's a piece of a wooden Africa puzzle – no surprise there – and it's Somalia, one of the pointier-shaped ones. God, it's painful! I'm sure it's left a mark. Maybe even drawn blood. Why couldn't it have been a curvier one – Sudan, or maybe Nigeria?

Rolling over, I see that Jack is awake. He's standing in his cot, his little hands clamped on the rail, staring at me in silence.

'Good morning, sweetie,' I croak. He smiles a gorgeously gummy smile, then slaps his hands on the rail excitedly, his way of saying hello.

He's sweet, adorably so, which is the opposite of what I thought at two o'clock in the morning when he was screaming like an apparition from the underworld. He's teething, or at least that's what Dr Google led me to believe in the middle of the night, but I wasn't convinced. His behaviour suggested that he'd been possessed by something wholly *unholy*, but without the number of a local exorcist to hand, I decided to treat the possession with Calpol and hope for the best.

I'm tired now; not just any sort of tired, but the real debilitating kind where your limbs feel as heavy as sandbags. The sort where your brain has turned to mush and you can't remember how old you are. Where you've lost the ability to speak your native language.

Last night, I'd been working until late at Kensington Palace with my best friends Charlie and Jen. We'd been booked to perform string trios at a posh dinner, and although I'm not usually all that enthused about churning out Mozart for rich people as they shovel down caviar, our agent, Miguel, said that dinner would be provided for us during our break. It's not every day that musicians get to dine out in a palace, especially with their friends by their side, so I'd eaten like a bird all day to save myself for it. But, in the end, we weren't served the 'Angus beef tournedos with mousseline potatoes' as the guests were. Instead, we were each handed a brown paper bag which contained a squashed tuna sandwich wrapped in cling film, a packet of ready salted Golden Wonder crisps and a banana that looked like it had done ten rounds in the ring with Mike Tyson. Charlie, pregnant and emotionally volatile, was already foaming at the mouth with rage, but once we'd realised that Miguel had only allocated us two five-minute breaks, we were all positively murderous. Our brown paper bags of sadness remained untouched, and other than a glass of sparkling water, nothing passed our lips all night.

When I dragged my cello through the door past midnight and saw the state of the flat, I was categorically hangry. The kitchen was trashed, dirty pants and socks were scattered all over the floor, and the bin was bulging full of wet nappies that were exuding a dreadful stink. Worst of all was the discovery that Ed had taken himself off to bed without preparing Stanley's things for school in the morning, so as usual, it was down to me to sort it.

Sighing heavily, I delved into Stanley's rucksack and pulled out his lunchbox. I binned the carrot sticks coated in cheesy Wotsits dust, along with a ball of soggy bread and yoghurt-smothered grapes, then set about preparing the same food for the following day. Of course, it was a pointless task. Aside from half of the sandwich and the crisps, nothing else would be touched, but it was important to me that the dinner ladies knew I'd made an effort. Once the lunch was made and chilling in the fridge, I reached back into the bag to retrieve Stanley's jumper and found a bit of paper soaked in orange juice at the bottom. I gently opened it, but it split into four bits, which I pieced together and laid out flat on the kitchen counter.

Dear Parent,

Tuesday is Fairy-Tale Day. All of the children are invited to come dressed as their favourite fairy-tale character. Time to get creative! Prizes will be given for the best costumes. Please contribute £1 per child. All funds raised will be invested in new equipment for the school playground.

Kind regards,
The Reception Team at Ealing Primary School

I quickly counted the days of the week with my fingers, but kept getting different answers. I tried again, only much slower, saying the words out loud to guarantee accuracy. *Saturday, Sunday, Monday … Shit! It's tomorrow! Okay. Think, dammit! Something with tin foil? An old bed-sheet? Binbag? Shit! Think!*

Nearly seven full weeks of being a school mum had passed, and despite trying my best to hop, skip and jump over every obstacle that had been thrown in my path, I still hadn't managed to get through one full day without falling on my arse.

Pinocchio! Shorts, T-shirt, braces, red lipstick circles on his cheeks, plus I'll make him a long nose. Pinocchio!

By this stage it was almost 1 a.m. I was desperate to pull on my jammies and collapse in bed, but first I had to fashion a long nose out of thin air. I shoved two bits of bread in the toaster, and while I waited, I raided the fridge and stuffed my cheeks with whatever I could find (a few slices of sweaty salami, a handful of olives, two Babybels and a fun-size Mars bar) As I chomped, I washed out Jack's bottles that were floating in grey dishwater in the basin, then made a start on the mountain of plates that Ed had left stacked on top of the dishwasher. I didn't stop until the kitchen was gleaming – I couldn't – and as soon as order had been restored, I abandoned my stone-cold toast and headed outside in the rain to rummage through my neighbour's recycling bins. Returning with armfuls of damp Amazon boxes, I crept around the flat looking for glue sticks, felt pens and scissors, trying my best to keep the noise to a minimum and not wake Jack up. A while later, I had a passable (if a little wonky) cardboard nose and my work for the day was finally done.

Trudging down the hall, I pushed open the bedroom door and waited for my eyes to adjust to the darkness. And there, I saw him ... the impostor lying on my side of the bed. Stanley wasn't tucked up in a little ball, but spread out face down like a huge starfish and taking up two-thirds of the mattress. The remaining third had been invaded by several large pieces of an alphabet floor mat, underneath which was buried a snoring husband.

Another night in a child's toy-filled bed was upon me.

Now it's 6.48 a.m. and I'm gearing up to face the long day ahead. Stanley must be dressed, fed and coerced through the school gates, then I have to battle London's rush-hour traffic and make it on time to teach my first student. But crushing fatigue will not stop me, not today, because there is light at the end of the tunnel. Three days from now, I'll finally be able to drop off the spinning hamster wheel and catch a breath. Because in three days' time, I'll be out of here, away from London and all the stress that it brings, cosied up with my gorgeous little family in a caravan in Cornwall.

It's the final countdown to half-term.

2

Sixty, Fifty-Nine, Fifty-Eight ...

'Mummy. Mummy. Mummy. Mummy,' comes my usual wake-up call from outside the bedroom door. It starts quietly, purring rhythmically like a washing machine mid-cycle, and I let it whir away, allowing myself some time to wake up a bit.

But the washing machine soon starts to crescendo, morphing rapidly from a gentle hum to a percussive racket. 'Mummy! Mum-EE! MUMMY!'

'Okay, Stan! Give me one second.'

'One!' He throws the door open so hard that the handle smacks against the corner of Jack's cot. 'I gave you one. Now, I want my apricot yoghurt, my chocolate pancake and my banana. In semicircles.'

'In semicircles, *please*,' is my automatic response.

'In semicircles, *please*,' he repeats, 'and then I got to put on my pants, then my socks, then my ...'

I wait for him to list every item of his uniform, as I do every morning without fail.

'... then my jumper. And then, I have to go to school, or I will be late and I will not get 100 per cent, Mummy.'

Yawning deeply, I stretch my arms out as far as they can reach and feel the glorious relief of warm blood rushing down my veins to my fingertips. My aching joints slowly start to come alive, ready to face another long day ahead.

'Mummy!'

'Yes, I *know*. I'm coming.'

'MUMMY!' he yells again, grabbing my attention by the short and curlies.

'Yes, Stan. Your clean socks and pants are in the usual place. Can you go and put them on, please?' I avoid mentioning the Pinocchio costume. A strong coffee needs to go down the hatch before I can broach that topic. 'Off you go. Quick as you can. I'll come and get your breakfast in a minute.'

He starts chanting, 'Sixty, fifty-nine, fifty-eight, fifty-seven…' before swivelling around and stomping down the hall towards the living room. Instantly regretting my choice of words, I lift Jack out of his cot and take him through to Ed next door, then I dash to the kitchen to whip up breakfast in fifty-six seconds.

'Three, two, one,' I hear as I skid around the corner into the living room with a plate of pancakes and semicircular bananas. Stanley is standing naked in front of the TV, transfixed by a YouTube video about one of his latest passions, the continental drift. 'Mummy, did you know that Africa and South America were stuck together in one big bit?'

'Stan,' I say with a sigh. 'You haven't put your pants on. Come on, now.'

'And did you know that three hundred millions years ago, they had a really big super-con-tin-ent and it is called Pangea?'

I put his breakfast on the coffee table and grab the pants that have been tossed on the floor.

'And then it got broken up into bits and now there are seven con-tin-ents,' he continues.

'Okay, pop your feet in here, please,' I say, holding the pants out ready for him. 'We don't want to be late. You want your 100 per cent certificate, don't you?'

'The biggest bit is Asia,' he says as he steps into his underwear. 'Then the next biggest is Africa, and then the next big...'

Up until recently, human anatomy was *the* hot topic in this household. Our living-room floor was decorated with rows of miniature rubber organs, and the whole family was subjected to constant reruns of YouTube videos about gall bladders, pancreases and intestines. Nothing else was permitted to be played on our telly.

'Have you seen the new series of *Bridgerton* yet?' Charlie would ask, and my reply would be a flat-out no. 'What about *Normal People* on iPlayer? There's loads of hot sex in it, Luce. And the book is even better!' And my response: 'Of course I haven't seen the hot, sexy BBC drama that *everyone* is talking about, Charls. And I definitely haven't read the book. But d'you know what? I know the "Gallbladder Song" off by heart and I can tell you a helluva lot about hepatic ducts and bile storage.'

Just as I'd reached the point where I'd absorbed enough information to qualify as a lecturer in human biology, a trip to the pub changed everything. It was my mother-in-law Judith's sixty-seventh birthday, and to celebrate, we took her out for Sunday lunch in a new gastropub in Ealing. The roast-beef dinner didn't interest Stanley one bit, but the globe that was sitting on a bookshelf in the corner immediately caught his eye. He abandoned the table and spent all afternoon playing with it, and by the end of the following week, gall bladders were out and maps were very much *in*.

Ever since that roast dinner, the vacuum cleaner has barely left the closet. I daren't disturb the fifty-four pieces of his favourite African-map puzzle that live on the rug in the lounge (all except Somalia, which, as I've just learnt, had the privilege of sleeping in his bed last night). The country-shaped pieces have been organised in order from smallest to largest and if moved, even by one centimetre, Stanley knows, and his reaction is usually explosive.

I pull up his pants then reach for his socks as he pauses the TV and redirects his attention towards his puzzle on the rug.

'Africa is my favourite con-tin-ent,' he says.

'I know, sweetie. I know.'

'Algeria is the biggest country in it, and he looks like paper that is ripped. And the next biggest is Democrapic Repabick of the—'

'It's Demo-*cratic*, Stan. The Democratic Republic of the Congo.'

'Democra-tiCK Repub-LICK of Congo. And Mummy, she looks a bit like a fallen over Stegosaurus.'

'She sure does,' I reply as I wrestle the socks over his toes.

'The smallest is Seashells and she looks like a leg and a foot.'

'It's the *Seychelles*.'

'The *Seychelles*,' he repeats.

I glance over at the Pinocchio costume hanging on the door handle. He's distracted, so now might be a good time to casually mention that, after wearing his uniform for all these weeks, he's now expected to dress in something completely different.

'Um, Stan. I don't know if Mrs Merryweather told you, it's fancy dress at school to—'

'SOMALIA!'

The volume of his outburst pierces straight through my eardrums. 'Stan, please don't shout like that.'

'But he is gone! Somalia is GONE!'

'I know where he is,' I say calmly, but my words go unheard. 'Wait one second and I'll go and get him.'

Stanley bellows, 'One!' as I run off to his room to get the jagged little punk that almost severed my spinal cord during the night. As soon as it's back in line between South Sudan and the Central African Republic, peace is restored.

Time to try again. 'It's dress-up day at school today,' I say bravely. 'And I thought you might like to wear a Pinocchio outfit that I made for you.'

'No!'

'But you just have to wear shorts and a T-shir—'

'Shorts are for hot days, Mummy. Trousers are for cold days, and today is a cold day.'

If he won't wear shorts and a T-shirt, then there's no way that I'll convince him to strap my cardboard creation on to his face. I decide to stick it in a bag and take it into school, so at the very least his teacher will see that I tried. Yesterday's white polo shirt is retrieved from the dirty laundry basket – the collar wet and chewed to pieces. I lay it on the kitchen counter, plug in the hairdryer and set to work drying it out and making it wearable. Minutes later, Stanley is dressed and settled back in front of the telly with his breakfast. Result!

'Morning, love,' says Ed lazily when I zoom into the bedroom at a hundred miles per hour. He's propped up in bed, skimming through a thick folder of sheet music, as Jack lies next to him whingeing. It hasn't occurred to Ed to get Jack's bottle of milk because he has a show tomorrow – his first ever performance of the new Michael Jackson musical in the West End – so, like a horse with blinkers on, that's all he can see. All he can think about.

'You didn't check Stan's bag,' I say, panting like I've just run up twenty flights of stairs. 'I've been up most of the night making a fancy-dress costume.'

He says nothing, so I snatch the folder out of his hands to get his attention.

'What did you do that for?' he huffs. 'Give it back! I'm working here.'

'I said it's Fairy-Tale Day today, Ed, and I've been up *all* night making a Pinocchio costume for Stan.'

'Pinocchio?' He leans forward and tugs the folder out of my clutches. 'That's not a fairy tale, is it?'

'It is now.' I bite down on my lip to calm myself. 'Did you at least wash his hair last night?'

His eyes drop, his silence giving me the answer I don't want. 'Well, that's great. I'm going to have to dry shampoo him again now. You know how he hates the smell.'

'But I was practising,' is his defence. 'I still haven't nailed number forty-one. And the overture is really fiddly. What if I get "never-agained"?'

'There's *no* way you'll get never-agained, love,' I say, softening. 'Have a little faith in yourself.'

His eyes suddenly widen. 'Take Jack for a minute,' he says, his stomach audibly gurgling. 'I need the loo.'

'I can't. I'm running late and I've got to leave extra time for a probable Pinocchio meltdown. Can't you wait?'

But the en suite door is slammed in my face, so the answer is no. His bowels can't wait, but neither can I.

Lifting Jack, I hurry to the fridge to get his milk, and once he is content lying back on our bed draining his bottle, I throw on some leggings and a baggy black jumper that I find strewn on top of a mountain of dirty clothes on the chair. A quick smear of foundation and a squirt of drops into my bloodshot eyes later, I drag a comb through my knotted hair then call Stanley through to get his sorted. I spritz him with dry shampoo which, as expected, is met with resistance, but given that he's squealing anyway, I go ahead and give his hands and face a once-over with a baby wipe while I'm there. Just shoes, coat and bag to do and then we're ready to go.

'Ed, are you done in there?' No answer comes so I knock on the bathroom door with a balled-up fist. 'Ed!'

'Gimme a minute!'

'I don't have a minute!' I push open the bathroom door and find him parked on the loo reading the back of a shampoo bottle. 'For God's sake, man.'

There's only seventeen minutes to get to school before the gates close and Stanley loses his chance of getting a certificate for 100 per cent attendance. I *cannot* let that happen. I've managed thirty-something straight days of being on time, and I'll be damned if I'm going to fall at the last hurdle.

'Drop the bottle, buddy, and come take your son. I've got to run.'

3

The Run

'Come on, Stan, as fast as you can,' I say as I pull him along the pavement.

'Mummy, I like Africa.'

'I know you do. It's great. Just keep walking. A bit faster, come on.'

'I want to holiday in Libya because he is my favourite shape. He looks like a wonky heart.'

It's late October, and although there's a fierce chill in the air, thick drops of sweat are running down my cleavage. It's so hot and greasy in there that you could crack an egg in it and it would probably fry.

'Mummy, I want to go to Lib—'

'I know, but we are going to Cornwall on Friday, remember?'

He stops in his tracks and writes the word 'LIBYA' in the air with his index finger – a silently delivered protest which loses us a precious forty-five seconds.

'Don't forget you want your 100 per cent certificate,' I say calmly out loud, even though I'm screaming it inside my skull.

As we turn the corner onto Oxford Road, I see Marsha Dunn and her gang of mum friends waiting in their favourite spot directly outside the school gates. Marsha is at the centre of the huddle, nothing unusual there, but what sets her apart from the rest is the six-foot-tall, green papier-mâché sculpture that she is holding in her arms. It's a striking piece – less of a kid's costume accessory and more like something you'd see on display at the Tate Modern. She waves in my direction when she sees us, and Stanley's grip instantly tightens.

'What do you think, Lucy?' she calls out as we approach. 'We've gone for Jack and the Beanstalk.' She gently strokes her masterpiece, then leans it in my direction, like she's presenting her newborn baby for the first time. 'I managed to whip it up last night ... but only just.'

'Very impressive,' I say, but those two words are two too many. Stanley yanks my arm and drags me past the group towards the school caretaker's white van that is parked several feet away. I turn back and smile apologetically but it goes unnoticed. 'Wow!' says another woman who has stopped to admire the work of art. 'You should start a costume business, Marsh,' says another. 'I'd *definitely* pay money for something like that.'

Marsha's son, Hugo, is swinging on the gate with a couple of other kids. He hasn't acknowledged Stanley, who is standing quietly beside me squeezing my hand, but I can't really blame him. He has never responded to Hugo's countless efforts to talk to him over the years, so it's not surprising that Hugo has stopped trying altogether. Unless Hugo suddenly develops a passion for Africa or the continental drift, then the two of them are unlikely to ever become friends.

Marsha's attention eventually returns to us. 'And what have you come as today, Stanley?' she calls out. The eyes of all of her friends are on us, far *too* many eyes, and he ducks in behind me and tugs sharply on the back of my coat.

'He's a schoolboy,' I reply. 'But we have a Pinocchio outfit here in case he feels like wearing it.'

'Pinocchio?' An irritating giggle escapes her lips. 'He isn't a fairy-tale character, is he?'

I quickly wipe the sweat from my upper lip with my sleeve. 'He is now,' I say, smiling as I imagine my hands wrapped around her gullet.

'Aren't you going away this week, Lucy?'

'Stop talking!' shrieks Stanley, but I persist.

'Yep, on Friday. We're heading down to Cornwall for the weekend.'

'On Friday?' Marsha's eyebrows spring up to the middle of her forehead. 'And when are you back?'

'Sometime on Monday.'

'So you're taking Stanley out of school for two days? Naughty girl!'

There's no time to defend myself because something more pressing has caught her eye and within seconds, she's up on her tiptoes, waving. 'Heidi! Heidi!'

I turn around and see the head of the PTA approaching. She walks briskly, with her pregnant belly protruding through the gap in her raincoat and her three kids scooting closely behind her. Heidi's twin girls look a year or two older than Stanley, but her son, Patrick, is in his class. Today, the twins are dressed in pink leotards and wear hairbands with glittery pointed ears attached, and Patrick has a brown feathery mask dangling off his handlebars. Three little pigs and a scary wolf, I'm guessing, minus one pig.

'How ad-*or*-able!' Marsha steps sideways and repositions herself directly in front of the open gate, forcing Heidi to stop.

'Thanks,' I hear Heidi say. 'Look, I can't stop. I've got a meeting—'

'Let … me … guess,' says Marsha, painfully slowly. 'Hmmm. Two little piggies, and …' She leans down to examine Patrick's costume, whacking the woman standing next to her in the face with her beanstalk as she goes. 'Hmmm … maybe a—'

'He's the wolf,' Heidi interrupts. 'Anyway, can we catch up later? I've—'

'But where is the third little pig then?' Marsha continues relentlessly. 'I can only see two.'

'Penny, show the ladies Percy, quickly!' says Heidi, and the little girl delves into her pocket and pulls out a small plush pig toy.

'It's such a clever idea!' says Marsha. 'Simple, yes, but very effective.'

'It's not quite my usual standard. I've sort of had my hands full with this one lately.' Heidi rubs her swollen belly. 'The heartburn is keeping me up all hours.'

'Oh, you must try my acupuncturist,' suggests the redhead who Marsha has just assaulted with her sculpture.

'No! There's a *wonderful* homeopath on the Broadway,' Marsha cuts in. 'I have his card here if you like. Hold this.' She shoves her beanstalk into the redhead's arms, then drops to the floor and starts rifling through her handbag.

'Don't worry about it, Martha,' says Heidi, clearly losing patience. 'I really do have to dash. I've got a meeting with Mr Muhley.' With the entrance gate now clear, she seizes the opportunity to escape, leaving red-faced 'Martha' on her knees.

Moments later, Mrs Merryweather appears on the far side of the playground to call the children into class. Hugo and Patrick run straight in without any fuss and Marsha follows, awkwardly dragging her sculpture across the playground like she's on her way to dispose of a dead body.

I kneel down to speak to Stanley who, whilst my attention was elsewhere, has curled himself up into a ball on the pavement. I discreetly pull the nose out of the carrier bag. 'I made this for you, little man. Do you want to see it?' I say, but his head stays buried under his arms. 'It's Pinocchio's nose. It's really funny and I think that the other boys and girls might like to see it, and so will Mrs Merry—'

He lifts his head just long enough to bark, 'P for Pangea! Not P for Pinochicko!'

I gently take him by the elbow and encourage him up onto his feet. 'Are you sure you don't want to take it? Just in case you change your mind?'

But his index finger comes out once again and he hurriedly scribbles 'PANGEA!' in the air. So that's a firm no.

At a loss as to what to do, I wrap my arms around him and whisper reassuring words in his ear. I tell him that he'll have a lovely time today, and once I've picked him up later, we can watch videos together and eat smiley faces and chicken dippers for dinner. But anything I say is met with a deafening 'NO!'

Parents soon start to spill out of the gates with their heads down, afraid to make eye contact with each other, as they're in a hurry to get off to work. Before long, the playground is mostly empty, except for Marsha, who is loitering behind to watch the show with whoever else has no place better to be.

I remain glued to the spot, waiting for a miracle. And eventually, she comes.

'Hello, Stanley.' Mrs Beard, the classroom assistant, approaches. She smiles at me, her finest 'I've got this' smile, and my shoulders unclench and fall to their normal position. 'Do you want to come inside and do the weather chart?' she asks him sweetly.

He ploughs his face into my belly, winding me instantly.

'But you are the only one who knows how to do it.'

A muffled, 'No! NO! Go away!' follows, but Mrs Beard doesn't break. She never does.

'I know!' she says. 'How about if we both go inside and draw some more of your map?'

The pressure of his head nuzzled into my guts lessens slightly, so I take the opportunity to break free. Aware of Marsha's close proximity, I bend down to speak to him in private. 'Stan, you could even draw Pangea and tell Mrs Beard all about it?'

Thankfully, that does the trick. He shuffles towards her and reaches for her outstretched hand.

'Say goodbye to Mummy,' Mrs Beard says, but he won't even look at me, let alone speak. He follows her in through the gate and I'm left behind holding the crappy cardboard nose, racked with such intense guilt that I feel the walls of my heart crumbling.

'Have a good day!' I call out.

'No!' he bellows vehemently. 'I will not!'

He walks away, his hand in hers, and before I know it, he is gone.

It starts to rain on the way back, and by the time I reach the flat, I'm drenched to the bone. I dump the nose in my neighbour's recycling bag, and with a heavy heart, I head upstairs to dry off and get ready for work.

4

The Jam

'Did you get the money?' Mum says over the loudspeaker. 'Your father sent it on Monday and he's worried the postman is going to pinch it.'

The North Circular is gridlocked and the chances of being late for my first student are growing higher by the second. The right indicator has been flashing for well over five minutes, and my eyes are glued to the wing mirror, patiently waiting for someone to let me pull out. I learnt to drive in the narrow lanes of a small Welsh village where herds of cows, gossiping joggers or runaway sheep blocking the road were all I had to worry about. But this is London, and unless you have the driving skills of Michael Schumacher combined with a turbo engine and a 'fuck you all' attitude, pulling into the fast lane of a major London A road is impossible.

God, I wish I'd had a wee before I left the flat.

'Are you still there, love? Hello? ... Roger, this bloody phone is playing up again.'

'I'm here, I'm here. Sorry, I'm just—' I roll down the window '— in, uh, the ... car.'

'Och, there you are. I can hear you now. So, did you get it? The money?'

'I did. Thanks so much. And can you thank Dad for me too?' I poke my arm out and start waving it around, hoping to up my chances of pulling out.

'There should be enough there to buy yous a wee meal and some treats for the boys.'

'Lush. Thanks, you're a … JACKASS!'

'Lucinda Wright!' she scolds. 'Wash that mouth out!'

'Not you, Mum! Some motorbike guy just nearly took my arm off.'

Her tone instantly softens. 'Och, you be careful now. You need that arm to play your cello.'

A silver Audi flashes its headlights to let me out. A miracle! I quickly spin the wheel, slam my foot down and manage to reach a speed of fifteen miles an hour before grinding to another halt seconds later.

'Hello? Can you hear me? Roger, this phone is—'

'Yep. I'm, um, I'm driving right now, Mum. Look, can I just call you guys later?'

A quick scuffle follows, and the next thing I know, Rachel is on the line. 'All packed for Cornwall, then?' she says, her voice muffled. She's blatantly scoffing something – probably one of Mum's home-made bacon and egg McMuffins.

'Ask her if she's got herself a new wee swimsuit yet?' Mum calls out in the background amongst the sound of clattering dishes and Dad yelling, 'Drop it, Poppy! DROP. IT!' at their elderly Shih-Tzu.

'Have you got a "new wee swimsuit"?' Rachel says, mimicking Mum's Belfast accent perfectly, and before I can answer, Dad butts in with, 'Has she got the money? Those London posties are robbing eejits.'

'Both of you shut up!' Rachel snaps. 'I can't hear a word with you both yabbering. She's just said she doesn't need a swimsuit. She's staying at a nudist campsite. And yeah, Dad, the postie has nicked your cash, and he's cleared off to Benidorm with it.'

'Rachel Byers, you're so bad.'

'I know, I'm so naughty.' She laughs. 'So go on, are you excited?'

'Not really. It's just Cornwall, Rach.'

'A holiday's a holiday, isn't it? Four days sleeping in a posh tin box is still better than being in shitty London.'

'Yeah, but I bet it'll be pissing it down, and freezing.'

I'm downplaying it, but in truth, I couldn't be more excited. Sure, it's no five-star trip to the Bahamas, but for us it may as well be. Life has been hard lately – too hard – and I've been champing at the bit for us all to escape London for a while. Ed was away on tour for most of August, so instead of jetting off to an exotic destination to drink piña coladas by the side of a pool, my summer was spent stuck in the flat trying to get my head around some huge news that had hit our family.

At the end of July, a routine appointment with Stanley's paediatrician ended with me being given an A4 piece of paper saying 'Yes, your son is autistic'. Although the diagnosis came as no surprise, and was in many ways a relief, I was still left feeling very overwhelmed by it. I'd read so many articles about autism emphasising that 'early intervention is key' and how an official diagnosis is essential if your child is ever to be eligible to access support. But I left the children's centre that day with no information whatsoever. Stanley was instantly discharged, not just from the paediatrician, but from the speech therapist and occupational health services too. It was literally a case of, 'Yep, he's autistic, now feck off and don't let the door hit you on the way out.'

No one was going to intervene, that much was clear, and any chance that Stanley had of succeeding in life would depend on me and Ed alone. This in itself was tough to digest, but to make matters worse, things between me and Ed had hit a brick wall. He was on tour in America when all of this was happening. I needed him, we all did, but despite my frequent attempts to contact him, he wouldn't answer his phone. He didn't find out about the diagnosis until he came home, and his reaction was so frustratingly underwhelming that a huge blowout between us ensued.

All of the things that had been niggling me in our marriage came to the surface – how I felt invisible, how I didn't feel listened to or supported and how he seemed to care more about the order of his DVD collection than he did his own family. It was only when he packed his bags and went off to stay with his mother for a few days that I had the headspace to mull everything over. And that was when it struck me like a bolt of lightning: Ed was autistic too. Once I'd seen it, I couldn't unsee it. Everything made sense – *he* made sense, as did our relationship, and all I wanted was to have him back home in my arms.

A few days later I sat him down and told him that I thought he might be autistic. It wasn't an easy thing to say, far from it, but if we were to move forward I knew that I had to be honest. He reacted in the same way he always had whenever I'd delivered life-changing news: by saying nothing. But deep down, I knew that the cogs in his brain were turning and he was processing what I'd said in his own time. Sure enough, following a restless night a few weeks later, he came to me one morning and told me that he'd filled out several detailed questionnaires online. The verdict, he said, was unanimous: he is autistic.

It was impossible to know his true feelings about the outcome. Ed had never been one to pour his heart out, and when it came to anything even vaguely emotional, he was very much a closed book. The most he had to say was that it 'sort of made sense'. He admitted that he'd always felt different to everyone else, that from a young age he'd struggled to fit in, but he could never pinpoint why. Other than that, he said little else. He was more of a thinker, I knew this, so I gave him the space he obviously needed to get his head around it. In the meantime, I took to the internet and poured all of my energies in to research. I read up about common triggers, sensory overwhelm and how to manage meltdowns, and I joined Facebook groups run by autistic adults to ask for their advice. I learnt that things needed to change, I needed to change, because if autism was in our lives to stay, I needed to know how best to support my son *and* my husband.

Rachel was my rock, and she assured me that everything was going to work out. She couldn't possibly know that it would, but with me in turmoil about what the future held for my family, she promised that once Stanley started school things would get easier.

'It'll be a fresh start. And not just for Stan, but for all of you. You'll meet new people, and you'll find your tribe like I did,' she said. 'And you'll have lots more free time on your hands. You can work through things with Ed, take on more gigs and get some more money coming in.'

I had no reason not to believe her. She'd been and done it all a few years earlier with my nephew George, and although he got off to a bumpy start when he started reception, he soon settled in after he made a few friends. She met tons of mums in the playground too, and her hectic work life really did get so much easier to manage with George being out of the house six hours a day. Time was what I craved more than anything – time with Ed, time with Jack, who'd always

23

come second to Stanley and his complex needs, and time to work and help ease the pressure on Ed to be the main breadwinner. Time, I was certain, would fix everything.

But when Stanley started school, I realised just how wrong Rachel had been.

Life didn't get easier, quite the opposite.

Our little boy, precious and vulnerable, was gone, and instead of relishing the peace and quiet, I was utterly bereft. He'd been glued to my hip for almost five years, and suddenly he was by Mrs Merryweather's side every day – a woman who was a total stranger. The flat was quiet, eerily so, and when I wasn't working, I couldn't do anything other than mope around with Jack and obsess about Stanley. Was he okay? Did he stop screaming after I left him at school? Or was he standing alone howling for me to rescue him?

I yearned for him to interrupt me on the toilet to tell me the population of Ghana, or for him to shout at me for not cutting his sandwiches into the right kind of triangle. I even missed hearing the same Africa videos blaring out of the TV, and him relentlessly chanting the names of countries in Jack's face in the hope that he would repeat them back. Most of all, I missed the stiff hugs which always came just after I'd helped him put on his T-shirt in the mornings. Stiff hugs that stopped the day he started school.

We didn't meet new people either, nor did we make friends and embed ourselves in the centre of a warm and loving new community. Not even close. For Stanley, school was, and still is, terrifying. It's noisy and busy, and it's full of strangers who he still can't bring himself to speak to. Even now, all these weeks since he started at Ealing Primary School, he doesn't know the names of any of his classmates aside from Hugo, and I'm yet to say more than two words to any of their mothers because he won't allow it. We haven't found our tribe. It's just him and us, and once I've dropped him at school and he has been lured from my arms, it's just him. He's all alone in there, day in and day out.

This mini break, low key as it may be, will be the first chance that we've all had to be together as a family in ages. I need it – we all do.

'I didn't shell out for the deluxe caravan in the end,' I say to Rachel. 'It was mega bucks, and I figured we won't be in it much. I've settled for the standard two-bedroom one, and it comes with absolutely no frills.'

'Well, in that case, you've got to pack the lot. Decent cutlery, a bottle opener, tea-towels and cleaning stuff. And don't forget binbags.'

'Seriously? I'm already taking the whole of Africa. Tea-towels and binbags will push me over the edge.'

'Just get Ed to help you. Delegate, innit.'

'That's *not* happening, Rach. He's got his first show tomorrow and he's looking after Jack today too, so he's a wreck.'

'Poor fella.' I hear her slurp a drink, then take another bite of what I've decided is definitely a home-made bacon and egg McMuffin dripping in butter and HP sauce.

God, I wish I'd eaten something before I left the flat.

'Can you not eat down the phone, Rach? It's minging!'

'Shut up and listen.' I wait for her to swallow and clear her throat. 'I've got news. Guess who's moved onto my street?' A dramatic pause follows. 'The Don!'

'What? As in *your* Don?'

'Yep. And d'you know what, Luce? He is looking g-ooo-d.'

Jason Donovan – known back in the day as 'The Don' – was the most beautiful boy that ever set foot in our village. He only joined Tref Y Glaw's comprehensive school in year ten, but his jaw-length rockstar-esque hair, his cool demeanour and the fact that he could play the guitar propelled him to the status of 'Most Wanted' the moment he arrived. His mum had named him after *the* Jason Donovan (who in 2002 was considered prehistoric and borderline repulsive), but that didn't matter. He was quite literally 'too cool for school' and every girl in the school was desperate to snog him.

The moment Rachel had clapped eyes on him, she was smitten. He might have been two years younger than her, but he was hot and, more importantly, he could play the solo from 'Purple Rain' on the electric guitar. They dated for six months before she dumped him for Rhys Jones who, despite being *far* less good-looking, was older, and this gave him a serious advantage. For starters, Rhys had a fake ID and could pretty much get served anywhere he went, so for Rachel and her friends, there was no shortage of Bacardi Breezers and bottles of Smirnoff Ice to be had. Better still, he had a driving licence and free rein to use his mum's Corsa (cue lunchtime trips to the McDonald's Drive Thru – the key to every teenage girl's heart).

'Oh my God! Is he married? Kids?' I ask.

'None that I can see so far.'

'Had the binoculars out, have you?'

'No need. He's moved into the three-bed semi opposite Auntie Dilys, so she's been keeping us all in the loop.'

Nothing gets past Auntie Dilys. By now, she'll have his full relationship history, details of his job and financial status and, following a rummage through his recycling bins, she'll be able to give us a full and accurate report of his dietary habits.

'Have you spoken to him yet?' I ask. 'Or popped over with a "welcome to the street" crate of beer and a box of condoms?'

'Hell no! I need to lose a stone first.'

The BMW in front slams on his brakes and I manage to do the same, narrowly missing colliding into his WE11 JEL number plate. 'Jack ASS!'

'What? You okay?'

'Look, Rach, I need to concentrate on the road. My first student is at ten and I've still got to tackle the M1 and find a parking space. To be continued, yeah?'

'Ask her what Stan wants for his birthday!' Mum calls out just as I'm about to hang up the phone.

'Just tell her that she can't go wrong with a map puzzle,' I reply, 'or anything to do with the alphabet, colours or shapes.'

'Cool. And what's his favourite colour now?'

'Cyan ... which is a posh way of saying greeny-blue.'

'And favourite shape?'

'Squares. Four sides because he's four, of course. But I'm guessing he'll move onto pentagons the moment the clock strikes twelve on his birthday.'

She takes another bite of her muffin. 'Okay,' she says, squelching as she chews her food. 'We're on it.'

'Stop eating, minger!'

5

The Ticking Clock

Three excruciatingly long hours later, I'm slumped over my cello in a cramped, dimly lit room watching the minute hand on the wall clock, which I'm convinced is moving backwards.

'Oscar, do you promise me that you will practise every day this week for ten minutes?'

The boy doesn't respond because he can't. His mouth is packed full of the crisps which he has been surreptitiously slipping past his lips since the start of his lesson. I haven't said a word about it. He must think that he's got away with it, but the air reeks of pickled onion Monster Munch, and in a tiny room with windows that are nailed shut, you'd have to be severely nasally challenged to miss it.

I have no intention of telling Oscar off. I'm actually quite impressed by his mischievousness. Impeccable behaviour is expected from all students at all times here at this thirty-grand-a-year boys' school, and sometimes it's hard to believe that the students are just children. Any time I go to a classroom to collect a child who hasn't shown up, I'm always a touch saddened when I peer inside and see the rows of little boys, all dressed in grey pin-striped suits like miniature businessmen, working in absolute silence as though they're in an office. Any other teacher here would scold Oscar and confiscate his crisps right now, but I'm not that teacher. He is just a kid, and in my lessons, I let him behave like one.

'Young man, your Grade 2 is really soon and you still don't know your scales. You promise me that you'll learn them?' I say on autopilot because my brain is too busy making a list of everything I need to pack for the holiday.

Stan's alphabet duvet cover, his tablet, extra chargers, nappies, armbands, rubber ring, swimming suits … where the feck am I going to find a swimsuit?!

Oscar swallows and quickly licks the salt off the tips of his fingers. 'Yep, miss. I promise.' He practically throws his cello down on the floor and trips over it as he makes his way over to me. 'Pinkie promise,' he says, dangling his little finger in my face until I'm forced to link mine with his. The deal is sealed, and the moment he leaves, I wash his salty saliva off my hands with sanitiser, then I grab my phone and quickly jot down the list that I've just spent the last half an hour compiling in my head before my next student arrives.

Print booking confirmation, fill up car, get snacks and toys for the journey.

I've spent the last year at home on maternity leave itching to get back to work, and now that I'm here, I just want to run home to be with my babies. If I could, I'd zoom back to the days when Jack screamed for five long hours – between 6 p.m. and 11 p.m. every single night – and I'd tell myself to cherish it. By comparison, those days were far easier than suffering being here at work.

Arriving twenty minutes late this morning meant that I missed my first student's entire lesson, so at some point, I will have to make it up on my own time. That already put me in a grump, but then Lenny Sayers, my next student of the day, failed to show up and I had to trawl the entire campus looking for him. By the time I'd extracted him from maths and escorted him the best part of half a mile back to the music block, there was only five minutes of his lesson left. Fergus Gallagher was next and spent his lesson describing in minute detail the new skin that he'd bought on Fortnite, and following him was Mahesh Kumar who didn't play a single note. He absolutely *had* to go and see the school nurse on account of an agonising paper cut on his finger and never returned. Either he'd got lost or he'd been airlifted to Great Ormond Street Hospital for emergency surgery to save the digit, but whichever the case, I didn't hear any of his scales. His pushy mother will probably put in a formal complaint about me when he fails his approaching exam.

Cutlery, binbags, tea-towels, bottle opener.

The clock is ticking, I have so much to do and I know that Ed isn't going to chip in and help because he is practising all hours. I quickly text him to ask how it's all going, then take a swig of cold coffee, force a smile on my face and head to the door to welcome my next student.

The corridor outside my room is empty. There's no Louis Robertson-Wade in sight. Sighing, I venture to the shelf to find the book of student timetables, then brace myself to trek across the campus once again and coerce him back here to scrape through 'The Can Can' at the speed of a geriatric turtle.

My phone starts to vibrate just as I'm flicking through my monster file of timetables. On the screen flash the three words that parents most dread to see:

INCOMING CALL
School

Oh God! What now?

The first call came just one week into the start of the term, and I totally freaked out. Had Stanley had a meltdown? Hurt himself? Run away? But it was nothing nearly as extreme. I was told that he'd forgotten his book bag and he was 'upset' (which I knew meant hysterical) and I was asked to bring it down as soon as possible. The second call came on a Tuesday when I was here in the middle of teaching Oscar, twenty-two miles away from home. This time, my horrendous failing was that I'd packed orange juice in his lunchbox (a drink strictly reserved for Mondays, Wednesdays and Fridays). He wouldn't touch his lunch until he had his apple juice (a *must* on Tuesdays and Thursdays) and I had to call Ed and get him to run down to the school with it. On another occasion, I'd forgotten his PE kit, on another his socks were hurting, and on another, I'd put the wrong-shaped sandwich in his lunchbox, and I had to wake up Jack from his nap and dash back out in torrential rain to deliver the right sarnie.

I answer the phone expecting to be informed of yet another fuck-up, and true to form, it's the school receptionist, Mrs Abel, ready to rain down her judgement upon me.

'Hello, Mrs Wright. Stanley has forgotten his fancy-dress costume for Fairy-Tale Day. He is the only pupil not wearing one and he is *very* distressed.'

I don't waste any time trying to defend myself. I just say, 'I'll get my husband to bring it down, no problem,' then get off the phone as quickly as possible and call Ed.

'You're kidding!' he snaps. 'Jack has been whingeing since you left and I've only just settled him and started practising. I've still got fifteen pages left to cover until I'm allowed a break.'

'I know, love. I hate to ruin your flow but Stan's freaking out. Just run down to number 24's recycling bag and find the nose. And pray to God that the binmen haven't been, or you'll have a real problem on your hands.'

He mutters a few obscenities before reluctantly agreeing to do it.

I hang up the phone and head out into the corridor to find Louis sitting on the floor watching YouTube videos on his phone.

'Louis, you're here,' I say. 'Where's your cello?'

Without looking up, he says, 'Forgot, miss.'

I exhale sharply. 'Well, I guess you'd better come on in and borrow one then.'

6

Bear Hugs

'Wallet? Fuck's sake, where is it?' Ed mutters to himself.

The dreaded day has arrived, the day of Ed's first show, and he has barely had a wink of sleep. An almighty bang woke us at three o'clock in the morning, one so terrifyingly loud that Ed was convinced we had an intruder. He grabbed a can of air freshener and bravely tore down the hallway to blast the baddie in the eyeballs, but found Jack. He had somehow climbed out of his cot and was sitting on the kitchen floor amongst the pots and pans with a cheese grater just inches from his cheek, poised to give himself some DIY microdermabrasion. There was no getting back to sleep, not after that.

'And my charger? My battery's 9 per cent.' Ed dashes past me into the living room and starts tossing all the cushions off the sofa.

'Relax, love,' I say with the tranquil tone of the Dalai Lama. Having just returned from another distressing school run, I close the front door, shake the water off my brolly and kick off my shoes. 'I've got it covered. It's all in your bag.'

He skids back into the hallway. 'Where?' His bloodshot eyes dart around, failing to focus on anything. 'Where?'

I pull off my coat and hang it on the back of the door before lifting the rucksack that's sitting right beside his feet. 'Here. You have to calm down, love. You'll be great. I know it.'

'What about my charger?'

'It's in there with your black shirt and trousers, in-ears, spare batteries and strings. I got it all ready for you last night. You just need your folder and you're good to go.'

'Uh, okay. Okay.'

'And I've popped three bananas in – one for the journey, one for just before the show and one for the interval to get you through to the end. Make sure you eat them – they're great for taking the edge off stage fright.'

He kneels down and starts rifling through the bag, the sweat running down his face.

'Ed, hug.' I reach over and tug the collar of his jacket. 'Get up here.'

One brief but firm bear hug later, he shoves his folder in the bag, grabs his guitar and dashes out the door, leaving his three bananas lying on the floor.

I can't wait for this wretched show to be over so I can get my husband back. Ed has been an anxious wreck ever since the regular guitarist, Jimmy Martel, got in touch a few weeks ago to ask him to cover the show today. Without running it by me first, Ed accepted. Considering our holiday is fast on the approach, I really wish he hadn't.

The build-up to our mini break was supposed to be exciting: the packing of the suitcase, the buying of delicious food to take with us to cook in the caravan, and the boozy evenings sitting up late googling pictures of the campsite and the surrounding area to really get ourselves in the mood. But there's been none of that. Our lives have been all about the show, and until the last note has been played, Ed will remain a snappy, hot-headed mess and there's nothing I can do about it.

Granted, the man isn't stressing out for nothing. Playing on a West End show isn't for the faint-hearted, and if the shoe was on the other foot, I would've had a brain bleed by now. Performing in a dark, cramped hole under a stage might not seem like a big deal, but what the average Joe doesn't realise is that working in a theatre pit is akin to spending three hours in a giant pressure cooker that's cranked up to the max. Every West End pit is filled with the finest session musicians in London. These are the same people who record the big movie soundtracks and albums at Abbey Road and Air Studios, and who perform in the house bands on shows like *Strictly* and *The Voice*. Playing a new show for the first time to a live audience is scary enough, but when you factor in the calibre of the musicians that Ed has to perform alongside, it's no wonder he's bricking it.

Ed has been a deputy (a 'dep') on lots of shows over the years, but each time he's put himself through it, it's *me* who comes out in hives from the stress of it. Deps never get the luxury of having months of rehearsals with the band beforehand, and given most shows usually run six days a week, Ed will be expected to turn up today and slot seamlessly into an established production. There's a lot to gain, but so much he could lose. If he plays well, he'll secure himself a permanent position on Jimmy's list of deps, and who knows, he might even get recommended for some big recording sessions and TV shows off the back of it. But make a mistake, and he's out. And if that happens, word of his fuck-up will spread across the West End circuit like wildfire and his reputation will be unsalvageable.

It sounds dramatic, but Ed and I have seen first-hand what damage can be done if things go wrong. A couple of years ago, Charlie was invited to dep on *Kiss Me Kate*, and halfway through her first show, she had a momentary lapse of concentration and came crashing in with a rather splendid

G major chord in the middle of a rest. She was 'NA'd' for that – 'Never-Agained' – and it was me and Ed who had to mop up her tears. We tried to reassure her by saying things like 'I'm sure it wasn't that bad' and 'Just wait and see – don't write yourself off', but we both knew that her days in the West End were over. To this day, she hasn't been invited back to play on *any* show, and unless she changes her name and has surgery to drastically alter her features, she'll probably never set foot in a theatre pit again.

Aware of the cut-throat competition, Ed has pulled out all the stops over the last few weeks to ensure that he doesn't get NA'd. He has barricaded himself in our bedroom with his guitar for hours on end, practising until his fingers split and bled all over the duvet cover, and other than popping in to give him cups of tea, beer, snacks and words of encouragement, me and the kids have barely seen him. All household chores, school runs and nocturnal screaming fits have been left to me (and all of this on top of my own work and practice schedule).

In the past, I would have totally lost it with him by now. I would have told him to get a grip, put the guitar down and come and help me bath/feed/change/raise *his* kids. But there has been a seismic shift in my attitude since I've realised that he's autistic. I've made some changes, just small ones, but ones that have already made a big difference to our relationship. When he comes home from work, I've learnt not to bombard him with questions about his day. I know not to bust his balls for forgetting to call, and not to punish him for leaving me alone all day by dumping a crying Jack in his arms before locking myself in the bathroom to scoff a box of doughnuts. After a long, over-stimulating day, I accept that he needs space to be alone – to decompress, to refuel – and I give it to him. If reorganising his Action Man collection is what it takes for him to feel calm, then so be it. It might not make sense to me, but to him it does and I don't question it.

I'm also much more aware of his triggers – busy places, queues, dealing with people on the phone and writing work emails, so I help him. If there's a queue, I will join it. If British Gas are ripping us off, I'll call the arseholes and argue with them. If he has to fill in an application form for an American visa before a tour, I will log on, trawl through the tedious forms and get it done. And when it comes to preparing for a new show, I now understand that Ed has a process that *must* be followed. It's not enough for him to practise the part along to the recording until he feels like he has it all under his fingers. For him, the entire show has to be memorised – all one hundred and thirty-two pages chiselled into his brain – before he can feel truly prepared. If that's what it takes for him to shine, then that's what it takes and I'll support him.

It's taken me years to see that we *are* on the same page, but we just see the page differently.

7

Brian May

'Okay, sweetie. Which one next? The turquoise or the stripey blue?' I hold up a couple of swimsuits to show my sixteen-month-old shopping companion, but he's too busy gumming a chunk of baguette to answer. Not that he can talk.

While Ed is hopefully nailing it in the West End, Jack and I are blitzing the shops to buy all the last-minute bits that we need for our trip. Preparing for a five-hour car journey with two young children is stressful enough, but what's really dominating my thoughts right now is the realisation that in a couple of days' time I'll have to strip off my baggy black winter clothes, don a swimming costume and parade my body around the pool in front of total strangers. Ugh! The horror of it!

Despite my best efforts, the baby weight hasn't budged an inch and I still have lumps and bumps in all the wrong places. In the run-up to Jen's summer wedding, I managed to shed seven pounds and squeeze into the satin bridesmaid's dress, but this miraculous loss wasn't from depriving my body of cakes, crisps and beer – it was down to stress. By the time Jen was back from her honeymoon, I was all cried out about Stanley's diagnosis and far more accepting of the news. Life carried on and old habits picked up where they left off – a sneaky glass of wine at the end of a challenging day, or a Chinese takeaway when I couldn't be arsed to cook

– and before long I was back to square one. Flabby, saggy and full to the brim with self-loathing.

Standing in the changing rooms of Primark gazing at my reflection in the full-length mirror, I see just how far I've let myself go. All of the bikinis that I've tried on have made me look enormous, and while I know that I'm no *Baywatch* babe, I'd still like to look respectable.

The first one was so hideous that it reduced Jack to tears. It was an 'Itsy-Bitsy-Teeny-Weeny-You're-Gonna-Knock-Yourself-Out Bikini'. It didn't matter that I'd opted to try a size 18, because the two tiny triangles of Lycra barely covered my nips, and my boobs escaped below the string like a pair of mad cows charging through a barbed-wire fence. The accompanying bottoms were equally hideous and wholly unsuitable for any woman with an arse even slightly larger than that of a toddler. In metaphorical terms, if your arse is the size of a football pitch, then these bikini bottoms were designed to cover the surface area of an NCP parking space. The bandeau style was even worse. Unable to cope with the force of my heaving bosoms, it made a run for it, dashing down the mighty hills at warp speed, and ended up wrapped around my waist like a belt. And the tankini was just as disastrous, as my boobs spilled out *under* the designated cup-holders.

It didn't take a genius to see that none of the bikinis was going to cut it, so I asked the dressing-room assistant if she would mind grabbing me a selection of one-piece costumes to try. She poked her arm through the curtain a few minutes later with several options in her hand, each one more horrendous than the last.

Firstly, a suit with a plunge neckline. On the hanger, it looked like an exact replica of Borat's mankini, but the tag pictured a model with a substantial set of puppies similar to my own, so I thought that it might well do. After squeezing it on, though, my puppies ran away, disappearing under my armpits, and I was left with a chest flatter than a twelve-year-old boy's. My arse fell out of the black and gold one, my side-boobs slipped out of the red one and the floral one gave me a frontal wedgie. Worst of all was the 'swim dress', which aimed to disguise one's lumps and bumps under an abundance of fluorescent pink and yellow frills. I must admit that there was a level of ingenuity to the design, but rolling up to the pool house dressed like a character from Sesame Street wasn't part of my plan.

My last two options are in hand, and if neither of these looks decent, I'll have to pack my old maternity swimming suit that I haven't worn since I was pregnant with Stanley.

'So, which is it, sweetie?' I say to Jack. 'Turquoise or stripey blue?'

He spits out a lump of soggy dough that hits my left foot, and I take it as a sign to try on the turquoise one, which I'm holding in my left hand. I say a little prayer and bend down to pull it on. I've just squeezed my football-pitch arse into it when I hear a familiar voice from the other end of the changing room.

'Luce, you in here?' It's Charlie. She and Jen have arrived early to meet me for lunch.

'Yo ... over here!' I stick my hand out from behind the curtain and give them a quick wave. 'I won't be a minute, girls. Wait there.'

Nanoseconds later, the curtain is whipped back and my friends get an eyeful of unpleasantness.

'Jesus!' squeals Charlie, her voice piercingly shrill. 'My eyes! MY EYES!'

At five months pregnant, Charlie is like a perpetually erupting volcano. Her hormones bubble under the surface of her skin like hot lava and it doesn't take much for them to come flying out. When they do, they usually spew from her mouth without any regard for the damage that might be done.

'For starters, Luce,' she says, 'Primark is *not* the place to buy a bikini.' She takes a sip of her soda water. 'Not if you have a set of knockers like yours.'

'They're not *that* big, are they?'

'They're huge!' says Jen.

With the palms of my hands, I push my boobs together and lift them up high as they'll go, then let them drop back down to their natural position. They smack the table with considerable force and Charlie grabs hold of it to stop our drinks from spilling.

She and Jen shoot me an 'I told you so' look and I shrug my shoulders in acceptance.

'Yep, and they deserve to be displayed honourably – *not* strung together with a cheap bit of Lycra,' Charlie adds. 'And I'm not being funny, Luce, but you've got *much* bigger fish to fry than worrying about swimwear.' Her eyes wander down under the table to where Jack is sitting on the floor helping himself to the contents of my handbag.

'What, Jack?' He tears open one of my tampons and puts it straight in his mouth. 'Yeah, I know. Don't worry,' I say as I reach down and take it off him. 'I'm going to stock up on loads of snacks to keep him entertained in the car. Or by the looks of it, he'll be happy with a bumper box of Tampax all to himself.'

'Nope. Not Jack. I'm talking about the fact that you have Brian May rocking out the sides of your costume!' She laughs unashamedly. 'You nearly poked my eyes out when I pulled that curtain back in the changing room earlier.'

'Charlie!' says Jen. 'Don't be mean!'

But Charlie isn't holding back. 'I want to break free-eee,' she sings, wiggling all ten of her fingers at the sides of her crotch. 'I want to breeeaaaak freeee!' Her fingers dance up into the air and land on the table, where they scamper in all directions. She explodes into a raucous laugh so infectious that we're all instantly in hysterics.

'*Obviously*, I'm going to have a trim before I go, Charls,' I say once I've managed to stop snorting like a pig.

'Sorry, love, but a "trim" ain't going to cut it,' she says, the hot lava spewing mercilessly out of her mouth. 'You're going to need some *serious* tools to tackle that beast of a bush if you plan on getting some action on holiday.'

'Hold on a minute. I thought you were a feminist?' I say.

She glares at me. 'I *am*.'

'But you're telling me to hack off all of my natural body hair just to please Ed? How is that "for the women"?'

'It's not for him, Luce. It's for *you*.' She slides her drink out of the way then lays both elbows on the table and leans in towards us. Jen and I huddle in closer, intrigued to hear what she has to say.

'Look. Ed is a typical lazy man, right?' she says.

'Of course. And?'

'Well, most blokes don't know where the clitoris is, to start with, so he'll have a cat's chance in hell of finding yours if Brian May is blocking his way.'

I'm lost for words.

Is it really that bad? A Brian May? Surely, it's no more than a Bruno Mars, tops.

'Charls, it's not like I'm off for a dirty weekend in Paris. I'm staying in a low-budget caravan *with* my kids, who sleep in our bed almost every night of the week. I doubt we'll even have sex.'

'Rubbish, Luce! I'm telling you that once you get a whiff of that sea air, you'll be gagging for some action. You can bonk in the bathroom if you have to, and when the time comes, which it *definitely* will, you'll need to make the path to your pleasure pip less treacherous for Ed.' She leans back in her chair and nods sagely. 'Actually, don't worry. I'm on it.' She lifts her phone off the table and suddenly disappears to the toilet. 'Back in a minute. Need to wee, again!'

Our food arrives at the table in the time that she is gone: a double cheeseburger and chips for her, a mushroom risotto for Jen, a bowl of chips for Jack and a sad-looking ham salad for me. Obviously, I wanted to order the scampi with an extra-large side of curly fries, but I'm glad I didn't. With thoughts of Ed going on a quest to find my 'pleasure pip' now embedded in my mind, I should try and shift a couple of millimetres off my waistline to prepare for it.

Charlie returns a few minutes later waving her phone in the air. 'Right. You owe me one, Luce. I've got you an appointment tomorrow at two thirty with Bonnie. She's squeezing you in as a favour.'

I look at her like she has ten heads. 'Uh, who's Bonnie? And what exactly is she squeezing?'

'Bonnie is only *the* best fanny-waxer in Ealing! She'll sort you out and Ed won't need a compass to find his way in the jungle.' She lifts her burger, takes a hearty bite and smiles deliberately wide so we can see the mayonnaise trapped in her teeth.

'Waxing?' I shudder. 'But does it hurt?'

'Of course it hurts, Luce.'

'But no more than pushing two babies out,' adds Jen.

Charlie reaches over and pats me rather hard on the shoulder. 'You'll be fine. Trust me. And even if you're not, I've already paid the booking fee and it's *non*-refundable, so there's no backing out.'

'Bonnie is brilliant, you'll love her,' says Jen.

'What? You know her too?' I say.

'Oh yeah. Charlie bought me a wax as a wedding pressie, and Will was a big fan of Bonnie's work. I see her regularly now.'

'See,' nods Charlie. 'Told you. The woman is an artist.'

'Okay, so I have a question ... how come Jen gets a bikini wax for her wedding gift but I got a gravy boat?'

'Not just *any* gravy boat,' she says with a smile. 'That was a very special one that I pinched from a gig at Claridge's, thank you very much.'

'I'm touched. Really, I am.'

The state of my pubic hair is not the only issue up for discussion. As we chew the fat (or rather, as I nibble a stick of cucumber) Charlie reveals that she has a potentially bigger problem that no amount of hot wax can solve. Simon Monroe, London's biggest pop music agent, has asked her to audition for The Fierce's European tour.

'The Fierce? Who are they?' asks Jen. I'm glad, as I was thinking the very same thing.

'They're some manufactured boy band assembled by a music industry mogul to rake in millions,' replies Charlie. 'I've googled them and they're all over YouTube, averaging ten million hits per video.'

'Standard,' says Jen matter-of-factly.

'I reckon it'll be a big-budget tour.' I can practically see the pound signs glistening in Charlie's eyes. 'And it won't start until the baby is around three months old. So, what do you girls reckon? Is it mental to go for it?'

A lump rises in my throat, then a sharp stab to the chest follows – the vicious attack of jealousy. Simon Monroe has asked her to audition, but why not me? I did a patch of work for him on BBC Radio 2 a couple of months ago, but I haven't heard squat from him since. It's been radio silence. For me, at least.

The internal descent into self-doubt and misery follows, which is totally undetected by Charlie as I have a big smile plastered on my face.

Did I fuck it up? Have I been scrubbed off his list? Or am I just too fat for a live tour? Too mumsy? Too teacher-ish? Oh God! It's my gut. My bingo wings. My double chins!

'That's amazing!' Jen gushes. 'You *have* to go for it, Charlie.'

Despite making a joyful fuss about Charlie's news, I notice that the corners of Jen's mouth are ever-so-slightly curled downwards – a subtle indication that she too is experiencing the typical 'why not me' thoughts. It's only natural. Jen's career might be more focused around performing classical music, but that doesn't mean she wouldn't like a shot at auditioning for a well-paid pop tour. It's much less pressure than her usual gigs, where she plays symphonies for peanuts, but through no fault of her own, pop music opportunities have never really come her way, whereas Charlie has always been drowning in lucrative offers. They might be best friends, but they are also both professional violinists working in London, so whether they like it or not, they're in direct competition with each other for every gig that's going.

Trying my best to be supportive and give some realistic advice without sounding like a Debbie downer is tricky, but as the only mother of the group, I have to be honest with her.

'The money will be amazing, Charls,' I say. 'And I don't want to piss on your fireworks, but if you got the gig, how would you do it? Taking a baby on tour isn't really the done thing.'

She dips a bunch of fries in a tub of ketchup then shoves them all in her mouth in one go. I watch them swirl around like wet clothes in a washing machine as she continues to talk. 'My mum said she'll help out where she can.'

'But doesn't she work full-time?' asks Jen.

'Yep,' she replies casually. 'It's no biggie. Stevie and Dan will be around.'

Charlie's flatmates Stevie and Dan are lovable boys, but they aren't exactly suited to raising a newborn baby. Dan is pretty responsible, I will say that, but Stevie is a disaster. He and Charlie have known each other since school and have been flatmates for years, and in that time, he has set fire to their flat twice – the first time after leaving his hair straighteners on (on top of a towel!), and the second from overdoing it on the peach schnapps, falling out of the shower and knocking over half a dozen Yankee candles that he'd lined up across the bath mat. Aside from being a bit of a firestarter, Stevie is always in the throes of a major crisis and is forever in tears. Admittedly, he has calmed down a bit since boyfriend Dan moved in last year, but he is still extremely sensitive, and there's no telling what might set him off. I once saw him cry because he'd ironed a hole in his cashmere hoodie, and on another occasion, he was hysterical after he found a tiny zit on his forehead the day before an audition for a TV commercial. Another time, he threw a fit because Dan had bought him a low-fat microwave meal for his dinner, which he took to mean that Dan thought he was fat.

They both work as dancers on a West End show – nine shows a week, all of them in the evening, bar two matinees on a Wednesday and Saturday. They never come home straight after the show, but usually hit the bars and clubs along the Strand to party until the early hours of the morning. They are creatures of the night, like vampires (not the blood-sucking kind, but more the Bloody Mary-sucking-through-a-curly-wurly-straw kind), and I can't imagine either of them hurrying back to feed and burp a screaming baby at 4 a.m. And nappies? Not happening. I mean, Stevie gets emotional if he finds a hair in the bathtub, so there's no way he'd cope when faced with a newborn's poonami.

'What about their shows?' I say gently, trying to keep the panic out of my tone. 'Who will do the evening shifts?'

'*Chill*, Luce. I'll get a nanny or an au pair or something.'

'But nannies cost a mint, love, and there's loads of things that you'll need to have in place before you can hire an au pair. You'll need a spare room, possibly a car and all sorts of—' I stop the rant abruptly, fearing that I might push her to full eruption.

'What about Tom?' Jen asks tentatively. 'Can you maybe ask–?'

'And why would I want to do *that*?'

'Because he, um, he's the baby's father.'

I can't believe Jen has the balls to say the T-word out loud, knowing the bitter reaction that normally ensues. Catching Tom, her doctor boyfriend, with his tongue tickling another woman's tonsils was upsetting enough for Charlie, but a few weeks after discovering that she was pregnant, she did a little cyber stalking and learnt the full extent of his betrayal.

'That man was L-wording me but boning half the nurses at the hospital behind my back, girls. I'm not sure why the pair of you are so keen for me to play happy families with him.'

'We're not,' Jen and I say in unison.

'You are!' She wipes the ketchup off her mouth, then crumples her napkin into a tight ball and throws it onto her plate.

I jump in and change the topic, terrified that if I don't I'll get burnt to a crisp by the magma that's seeping out of Charlie's mouth.

'What about you, Jen? Any news to share?' I glare at her in desperation and she takes her cue.

'Not much, really, except Will's car went up in flames.'

'No! The Fiat Panda? It wasn't Stevie, was it?'

'Nope, Stevie is off the hook for this one.' She laughs. 'Yeah, it happened up north somewhere. Will stopped for a fry-up in the Little Chef on his way to a gig and he looked out of the window, and there it was … on fire.'

'I bet he's gutted,' I say. I am too, if the truth be told. That shitty red car might have been a death trap, but for all its faults, it was the chariot that got me to hospital when I was in labour with Jack. 'We'll miss her. She did us proud, Jen.'

'She sure did.' She smiles fondly. 'He's got another one now – some banger that he found on eBay for five hundred quid. He is so chuffed with it but—'

'I've got no problem letting Tom see the baby,' Charlie interjects, having not heard a word of what Jen has been saying. 'But it'll be a cold day in hell before I let him take her for weeks on end … not when he has a load of slappers wandering in and out of his flat all hours.'

The only T-word that truly matters to Charlie is trust, and rightly so. I can't even begin to try and defend the man. He really is a total dickhead and, who knows, if I was in her shoes, I'd probably react just the same.

'Anyway, fuck all that. I'm going to say yes to the audition. I'm doing it,' Charlie says firmly. 'It's the week after next so I'll probably be a bit bigger by then. Reckon they'll notice?'

She stands up, pulls her black dress taut to her stomach and looks down to gauge our reactions.

At five feet and nine inches tall, she is blessed with a long narrow torso and, from where I'm sitting, her bump looks no larger than your average post-Christmas cheese and chocolate pot belly. It helps that as her body has swelled she's had a cunning rethink of her wardrobe, swapping her usual skinny jeans and tight off-the-shoulder tops for short, dark-coloured smock dresses which hide her midriff well. If you didn't know her, you'd probably never suspect that she's pregnant.

'Actually, Charls, I reckon you'll get away with it for now,' I say. 'But if you get the gig, then you'll have to explain seven months from now why you have a screaming baby in the green room of the O2 ... and a set of hooters bigger than Kim Kardashian's. Perhaps more of an issue.'

'Nah. I'll deal with that as and when,' she says casually. 'Needs must, girls. I need the cash and that's that.'

'If you say so,' Jen says. 'But perhaps you should—'

'Do you really think I'll have a set bigger than Kim's?' Charlie interrupts, her eyes wide with delight.

'Yep.' I lift a cherry tomato off my plate then pop it in my mouth.

She crosses her arms over her tiny breasts and cradles them. Smiling dreamily, she says: 'Finally, I'll have a pair to call my own.'

8

Brain Pain

I'm a master multitasker, proactive and efficient, a powerhouse of a woman who, no matter how tired, can keep going and going like the Energizer bunny on speed. Our trip is just twenty-two hours away and since no one else is going to say it, I will. I'm magnificent!

Despite the crushing disappointment of not being asked to audition for the tour, I've given myself a firm talking-to and I've managed to pull myself together. A large injection of cash into our joint account would be more than welcome, but if it means abandoning my children and disappearing for weeks on end to get my hands on it, then it's not for me. My days of gallivanting across Europe with burly young pop stars are over, and that's okay. There's plenty more work out there, work on home soil, and I just need to get off my arse and claim it.

Having managed to suppress all feelings of despair, I've directed my attention towards someone more miserable than me: Ed. His first show went well (or at least that's what he said when he rolled through the door pissed out of his skull last night), but by lunchtime today he still hadn't received any feedback about his performance from Jimmy Martel or the show's musical director. As time has dragged on, paranoia has totally consumed him and he is now convinced that the entire show was a 'fucking disaster' and that he has definitely been 'never-agained'. Most musicians in a similar boat would probably block out the paranoia by hitting the pub, but not Ed. He has chosen to handle the blow by burying himself under the duvet in our room, torturing himself by carefully analysing all one hundred and thirty-two pages of the music pad to decipher where he might have gone wrong.

Lord knows I've tried to pull him out of his funk. I cooked bacon and eggs and delivered it to him in bed, and after Jack went down for his mid-morning nap, I even danced into our bedroom to flash him my boobs, but nothing I have said or done has made any difference to his mood. The man is in full shut-down mode, and until he hears from Jimmy, he's never going to perk up. So, while he is wallowing in misery under the duvet, I've thrown what's left of my energy into packing for our trip and praying that Jimmy comes through for him. If he doesn't, our holiday will be ruined.

My morning has been spent single-handedly sorting out everything that we need for our break. All of the family's clothes have been packed, and I've stockpiled all of Stanley's and Jack's go-to foods in case there isn't a decent supermarket nearby. The car has been filled with petrol and the tyres pumped up. I've downloaded a map so that we can find the caravan site without Ed calling Jane (our well-spoken and highly patronising sat nav) a 'stupid cow'. Not only have I done all of these things without complaining, but I've also managed to do them whilst being inundated with messages from Ed's mother, which have been coming thick and fast since 7 a.m.

Ping!

Don't forget to pack extra inhalers, Lucy.

Edward's chest can play up by the sea.
Judith xx

One hour later ... *Ping!*

Don't forget to water your plants before you
go. Your peace lily was very dry and wilted
the last time I saw it. Judith xx

And ten minutes after that ... *Ping!*

Have you packed hand sanitiser? There was
an article in the paper about how filthy those
resorts are. Judith xx

As grating as these messages are, I'd take them any day over having to see her in person. Since embarking on a romance with our neighbour Alan, she has developed an inconvenient habit of turning up on our doorstep unannounced. 'I just happened to be in the neighbourhood,' she will say, but one glance at her new blouse and her professionally blow-dried hair is all it takes to expose her underlying motives. It's obvious that she just wants to leave her car on our drive and avoid paying extortionate parking fees to schmooze with her beau from number 27, and after spending one obligatory hour with the kids, my suspicions are usually confirmed when she vanishes 'to the shops' and we don't see her until she's reversing her car out of our drive at the end of the evening. As long as she is drawn to Alan and his irresistible collection of pastel-coloured V-neck jumpers, these impromptu visits aren't going to stop. If we weren't going away tomorrow, I suspect that she'd be knocking on the door right now after having made plans to sneak off to Café Rouge with him.

PING!

> Did you get that article link that I sent about
> the boy that got mauled to death by a dog in
> a caravan? J xx

Feck's sake!

After lunch, Amy, our wonderful babysitter, arrives to look after Jack so I can attend my appointment at the waxing parlour. It might be extravagant to shell out money on childcare just so I can beautify my genitals, but Charlie has shamed me into it. If I want to feel vaguely attractive on holiday, perhaps even get some hot action, then Brian May needs to go.

Halfway down Windsor Road, my phone starts to ring. I pull it out of my pocket, glance down at the screen and see the dreaded three words:

> INCOMING CALL
> School

I answer expecting it to be Mrs Abel as usual, but it isn't. It's Mrs Beard. She tells me that Stanley is having a rough day and she feels that it would be best if I came and collected him.

The words 'rough day' can only mean one thing: he has had a meltdown.

I am told that during morning break a group of kids were playing cops and robbers and one boy told Stanley that he was going to shoot him. It didn't matter that the boy was wielding an imaginary weapon, because being the most literal of children, Stanley believed that his death was imminent. Mrs Beard tried and failed to calm him down, but I can't say that I'm surprised. If I thought that I was about to be shot at point-blank range by a five-year-old kid, I'd be absolutely hysterical too.

Stanley is sitting in reception rocking gently on his seat when I arrive to collect him. His little legs are dangling in mid-air, his eyes are red and swollen and his hair dishevelled, but emotionally, he appears to be much calmer than I was expecting.

'Hello, little man. I'm here.' I reach down to hug him and his body stiffens. He pulls away from my arms and slips off the chair and begins to pace back and forth.

'Excuse me, Mummy, excuse me. He said "kill you". He said "kill you", "kill you", "kill you"!'

'I know, Stan, but it was just pretend. Not a very nice kind of pretend, but I'm sure he didn't mean it.'

Mrs Beard pops her head around the cornerand greets me with a sympathetic smile. She offers her apologies for failing to defuse the situation, then assures me that she will ask Mrs Merryweather to have a word with the class about more appropriate games for the playground.

'We thought that it might be best to take him home so that he has a chance to unwind before he goes away tomorrow,' she says to me, then she bends down to speak to Stanley. 'And I know how excited you are to be going on holidays, Stanley.'

He blanks her and paces to the door, then springs up on his tiptoes to try and reach the lock.

'Wait a minute, please, Stan. I'm still talking to Mrs Beard,' I say. 'Away from the door, please,' but he ignores me and jumps up and down on the spot trying to grab the bolt.

Mrs Beard steps in. 'Before you go, Stanley, I have something for you, and it's something that I know will make you very, very happy!' Straight away, she has his attention. He turns around and stares at her intensely as she reaches over to Mrs Abel's desk and lifts a brown envelope with his name written on the front in block capitals.

'Open it,' she says, and his face beams when he sees what's inside. It's a handmade certificate saying, 'Well done, Stanley, you have 100% attendance!' Stars, hearts and smiley faces are drawn around the border, and the '100%' has been written in large rainbow-coloured bubble writing. I can tell instantly that it is her work. My instinct is to dive on the woman, to hug and squeeze her until her head pops off, but not wanting to come off as a total nutter, I simply say thanks and decide to buy her a posh bottle of wine for Christmas.

We leave the school with just ten minutes to go until my appointment at the waxing parlour. I really should cancel, I want to, because for the first time in ages I have my little boy all to myself. Jack is in good hands with Amy, so why not take Stanley out for a treat? We could go for ice cream, perhaps buy a new puzzle to cheer him up, or head to Ealing Library and let him go wild flicking through all of their atlases like we do most weekends. But then I remember Charlie's harsh words about the state of my bountiful bush and I cringe at the thought of exposing it to my poor, suffering husband. Plus she has already paid a deposit, hasn't she?

'Stan,' I say, 'I have to go to the hairdresser's now.'

'Why?'

'Because I want to change its shape.'

'Why?'

'Because I want it to look nice on holidays. Shall I quickly take you home to play with Amy and Jack, or do you want to come with me?'

He replies instantly with an answer I wasn't expecting. 'Come with me.'

'But it won't be fun. It'll be really *really* boring. Let me just take you home quickly.'

'Come! Come! I like to come!'

I don't have time for a debate, and definitely not one that might escalate to a meltdown. 'Okay. You can play maps on my phone while you wait,' I say as I take him by the hand. 'And if you're really good and sit quietly, we'll go for ice cream and buy a new puzzle afterwards.'

His eyes light up. 'Mummy, okay. That is very okay.'

With just minutes to spare, we jog up to the High Street hand in hand and take a left by Pret a Manger. We're making good progress and the parlour is in sight when Stanley suddenly stops, jolting me backwards and jerking my neck. 'Ouch! Stan! Don't stop!'

He looks up and frowns intensely as he examines my face. 'What shape are you going to have?'

'Shape? What do you mean?' I rub my neck, trying to cure what feels like whiplash. 'Look, we're going to be late. Come on.'

'What shape?' he persists, pointing at my head. 'What SHAPE?'

'Oh.' I hesitate briefly. 'Um, I don't know. I can't think just now.'

'I think like Libya,' he says decisively. 'Because Libya is my favourite shape.' He then draws what I assume is the shape of Libya in the air with his index finger.

Although I admit it's a rather nice shape, having my bits waxed to resemble one of the most hostile, war-ridden territories on the planet isn't quite what I had in mind. I want to entice Ed, not repel him. I need a style that says 'Welcome, come on in' and *not* 'Danger! Run away! Save yourself!'

I stifle a laugh. 'Maybe, Stan. Come on, let's get going.'

Waxing Lyrical

I'm sitting in the waiting area of Waxing Lyrical with my legs crossed, waiting to be tortured in the name of vaginal beauty. Stanley is pacing back and forth in front of me, happily entertained by typing random countries into Google Maps on my phone, then telling me how long it takes to get there by foot.

'Have you looked at the menu?' asks the receptionist, a thin brunette with gold dangly hoops that almost touch her shoulder blades.

'There's a menu?'

'Oh yeah. We do all sorts in here.'

'Spain takes eleven days and nine hours,' interrupts Stanley in his standard 'outdoor voice'.

'That's very far away,' I whisper. 'What next? France?'

'No, *not* France. Portugal!'

'Stan, can you try and speak a bit quieter? That man is trying to concentrate on reading his magazine over there.' The handsome man in the corner peers over the top of his copy of GQ and smiles gratefully. I turn back to the receptionist. 'Sorry, you were saying something about a menu?'

'I've got you down for a bikini wax, yeah?' Like Stanley's, her voice is at least twenty decibels louder than I'd like. She tugs a thick leather-bound ring binder off the shelf and totters over in her excruciatingly high heels like a wounded deer.

'Mummy, it says Portugal takes fourteen days and eleven hours.'

The girl smiles at him, albeit strangely, then opens the binder and lays it down on my lap. 'Have you thought about what kind of style you'd like?'

'Style?'

'Yeah, like a Brazilian or a Hollywood?'

The heat hits my cheeks when the attractive man in the corner looks up once again, but before I can find any words to respond, Stanley cuts in. 'Brasilia is the capital of Brazil, and Hollywood is in Califormia.'

'Califor-*nnnnia*, Stan,' I correct him, then I turn to the girl. 'I'll just look at the list. Thanks.'

I bury my face in the ring binder like a humiliated schoolgirl, only to be thrown into a world I never knew existed.

Waxing Lyrical

Bikini Treatments

CHLOÉ
Classic bikini wax: knicker line and crease of leg
£40

ROXANNA
A high-leg bikini wax, extended to top and underneath **£45**

JASMINE

Our popular Hollywood style that removes everything

£58

ARIANNA

A Brazilian wax which includes butt crack, inner and outer labia, leaving a small strip **£58**

Buttocks

N.B. Shaded areas reflect hair removed

JENNIFER

Full buttocks **£30**

KIKI

Butt-crack only **£22**

Just five seconds looking at the first page of the 'menu' makes my pelvic-floor muscles shrivel all the way up to my throat.

Butt-crack only? Inner labia?!

The explicit descriptions of the treatments are one thing, but the accompanying illustrations and hefty price tag attached to each one make me want to throw Stanley over my shoulder and make a run for it with my inner labia still intact. But it's too late.

'Lucy?'

A plump woman is standing over me, her peroxide blonde hair stacked in a spiky pile on her head like the crown of a pineapple. Her face is an explosion of colour. Lilac eyeshadow is dusted across her eyelids, her lips are a glossy coral, and aside from the circles of salmon-pink powder on both cheeks, her skin is a solid canvas of orange from wearing liquid foundation that's at least four shades too dark.

'Charlie's mate, right?' she says in a sweet, high-pitched cockney accent. 'I'm Bonnie. Come on through, luvvie, and we'll get you sorted.'

Stanley hasn't acknowledged Bonnie standing right beside him. 'Belgium is two days and twenty-one hours to walk.'

'Belgium?' Her eyebrows raise ever so slightly, but not as much as they might do if she wasn't Botoxed up to the hilt. 'I've been there, sweetie, and they've got the *best* chocolate in the world.' She turns to me and adds 'and beer' under her breath followed by a cheeky, unwrinkled wink.

'I *don't* like chocolate and I *don't* like beer!' protests Stanley.

'Oo-er! Well, that told me!' She chuckles and slaps her hands together jubilantly. And that's when I notice her nails – inch-long, shiny, sharp talons, painted blood red.

A bush trimmer with shears for fingers … Oh God! She's Edward fecking Scissorhands!

'Right then, let's crack on,' she continues. 'I've got just two more of you to go and then I've got to leg it. I've got a late lunch date at Greggs with my fella.'

Still lost in thoughts of the horror of my impending shearing, I silently stand up and hold my hand out to Stanley and wait for him to notice it, but the phone has his full attention.

'Your little fella can stay out here if he likes? Michelle's good with the kiddies,' says Bonnie. She bends down to speak to Stanley. 'She might even have a lollipop for you if you want?'

He steps in behind me and presses his face into my back.

'Actually, can I bring him in? He'll be happy playing with my phone. Have you got a curtain or something in there?'

'Yeah, I've got a screen, luvvie. Is that all right?'

'Perfect. Thanks,' I say, before guiding Stanley by the elbow through the door and down the narrow corridor behind her.

In the centre of the small, dimly lit treatment room is a high metal-framed bed with a roll of white paper towels laid out across it. The bed is similar to what you'd see in a doctor's office, but I'm relieved that there aren't any stirrups attached to it, nor is there a lamp hanging from the ceiling to provide an unwelcome spotlight. The walls are filled with floating shelves which are stacked with bottles of fancy lotions and bundles of lemon-yellow hand towels, and wafting from a scented candle is the faint smell of lavender, which isn't nearly potent enough to mask the overwhelming scent of disinfectant.

Bonnie ties a plastic apron around her waist, then takes a swig from a can of 7up and dumps it down on the nearest shelf. 'So, what are we doing for you today, luvvie?'

I'm hovering by the doorway behind Stanley, my knees knocking together as I clutch his shoulders and pull him closer to my body like he's a human shield. 'To be honest, I've never done this before, so I'm really not sure. What do you suggest?'

'We do all sorts in here, m'love. Hollywoods, Brazilians, nips, bums, tums ... the full monty! I did a heart yesterday, and I ain't even kiddin' but last week a lady asked for a thunderbolt.'

'Mummy wants a Libya shape because Libya is my—'

'A thunderbolt?' I quickly interrupt. 'Seriously?'

Bonnie nods emphatically, then lifts a long spatula and starts stirring a large bowl of what I assume is the wax.

'Yep. City girl, she was. Had on one of those posh suits and carried a briefcase and all. But y'know what, nothing fazes me these days.'

'I had no idea that people got so creative,' I say, genuinely surprised at the lengths that some women will go to to beautify their genitals.

'Oh, it's big business. And it's not just the ladies, y'know. A couple of weeks back, I waxed "Say YES?" onto a fella's chest. The question mark was a bit of a faff to do, but the message came across all right. He came in and told the girls that his boyfriend had said yes, so it must've been good enough.' She drags the bamboo screen over to the treatment table and opens it out, then places a chair on the other side for Stanley to sit on. 'So, what's it gonna be?'

My eyes have been opened to possibilities I never knew existed, but it's all so overwhelming. 'Well, what do *you* normally go for?'

'God no, darling! I tried it once, but I said to my fella that if he wanted me to do it again, then he'd have to get his—' she pauses and glances down at Stanley, suddenly aware that his little ears are pricking up '— um, to get his *plums* done first.'

I burst out laughing at the mention of 'plums'.

'Yep. That soon shut him up.' She snaps on a pair of pink latex gloves without any bother. 'Right, so I reckon a Chloe is the way to go for you, luvvie. Perfect for a first timer.'

I release my grip on Stanley's shoulders and bravely step forward. 'Okay. Let's do it.'

Ten minutes later, I'm not only halfway to having a beautiful new hairdo, but I've also made a cracking new friend. As Bonnie rips out my pubic hairs, she tells me everything, and I mean *everything*. Conscious that Stanley is sitting behind the bamboo screen, she chooses her words carefully, but she still manages to distract me from the agony of her assault by delivering an entertaining account of her life as a mum of two and wife to a bricklayer called Darren, a man who has quite the sexual appetite.

'The man's got his sword in his hands twenty-three hours a day and he's always fixing for a *fight*.' She winks at me and waits for me to signal that I understand what she's talking about. I smirk and quickly return the wink, giving her the green light to continue in a similar child-friendly fashion. 'I swear to Jesus that I only come to work to give my *fairy* a rest.'

Aside from a sword-fighting husband and an exhausted fairy to contend with, she tells me that she has a nineteen-year-old daughter called Britney and a ten-year-old son whose name I don't catch because she only refers to him as 'our little accident'.

'Britney's was bad, but *his* labour was off. The. CHARTS! Seven hours it was, puffing and panting in one of those paddling pools, and you'll never guess what happened?'

'What?'

She calmly smears the sticky wax across the creases of my leg and pats down a strip. 'Well, the midwife said to push and so I did, yeah, and then, I'm not kidding, but a couple of *chicken nuggets* slipped out!'

'Nuggets! No!'

'I ain't lying, babe! It was proper bad. And the midwife – hilarious, she was – made Darren scoop them out with a fishing net!' The strip is torn off in one swift motion and the sound of my gasping is totally buried under her shrill guffaws. 'He wouldn't go near me for months after that. And it made me think that maybe I should have *chicken nuggets* in the bath more often!'

'Jack poos in the bath,' interrupts Stanley, alerting us to the fact that he has managed to crack Bonnie's code. 'Mummy takes it out of the tub with a yoghurt pot. But not a full one. An empty one.'

Bonnie explodes once again, her laughter so physically raucous that she has to sit down for a moment to regain her composure.

By far the best discovery I make is that her 'little accident' goes to the same school as Stanley, meaning that she is seriously clued-in on both the classroom and playground politics.

'That Mr Muhley has got no *plums*, and take it from me, if you want anything done, you've gotta go through his secretary.'

'Mrs Abel, right?'

'Yep. That's her. She's been there donkey's – since Muhley was in nappies, I reckon. She wears the trousers, all right. I mean, he can't fart without asking her first. Oh, and there's Heidi. Have you met her yet?'

'PTA Heidi?'

'Yep … *total* fruit-and-nut bar, that one.'

'Really?' I'm practically salivating as I wait for her to dish the delicious dirt. 'Go on. Hit me.'

'Well, she's always shooting out kids one after the other and now they're like the blimmin' Von Trapps, so they are, getting up in every school concert to play guitars and bongos together. I mean, use a condom, love. Give some other kid a chance, eh?'

My cheeks throb from smiling so much. 'How many does she have, then?'

'She's got those twins, Penny and Polly. Then she's got Pascal in year six with my boy, and there's an older one …

Perry or Parry or something. And she's cooking another one, ain't she? So nearly five in all.'

'And she has a son in Stan's class. Patrick,' I add. 'So that's soon to be six, right?'

'Gawd, what a mouthful! Can you imagine her calling them down for their tea? It'll be like that "Peter Piper picked a peck" thing – "Penny, Polly, Pascal, Parry, Peter … your pizza is ready." *Total* nutter!' Bonnie scoffs.

She goes on to tell me that Mr King, the PE teacher, is 'built like a Chippendale' and worth a look on a dull day, and Mrs Beard, as I've already learnt, is the best member of staff in the school by miles. Her exact words: 'She's a good egg, that one. A total legend, through and through.'

It's fair to say that I've learnt more about Stan's school in twenty minutes than I have in nearly seven weeks, and although having my pubic hair ripped out of its sockets is a less than desirable way to get this information, it's all worth it.

'So, have you got any pals down there? Found your tribe?' Bonnie asks.

'Not quite,' I reply, suddenly saddened by the 'T' word, which feels as unachievable for me as winning the lottery. 'I know one mum from my pre-baby days, but she's a bit of a, um, a …'

'Duckhead?' Bonnie winks exaggeratedly.

'Yep, actually. She's a major duckhead. Like a front-runner in the duckhead-lympics.'

'Hilarious, babe!' she roars, then tears another strip off my fairy. 'Well, stay away from her and find another crowd.'

'Easier said than done.' I sigh. Stanley's antics at the school gates during the first few weeks have extinguished any hope of making friends. The crying, screaming and attempts to do a runner at every single drop-off meant that I didn't get a chance to introduce myself to any mums, and now that he has calmed down a bit, the opportunity to befriend anyone has long since passed. Clusters of friendships have already formed which are impossible to infiltrate, especially as Stanley won't enter the playground unless it's empty. Until he musters the courage to go inside where all the action is, I'm stuck on the street, standing by the caretaker's white van, listening to Marsha and her usual bullshit by the front gates.

Several minutes of ripping and stripping later, Bonnie's masterpiece is finished.

'Right, that's you ship-shape and shiny, luvvie.' She tugs off her latex gloves and takes a quick swig of her 7up. 'Wanna 'ave a look?'

'God, no!' I say. 'As long as it doesn't look like a plucked chicken then I'm happy.'

'Hil-ARIOUS!' she squeals again. 'Well, have a lovely time on your holidays. Oh, and top tip, if your man is batting down your door for a sword fight just crush a few Kalms and mix them in his pint. They knock my Darren right out every time we're on holibobs ... then I can sit on the balcony with me book in peace.'

'Top tip! Thanks.' I quickly climb off the bed and manage to pull on leggings before Stanley emerges from behind the screen.

He stares at my hair in bewilderment. 'Excuse me, Mummy, but it looks the same. And there is no Libya!'

'Let's go buy a new map puzzle, shall we?' I grab his hand before he can say another word. 'Quick, before the shop closes!'

As I'm standing paying the receptionist, I hear Bonnie

call in her next victim. 'Brad, it's your turn, my luvvie. A Kiki as normal, yeah? Come on through.'

Brad lays down his copy of GQ on the empty seat next to him, then slowly uncrosses his legs and stands up. With his buttocks clenched in trepidation, he follows Bonnie into the treatment room.

10

SOMALIA!

'Cheers!' I hold my drink up to toast Ed's, but his head is drooping down towards his phone and he fails to notice.

'Ed! Cheers. I said, cheers!'

When no response comes, I lean across the table and clink my glass against his. He looks up and smiles half-heartedly before returning to his phone.

His joyless demeanour means I already know the answer to my next question, but I ask it anyway. 'Any news from Jimmy?'

He shakes his head sadly then lays his phone face down on the table. Lifting his glass, he leans back in his seat and downs the remainder of his beer in one go.

'Just text him,' I yell over the sound of Stanley, who is spinning around in a circle chanting 'A for Angola, B for Burundi, C for Chad' at deafening volume. 'Ask him for feedback.'

'No way,' says Ed. 'That's not the done thing.'

'D is for Democrapic Republic of Congo ...'

'Democra-*Tic*,' Ed and I say in unison.

'*Democratic* Republic of Congo, E is for Egypt ...' Stanley continues.

With Ed's glass now empty, there's nothing else for his fidgety hands to do but check his messages again. I reach over and grab the damned phone off the table before he can get to it. 'You can't go on like this, love. You'll drive yourself insane.'

I'm trying my hardest to be patient, but this self-indulgent misery has been dragging on long enough. Our first day in Cornwall is almost over and not one drop of relaxation has been had.

'L is for Libya, M is for Mali, N is for Nigeria ...'

'Just cheer up, love. Look where we are! Soak it all in and try to enjoy it.'

But our immediate surroundings aren't anywhere near what I'd pictured when I booked it. Online photos of the holiday park showed lush green fields with a stunning lake at its centre, where fluffy ducks tottered about, even a swan or two. There was so much to do: bike trails, a nature reserve, an adventure playground and a private beach all within walking distance, plus a large pool with two slides and an onsite shop, pub and chippy. By night, the clubhouse had all sorts of child-friendly entertainment on offer, and with all of that going on, I figured that we wouldn't be in the caravan much. That was why I'd booked this one – the 'standard' caravan – which I've now discovered means the 'way-below-standard' one.

It's small – shoebox small – and there's barely enough room to swing a cat let alone accommodate a spinning four-year-old and a sixteen-month-old toddler. There's no Wi-Fi (disaster!), the walls are made of cardboard (quite literally 'paper thin') and it stinks of wet dog and damp towels. There *are* two bedrooms, I'll give it that, but neither are big enough to fit Jack's travel cot. He will have to sleep here in the lounge where the windows only have cheap yellowing net curtains to keep out the sun. Some very early starts are on the horizon.

I could slap myself silly for not reading the small print before hitting the 'book it now' button, but there's nothing we can do other than make the best of it.

'Crazy day, eh?' I say to Ed as I pour him another beer, but his mind is still lost in thoughts of West End shows and guitar chord charts and he doesn't say a word.

'Crazy day' doesn't even begin to cover it. The ordeal. The stress. The vomit.

The traffic had been minimal when we left London at the crack of dawn, and we managed to cover a good hundred or so miles with Stanley quietly watching his tablet and Jack snoozing in his car seat. Ed was in a grump and made it clear that he wasn't up for chatting, so I pulled the lever on the passenger seat, lay back and delved into the erotic novel that Charlie had lent me ('for inspiration').

I managed to read all the way to chapter eleven without any interruptions. The fiercely handsome duke had cornered the timid maid in the kitchen where he had her pressed up against the wall, breathlessly yearning for his 'throbbing sceptre'. He was kissing her neck – softly, tenderly, at first, but as the hunger for her flesh consumed him, the kisses hardened and turned to passionate bites that made her groan with pleasure. He bit. He sucked. He drank in her 'sex' harder and harder. Then, when he was moments away from ripping open her corset and ravaging her in the pantry, all hell broke loose.

'Somalia!' screeched Stanley at the top of his lungs.

The shock of the outburst caused Ed to swerve the car. In a panic, I tossed my book, undid my seat belt and turned around to see what was going on.

'He is GONE!'

The whole of Africa was strewn across the back seat. All

71

of it, bar one essential piece: Somalia. Stanley was screaming like he'd been set on fire, and the hysteria escalated so rapidly that he vomited everywhere. Hot chunks of partly digested banana and chocolate pancakes sprayed across the back of the car, saturating everything in its path: the puzzle, the snacks, the blankets, the seats and, worst of all, Jack, who started bawling from the shock of it.

'What's going on back there?' Ed barked furiously.

'Ed, pull over!'

It was a disaster. Somalia was missing, and if my instincts were right, it was tucked up in its usual place under Stanley's duvet. There was no getting out of this one. Regurgitated banana chunks I could handle, but a missing Somalia? No.

Ed pulled onto the hard shoulder and got out of the car to have a breather. While he paced back and forth on the hard shoulder of the M3 in the rain, I climbed into the back seat to sit in a pool of vomit and hug my babies until they calmed down. Which, eventually, they did.

Ed returned dripping in rainwater, but visibly calmer.

'Let's just turn around and go home, love,' I said defeatedly. 'We've got to go back for it.'

'Actually, I've got an idea.'

'No, Daddy! Go back home!' Stanley was already riling himself back up into a state.

'Stan, let's *make* Somalia,' Ed suggested. 'I'm serious. We can stop at the services and make a new one.' It was a bold move. Some might say a stupid one. But amazingly, it worked.

'But it *has* to be green, Daddy! It *has* to be like the other one at home and he is green.'

'No problem,' Ed said confidently. 'One green Somalia coming up.'

We pulled up at Fleet Services half an hour later, and whilst I took the kids to the toilets to clean up, Ed dashed to WHSmith with a wallet full of cash and a heart full of hope. He returned to the car with a stack of empty Costa cups, a pack of Crayola pens, Sellotape and a pair of nail scissors from a travel manicure set, then got to work. Using a picture of Somalia on Google Maps, he drew the outline onto a thick wedge of flattened cups, cut them out, coloured the top piece in green and then taped them all together and presented it to our bereft son.

'I love him! I love him 100 per cent' was Stanley's reaction, and once we were back in the car and on our merry way, I leant over and whispered very similar words in Ed's ear. The man is a crafting legend.

By the time we arrived at the camp site, we were all exhausted, smelly and starving, so before checking in, I suggested that we head straight to the pub to have lunch and a pint of the strongest beer on tap. Lord knows that we both deserved to claim our gold medal at the end of what had been a marathon of a journey. But we never got our glorious glass of thirst-quenching lager, because blocking the path to the pub lay Cornwall's answer to Disneyland.

The amusement arcade.

Ed was the first to get hooked in – 'Look, Stan! *The Empire Strikes Back!*' – veering off course and straight over towards a massive black box with red and blue lightsabers emblazoned down both sides of it. Seconds later, his wallet was out, his coins were pumped into the slot and he'd transformed from a forty-three-year-old knackered dad of two into Luke Skywalker.

Naturally, it didn't take long for the kids to follow in their father's footsteps, and there was nothing I could do to stop it. Everything that a child could ever wish for was there: air hockey, mini basketball hoops, toddler rides, claw grabbers, candy floss machines and giant red race cars with real seats and steering wheels. It was an open-plan paradise, an irresistible maze of attractions designed to lure innocent youngsters in like moths to flames. And our kids were no exception.

Stanley was instantly besotted with the coin-dropper machine. The simple act of pushing a twopence coin into a slot and watching it fall onto a moving platform was totally mesmerising to him, but he wasn't in it for the money. Once he'd clocked a teenager pulling a reel of paper tickets out of the neighbouring machine – tickets that could be exchanged for prizes – that was it: he was obsessed.

In the absence of any identifiable structure, he has channelled all of his anxiety exclusively towards winning as many tickets as possible, and knowing my son, it's a dead cert that we won't be leaving this place until he has bled the ticket dispenser and our bank account dry. Our relaxing break will go as follows: Wake up – 'I want tickets.' Have breakfast – 'Tickets!' Suggest going to the pool, the beach or for lunch – 'Tickets!' For a nature walk – 'TICKETS!'

And we will do exactly what he wants, because he is our world.

11

PEACE AND QUIET

It's our second night in beautiful Cornwall and, as predicted, I haven't seen an inch of it beyond the arcade and the clubhouse. We haven't walked around the local town, nor have we set foot on the beach and inhaled the fresh sea air, and not a single morsel of locally sourced cod and chips has passed my lips. To top it all off, the misery of swimsuit shopping and the agony of deforesting my Brian May were all for nothing. As it stands, there's plenty of slots getting stuffed on this holiday, just not the one I had in mind.

But all is not lost. Ed is up to level sixty-one of *The Empire Strikes Back* and Stanley, to his delight, has amassed an impressive collection of three hundred and thirty-nine tickets. Jack has also been having the time of his tiny life, and I've been folded over like the Hunchback of Notre Dame since we arrived, holding his hand and being dragged in the direction of anything with sparkly lights. Which is *everything*.

'Tickets!' comes the cry for the four-gazillionth time today.

We are in the clubhouse, where hundreds of Brits are packed-in like battery hens around the edge of a small semicircular dance floor, sucking up their overpriced drinks as they watch the mini-disco. Barney Bear, a six-footer of matted brown fur with a thick Liverpudlian accent, is busting his moves on stage, leading the crowd in a dangerously overchoreographed rendition of 'Heads, Shoulders, Knees and Toes'. Arms and legs are flying about, the fuggy air stinks of chips and the sweat of a hundred pits, and at any moment, it's likely that someone is going to get knocked out cold by an overly enthusiastic elbow.

'Stan, why don't you go and have a dance? It looks fun,' I say, because it's worth a try.

'Tickets!'

'Go on. Daddy will go with you and you can both have a boogie!'

'Tickets!'

'And once Jack wakes up, we can all have a boogie together.'

The blaringly loud music stops just as he screams 'TIIIIICCCCCCKKKKKETS!' with the shrillness of an air-raid siren.

With every eyeball in close vicinity on us, Ed is quick to cave in. 'Okay, okay. Let's go to the arcade, little man.' He leaps out of his seat and grabs his wallet off the table.

'Ed, no. We can't keep giving in!' But my attempt at responsible parenting is overshadowed by the bellowing – 'TICKETS! TICKETS! TICKETS!' – and as always, I back down. 'Fine, just take him. I'll stay here with Jack,' I say. 'It's easier.'

Off they disappear down the stairs towards the arcade, where they will no doubt remain until Darth Vader has been defeated and Stanley is wrapped in more strips of paper than an Egyptian mummy.

With Jack still snoozing in my arms, his soft cheek nuzzled into my cleavage, there's not much else to do other than mess around with my phone. There hasn't been an opportunity to turn it on since being woken up by a flock of seagulls dancing on the roof of our caravan at 4 a.m., so now's my chance. Leaning back in my seat to take the strain of Jack's weight off my back, I reach for my phone, switch it on and wait for it to boot up. WhatsApp and text-message notifications fly into my inbox at such a rate that my phone starts to vibrate furiously and persistently, like a Rampant Rabbit cranked up to the max.

The first message is from Judith:

> Hi Lucy. Hope you're all having a lovely time.
> I can't stop thinking about your sad little
> peace lily. Did you remember to water it
> before you left? J x

I delete it straight away and move onto the next one from Charlie:

> Luce. I just told a pigeon to 'Fuck off' and
> then cried about it for 10 minutes. WTAF! x

Another one from Judith follows, sent only five minutes after her previous one.

> Lucy. Did you get my message about the
> peace lily? Did you water it? J x

Then Charlie again:

> Urgent pregnancy question: how big are
> these nipples going to get? They're the size
> of dinner plates!

And directly after that comes *another:*

> OMG! Just found a pube. On my NIPPLE!

And another:

> What do I do? Shall I pull it out? Or will doing
> that make fifty more grow?

Then another:

> It's BLACK! And THICK! And long enough to
> hang my washing off! HELP!
> PS. Did Ed find your pleasure pip?!

Fully intending to offer Charlie support at this difficult time, I start typing a reply but only get as far as 'Hi love' before a waitress stops at the table next to mine. I wave to get her attention and mouth the words 'Can I have a pint of lager, please?' and once she gives me the thumbs up, I lay my phone on my lap to have a quick breather.

Charlie's gigantic hairy nipples are at the forefront of my mind. If I was a terrible friend, I'd spill the beans and let her know the full extent of what is in store for her body once her baby is born. Two pregnancies have left me with a moustache, a goatee and hairier nipples than King Kong. If you throw the purple wormy veins down the backs of both thighs and the cellulite and stretch marks onto the pile of post-pregnancy fallout, I'd happily trade it all in for her solitary washing-line nipple hair. In fact, I would welcome the extra space to hang the insane amount of washing that has landed in my laundry basket since becoming a mum.

My pint arrives moments later. I take a quick sip then assure Charlie that a pair of tweezers will solve her heinous problem in a flash. Next, I drop a message to my mum and dad, Rachel, my Auntie Dilys, Big Nan and my Auntie Glad, who have all requested a holiday update. Naturally, the words 'having a ball' and 'never felt so relaxed' are used, then I move on to my text messages.

The first one is from my cellist friend, Emily:

> Hi Luce. Archie has a high temperature and
> I can't leave him. Any chance you're free to
> cover me tonight for a gig at the Savoy? 6—9
> p.m. Masked ball. £175 and dinner included.
> Em xx

It's so typical that work comes in on the one weekend in the year that I'm away, but it's no biggie, because after declining her offer, an even better one pops into my inbox.

> Hello Lucy. Meredith here. Can I heavy pencil
> you in for *X Factor* results show tomorrow
> night? 3 p.m. call. LH2 Studios. Cleared by
> 10 p.m. And can you confirm your dress size
> and shoe size for wardrobe?

My brain quickly launches into business mode. *A 3 p.m. call? That's doable if we pack up the car tonight and leave the caravan by 8 a.m.*

Undeterred by Meredith's request for my dress and shoe size – neither of which are favourably low numbers – I take the bull by the horns and accept. Ed is having a miserable time anyway, and Stanley has been out of sorts since we arrived, so leaving early won't be a big deal, surely? It's Meredith Foster, a woman you *don't* say no to, and it's live television, performing to eight million people on the UK's biggest show. Ed will understand. He has to.

But the opportunity is snatched from my grasp.

Buzzzzzz.

> *X Factor* has already been sorted.
> Apologies. M

Hired and fired in the blink of an eye … same old, same old. The sting of rejection never gets easier to take, even after all of these years of hard grafting.

Desperate for a distraction, I gulp my beer and move on to Facebook. Seventy-two notifications are waiting to be acknowledged and top of the list is one from Marsha:

Marsha Dunn is at **St Stephens Church**, Ealing with **Nicola Fry** and 26 others.
4 November at 17.34

Brilliant day! Thanks so much **Nicola Fry** for inviting us to Monty's birthday party. Hugo had the BEST time! He loved being a tiger. Hope Monty liked his present. xx

No good can come of clicking on the photos attached, but curiosity takes control. Scrolling through every picture, my eyes home in on the painted faces of Stanley's classmates – tigers, monkeys, glittery unicorns and zebras – dancing and jumping on bouncy castles, scoffing cake and kicking balloons across the dance floor. There's so many kids, too many to count, but no Stanley.

Maybe he wasn't invited because Marsha told people that we were going away? But my instincts tell me otherwise. We've been here plenty of times before, and it's *never* the case. Party invitations are as mystical to Stanley as unicorns.

Mere seconds away from bursting into tears … *Buzzzzzz.*

> Hi Lucy. Just to say that I've popped over to water
> your peace lily. It's looking much healthier now.
> Did a bit of washing too and managed to get rid of
> that awful smell in your washing machine. And the
> electric bill has arrived. £183. So expensive! Much
> love to you all. Judith x

Lucky for Ed, he's busy stuffing what's left of this month's mortgage money into coin slots. He must have given Judith a key to our flat, and if he was within arm's reach I would strangle him dead.

As I cringe at the thought of Judith reading through our bank statements, her lips shrivelled in disgust … *Buzzzzz.*

> Hi Lucy. Are you free to audition for a UK/Europe
> tour? THE FIERCE. 13 weeks starting March.
> Audition next Wednesday 8 November, Kensington.
> 10.30 a.m. Pls confirm receipt ASAP. Will send
> more details upon confirmation. Best. SM

'Holy shit!' I leap out of my seat, startling Jack awake.

'Can you watch your language, please?' snaps an old woman at the neighbouring table. 'There are children present!'

But there's no time to apologise, because I'm already hotfooting it down to the arcade with Jack in my arms.

I find Ed queueing up for the *Star Wars* game, holding a monstrous bucket of popcorn and a half-eaten hot dog, with a pink unicorn plush toy wedged under one arm.

'Ed!' I dive on him and shower his bald head with kisses. 'I got an audition! I got one!'

12

The Time of My Life

It's our final evening and, true to form, we've spent most of the day in the arcade. A brief visit to the pool did happen after lunch, but the thick scent of the chlorinated water proved to be too overpowering for Stanley. There's only so many times one can let their child shriek 'It stinks! It stinks!' in a pool full of strangers before feeling compelled to leave.

Leaving early was a blessing. My time was spent in the toddler zone with Jack, who only wanted to walk in circles around the edge of the shallowest of pools. Standing up *and* bending over in an old maternity swimsuit, flashing my wobbly bits to all and sundry, isn't exactly my favourite pastime, so I was more than relieved to put my clothes back on and get dragged back to the claw grabbers.

To celebrate our final night, we're in the clubhouse watching the cabaret show *A Tribute to Dirty Dancing*. Bribing Stanley with a ten-pound note did the trick. He is perfectly content sitting at his own table in the corner counting all the tickets that he has amassed, and Jack is bouncing happily on my lap as he ploughs his way through a cone of soggy chips that cost almost as much as my monthly phone bill.

I'm in a brilliant mood. The offer of an audition has given me a long overdue boost, but I'm being extremely careful to downplay my elation, as poor Ed still hasn't heard from Jimmy. We have gin and tonics in hand, gin that we smuggled into the clubhouse inside an empty Evian bottle. I don't feel a shred of guilt about it. The arcade has already robbed us blind, so I'll be damned if I'll pay the extortionate bar prices and allow ourselves to be rinsed of our last few pennies.

The evening show so far has been an unexpected but very welcome feast for the eyes. Barney bear – the host of the mini-disco – is actually a bear of *many* talents. At 6.30 p.m. each night, directly after the bingo, Barney is just a fluffy irritation who riles up little kids, but at 8.30 p.m. on the dot, he magically transforms into 'Jonah' – a hot, muscled and deliciously flexible specimen of humanity.

Clothed in a skintight white vest and black leather trousers, he strides across the stage in time to 'Hungry Eyes'. He takes the hand of his svelte blonde dance partner, pulling her in close to his pouting lips, thrusting his pelvis and spinning her backwards just before their lips dare to touch. Suddenly, I'm aware that my tastebuds are watering, my palms are sweating, and my heart is throbbing as I soak in his magnificent physique like some Grade A pervert.

As the gin slides down my gullet, a pleasant heat begins to spread through my body. It starts in my cheeks but by the time the production reaches 'She's Like the Wind', the heat has intensified and spread all the way down to my loins. I had assumed the high-quality gin was to thank for this pleasant sensation, but I now realise this isn't a gin rush, but a Jonah one. With every rugged thrust of his manhood, a bolt of electricity strikes my pants (Oh God!) and when his partner swings one leg around the back of his waist and reels him in close to her body, my fanny practically bursts into flames.

'Ed. Let's go back to the room!' I say with extreme urgency.

He is face down, staring at his phone, as he has been since the show started.

'Ed!'

Still no response.

'Look, this is getting out of hand. Just send Jimmy a text and ask him for feedback, will you?'

'No,' he says firmly. 'I just have to wait.'

'Ed, there's a semi-naked woman with legs up to her armpits on stage. She's smokin' hot and very bendy and you're missing all of it!'

He briefly glances over at the girl then flops back in his chair, uninterested.

'A quick text is all it'll take. The man is probably busy and hasn't had a chance to contact you. His phone might have been stolen, or maybe he's got the shits or something. There'll be an explanation. Just text him. I beg you.'

Ignoring me, he slides his thumb across his phone screen.

There's nothing I can do. Ed would rather stew in his sadness and ruin what's left of our minibreak than send a simple message. The temptation to wait until he goes to the toilet and text Jimmy myself is overpowering, but my conscience won't let me. There are plenty of things I can do to make Ed's life easier, but this isn't one of them.

The most anticipated song of the evening starts to play, 'I've Had the Time of My Life'. The crowd erupts into raucous wolf-whistling, applauding jubilantly as Jonah somersaults diagonally across the stage towards his partner. Upon reaching her, he lunges into a handstand and settles on his head. He splays his legs wide open and starts to spin, drawing my eyes towards his dinger, which casts a large spinning shadow across the stage like some kind of mesmerising merry-go-round.

I slam my glass down on the table. 'Ed. Let's get a drink!'

'I've already got one.'

Leaning across, I pull his phone out of his hand. 'Look at my face, love. I said, how about we go back to the caravan and have a "drink".' I air-quote the word 'drink' with one hand because the other is trying to hold my necklace out of Jack's reach. 'Or maybe we can have a drink in the bathroom?' I wink exaggeratedly, but his blank expression tells me that he is not even close to cracking my code.

Moments later, the crowd goes wild when Jonah's biceps practically burst through his skin as he hoists his partner up over his head to execute the famous final lift.

I'm straight up on my feet. 'Ed! Kids in bed. Gin. Shag. Let's go!'

This does it. His eyes light up and he's out of his seat in two seconds flat.

'You take Jack back and start getting him settled,' I say as I hand him over. 'I'll handle Stan.' He straps Jack in his pram and races out of the clubhouse at such a breakneck speed that I'm certain he has left skid marks on the carpet.

When I arrive at the caravan forty minutes later, my arms laden with popcorn boxes and another tenner's worth of paper tickets, Jack is fast asleep in his pram and Ed is nowhere to be seen. Assuming that he has steered off task as usual, I tell Stanley to put on his pyjamas and I go to find him.

Before I reach the bedroom door, an almighty ruckus penetrates the atmosphere.

'I'm IN! Love, I'm in, I'm in!'

Ed bursts out of the bathroom wearing nothing but his boxer shorts. With a toothbrush in one hand, a phone in the other and an expression of pure glee on his face, it's clear that the golden text of approval has arrived in his inbox at last.

'Jimmy's texted?'

'Yep, and he's asked me to do two full weeks in December, plus Christmas Eve and Boxing Day, and there's double time on Boxing Day.'

'Amazing!' I squeal, choosing to ignore the bits about Christmas Eve and Boxing Day. It's bad enough that he's going on tour to Australia for the whole of January, but now he'll miss a huge chunk of Christmas too. Yet he's out of the gutter of despair, for now at least, and I'm determined to make the most of it while it lasts. 'I told you, love,' I say. 'I told you that you'd nailed it.'

'And he hadn't been in touch sooner because his wife had gone into labour, so there you go.'

'Right, this calls for a celebration! You sort the drinks; I'll sort the kids. I'll meet you back here in ten minutes.'

Fuelled by desire, I'm more than motivated to execute my motherly duties as quickly as possible so we can get down to business. Jonah's athletic prowess has inspired me and I'm hopeful that, if Ed's biceps are up to it, he too might throw me around the caravan like a rag doll.

Jack remains asleep during his nappy change, which is performed with the stealth of a bomb-disposal expert. Even when I transfer him to his travel cot in the lounge he doesn't stir, but Stanley is harder to settle.

'Mummy, crisps!'

'"Mummy, *please* can I have some crisps" you mean?'

He repeats my words without breaking his focus on the tablet, which he is struggling to turn on. I place a small bowl next to him and stand over him, drumming my fingers on the cardboard wall as he meticulously licks every grain of salt off one crisp.

He slaps the tablet in frustration. 'Mummy, I want Africa!'

'An Africa *video*, *please*, Stan.'

'AN and VIDEO and PLEASE!'

'Fine!' I switch on the tablet, find his favourite video, then suffer a full five minutes and twenty-three seconds of geographical torture as he licks the salt off two more crisps.

'Right, that's it. No more videos. Time for teeth and wee-wees.'

'Get me drink!'

'Stanley Wright. That's enough, it's bedtime!'

'Drink, drink, drink, drink!' comes the monotonous chant.

'Sshhh! You'll wake your brother.'

'DRINK!'

Trying my hardest to keep my cool, I grab a bottle of water off the unit, dunk in a straw and hand it to him.

'Juice in cup!'

'Just take this. Hurry up now.'

'Don't shout!'

'I'm not,' I say because I'm really not. 'Just have a sip of water and let's get you to bed. You don't want to be tired for the arcade tomorrow, do you?'

He snatches the bottle and wedges it between his legs. Ten excruciating minutes pass where each and every crisp is licked clean and placed back in the bowl, and at no point does he touch the water. I can actively feel my virginity growing back, and if some quality time with Ed is to be had, there's no choice but to give him what I know he wants. So, against my better judgement, I head to the kitchen to wash out his favourite cup and fill it with blackcurrant cordial. Once he has it, he drains it in one go.

But not even that is enough.

Four Africa videos, two Asias, two wees and a laborious toothbrushing session later, he finally climbs into bed and eventually falls asleep with a thick reel of arcade-game tickets clasped in his tiny hand.

I find Ed on the sofa, head tilted back, mouth wide open. I gently shake his arm, but when he doesn't stir, I do it more vigorously. 'Love, wake up. Come on. Wake up.'

He opens his eyes and squints at me, totally disorientated, then lets out a dry hack of a cough.

'The kids are down. Get out your lightsaber and I'll meet you in the bathroom?' I wink. 'What I've got planned can only take place behind a lockable door.'

'Uh, what time is it?'

'Time to take *me* dirty dancing!'

He wipes the dribble off his chin with the back of his hand. 'Uh ... okay. Let's go.'

Five minutes later, my loins and I are having the time of our lives on the toilet seat. And it really is 'The Time of My Life' because it's the longest that we've sat down all weekend.

13

Trigger-Happy

*C*lick, click, click.

The sound is familiar, but in my semi-conscious state I can't quite place it. Figuring that it must be Ed grinding his teeth in his sleep, I roll over in bed and gently tap him on the shins with my foot. But the sound persists.

I kick him again, only a little harder, but out of nowhere a far more irritating noise trills through the air.

'Good morning, everyone!'

I jolt upright and, to my horror, I see Judith standing at the foot of our bed with her phone in hand.

Click, click, click.

'You all looked so peaceful, so I thought I'd take a picture!' she chirps.

'Judith! What are you do–?'

'Breakfast is ready,' she interrupts. 'I've got some nice fresh fruit and yoghurt. I thought that you might want something healthy after your weekend of indulgence.'

'Judith! Can you please get ou–?'

'It looks like you might need your pyjamas back, Lucy!'

I snatch the covers and pull them up over my head and wait for the squeaky giggle which I know is coming. 'I'll wash them for you now,' she says before casually strolling out of the room and giggling all the way down the corridor. Squeakily, of course.

We'd arrived home late last night to find her waiting for us in the flat. The peace lily was her excuse for being here ('It was gasping for a drink!') but I knew that she'd been out with Alan and probably couldn't face driving home in the dark on her own. Nothing new there.

The traffic on the M3 had been diabolical and our journey back had taken almost seven hours. With Stanley chanting lists of countries for most of it and Jack crying for nursery rhymes to be played on loop, Ed was riled up and ready to blow by the time we rolled up on the drive. The presence of his mother was just too much for him to handle, so I did the noble thing and gave him the green light to escape. I sent him to the shower to scrape the smell of the journey off his skin and I dealt with Judith alone. As much as I would have liked to, I couldn't exactly throw her out at 10 p.m., so I ended up lending her some of my pyjamas and making up the sofa bed in the living room.

I shake Ed awake vigorously. 'Your *mum* was just taking pictures of us!'

'Uh?'

'Ed! Get in there and sort her out now, before she loads them up onto Facebook and ruins our lives. This wouldn't be happening if you didn't give her a fecking key!'

He doesn't budge, so I throw on a nightie and storm out of the room, slamming the bedroom door behind me.

Judith is in the living room, lounging with her feet up on the recliner as her index finger glides across her phone screen.

'You're not posting anything, are you, Judith?'

Entranced by the irresistible glow of her phone screen, she doesn't reply.

'Judith! What are you doing?' I snap, perhaps more harshly than I intend to.

'What?' she retorts defensively. 'I'm not doing anything.'

My gut tells me not to trust her. Knowing how trigger-happy she can be with the Facebook share button, fast action is vital. I stomp over, and just as I'm about to snatch her phone, she holds it up at arm's length in my face.

'If you don't believe me, look!'

Surprisingly, on the screen is one of those quizzes that you find on Buzzfeed: *Which Harry Potter character are you?*

'Is it your time of the month, Lucy? Because I must say that you're being *very* hostile right now.'

Seething, I back out of the room in silence and head to the kitchen. I need coffee. And lots of it.

'I'll just be a minute, then I'm going to sort out your laundry,' she calls out. 'There's dirty pants and wet towels all over the hallway floor. Didn't they have any radiators in your caravan?'

I return a few minutes later with a cup of peppermint tea and hover over her, waiting for her to take it, but my presence is ignored. As my hand starts to burn, she casually presses a few more buttons, then pauses to wait for her results.

'Rubbish!'

'Who did you get?'

'Can you explain to me why liking salad, reading historical romances and watching *Sherlock* make me Hagrid? He's that big hairy oaf character, isn't he?'

'Yep.' I swallow my laugh. 'He's the gentle giant.'

'Well, I'm *nothing* like him!'

I drag the coffee table over and put her tea down. 'It's all for clickbait, Judith.'

'Click-what?'

'Those quizzes are full of ads. They're designed to make you click on them so big companies make money.'

She sighs exaggeratedly then tucks her phone down the side of the recliner, sulking that she'd allowed herself to be tricked.

Judith and a smartphone make for a dangerous combination. Ever since upgrading from a prehistoric flip phone to the latest iPhone last month, she has been introduced to the wondrous world of social media and, like most people, she has become totally obsessed with it.

'Did you see the pictures of Erica's baby? He's got his father's nose.'

'Has your friend Charlie put on weight? She's looking a little tubby around the middle.'

'Oooh! I've got fourteen likes for that picture of my begonias.'

The running commentary is hard enough to tolerate, but lately I've had to start policing her Facebook page on a daily basis after she posted a wildly unflattering photo of me. It was taken a few hours after Jack was born – me in the hospital bed, one boob out, hair a huge ball of frizz, black eyeliner staining my cheeks and with the spotty complexion of a pubescent teenager. Thankfully, the picture had only generated nine likes by the time I'd seen it, but I'm all too aware that once she learns how to tag people, she'll have the potential to cause massive damage to my reputation at the click of a button.

Other than posting hideous photos that are not meant for the public eye, she has developed a penchant for sharing articles on her feed that I just know are aimed at me. 'Marie Kondo's Top Tips to Keep Your Home Tidy' and 'Top Five Calorie-Burning Exercises to Help You Lose Belly Fat' are pretty standard, but every so often, she'll post something that makes my blood boil – 'Autism Can Be Cured ... A Study Finds'.

Despite reading Stanley's diagnosis report from the paediatrician with her own eyes, Judith will not accept it. 'They never had anything like that in my day' is all she ever has to say about it. I've patiently tried to explain that due to the huge advances in medical research over the last twenty years, more and more children are being diagnosed as autistic, but her ignorance knows no bounds. 'Lazy parenting' is to blame, pure and simple. 'If boundaries are not made, rules not enforced and manners not taught, then it's no wonder that the youth of today have troubles.' Obviously, I've wanted to scream at her. To point out that her own son is in all likelihood autistic, but I know her too well. Anything I say will either fall on deaf ears or fuel a fire that will be impossible to extinguish. She will never side with me – not about this or anything else – so, for Ed's sake, I've forced myself to bite my tongue and keep the peace.

Naked Stanley wanders into the room ready to start his morning routine.

'I want my apricot yoghurt, my chocolate pancake and my banana. In semicircles,' he says before reaching for the remote control.

'Why does nobody wear clothes in this house?' Judith scoffs. 'Stanley, go and put some pants on, please.'

He blanks her, parks down on the rug and starts scrolling through YouTube. I duck out to the kitchen, relieved to have an excuse to escape.

'Lucy,' she calls out. 'Where are Stanley's pants and socks, please? And his uniform? He is going back to school today, isn't he?'

'Stop talking!' Stanley shrieks. 'I can't hear my video.'

She reprimands him for interrupting adults while

they're talking, and before I know it, she is behind me, standing so close that I can feel her hot breath on the back of my neck.

'Lucy, where is his uniform? Didn't you get it ready last night?'

I step sideways. 'Nope. I'll do it in a minute.'

'But he's naked in there! Goodness me, I'll just go and get it.' She leaves and my stiff shoulder blades immediately unclench. 'By the way, I cleaned out all of your cupboards yesterday afternoon,' she yells from the other end of the flat. 'I thought that the pots and pans would fit better in the top cupboard.'

Abandoning my banana-chopping duty, I open each of the top cabinets to see which one she is talking about, and lo and behold, there are my pans stacked at the top of the tallest cupboard in my kitchen ... one so high that I'll need a stepladder to access it.

'Oh, and some of your plates had cracks in them, so I wrapped them in newspaper and put them in a binbag.'

Sighing, I pull the dish-cupboard door and discover that she has thrown away over half of my dinner plates.

'And you have so many carrier bags stuffed under the sink. You really should free up some space and get them recycled.'

'But with no plates, I need something to serve dinner on,' I mutter, scowling, under my breath.

'Sorry?' she says as she enters the kitchen with Stanley's uniform in hand.

My shoulders re-stiffen. 'Nothing. Um, so what are your plans for the day, Judith? What time are you heading off?'

'Sometime later. I don't know. Why? Looking to get rid of me already?'

'No,' I say, but the voice inside my head screams the opposite.

'I might even stay another night. I'm not sure yet,' she continues, which loosely translated means that she is waiting for Alan to get back to her about another possible date.

'But I'm not going to be around today, Judith. I've got a big audition tomorrow and I need to prepare.'

She claps her hands together joyfully. 'Perfect! Then I can help out.'

14

Smize

'Lucy, have you seen how much sugar is in these Petit Filous?'

'Lucy! When was the last time you cleared out your spice rack? I've just found some cumin and star anise in here that went out of date three years ago!'

'Where's your sewing kit? Half of Stanley's socks have great big holes in them. When did you last cut his nails?'

I'm ready for jail. I don't care any more. I mean it. A life behind bars would be easier than another day spent tolerating any more of Judith's abuse. All morning, she has been following me around, providing a critical commentary of my every move, and if she says one more thing out of turn, I'll just have to go ahead and whack her across the noggin with a frying pan.

To avoid giving in to my violent streak, after I pick up Stanley from school I grab my cello and escape to Charlie's flat, claiming that I have to practise for our big audition tomorrow. Simon Monroe hasn't emailed any of the details yet, but Judith doesn't need to know that, and neither does Ed. If he hasn't got the balls to tell her to leave, then he can deal with her and the kids by himself for a few hours.

'Taking pictures of you sleeping? What a fucking nutter!' Charlie gasps immediately after I've filled her in on this morning's events. 'It's like something from a horror film!'

'And I had no jams on, so I was fully topless. Proper tits ahoy!'

'Don't worry about that, you've got lovely hooters,' she says. 'If I had a set like yours, I'd totally be up for a topless shoot ... even with Judith behind the camera.'

'And when I got angry, she asked me if I was on my period.'

'Bitch!' she spits. 'Call a hit-man. It's the only way out of it, love.'

With no clue as to what to prepare for the audition, we lounge about on the sofa for an hour drinking tea and catching up on the latest news. Aside from the trauma of ever-expanding nipples and the inconvenience of having to pluck jumbo black hairs, Charlie tells me that she received a call from Olivia, Tom's mother. Apparently, she was all sweetness and light, saying she wants to be involved with the baby even though Charlie and Tom aren't together, and to show her support she has offered to buy a pram and a high chair.

'Ah, that's nice!' I say.

'Not really. Considering she's filthy rich, she could at the very least buy me a flat.'

'Prams can cost up to a grand, Charls. So that's pretty decent of her, and far more generous than anything Judith would offer. I'm only ever given bottles of Mr Muscle, laundry detergent or new Marigolds – and I'm married to her only son.'

'Well, she should just hand over a grand and I'll carry the baby.'

'And what about him?' I ask cautiously. 'Has he, uh ... has he been in touch to see how you're doing?'

'Why are you so interested, Luce? The man's a waste of space. Accept it, because I have.'

This beautiful, talented girl sitting in front of me shouldn't be in this situation. She deserves none of it, and where she might be managing to hold back her anger, for me, it's impossible.

'How about I fashion a Tom-shaped voodoo doll and get to work on it with the sewing kit?' I say.

'What? You own a sewing kit?'

'Nope. But I could buy one. Or, better still, I could sneak into his hospital and hide poison ivy in his scrubs? Like that girl does to the pervy priest in the *Magdalene Sisters*.'

'And start chanting "You are not a man of God" in the maternity ward of Queen Charlotte's as his skin ruptures into sores?' Charlie laughs. 'Nice idea, Luce, but a tad over the top.'

We sit in silence for a moment, my brain conjuring up a whole list of punishments that we could inflict on this awful man. 'Wait! I've got it!'

'Got what?'

'We can call up Ed's buddy in the Japanese mafia and get him to pay the jackass a visit.'

'Hold up!' The end of Charlie's biscuit drops into her tea and she flinches, spilling it onto the arm of her chair. 'Ed knows people in the Japanese mafia?'

I remind Charlie of the time that Ed befriended a guy at a backstage party when on tour in Japan some years ago ... a guy who turned out to be high up in the Japanese mafia. He took a shining to Ed (I think he was a sucker for a bald head) and they sank a whole bottle of sake together. By the end of the night, he'd given Ed his business card and mentioned that he had 'contacts' all over the world. If Ed ever needed a 'problem' solved, then he only had to pick up the phone.

'Fucking hell! I didn't remember that at all. Insane!'

'I know, right? And quite handy too. So far, we've got five or six people on our imaginary hit list.'

'Is that it? I've got, like, a hundred.' Sitting up straight in her chair, she tots up her hit list on her fingers and calls them out. 'That bitch receptionist from my surgery, for starters. Then the usuals: Piers Morgan, Trump, Harvey Weinstein, *all* of the Kardashians, *all* of the cast of *Love Island*. Oh, and … Keira Knightly. No question.'

'Why her?'

'That *pout*, Luce. I mean, the girl is just begging for a karate chop to the face.'

We double over laughing and waste the next ten minutes compiling an extensive list of people in our lives who deserve an unwelcomed visit from Ed's Japanese connections. Every ex-boyfriend and cheating lover that we've had makes the list, along with a bunch of scumbag agents who'd ripped us off, a dodgy lecturer with wandering hands from college and a couple of violinists and cellists who, if taken out of the picture, would up our chances of being booked for more gigs.

'And Judith, obvs,' adds Charlie upon reaching the end of our list.

'Nah, Charls. Annoying as she is, I have a soft spot for the old bag. Judith stays.'

Jokes aside, Charlie's situation is keeping me up at night. When it comes to her pregnancy, she can't see further than her giant hairy nipples, but there will be so many more hurdles in her future that will feel impossible to leap over. Her life as she knows it will be blown apart. Boozy nights down the pub will vanish, as well as dalliances with sexy drummers who she meets backstage. Her work will suffer too. Touring will be difficult, as will last-minute gigs, and money will be tighter than she's ever known. She is not prepared – mentally, physically or practically – and as far as I can tell, she thinks the baby will just slot into her life and everything will carry on as normal. A big shock to the system is on the horizon.

'You *do* need your own place,' I say. 'I mean, how do Dan and Stevie feel about bringing a baby into the fold?'

'You're kidding, aren't you? They're ecstatic. They want us to raise her together. We've planned it all out.'

'Seriously?'

'Yeah. They're always home in the day, except for when they have matinees, so I can pop out and do recording sessions or background gigs, and as long as I'm back by 5 p.m., they'll be here to look after her.'

I glance down at my watch. 'But it's one o'clock now and they're not here, Charls.'

'Stevie's having a facial, and Dan is probably still in bed. The producers of his show are over from the States and he had a company party last night. But don't worry, they've both promised to help when the time comes. They've always wanted to be dads.'

The woman won't push for help from the baby's biological father, a wealthy obstetrician with super-rich parents, but she'll put her faith in two dancers who blow their money on facials and stay out drinking until all hours. No matter what I say, she'll do things her way, the unconventional way, but if it all falls apart, I'll just make sure I'm waiting in the wings to support her.

My phone buzzes. The long-awaited email from Simon Monroe has just popped into my inbox. Charlie's phone pings milliseconds later.

'Finally,' she tuts. 'Better late than never, eh?'

<u>The Fierce Audition</u>

Ladies,

Details for tomorrow:

Arrive 10 a.m. Wired Studios, Holland Road, Kensington.

Prepare from memory the track attached: 'Sorry Seems to Be the Hardest Word'

NB. It's mainly just choruses where the strings are playing, but prepare the whole thing as they'll want to see how you move in the verses.

Dress code: smart casual.

Please confirm receipt of this email ASAP.

Best,

SM

I cringe heavily as my eyes focus on the words 'they'll want to see how you move'.

Oh God! Oh God! Oh God!

Charlie butts in and interrupts my inner monologue of despair. 'An Elton John cover? God, how original,' she scoffs.

'Isn't that quite a slow track, Charls?' I'm horrified. 'I mean, we'll have to dance around to it … Potentially in front of the hot young band members and their oil-slathered six-packs!'

'No biggie, Luce. Calm yourself. We'll have this nailed in five minutes.'

Clutching the arms of the sofa with both hands, she pushes herself up then tugs her vest top back down over her pregnant belly. 'We're nothing if not sexy.'

As usual, there's no mention of money in Simon's email. Musicians are rarely told what they'll be getting paid, but Charlie points out that, given the hype surrounding the band, the fee should be handsome and well worth fighting for. She connects her phone to her Bluetooth speaker, hits play and we get to work.

Memorising the music is the easy part. We both trained at a world-class music college so that side of things is no big deal, and between us, it takes less than ten minutes to commit the entire song to memory. But this audition has little, if nothing, to do with how well we can play. It's going to come down to how good we look on stage, and specifically how sexy we can be as we gyrate with our instruments behind Europe's biggest boy band. Where memorising music is a skill we were trained to do, dancing sexily to a slow beat with a pregnant belly and a post-minibreak beer gut was *not* on the syllabus at the Royal Academy of Music.

'Okay,' says Charls, her tone authoritative and a tad scary. 'We just need to go in there tomorrow and pretend we're in our bedrooms, buck naked, trying our best to seduce Tom Hardy.'

My knees are already knocking together at the thought of it. I have the potential to get quite creative, especially with Tom in mind. But can I really do this in front of other people?

With her violin propped up on her shoulder, ready to start, she hits play once again and cranks up the volume to maximum. The track starts and the room fills with the introduction of high-pitched pianissimo violins. The piano part then enters, followed by my part, which is no more than two bars long, then nothing. There are no strings for a whole verse, so at a loss for what to do, I stand glued to the spot and rock awkwardly from side to side like a middle-aged dad at the school disco.

Charlie slips into full Jessica Rabbit mode and struts seductively down the middle of the room in time to the music. Her lips are fixed in a loose pout, her eyes squint sexily, and her shoulders are pinned back to exaggerate her breasts. If she wasn't wearing a faded pink vest top with a large ketchup stain down the front, then her performance would be on par with something you'd see in a Katy Perry video.

She pauses the music. 'Now you, dahling.' She restarts the track from the beginning. 'Show me what you've got. Pout, woman! That's it. Madonna-up! Strike a pose!' With her violin still under her chin, she slips one leg over to straddle a chair then puckers up her lips and throws her hair back.

Laughing hysterically, I lift my cello and begin my sultry strut.

'*Smize*, Luce. Smize!'

I have no idea what she is talking about, and my gormless expression must indicate as much.

'Smile. With. Your. Eyes. *Smize!* Think Tyra Banks. *America's Next Top Model*, baby. Work it, own it, TAKE IT!'

Over time, Charlie's passionate interjections of encouragement work their magic, and gradually, my inhibitions fall away. Before I know it, my leg is wrapped around my cello, I'm 'smizing' up a storm and giving Madonna a run for her money.

'If we do this tomorrow, my friend, the tour is in the bag,' announces Charlie with unshakable confidence. 'We are sexy muthafuckers!' And with that, a massive burp escapes her mouth. 'Grab me some Gaviscon from the bathroom will you, Luce?'

15

Cakes, Bunions and Uteruses

'Well, don't you look all dressed up?' Marsha scans the full length of my body as I approach. 'I don't think I've ever seen you in heels, Lucy, or a skirt. To be honest, I didn't even realise you had legs.'

All eyes are on me as I walk past, but instead of basking in the attention, I let go of Stanley's hand, pull my coat around my body and secure it shut with folded arms.

We reach our usual spot by the school caretaker's white van. 'I've got an audition,' I say.

'Audition?' says Marsha's blonde friend. 'What for?'

'It's—'

'Stop talking!' barks Stanley. I pull my phone out of my pocket and load up Google Maps, hoping to buy myself peace to talk, and it works.

'Yeah, it's for The Fierce,' I reply to the blonde.

Marsha says, 'Well, after my run, I'm going shopping to get edible flowers for my cupcakes.'

'I'm doing Rolo brownies,' says a sour-faced brunette, then a redhead wearing a polka-dot rain mac pipes up something about rocky-road flapjacks.

'What's this for?' I ask, clueless as usual as to what they're talking about.

'The annual bake sale tomorrow,' says Marsha. 'There *was* a reminder sent out over the weekend. And it's all over the class WhatsApp group.'

'There's a WhatsApp group?' I say, trying to contain my surprise.

'Um, yes. Yes, there, um, is,' she stutters pathetically. 'Aren't you in it? Actually, um, I don't think I had your number to add you, Lucy. I mean, I *did* have it, but I changed phones and I must have—'

'No problem,' I cut in, ignoring the stench of bullshit exuding from her mouth. 'I'll just call you now, and then you can save it.' Without waiting for a response, I take my phone from Stanley and, while he screeches for it back, I calmly scroll through my contacts, find Marsha's number and press the call button. The sound of her high-pitched ringtone coupled with Stanley's incessant shrieking propels her into a hot fluster. She rummages around in her pocket, flaming red with irritation, and when she finds her phone, she quickly terminates my call.

'There you go,' I call out to her. I hand my phone to Stanley, who quietens down instantly. 'If you could add me to the group now, that would be great.'

'Of course,' says Marsha with a sour smile. I walk across and hover over her as she swipes her finger across her phone's screen. Seconds later, I become a member of the class WhatsApp group ... several weeks after it was started.

'Thanks, Marsha. That's perfect.'

I did ask both Ed and Judith to do the school run today, but Stanley wouldn't have it. 'No! You, Mummy, you!' were his exact words, so now I'm standing in the street at 8.35 a.m. dressed like a high-end escort, willing him to go into school without a fuss so that I can leg it to Kensington for my audition.

I *have* to nail it today. I have to give it everything I've got, no matter how humiliating. If Ed and I are ever going to get out of our overdrafts, that contract needs to be mine. But even with all of these pressures weighing on my mind, getting in with these women somehow feels like more of a priority. Until the day comes, if ever, when Stanley will agree to wait inside the playground with the other parents and kids, these pavement-loitering mums are his only ticket to making some friends.

'So, what do you need me to make for this bake sale then?' I ask.

'You've only just found out about it, Lucy,' sneers Marsha. 'Just leave it. Really. We all have it covered, and you're obviously busy.'

'I've got time!' I pipe up enthusiastically. 'I'll sort out a cake or a few muffins or something.'

Marsha is barely able to contain her surprise. 'Are you sure?'

'Yep. No problem. I'll whip up something chocolatey,' I say casually, like it's something I do all of the time.

She hesitates briefly. 'Okay. Fine. If you say you can do it, Lucy, then I believe you. I'll WhatsApp Heidi to let her know that you want to contribute.'

It's harder than usual to fake pleasantries with Marsha and her gang because Mother Nature, my least favourite of imaginary icons, decided that today was the perfect day to gift me with my period. And it's not just a regular period, but one that is currently registering 9,000 on the Richter scale. So, thanks to her, I now have suck-in pants, tights, a contracting uterus *and* leaking tampons to deal with.

To make matters worse, every muscle in my body is aching like I've been assaulted with a baseball bat. It's all Stevie's fault. When he returned from his facial yesterday, he caught me and Charlie trying to dance sexily in the living room and was so horrified by what he saw that he and Dan insisted on giving us an intensive masterclass.

'For a tour with The Fierce you're gonna have to work it a lot harder,' Dan said. 'Shoulders back, chin up, belly in … No, Charls, I said belly in!'

'I'm pregnant, you dick. It can't go any more *in*!'

'Well, you're going to need some suck-in pants, darling. Pop stars *don't* protrude.'

Dan wasn't any kinder to me. 'You move like an old biddy pushing a trolley around Asda, Luce. Come on, free up those hips! You're so wooden. And what's *that* on your chin? Oh, God! It's a zit. Stevie, get the witch hazel. Quick, before it gets any bigger!'

A lengthy fashion show followed where Charlie and I tried on every outfit in her wardrobe and the boys scored us out of ten. I left with a 6.5 outfit: a short black maternity dress, a pair of Spanx, knee-high *mega*-high leather boots, a leopard-print scarf and a stick of organic witch hazel. It was the best outfit from a bad bunch, but according to Stevie I looked 'doable', which I guess is the ultimate compliment coming from a gay man.

Now, everything hurts from yesterday's overexertion, and my bunions are throbbing from being crammed into a pair of ridiculously high boots in an attempt to look taller and thinner than I actually am. I'm pumped full of paracetamol to take the edge off the cramps, stuffed to the gills with bananas and have layered on half a tube of foundation to cover the zit on my chin which overnight has mutated into a volcanic boil.

Marsha is still blathering on about cake, Stanley is pulling on my arm, and all I want to do is run home to my bed. But instead, I'm off to Kensington to convince a bunch of hot pop stars that I'm sexy enough to stand behind them on an international stage. And once the ordeal is over, I'll be stopping off at Tesco to buy ingredients for a cake, jumbo sanitary towels, hardcore painkillers and bunion supports.

Because that's what all pop stars do, right?

16

Bats In The Cave

Charlie practically has an orgasm when she sees who is standing outside the entrance to the studio. 'Oh my God! That's him, right? That's Harry Jarvis.'

'You're asking me?' I look at her, dumbfounded. 'If it is him, he looks nothing like his pictures.'

Charlie squints. 'Yep, it's him. Definitely him. God, he's *delicious*. Stevie would blow his load if he was here right now.'

'Or he'd cry, more like.' I snigger.

We did a little internet research last night to familiarise ourselves with the members of The Fierce and we learnt that Harry Jarvis is the front man. Exceptionally handsome with dark wavy hair and piercing green eyes, he has one of those smouldering pouts that can erect the nipples of *anyone* he chooses to unleash it on. Stevie was beside himself when he zoomed in on a topless picture of Harry on Instagram. 'Look at that Adam's apple. The things I could do to *that*!' he said, licking his lips like he'd just been served a T-bone steak.

But in the harsh light of day, I'm not sure that Stevie would have such a heart-thudding reaction. From where I'm standing, Harry and his Adam's apple are nothing to write home about. Dressed in ripped jeans and a wrinkly off-white T-shirt, with damp dishevelled hair and thick dark whiskers lining his jaw, you'd never guess he's a multimillionaire and that his picture is every teenage girl's screensaver in the country. Based on his current appearance, I'd sooner believe that he's a handyman who gets by on a modest wage, one who drinks pints of cider down his local every Friday night with the lads.

He looks up from his phone as we approach and mouths 'Hi'. I smile in return, and just as my lips part to make an inane comment about the weather, he speaks.

'Either of you have a light?' he says, his emerald eyes boring into my soul.

'Nah, mate,' Charlie replies casually. She flicks her fringe back off her face. 'I quit.'

'No worries,' he replies coolly. He wanders over to a couple of young guys, presumably techies, who are standing smoking in a huddle next to a large truck in the car park.

'God dammit!' Charlie mutters the moment he is out of earshot. 'Why, of all days, do I have to be pregnant right now? The inconvenience of it!'

'Yeah, Charls, cos if you weren't, you would have had a lighter in your bag, right?'

'Exactly.'

'And what then? He'd be so grateful to you for lighting his fag that he'd fall instantly in love with you? Maybe ask for your hand in marriage?'

She smiles dreamily. 'Maybe, actually.'

'Then you'd tell the grandkids that you met over your shared love of Marlboro Lights?'

She slaps my arm. 'Fuck off, Luce.'

'Just focus, woman,' I say. 'Get your head out of the clouds and let's get in the zone. How's my chin?'

She leans in close to inspect the mother of all zits. 'Yeah, it's covered, but it's got the potential to blow. Maybe don't talk for now. You don't want that thing erupting.'

I self-consciously pat my throbbing boil and consider another blitz of my cover stick, but I quickly decide against it through fear of over-caking it. 'What about my hair?'

'Hold on.' She spits on the palms of her hands, rubs them together and smooths them down both sides of my head. 'Okay. You're all frizz free. But you've got a bit of eye poo, though.' Next thing I know, her index finger is in my eye, digging out a black blob of mascara gloop. She examines the extraction up close, declares it to be 'Gross.' then wipes it on my jacket sleeve. 'So what about me? Any eye poo?'

'Thankfully, no.'

'What about bats in the cave?' she asks, tilting her head back and flexing her nostrils so wide that I swear I can see her brain.

'Nope. You're booger free, my friend.'

'Excellent. So it's just the girls to fix and we're good to go.' She turns to face the wall and hoiks and pokes around under her leather jacket as the smokers by the van watch her from a distance.

'Charls,' I whisper. 'What are you *doing*?'

Swivelling back around, she says, 'Okay, girls, you're looking good,' to her breasts, which now bulge magnificently out of her V-neck dress. Satisfied that we are as sexy as we can possibly be, me, Charlie and her girls push open the glass door and step into the foyer ready to face our destiny.

The scene inside is pure mayhem. All of London's finest artists have descended, ready to fight to the death for their place on the tour. Dancers in patterned leggings and crop-tops clog up most of the foyer's floor space, stretching out their svelte limbs in an exuberant fashion to show off their attributes. And backing vocalists – true wannabe pop stars – pace up and down, their hands dancing through the air in sync with the arpeggios that blast out of their mouths. Everyone in the building is going all out to *stand* out, the atmosphere stifled by the overwhelming clash of egos. Wardrobe assistants push rails of clothes in and out of the various studios, and brass players casually lean against the wall, failing to notice all of the gorgeous dancers stretching beside them as they're too busy warming up.

A young girl in a tight black catsuit waves her hand through the crowd. 'Strings?' she shouts from six feet away. Charlie gives her the thumbs up and the girl beckons us over. 'Studio 4, ladies. Last one on the left.'

We make our way down the corridor, stepping over two dancers who are sitting on the floor in the lotus position, a look of forced calmness on their faces. We pass the bells of the brass boys, who mercilessly continue to blow their trumpets with full force, then we squeeze through a queue of scantily clad twenty-somethings who are waiting to access the disabled toilet to touch up their make-up. Upon reaching the door marked 'Studio 4', Charlie runs the palms of her hands down the sides of my head for the last time. 'Smooth. Sleek. GORGEOUS!' she announces before scooping her girls up once again and readjusting them to their former stage-front position.

She steps to one side. 'Okay. After you, Luce.'

'No, *you* go first.'

'*You!* You're my bump hider.' And before I can retaliate, she pushes me through the door.

Within seconds of stepping inside, I know that I've lost.

This tour will never be mine.

17

It Could Be You

'Luce!' comes an excitable yelp from the far end of the studio.

It's Celine. My oldest friend, esteemed colleague and arch-nemesis rolled into one beautiful, olive-skinned, tiny-waisted, naturally flawless package.

I should have known she'd be here.

She leaves the gang of string players that are mooching about in the corner and bounds over with an almond croissant clamped in one hand. She throws her arms around me and I hug her tightly, burying my face in her thick blonde curls, which are still damp from her morning shower.

'I 'aven't seen you in ages!' Her sexy French accent glides over my eardrums like silky chocolate dripping off a spoon.

'How come you're here?' I say, trying to sound upbeat. 'I thought you were in the States?'

'Ah, no. I'm back.' She swallows the lump of croissant in her mouth and clears her throat. 'The schedule was crazy. A different city every day, and so many parties and wines and cigarettes, but we had the best time!' A yawn escapes her mouth – a sexy yawn, if such a thing can actually be said about a yawn. 'We only got home at 4 a.m. this morning,' she continues. 'I 'aven't been to bed yet.'

'So how come you look so lush? You arsehole.'

She laughs, and even *this* sounds sexy. 'What? No make-up, dirty clothes that I wore on the plane, plus I 'aven't even dried my 'air.'

She takes another bite of her croissant and I hold my breath, terrified that just one sniff of it will make my gut expand over the top of my suck-in pants and send them rolling back down.

'So how are the boys?' she asks. 'I found a really cool map puzzle of America in San Francisco for Stan. I wish I knew that you would be here and I would have brought it along.'

Try as I may, it's impossible to hate the girl. I've known her for a decade, and since sitting next to each other in the induction meeting on our first day at the Royal Academy of Music, we've been good friends. We've sort of grown up together, taking the same turbulent journey from being naive small-village dwellers to big city girls, and we've powered on through some pretty hard times together: college exams, auditions, multiple rejections, boyfriend break-ups and student money worries. She's a brilliant cellist, a total stunner with a heart of gold; a girl who would give you her last Rolo without a second thought, or even a kidney if you needed it. It comes as no surprise that she took time out of her tour schedule to trawl San Francisco looking for a gift for Stanley. She's that sort of girl. A straight-up legend.

We chat about utter nonsense, neither of us fully concentrating on what the other has to say. Celine is distracted by her croissant, and I'm using my last few precious minutes before we start to size up the rest of the competition. I count four cellists here in total – Annabelle, Aoife, Celine and myself – which if we were competing on a level playing field would give me a 25 per cent shot at victory.

But the playing field isn't level, *far* from it.

With long, glossy brown hair and legs up to her armpits, Annabelle Marsden is never short of a gig or two. She was a child prodigy and used to fly all over the world playing concertos, but in her early twenties, she switched paths, and these days, she only does recording sessions and the occasional pop gig. Aoife Sexton, rival number four, is a blonde bombshell who could turn the heads of anyone she chooses. She is currently engaged to the lead singer of an Irish boy band and their engagement party had a four-page spread in *OK* magazine six months back. So she is no stranger to the celebrity lifestyle.

All three cellists are long-standing friends and all of them regular faces on the pop music circuit. Hardly a week goes by when I don't see one of them bowing their cello behind whoever is on the *X Factor* or the *Jonathan Ross Show*. Between them, they've played with everyone: Michael Bublé, Sting, Beyoncé, Rod Stewart and Tom Jones. In any normal situation, I'd be rooting for them all to win the audition. That's what friends do for each other, right? Cheer each other on? But the music business is nothing close to normal. It doesn't allow for such niceties. No matter what great friends they are, I'm in a position where it's them or me.

It's worse than 'dog eat dog' – it's more 'cat mauls cat' – and by lunchtime, it's a given that one of us will be crowned 'winner' of the tour and the remaining three will be sulking off to the pub at the end of the street to drown our sorrows.

'Ladies, please get your instruments and come and sit on the hot seats.'

A slim bald man wearing a white vest and pea-green leggings calls out to us from the coffee station at the far side of the studio. He struts towards us like a model on a catwalk, his red silk scarf wafting behind him. 'Quickly now!'

he says, clapping his hands. 'We're running behind. We've got the dancers scheduled in half an hour, so we have to push along.'

We take our instruments out of their cases and walk over to the row of eight plastic chairs lined up in the centre of the studio. Everyone around us waits in absolute silence. There must be over twenty spectators – tour managers, techies and record-label representatives, all of whom are sipping coffees and already making their judgements as they watch us take our seats. Last to arrive are the members of The Fierce themselves ... all looking pale and withered, like they'd rather be anywhere else but here.

'Right, ladies,' says the red-scarfed man. 'I'm Marvin, choreographer. We are going to pair you up. Four groups of two. Then we'd like you to play the track.'

His sentences are short and snappy, an indication that he's already irritated.

'Violins, we want flamboyant moves with the bows. And cellos, the same, and we want you standing up for this. Thank you very mu-CH!'

The 'ch' is so over-articulated that if he stood any closer, we'd probably all get showered with his spittle.

'Right, and who is first?' he says to himself as he surveys the line-up, strutting past us like a military drill sergeant carrying out an inspection.

I'm nearly sick in my mouth. My hands are sweating, my feet numb, and my knees smack together like a pair of castanets. My instinct is to bolt out of the door, but there is no time to escape because Marvin's finger lands on me.

'You,' he says authoritatively.

I almost leap out of my seat and shout, 'Sir, yes, sir!' But I sit tight and wait.

'And …' He pauses for so long that I can hear the heartbeat of the girl sitting next to me. 'You. Yes, you.'

He points at Carmel Ryan, a stunning Irish violinist who is a foot shorter and at least three dress sizes smaller than me. I instantly regret every Big Mac that I've ever consumed, every Steak Bake and every family-sized bag of Doritos that's been stuffed down my gullet without any thought for the damage it would do. If only I was a chickpea enthusiast, a salad lover and a drinker of beetroot smoothies, I might stand half a chance.

The two of us rise from our chairs, take our instruments and walk with trepidation towards where Marvin is now standing.

'Quickly!' He claps his hands together urgently. 'We're on a tight schedule, ladies.'

Work it! Suck it in! Pop stars don't protrude! Pop stars DON'T protrude!

The track starts and it's so loud that I'm momentarily paralysed like a rabbit in the headlights. But Carmel is straight in character, tossing her dark wavy hair back over her shoulders, lifting her violin up to an unnaturally high position and wielding her bow flamboyantly through the air like a dominatrix cracking a whip.

All eyes are on us – not just those of The Fierce but of every single one of my colleagues who are sitting behind me secretly wishing for me to fall over.

'That's enough,' declares Marvin after witnessing just fifteen seconds of my awkward gyrations. He turns his back on us and strides over to consult the boys, who look even less enthused than they did before. Like a bunch of bitchy schoolgirls, they all huddle up and whisper their thoughts to each other whilst Carmel and I stand there waiting to be dismissed.

'And now the next combination,' Marvin says, returning to the rest of the girls, who are all propped up in their seats like meerkats, anxiously awaiting their turn.

'Let's have … you.' He points at Charlie, then turns his finger towards Celine. 'And, um … you.'

I sit through every audition, my confidence crumbling away as I watch my friends execute their finest bow swings and seductive pouts. Charlie is great – sexy, confident and eye-catching – and Celine, as always, is so comfortable in her own skin that she quite literally dances like there's no one watching. Marvin doesn't stop them until the end of the four-minute-long track.

After we've all had a turn, another whispered chat with the boys follows. Marvin struts back over to the line with his index finger already extended ready to make his choice.

'Right, and this is by no means the final combination, but we'd like to see …' He pauses for an excruciatingly long time, his finger hovering over our heads like the giant finger from the National Lottery advert.

'You!' he says, his finger landing on Charlie. 'And …' The finger glides slowly down the line, passing over Annabelle's head, then Aoife's. Then… 'You!'

The finger is on me!

Oh God! Oh God! Oh God! Oh God!

'You and you,' he says, wafting the back of his hand down the line. 'You are free to leave.'

And just like that, fifty percent of my competition is dismissed on the spot. Annabelle and Aoife put their cellos away and leave, but not before executing the most noble of 'gracious loser' smiles that I've ever seen.

Six of us remain.

Charlie and I silently take our positions in the centre of the room, ready to swing our hips like our lives depended on it. Our bows are on the string, our shoulders are back, and our beer guts and baby bellies are sucked in as much as physically possible. This is it, our chance. Right now, right here … We can do this!

'Track,' orders Marvin as he snaps his fingers in the air once again.

The track starts.

'Stop! Stop, stop, stop!' he squeals. 'Not you!' The music stops abruptly. 'My mistake,' he says, 'I meant … you.'

I look up and see that his long bony finger is no longer pointing at me.

It's on Celine.

18

Pillocks!

'Are you still there, love? I said pillocks. They're a big bunch of pillocks!'

'The Fierce aren't pillocks, Mum. They seemed like pretty nice guys. Quite down to earth, y'know.'

'How could they not choose my beautiful wee girl? Did you have your lipstick—?'

I'm on my way to my teaching job again, stuck in the usual traffic jam with my arm out of the window, waving for someone to let me pull out into the fast lane. A quick scuffle follows and Rachel takes control of the phone. 'Who got it then?'

'Ask her if she had her wee lipstick on,' Mum calls out in the background.

'Mum wants to know if you had your wee lipstick on?'

'And ask her what she was wearing,' Mum yells again.

'Rach, tell her that I had no lipstick on and I was wearing a binbag,' I say, 'and *that's* why the boys didn't pick me. They said so themselves.'

'So who got it then?'

'Celine.'

'Course she did. Bitch!'

'I know. Gorgeous, lovable bitch. But what you gonna do?'

'Poison her with ricin,' she suggests. 'Walter White did it on *Breaking Bad*. Subtle and very effective.'

'Tell her that your father says they're all pillocks,' Mum interrupts, then Dad reiterates – 'Pillocks!'

'All right, shut it! Both of you,' Rachel scolds. 'I'm talking here.' Another scuffle follows then she's back on the line. 'Okay, Luce. I've taken you into the living room. Hit me. Tell me *everything*. Did you meet Harry?'

'Yeah. Sort of. He asked us for a light.'

'He didn't!' She squeals with delight. 'That's sooo exciting! Was he hot? How tall is he? Did you smell him?'

'Since when have you been a fan of Ha—'

'Hold on, he doesn't smoke, does he? I've read somewhere that he quit on his twenty-fourth birthday.'

'Sorry to shatter your illusions, Rach.'

'You know what? I forgive him … I mean, with that face, he could be a full-blown heroin addict and I still wouldn't kick him out of bed,' she says. 'So did you say anything to him? Did you touch him?'

'No and no.'

'What? What am I going to tell the girls in the office, eh? They're all desperate to know what happened.'

'I couldn't exactly throw him on the floor and straddle him, Rach. There were people around, so I deemed it inappropriate.'

'Don't worry,' she says dismissively. 'I'll make something up. And what about my autograph?'

'Sorry, but no. I couldn't get it. It would have been weird to ask.'

'You're dead to me,' she spits. 'DEAD!'

'Chill, jeez. I'll ask Celine to get it for you. She'll be working with them soon enough.'

'Okay. Better hold off on the ricin plan in that case … at least until I've got my autograph. Shhh! Okay, Mum. *Wait.*

Luce, Mum's back in the room. I'm handing her over.'

'Are you okay, my wee sweetheart? Want to bring the boys home for the weekend and we can all cheer you up?' Mum says.

'I'm not sad, Mum. I'm fine. No cheering up required,' I say, trying to sound upbeat. 'A tour would have been a nightmare to organise with the kids anyway, so it's for the best that Celine got it.'

'Pillocks!' shouts my dad once again.

'Look, I've gotta go. I'm hitting the M1 in a minute and need to keep my eyes on the road.'

'Okay. Call me later. And chin up,' she says. 'Love you.'

'Love you too.'

Five minutes drag by. I've only crawled two metres across the tarmac and I'm still listening to Mum chatting with Rachel and Dad. Typically, she hasn't pressed the red button on her phone to terminate the call, so I listen in amusement to Rachel gush about Harry, then roll my eyes at Mum's protestations. She cannot fathom why Celine was picked over me, her 'stunning daughter', and come lunchtime, every resident in Tref Y Glaw will know of my rejection. As the village surgery's nurse, she will tell them all about it as she lances their boils and redresses their wounds. The Fierce's reputation will become mud. And Harry Jarvis? Well, I'm pretty sure that I'll have the *Daily Mail* banging down my door tonight after my sister has told everyone in her office that I shagged him in the middle of the street.

Several hours later and I'm with Oscar, my last but one student of the day. Today, his illicit snack of choice isn't pickled onion crisps. There's a slight but noticeable deposit of brown residue in the corners of his mouth, and his chubby cheeks are drawn in like a deflated puffer fish. My guts tell me that he's sucking something chocolatey, and if I was a betting woman, I'd put all my money on Maltesers.

'Right, hand them over, please,' I say firmly. 'You can have them back at the end of the lesson.'

Having just listened to his catastrophic rendition of 'The Pink Panther', I've decided to take a hard approach – brutal if needs be. His Grade 2 is just a few weeks away, and if he fails, *I'll* fail. Lord knows I don't want his international powerhouse business-parents on my back.

Without meeting my eyes, he pulls the bag of Maltesers out of his blazer pocket and gives it to me.

'Oscar, this is simply *not* good enough,' I say in my finest I'm-very-disappointed-in-you tone. 'Have you practised at all since last week? Because it's clear to me that you haven't.'

He hangs his head in shame and remains mute.

My patience is wearing thin. I've already broken up a cello-bow sword fight between two year fives and walked miles around the campus collecting kids who didn't turn up. To add fuel to the fire, I've had a grilling from my boss because I still haven't handed in my termly reports.

'Did you even take your cello home?' I ask.

'I couldn't,' he replies, his voice small and loaded with remorse.

'And why not?'

'Because Lisa was picking me up and she doesn't have a car, and we had to go on the bus. And it's always too busy to fit the cello with my hockey stick and my art folder.'

'Who is Lisa?'

'My new nanny.'

I've emailed Oscar's parents on many occasions over the years – 'Oscar hasn't shown up to his lesson today,' 'Oscar has forgotten his cello for the third consecutive week,'

'Oscar has lost all of his cello music' – and any replies have always come from a nanny. There's been quite a few who've come and gone in a reasonably short amount of time – a Mona, a Lulu, a Samira, a Trixie and, the most recent, a Rapunzel, if you can believe it (and no, she didn't have thirty-metre-long hair, but a modest bob).

'Oh. So what happened to Rapunzel?'

'She had to go back to Germany,' he says matter-of-factly.

'Well, if you don't practise this week, I'm going to have to call home and speak to your mother about it.'

'She's in Dubai.'

'Okay, your father then.'

His bottom lip wobbles. 'He's in New York.'

'Okay. Okay, not to worry, young man.' I'm suddenly soft and gentle, morphing from Cruella de Vil to Mrs Doubtfire. 'I know you'll try harder this week.'

The kindness backfires on me. The boy ducks behind his cello to mop away the tears that are running down his cheeks.

'Cheer up. It's okay.' Desperate to stop him crying, I pull the confiscated chocolates out of my bag and give them back to him. 'Go on. There's only a few left so you may as well finish them off.'

Yesterday, I was dancing in front of pop stars with the exciting prospect of earning thousands of pounds doing what I love, and today, I'm picking on a defenceless eight-year-old boy who, by the sounds of it, hasn't seen his parents in weeks.

I disgust myself.

My mood is worse than usual because I'm exhausted from attending yesterday's 'no hard feelings' drinks with Celine and Carmel. They were the audition winners, and in the spirit of being good sports, Charlie and I went out in Kensington with them to celebrate their victory. In a way, I was the lucky one. It's much easier to feign enthusiasm for others' achievements with a pint of beer in hand, but Charlie was stuck with a soda water and sought comfort in three packets of Kettle chips and a bag of pork scratchings. After leaving the pub, she made me stop off at McDonald's on the way home where she ordered a Big Mac, a box of twenty nuggets and a large chocolate milkshake, and even then, she didn't feel any better about the rejection.

My last student of the day fails to show up, and instead of scouring the grounds looking for him, I slip out early. It dawned on me over lunch, as I watched Dr Houston, the head of chemistry, dabbing the remnants of his chocolate cake and custard from his chin with a handkerchief, that I'd forgotten about the school bake sale this afternoon. There is one hour to solve the problem, and even if leaving work early gets me fired, it'll be worth it to keep on side with the PTA and, more importantly, help Stanley get a party invite or a playdate at some point in the future.

Stopping and starting down the North Circular all the way home, the full weight of the rejection engulfs me. My life for the foreseeable future will be this: traffic jams, cello-bow sword fights, Grade 2 scales and lunches with chemistry teachers clothed in plaid blazers. While Celine gallivants across Europe with the UK's most famous boy band, I'll remain trapped in that dingy teaching room with no natural light, attempting to inspire my students to aim for the stars – stars that for me are unreachable.

And just as I pull up the handbrake for the fiftieth time, it occurs to me that my mum was spot on. The Fierce really are a bunch of pillocks.

19

A Quick Word

Gooey triple chocolate, red velvet and lemon drizzle cakes, tiers of butterfly rainbow cupcakes, fruity flapjacks, toffee apples and chunky home-made cookies: it's all here and it *all* looks delicious. With my plastic tub tucked under my arm, I keep my head down and make a beeline for the table in the far corner of the hall, and when I get there, I slip it down behind a Tupperware box full of blueberry muffins where it will hopefully garner minimal attention.

Marsha is on top of me in milliseconds. 'So, what have you got for us, Lucy?'

'Just a chocolate cake,' I reply.

'Well, open it up then, don't keep me in suspense.' She peers at my box, practically salivating as she waits for me to wrestle off the lid, and when she sees what is inside, her thin lips draw in tight until they resemble a cat's bumhole. She stares at me straight in the eyes, daring me to turn away first. But I don't budge.

'Well, is it nut-free, at least?'

I hesitate briefly, foolishly showing weakness. 'I think so.'

'Well, best check the box when you get home, Lucy, and let me know, eh?' She throws her head back and squeals like a hyena, then pats me on the back and saunters off towards Heidi, who is setting up the main table in the middle of the hall.

In just one hour, I've hauled my arse down the M1, snatched a cake from a petrol station on the North Circular and dashed home to customise it. I've scraped off the 'Happy Birthday' sign, sieved icing sugar over it and re-boxed it in an empty Jacob's cracker tub, and I've still managed to make it here by 3.15 p.m. Medals should be handed out for such achievements. Magnums of champagne, even.

I slip out of the hall and into the playground to wait for Stanley's class to be released. It's pouring down and icy cold, but I'm sweating buckets and welcome the opportunity to cool off. Pulling down my hood, I let the rain hit my face, not caring for once that my hair will blow up into a mass of frizzy curls. Feeling better, calmer, I worm my way through the crowd, dodging the umbrellas as I go, and squeeze into a gap at the front where Stanley can see me through the window.

A meaty hand lands on my shoulder. 'There she is!'

Startled, I swivel around to find Bonnie, the fanny-waxer, holding a bright-pink umbrella in the shape of an upside-down flamingo.

'You scared the shit out of me!' I shriek without thinking.

'Sorry, luvvie,' she says. 'My Darren always tells me off for sneaking up on people.'

A wholesome-looking mum in a flowery rain mac gives me daggers, unimpressed by my uncouth outburst.

'"Bull in a china shop" he called me once,' Bonnie continues, 'but *never* again. I told him, "I'm not a bull, I'm a FOX!"'

'That you are!' I laugh. With the leopard-print rain mac coupled with the faux fur pink scarf and the flamingo umbrella, the woman is definitely an animal. But a fox? I'm not so sure.

'So how was your holibobs?' Her eyes gesture down towards my crotch. 'Did your fella like my artwork?'

'He sure did. He said it was on a par with a Monet.'

She squeals with laughter and slaps me on the back so firmly that I stumble forward into a puddle.

'Oh, sorry, luvvie!' She grabs hold of my elbow to steady me. 'I don't know me own strength. Darren's always saying I should join the arm-wrestling team down at the social club. He reckons I can take on most of the blokes in there, and there's big bucks in it and all.'

The eyes of everyone around us are burning a hole in my back, but Bonnie couldn't give two hoots about who's listening in. With a voice that could shatter a double-glazed window, she blathers on about all the new styles that she's given her clients' genitals since I last saw her, and in return, I fill her in on the highlights of my holiday. I start off with the usual chit-chat about the weather and the quality of the caravan, but she soon breaks me down and gets me talking about oh-so-hot Jonah and the ensuing lightsaber duel with Ed on the toilet seat. She guffaws away, continuously slapping me on the back with such force that I'll probably have to ask Ed to rub some aloe vera on it when I get home.

'You going to this bake sale, then?' I say, failing to conceal a hint of desperation in my voice.

'Nah,' is her blunt reply. 'I'm going straight home to get into my jim-jams and catch up on *Love Island*. I'm not even supposed to be here, luvvie. My girl does the school run for me, but she's got a date with a lad called Orlando.'

'Orlando … as in Bloom?'

'Yeah, I know. With a name like that you'd think he'd be a looker, but let me tell you, that boy is punching. I reckon she's only with him 'cos he drives.'

'Wheels are often the way to a girl's heart, Bonnie,' I say, remembering the day that Rachel was knocked off her feet when Rhys Jones pulled up on the drive in his mum's brown Corsa to take her to KFC on a date.

'But this one's got a moped. A *yellow* moped! I mean, I clearly ain't raised her to want much from life, eh?' She flicks the water off her umbrella and soaks a woman standing next to her. The woman eyeballs her – a real menacing glare – but it goes unnoticed because Bonnie is too busy ranting about Orlando's zits, his gold earrings and his dirty fingernails, and how she is determined to split him and her daughter up.

'Oh, Bonnie, *please* come into the bake sale with me,' I plead once she's come to the end of her colourful rant.

'Never gonna happen, luvvie,' she says. 'I'm done with spending two quid on a box of cherry Bakewells only to be charged double to buy them back. That PTA are robbing bastards, and I'm not getting sucked in any more.'

Discussing pubic hair, zitty teenagers, cherry Bakewells and corrupt PTA officials in the rain is not only the most fun I've had all day, but it's the most comfortable I've ever felt on the school run. Friendly, no-bullshit women *do* exist within the perimeters of the school gates, and finally fate (and hot wax) has brought us together.

I decide to brave it and make my move. 'Okay, I'll let you off today. But how about next time you do the school run we get together for a coffee?'

'Nah. *Never* going to happen,' she says cuttingly. I can't tell if she's kidding – the Botox in her forehead having rendered her face totally expressionless. But before I have a chance to flush red with humiliation, she adds, 'A bottle of Lambrini more like. Deal or no deal, babes?'

'Deal!' And just as I reach for my phone to store her

number, Mrs Merryweather pops her head out of the door and mouths 'Can I have a word?' in our direction. I turn around to check if there's anyone standing behind me, but there isn't. Her eyes are fixed on me, and now her finger. I've been hooked in and there's no escape. Without saying goodbye to my new friend, I'm reeled in towards the classroom, dreading what I'm going to find.

Stanley is standing facing the wall at the other end of the classroom where he is examining the weather chart. He doesn't acknowledge me when I enter, but that's nothing new.

'Hello, Mrs Wright, don't worry. Everything's okay,' Mrs Merryweather says, her soft Scottish accent immediately melting away the anxiety welling up in my chest. 'I just wanted to have a quick word. Please, take a seat.' She sits down at her desk, and with no other adult-sized chair in the room, I balance one butt cheek on a red chair that was designed to accommodate the rear of a four-year-old. I hold my breath, bracing myself for what's coming.

'I just wanted to ask if Stanley has any noise-cancelling headphones that you could bring in?'

'Um, no. He doesn't. Why?'

'Well, he's been struggling a bit with the classroom noise and I thought they might help him.'

Stanley sat through the mini-disco on holiday without any trouble, and most days, he spends hours glued to YouTube watching geography videos at a blisteringly loud volume. None of what I'm being told makes any sense. 'What makes you say that he's struggling?'

'It's just that he has run out of the classroom a few times this week, and he has told us that it's because everyone is too loud.'

'Really?' I twist around to speak to Stanley. 'Stan, do you find the classroom too noisy?'

He doesn't answer, so I ask him again, marginally louder.

'Stop shouting at me!' he barks, instantly proving Mrs Merryweather right and me, his mother, wrong.

'But I'm not shouting, Stan.'

'Stop it! Stop it right now!'

Mrs Merryweather cocks her head to one side and lowers her voice. 'As you know, it's just Mrs Beard and myself working in the class, so it's difficult to manage if he keeps running out.'

I understand, I really do. Looking after two children is hard enough for me to handle, but Mrs Merryweather and Mrs Beard have to educate, nurture *and* discipline thirty four-year-olds with thirty different wants, needs and personalities. As if this wasn't enough, they also have pushy parents, never-ending paperwork and Ofsted inspections to deal with. I'm in no position to criticise how they do their jobs, nor would I ever want to. These women are the heroes of our society.

At a loss for what to say, I eventually pipe up with a suggestion. 'Um, what about if we got him a one-to-one assistant?'

'Honestly, I don't think that's a possibility.' She breaks eye contact, shifting uncomfortably in her chair. 'I did have a word with our SENCO about it, but she doesn't think that his challenges are complex enough to apply for a one-to-one. He's quiet in class, he follows rules and instructions, and he does his work to a good standard. On paper, he's coping rather well in a mainstream setting without additional support.'

From my perspective, I'm not nearly so sure. Stanley returns from school each day pale and withdrawn, his collars and sleeves chewed to pieces. Most days, he erupts the moment he walks through the door, and sometimes it takes hours for him to calm down. But Mrs Merryweather obviously doesn't see any of this, so I tell her, and she nods sympathetically, her expression one of genuine concern.

'Can we just apply anyway?' I ask. 'See what happens?'

'We can, yes, but I want to manage your expectations. In my experience, the council only allocates additional support for children who have *significant* problems,' she says. 'Stanley has had a few bumps in the road, but I have a feeling he'll get there.'

'Okay,' I say, trying my best to take her word for it, although I'm far from convinced. 'Has he started interacting with the other kids yet?'

'Since the cops and robbers incident, he prefers to draw and he mostly stays inside at playtime.'

A sudden sadness engulfs me.

'But don't worry,' she continues, 'children don't tend to form close friendships at this young age. Parallel play is more what we'd expect at the start of reception year.'

This might be what the child-development textbooks say, but I've seen different in the playground. Day after day, I've watched Hugo and the other boys in the class running around together, kicking balls, jumping, laughing, playing.

I swallow the words that I want to say, words telling her that she's wrong. 'So is he doing that at least? The parallel play?'

'Not quite,' she says. 'But I will say that he seems happy enough in his own company. And actually, you'll be amazed by what he has drawn.'

She rolls back in her wheely chair, pulls a huge sheet of white card out from under her desk then awkwardly flips it around for me to see.

And it's incredible. An intricate hand-drawn map of the entire world with twenty or so countries and oceans labelled in multicoloured writing: Bra zill, In gland, Ch i naah, Rush ah, Spane, Amerika, Frans, A frika, Hawaiieeey, Atlandtik Oshin, Pasifik Oshin.

'He drew that?'

'Yes. He's spent every breaktime doing it, and without even looking at a proper map.' She gazes at it for ages, spellbound by its marvellousness. 'I can honestly say that I've never seen anything quite like this in my entire career.'

I push away my sadness about Stanley's isolation at playtime and force myself to focus on the positives. 'Stan, did you draw this map all by yourself?'

Turning around, I watch him tip a large plastic tub full of Duplo bricks all over the floor. 'Stan. Are you listening? I said that this map you drew is brilliant!'

'It's *not* brilliant!'

'But it's so clever,' I gush. 'I didn't know you knew all of the countries in the world.'

'Stop! STOP!'

I back down instantly. Compliments are never taken well, and I should know better than to give them.

'I want Libya cake,' he says, still with his back to us.

'I don't think they have any of those at the bake sale.' I stifle a smile just in case he turns around and sees me. 'I did see a really delicious-looking rainbow cake, though. Do you want to try it?'

'Not bake sale. My party! I want Libya cake at my big party.'

'Your party?' I say, confused and borderline alarmed as to what he is talking about.

He turns around and bellows, 'Yes! My big birthday party!' from the other side of the room.

The only party he has ever been to was Hugo's last July, and it ended in total disaster after Marsha had run out of chocolate fingers. He had the most awful meltdown that I've ever seen, one where he punched me in the car park of St John's church as all of his peers and their parents watched.

'But I didn't think you liked parties, Stan?'

He's instantly furious. 'I do! I do! I DO!'

And in the space of five minutes, my brain is reeling with a dozen bits of information that are impossible to process: my son can't handle noise, he spends playtimes alone, he's a cartographer child prodigy, and he's insisting on having a 'big' party for his birthday next week. And the cake?! I'm going to have to seriously up my baking skills if I'm to produce one in the shape of Libya. A petrol station is definitely *not* going to save my arse on this occasion.

'Oh, and there's one last thing before you go,' says Mrs Merryweather. She leans in close, her voice shrinking to no more than a whisper. 'Mrs Beard noticed that Stanley has been scratching a lot today. She took him to one side and did a little investigating, and I'm afraid to say that ... unfortunately, she found ... um ...'

'Found what?'

'Nits. He has nits.'

20

'Little Bastards'

'Got the stuff!' Ed skids past me into the living room, his forehead dripping with a mixture of rain and sweat. He throws himself down on his knees and shakes his bulging carrier bag upside down until all of the contents have spilt out on the floor.

'Take a breath, love,' I say, hovering in the doorway with a cup of coffee. 'Just slow down a bit. You're going to keel over if you're not careful.'

He ignores my advice and lines up his purchases in a neat line across the coffee table whilst telling me what each one is. 'I've got the Hedrin spray, the Hedrin shampoo, two Nitty Gritty combs—'

'*Two?*'

'Yeah, in case one breaks ... disposable gloves, surgical masks, hand sanitiser—' he pauses for a beat to gasp '—and Dettol. Both the spray and the wipes.'

I stifle a laugh. 'Jesus! All that's missing is a flamethrower.'

When I first said the 'n' word out loud half an hour ago, Ed actually retched. One minute he was chilling in the recliner watching *Star Trek*, and the next, he was bent over the kitchen sink hacking up his lunch. Once he'd regained his composure, I calmly pointed out that as a bald man he had no reason to be such a drama queen. He was one of the lucky ones, as he had natural immunity to this particular kind of infestation. Unless nits were attracted to back or ball hair, then he was perfectly safe. But nothing I could say made a difference. He wasn't going to relax until every single nit had been eradicated, hence why he bolted straight down to the chemist without changing out of his pyjama bottoms first.

'And I've got some conditioner made especially for kids,' he continues. ' Apparently, the comb works better if you use it first.'

'Cool. So what's in there?' I ask, eyeballing a Tesco Bag for Life sitting on the rug by his feet.

'Beer. They need to go in the fridge, though. Want one?'

'You're all right, love. It's a little early for me.'

He shrugs then cracks open a can of warm Heineken and gulps it down without coming up for air. I watch in amusement as he tears open the packet of rubber gloves with his teeth. He snaps one onto each hand, then completes his look with a light-blue surgical mask.

'I'm ready,' he announces bravely. 'Let's annihilate the little bastards!'

'Okay, Rambo. Let's go!'

I haven't been near poor Stanley since we left his classroom earlier. Following Mrs Merryweather's disgusting diagnosis, I told him to put on his coat, pull up his hood and fasten it closed with the popper, which he miraculously managed to do without asking for help. We then made a run for it, darting through the playground to avoid the surge of parents heading into the bake sale, and when the coast was clear, we slowed right down and walked at arm's length all the way home. He has been playing in his room ever since, and I've been hiding in the living room with Jack, anxiously waiting for Ed to come back from the shops with nit killer.

And now here we are. Two grown adults, suited and booted like a pair of top-grade virologists, tiptoeing down the hall towards Stanley's room.

I push Ed ahead of me. 'You go first.'

'But your eyesight's better than mine!' he hisses.

'But you're bald! I have hair, Ed, lots and lots of hair that you lie next to every night in bed. Think about it. If I get infected, they'll be running all over our bed, maybe even inside your ears, swinging on your ear hair like mini Tarzans in the jungle.'

For a moment I fear that he's going to be sick again, but he manages to hold it in. 'Fine! I'll do it!'

He opens the door and steps inside.

'Hi, little man, I just need to have a look at your head if that's okay?'

Stanley is so engrossed in a puzzle that he doesn't seem to notice we're in the room. Ed creeps towards him, crouches over and, using just one stiff thumb and index finger, cautiously lifts Stanley's floppy blond fringe. In an instant, Ed's hand shoots up in the air as if he's been shocked by a live wire. 'Get the stuff ! Get it now!'

The next few hours are beyond challenging. Ed and I start off taking it in turns to scrape the brown creepy crawlies and unhatched eggs off Stanley's hair follicles, but with every scrape, Stanley throws a hissy fit and Ed's choice of expletives shoots rapidly up the scale from colourful to psychedelic. To spare our children from learning expressions like 'Die, you little bastards, DIE!' I end up sending Ed off to the kitchen to unload the dishwasher, and I tackle the army of pests alone.

With a large bag of Haribo to hand, I power on, slipping gummy hearts and fried eggs into Stanley's mouth to silence the screaming that follows every torturous tug of the comb. Thankfully, Jack's scalp is all clear, and after tucking the kids into bed a while later, I summon Ed in to perform the final examination, which, unfortunately, can only be done by him. He straps on his surgical mask and gloves once again and, with a set of kitchen tongs in each hand, he cautiously approaches my scalp.

Milliseconds later, he chucks the tongs and bolts out of the room, retching like he has just stumbled across a mutilated corpse.

From a safe distance, he delivers my diagnosis.

'Eggs!' he heaves. 'There's hundreds!'

21

Going Big

It's almost midnight and I'm hunched over the dining table stuffing sweets into cellophane cones as I wait for Ed to come home. He has been up in Manchester for most of the week depping on *The Book of Mormon*, and by accepting the work, he dodged round two of the nit killing and all of the hysteria that came with it. I kept Stanley off school and soldiered on alone, single-handedly wiping out entire generations of creepy crawlies from his scalp and my own until none were left standing. The real work was then done last weekend, when I spent hours bleaching surfaces, washing bed-sheets and steaming upholstery. It's only now, a whole week after the invasion, that I'm confident to say that our flat is at last a nit-free zone.

The fallout at school, however, is still ongoing. Understandably, Mrs Merryweather was obligated to inform the other parents of the outbreak, and a note was sent home in every child's bag on Monday afternoon. The notifications on the class WhatsApp group have been pinging relentlessly ever since and they show no signs of dying down.

Oh God! Gross! I can't stop itching now ... LOL! Do we know who has them?

Imran is clear. Just checked x

Not Scarlett!

Nothing on Hugo ... Thank GOD! Going to bleach
the house to be sure!

Naturally, I replied with 'Stanley's all clear too', but his absence from school last Friday was bound to have set tongues wagging. To stop the paranoia from escalating, I temporarily muted the notifications on the group, as I just didn't have the headspace to worry about it. With a last-minute birthday party to organise, I had bigger fish to fry and I needed to keep focused.

When Stanley first mentioned that he wanted a party, I practically had an embolism. There wasn't nearly enough time to throw together anything decent from scratch. Even if I lucked out and managed to find a venue, then hire a bouncy castle or a magician or whatever, there was still the issue of the guest list. Who was going to come? Besides Hugo, Stanley still can't tell me the names of the kids in his class, nor I their mothers', and after Mrs Merryweather disclosed that he spends most breaktimes alone, I wasn't confident that anyone from school would make the effort to come. But with the nits threatening to alienate him further, something major had to be done to turn things around. He wanted a big party, and with Ed away, it's been down to me and me alone to give him one.

Not having the first clue how or where to start, I called Charlie at the crack of dawn on Monday. As the queen of hosting stonking parties, she'd tell me what needed to be done.

'Go big or go home,' was her sage advice. 'It has to be so outrageously fun that *every* kid in his class will talk about it for the next ten years. You've gotta out-shine Santa Claus on this one, Luce ... like, properly take the old fat man down!'

'But it's on Saturday, Charls,' I told her. 'Everything will be booked up by now, won't it? And Ed is away until Thursday, so it's all on me to pull it off.'

'Just cool it, Luce. We'll get it done.'

'What, you'll help?'

'You're kidding, aren't you? This is my chance to shine.'

The pressure to pull it out of the bag has been intense, but Charlie took hold of the reins and recruited Jen, Stevie and Dan to assist. Securing a venue was Charlie's job, but by Tuesday lunchtime, she'd called over a dozen places and was still hitting a brick wall. The hall at St Mary's had been booked up months in advance, same for the halls at All Saints, Ealing Green and St Stephen's. She even tried the local pubs, but the function rooms at The New Inn, The Grove and The King's Arms were all out of action. The football was going to be on and crowds of lagered-up Liverpool and Chelsea fans were expected to take over every pub in Ealing, so Charlie had to abandon that idea altogether. On Tuesday night, she ventured down to the evening service at St John's and befriended a member of the church committee. Several hymns, two cups of tea and a long chat about the Good Lord later, she'd signed up to attend the weekly Alpha Christian course and put her unborn baby's name on the waiting list to be baptised. That did it! The deal was well and truly clinched and a two-hour slot on Saturday afternoon was secured (prime-time jackpot!). She even got complimentary paper cups and plates thrown into the deal.

Food, decorations and invitations have been my responsibility. After giving the other mums a heads-up about the party on the WhatsApp group, I asked for a list of the class's names from Mrs Merryweather. I wrote thirty personalised invitations in my finest handwriting, making sure to accentuate the RSVPs with a red Sharpie at the bottom of each one, but twenty-four hours after the kids received them, I'd had no replies. Not a single one. I powered on regardless and dashed out to Asda during my lunch-break to load up my trolley with every Jammie Dodger, chocolate finger and party popper in stock.

Jen has been assigned to entertainment, and she managed to hire the last available bouncy castle from a local company that she found on Facebook. Stevie has been bribed with vodka and Yankee candles to do the face painting, and Dan has offered to dress up as a giraffe (a costume which he has borrowed from his friend who is the wardrobe assistant on the *Lion King*). Jen's husband, Will, has called in a favour from a friend and borrowed an amplifier and some disco lights. After a little persuasion (aka Jen threatening to cancel their subscription to Sky Sports), he has agreed to ditch football practice and keep Saturday afternoon free to be the DJ.

Thankfully, the replies have started to trickle in. Marsha and three others have confirmed that they'll bring their kids, and one mum has said that she and her daughter will try to stop by on their way back from a piano lesson. The response hasn't been exactly mind-blowing, but it's a solid start. There's still a chance that replies might flood in at the last minute, so to be safe, I'll keep filling up party bags. If hardly anyone turns up, I'll drag in strangers off the street to come and sing 'Happy Birthday' to our little boy. If it needs to be done, I'll do it without hesitation.

*

I hear the key in the lock just shy of 12.45 a.m. Ed is back at last, almost an hour later than expected.

'In here,' I call out from the front room. 'Train delayed, was it?'

He trudges in with a wheelie suitcase and his guitar strapped to his back. He looks absolutely shattered.

'What's all that?' he says, his eyes homing straight in on the mounds of fizzy cola bottles, gummy cherries and mini marshmallows scattered all over the dining table.

'Uh, where's my "hello, my beautiful wife"?' I say. 'And my kiss?'

He leans over, bypassing my puckered lips and pecks my cheek lightly. It's not quite the passionate embrace that I was hoping for after being apart for almost a week, but it's all I'm getting by the looks of it.

'Did you get food on the train? Or shall I make you some crumpets or something?'

He's still gawping at the sweets.

'They're for the party bags,' I say, pointing out the obvious. I seal a cone closed with a strand of spotty blue wire and attach a 'Thank you for coming to my party' sticker on it. 'I was going to go for small toys and balloons, but this is the done thing these days. And I've discovered that if I half-fill each one with marshmallows, it keeps the cost way down.'

His expression remains blanker than blank.

'Gawd, you're out of it, man. Have you been shot with a tranquilliser dart or something?'

'Shit journey,' is all he says.

'Why don't you get your jams on and grab us both a beer. You can keep me company while I finish these off.'

'Finish what off?'

'The *cones*, love.'

'Cones?' he repeats, like he's never heard the word before.

'Yep. They're for the party.' I hold a filled one up to show him. 'They look pretty, right?'

His forehead crumples like a piece of paper. 'Uh ... what party?'

'Your son's birthday party.'

'Stan's? But he hates parties.'

'No, no, it's all fine.' I bat my hand reassuringly in his direction. 'He likes them now. Me and the girls have sorted out a fabulous bash for him.'

I fill half of the next cone with marshmallows then layer on the cola bottles as I fire out all of the details at him. 'So, we've got St John's hall booked for Saturday, and Jen has sorted us out with a bouncy castle. It's a hundred and twenty-five quid for two hours, mind, but we're lucky that we got one at all this late in the day. And Will's got us an amp and some lights, so I thought you could help him out with the—'

'Cancel it,' he interrupts abruptly.

'Ha! Yeah, good one!' I shriek, wildly amused by his witty interjection. But he doesn't laugh along with me. He's not even smiling. 'What? You're serious?'

'Yeah ... I am. I'm *deadly* serious. Stan doesn't like crowds. We should definitely do something more low-key.'

'Like what?' I snip. 'Just stay home and watch him play with his puzzles like we do every other day of the year?'

'Yeah,' he says. 'And we could take him to McDonald's for lunch then bring him back here for cake and a chill.'

I shut him down with a scorching hot, 'No!'

'What about if we drive to Wales to see George? He'll love that.'

'No, Ed. Hear what I'm saying, will you? He wants a proper party this year, and that's what he's getting. It's his chance to finally make a few friends here.'

'But maybe he doesn't want to make friends.'

'You're kidding, right? Everyone wants friends. I'd be lost without mine.'

His voice is suddenly much quieter, cautious. 'He's not you, though. He's him.'

'Enough!' I erupt, unable to contain my frustration one second longer. 'Why are you picking a fight? It's not my fault you've had a shit journey, so don't take it out on me.'

'I'm not.'

'You are. Look, our son has asked for a "big party". They were his words, not mine.'

He pulls his guitar off his shoulders, leans it against the wall then leaves the room in silence. I exhale loudly, expelling my agitation with one voluminous gush of air, then return to my candy-cone duties. I've done twelve so far with eighteen left to go, and I'm determined to finish before bed.

Ed returns a few minutes later wearing his pyjamas. In his hands are two beers, which I assume is a peace offering. But I'm wrong.

'His idea of a big party might not be the same as yours, though,' he says. He takes a swig of his beer.

'Oh God, why are you still going on about this?'

'I'm just saying—'

'*Don't* just say … really, don't. You haven't been here to help. You haven't even answered my calls, so it's a bit late to throw your hat in the ring.'

'My phone's been on silent,' he mutters shirtily.

'Save it,' I hiss. 'It's going ahead. I've paid deposits, and me and the girls have lost hours of our lives to this. It's what he wants.'

He dumps a beer on the table in front of me then flops down into his chair. 'Whatever,' he mumbles before switching on the TV. 'You know best.'

22

Go Home

Not another word is exchanged between me and Ed before bed. As he reclines in his chair, watching *Star Trek* and working his way through a four pack of Heineken, I finish making all of the party bags without so much as looking at him. My chest is tight, my tear ducts are swelling, and I can't tell if I'm going to lose it and shout or bawl my eyes out. Either way, something is brewing and it's not something good.

Luckily for Ed, Jack beats me to it and starts crying. I leave to go and tend to him, grateful to escape the palpable tension. One nappy change, half a bottle of milk and countless whispered renditions of 'You Are My Sunshine' later, he eventually drifts back off to sleep in my arms.

I'm far too agitated to sleep right now, too angry, so I decide to stay put on the rocking chair. Jack's warm cuddles will hopefully calm me down.

'*Cancel it.*' Pah!

Ed doesn't get it, that much is clear. He has no clue about the lengths we've all gone to to make Stanley's birthday special. The incessant phone calls, the supermarket sweeping, the tedious WhatsApping and the nocturnal sweet-stuffing sessions have been a big stress, but all of it has been served with a generous side order of anxiety.

What if all of it has been for nothing? What if we turn

up on Saturday and find the hall empty? How will our son feel then?

I've wrestled with these kinds of negative thoughts for days, but my faith in humanity has just about won the fight. People will come. Stanley will have a good time. He will make friends. And now that the finishing line is in sight, Ed has waltzed in and wrecked everything with two short words: 'Cancel it.'

I rock gently back and forth in the chair as Jack's warm, light breaths blow softly on my neck. They're soothing, like being tickled by the wings of a butterfly. Closing my eyes, I mimic his breathing. In and out. In and out. Rhythmical. Peaceful.

And before long, I doze off.

'What is your favourite country?!'

I jerk upright and swing forward, instinctively slamming my feet flat to the floor to steady my body. It takes seconds to realise that I'm still on the rocking chair, and Jack, thankfully, is still fast asleep on my chest. Thank God I haven't dropped him.

'I said, what is your favourite country?' comes again, only this time it's accompanied by a stiff finger to my temple.

'Stan, why are you up? It's the middle of the night.'

'Favourite country, Mummy,' he persists, and while my brain is scrambling to find the name of a country, *any* country, he spits his dummy out and yells, 'You have to say your favourite!'

'Shh! *Whisper*, please, or you'll wake up Jack.'

'Fav-our-ite,' he demands, now with an articulated whisper.

'Umm. It's Ja– Ja–' I stutter pathetically, 'Ja– PAN! Yes, Japan.'

'My favourite is Libya,' he says. He starts to pace back and forth, his arms swinging erratically by his sides as if they're boneless. He's anxious, this is obvious, but I'm unsure why.

'Let's get you back into bed,' I whisper. 'It's not wake-up time yet.'

He grinds to a halt directly in front of me and pokes my forehead once again. 'Excuse me, Mummy, but can I have a Libya cake for my big party?'

I reposition Jack to free up one hand and take hold of Stanley's. 'Is that what you're thinking about, little man? Your party?'

'My Libya cake. Can I have it?'

The cake is the one thing that he has asked for, the only thing I have failed to organise. I've totally forgotten about it, but this is not the time to disclose the truth.

'Yes. You'll have a lovely cake.' He tugs his hand free and resumes pacing. 'And do you know what else, Stan? You're going to have a big bouncy castle and a disco, and Uncle Dan is going to dress up as a giraffe. And you'll have all of your favourite snacks and treats, and some of your friends from your class might come and sing "Happy Birthday" to you.'

'No singing!'

'Shhh. We mustn't wake Jack, remember?'

He stamps his feet in protest. 'No singing! No singing!'

'Shhhhh! Okay, how about blowing? You can blow your candles out and then we can cut the cake and share it with your friends. Does that sound better?'

He stops and leans in close to my face. 'Can George share my Libya cake?'

'George is back in Wales with Auntie Rachel, so I'm afraid he can't.'

'Can Auntie Rachel?'

'Um, sorry, Stan, but she'll be in Wales too with George.'

'Can Nanny and Bampi share my—?'

'They can't come. But we can send them a piece if you like?'

'No Nanny and Bampi at my big party?'

'Not this time, hun. But Daddy and me will be there. And Jack too, and Auntie Charlie and Auntie Jen, and Scarlett and Hugo and a few others from your class. It will be so fun.'

But all he says is 'Who is Scarlett?' and I can't answer that question, because I literally have no idea.

Come 5.30 a.m., I'm back in my own bed with two small children and one snoring husband lying beside me. There's no chance of getting back to sleep because there's still so much to do. I've already emailed the bouncy castle company and the church, and I've messaged Charlie, Jen and the school mums to apologise and tell them about the change of plans. Now, I need to send the most important message of all to my mum, dad and Rachel.

> Guys, we're coming home for Stanley's birthday. He wants to spend it with you all. Hope that's okay?
>
> P.S. Any chance we can rustle up a cake in the shape of Libya between us? L xx

Ed was right. Going big is the wrong move. Instead, we're going home.

23

McMuffins

The front door is yanked open before I've even had a chance to ring the bell.

'That's *my* cardigan,' Rachel snaps furiously. 'Thief!'

I glance down at the rather distinctive black lace-trimmed cardigan and realise that I've made a whopping little-sister mistake. 'It's not!' I pull my coat closed and step back. 'It's *mine*. I've got the same one.'

'Save it! It's mine, and I want it back.'

'Fine!' I take off my coat and dump it in her arms. Then, in a deliberately slow manner, I unbutton the cardigan – *her* cardigan – and when it's fully undone, I peel it off my arms and shudder dramatically like I've already been consumed with hypothermia.

'Twat! Not now.' She flicks my temple and I retaliate with a soft punch to her arm.

She peers over my shoulder and I seize the opportunity to sneak her cardigan back on. 'Where's the kids then?'

'Still in the car. Senegal is missing and Ed's in charge of finding it, so we've got about ten hours.'

'Cool. Come and see what we've done then.' She beckons me inside. 'Quick.'

The house is a geographical haven. Metres upon metres of flag bunting is dangling from the living-room ceiling, and a huge map of the world is taped over the mirror above the fireplace. Multicoloured balloons matching the colours of the Libyan flag are scattered all over the floor, bowls of salty and sweet snacks are dotted about on Mum's nest of coffee tables, and playing over the speaker, albeit quietly, is Toto's 'Africa'.

'The flags! Amazing, Rach! Where did you find them?'

'Dad borrowed them from Jeff at The Farmer's Arms. He's had them in storage since the last World Cup. And that big map by there is an Amazon Prime jobbie. It literally arrived half an hour ago.'

'I'll totally wire you over the cash for all of this in a minute.'

'Forget it,' she says. 'It's pennies. Oh, and don't even try and give Mum anything for the buffet. She won't have it.'

'There's a buffet?'

Rachel gives me one of her 'duh!' looks. 'You're seriously asking me if our mum – the feeder – is doing a buffet?'

'Fair play. Dumbass question.' I step back and take in the room once again, flabbergasted by how perfect it all looks. 'God, Rach. He's going to go nuts when he sees all of this.'

I lean in to hug her but I am, of course, slapped away.

'Keep your nits away from me!'

'They're long gone,' I tell her but her face is still a picture of disgust.

'I'm not taking any chances. I've been itching non-stop since you told me, so keep your filthy head away from me and let me crack on and tell you the plan.'

Rachel has thought of every little thing. She tells me that Ozzy, owner of the local sandwich shop, has made a Libya cake and will drop it over later. And for entertainment, she has bought a piñata from the party shop on the industrial estate and filled it with whatever sweets were on offer in the Co-op.

'I've not sealed it yet,' she says, 'so if there's anything else that you want to stuff in there then there's still room.'

'Yep. I'll put his new USA puzzle inside. He'll love it!'

Knowing how attached Stanley can get to balloons, she has even bought two packets of back-ups in case we experience any tragic popping incidents. I am told, however, that she has more than fulfilled her balloon-blowing quota for the day, and if any more inflating is required, it'll be down to my and Ed's lungs to do it.

'Me and Dad did these ones at the arse-crack of dawn. He nearly had an asthma attack, and I had to change my pants ... twice.'

'Ew! Minging! I'm not hugging you ever again now.'

Her warm, squishy welcome hug finally comes, and just as I'm shrieking, 'Get off me, Piss Pants!' Mum comes through from the kitchen with a bountiful platter of bacon and egg delights.

'Och, look at you all skin and bone!' she blurts out dramatically as if she's just clapped eyes on Kate Moss standing in her living room. 'Here, get a couple of these down you, love. I've made McMuffins.'

'In the new air fryer,' Rachel mutters.

'In my new air fryer,' Mum says a split second later. 'Your father found it in the middle of Lidl on Thursday and it's a—'

'Brilliant wee thing,' Rachel finishes, obviously having heard the story a hundred times already.

'Thanks, Mum.' I kiss her on the cheek and reach for a muffin. We stopped at services less than an hour ago, where I scoffed a sausage roll and a doughnut, but that's neither here nor there. It's practically lunchtime and I'm all 'skin and bone', right?

'Got any washing?' are the next words out of Mum's mouth. 'I'm about to put on a dark load.'

'No. Thanks, Mum. I've only packed the bare minimum and it's all clean.'

She almost looks disappointed.

'So who all's coming today?' I sink my teeth into my muffin and feel the endorphins flood my bloodstream as the delicious salty bacon and runny yolk hit my tastebuds.

'Just us lot and Big Nan,' replies Rachel. Her hand hovers over the platter trying to decide which muffin takes her fancy. 'We've kept it on the lowdown, just like you said.'

Ed appears moments later. Jack wriggles free from his arms, and once he's on the floor, he crawls straight towards a box of tissues sitting on the coffee table.

'Did you find it, love?' I ask.

'Yeah, in the boot,' Ed replies wearily. 'It must have slipped through a crack in the back seat.'

'There he is! My wee grandson,' Mum says softly when she sees Stanley hovering in the doorway behind Ed. She gives the platter of butties to Rachel and, with outstretched arms, bends down and waits for a welcome hug. Transfixed by the awesomeness of the African surroundings, Stanley doesn't budge, so she redirects her arms towards Jack and pulls him off the floor along with a reel of tissues in his grip. An automatic bum-sniff follows, and without saying a word, she takes him off to the bedroom to change his nappy.

Straight away, I know that I won't have to lift a finger all day. Everything, and I mean *everything*, will be taken care of.

'So what do you think of your party room?' asks Rachel. 'We've got all the flags of the world and balloons in the colours of the Libyan flag. And we've got all your favourite treats for a feast later, and a piñata and—'

'Excuse me,' he interrupts. 'Excuse me, but there is no Gabon flag up there. Or Eritrea. Or Namibia. Or—'

'Oh, sorry. My bad!'

'Or Mali, or Burkina Faso, or—'

'There's Libya ones, though, Stan,' I say. 'That's still your favourite country, right? So make sure you say thank you to Auntie Rachel for doing all of this for you.'

Before a word of thanks can pass his lips, George, Stanley's seven-year-old cousin, comes charging into the room with a giant number 5 balloon.

'Happy birthday, Stannie!' he cries. 'Let's go and play with this in the garden.' And in an instant, Stanley is all smiles, the missing flags forgotten.

A beer lands in my hand seconds later when Dad emerges from the kitchen. 'Cheers, guys!' he says after he plonks another one into Ed's.

The party has officially started.

24

The Descent

By 6.30 p.m., half of Tref Y Glaw have rolled up uninvited and my parents' tiny bungalow is full of people stuffing their faces with burgers and hot dogs and drinking my dad's booze cabinet dry.

Auntie Dilys, my parents' next-door neighbour, was the first to pop in at around three thirty. She had a copy of the newspaper that she'd kept to pass on to Dad, but once she realised there was a party on the go, that was it. Off came her pink moccasins and down went her arse onto the sofa, clutching a paper plate stacked with sandwiches and vol-au-vents to keep her jaws occupied while she waited for the barbecue to start. She didn't move from her seat all afternoon, as there'd been no need with my dad around. Whenever her glass was getting a little low, he was straight over to refill it, making sure to serve her Malbec just how she likes it – with a hefty dash of Coke, ice and a wedge of lemon. 'Stop making fun, Roger,' she kept saying every time he teased her about the ice and Coke in her red wine. 'It tastes like sangria this way, and it makes me feel like I'm on the Costa del Sol.'

Within half an hour of her arrival, word of the party had spread across the village like wildfire. Uncle Gwyn soon rolled up with a six-pack of Strongbow and a five-pound note for Stanley, and Auntie Glad followed with a platter of corned beef sandwiches and a bottle of Blue Nun. Big Nan was the last to get here because Nick the Shit, local taxi driver and infamous wheeler-dealer, got waylaid doing one of his dodgy deals out the back of his cab in the Co-op car park. She hobbled through the door with her arm looped through Nick's and greeted Stanley with a bag of gifts that I knew she'd assembled from the contents of her home. I discreetly slipped the bag under the table whilst she was busy planting a wet kiss on Stan's lips – one that he immediately wiped off. Undeterred by his repulsion of her moist welcome, she went on to greet the rest of us in the same way, leaving bright-pink lipstick smeared across every pair of lips in the house.

As usual, all of the men have gathered in the garden to keep Dad company while he torches sausages and burgers on the barbecue. The torrential rain isn't going to stop him. Not even a blizzard or a tornado would, and as long as he's wearing his Lidl rain mac and has a pint of Guinness on the go, he's always happy to suffer the elements to ensure that there's an abundant pile of meat at every family do.

As I pick at my plate of food, I watch Ed through the conservatory window, marvelling at how sociable he is being. He is midway through telling his favourite anecdote: the one that happened when Stanley was just a newborn, and Ed was so exhausted that he fell asleep on the toilet at the BBC and had to be woken up by a cleaner at 7 a.m. 'And my pants were around my ankles!' I hear him say. 'She thought I was some kind of pervert.' Nick the Shit and Uncle Gwyn are belly-laughing, and Dad has even turned his back on the barbecue to listen.

No one would ever believe that Ed spends hours of his life in solitude – that he hates small talk, always has, and if given the choice, he'd rather lock himself in Mum and Dad's bathroom and spend the rest of the afternoon bidding for Action Man figures on eBay. But right now, he's the life and soul of the party, one of 'the lads' – and by the look of it, he really is enjoying himself.

A while later, I'm in the living room blowing up extra balloons when Ed comes in from the garden.

'Hey, love. Are you okay out there with all that testosterone flying about?'

'I was,' he replies. 'But not any more.'

I turn around to face him, and that's when I spy a bundle of fabric rolled up under his arm. 'Oh God … what's that?'

He exhales the words, 'Designer T-shirts.'

'Oh no! Have you been Nick the Shitted?'

Ed nods in defeat. Nick the Shit had hooked and reeled him in, and before he knew what had hit him, it was too late. His wallet had been ripped wide open and gutted.

'How much did he get out of you?' I ask, afraid to hear the answer.

'Twenty.'

His left eyebrow is twitching – his lie-brow, as I often call it. 'How much, really? Just tell me.'

'Forty-five,' he mutters sheepishly. 'He said they're Ralph Lauren, though.'

I tug the pink and mint-green polo shirts out from under his arm and hold them up to inspect them. I start at the logo, which is supposed to be a polo player on a galloping horse, but it looks more like a stickman riding a pig, then I move on to the label inside – ROLF LAUREN. MADE IN CHINA.

'You'll just have to sell them on eBay, love,' is all I say to Ed. That and, 'Just stay away from Nick the Shit!'

He slips off to the toilet, and when he returns, he assumes

his favourite role in family parties such as these: child entertainer. The piñata is smashed to bits, then Ed shares out the sweets and the USA puzzle pieces that were stuffed inside. Stanley and George choose Texas, Washington, Florida and Idaho to be the 'baddies'; the remaining forty-six states are the 'goodies'. Once I've cleared away the piñata carcass and made some floor space, a thrilling game called Superhero States is born.

Exhausted from the long car journey and an afternoon spent decorating the house in ripped tissues, Jack falls asleep on Mum's boobs, meaning that I'm hands-free for a while. I plonk down next to Rachel in the conservatory, finally able to relax and catch up with the ladies. The drinks are flowing, as is the local gossip – which, as always, is more entertaining than anything you'd see on Netflix.

Apparently, Jason Donovan, Rachel's former teenage boyfriend and the newest addition to the street, is having a new kitchen installed.

'I saw the delivery van,' says Auntie Dilys. 'He got it from Leekes!'

Everyone gasps, and for good reason too. A bog-standard tap in Leekes will set you back a few hundred quid, so an entire kitchen is something to talk about.

'He must be loaded,' says Big Nan.

Mum's eyes are sparkling with delight. 'You should go and knock on his door and say hi.'

'And ask him to marry me, is it?' Rachel replies snarkily.

'Not at all!' Mum dismissively bats the back of her hand in Rachel's direction. 'Just a wee hi and welcome to the street, that's all.'

But Rachel isn't stupid. She knows that everyone in the room is already planning their wedding outfits, deciding if it will be a big-hat affair or more of a low-key fascinator one.

'I'm just saying that a wee bit of company will do you good,' Mum continues.

'If it leads to a wedding, I'll need two years' notice,' says Auntie Dilys. 'Rodrick at Slimming World says that at the rate I'm going it'll take me that long to shift these boys.' She pats her heaving breasts — her 'bastards' as she often calls them — and releases a gassy sigh.

Talk of Rachel and The Don's future wedding soon fizzles out, and we move on to the next piece of juicy gossip: Bungalow Baz (the local handyman, fondly known for having 'nothing upstairs') has started dating a widow — some woman from the neighbouring town called Pam. They'd first met down at the quiz night in The Farmer's Arms, but Mum tells us there's been growing concern amongst the regulars that this Pam woman is just using Baz for his DIY skills.

'They've only been together a few weeks and he's already built fitted wardrobes and landscaped half of her back garden,' Mum tells us.

'He's not a bad-looking boy,' Dilys says. 'I'd give him a cwtch for hanging a few shelves and sorting out the leak in my garage.'

Rachel points out that a cwtch (aka a hug) isn't all that Baz is after and informs Dilys that she'd probably have to offer up a *lot* more in exchange for his services.

'Oh *no*! No thank you! I haven't touched one of *those* in years,' she scoffs, appalled at the suggestion.

'Neither have I,' says Rachel.

'Nor me,' says Glad, and Mum smirks as she nods along.

'I'd rather have a nice mug of tea and a good fruity book of an evening,' Big Nan says. 'Much better to keep a safe distance from those things if you ask me.'

Just as I'm gearing myself up to break it to the boys that it's time to finish their game and put their jammies on, Ozzy and Claire arrive with the birthday cake. Not one to do things by half, Ozzy bursts into the conservatory wearing a skintight The Fierce T-shirt, singing what I assume is one of their hit songs at full pelt.

'*Girl, I want your body. Girl, I need it now,*' he sings as he dances over with his finger pointed at me. His wife, Claire, follows him holding the boxed birthday cake, already mouthing the word 'sorry' on her husband's behalf.

He sings so close to my face that I can smell what he had for dinner. '*Girl, I want to drive you wild. Take my hand and show me how.*'

Rachel mimes a throat-slitting action at him, but her heads-up goes unnoticed. He isn't going to stop until the chorus is over, so we all wait patiently for him to finish and applaud when he finally does.

'All right, all right, all right, girls!' He takes an elaborate bow, and when he returns to an upright position, his T-shirt has rolled up, exposing his hairy pot belly. 'We've got a delivery here for The Fierce's right-hand girl.'

Claire lays the cake box down on the table. 'Sorry we're so late, Luce. We had a problem getting the west coast to look ri—'

'How's your new best mates, Luce?' interrupts Ozzy. 'You're getting us tickets for Cardiff arena, yeah? And backstage passes? Do Harry and the lads like brownies, 'cos I can bring a few boxes down?'

'I didn't get the tour, Oz,' I say once he's shut up long enough for me to get a word in.

'What?' His jaw drops open. 'How come?'

'They went another way, a sexy French way, but it's cool.'

Without saying another word, he pulls his T-shirt up over his head and throws it at Auntie Dilys, who is already wolf-whistling. 'That's it! Harry's dead to me!'

'Oz, put your clothes on, for God's sake!' orders Claire. 'No one wants to see that belly of yours.'

'I won't. The Fierce are *dead*!'

'Oh, Ozzy, I've got a few shirts in my boot that you might like better?' offers Nick the Shit, the pound signs flashing in his pupils. 'Rolf Lauren ones, they are, mate.'

Ozzy gives him a knowing smile. 'Nah, you're all right, mate. I'm wearing a pair of those *extra*-large Calvin Klones you sold me, and I'll tell you for what, my nuts are flat-packed like an IKEA unit.'

Claire slaps him on the arse. 'Shut it, Oz! No one wants to hear about your nuts. We're here for the cake. A *child's* birthday cake, remember?' She opens the box and beckons me over to have a look.

The cake is sheer perfection: a double-layered vanilla sponge which has been carved into the exact shape of Libya and decorated with black, red, white and green buttercream to match the colours of the flag. I'm so overwhelmed that I throw myself on top of Claire to express my gratitude, nearly knocking her clean off her feet.

'All right, hands off my wife!' Ozzy smiles naughtily. 'But I'm happy to share. If you fancy popping over later, you can join us both for a spit roast?'

Claire slaps him again, only a lot harder than before, judging by the handprint she leaves on his arm.

'It's amazing, love!' I gush, totally ignoring Oz and his usual filth. 'I can't believe you knocked this up so quickly. How much do I owe you guys?'

'Nothing,' replies Claire at the exact same time that her husband is saying he'd 'settle for a blowie'.

163

At around 11 p.m., long after Libya has been demolished and the kids are fast asleep, Dad's kilt is on and his bagpipes are out. The conservatory table is pushed to one side to make room for a dance-off, and almost everyone, including my nan with her dicky hip, is showing off their best Michael Flatley moves as Dad blasts out every Scottish reel in his repertoire.

Auntie Dilys is the only one to miss out on the action. Despite the racket, she falls asleep on the sofa with a cold hot dog resting on her breasts. In the end, her unconsciousness is a blessing in disguise, because when the party is over, she's the only one who leaves wearing the clothes that she arrived in.

The rest of us aren't so lucky and fall into bed wearing our brand-new Rolf Lauren polo shirts.

25

Being You

URGENT! Are you free for an *X Factor* results show tonight with The Fierce? Call time 3 p.m. Live at 8.45 p.m. Clear by 9. Can you confirm dress and shoe size for wardrobe?

The text from Meredith Foster comes at 3.59 a.m. when I'm giving Jack his bottle. It's laughable. Rejected one week and offered a gig with the *same* group the next. You couldn't make it up.

Of course, I want to say no. I have my pride and don't see why I should jump to Meredith's attention like a little lapdog desperate for a treat. I've already made plans to lounge around with my family in our matching Rolf Lauren shirts and soak up the excess alcohol in our systems with another one of Mum's McMuffins. A Sunday roast is on the cards too, maybe a little afternoon nap whilst Stanley and George play together, then we're going to drive back to London in time to bath the boys and put them to bed.

But Meredith's text has got to me. The tour audition didn't go my way, but I can't escape the niggling thought that perhaps I'm being offered a second chance. If I help Meredith out of a hole, she might be so grateful that she'll bump me up to the top of her list for the next gig, and this might help me slide through the golden gateway into getting more pop work. This is how Charlie started out, after all. For her, a TV mime here and there soon snowballed into being offered recording sessions. That's where the real money starts coming in, and Ed and I really could use it.

What if I decline the offer? Will I slip off the ladder altogether and disappear into the oblivion of musician has-beens? Go bankrupt? End up penniless, homeless and feeding the family from the remnants of street bins? Whether I like it or not, Meredith has me under her control. All agents have musicians under their control. But Stanley won't want to leave early. I know this much. George is his hero, and he'll want to have as much fun with him as he possibly can before going back to his lonely life at school tomorrow.

My brain is working on overdrive weighing up the pros and cons when the door squeaks open and Mum creeps in. Her short wiry hair is stuck up on end, her eyes are half-shut, and her big boobs are swinging freely under her tight polka-dotted nightie.

'Look at the danglers on you!' I whisper. 'Dad's a lucky man.'

Still half-asleep, she doesn't register what I've said. 'Want me to take him, love?' she whispers. 'You go back to bed and I'll finish up with his bottle.'

'It's okay, Mum. I'm up now. I'm just sorting out some possible work.'

'What?' She tiptoes over to avoid waking Ed, who is flat on his back snoring. 'Did you say you've got work?'

When I tell her about Meredith's text, she immediately wakes up. 'You have to do it,' she says. 'Just get down there and show those Fierce boys what they've missed out on.' She lifts Jack out of my arms, sniffs his bum then lies him down on the bed to change his nappy. 'Text back with a yes now.'

'What about Stan, though?' I say. 'He won't want to go.'

'He'll understand. He loved his party, and sure you'll all be back here for Christmas soon enough. You're a fab wee mum, but you're a cellist too, so go and be one.'

With Ed fast asleep and unable to offer a second opinion, I go ahead and do it.

I'm free. Thanks, Meredith. Size 14 dress, size 8 shoes. x

And miraculously, Meredith is undeterred by my measurements and replies instantly.

Confirmed. M.

Our bags are packed, the McMuffins made to-go, and we're on the road back to London by 7.30 a.m. Ed is disappointed to leave early. He had been looking forward to taking a drive down to the beach with my dad after breakfast, but I assure him there will be plenty of time when we come back for Christmas to get his fix of Welsh sea air. Stanley, on the other hand, takes the news of our early departure well. He is full of beans following his party, and while Jack snoozes next to him in his car seat, he spends the first half of the journey scrolling through the pictures that I'd taken on my phone.

'Daddy, look! That's me and you, and George, and Idaho, and Texas. And that's George and you, and my number 5 balloon!

'And, Mummy, that's my Libya cake. And, Mummy, that's Nanny and Jack having a hug. And there is George with …'

I've never seen him so chatty, so enthusiastic, so happy. As I sit listening to him, I can't help but wonder what might have happened if we'd gone ahead with the party in London. Would he have played with his classmates? Would he have even set foot on the bouncy castle? Or had his face painted? Would he have danced or sat at the table with the other kids and eaten party food? Would he be as happy as he is right now?

And the answer is no, to all of it. It would have been a disaster, I see that now. Thank God Ed made me see sense before it was too late. If it wasn't for him, we wouldn't be listening to our little boy jabber on and on about his flag bunting and his Libya cake or the piñata and the Superhero States game that he loved. He wouldn't have played with George or spent quality time with Rachel and my parents, and he wouldn't have felt comfortable to be himself.

'Look! That's Big Nan and her pink lips!' Stanley continues.

'Oh, Stan, you've just reminded me,' I say. ' Big Nan gave you a bag of presents that you haven't opened yet. Do you want to take a look and see what she got you?'

'Yes!'

I pass the bag through to him and he delves straight in. Most are fairly standard items for my nan to lift out of her cupboards and bag up as gifts (a packet of lemon sherbets, some after-dinner mints, £2.63 in loose change, a wooden ruler, some lavender talcum powder and a box of cheese twists), but to my total surprise, there is a remarkably fitting gift.

'Look! Maps! Look. Mummy, LOOK!' Stanley screeches when he pulls the final item out of the bag: the AA Roadmaps of Great Britain (1982 edition).

'Big Nan knows that I like maps!'

And I smile to myself at his remarkable good fortune. He could have just as easily ended up with a copy of the Argos catalogue from 1975.

Just before lunchtime, we roll up on the driveway, and as soon as the car has come to a complete stop, I undo my seat belt, lean across and kiss Ed on the cheek.

'Thanks,' I say.

He is momentarily taken aback. 'Uh, what for?'

I kiss him again, only this time on the lips. 'For all of it. But mostly for being you.'

It has been the best decision taking Stanley to Wales for his birthday. With a family like mine, both flawed and perfect in equal measure, it's easy to let loose and be yourself. And let's face it, with my nan and her slobbery pink lips, crazy Ozzy, Nick the Shit and Auntie Dilys with her Malbec and Cokes and her heaving 'bastards', Stanley's autistic quirks barely got a look-in.

If there's any place on earth where you can be your true self, it's in the company of my mum and dad.

26

Five Decades Of Fame

I wake with a jump. My eyelids are stuck together with last night's mascara, and following a long and satisfying rub, I roll over onto my side and notice that, for the first time in ages, I'm in my own bed and Jack is not lying next to me. Something is very wrong.

An array of horrifying thoughts flood my mind.

He has suffocated in his sleep! Or he has climbed out of his cot again, eaten one of Stanley's puzzle pieces and choked to death! Or maybe his fingers have made their way into a live plug socket! Or someone has broken in and KIDNAPPED him! Oh God! OH GOD!

All of these thoughts might seem ridiculous, but they're more believable than the alternative: that he has actually slept through the night.

Before succumbing to my darkest fears and dashing to his room to investigate, I reach for my phone to check the time. Winter has fully kicked in, so there's no distinguishing day from night. It might not even be morning yet, and it's conceivable that I'm getting myself in a tizz over nothing.

I plant my thumb flat on the sensor. The screen lights up and I wait for my eyes to adjust to the brightness. It's 3.48 a.m.

Phew! He's alive!

Lately, Jack's nocturnal screaming has let rip at 3.59 a.m. on the dot, regular as clockwork, so like an infant in primary school, I use my fingers to count how many minutes I have left until it all kicks off.

Seven, eight, nine, ten, ELEVEN! Eleven! Eleven juicy minutes of peace until all hell breaks loose and I'm up for the rest of the day.

When granted a window of freedom, no matter how small, every mum knows that it's best to use it wisely, so I consider my options carefully. I could have an eleven-minute power nap or perhaps read a bit more of the raunchy novel that Charlie lent me. Better still, I could hotfoot it to the kitchen and make myself a cinnamon and raisin bagel layered up with butter and cream cheese. There's just enough time to cram it down if I get going now.

But I don't do any of these things. Instead, I end up having another crack at level 567 of Candy Crush.

I've been stuck on this 'fiendishly difficult' level for ages, but I will not be defeated – not by the ticking time bombs, nor by the flurry of menacing chocolate bars that spread rapidly across the grid like a malignant cancer. It's a profound waste of precious time, and I know that in the hours I've spent reaching level 567, I could have completed a degree in astrophysics or read *War and Peace* cover to cover. But I'm hooked. I have to level up. At this point in my life, I *need* to.

No more switching possible. Level failed. You are so close, buy extra moves.

In a huff, I shut down the app after several failed attempts and turn to Facebook for entertainment. Something interesting must have happened since I last checked my feed, and I have just four minutes to find out. A baby must have been born somewhere, someone has inevitably posted a picture of their dinner, or an amazing gig must have happened – one in which the whole of the London music scene has been tagged (everyone but me, as usual).

But I can handle reading about other musicians' successes because I've just done a vaguely interesting gig for once. Miming behind The Fierce on the *X Factor* might not be a life-changing advancement in my career, but it still beats troughing a bottle of wine in front of Netflix whilst I fold school uniforms, like I do most evenings.

I click on the icon and my feed loads.

127 notifications

A surge of adrenaline floods my system. I quickly flip onto my front, turn up the light on the screen and click the notifications button.

Ozzy Jones has tagged you in a status

Oh God! This can't be good.

On the screen is a picture of me playing on last night's *X Factor*. It's an extreme close-up, *full* frontal shot. My head is up, my lips stiff, my jowls pronounced, and my dark baggy eyes are gawping across at Harry Jarvis like a gormless moron.

But that's not the worst part.

There's no sight of the hideous dress that they made us wear. Just a bare chest, bare arms and bare legs poking out from the sides of the cello.

In short, I look like I'm stark bollock naked.

Ozzy Jones is at The Farmer's Arms, Tref Y Glaw with Lucy Wright and 14 others

20.37

Well, shit a brick! Is that our **Lucy Wright** naked on the telly!? We're all here watching you, Luce, and I don't know if you're happy about it, but Bungalow Baz has got a big stiffy by yer!!

Barry 'Bungalow Baz' Jenkins: No, I don't Luce! Ozzy's a twat.

Charlie Danvers: Nice pins, friend. I'd do you! xxx

Dilys Griffiths: Did you give Harry a cwtch?

Ozzy Jones: Baz wants to know if you're up for playing naked in the Christmas fair?

Claire Jones: Ignore my husband, Luce. You look LUSH! Mega proud of you here! xx

Jen Langridge: There she is! Lovely pic. Love you, bestie xx

Rachel Byers: Jesus, sis! My eyes!

Judith Wright: Oh dear!

It's not just half of Tref Y Glaw who have chipped in to rip the piss out of me, but my naked stint on the UK's biggest TV show has attracted the attention of half of the London music scene. Simon Monroe – number-one London agent – has written just 'Ha ha!', Rhodri Lewis, the first boy I ever snogged, has proposed marriage, and my mum, as usual, has used the public platform to gush in her typical non-punctuated way.

So proud of you wee woman our beautiful clever daughter love mun and dad? zzzz ☹

The gig had been a traumatic one. Not because I had to perform with a band who'd rejected me just weeks before. Not because I had to perform alongside eleven other girls who looked about half my age and size. But because of the dress.

The mini *white* boob-tube dress.

None of us looked good, not even Antonia Brookes, and she is two or three sizes smaller than me. The only saving grace was that Charlie was there. She'd received the same last-minute text from Meredith, so at least she was by my side to share in the white boob-tube humiliation.

The wardrobe assistant (some twenty-something called Jodi) didn't attempt to hide that Charlie and I were a massive inconvenience to her. Where the other girls slipped effortlessly into their tubes and made their way to the stage for the camera rehearsal, Charlie and I were lagging behind in the dressing room, causing a delay to the entire production schedule. We did our best to squeeze ourselves into the pathetic sliver of fabric that Jodi had given us, but neither of us was even close to getting it on. Charlie's wouldn't budge over her bump, and my tits and back fat were hanging over the edges of mine like excess toothpaste bursting from the end of the tube.

'But I've got you down here as being a size 10–12?' Jodi said, her eyes switching back and forth between Charlie's bulging midriff and her clipboard which detailed all of our measurements.

'That's right,' replied Charlie matter-of-factly. With her hands planted on both hips, she took a step towards her, and towering confidently over her in a pair of stilettos, she continued to act like her pregnant belly was a figment of the girl's imagination. 'Look, is there some sort of problem here?'

'Not at all,' Jodi replied. But her scowling expression suggested that there clearly was.

She turned her back on us and pulled off the walkie-talkie that was clipped to her belt.

'Belle, come in, Belle. We've got a disaster here. I'm going to need you to run out to H&M and pick me up some bigger dresses for the strings. Get two size 16s, and—' she eyed up Charlie once again '— maybe an 18 just to be safe.'

Once she left the room, the tears slipped out. My confidence was shot, and I couldn't contain the misery.

'What am I even doing here, Charls?' I whimpered. 'I'm too old for this shit. I'm past it. I'm best off out of it.'

Charlie was patient at first. She gave me a there-there-now back rub of reassurance, as any friend would do in this situation, but when I fully let go and started saying things like, 'So much for getting my career back on track after having kids, eh? I mean, look at me! I'm too fat for pop, too rusty for orchestras ... All I'm good for these days is teaching the kids of rich arseholes. Maybe I should just accept defeat and get some more students,' she grabbed me by both shoulders and shook me into silence.

'Enough of the pity party, woman! Don't let a flat-chested bitch with a clipboard tear you down. You're beautiful *and* amazing, Luce, and you *can* have all of it if you want, but you've just got to stop whingeing and get out there and grab it.'

That shut me up fairly sharpish.

'Now get that fucking horrible thing off, put your jeans back on and let's go and mime behind some douchebags.'

So while a courier was sent out to the shops to buy clothes big enough to accommodate our bulging bodies, Charlie and I peeled off our dresses and did the rehearsal wearing the leggings and baggy T-shirts that we'd arrived in. I was beyond mortified, but when the stage manager sat me in the front row – right at the centre of the main camera shot – it was clear that the humiliation was going to intensify. And now that I've read Ozzy's post, I've seen that I was right. That five minutes of fame will haunt me for five decades.

Just as I begin to type a reply to set things straight with my friends, family and eight million others who watched the show last night, the clock strikes 3.59 a.m. and Jack starts to howl.

Right on cue.

27

The Cat Is Out

My stint on the *X Factor* might have garnered some unwanted attention on social media, but I'm not the only one who's been thrown into the limelight against their will. Thanks to Antonia Brookes, the cat is out of the bag and the whole world now knows about Charlie's pregnancy.

'I blame the dress,' she said when she called on Monday. 'I may as well have turned up to the studio with a tattoo on my forehead saying "Knocked up".'

Antonia, a killer session violinist and one of Charlie's biggest competitors, must have noticed the bump and decided to use it to her advantage. Instead of approaching Charlie and saying congratulations, as most decent people would, she kept schtum until she got home. Then out came her claws and down they went onto her keyboard, breaking the news to the music industry in the most efficient and damaging way.

> You looked so stunning tonight. Huge congratulations! You're going to be an amazing mum! Boy or girl, do you know yet?

That was the post shared on Facebook, and unfortunately, by the time Charlie had seen it, it was too late. Everyone knew and there was no going back.

'What a bitch!' I said. 'That was not her news to share.'

'You're telling me, Luce. My gigs are already going. Meredith's just rubbed me for another X Factor next week. That's not a coincidence, is it?'

'Probably not.' I sighed.

So much of my work vanished when I was pregnant with Stanley. The pop music industry is infamous for being the king of 'ist's – sexist, ageist, racist, weight-ist – if that's even a word. I could have sued tens of dozens of agents for discrimination over the years, but no good would have come of it. The bottom line is that TV executives don't want heavily pregnant musicians in PVC miniskirts waddling behind world-class pop stars on their shows. Show business is all about glitz and glamour, not swollen ankles, bloated bellies and stretch marks. I know it, and so does Charlie, hence why she was trying to keep her condition a secret for as long as possible.

'I was seconds away from taking the bitch down with a deliciously creative retort,' Charlie said. 'I was going to go for something like "It was so lovely to hang out again, Tony. Those herpes sores have healed up perfectly since I last saw you."'

'That would've been glorious!' I laughed. 'But you never would've posted that.'

'I would've.'

'You wouldn't, Charls. Because you're not a bitch.'

'I *am* a bitch, Luce ... when I have to be. God knows how many gigs her stunt will cost me. She's just lucky that the postman came when he did or else I would've gone ahead and ruined her.'

An unexpected letter had landed on Charlie's doormat on Monday morning, shortly after she had seen Antonia's post. It was a whopping cheque from Tom's parents – ten thousand pounds to put towards 'decorating the nursery'.

Although infuriating, it couldn't have come at a better time.

'It's guilt money,' was her initial response. 'A big, fat "I'm sorry our son is such a jackass" cheque.'

'True, but as gifts go, it's a pretty good one,' I said. A wad of cash, be it guilt money or not, wasn't to be scoffed at. 'Just stick it in the bank, Charls. It'll really help further down the line.'

'Fuck that! We're going to the Maldives,' she declared. 'Picture it: me, you and Jen. Baking-hot white beaches with palm trees and gorgeous waiters in tight trousers delivering us drinks with those tiny umbrellas in. Up for it?'

And she was serious too.

As usual, I had to be the voice of reason. 'Not to piss on your fireworks, love, but baby stuff is proper expensive. There's the pram, Moses basket, sling—'

'Nailed it already,' she butted in before reeling off a list of everything that she'd acquired from Facebook freecycle pages, Gumtree and Kensington charity shops. A Moses basket, an immaculate second-hand Maclaren pram, a changing table, an electric breast pump and a binbag full of newborn clothes: she'd sourced it all, and for less than four hundred pounds.

'How did you manage that?'

'I'm a hell of a haggler, Luce. You know this. So let's go for it and have one last splash-out before I pop.'

'Your generosity knows no bounds, my friend,' I told her. 'And as fun as it would be to lie on a sun lounger next to you on a luxury beach, necking cocktails as you watch me with your sad little pineapple juice, the Maldives is out.'

'Out? You're seriously saying no?'

'I am. You don't know what's around the corner,' I say. But I *do* know, and if her experience of juggling motherhood with the music business is anything like mine, the toughest of times await her.

'You overthink things, Luce. Sometimes you've just got to let go and chuck it in the fuck-it bucket.'

I stood my ground. 'If you want some pampering, just treat yourself to a fake spray-tan, then lie under your living-room lamp and read a trashy novel in your bikini.'

And following some huffing and puffing, she eventually agreed to bank what's left of the cash after she's bought herself a new pair of leather boots from Dune.

28

Woman Down!

*S*chool run, tick. *Leave cash and list of instructions for Amy, tick. Load dishwasher, tick. Get spag bol out of freezer for kids' dinner later, tick. Put wet clothes in tumble drier, tick. Sterilise dummies and bottles, tick. Set a reminder to text Ed to remind HIM to remember that he's doing the school pick-up later, tick. (WTF?!) Shower, tick. Hair, tick. Make-up, tick. Pack cello, tick. Spare strings, tick. Check there's no delays on the Bakerloo line, tick. Check again. Tick. And again. Tick.*

I have to leave in fifteen minutes for my first professional orchestra rehearsal in over four years, yet I'm still standing here in my bra and pants. Amy is due to arrive any minute to look after Jack, but here I am pulling shirts, jeans and dresses out of the wardrobe in a frenzy, dismissing everything that comes to hand and steering myself dangerously in the direction of having a panic attack.

Oh God! Need another wee!

Jane Montague, the contractor for the Philharmonia orchestra, got in touch on Friday asking if I would be free to do a patch of work. My initial reaction was one of pure elation, but crippling fear kicked in mere seconds later. My brain conjured up dozens of reasons to turn it down, most of which revolved around childcare, but ultimately, the issue was more down to my lack of confidence.

Jen, who was sitting opposite me in Costa when the email landed in my inbox, insisted that I do it.

'You've been wanting a way back in to real playing, and this is it. Say yes! Do it!'

'It's the Philharmonia, Jen. There's *no* way. I don't have time to get my playing up to standard.'

'You do. Just learn the parts, Luce. No excuses.'

One inspiring pep talk, two espressos and a quick call to book Amy later, I gave in and emailed Jane back to accept the work, then hotfooted it home to get my cello out. My body has since gone into shock from the intensive last-minute practice, leaving me with blistered fingers and burning muscles, but the music is all learnt and I'm in as good a shape as I'm ever going to be.

Now that the big day is here, I'm beyond frazzled and just want to go back to bed. I've been on the go since 5 a.m., spending every spare second either dashing back and forth to the living room to check on Jack or sitting on the toilet. It doesn't matter how many times I've been, my bladder is still telling me that it's about to burst. My stomach is in knots, my brain is working overtime, and the paranoia has invaded my every thought. What if I'm crap? What if I wee my pants on stage? What if I'm late? I've checked that the tubes are running countless times, and although the website assures me that there's a 'Good Service' operating on all lines, I still don't trust it. There's only one way to stave off these crushing nerves, and that's to pump my system full of vitamin B, so I force down a large bruised banana, gagging as I shovel it into my mouth, then check the TFL website again.

Need one more wee. Oh god, a poo. No ... a puke!

After regurgitating a belly's worth of bananas, I check

that Jack is still content in his high chair watching *Peppa Pig*, then I hurry back to the mountainous pile of clothes that I've tossed on the bedroom floor. My stomach is still gurgling, my hands trembling like an addict desperate for a fix, but the clock is ticking and I must get dressed. Delving into the pile, I pull out a chunky knit black jumper. *Smart, plain and inoffensive. This'll do,* says one half of my brain, but the other half jumps in with a *No! DON'T do it!* It's freezing outside, but by the time I lug the cello on a busy tube to the other side of London, I'll be sweltering hot and sticky. Gassing out the cello section of a major London orchestra with my honking armpits would be a big mistake.

It's a no to chunky knits and stinky pits.

Next, I grab a leopard-print shirt that I find rolled up in a ball. It's nowhere near the tacky sort of leopard print that the likes of Janice from *Friends* wears (or Pat Butcher behind the bar at the Old Vic, even) but a lot more subtle. With a light black cardigan over the top, it could even pass as being quite sophisticated.

Yes! This ought to do it.

I put on the shirt and start doing up the buttons, cursing at my trembling, useless fingers as I go, but reaching the button that sits level with my nipples, I stop.

No! DON'T do it! NO buttons!

The memory hits me like a high-speed train. It was a day when, at sixteen years old, I wore a buttoned-up crop top to youth orchestra to try and impress Andrew McDermott – the most beautiful principal violinist in the county. Turning up half-naked might have been a tad overboard for a Thursday-night rehearsal in the Tref Y Glaw rugby club, but I was hell-bent on getting Andrew's attention. And it worked. I caught him smiling at me halfway through the rehearsal, but not for the reason I'd hoped. The cello had tugged on my buttons and my top had come totally undone, exposing my 32D bra to everyone in the room – a bra that was stuffed with thick wedges of smoked bacon (let's just say that if Andrew was to cop a feel, I wanted them to feel real). In short, cellos and buttons *don't* mix. And yes, bacon has no place inside a bra. I know this now.

The leopard-print shirt is out. The same for skirts above the knee (definitely too slutty) and skinny jeans that might roll down when I lean forward in my seat. Exposing the crack of my arse to the entire double bass section wouldn't be a good move.

Shit! Better rethink my pants just in case.

Off come the off-white full briefs before I rummage around my underwear drawer, slinging knickers across the room like a stripper.

It's ridiculous to plan my outfit all the way down to the colour of my pants, but it's only wise. Jen is always gossiping about extra players who have been foolish enough to turn up to rehearsals in low-cut tops and tight fake-leather trousers. 'Why would you risk alienating every woman in the orchestra by dressing like a prostitute?' I've heard her say. First impressions last, and if I'm going to stand a chance of doing well today, it pays to overthink every last detail.

With my knicker drawer failing to deliver anything even vaguely suitable, I shuffle across to rummage through Ed's and settle on the next best thing to guarantee full coverage of my rear: a pair of his boxers.

Black, comfy, perfect!

I pull them on then dive back into the pile on the floor. I sift out yesterday's flowery top and stained black cardigan just as the front-door buzzer sounds.

Zzzzzzz. Zzzzz. Zzzz.

Amy has arrived. Shit! I grab my jeans that haven't seen the inside of a washing machine in weeks, then flip onto my bum, force my feet through the tight ends and spring up straight to wrench them over my hips.

I'm struck by lightning.

An excruciating surge of pain rips through my body and I collapse to the floor. The tears are instant and sting my eyes but I can't wipe them away. I can't move. Not a hand, an arm, nothing. I'm down – woman down – and with my jeans still trapped around my knees, I can't do anything but lie curled up in a ball, frozen in agony.

Straight away, I know what's happened. My back is in spasm. And what's more painful than suffering the involuntary contractions of my spinal muscles is accepting the truth: I won't be playing with the Philharmonia today.

Zzzzz. Zzz. Zzzzzz.

I have to get to the intercom now, before Jack starts crying to be lifted out of his high chair.

'I'm coming!' I call out, even though it's pointless. Amy is two flights of stairs and two locked doors away. And she doesn't have a key.

Taking a deep breath, I roll onto my front and begin to drag my body out of the room like a wounded deer crawling to safety. With each agonising shuffle, vomit smacks the back of my throat, hot tears stream down my cheeks. Kicking off the jeans would make it easier, but it's impossible.

Zzzzz … Zzzzz

Jack starts to cry. I keep going, pushing through the pain, crawling down the hall through the streams of bog roll and past the maps of America, Asia and Europe lined up all down the side of the wall.

'Mummy's on her way!'

Zzzzz. Zzzzzzzz. Zzzzzzzzzzz.

My upper arms tremble, threatening to give way, my spine on the verge of splitting in half. But I power on, determined, and eventually I make it to the intercom. One more deep breath and I hoist myself up on one elbow and reach for the button.

I'm so close, mere inches away from salvation.

Just one more push and ... blackout.

29

The Patient Patient

'What on earth? Darling, quick! Come and help me.'

The voices are muffled and distant, the colours blurred – hazy kaleidoscopic swirls of yellows, oranges and purples. I try to rub my eyes, but it's impossible. Movement is *impossible*. A towel drops down over the back of my body, then hands grip and pull me up off the floor.

'Quick, on the sofa! Hurry before I drop her – she is *very* heavy!'

I smell him first. The familiar scent burns the hairs in my nostrils, a musky nutmeggish smell, and when my eyes finally regain focus, the lemon V-neck jumper confirms it. It's Alan. And by his side, Judith.

'Lucy, you gave us quite a fright,' he says.

'Jack ...' I mutter. 'Is he okay? And Amy, where–?'

'Jack is fine, and I sent the girl home. There's no use all of us being here, is there?' says Judith. 'We only stopped by to water your plants, and thank goodness we did. Who knows how long poor Jack would have been crying, or how long you would have been lying on the floor in Edward's pants!' She giggles like a silly teenage girl and Alan joins in, throwing his head back to reveal his freakishly pin-straight, white teeth – teeth that probably had to be glued to his gums before he could eat his breakfast. An incoherent noise exits my mouth, then the room goes black.

I wake to the sound of the same irritating laughter. Judith and Alan are sat opposite each other drinking tea in the dining area, and the giggles are bouncing back and forth across the table like a ping-pong ball.

'Jack?' I say, my voice croaky. I try to pull myself up, but my muscles scream and my head drops down onto the sofa cushion.

'You're awake!' declares Alan.

'Where is he?'

'He is having a nap, Lucy,' says Judith. 'He was very worn out after all of that screaming.'

The panic suddenly engulfs me. 'Uh, what's the time?'

'How are you feeling? You gave us quite a fri—'

'Time? Judith, the time?!'

Alan casually rolls one sleeve of his lemon jumper up to his elbow and squints down at his watch. Years pass as I wait for him to move his wrist to a distance at which he can see. 'I make it eleven thirty-three,' he says. 'And now, wait a moment, wait, and now … it's eleven thirty-four.'

Judith erupts into laughter.

'The orchestra! I've got to call them. I've got to tell them—'

'No need,' Judith interrupts sweetly. 'It's all sorted. I spoke to a Jane something-or-other, and I told her about your situation. She was *very* understanding about it.'

'What?' The blood rushes to my cheeks. 'You mean the orchestral contractor, Jane? Jane *Montague* Jane?'

'Yes, that's her, Montague. Such a fancy name! Alan found her number on the internet.' She beams at Alan, who looks very proud of himself.

'It was actually very easy,' he says, looking over at me. 'We knew that you were playing with a big London orchestra, but weren't sure which one. I used the Google to find the numbers of the biggies, then Judith called each of them up and asked them if they were expecting you today. It really didn't take lo—'

'What did you tell her?' I cut in urgently. 'What?'

'Just that you'd had an accident in the kitchen,' Judith says. 'And I told her that I suspected you'd had a back spasm and you wouldn't be there today to play in the show.'

I cringe, mortified at her use of the word 'show'.

'And then she asked if you would be in tomorrow, but I said that with your history of back problems, I *very* much doubted it.'

'You didn't say that, did you?'

'Well, it's the truth, isn't it?' She lifts her tea, keeping her eyes fixed on me as she takes a long sip. 'The last time you had one, you were out of action for a very long time, if I recall.' She looks over at Alan for reassurance. 'Edward was in a terrible state about it. He had to work and look after Stanley all by himself,' she tells him, and he offers up an understanding nod.

If I could move, I would catapult myself off the sofa and shake the woman, but I'm stuck here, trapped in my useless body. Trapped in the company of the last people on this earth who I'd ever call in the event of an emergency.

'Right, so what needs to be done before I collect Stanley later?' says Judith, smacking the palms of her hands together enthusiastically.

'Ed's getting him today.'

'There's been a change of plan,' she says. 'He's stopping off at Waitrose to pick me up a few things, so I'm doing the school run.'

A wave of sickness hits me when I imagine Stanley

finding Judith waiting for him in the playground. What was Ed thinking? How could he change the plan?

'I think I'll start with sorting the clothes on your bedroom floor,' Judith continues. 'It's like a bomb site in there.'

Alan reaches over and strokes her forearm gently, gawping at her like a puppy does at its owner. 'And how can I help?'

'How about you sort out something for lunch? One of your mackerel and beetroot salads would be just the ticket. I'm really in the mood for one.'

'Of course.' He smiles. 'Wonderful idea.'

'Oh, but, darling, you might have to pop home and get some bits first. Lucy is not one to keep mackerel and beetroot in her fridge,' she says, as if I'm not in the room.

I squeeze my eyes shut, praying that when I open them this situation will be nothing more than a hideous hallucination.

But it isn't. It's real, all too real.

By the time Stanley arrives home from school, I am positively miserable. My breath stinks of smoked mackerel, I'm burping up peppermint tea, and I'm gasping for some codeine and a glass of Pinot to take the edge off my suffering. As Judith couldn't cope with the 'heavy lifting', Alan called in the cavalry after lunch to help move me from the sofa to my bedroom. His friends Trevor and Ibrahim cut short their daily game of golf to come over and help out. If I wanted some privacy, I had little choice but to accept their help, even if it meant them seeing me in Ed's pants.

Most of my afternoon has been spent lying on my back staring at a yellow stain on the ceiling that has been there since our neighbour's shower flooded two years ago. Charlie hasn't answered any of my calls, and Jen couldn't rescue me because she's in Portsmouth doing a concert, so the stain has become my only friend. If Stanley didn't come home when he did then I might have named it and started talking to it – like Tom Hanks does with his football, Wilson, in *Castaway*.

'Why did Grandma get me?' Stanley demands moments after he's barged into the room. His eyes are bloodshot and swollen from crying.

'Hi, little man. I've hurt my back and I need a big hug.'

'But, excuse me, but Daddy said he is getting me!'

'I know, I know he did. Daddy had to go to the shops and I couldn't get you because I can't move.'

I wait for him to process what I am saying, curious to see his reaction to the news that I'm temporarily paralysed from the neck down. But he just stands in the doorway staring at me for ages, his expression unreadable.

Eventually, he patters over and leans in close to my face. 'But you *can* move, Mummy.' His finger prods my cheek. 'Your eyes are moving right now.'

Midway through explaining the nature of a back spasm, Ed rushes in with half a dozen carrier bags from both Waitrose and Sainsbury's dangling from his hands.

'Hi guys,' he pants as he dumps them on the floor. 'Everyone okay?'

'Thank God you're back!' I say. 'Did you bring my–?'

'Daddy, you didn't get me!' interrupts Stanley.

'I know. I'm sorry, little man. I need a wee, just wait a second.'

Whilst I wait patiently for Ed to empty his elephant-sized bladder, Stanley rummages around the carrier bags, and when he doesn't find anything interesting, he marches out of the room chanting, 'Snack, snack, snack, SNACK!' Ed flushes the toilet, squeezes out a string of percussive farts, then washes his hands. After what feels like hours later, he emerges from the en suite bathroom wearing his Incredible Hulk pyjama bottoms and his tatty AC/DC T-shirt that I'm pretty sure I'd hidden in a black bag to be taken to the charity shop.

'So did you get my codeine?'

He looks at me blankly.

'My wine?' I watch the lines on his forehead shrivel into a helpless frown. 'Oh God! You forgot, didn't you?'

'Fuck it!' he snaps. He practically tears off his T-shirt and kicks his pyjama bottoms off, getting all the way down to his boxer shorts before scanning the ground frantically. 'Jeans? Where's my jeans?'

'They're probably on the bathroom floor. Why?'

'I'm going back out.'

'No, don't leave me here!' I plead. 'I beg you!'

In just his boxers, he stands frozen to the spot with a face like thunder. 'It's Mum's fault. She called asking for salmon steaks, but ones from the fresh counter.'

'What, *more* fish?'

'Yeah. I got off the tube early and went to the Waitrose in Westfield. But it was rammed! Then I lost my card at the till – it was in the wrong part of my wallet. Then as I was paying, she called *again* and asked for asparagus and a lemon, but I was already on the tube, so I had to go to the Sainsbury's on the Broadway.'

'Which I'm guessing was also "rammed"?'

'Yep, and then—'

'Forget it, love. Just get over here and hug me.' He leans over and gives me a limp one-armed hug, but it doesn't nearly hit the spot. Not for either of us.

'That's crap. Get on here and give me a real one.'

He climbs over and lies down beside me, his heart pounding from the sudden burst of stress that I've just accidentally caused.

I wait for the stiffness to fizzle away from his muscles and for his breathing to return to normal before I launch into a whispered rant about the Judithness of my day. If she wasn't shaming me about the bags of brown salad in the fridge and the furry cucumbers, she was passing comment on all of the DIY that needs doing in the flat. At one point, she found a bundle of unopened letters which she then saw fit to open and read to me as I lay frozen in agony on the bed.

'So, to sum up, the ceiling is about to fall down, we owe £316 to Thames Water, the car insurance renewal quote is scandalous, your current account is almost £1,200 overdrawn and, best of all, I'm due a smear test. Throw in the spasm, the traumatised toddler, the disgruntled babysitter, the collapse of my orchestral career, the peppermint tea and the cold fish, and I'd say that I'm pretty much ready for this day to end.'

He props himself up onto his elbow and flexes his nostrils exaggeratedly. 'Fish? What kind of fish?'

'Mackerel.'

'So *that's* the smell?'

'Well, it's not *me* if that's what you're thinking.'

A stiff knock on the door penetrates the atmosphere and Judith swans in without waiting for permission. 'Did you get my salmon, Edward? Oh, goodness! Am I interrupting something?' she says, failing to divert her eyes from where we are both lying semi-naked on the bed.

Ed leaps up, almost knocking me off the bed. He snatches his tatty T-shirt off the floor and pulls it on.

'Can I look now?' says Judith, even though she hasn't stopped looking. Not for a nanosecond. 'Well, I just wanted to tell you that I've got everything sorted. Stanley's lunch is packed for the morning, his uniform is clean, and the laundry basket is completely empty.'

'Thanks, Judith,' I reply with a forced sweetness.

'And Jack is eating his dinner. With a spoon, might I add.'

I can feel her eyes on me, waiting for me to gush with gratitude, but I can't bring myself to look at her let alone speak.

'Can you pop that salmon in the fridge for me, please, Edward? I don't want it to go off.'

'Yeah, yeah. Of course.' Ed does as he is told and leaves me behind to listen to the rest of her monologue of triumph as I stare at my new yellow friend on the ceiling.

'I didn't heat up that Bolognese that you left out for them, Lucy. It's been sat out all day, so perhaps it had gone off? It did smell a little strange.'

'Maybe that's the mackerel that you can smell?' I say snidely, because I just can't help it.

'And Alan brought over some bits for you,' she continues, ignoring my comment. 'Your fridge was almost empty – well, aside from some chocolate mousses and six half-empty jars of pesto. But now you have the essentials: wholemeal bread, milk and low-fat cheese, and lots of fresh fruit and veg. I'm determined to get some nutritious food into all of you this week.'

'Week?'

'I've made up the sofa bed and I've cleared my schedule. With Edward working, you're going to need me. So I'm here for the week, perhaps longer if you need.'

Her announcement hits me like a bolt of electricity and I shoot up, yelping as my pillow falls onto the floor.

'Don't be trying to get up, silly girl!' She rushes over and lifts the pillow then plumps it up and pushes it back under my head.

This is when I look at her. When I notice the skirt that she is wearing. My skirt.

'Is that mine, Judith?'

'Oh, yes. It is. What do you think?' She twirls around and the skirt springs to life, wafting a gush of air in my face. Air that is heavily fragranced with Marc Jacob's Daisy.

My perfume.

'It was in that bag in the hall along with some other lovely things. I assumed that they were for charity?'

'They are … for *charity*.'

'But some of it is just too nice to give away. Alan and I went through it all earlier and we had a bit of an impromptu fashion show.' A childish chuckle pops out of her mouth. 'I've picked out some nice black trousers from H&M. And there's some beautiful sparkly cardigans and so many pretty tops. Some of them still have labels on.'

This is when I notice the black glittery jumper that she's wearing. I bought it on sale in Zara the year after Stanley was born thinking that it would be perfect to wear for Christmas lunch at my parents' house. There was only a size ten left on the rail, but I still bought it. Christmas was five or six months away, so I figured I had plenty of time to shave off the baby weight. But I never did.

'My top looks nice,' I say through gritted teeth.

'Doesn't it? It's quite baggy around the middle, mind.' She pinches the rim of the jumper and stretches it out until it's taut then, after a quick sigh, she lets go and the fabric pings back to hug her tiny waist. 'I'm just not sure, but Alan loved it. He said that he wants an excuse to fatten me up with lots of romantic dinners, so I think I shall hold on to it.'

'Sure, knock yourself out,' I say, and mean. Quite literally.

'Perfect! There's no need for me to go home to get a change of clothes now. I'm all kitted out for the rest of the week.' She pauses briefly. 'But, oh … I will need some clean underwear.'

I glare at her in silence.

'Actually, not to worry. I suppose I could always borrow some of Edward's!'

She bursts into laughter and smacks her hands together repeatedly as if giving herself a round of applause, then swivels around and strides out of the door, blasting me in the face with fumes of Marc Jacobs Daisy and smoked sodding mackerel.

30

Cracks

'Why don't you just come home?'

'I can't, Mum.' I press the phone closer to my ear. 'I'd love to, more than anything, but I just can't,' I whisper.

Five painfully long days have passed, Judith's presence in the flat has wreaked havoc with our daily routine, and I've been counting down the hours, minutes and even seconds until she leaves.

At the start of the week, she had it all under control, and as I lay immobile on the bed, she took immense pleasure in popping in to tell me all the things that she'd done better than me. 'Stanley ate all of his dinner with a fork.' 'Jack does like carrots and peas – didn't I tell you?' 'We've just eaten dinner *at* the dining table together, no grumbling.'

But as the days have dragged on, the cracks have started to show, and there has been a rapid decline in her enthusiasm for playing the role of me.

The truth: Judith and autism don't mix. Her approach to raising children is at best prehistoric, but it's her total ignorance and her refusal to accommodate Stanley's rigid way of doing things that have made her presence so toxic.

Meals should be served at the dining table with the TV OFF, and if you don't eat what is served, then you DON'T eat. NO chewing with the mouth open, USE your cutlery, and DON'T answer back. Toys should be kept in the bedroom, and the communal living areas must always be immaculate. A bath is essential EVERY night, and a hair wash every other. And at the age of five, a child should be able to fold his own clothes, wipe his own bottom and flush the toilet.

And so on and on.

It's impossible for any child to fit the perfect template that she has etched out, let alone a sensitive autistic boy and an acrobatic toddler with a death wish, and her inability to adjust her approach means that all hell has broken lose. On Tuesday, she tidied away Stanley's maps, and when he came home from school, he had a huge meltdown that took three hours for him to come out of. By that point, I was still bed-bound, so she had to take control of the situation and he wound up more distressed than he was to start with.

The following day, it was Judith's turn to throw a wobbly, but she only had herself to blame. I warned her that Jack was going through a mischievous stage, that she needed to keep an eye on him at all times, but she didn't listen. While she was busy folding clothes in the kitchen, Jack helped himself to the contents of her handbag and fed the DVD player with her credit cards and whatever loose change he found in her purse. And it didn't stop there. That same day, he poured Fairy Liquid into her shoes, threw Stanley's magnetic letters down the toilet and emptied a box of basmati rice all over the kitchen floor. The hoover was back in the closet for all of fifteen minutes when she found the living room decorated in ribbons of toilet roll and the walls stained with orange spaghetti Bolognese handprints.

Later that night, Stan was screaming blue murder while she was trying to wash his hair, and I had to limp into the bathroom to break up the row. She also tried to take his tablet away when he was in the middle of watching YouTube before bedtime, a foolish error which resulted in him flinging it at the wall and cracking the screen. It was just a tiny crack, but for Stanley, it may as well have shattered into a million pieces. Judith was sulking, Jack was bawling, and I ended up taking several punches when trying to calm Stanley down. The only way to defuse the chaos was to hobble out to Argos to buy a new tablet. A decision that I'll no doubt be chastised for until my last days on this earth.

It's Ed who I've felt sorriest for this week. He's so anxious around his mother, so desperate to please her, that he turns into a totally different person when she is around. 'Yes, Mum, no, Mum, I can do that for you, Mum,' he says, jumping to attention every time she clicks her fingers. He has barely noticed the pain I'm suffering because she has commanded all of his attention, and it's only when she pops out to see Alan that he relaxes. It's like a switch is flicked and he turns back into the man I know and love. Witnessing their relationship so intensely over the last few days has really opened my eyes to how hard his childhood must have been. Playing the role of the perfect, dutiful son, having to mask who he truly is to his own mother. It's so very sad.

'Your dad and Rachel can come and pick you and the boys up,' my mum says. 'We'll all muck in and help you, then Ed can come down after his work is over and we'll have a lovely, relaxing Christmas.'

It sounds like perfection. Better than any codeine, ice packs or medicinal alcohol. But it can't happen. I still have a few gigs scheduled which I'm hoping to do, plus my students have their exams. Aside from all of my work commitments, Stanley can't miss school.

'I just can't. I've got work and Stan has his nativity next

week. He's learnt all of his lines already so I can't just pull him out. I'll have the cops on my arse and I'll wind up eating my Christmas dinner in jail.'

'Och, you poor wee woman.'

'What did she say?' Rachel calls out.

'She said she can't come home or she'll get in trouble with the police and have to eat her turkey in a cell.'

'That's bollocks! Give me the phone, Mum.'

Rachel comes on the line. 'Luce, you're on loudspeaker now, so watch your language 'cos George is in the room.'

'Sure,' I say, rolling my eyes. As if she, Miss 'Bollocks-Shit-Twat' is one to lecture *me* about bad language.

'Stan's only five,' she says. 'What's he going to miss? Colouring in Christmas trees and listening to stories about a little donkey being crushed by a heavily pregnant virgin? Pull him out and we'll come and get you.'

'What about the nativity? It's—'

'Before you start digging up more excuses, you should know that work sent me a Virgin Wine Christmas gift box ... another excellent virgin worth celebrating. I've got twelve posh bottles and a magnum of Prosecco. We can get stuck in and watch *Elf* and *Home Alone* and you can help me put my tree up. Y'know, get ourselves in the mood for the big day.'

'But what if the school call the police on me?'

'Well, better to go to jail for truancy than murder. If that joyless bitch pushes you any further then you're bound to snap.'

'Rachel!' my Mum interjects. 'Don't be unkind!'

'What? She is a joyless bitch, Mum. And that is being kind.'

'Actually, Rach, she might be a bitch, but she's definitely not joyless any more. Quite the opposite, thanks to Alan.'

'Oooh! What's happened?'

I fill her in on the juicy details of the past few days – days where I've had no choice but to experience first-hand the blossoming romance between Judith and her beau.

Every morning, Judith has come into my bedroom to ask my opinion of the outfit that she pulled out of the charity bag. 'Is it too showy?' 'Is it slimming?' 'Is it my colour?' These daily visits haven't been because she's genuinely wanted my opinion, but more that she's been after access to my make-up, jewellery and accessories, which are all kept in my bedroom. She wants it all – anything to make her outfit 'pop'.

And 'pop' it sure has, along with the lid off Alan's formerly dormant libido. Indeed, the man can't seem to keep his paws off her, and he's been on the doorstep at 9 a.m. every day, sniffing around her like a dirty old dog. Clothed in fifty shades of lilac, he has turned up bearing gifts of flowers or fresh breakfast pastries from the Polish bakery – the ultimate tools of seduction for a woman in her late sixties.

'How naughty of you! You must put those away,' I'd heard Judith say through the door, and, 'Oh goodness, Alan! It's so soft that it simply melts in your mouth.' Overhearing this particular conversation sent my imagination plummeting into the gutters of filth. To avoid having nightmares, I had to work hard to block out the hideous imagery that my brain had conjured up. Judith wasn't a sexual being. No. Just *no*. But when I hobbled into the kitchen the day after this conversation and busted her and Alan kissing behind the door – disgusting slobbery kisses which made me gag – I stood corrected. The woman *was* capable, and of far more than I dared to imagine.

'Gross!' says Rachel.

'And that's not the half of it. She keeps tapping him on the bum, and any time she is sat down, he makes a point of moving behind her to give her a massage.'

'Ah, he's one of those. The old wandering hands, eh? So do you reckon they're full-on doing it?'

'I dunno. Do old people actually do it?'

'Yes, we do!' I hear Dad call out. 'Every night at 7 p.m. before *Only Fools and Horses* starts.'

'Dad! I'm going to vom – stop!' squeals Rachel. 'Your grandson is sitting RIGHT THERE!'

'And sometimes we do it TWICE!' he carries on, before he is silenced by my mum yelling, 'Roger! Shut your bake!' and Rachel crying out, 'George, cover your ears!'

A few minutes on the phone to these nutters and my despair is obliterated. None of it matters: not the back spasm, the loss of my concert with the Philharmonia, the broken tablet or the fact that I haven't been able to hug my children all week without yelping out in pain.

For a brief moment, all of that is forgotten.

31

Operation: Christmas

'Dinner's ready!' I call out for the third time, but there's still no sign of Ed.

Judith left this morning, and to celebrate, I've cooked steak and home-made chips, and not just any steak, but fillet steak. *That's* how happy I am to see her gone. The moment her car reversed out of the drive, I grabbed my wallet and dashed straight out to buy supplies, stocking up on as much chocolate, meat and wine as my basket could hold. When back home, I cracked on some Guns N' Roses and moshed around the kitchen like a wild thing, devouring chunks of Dairy Milk and de-Judithing my kitchen to get everything back to where I like it.

After collecting Stanley from school, I took him and Jack to McDonald's and treated them to a Happy Meal while we waited for Ed to get back from his matinee. When he came home at around seven, we lounged around in our jammies – him and Stanley doing a World Flags quiz and me watching *Peppa Pig* with Jack. There's been no emotional breakdowns, no arguments, no throwing of tablets or fists, and it's been obvious that all of us are relieved by Judith's departure, not just me.

With the steak going cold in the frying pan, I head down the hall to get Ed, assuming that he's distracted reading a shampoo bottle on the toilet, as he often is. To my surprise,

I find him in the bedroom, sitting on the floor behind the wardrobe door, where he's organising his Action Man collection.

'What's wrong, love?' I ask.

He mutters, 'Nothing.'

One look at his pale face and it's obvious that something is on his mind. 'What's up? Just tell me and then we can eat. I'm starving here, man.'

'It's Ben and Niall,' he says, pausing to put a helmet on one of his figures. 'They've pulled out.'

'What? Of the tour?' My heart sinks. Suddenly, I'm not the least bit hungry any more. 'But why?'

'Ben's just been offered the *Mamma Mia!* gig, and Niall's landed himself a cushty teaching job, so he's staying put.'

'I'm so sorry, love.' I lean over and stroke the top of his bald head. 'Have they said who's doing it instead?'

A sad 'nope' slips out of his mouth.

Losing Ed for the whole of January is bad enough, but learning that his best friends won't be touring Australia with him any more makes me uneasy. Ben and Niall know him inside and out, and they've always had his back when they've been away together. On the many occasions that Ed has overslept on tour, they've saved his arse and banged on his door to get him up for an early lobby call. If he's had one too many pints, they've escorted him back to the hotel, and if he's forgotten to charge his phone, which he always does, they've answered my calls to let me know that he's okay. As long as they've all been together, I haven't had to worry, but now that's all about to change.

'They might book other people you know,' I say, forcing myself to sound upbeat.

'What if they don't? What if they book a bunch of young dickheads and I'm trapped with them on a tour bus for a month?'

'Just pull out,' I say without thinking. 'Fuck it!'

'I can't, can I? We'll be skint after Christmas, and I've got my tax bill coming up.'

My phone isn't exactly ringing off the hook with work offers, and our credit card has already taken a hammering from buying Christmas presents for the boys. But when it boils down to it, Ed's well-being is more important than money.

'We'll find a way, love. We always do,' I say, albeit with false confidence. 'I'll call Miguel and see if he's got any quartet gigs in the pipeline. And you never know, maybe some more shows will come in from Jimmy.'

Jimmy Martel has been on annual leave over the last couple of weeks, and he'd booked Ed to cover all of his shows. It's been a total game-changer, not just for Ed, but for both of us. Most nights he has returned home on brilliant form, and he hasn't needed to hide in the bedroom to decompress from the stress of his day, like he is doing right now. Not even Judith's presence this last week could bring him down. He's made the effort to sit and drink herbal tea with her, and as soon as she's cleared off to bed, we've cracked open the wine and snuggled down on the sofa together to watch Netflix. Working on a show suits him so much better than schlepping all over the place on tour. Leaving the house at the same time each day, boarding the same tube and heading to the same theatre to perform the same music has made a massive difference to his anxiety. And the regular pay has been a godsend.

'He's already said that he's not taking any time off until mid-February, so that's out.'

There's nothing else I can say. Only a lottery win will save us now, and the chances of that are pretty slim given that I always forget to buy a ticket.

'Don't worry about it for now. Just wait and see what happens and we'll deal with it then,' I say before kissing him on the cheek. 'Come on. Let's have our steak and watch *Ozark*. It'll cheer you up.'

By 11.45 p.m., we've stuffed ourselves silly and drunk our way through a bottle and a half of red wine, but not one minute of *Ozark* has been watched. Instead, I've made Ed sit through *Elf* and now, much against his wishes, his arse is up a stepladder digging out our Christmas decorations from the cupboard in the hallway.

'Why does this have to be done now?' he grunts, pulling binbags full of baubles and tinsel down from the top shelf and dumping them in my arms.

'Because it does. The mood has taken me.'

'But it's the 29th November. It's bad luck.'

'Our luck is shit anyway,' I say. 'So we may as well chuck the tree up and have something pretty to look at while we suffer.'

Carrier bags and heavy boxes are handed down to me, and like an impatient child, I can't resist delving in and pulling out strings of tinsel and baubles as we go.

'Look! It's the bauble that Charls stole when we did that gig.' I smile fondly as I recall witnessing Charlie stealthily slipping a few fancy baubles into her handbag at the Harrods staff Christmas party. 'Oh, and here's Big Nan's one-winged angel. She looks a bit knackered, but I reckon she'll do another year.'

The hallway is a total mess, but I can't seem to stop myself. 'Ah, look at this. It's the one from New York! Do you remember the day we got it? When those dodgy guys in Times Square conned you out of a hundred bucks, and you got the NYPD involved and—?'

He glares down at me from the top of the ladder, really not amused.

'Sorry!' I've touched a nerve, so I move on quickly to the next item in my hand. 'Look!'

By the time Ed climbs back down the ladder, every box and bag has been opened and I'm buried under a mound of glittery tinsel, joyfully thrashing around in it like a toddler in a muddy puddle.

'Oh gawd,' he sighs when he surveys the wreckage.

'Come on! Live a little!' I pull the Santa hat off my head, then leap up and start swinging it in the air like a lasso.

'Stop! Stop it!' he shrieks as I whip him on the arse with it. 'Stop!'

'Excuse me, Mummy, but what are you *doing*?'

Caught up in the thrill of the moment, I haven't noticed that Stanley is standing outside his bedroom door. 'Mummy, is that the Christmas tree?'

'Yes, it is!'

'But it is November.'

'I know, but I'm too excited to wait. We're putting it up now. Do you want to help?'

'Uh, it's nearly midnight,' says Ed, looking at me like I've lost my mind. 'He's got school tomorrow.'

'So what. It's CHRISTMAS!'

Our artificial tree takes just minutes to erect, but half an hour later, it's still bare. Ed is elbow deep in a bundle of tangled lights that I specifically remember telling him to pack away neatly last year, and we can't proceed with the tinsel until he's sorted them.

Where he's busy trying to undo knots, I've been tying myself up in more.

'Mummy, how can Santa fit down a chimney when he is so fat?'

'Because, um, he can. He has magic powers.'

'But why, Mummy? If he has magic powers, why is he fat? Why can't he magic his body small?'

'I'm not sure. Maybe he likes being fat? It's really cold in the North Pole, so I guess his big belly helps him keep warm.'

'But he has a red coat. Why does he wear a coat if he is so fat and so hot?'

The questions haven't stopped, and with no time to prepare decent answers, I've ended up telling our child all sorts of ridiculous things that I'll probably have forgotten by morning.

If I am to be believed, Santa is older than Jesus, but he isn't dead because he 'drank a magical potion that will keep him alive forever.' He has X-ray vision, and if he so chooses, he can check up on any child in *any* part of the world and see if they're behaving nicely ('Yes, even in Libya'). If there's a house with no chimney, he can walk through walls so that's no bother. And no, he'll never explode from eating millions of mince pies in one night, because every time he eats one, he farts it out and the gust of air is what makes his sleigh fly. Fart energy – who would have thought I'd be capable of solving the world's energy crisis at midnight on a school night?

'And, Mummy, how will Santa know what I want for my presents?' comes next.

'Well, that's an easy one. You have to write him a list and put it in a postbox and send it to the North Pole, Stan.'

'But, Mummy, when?'

'We can do it tomorrow, if you like?'

'No! Now!' he yells. 'Now! Now! Now!'

I try to persuade him to wait, but it's too late. He, too, has been possessed by the Christmas spirit, and it's not within my power to exorcise it. Out come the pens and paper, and at almost one o'clock in the morning Stanley presents us with his finished list.

Deer Santah

Mi naym iz Stanley and i am
a veree gud boy.

GET ME

Numbur 1. Holly day to Libeeya

Numbur 2. A frika puzzell

Numbur 3. A frika T shurt

Numbur 4. Alfabet puzzell

Numbur 5. Numbers puzzell

Numbur 6. Fiyer ex tink wish her.

From Stanley

Just as Ed has finished detangling the lights, I zip up my coat over my pyjamas and head out in the dark to the nearest postbox.

32

The Messy-Ah

'Stan, you are looking at your feet. Try holding your face up so everyone can see how handsome you are,' I say.

'I am *not* handsome!'

'Of course not.' I cower behind a cushion to hide my smile. 'You are not handsome at all. I just meant that if you hold your face up, people will hear you better.'

He looks up at the light fitting dangling from the ceiling and tries again. 'Today, in the, town, of, Saint, Da-vid, a savoury, has, been born.'

Ed butts in. '*Saviour*, Stan. It's sav-i-our.'

'Sav-i-our,' Stanley mimics before continuing in his standard monotonal fashion. 'He, is the, messy-ah, the—'

'*Messiah*,' Ed interrupts again. 'Mess-i-ah!'

'MESS-III-AAAH! He is the messy-ah!'

And before I can stop him, Ed's on his case again. '*Messiah*! It's messiah! And make sure you look at us when you are talking,' he huffs, the vein on his forehead purple and pulsating.

'I don't like looking at people!'

'It's okay, Stan. Why don't you pretend that your audience aren't people?' I suggest. 'In fact, do you know what me and Daddy do when we have to get up on a stage to perform? We pretend that the audience are just a row of cabbages.'

But it's the wrong thing to say.

'No cabbages!'

'Okay,' I say calmly. 'How about … um …' My brain scrolls through my catalogue of vegetables: cauliflower, turnips, Brussel sprouts, aubergines – no. None of them are going to cut it.

'Bananas?' offers Ed.

'Yes, Daddy. Brilliant idea! Stan, you could pretend that they are bananas in pyjamas!'

He stares at Ed and me like we have suddenly sprouted horns, then after a brief pause to consider our suggestion, he nods. Cabbages are out, bananas are in. He tries again, his voice barely audible under the sound of Ed's heels drumming on the laminate floor.

'Today, in the, town, of, Saint Da-vid, a savoury, has, been born.'

I shoot a look at Ed and shush him before he dares to say a word. 'That's much better, Stan. Well done. Now let's do it again and try saying your lines a bit louder. The old ladies at the back won't hear you,' I say. 'They might have to turn up their hearing aids.'

A ten-minute conversation ensues about the degeneration of the human ear, but Ed doesn't stick around to participate. His patience has long gone, and in all honesty, mine has been whittled down to virtually nothing too. But for Stanley's benefit, I must power on.

Over the last couple of weeks, the notifications from the class WhatsApp group have been pinging incessantly like hot popcorn exploding from a lidless pan. This nativity is driving all of the mums crazy, the costumes being *the* hot topic for discussion. Some, like Marsha and her friend Nicky, are making their own, and they've uploaded photos of their handiwork for everyone to admire. Others have scoured the internet, then panicked themselves stupid that the Christmas post might delay the arrival of their camel and donkey outfits which are being shipped from the depths of mainland China.

But I couldn't give a shit about any of that.

I'm more worried about how my boy will cope when under pressure to perform. Or how he will react to the sheer volume of people that will be watching him – the unfamiliar faces, the sounds, smells and colours – all of which are like red flags to a bull for him.

Every time I picture the scene, a wave of nausea comes over me. Our sweet little boy comes out on stage, his heart racing, his limbs stiff. He looks down to see Marsha parked in the front row with all of her PTA buddies, their camera phones suspended in the air ready to start shooting. He panics. Overwhelmed by the eyes of a hundred strangers boring into him, his legs give way and he throws himself down on the stage. The kids and parents stare in shock, and rightly so because it is shocking to see a small child in the throes of an autistic meltdown. Mrs Merryweather tries to calm him, but she doesn't know how. Only I can rescue him, but he's out of reach. I'm stuck at the back of the hall, desperately trying to push through the crowd to save him before Marsha films the whole scene on her smartphone.

Oh God!

But what can we do? Pull him out and have him miss the opportunity just because he is autistic?

No. Hell *no.*

Stanley wants to do it, and even though he has no idea quite what 'it' entails, it's our job to guide him. No matter what happens.

'Let's try it one more time, Stan, and then we can have some Wotsits and orange juice. Good idea?'

He nods stiffly. 'That sounds very okay, Mummy.'

'Good, go for it then. Nice and loud, okay?'

He drops his head towards the floor. Then, with the quietest indoor voice I've ever heard, he has another try.

'Today, in the, town, of, Saint, Da-vid, a, sav-our-y, has, been born, He, is, the, messy-ah.'

33

The Nativity

When we turn the corner onto Oxford Road, disaster strikes.

'Fuck's *sake*,' mutters Ed when he sees the size of the queue. 'It doesn't even start for another half an hour. You'd think we were going in to watch the FIFA cup final.'

For once, he isn't exaggerating. Every mum, dad, granny, grandpa and younger sibling in the borough of Ealing has descended to watch their darlings perform, and the queue is spilling out of the school gates and all the way up the street. It's pouring, and Jack, who refused to get in his pram, is pulling relentlessly on my arm and dangerously in the direction of giving me another back spasm.

Ed huffs and puffs as we approach the queue, growing increasingly more agitated.

'It's annoying, I know,' I say. 'If I could have bought fast-track tickets and had us escorted to a private box to watch it, then believe me, I would've done it, but this isn't the O2 arena. It's a primary school, and they don't sell VIP tickets.'

'Well, they *should*.'

I swallow my frustration and try to be understanding. 'Look, I don't mind going by myself if you want to bail?'

'No.'

'Are you sure? If it's too much, you can just leave it.'

'No. I want to see Stan.'

'Well, how about I handle the chit-chat and you take charge of Jack?'

'Okay. Fine.'

I plonk the bag of snacks and toys on his shoulder, and he takes Jack's hand and walks on ahead, granting me a few seconds to stretch my spine back out to its formerly 180° angle.

When we reach the back of the queue, the plan goes straight out of the window. Ed – Mr self-professed 'I hate chit-chat' – instantly switches into his mega-sociable mode and starts jabbering to the first stranger he sees. That person is Dave, a six-foot-tall brute with a thick mound of curly ginger hair and a bushy beard to match. All I manage to learn about Dave before having to run off and stop Jack from lying face down in a puddle is that he's a cab driver, and that he's here to see his little girl playing the role of a donkey. By the time we enter the front door, Ed has extracted Dave's full life story from him and has divulged every detail of his own, whether Dave wanted to hear it or not.

We are all herded into the hall like cattle by Mr Muhley and his ice-queen receptionist, Mrs Abel. I try to duck out of the line and slot in between two women who are leaning against the wall by the entrance, but Mrs Abel moves me along. She says something about health and safety hazards, and as much as I want to stand my ground, Jack is pulling on my coat and whingeing to be picked up so there's no time to argue. We end up squashed in the far corner of the hall behind Ed's new friend, Dave, and his bountiful head of hair, which, thanks to the shitty weather, has frizzed up and added an extra five inches to his already towering stature. Shoulder to shoulder, we stand in our winter coats next to a blisteringly hot radiator, saturated in rainwater and asphyxiating in the damp, stuffy air.

'I mainly do Heafrow drops, mate,' says Dave. 'Sometimes I do a bit of Ga'wick, but I try not to take those fares 'cos I can't be bovvered with the M25.'

'I know what you mean, mate,' Ed replies, his accent suddenly turned cockney to match Dave's.

'And I won't take on the M4 after 7 a.m. It's usually stuffed, so I stick wiv the A4 where I can.'

Ed and Dave's tedious banter is hard enough to tolerate, but *We Wish You a Merry Christmas* is being played on the PA system, whingeing babies and toddlers are letting rip, and Jack is gearing up to make a run for it. The snacks I've packed aren't distracting him, nor is Sophie the Giraffe or his toy flip phone. I should've packed something more effective. Some rope, or handcuffs even.

Marsha waved at me on our way in. As expected, she has landed seats on the front row next to Heidi and the other PTA mums, but instead of bringing a phone to record her little Joseph in action, she has set up a swanky video camera on a tripod.

Just brilliant.

The longer I stand waiting for the show to start, the faster the knot in my stomach unravels and I don't know what to do. Should I grab Stanley from his classroom and do a runner? Spare both him and me the stress? Or shall I stay put, keep the faith and see how it all pans out? Fight or flight?

I'm busy weighing up the options when the crowd starts to applaud. It's too late. The house lights go out, the spotlight kicks in, the music starts and hundreds of camera phones click into action.

'*Little Donkey, little donkey, on the dusty road …*'

On tiptoes, I shuffle left and right behind Dave's back, trying to see something. The top of Stanley's head will do, his arm or his shoulder even, but Ed has befriended the broadest, hairiest, most ogre-like man in the building and I can't see a thing. Why couldn't he have buddied up with a four-footer? Maybe a nice old lady with an unfortunate curvature of the spine? Then at least I'd have a shot at seeing something.

I briefly contemplate kicking Dave in the back of the knee – a little trick that I learnt in a self-defence lesson back in my college days – but there's no need, as Jack goes ahead and clears the deck for me. Pulling free of my hand, he drops to the floor and pushes his way through the gap between Dave's feet, thundering on all fours in the direction of the stage. Startled, Dave immediately shifts out of the way and Ed springs into action to fetch him.

At last, I have a visual.

Stanley walks on to the stage holding Mrs Beard's hand, and once he has lined up next to his peers, who are all singing their hearts out, she lets go and retreats to the side. The whole scene is incredibly sweet. Mary and Joseph are in the centre holding baby Jesus, the three wise men and Angel Gabriel are on either side of them, and there's a whole selection of singing animals decorated in multicoloured tinsel: camels, sheep, cows and one very proud-looking T-Rex. The rest of the class, who I assume have been cast as narrators like Stanley, are dressed in their best Christmas-party outfits. Little girls wear sparkly pink and red frocks, a dozen others have light-up Rudolf and Santa jumpers on, and there's one very dapper little fella dressed in a white tuxedo with a red bow-tie. Stanley is the only one in school uniform, and the string of red tinsel that I spent ages convincing him to drape over his shoulders this morning is gone.

Mrs Merryweather is positioned in the middle of the audience, where she exaggeratedly mouths lyrics and throws out choreographed arm actions like an aerobics instructor. The kids copy her, their eyes fixed on her every move, but Stan's lips remain clamped shut as he scans the crowd looking for a face he recognises.

The fuse is lit, and there's just seconds before the bomb goes off.

I start to push my way to the front. Ed is crawling on the floor somewhere, so it *has* to be me. I duck through a gap in the crowd, whacking an old man on the head as I go, but I don't waste time apologising and keep moving, twisting through the obstacle course of arms, legs and pushchairs before finally making it out into the open.

I'm in his eyeline at last.

I jump up and down on the spot, waving both arms in the air like a stranded survivor, and eventually he notices. 'Mummy!' he squeals, pointing at me with a huge smile on his face. I blow him a kiss and he catches it, then he starts to sing along, keeping his eyes fixed solely on me, as though there is no one else in the room.

His big moment comes right after the song. Stepping forward, he turns his whole body to face mine and lets rip.

'TODAY, IN THE, TOWN OF, SAINT DA-VID, A SAV-OUR-Y HAS—'

He stops abruptly, squeezing his eyes shut and dropping his head down.

Oh God! Tick, tick, tick …

Then he looks up directly at the audience. 'Excuse me, but can the old ladies at the back hear? Or do you have to turn up your hearing machines?'

The crowd erupts into laughter, but he stands there patiently awaiting an answer.

'I SAID, DO YOU HAVE TO TURN UP YOUR HEARING MACHINES?'

'It's okay, Stan!' I shout over the guffaws. 'Carry on, we can all hear you!'

And without waiting for the laughter to disperse, he picks up exactly where he left off.

'—BEEN BORN. THEY CALL HIM THE MESSAY-AH,' he bellows as I weep juicy, thick tears of overwhelming pride.

34

All He Wants For Christmas

It's my last day of teaching before the holidays, and I'm absolutely bursting with excitement. Stanley's nativity has really got me in the festive mood. Nothing, and I mean *nothing*, can bring me down: not the lingering pain in my back, not the massive traffic jam that I'm trapped in and not the fact that the car radio is malfunctioning and switches itself off every time I turn left.

The jingle bells are ringing, Santa is on his merry way, and I can practically smell the turkey browning in the oven. Ding fecking dong!

'Ask Lucy what veg she wants,' Mum says in the background. 'And if she's happy with lamb, turkey and beef.'

'Did you hear that, Luce?' Rachel says. 'Mum's trying to lock down Christmas dinner.'

'Uh, yeah, I heard her. Just tell her that I don't know what I'm eating tonight, let alone a week from now.'

The loudspeaker is deactivated and Mum comes on the line. 'I'm doing a joint of lamb for your father and Rachel, because they hate turkey. But I know Ed is a big turkey man, so I've ordered a medium-sized one from the butcher for him. Glad and Gwyn won't touch it, and Glad doesn't believe in eating lamb, so I'm doing a beef too.'

'Glad and Gwyn are both coming?'

'Oh yes. They'll be on their own otherwise and I won't have that.'

I smile, my mother's heart of gold radiating such warmth that I can feel it pouring out of my phone and heating up my cheek.

'So, veg wise,' she continues, 'Rachel wants carrots and broccoli but won't have the sprouts. But I love them, y'see, and so does your father and Big Nan, but we've to keep them away from her. Y'know her bowels can't take them.'

'Oh, I *know* all right. Don't forget I was sat next to her last year, Mam.'

'Och, course you were. Hard times, they were.' She pauses briefly. 'And Glad is after mushy peas ... but who puts mushy peas on a Christmas dinner?'

'People with dodgy teeth, I'm guessing.'

'But her teeth are good. They're her own, which at her age is a blessing. So I'm going to do a wee bowl for her because no one else will have them.'

'Good plan,' I say. 'And I'll eat whatever is going, just so you know.'

'Okay, so it's just the boys now. Jack will have a wee bit of dinner, won't he?'

'Yeah, I think so. He's pretty adventurous with his food at the moment. He ate a tomato the other day!'

'Did he, now? That's great. And what about my Stanley? What will he have?'

I could say anything right now: smiley faces and chicken dippers, or a slice of turkey carved in the shape of Libya. Whatever I say, she will do it, without any fuss or judgement. Not just because she loves him, but more because she *gets* him.

Several hours later, I'm sitting playing Candy Crush as I wait for Oscar, my last student of the day, to arrive. The back spasm meant that I didn't make it in to teach him before his exam, but Mrs Morecombe, the piano accompanist, said that my students all managed to get through their exams relatively unscathed. There were 'a few minor hiccups', but a minor hiccup here and there is far better than an explosion of belly-burning belches, so I'm happy enough. Everyone should pass, their parents will keep off my back, and come the New Year, I'll hopefully still have my job.

Oscar turns up fifteen minutes late without his cello, but I can't tell him off as he has brought me a box of Quality Street and a lavender candle. A bag of cash and plane tickets to Hawaii would have been preferable, but the kids of millionaires aren't as forthcoming with the extravagant Christmas presents as one might think.

'Mrs Morecombe said that your pieces went well, which is great!' I say to him. 'But what about your scales? Which ones did the examiner ask you to play?'

'The one that starts on this string.' He twangs the C string of the cello that I've loaned him with such force that it almost breaks. 'And the one that starts on this finger,' he says, innocently giving me the middle finger.

'Good. And did you play all of your pieces without stopping?'

'Yep.'

I punch the air excitedly and let out a little cheer. Considering he couldn't get through two lines of his pieces without stopping for a chat, this news borders on miraculous.

'Actually, miss, I did have to stop in the second song because the page fell on the floor and I had to pick it up.'

My heart sinks. He'd obviously used a photocopy after I'd explicitly told him not to.

'Didn't your mum buy the proper book to use in the exam? I emailed her to remind her.'

He casually shrugs his shoulders, oblivious to the possibility that I might be sued for breach of copyright because his mother didn't get her act together.

'Never mind. The exam is out of the way, so let's forget all about it and play some Christmas carols.'

I'm wearing my Santa hat and I have a sack full of selection boxes on the floor by my chair, which I've been dishing out all day to the kids. At this point, I couldn't give a shit if I end up being taken to court for photocopying 'The Drunken Sailor'. Christmas is around the corner and I can almost taste my mum's pigs in blankets, not to mention my dad's infamous snowballs, which he always beefs up with an extra glug of brandy.

'What about "Rudolph the Red-Nosed Reindeer"? Or I have "Silent Night" and "We Wish You a Merry Christmas". And as it's the last day before we break up, I've brought lots of …' I drum my fingers on my cello, bigging up the drama for the grand reveal. 'CHOCOLATES!'

Oscar gives me a watery smile. Every other kid that I've seen today has practically snapped my arm off to get at my chocolates, but not him. He is so unenthused that I may as well have offered him a bag of cold broccoli and farts.

'Aren't you excited for Christmas?'

He shakes his head but doesn't say a word.

An uncomfortable silence follows, one that I'm desperate to fill. 'I know, tell me what you've asked Santa for? An Xbox, or a bike, or some Harry Potter Lego?' I ask, knowing that he probably has all of these things a hundred times over. His dad owns an international electronics company and divides his time between his New York and London offices, and his mum is a high-flyer in the business world too. According to Oscar, their Hampstead home has seven or so bedrooms, an indoor pool, a cinema room, a sauna and a gym, plus he goes to this school, one of the most expensive in the UK. What can Santa possibly bring a boy who has everything?

'What about a trampoline?' I continue. 'Or an electric scooter?'

It's only now that I notice his bottom lip is trembling. Quickly laying my cello down, I reach for the sack of chocolate. 'Here, quick! Tuck in!' I say, but it's too late. The tears have fallen. 'Oscar, what's wrong?'

He can't speak, only sob.

'Are you poorly? Shall I call Mum and ask her to come and collect you?'

'She's ... at ... at ... at work.'

'I can still call her at work, no problem.'

'In Dubai!' he shrieks.

'Oh,' is all I manage to say. I want to hug him, but I'm not allowed to. Inhumane as it might be in these circumstances, physical contact of any kind is against school policy. 'Shall I call your dad, then? Or is there someone else?'

'Lisa.' The snot drips out of his nostrils. 'But I don't want *her*!'

This child needs a hug, and he needs it now. *Sod it!* I get up and put my arms around him and he totally lets go, his little body convulsing as the tears continue to fall.

'Has something happened?' I ask, gently rubbing the back of his head as I wait for him to calm down.

'Santa won't ... find ... me,' he splutters.

'Of *course* he will.'

'No, he won't, because he won't know where I am!'

It takes a while for the full story to come out, and once I've heard it, I understand why he's so upset. He won't be celebrating Christmas at home this year as planned, but instead he will be going to Dubai because his mother has to work.

'But how are you going to get there? Isn't your mum already out there?'

'Lisa is taking me. And we all have to stay in a hotel, and they don't have chimneys in hotels, and Santa won't know where I am!'

'He definitely will,' I say, my heart breaking for him. 'You do know that he has X-ray vision, don't you? And that means he can find you anywhere in the whole world ... even Libya.'

'Really?'

'Absolutely! And I bet he'll love going to Dubai to find you. It'll be sunny there, won't it?'

'But Granny won't be there. Or my Xbox. And Theodore will be lonely without me.'

'Who's Theodore?'

'My hamster. He's very old and he might die soon.'

The tears continue to fall, and nothing I say makes him feel better. All he wants for Christmas is to be home, and I understand that more than anyone. Because for me, there's no place on earth I'd rather be.

35

Christmas Eve

'That poor wee soul! Fancy spending your Christmas stuck in a hotel room on the other side of the world. That's shocking!'

'It'll probably be a five-star one, Mum,' I say. 'He's not exactly going to be slumming it.'

'I'd go in a heartbeat,' adds Rachel. 'Sunshine, pools and cocktails. It beats freezing our nuts off here.'

Mum's not having it. 'I'm sorry, but kids want to be in their own homes, with presents around their own tree … not eating turkey in the sweltering heat with sunglasses on,' she insists. 'You should have just stuck him in the car and brought him back here with you.'

'Um, that's kidnapping,' says Rachel, smirking.

'I don't care! The wee soul would have had a lovely time here.'

My mother isn't wrong. We might be in a modest two-bedroom bungalow on an ordinary street in Wales, but for a young boy, rich or otherwise, my parents' house is possibly the most magical place on earth to spend Christmas. Stanley exploded with excitement when we arrived a few days ago, and he's yet to come down from his high. He still can't believe that there's a Christmas tree in almost every room of the house, and what's more, that each one is covered with candy canes and chocolates on golden strings that are free for the taking. 'Chocolate for breakfast! I like this house lots!'

Fairy lights and foil garlands hang from every ceiling, stacks of presents are piled up all over the floor, and fake snow is sprayed on the windows. Walter – the light-up snowman – is parked in his prime position in the front garden next to the 'SANTA, STOP HERE!' sign, and there isn't a doorknob, curtain pole or an ornament inside that doesn't have tinsel wrapped around it. Even the toilet-flush handles have been adorned with red glittery baubles.

It's safe to say that if I had kidnapped Oscar and brought him here for Christmas, he would have had the time of his life, because Stanley certainly is. George has been over every day to play with him, and between them, they've polished off nearly two tubs of Celebrations and watched *Elf* about fifty times. George has taught Stanley to sing '*Jingle bells, Batman smells, Robin flew away, Uncle Billy lost his willy along the motorway, Hey!*' This been the theme tune to our holiday, and the pair of them have erupted into belly laughter every time they've reached the word 'willy'.

Stanley now knows what a whoopee cushion is, and he can also burp on demand and flick a bogey an impressive distance. Aside from all of the festive farty fun, George has bagged up all of his toys and brought them over to play. Nerf guns have been firing at all hours, elaborate Marble Run structures have been built, and Spiderman has defeated Dr Octopus, Electro and the Green Goblin in many ferocious battles. Stanley's puzzles haven't had a look-in – last time I checked, they were still in his rucksack in the bedroom, which in many ways is a good thing. Spending time with his cousin has been so good for him, and I've noticed that his confidence has really soared these last few days. That being said, Santa is soon to squeeze his fat arse down the chimney to deliver a very expensive set of handmade wooden puzzles of the entire world, so I'm hoping that he is still a geography enthusiast come morning.

Jack has had plenty to keep him occupied too. If he's not trying to pull down the Christmas trees, he is trying to eat the baubles, and we've had to make some necessary readjustments to the decorations to spare him from winding up in hospital with glitter poisoning. Yes, he has acted up, but his little outbursts of frustration have been much easier to deal with – partly because my family is around to help, but mainly because I've had either a snowball in my hand or a wedge of cheese on the go since I arrived. It's impossible to feel stressed when your liver is soaking in advocaat and your belly is full of Brie, and so far, the only genuine stress that I've experienced is trying to grab a few Maltesers from the tub of Celebrations before they all get scoffed and nothing remains but Bountys.

The oven has been blazing all hours, as has the slow cooker, and I've watched Mum pull out joints of beef, pork, lamb and ham, not to mention meringue nests, apple crumble and home-made sausage rolls. And the insane production of food hasn't stopped there. In keeping with tradition, Dad has fired up the barbecue every lunchtime and has been out in the rain with his Santa hat on and his can of Guinness, torching Cumberland sausages to make hotdogs. Ed has stayed back in London to do one more matinee, and he isn't due here until later this evening, but come tomorrow, I know he'll be next to my dad in the garden, gnawing on burnt sausages with a can of Carling on the go.

'So, Rach, what are you wearing later?'

'No! Before you ask, you can't borrow my red cardigan.'

'I wasn't going to ask!' I say sharply, because it's true. I was just going to take it, but now that option is off the table. 'Are you going for a festive dress? Or jeans and a sparkly top? What are you thinking?'

'It's the Christmas fair, Luce. Do you even need to ask?'

Every year it's the same. Bungalow Baz will be in his threadbare Santa outfit, Ozzy will have a garish Christmas jumper on that is four sizes too small, and Claire will be a sexy elf. The rest of the village will be wrapped up in their thick winter coats because it will be icy cold and raining. This is Wales, after all. No matter the time of year, it's always icy cold, and it's *always* raining.

'A thermal vest, two jumpers, a cardigan and a coat it is then,' I say. 'And what about food? Are we eating down there or getting a Chinese later?'

'Ozzy's got a new sandwich on the menu this year,' says Mum. 'It sounds nice too. Turkey, pigs in blankets, stuffing and a layer of gravy bread served inside a huge roll. He's calling it the Moisture Manger.'

'Do you mean Moist Maker, Mum? Like Ross's sandwich in *Friends*?'

'Yeah, it is, Luce,' says Rachel. 'I'm so having one of those bad boys.'

Hot dogs for brunch, a block of cheese and a box of Quality Street for dessert, and now, for an afternoon snack, a massive bap loaded with turkey, stuffing, sausages and a slice of extra gravy-soaked bread. Perfection!

'Maternity jeans,' I announce decisively. 'That's what I'm wearing later.'

36

The Fair

The residents of Tref Y Glaw sure know how to throw a party. Old or young, it doesn't matter: everyone has got their Santa hats and Rudolf antlers on, and the small square outside Ozzy's sandwich shop is crammed full of festive-fun seekers. Rugby lads stand around drinking beer from plastic cups, pensioners in wheelchairs swing their arms in time to the live music, and excitable kids inhale sweets from cellophane candy cones and jump around like they're on pogo sticks.

Small gazebos are erected in the corners of the square, each one drawing a large crowd of locals. Ozzy and Claire are manning the hot-food station, Gary and Ange from the Greenacre village shop are selling sweets, crisps and drinks for the kids, and the alcohol is being served at my dad's favourite drinking establishment, The Tafarn Cwtch – shortened by the locals to just The Cwtch.

Bungalow Baz's gazebo is by far the most popular attraction. He is Santa Claus, and for the price of one pound, the kids get to sit on his knee, assure him that they've been very good and then choose a present from his sack of surprises (a black binbag filled with whatever sweets were on offer in the Spar or the Co-op). With his skinny limbs, his bleach-blond eyebrows and his straggled muddy fair hair poking out from beneath his hat, Baz isn't the most convincing Santa that I've ever seen, but the kids don't seem to care. They just want a present, and if that means sitting on the lap of a stick-thin Santa with a broad Welsh accent, a Santa whose beard is held on with a string of green elastic, then that's what they're going to do. No questions asked.

The delicious smell of roast turkey and thick-cut chips wafting from Ozzy's gazebo has my tastebuds screaming for a sample. 'Rach, I'm starving. Dad is at the bar, so if you get in the queue for the food, I'll take the kids to meet Santa. Deal?'

'Okay. Meet you back here in ten,' she says before pulling her wallet out of her handbag and charging off through the crowd.

I kneel down to speak to Stanley, who has been hiding under my coat since we arrived. 'Stan, do you want to come with your brother and George to meet Santa?'

He looks over at Santa, who at this very moment is taking a monstrous bite of a Moist Maker. A dribble of gravy slips out and splashes his beard, but it's quickly mopped up by a silver-haired lady who is hovering behind him with a wedge of serviettes. Judging by how she lovingly dabs his beard, I surmise that she must be Baz's new girlfriend. Either that or his mother.

Stanley is no fool. 'That's *not* Santa!'

'It is!' shrieks George.

'It's *not*! His beard is not real. And he is *not* fat!'

I glance over just as Santa is gulping his pint. There's no coming back from that. 'Okay, Stan. You're right. He's not the real one, but he is *best* friends with the real Santa.'

George is horrified by the revelation. Rachel is going to flatten me unless I dig my way out of this one. 'It's all right, boys. He's helping out today because the real Santa, is, um …

busy. He's packing up his sleigh before he sets off around the world tonight.'

To my relief, George takes me at my word and runs straight over to join the queue, but Stanley doesn't move.

'Are you coming then, Stan?' He stares at Baz through the crowd, lost in thought. 'Can you hear me? Shall we go and—?'

'Uncle Baz is best friends with Santa?' he butts in.

'Yes, he is. So we should tell him how good you've been, then he can pass the message on to Santa later. Shall we do it?'

After careful consideration, he agrees.

Jack's turn on Santa's lap lasts mere seconds before he bursts into tears. Mum swoops in to get him and his head is now resting on his favourite comfort pillows. George is next, but he doesn't hang about. He barely manages to tell Santa his name before jumping off his knee and diving into the sack to pull out the biggest parcel he can find.

It's now Stanley's turn.

'All right, buddy. Want to hop up by yer?' Baz pats his bony leg, but Stanley is fixed to the spot with his attention focused on Baz's questionable beard. At a loss for what to do next, Baz tries again. 'Come on 'en, up by yer, then you can have a pressie from my sack.'

'Excuse me, but what language are you speaking?' asks Stanley.

'Um, it's okay, Santa,' I intervene with a wink. 'I think that he's happy standing for now. Just carry on.'

'No worries. Dim problem,' Baz says returning the wink. He turns back to Stanley and tries again. 'So, what's your name then, buddy?'

'It is not Buddy, it is Stanley. And I know yours, and it is not Santa. It is Barry!'

An awkward 'Ho, ho, ho!' slips out of Baz. 'No, I'm *Santa*, so I am. And I yur you've bin a very gud lad this yur.'

'Barry! Barry! Barry! Your name is BARRY!'

'Okay, Stanley, that's enough,' I cut in sharply. The hopes and dreams of every little believer standing in the queue behind us hang in the balance. 'Just tell Barry what you'd like for Christmas,' I whisper in his ear, 'and then we can go and get some sweets from the shop, okay?'

He exhales noisily then starts strutting back and forth across the small patch of artificial grass that's been laid underneath the gazebo.

'Excuse me, *Barry*, but what I want for Christmas is: number one, a Celebrations chocolate box; number two, a talking Spiderman; number three, Doctor Octopus; Number four, a whoopee cushion.'

Baz's eyes glaze over, but mine do the opposite and virtually burst free of their sockets. 'But what about map puzzles, Stan?'

'Number five, slime; number six, a Green Goblin; number seven ...' he continues, shouting his list to ensure that both Barry and the real Santa can hear him all the way from the North Pole.

'Did you hear what I just said?' I huff.

He ignores me and ploughs on calling out the names of almost every toy that he and George have played with over the last few days – 'Number eight, a Nerf gun; number nine, a walkie-talkie machine; number ten, a Marble Run set' – none of which he'll be opening tomorrow. By the time he gets to number fifteen, pins and needles have invaded my limbs, my toes are frozen together in one clump, and I'm ready to throw in the towel and cancel Christmas.

'Stanley Wright, you told me that you wanted new map puzz—'

'And the last one is number seventeen.' He stops pacing and turns to look me straight in the eye. 'And it's a best friend.'

I'm momentarily winded. 'Um, what did you just say?'

'Mummy, I said that I want Santa to get me a best friend.'

'What's wrong love?'

'Nothing, Mum,' I sniffle quietly. Glancing behind me, I check that Stanley is out of earshot, then lean in close to her. 'He's just said that he wants a best friend for Christmas.'

'Gawd bless him.' Tears are already gathering on her eyelashes. She quickly offloads Jack into my arms and reaches for her bag. 'Stop your crying, now.'

'You stop yours!'

She gives me a tissue and takes one for herself. 'What a right pair we are, eh?'

Dad returns from the bar with a tray of pints, which he sets down on the small wall behind us. 'For gawd's sake. What's wrong with you two?' he says when he sees our teary faces. 'I've only been gone five minutes and everyone is crying.'

'It's nothing. Shut it, Roger.' Mum blows her nose and scrunches her tissue into a ball. 'What did you get me?'

Dad lifts a pint off the tray and gives it to her. 'Here.'

'Och, what do you expect me to do with this?' she says, aghast at the size of the glass that she is being offered. 'I only wanted a half.'

'It's all they had, Linda,' he huffs. 'Just get it down you.'

234

She lifts the glass with both hands and waits for Dad to turn around before pouring a quarter of it away and setting it back down on the wall. I watch her reach into her handbag and pull out a small plastic tube filled with a yellowy-green liquid. Intrigued, I lean in closer to get a better look and immediately realise that it's a urine sample pot.

'Mum! What are you doing?' I shriek as I watch her calmly unscrew the lid and pour the putrid liquid into her glass. 'Is that—' I lean in closer still and hiss the word '— wee?'

'Don't be silly, you eejit! It's lemon and lime. I can't be drinking this big brute without a wee dash of it.'

I burst out laughing, blowing the last of my tears away. 'But why's it in a piss pot?'

'I pinched a few from the surgery. They're handy, so they are. Great for spices, condiments and the like.' She sips her beer and smacks her lips together in satisfaction. 'Lovely. Now where's your sister? Och, is that her over there? It is! That's Jason Donovan she's talking to, isn't it?'

Rachel is leaning against the wall chatting to a tall, broad fella who's wearing a light-up Santa jumper. He has a little less hair than the last time I saw him in 2016, but I'd recognise him anywhere with that killer smile. It's him. It's The Don.

'The rascal!' I say. 'She looks like she's *well* in there, Mum.'

'She does, doesn't she?' Mum is practically salivating.

Intent on watching the drama unfold, we decide to reposition ourselves and perch on the wall facing the lovebirds to get a better view. When Rachel finally returns, she has a huge grin on her flushed face. There's not a Moist Maker to be seen, but I know why. Nothing kills a good old flirting session more than eating something messy in front of a potential suitor. I might starve to death, but it'll so be worth it if she gets a good shag in before the New Year.

'I got his number,' she mouths discreetly.

Both Mum and I yelp.

'Sshhh! Cool it!' she hisses. 'He might be looking.'

Dad, blissfully unaware of what is going on, lifts a pint off the tray and gives it to her. 'Here, love. Get this down you.'

Rachel automatically pours a quarter of the pint away and, with an extended arm, waits for Mum to delve into her bag and hand over the piss pot. She unscrews the pot with her teeth then casually pours the cordial into her glass.

I only hope that The Don isn't watching.

37

He Has Been!

'Rudolf didn't eat his broccoli!'

That is how Christmas morning kicks off. Following Ed's announcement of the three glorious words that most youngsters wait all year to hear – 'He has been!' – Stanley bolts into the living room, bypassing mounds of presents, and heads straight towards the fireplace to inspect the plate of treats that he'd left out for Santa.

'But why not?' he demands. 'Why did Santa eat his Twiglets and drink his Guinness, but Rudolf didn't eat his broccoli?'

'I guess he wasn't hungry,' I say, glaring across at Ed, whose only job was to clear the plate before coming to bed. He'd arrived from London at gone 11 p.m. last night, and while I wrapped all of the kids' presents, he stayed up drinking whisky with Dad in the conservatory. It was obviously a big mistake leaving them unsupervised. Ed's peaky complexion indicates that things got out of control, and my dad's bloodshot eyes confirm it. They'd got hammered.

Stanley persists. 'But—'

'Quick, let's look at which presents are yours, shall we?' Ed interrupts.

But he isn't interested in presents. 'I want my pancakes and my banana in semicircles,' he says. 'And I want to watch my videos.' Ed tries to steer him towards his stocking, which is bursting at the seams with presents, ones that he'd been bidding for on eBay for the last six months in the lead-up to this very moment, but Stanley isn't fussed. 'Pancakes. Banana. Semicircles,' he says, obliterating Ed's enthusiasm with three short words. He isn't going to budge, so off I go to the kitchen to prepare his breakfast in the same way that I do on any ordinary day of the week.

By 11.30 a.m., Ed and Dad are effing and jeffing under their breaths as they attempt to assemble a Fisher Price car ramp that has an instruction manual as thick as the *Yellow Pages* – a manual that neither of them has the patience to read. Jack is happy playing inside the huge box that the ramp came in, but Stanley's presents are still untouched. With Dad itching to fire up the barbecue, and Mum harping on about having to stuff the turkey and glaze her ham, Ed and I decide to step in and help get things moving.

'Look, Stan, a slime-making kit! Look, colouring pens! Look …' Ed squawks at regular intervals as he tears through the stocking fillers at the slick speed of a till operator at Lidl. Mum and I join in with a variety of 'wow' noises as and when required, but Stanley's attention is fixed on his trusty Africa puzzle, which he's busy organising in alphabetical order on the coffee table. Even when Jack crawls out of his box and rips open one of Stanley's gifts, he doesn't bat an eyelid. But I, on the other hand, do.

The gift in question is from Judith, who, despite being two hundred miles away in London with Alan and his sizeable collection of high-waisted tartan trousers, has still managed to find a way to piss me off. It's a packet of socks. Not just *any* socks, but ones with the days of the week written on them. Judith's contempt for my growing bag of odd socks has incited intense friction between us over the years, and by giving Stanley these, I know that she is intent on setting me up to fail. I can already imagine the stress that these socks will invite into my life – having to ensure that they're matched up and, worse still, that the correct ones are clean and ready to wear on the correct days because Lord knows it will be insisted upon.

Of all the brilliant things that Stanley has received, it's the wretched socks that catch his eye. He abandons his puzzle to lay them out on the floor, then proceeds to tell us which pair he will be wearing on each of his birthdays until November 2032. Dad has slipped into his chair and drifted off to sleep, and Mum has taken to peeling a monstrous bag of carrots on her lap as she waits for Stanley to finish listing his sock-wearing schedule for the next decade.

Stanley's monologue is cut short by the dramatic yelp of his father. Ed has been shot in the forehead – not a self-inflicted injury, but one caused by George, who comes bounding into the house wielding a turbo Nerf gun. Like Al Pacino in *Scarface*, he vigorously unloads his weapon on every adult in the room, and by the time his chamber is empty, my boobs are stinging from the assault and Mum is cowering behind her carrots.

'Stop it, George! *Stop!*' growls Rachel. She limps in behind him, her arms laden with bags of presents, but it soon becomes clear that the reason for her limp isn't down to the heavy bags that she is carrying. 'I've been shot,' she says. 'About fifty rounds on the arse, and I'm not sure, but I might need an X-ray.'

'Want me to take a look, love?' Mum offers.

'Nah, Mam. You're off-duty today.'

My mum, the devoted nurse, almost looks disappointed. She's forever offering up her skills – an ear syringe here or a tetanus jab there – and we're usually happy to accept given how difficult it is to score an appointment at a surgery. She has even offered to do our smear tests from the comfort of our own homes before now, but Rachel and I have drawn the line at that one. Poking around our ear canals is one thing, but some orifices aren't meant for your own mother's eyes.

'What time was he up?' I ask as I watch George scamper around the floor searching for bullets.

'Five a.m.,' Rachel replies wearily. 'And he's got two full selection boxes surging through his digestive system, so if I were you, I'd give him a wide berth until he's come down from his sugar high.'

'And what about you, love? Have you eaten?' Mum says, already gearing up to dig out the air fryer and whip up some of her special breakfast muffins.

'Not yet, but I'm fine, Mam. Sit your arse down and take a load off. I'll wait for the hot dogs,' Rachel says. 'Truth be told, I'm more after a good stiff drink.'

'Rach, it's not even noon yet.'

'Shut it, Luce. I need something to take the edge off my pain. It's Christmas!'

The one thing we all need is a good stiff drink to get this painfully slow show on the road. 'Okay, but let's just get these presents done first, yeah.'

Before George has a chance to reload, he sees the pile of unopened presents and is flabbergasted by it. 'Stannie! You've still got loads left to open!'

'Yes, I do,' he replies flatly.

'Are you going to do it?'

Stanley looks across at me, an expression of pure bewilderment on his face.

'I'm going to help you. Come on,' says George, instinctively taking the lead, and before I know it, Stanley has snapped out of his rigorous morning routine and he and George are drowning in a sea of torn wrapping paper. The most anticipated gift of the day is opened last. 'It's the whole world!' Stanley squeals when he wrestles the paper off his new collection of handcrafted wooden map puzzles. My relief is immeasurable. He is absolutely ecstatic, as am I by his reaction.

Even George finds a way to get excited about them. 'I know! We can go outside and shoot your countries with my turbo gun,' he suggests.

'But they will get wet.'

'Upstairs, then. Come on!' he says, taking Stanley by the hand and dragging him off to play.

'Who's for a drink then?' Dad has suddenly woken from his coma and leaps out of his chair like a Jack-in-the-box. 'Ed, get the sausages from the fridge in the garage. I'll get the Guinness and meet you out back,' he orders, and Ed does as he is told. Us girls are left to open the Buck's Fizz, tidy up the living room and help Mum stuff the turkey's cavities (not that she needs any help with the latter given that it's not so different to what she does on a regular working day at the surgery.)

It might have got off to a slow start, but Christmas Day is in full swing by 3 p.m. Our guests have arrived – Nan, Uncle Gwyn and Auntie Glad – and just as we are tucking into our feast, some old boy called Ivor rings the doorbell.

It's not unusual to answer the door on Christmas Day and find a random stranger standing there with a bottle of wine and an anxious smile, so I'm not all that surprised to meet Ivor. His wife had recently left him (Mum suspects on account of his drinking) and his kids aren't speaking to him, so with no place else to go, he was invited over. He's tried to make the effort, dressing himself up in a dark-green shirt, a red bow-tie and a tatty blazer with a big hole in the sleeve, but he stinks of old sweat and liquor and his teeth are stained brown with tobacco. It's obvious that he hasn't been taking care of himself, and if we weren't in the middle of dinner, Mum would've quite literally had the shirt off his back and in the washing machine the moment he got here. The sewing kit would be out to fix the tear in his blazer too, but with so much going on, she just plates him up a dinner and gives up her seat at the top of the table.

Over the years, we've had all sorts of lost souls drifting over to share our turkey on Christmas Day. This, in fact, is how Big Nan came to be my nan. My parents met her down the pub and sort of adopted her when her husband died. She is very much a part of the family now, as are Auntie Glad and Uncle Gwyn, who came into our lives in a similar way. With most of our real family living in Northern Ireland and Canada, there's always space around the table, and my folks never have any problem filling it.

Ten of us are squeezed around a dining table designed to accommodate six, and we are sitting on whatever chairs we managed to borrow from the neighbours. There aren't enough dinner plates or cutlery, so some of us are eating out of pasta bowls with plastic forks, and others have their dinner piled high on those colourful kiddies' plates from IKEA. The table setting isn't exactly Pinterest perfect, but it doesn't matter. To my mind, it's a work of art, and the artist responsible is Mum. She doesn't take her apron off all afternoon and remains flushed and sweaty from glazing, slicing, stuffing, chopping and plating up four different joints of meat and vegetables to suit everyone's taste.

Aside from the turkey, which is as dry as the Sahara, it's all cooked to perfection. Dad and Rachel get their lamb with Yorkshire puddings. Auntie Glad – a true patriot who doesn't condone eating Wales's national treasure – gets her beef and mushy peas. The rest of us have an entire turkey and joint of ham to ourselves, and Stanley is delighted with his chicken dippers and potato waffles which he eats with George in front of the telly.

Just as the Christmas pudding lands on the table, Ed is accosted by the kids. They're desperate to play the Superhero States game that he invented at Stanley's party last month, and they're not going to let up about it. Ed is the lucky one. By ducking out early, he is spared having to do the dishes, which ultimately falls on me and Rachel. Knowing my sister, she will hide in the conservatory with her glass of wine and wait for the dishes to drip dry if I let her. I'm no fool. She used the same devious tactic when we were teenagers, leaving me to do all the hard work while she hid in her room chatting to her boyfriend on the phone, so today, *she* is the washer, and I'm the drier. The older generation retires to the conservatory with wine and cheese to watch the King's speech on iPlayer, leaving me and Rachel to get on with it.

Mum is in her chair for all of fifteen minutes before she's back in the kitchen to make a start on the buffet. We've barely made a dent in the dishes, and any bowls and plates that have been washed are taken straight from my hands and refilled before I've had a chance to put them back in the cupboard.

The spread, as always, is magnificent – Mum's home-made sausage rolls, turkey and ham vol-au-vents, lamb sandwiches, mini quiches and platters of frozen nibbles from Iceland. All of this food might seem excessive, but this isn't Mum's first rodeo. Experience has taught her to be prepared to feed the masses, and sure enough, within the hour, the tiny house is packed with people who have stopped by for a Christmas drink.

Mike and Gwenllian from number twenty-three come over with their kids, Ozzy and Claire too, and Auntie Dilys is the last to arrive with her karaoke machine. Once the microphone is plugged in and the glasses are filled, the buffet is declared open and Mum finally takes her apron off.

Her work is done.

38

Crappy New Year

The smell hits my nostrils and it's strong; strong enough to overpower the stench of Jack's nappy. 'Ed.' I try again, only louder. 'Ed!' And again, louder still. '*Ed, check the lasagne!*' And again, foghorn loud. 'LASAGNE!'

But nothing.

'Stan! Get Daddy! The food is burning.'

I quickly wrestle a clean nappy around Jack's wriggling body, seal it shut, then plonk him in his cot and leg it to the oven before the flat goes up in flames.

'Stan, where are you?' I pull open the oven door and a blast of thick cheesy fumes scalds my face. Dumping the steaming Pyrex dish on the hob, I flick on the extractor fan and open the kitchen window, desperate to let some fresh air in.

Coughing and spluttering like a cat hacking up a fur ball, I grab a tea-towel and whip it around to waft away the fumes. It's only when the worst of it has dispersed that I see Stanley standing in the doorway naked.

'Excuse me, Mummy, but where is my best friend?' he says.

'Stan! You shouldn't be in here. It's a bit too smoky. Go to your room and put some pants on.'

'Mummy, Santa didn't bring me—'

'Quickly, now! Nana will be here soon.'

'But he did NOT bring me a BEST FRIEND!' He slams his fist down on the kitchen counter. 'Why didn't he get me one, Mummy?' he says, his voice now small.

My heart splits in two. 'Oh, Stan, I'm sorry.' I lean over and brush his soft blond hair out of his eyes. 'It's very disappointing, I know, but sometimes even Santa can forget.'

He steps back into the hall and looks at me quizzically. 'Can he really?'

'Oh yes, definitely. I once asked him for, uh, for a ... puppy. And he didn't bring it to me.'

'He didn't?'

'No. And it wasn't because I'd been a naughty girl, because I was always very good. It was only because he had forgotten. You must remember that he is very old—'

'Older than Jesus,' he adds.

'Exactly. He's much, much older. So it's no wonder he can be forgetful. Do you understand?'

'I think yes,' he says. 'But did you get your puppy when he remembered?'

'I did. And it was worth the wait.' His expression instantly brightens. 'Look, are you hungry? We're having ...' I straighten up and glance back at the blackened slab of torched cheese and crusty pasta sizzling on the hob. Honestly, it reminds me of Freddie Krueger's face, and if I can't stomach eating it, he definitely won't be motivated to put some clothes on and sit down to have some. I grab a packet of Wotsits out of the cupboard and dangle them over his head. 'How about you go and put your pants on, then you can have these as a treat?'

He nods stiffly and wanders off to find his pants, leaving me behind to swallow down my tears.

With Judith and Alan due within the hour, this is not the

time to get emotional. The bathroom needs wiping down, the living room needs hoovering, and now lunch is ruined. Alan will struggle to get his dentures through it, and Judith? Well, she'll not let this slide.

Oh, how I wish we were still in Wales. Stanley would be playing with George, not sitting all by himself wondering why he doesn't have any friends. Jack would be snoozing on my mum's chest, Ed would be down the beach walking Poppy with Dad, and I would be at peace. The kitchen wouldn't practically be on fire, and my stomach wouldn't be contorted in knots at the thought of Judith coming over for lunch.

'Ed!' I storm towards the bedroom and push the door open with more force than I intend to. It whacks the wall and flings back, nearly taking my nose off.

The room appears empty at first. My eyes are drawn towards the bed on which sit several piles of clean clothes, Ed's guitar, a jumble of wires and strings and an empty suitcase laid open waiting to be filled. But then I notice a Spiderman slipper poking out from underneath the open wardrobe door, and I know exactly what he's up to.

'Is now a good time to be playing with your toys? You're supposed to be packing!'

Since we've been back, I've busted a gut to get everything ready for his tour. The washing machine has been on constantly, the tumble drier too, and the flat has been sweltering from all the laundry action. I've dragged my arse out in the rain to buy the essentials: painkillers, diarrhoea pills, antiseptic wipes, sun cream and plasters (in case he gets bitten by a tarantula or a koala). All he has to do is put it all in the case.

'Your mum is coming soon. Are you listening? I asked if this a good time to be playing with toys?'

'I'm not playing with them,' he says quietly. 'I'm tidying them up.'

Peering around the wardrobe door, I find him kneeling beside several half-naked Action Man figures, carefully manoeuvring a camouflage jumpsuit around the muscled arms of the one in his hands. He's not tidying them up. He's dressing them up.

'Did you find your passport and the visa?'

'What do you mean?' he mumbles, his gaze fixed on his figure.

'Your passport. And your visa. I left them out for you to put in your hand luggage. Did you pack them? And your extra phone charger? I'm not spending a month stuck here with you not calling because your phone is dead. I need to be able to reach you day or night.'

He is too engrossed in strapping a gun belt around his Action Man to hear me.

Ben and Niall's places on the tour have been filled. As predicted, the gig has been offered to a couple of younger guys he has never worked with before, and this is why Ed doesn't want to go. The thought of schlepping across Australia with a bunch of strangers is daunting – I get it, I really do – but he's incredibly lucky that he has any gigs in his diary at all. January is always a very dry month for musicians, and with our tax returns due to be filed and the ensuing bills settled, we need all the cash we can get.

As tempting as it is to lose my cool, I know that he isn't deliberately trying to aggravate me. Insurmountable stress awaits him tomorrow: traffic jams, queues at check-in desks and long-haul flights sitting next to strangers. He won't see his family or sleep in his own bed for a month, nor will he have anywhere familiar to escape to when he feels overwhelmed. He has always been severely anxious in the run-up to a big tour, but it's only after realising that he's likely autistic that his behaviour makes sense. Right now, he's doing what he can to calm himself down. For Stanley, map puzzles are his stress busters, and for Ed, it's 'tidying up' his Action Man figures.

There's only one way to handle this.

'So, who's this guy, then?' I say, parking myself down next to him and lifting the nearest figure to hand.

He looks up. 'Him? He's a field commander. The 1974 edition.'

'Is he, um … is he worth a lot?'

'Yeah. About four hundred quid, if you have the original box, which I do.'

I select another one from the line-up – a mean-looking fella dressed in jeans and a brown faux-leather jacket with a shaved head and a large scar down the side of his cheek. 'What about this one?'

'He's an undercover CIA agent,' he replies. 'He's quite modern, though, so he's only worth about fifty quid, maybe seventy on a good day.'

'Oof! He sort of looks like Jason Statham.'

'Kind of. I guess.' He shrugs.

'So you're selling him then? For seventy quid?'

'No way! I'm *not* selling. I'm saying that if I ever did decide to, then I *might* get seventy quid for him. On a good day.'

'Fair enough.' I lean back against the chest of drawers and examine the CIA agent's features up close. 'Okay, so I've got a question.'

'What?'

'Does he have a big dinger?'

Ed rolls his eyes. 'See for yourself.'

To my disappointment, I pull down Mr CIA agent's trousers and discover that he's as flat as a pancake. No throbbing manhood in sight. But it's not all bad news. A quick undo of his shirt reveals a rather splendid six-pack and an Adam's apple that would drive Stevie wild.

'Okay, so I've got another question for you.'

'What?'

'Where are the women? I mean, you've got all the lads here dressed up and ready for action, but no girls. It wouldn't hurt to have a few leather-clad Barbies in here, y'know, for inclusivity?'

'No way!' He laughs. 'Malibu Barbie has no place here.'

My creativity blossoms. 'This guy here, he's Dave, and he has a secret passion for old musicals. And when he gets home from a long day of gunning down terrorists, he cosies up on the sofa with his cat, Muddles, and watches *Funny Girl*.'

'He's not a Dave,' Ed objects, laughing. 'He's more cool … maybe a Clint or a Pierce.'

'Nah. He's a Dave all right. Or a Doug at best.'

'And this one,' I say, selecting an Asian streetfighter from the row, 'he's definitely a Billy, and he's seeing a therapist once a week because he hates his job.'

'No way! He's a Bruce, and he's a badass.'

'*Nope*. He's Billy, and he was forced into streetfighting by his father,' I tease. 'But secretly, he wants to be a flower arranger, and—'

'I'm going to ban you from playing in a minute.'

'— one day, he'll finally stand up to his dad. He'll put down the machete and open up his own flower shop.'

Jack starts to whinge. I've totally forgotten that I'd left him in his cot. Ed pops in to get him, and he's happy to sit on the floor pulling wet wipes out of a packet while we finish up our game. Once we've dressed the entire troop and accessorised them with guns, hand grenades, robust boots and protective helmets, Ed puts them back in their pristine boxes and packs them away at the bottom of the wardrobe.

'Right, I'm off to give the lasagne an extreme makeover,' I say. 'It's going to need a chemical peel at the very least, but if that doesn't work, I'm going to have to operate.'

'Why don't you just scrape out the sauce and serve it with spaghetti?' Ed suggests.

'Genius!' I plant a wet kiss on the top of his bald head. 'So do you maybe want to pack a bit now before your mum comes?'

'Yeah, in a minute,' he says before disappearing into the en suite bathroom and locking the door behind him.

Judith and Alan ring the buzzer a short while later. The lasagne has been scraped, the burnt sheets of pasta binned and I'm in the middle of throwing a salad together. I quickly stuff the empty salad bag at the bottom of the bin, then head to the hall to buzz our guests up.

An afternoon of criticism awaits me. Stanley is still naked, our bedroom is covered in baby wipes, the recycling box is full of empty wine bottles and Ed is still on the toilet, probably reading the back of a shampoo bottle and reflecting on the meaning of life.

'Helllooo!' Judith trills from the bottom of the stairs, and Alan contributes with a 'Happy New Year, ladies and gents!'

'Hi guys,' I call back half-heartedly as I wait by the front door, already dreading Judith's reaction when she sees the disgrace of a meal that I'm about to serve her.

'Get the boys, Lucy. I have news!'

Her hand appears around the corner first, suspended dramatically in the air, and when I see the gleeful expression on her face, the dread intensifies.

'Alan and I are married!'

39

New Year, Same Me

The removal van rolled up on 3 January and I watched from the window as Judith's worldly possessions were loaded into Alan's flat across the street. By lunchtime, that was it, she was in. She was here to stay and there was nothing I could do about it.

'We just thought that we'd go for it,' she'd blurted out moments after showing us the ring on New Year's Day. 'We've both been married before, so we didn't need a big fuss.'

I was stunned, not about the wedding itself, but more that it happened in secret. I would have pegged Judith to be the sort to announce her engagement in the national newspaper, to insist upon a lavish church wedding with a horse-drawn carriage, a bunch of white doves and a five-course dinner with all of the trimmings. But I couldn't have been more wrong.

Over lunch, she had filled us in on the wedding, which was held on 27 December in a registry office in Hertfordshire. Other than Alan's two golfing friends, Trevor and Ibrahim, who were only invited to serve as witnesses, not another soul knew about it. There was no drinks reception or fancy dinner. No flowers. No frills. No fuss. 'We just wanted to make a commitment to love each other for the rest of our lives,' Judith said, 'and we didn't need an extravagant affair to do that.' It was a touch sickly, but admittedly kind of sweet.

Ed made all of the right noises – 'That's brilliant, Mum!' 'Congratulations!' – but once he'd sat through lunch and picked through the remodelled lasagne, he couldn't get out of there fast enough. He disappeared, claiming that he had to pack for his tour, but I found him hiding behind the wardrobe door some hours later practising arpeggios in his pants. I tried to talk to him about it, but he was very stressed and not in the mood to discuss anything, let alone his mother's shocking news. In the end, I let him practise and I packed his suitcase for him. By 9 a.m. the next morning, he was on a plane to Sydney, and I was left behind to deal with our heartbroken children and new neighbour.

With no gigs on the horizon and not much else to keep my mind occupied, I began to obsess over the Judith situation. Of course, part of me was happy for her. After fifteen years of being single, the woman had found a new partner in her sixties, and as love stories go, hers is nothing short of inspirational. My single friends have trawled internet dating sites for years without getting any bites, but Judith had bagged herself a wealthy husband from across the road in under six months. That being said, the thought of her living under our noses gave me rapid palpitations every time I thought about it. Her impromptu visits have always been taxing enough, but now there would be no escaping her. Even if she didn't burst through our door every day, I could just picture her gawping out of her living-room window into ours, with a set of binoculars and a box of doughnuts, like a police officer on a stake-out. Big Brother was going to be watching us night and day, and I was never going to feel comfortable in my own home. Not ever.

But to my absolute astonishment, ten full days have passed since she moved in, and other than a cup of tea here and a brief lecture about my odd-sock collection there, I haven't seen much of her at all.

'I bet she's been busy christening every room in her flat,' says Charlie down the phone.

'Don't say it!' I shriek. 'Don't even think it!'

'She is a woman, isn't she? And she *does* have needs ...'

'There's no way, Charls. I reckon it's more likely that she's been busy reorganising all of Alan's furniture the way *she* wants it, or busting his balls for folding the tea-towels in the wrong way.'

'Well, whether she's shagging herself senseless or not, just be grateful that she isn't hanging around your flat ripping holes in you.'

'I know. But how long will that last?' I've figured not long.

'She's got her own life now, Luce – a new life with Mr Dull Nuts. Maybe she'll keep away.'

I wish I could believe that to be true, but I know Judith. Once the dust has settled, she'll be straight over here to stir up trouble. She won't be able to help herself.

'And on the bright side, you've got unlimited free childcare right across the road,' Charlie continues. 'That can't be a bad thing.'

But it really could. Judith has a knack of bringing out the worst in all of us. Ed becomes a pandering idiot in her presence, and poor Stanley is constantly scolded for anything and everything. As for me, I'm not an inherently violent person, but if I spend any longer with her than is absolute necessary, she might well end up with a saucepan to her temple.

'Anyway, can we stop talking about Judith, Luce? It's making me nauseous.'

'Still feeling sick?'

'Yep. It comes in waves, and all this talk of old people bonking isn't helping. Why don't you fill me in on your sister instead,' she says. 'Has she nailed that old boyfriend of hers yet?'

Rachel and The Don had their first date a few weeks ago. He texted her on New Year's Day and invited her out for a few drinks down at The Cwtch. It was on a Thursday, a school night, so she couldn't exactly go crazy, but George was staying over at his dad's house so it was her only chance to get out. Those few drinks ended in a snog, and one far more passionate than any she'd ever had with him when they dated many moons ago. He has since stopped over to visit her a few times after George has gone to bed, and as far as I can tell, she is enjoying his company, amongst other things.

'There's been a bit of kissing, but nothing else yet,' I say.

'What? Not even a cheeky finger?'

'Nope. Not even close. She says that she has to lose a stone before she'll let him anywhere near her.'

'That's bollocks.' Charlie tuts. 'And it sounds like far too much effort to go to for a shag. No man is going to give a shit if she's packing a few extra pounds. She should just hop on and enjoy herself.'

'You have to bear in mind that it was nearly twenty years ago since he last saw her naked. That's one baby, two stone and a million stretch marks ago. So we're now both on diets. But she's doing it to get a shag and I'm doing it to get Judith off my back.'

Judith's Christmas gift was a six-month subscription to a new dieting programme that promises to 'retrain the brain and permanently change unhealthy attitudes towards food'. She cornered me in the kitchen on New Year's Day and gave it to me just as I was plating up the cheesecake for dessert. 'It's designed by real psychologists, and you get your very own diet coach to guide you,' she said excitedly when I opened the envelope and found the subscription certificate inside. 'Mary's daughter has already lost eleven pounds on it – that's six inches off her waist!' After reading what she'd written in the card – 'New year, new you. Give it a go, love J. xx' – it took every shred of self-control not to tear up the certificate and shove it in her mouth.

'How's the diet going then?' Charlie asks.

'I'm zero pounds off,' I confess. 'But I lied and told "Travis in Michigan" that I lost half a pound. He sent me a harsh message last night saying that I need to seriously rethink my meal planner.' I look across at my sad glass of soda water sitting on the coffee table, flat and tasteless and crying out for a shot of vodka and lime to liven it up.

'This Travis guy isn't real. You know that right?'

Travis is the 'personal weight-loss specialist' who has been assigned to support me on my journey back to a size 10. He allegedly lives in Michigan, and his avatar shows a muscly, tanned guy – the sort who does five hundred press-ups before breakfast – and since I downloaded the diet app, he has sent me countless messages asking for details of every bite of food that's passed my lips. Although I've sworn that I'm eating all of the right things, I don't think he's buying it. The man has a nose for sniffing out bullshit, and I'm almost expecting him to make me send him a stool sample in the post to expose my deceit.

'I know he's not real,' I say. 'He's probably a bot. But he's a good-looking one with a killer body, so I have to do what he says.'

'I bet he's a twenty-five stone, middle-aged bloke called Gary,' she says as she chomps something crunchy. 'And I bet he's messaging you from some office in Glasgow while he's inhaling a multipack of Greggs sausage rolls on his lunch-break.'

'Maybe. But it doesn't matter either way. I'm going to have to get my shit together and do what he says.' I reach for my glass of soda water and force a few sips down. 'Judith will emerge from her sex dungeon soon, and when she does, she'll be straight over with a tape measure to check if my gut is shrinking.'

'Well, get on it. And if this Travis is any good, he can help me lose the weight once this baby is out.'

If it wasn't for these daily calls from Charlie, I would've lost the plot by now. Like me, she has no work in the diary either, so she decided to hang back at her mum's house after Christmas to enjoy a bit of TLC before the baby comes. Since Ed left, I've hardly conversed with any adults besides her. Jen has been practising all hours for an audition, and now that Rachel has started dating The Don, I've been trying to give her some space and not harass her every five minutes to ease my loneliness.

So far, January has been all about hibernating indoors with the kids, leaving only to go teaching and do the school run. Every spare minute I've had has been spent sorting through receipts to finish off my and Ed's tax returns, which are due in by the end of January. My own receipts were filed neatly in a pretty floral folder, but his are scrunched up in balls or folded in thick wads. Most of the ink has faded, meaning that vital information is impossible to read, and he has been of no help at all. His phone has been off – no surprise there – and apart from a couple of brief WhatsApp messages to tell me he is alive, I haven't heard much else from him. His mind is focused on his tour, and in a way, his lack of contact is comforting. It must be going well or else I'd know about it by now. Hopefully he has settled in, connected with the new band members and is having a good time. One of us in the family may as well be.

A text-message alert rings in my ear as I'm midway through listening to Charlie whinge about her chronic constipation.

'I've eaten a shit ton of apricots, I've drunk a litre of prune juice and downed a whole bottle of lactulose, and still nothing, Luce. I mean, what's it going to take?'

'Oh God!' I interrupt her. 'Travis has just texted.'

'No! His ears must have been burning. What's he said?'

'Wait a sec.' I slide my finger over the phone screen to load his message. 'Classic! It says "Hey, Lucy, greetings from Michigan. How's it all going over there? Here's ten top tips to help you become the *new* you." And there's some bullshit link attached with a picture of an avocado on it.'

'New you? That's freaky! Maybe "Travis in Michigan" is actually "Judith in Ealing Broadway"?'

'Oh God, can you imagine?'

'New year, new you …' she teases, mimicking Judith's whiney tone perfectly.

I get up and head towards the fridge. 'More like new year, *same* me.' I pour myself a large glass of Pinot Grigio and tear open a Snickers bar with my teeth.

40

Tails

'What do you think your parents will say?' I ask Oscar. 'I bet they'll be really pleased.'

An envelope full of certificates was waiting in my pigeonhole when I arrived at school this morning. My students have all passed their cello exams, and quite miraculously, Oscar managed to get a merit for his Grade 2, which is cause for a huge celebration. If he wasn't eight years old, I'd be taking him down the pub to fill him full of Prosecco. *That* is the extent of my utter elation at his results. Instead of a good booze-up, he has to make do with whatever was in my handbag as a congratulatory gift. As it happens, it was a maxi bag of Monster Munch. Pickled onion flavour, his favourite.

'They will be happy, I think,' he says as he licks the salt off his fingers and delves back into the packet. 'My mum said if I get a merit, she will take me to Harry Potter World when she gets back.'

'Oooh! And what would you have got if you scored a distinction?' I ask, genuinely intrigued.

'Fifty pounds of Robux for a pass, two sleeps at Harry Potter World for a merit and a hot tub for a distinction.'

'A hot tub? Wow!' I got the new Aerosmith album and a trip to the Harvester for a Rocky Horror Sundae when I got a distinction, and that was for my Grade 8. 'Well, I guess it's a shame you didn't get six marks more in that case.'

'No, miss. It's okay.' He shrugs. 'We have a pool already. What I really want is a magic wand. And you can buy the real ones at Harry Potter World.'

'Fair enough,' is all I say, acting like it's perfectly normal for a child of his age to have a swimming pool in their house. 'It's all worked out well then.'

The rest of his lesson is spent eating crisps and chatting about his Christmas trip to Dubai. The cello stays lying on the floor in its case, but with a certificate saying MERIT on it, the pressure is off and I'm happy to take it easy. My day started with Stanley having an awful meltdown at the school gate, so hearing about Oscar's luxury hotel in Dubai – with four swimming pools, a water park and a full-sized cinema – is a far better way to lift my spirits than making a scratchy start on 'The James Bond Theme'.

'And, miss, in case you were wondering, Theodore was still alive when I got home.'

'I'm so glad to hear it,' I say.

'His teeth are more yellow than before, but Lisa said that we can give him cucumber and it might clean them a bit. And Mum says that if he dies, we can get a new one when she comes home.'

'And when is she coming home?'

'Eight more sleeps,' he replies, his voice suddenly a touch wobbly.

'That's not long at all!'

It's only when driving home at the end of my working day that it hits me: I know my students far better than I know my own son.

In bursts of half-hour slots today, I've learnt that Mahesh has a new baby brother and he hasn't slept properly in weeks, and Fergus has a big football match on the weekend, but he has a sore knee and he's worried he'll get benched. Lenny is excited for his thirteenth birthday party and is hoping he'll get a quad bike, and Louis had a bollocking from his maths teacher for talking in a test. And then there's Oscar … a boy who I know inside and out. From how much he misses his parents to how Lisa, his nanny, has bad breath and a weird collection of porcelain dolls in her wardrobe. I even know about Theodore, his elderly hamster with dental hygiene issues. But *my* son. Am I there for him in the way that he needs me to be?

Stanley has been very down since coming back to London, and his anxiety has been at a record high. Returning to school after a two-week break has been very unsettling for him, and I've had to start setting my alarm half an hour earlier to leave time to defuse his explosions. If it's not his socks feeling 'crunchy', it's his school T-shirt that 'smells funny'. To make the morning routine even more challenging, a new and rather unusual phobia has appeared out of nowhere. I have no idea where it came from, but he is suddenly repulsed by the sight of a tail. Be it the tail of the cartoon elephant on his breakfast plate, or that of Peppa Pig and her chums on our TV screen, or the one on Jack's favourite cuddly tiger, if Stanley sees one, he starts to physically gag. The living room has now become a tail-free zone at meal times. Peppa Pig has been banned from *all* screens, and Terry the Tiger is no longer welcome – two new rules that have not gone down at all well with Jack who, unlike his brother, is a devout lover of animals with tails.

By the time we're ready to leave for school, all three of us are in a total state. Jack is red-eyed and blotchy over crying for Terry, Stanley is irritable because of said crying, and I'm hanging onto the last few threads of my sanity. Upon reaching the school gates, the last threads slip from my grip as Stanley refuses to go into his classroom. It's like day one of school all over again, and I end up standing in the rain, bear hugging him as he punches me in front of all the other mums and their kids. Mrs Beard comes to my rescue and manages to coax him inside, then I leave the school grounds in tears. I roll Jack home in the rain, having to duck down as I pass Judith's window, and I return to a cold empty flat because Ed is on the other side of the world, miles away from where he is needed.

And I have no idea how he is either, because he still hasn't called.

41

The Wet Patch

The patter of little feet smacks across the laminate floor as Stanley makes his way over to my side of the bed. It might be the middle of the night, but I'm already awake. His little brother has seen to that.

'What is your favourite country?' Stanley leans in so close to my face that I feel the ring of his dummy knocking my cheek. Without waiting for my answer, he immediately asks again. 'Mummy, what is your favourite–?'

'Back to bed, Stan,' I say, because it's worth a try.

Jack stirs next to me. He has only just settled back to sleep, so I stroke his hair gently, praying that he won't wake up and resume screaming.

'Mummy, favourite country?'

'I think it's … um … Africa,' I say with a whisper, because that's what I said last night. And the night before that, and that.

'That is not a country, Mummy!' Stanley laughs, knowing that I'm joking. 'That is a continent!'

Playing along, I read the lines from my invisible script. 'Sorry. I meant, um, I meant to say … The Congo.'

'Mummy, it's the Democrapic Republic of Congo,' he states matter-of-factly.

'Democra-tic.' I pull my phone free from the charging cable on the bedside table. Unbelievably, it's 4.38 a.m. on the dot – *exactly* the same time as all of the other nights that he has turned up in my room to quiz me about countries. 'Look, just climb in here and let's go back to sleep for a bit.'

'Why?'

'Because it's still night-time.'

'No, Mummy! Why Congo? You have to say why, remember?' he demands far too loudly.

I quickly shush him. 'I guess because it sounds like a funny word. Like a bongo with a C.'

'My favourite is Libya.'

'I know, love.'

'Because it has a nice shape and because it—'

As he rattles off his list of reasons why he is hopelessly in love with Libya, I pull back the duvet and pat the mattress, encouraging him to hop up into the bed. It's only when he does that I notice he's naked.

'Where are your jim-jams, Stan? You're going to be cold.'

'My next favourite is Somalia, and my next is Senegal ...' he continues, oblivious to what I've just asked him.

His pyjamas are probably lying on his bedroom floor, but my eyes and nose feel like they have icicles dangling off them. I can't bring myself to leave my cosy bed and face the fierce winter chill in the air, so I decide to stay put. He'll be warm enough snuggled up next to Jack, and the heating will have kicked in by the time we have to get up for school.

'Okay, let's get some sleep, little man. Goodnight now.'

But just like every other night that has preceded this one, he has other plans. 'What is Daddy's favourite country?'

'I don't know. We'll have to ask him when he gets home.'

'No! Now! Let's ask him now!'

Having called Ed a gazillion times in the last week and been greeted with his answerphone on every occasion bar one, it would be quicker to drag my arse to Australia and ask him in person rather than call.

'Oh, wait, I do know what his favourite is,' I say. 'It's Bahrain.'

Stanley sits up in the bed, eager to know more. 'Why? Mummy?'

'Um, because Daddy hates the rain. So he says, "Bah! Rain!"'

He laughs. Mission accomplished.

'I like California also because she has a nice shape. And my next favourite is Seashells—'

'The Seychelles,' I correct him.

'Yes, Seychelles, and my next favourite …'

And on he goes until, eventually, we both fall asleep.

When I wake, daylight is peeking through the curtains, the dreaded signal that a new day has begun and it's time to get up. I roll over and find that Stanley is still fast asleep, curled up around Jack, who is sat upright, bright and alert but quiet as a mouse. He claps when he sees me and holds out his arms, waiting for me to lift him. I climb out of bed and pull him up into my arms, which immediately wakens his big brother.

'No!' Stanley shrieks. 'I have to get out first! Not Jack, I do! Put him back!' He scrambles out of bed and over to the door, then closes it, leaving me behind wondering what on earth is going on.

'Are you back in?' he calls out.

Perched on the edge of the bed, I answer 'yes' and brace myself for whatever is coming next.

He taps on the door. 'Mummy. Mummy. Mummy,' he chants, his voice getting a tad louder each time. 'Mum-EEE!'

'What? What's going on?'

He throws open the bedroom door. 'No, that's not what you say!'

'What do you want me to say?'

'You have to say, "Give me one second," and then I have to say, "One." And then I have to tell you that I want my apricot yoghurt and my chocolate pancakes and my banana … in semicircles.'

'Okay.'

'And then you say, "In a minute," and I have to start counting backwards from number sixty, and you have to go and get it!'

I suppress a smile. 'Of course! Silly me. Okay, let's start over.'

He closes the door then resumes tapping it whilst chanting out my name.

'Stan! Give me one second!' I say, as instructed.

'One!' He pushes the door back open and recites his lines in the same order as he does every morning.

'I'll be there in a minute!'

'Sixty, fifty-nine, fifty-eight, fifty-seven …' begins the countdown as he swivels around and marches down the hall to wait for me in the living room.

Once his breakfast is delivered on a plate with no tails and Jack has his warm milk, I head to their bedroom to get Stan's uniform and the pair of THURSDAY socks. Upon entering the room, I notice straight away that something is off. Hand-drawn maps and alphabet jigsaw pieces are scattered in disarray across the floor, not laid out in their usual perfectly straight lines, and Stanley's pyjamas and duvet have been rolled up in a ball and shoved inside Jack's cot. His fitted sheet is missing too, and in the centre of the bare mattress is a large circular wet patch.

My heart sinks.

Without lifting a finger to clean up, I go straight back to the living room to ask my little boy a very important question.

'Stan. How about we take the day off school and do something fun together?'

'Today? But it's Thursday.'

'Yes, I know. No school for one whole day.'

He pauses YouTube and looks up. 'But my 100 per cent!'

'Well, you have two choices. Number one, you can go to school and get your 100 per cent, or, number two, you can come with me and Jack to the library to play with the globe, then have a McDonald's for lunch. What do you say?'

'Number two! YES – 100 per cent yes!'

42

The Fart Machine

While most kids are at school plugging away at their phonics, we skive off and spend a couple of hours in Stanley's favourite building in the world besides home: Ealing library. Jack is happy to sit on my knee for the most part, working his way through a whole stack of *That's Not My* ... books. Aside from five minutes of madness where he slips out of my sight and empties an entire shelf of encyclopaedias all over the floor, he is surprisingly content. Stanley's time is spent playing with the globe that sits on a shelf on the far wall near the history section. He spins it over and over again, flapping his hands as he watches all of the countries whizz past before his eyes. Every now and then, he stops the spin with his finger and shrieks out the name of the country that it has landed on. 'Germany!' 'China!' 'Australia – look, Mummy. I got Australia where Daddy is!'

I should feel guilty about calling in sick to my teaching, but I don't. I'm not exactly in a financial position to lose a day's wages, but Stanley needs me. The signs of his distress are obvious and I can't ignore them. Appearing in my room night after night isn't so unusual, but the bed wetting is, and I need some time to figure out what's bothering him. Like Ed, he's not a talker, so I must find a way to show him that he is not alone – that he has me by his side whenever he needs me. Mahesh, Fergus, Lenny and Oscar have had more than enough of me lately. It's my son's time now.

Jack starts to fidget after a while, and to spare him emptying any more shelves and getting us banned from the library, I manage to persuade Stanley to leave early and head over to McDonald's for lunch. It's not quite noon when we arrive, just ahead of the lunch-hour rush, and our favourite table by the window is available for a change. We order a very specific list of food on the self-serve screens, then take our seats and wait to accost an employee to bring us a red balloon – a must-have on every trip.

Our food arrives pretty quickly, and as I lay out Jack's nuggets on his high-chair tray, Stanley opens his Happy Meal and inspects the contents to ensure that everything is as it should be. The burger is plain – tick; the fries unsalted and served in a separate bag – tick; and the Sonic the Hedgehog toy is one that we haven't got – the most welcome tick of all.

'Where is your burger, Mummy?' he says as he lines his fries up on top of a napkin.

'I'm not hungry,' I lie, forcing myself to look away from his fries and swallow the saliva that's gathered in my mouth. 'I'm just having coffee today.'

'Excuse me, but you never have coffee in a cup! You have a Big Mac with extra pickles, and then you have a big box of fries and a big cup of Coke. And sometimes you have apple pies and sometimes you have chocolate doughnuts.'

A couple of young mums on the table opposite chuckle as Stanley bellows the full truth of my formerly sinful behaviour.

'I know,' I say under my breath. 'But today I'm having something different. I don't like to have the same thing every time I come here.'

'But why, Mummy?'

'Actually, today I am trying to eat healthily because I've made a list of New Year's rules. And if I follow them, these rules will hopefully make me feel happier.'

Like his father, Stanley is an avid fan of lists, and he wants to know the full details.

'What is number one on your list, Mummy?'

'To eat more vegetables.'

'And what is number two?'

I divulge my plans to drink more water, watch less television, practise my cello and take extra care to add one that will hopefully strike a chord with him.

'And number five on my list: to make sure that I talk to my friends when I am feeling sad.'

His eyes widen. 'Why?'

'Because if I tell them what is worrying me, then they might be able to help me feel better.'

He puts a chip down on the napkin, slides back in his seat and looks at me directly in the eyes. 'Mummy, who is the friend that you tell your worry things to?'

Now is my chance. 'Well, the first person I call is Auntie Rachel.'

'But she is a sister. Not a friend.'

'She is my sister, true, but she is also my bestest friend in the whole world. And do you know who else is one of my bestest friends?'

'Who?'

'Nanny.'

'But she is your mummy.'

'You're right, but she is also a very important person who I can say anything to.'

He falls silent, his little brain trying to compute what I've just said. Eventually, he lifts the half-eaten chip, and just before he takes a bite he says, 'Do I have two best friends?'

It's worked. 'No, you have so many more than that! You have me and Daddy and Jack. And Nanny and Auntie Rachel and Bampi and George. So many best friends!'

He looks across at Jack, who at this moment is smothered in ketchup, which starts on his eyebrows and ends in his hair. 'But Jack is boring. He cannot talk. And his bum always smells bad. And he likes Peppa Pig and I don't like tails. And he can't even say Califormia yet.'

'Califor-nia,' I correct him without thinking. 'And he can't say it yet because he is still so young. But one day, he will. Why don't you try and teach him to say some easier words – like how to count and how to say his letters?'

'But George is much more fun because he can talk. And he likes farts and boogers and Spiderman.'

'But Jack loves farts too,' I say with a smile. 'He is the best farter in our house, isn't he? And let's face it, his farts definitely stink the most.'

Stanley laughs. 'They do! They stink so bad ... even badder than yours!'

I blush as the young mums opposite look over at me – the Big Mac addict with the smelliest farts around – and once the shame has subsided, a brilliant idea pops into my head.

'Finish up your lunch and then we are going to the toy shop to buy something very special!'

'A new puzzle?'

'Nope. But it's something even better than that. Come on, let's hurry so we can go.'

An hour later, we're back home tearing the packaging off our new toy: a shiny-blue Minions Fart Blaster gun. I'd given one to George for his birthday a few years earlier when *Despicable Me 2* was all the rage, and I remember how much he loved it. By the looks of it, my boys do too. With every press of the button, both Stanley and Jack erupt into raucous laughter, experiencing the full repertoire of fart noises, and I sit back and watch their friendship begin before my very eyes.

After dinner, the boxes of alphabet and number puzzles are emptied onto the rug, and Stanley gets to work barking letter names in his baby brother's face.

'Say A, Jack ... A.'

And Jack actually says it.

Stanley flaps in excitement then moves on to B. Then C and D. And once the alphabet has been chanted to death, he makes a start on numbers.

A while later, they fall asleep in my bed, snuggled up to each other with a stack of foam letters by their sides.

Stanley's best friend was under his nose this whole time. And now he can finally see it.

43

Whats-Arghhhh-Pp!

'Helllooo, Lucy. It's me. Buzz me up, will you?'

'Okay, Judith, give me a sec.' I'm sweaty and bra-less, having just survived another diabolical school run. With no time to make myself look presentable, I quickly zip my coat back up and flatten down my damp, frizzy hair with my palms before pressing the buzzer to let her in. But my efforts were for nothing.

'Gosh! You look dreadful!' she gasps when she sees me waiting by the front door.

I'm not quite sure how to respond, but settle for a 'Thanks.'

''I've never seen you look so … um …'

Intrigued, I wait for her to find the word that she is looking for, but she comes out with something far more original than I was expecting.

'You're not—' she lowers her voice dramatically '—on *drugs*, are you?'

I burst out laughing. 'I wish, Judith. Caffeine isn't cutting it, so maybe it's time I found something stronger.'

'What on earth is going on then?'

'Two small kids who don't sleep, a teaching job, two tax returns to file and no husband to help. *That's* what's going on.'

'Oh dear.' She pushes past me and heads into the kitchen. 'Let's get a nice peppermint tea down you and get you hydrated. It's probably all of the caffeine that's doing that to your skin.'

Following yesterday's amazing day of fart-blasting fun, Stanley was back in my room bang on 4.38 this morning, but instead of pummelling me with geography questions, I was woken up by the sounds of squelchy farts being played directly into my earlobe. His noisy shenanigans woke Jack, and after that there was no settling either of them. Not when they were both in hysterics.

So, my day started with farts at 4.38 a.m., and they continued all the way through breakfast. They even accompanied us on the journey to school, as Stanley hid the gun under his coat, choosing to press the ON button every time we passed a stranger. I didn't mind that heads were turning, that passers-by assumed we were an uncouth trio of prolific farters, because it was funny – so very funny – and a welcome change from having to stop every few steps for him to draw Libya in the air with his finger.

But the laughter ended the moment we arrived at school. The playground was busier than usual, and the sight of dozens of people hanging about must have spooked Stanley. Without any warning, he pulled his hand out of mine and bolted down the street towards the shopping centre. I launched into a sprint, wheeling poor Jack at breakneck speed over the slippery cracked pavement, and managed to catch him right before he reached the stairs that lead up to the library. Jack was sobbing from the turbulent ride, and the noise of his piercing cries set Stanley off. From there, it took another half an hour to calm them both down before we could walk back to school.

The gates were locked when we arrived so we had to ring the bell and enter at the main reception.

'We'll be waiting for you when you're finished,' I said softly as Stanley gripped hold of my thigh. 'And when we get home, I'll make Alphabites for dinner and you can teach Jack how to say the letters again.'

'Okay,' he said. 'That is okay.'

Mrs Beard came to collect him and off he went to class, his little face soaked in tears and his head slumped in sadness.

'He's just overtired, Lucy. You must make them stay in their own beds or none of you are ever going to get a decent night's sleep,' Judith says after hearing a shortened version of the story. 'If you're not careful, they will still be in your bed when they're adults.'

She might be exaggerating, but I can't deny that I've often imagined how bleak my future might be in the bedroom department – where, thirty years from now, me and Ed are perched on the edges of our bed with our six-foot, hairy-chested sons lying in between us, sucking dummies and kicking us in the guts as they sleep.

'You're too soft,' she continues as she pours some boiling water over a tea-bag and puts the cup down in front of me on the counter.

'You're not having one?'

'Oh no, I can't stay. We are going to an antiques fair today. I'm after a dresser for the dining area.'

'That sounds nice,' I say, surprised that I feel a tad disappointed that she is not staying. 'So how's it all going with your new husband?'

'It's *very* busy. There's still so much to do in the flat, and we've booked a cruise, so I'd like it all done before we go.'

'Oooh, where to?'

'We're going to see the Northern Lights. It's in March. Twelve nights and all-inclusive.'

'A late honeymoon, is it?'

'Yes, I suppose so. And Alan has a flat in Tenerife, so we're back for a few days and then we're flying out there for a golfing tournament. I've seen the pictures and it really is *very* quaint.'

Charlie's comment about having 'free unlimited childcare' pops into my head. Oh, how wrong she had been. But then, so had I. All the worry about Judith invading our lives was for nothing. By the sounds of it, she's never going to be here at all. She has her own life now, just like Charlie said, and her new life is set to be far more exciting than hanging around here emptying soggy bags of lettuce and half-empty jars of mouldy pesto from my fridge.

'I only popped in to ask if you've heard from Edward?'

'Yes, I have. But only a text message here and there. I had one a few days ago and—'

'Well, I spoke to him last night,' she cuts in, 'and he sounded rather off. I just wondered if you knew what that was about?'

'I'm sure he's okay. His schedule is pretty hectic, I think. Lots of early lobby calls and airport check-ins. He's probably just tire—'

'I know my son, Lucy. Call it a mother's intuition, but something isn't right. Give him a call and see if you can get more out of him than I did.'

She lifts a cloth off the draining board and wipes up a small pool of water that's dripped from the kettle, then before I get a chance to ask her if she can babysit for me tomorrow night for a few hours, she leaves.

My plan to finish Ed's tax return has gone straight out of the window. Until I know what is going on, I can't concentrate, so I strap Jack in his high chair, put *Peppa Pig* on the telly then call him. Several attempts later, there's still no answer, so I search my emails to find his tour schedule. I realise that I have no idea what part of Australia he is in, and knowing very little about international time zones, it's best to check in case I'm calling him at God-knows-what-o'clock in the morning.

I soon discover that he's in Melbourne, and according to Google it's around 8.30 p.m. there and he has a day off so why is he not picking up? I try again and again, but nothing, so I WhatsApp him saying, 'Call me. URGENT!' That ought to get his attention. But it doesn't.

The day drags on by. I spend most of it with my phone in my hand and my heart in my mouth as my brain conjures up dozens of awful scenarios that Ed might find himself in. Has he fallen off the stage and broken his arm? Missed a lobby call or a flight? Got himself fired?

Once the kids are settled in my bed for the night, I open a bottle of wine to take the edge off my nerves and crack on with Ed's tax return, which I've been putting off all day. Charlie and Jen are coming over tomorrow night, and I don't want it hanging over me when I've made plans to enjoy myself. I sit at the dining table with piles of crunched-up receipts scattered all over the place. My neck is stiff, my vision is blurred, and my brain is telling me to ditch the calculator and hit the hay, but a £100 fine is in store if I don't file it on time, so I must power on.

After sorting all of Ed's receipts into categories – subsistence, travel, hotels etc. – I log on to his internet bank account to add up his income. That's when I see it ... a withdrawal made three days ago for £500. And it's not just the one withdrawal. Exactly the same amount is missing from our savings account, our joint account, and the same again from his credit card.

There's over £2,000 missing in total.

Judith was right. Something is wrong – very *very* wrong.

I immediately call him on WhatsApp, and when he doesn't answer, I slam my phone down on the table, cracking the screen.

44

Mr Tipsy

'So what did he have to say about it?' asks Jen.

'Nothing,' I reply. 'He still hasn't answered his phone.'

'Did you leave him a message?'

'Course she did,' scoffs Charlie. 'He's obviously avoiding her because he's scared shitless of how he is going to explain himself.'

Jen reaches over and rubs my knee. 'What do you think has happened to all that money?'

'I know *exactly* what's happened. He's done what he always does. He's Mr Tipsy, isn't he?'

For as long as I've known him, Ed's nickname amongst his friends has been Mr Tipsy. It's a particularly clever nickname because it has a dual meaning: when he is tipsy, he has a tendency to over-tip. It's not just bar staff or waiters that reap the benefits of his generosity, but after a few too many beers on a night out, he's the sort of man who will say things like 'Drinks are on me' and 'Nah, don't worry about it. I'll get this!'

When we first started dating, the Mr Tipsy part of Ed was all I was exposed to, and he seduced me with dinner dates at high-end restaurants and bought me expensive presents. I admit that I liked it at first. Until I met him, my idea of a posh dinner was splashing out on a Romana base at Pizza Express, and never in my life had a man sent a bouquet of thirty roses to my door with a note saying 'Thinking of you'. It was nice, special, and I felt like a million dollars, which I suppose was his intention. But a few months into our relationship, he left his credit-card statement lying open on the kitchen counter, and I know it was wrong, but curiosity got the better of me. I discovered that Ed was neck-deep in debt. Horrified that he'd run up such a horrendous bill just to impress me, I immediately confronted him about it. I told him to stop going overboard, that Steak Bakes from Greggs were as delicious to me as steak dinners in West End restaurants, that I loved *him*, wanted *him*, and not the contents of his wallet. It took a while for him to drop the act and be himself, and further down the line, I handed him some scissors and convinced him to cut up his credit cards. And together, over a bottle of cheap wine, we sat on his shabby old sofa and worked out a payment plan to clear the debt that he'd acquired from the girl he'd dated before me – a girl who had a penchant for Tiffany diamonds and designer shoes.

I can just imagine him in Australia right now, surrounded by people he doesn't know, insecure and socially paranoid and seeking acceptance from his colleagues. And what better way is there to make new friends than to call out the words 'Drinks are on me' at every opportunity?

'I don't want to talk about it any more, girls,' I say. 'It's making me sick to my stomach. We're already skint and I haven't got any work in my diary.'

'You can have that cash that Olivia gave me,' offers Charlie. 'It's just sat in a savings account doing nothing, so if you need it, it's yours.'

'No way! I'm not taking your money, Charls. That's for your baby girl. I'm not some kind of monster.'

Charlie shrugs. 'Suit yourself.'

'We'll be okay. And if the gigs don't pick up, then I can always take to the streets and become a hooker.'

'I tried that recently,' says Charlie, her expression totally deadpan. 'But I ended up owing the *clients* money.'

'Shurrup!' I laugh.

She lifts a handful of cheese balls from the bowl that is balanced on top of her ginormous belly and shoves the whole lot in her mouth. 'I'm serious. It's not my fault I could only manage a number 68, is it?'

We all erupt into hysterics, which instantly lightens the mood.

Charlie has only just arrived back from her mum's house. We're supposed to be having a fun girly catch-up over a few drinks and some snacks, but all I've done is whinge about Ed and his decision to buy cocktails for half of Australia with our savings.

'Right, Charls, it's nearly past your bedtime,' I say. 'So tell us the latest before you pass out, will you?'

'Stop taking the piss, Luce. I'm pregnant, not dead.'

Jen looks at her watch. 'But it is 8.45 p.m.'

'Is it? Shit! It's no wonder I feel like I've been out clubbing. I better head off in five.'

'Not without telling us your news first, woman,' I say. 'Just spill the beans and then be on your way.'

Through intermittent yawns, she updates us at warp speed. Her latest pregnancy symptoms are her main cause for complaint: the incessant peeing, the nocturnal bingeing and her new giant boobs that aren't as much fun as she thought they'd be.

'They hurt all the time. It's like someone's put them in one of those clamps that we had in Design Technology at school,' she moans. 'And if I catch one more jackass staring at them on the tube, I'm going to headbutt them!'

'That's the downside of owning a big pair.' Having caught many a stranger ogling my cleavage on the Central line over the years, I know what she means. 'And it's never the good-looking ones that want to stare at them, just the creepy old ones with dirty fingernails and ear hair.'

'Exactly, Luce. It's sick. Sick and wrong. And to top it all off, I'm pretty sure that I'm rocking a Brian May in my pants right now, but I can't get down there to check.'

'When's the last time you had a wax?' asks Jen.

'Ages ago … maybe months.'

'Then it's probably more of a Diana Ross by now, Charls,' I tease.

'Shut up, you arse! If you're not careful, I'll make you get down there and fix it.'

'Sorry, love. I don't have a garden – therefore I don't own any shears or a mower. You'll just have to go and see Bonnie.'

It's not her Diana Ross, her weak bladder or her bulging bosoms that we care about, but a body part far more vital to life – her heart. Jen was scrolling through Instagram a couple of days ago and found a post from Tom, who, unbeknownst to Charlie, we both still follow on all social-media platforms. The post pictured him standing outside a hospital in Edinburgh, beaming proudly as he held a lanyard up to the camera. The caption read, 'New job, new city, new life. Edinburgh, I love you,' and the sight of it had made Jen enraged.

'The absolute arsehole!' she spat down the phone. 'What are we going to do?'

'What can we do?' I replied. 'He doesn't want to be a dad.'

'But he's an obstetrician, Luce. How can an obstetrician not want to know his own baby?'

And I had no answer for that. Not one that made any

sense anyhow. 'How could *any* man not want to know his own baby, Jen? But plenty of men have fecked off, and Charlie knows that more than anyone. Her own dad was a serious disappointment.'

We'd decided to get Charlie over for drinks to ascertain if she knew that Tom had officially moved away for good. She would be furious if she knew about our clandestine surveillance of him, so our plan was to feign ignorance and see if she brought up the topic in conversation, poised to hug and support her if the tears started flowing. But so far, Tom hasn't had a mention. She has now moved on to gushing about Dan and Stevie, telling us how excited they are for the birth, how they've been reading all sorts of books to prepare for it.

'And Dan has given a month's notice to leave his show,' she says.

Jen's mouth drops open. 'So he's quitting the West End for good?'

'Yep. Dancers have a short shelf life anyway, so he'd have to give it up at some point. He says he wants to be around for me and the baby.'

'What's he going to do for money, though, Charls?' I ask.

'He's all set for dosh. The jammy bastard has been customising Nike trainers and selling them on Instagram.'

'What do you mean by customising?'

'Painting them in funky colours, basically,' she says. 'People literally pay hundreds for them, so he's raking it in! And the best part is he can run his business from the flat, so he'll always be home. I'm one lucky girl to have him ... and Stevie, obvs.'

As great as it is that Dan is prepared to quit his job and uproot his whole life to help raise his friend's baby, there is still a *very* big, practically gargantuan, elephant in the room.

And this elephant is wearing rubber gloves and a white coat and has a huge stethoscope around its thick neck.

I'm just about to stop beating about the bush and throw Tom into the mix when we are disturbed.

Fffffffrup. Bbbuuuuuurrrrrt. Thurrrrrp … sssssssspt.

Jen's eyes land on Charlie, the most obvious culprit out of the three of us. But pregnant or not, no human is capable of producing such a colourful variety of bum burps in one fell swoop.

Ffffffffup. Parrrrrrp.

'Stanley, what are you doing up?' Leaning over, I spy the fart gun peeking through the crack in the door. 'Just come on in, little man.'

The door creaks open and in runs a naked Stanley with his Fart Blaster in hand, giggling hysterically as he offloads a plethora of guffs into the atmosphere.

'It's bedtime, young man,' I say authoritatively. 'You should be fast asleep.'

He ignores me and runs around in a circle on the rug, squealing with laughter and knocking all of his Africa puzzle pieces out of order as he wildly fires his weapon. I let him carry on for a bit, but when he shows no signs of wearing himself out, I intervene.

'Come on. Let me take you back to bed.'

'Why?'

'Because it's late and little boys and fart guns should be fast asleep.'

'Why?' he says, his finger still holding down the trigger. *Paaarp, ffffffffrup.*

'Because I am trying to talk to my friends. Now give it to me.' I extend my hand, waiting for him to surrender his weapon. 'Say goodnight to Auntie Charlie and Auntie Jen and I'll take you back to bed.'

He drops the gun on the rug and turns around to face the girls. 'Excuse me, but do you know that you are not my real aunties?' he says, his eyes switching rhythmically between them. 'You are Mummy's friends, but you are *not* her best friends because Auntie Rachel is. She is her *real* sister, but she is her bestest friend too.'

Jen smiles. 'That's right. We are her second-bestest friends, Stanley.'

'No, you are not. Auntie Rachel is number one, and Nanny is number two. Does that mean you are number three?'

Charlie cuts in. 'No, Stan, *I'm* number three and Auntie Jen is number four.'

'Why?'

'Because I'm *much* nicer than Auntie Jen,' she says, smiling wickedly at us. 'But what about you, Stan? Who is your number-one best friend?'

'Jack is my number one. And he is my brother. My real one.'

'Okay, Stan,' I say. 'Come on. Let's get your jammies on and get back into bed.'

Jen pops her head through the bedroom door a while later. She finds me lying on my bed next to Stanley, trying and failing to get him off to sleep. We've covered all manner of topics. We've ranked my friends in order of favourites – the first, second, third and all the way to the fifteenth – and we've moved on to rating the countries of Africa. We dabbled in Asia for a bit, then discussed whether there will be another Pangea, where London breaks free from England and floats over to join Africa. And if that happened, would we be able to drive in the car to Libya for a holiday one day?

Jen whispers that Charlie has fallen asleep on the sofa. She has left her there with a blanket on and is heading off home to see Will. The dishwasher has been unloaded and she has wiped out Stanley's lunchbox, but she hasn't filled it because she wasn't sure what to put in it. She blows me a kiss and sneaks out the door just as Stanley asks me if he can watch his favourite Pangea video one more time before he closes his eyes.

45

The Attack

Stanley is out cold at last, but for me, sleep is impossible. Thoughts of financial ruin are plaguing my mind, and nothing has helped to distract me from them. Candy Crush only made me more wired, and watching cute pug videos and cookery hacks on TikTok didn't help either. Ditching my phone, I delved into the erotic novel that had been gathering dust on the bedside table since we returned from our caravan holiday. But fifteen or so pages later, I was still none the wiser as to what happened to the maid when she was cornered in the pantry by the duke and his 'throbbing love muscle'.

What was Ed thinking? He knows that splurging on Christmas presents has left us in the shit. And he knows that the tax man will want paying soon. I try to dig deep and find an excuse for his behaviour, to find some shred of understanding, but there isn't one. I've told him to be careful, I've warned him not to let people take advantage of him, but after all of these years, he still hasn't learnt.

I lift my phone and squint at the clock. It's 03.22 a.m., and before I know it, I'm drawn towards Instagram where I scroll mindlessly through my feed, looking at warped photos on the cracked screen. Most of the content is pretty standard for this time of year. There are friends who've started Couch to 5K, others who have joined a gym, and the recently turned vegans, of course. Countless pictures of roasted cauliflowers and lentil curries have been uploaded along with the most irritating of captions – 'nom nom'.

Worse than the posts from the vegans and the runners are the photos of Celine. She's back on tour in the States and is currently living it large in Los Angeles. She looks gorgeous as always – tanned, happy, thin – and I can't help but envy her, especially as my pasty-white flabby body is lying in bed with an empty diary and an emptier bank account.

To spare myself any more misery, I ditch Instagram and move on to WhatsApp. Two hundred and thirty-eight notifications are waiting to be acknowledged, and almost all of them come from the Ealing Primary Reception Class group. I'd muted the notifications a week ago as it was all getting too much, but the messages have obviously kept coming thick and fast. Knowing how mind-numbingly dull the content of the group usually is, these two hundred and thirty-eight comments are an absolute blessing. They're bound to send me off to sleep.

Marsha has commandeered the feed as usual, starting off with a major crisis that happened five days ago.

> Hi, ladies. Has anyone's child come home wearing Hugo's sock by mistake? It's the left one, grey and it has his name on it. Marsha Xx

Dozens of mums had taken the time to reply, and not just with a flat-out 'no' but with messages offering condolences and suggestions for how to find the missing sock: 'Oh no! I'll keep a look out!' 'Have you checked the lost property bucket?' 'Maisie hasn't got it, but I'll have a look in her PE bag when I get in tomorrow.'

It isn't just the sock that's headlining the news – one of the kids has been caught with a can of Fanta!

> Just a reminder, ladies, that EPS has a strict 'no fizzy drinks'
> policy. I'm not naming names, but a child was spotted with
> a Fanta at lunchtime today. For all of our children's benefit,
> can we stick to bottled water, please? Ta, Marsha x

Twenty or so replies follow this comment, mostly from Marsha's friends, who are as disgusted as she is that a can of Fanta had made it past the school gates, but the only impact it has on me is to make me crave something sweet. I bat the craving away, forcing myself to think of my 5K cauliflower friends and of Travis in Michigan, whose texts I have been avoiding for days. A sugar high is the last thing I need right now, so I must be strong.

Returning to WhatsApp, I catch up on the rest of the latest news from Ealing Primary School. One woman's daughter misplaced her My Little Pony flask on Tuesday, and a boy had lost his reading book (his mother made a point of saying which reading band it was so everyone would know how advanced her son was). The gossip that dominated most of the feed from Thursday onwards was the revelation that the PE teacher, Mr King, was taking the rest of the term off to have his bunions removed.

Everyone was heart sorry for the poor man and his terrible affliction, so Marsha took it upon herself to organise a collection for a get-well-soon present. Dozens of messages flooded in offering ideas including links to Best Teacher mugs on Amazon, pictures of engraved whisky flasks, cufflinks and rugby socks that could be personalised with his initials for an extra fee. A PayPal account was set up especially for the gift, and after Marsha posted the link, another gazillion or so messages followed, everything from 'All paid' to 'I'll give you the cash when I see you'.

My legs are restless, my eyeballs twitchy and, not surprisingly, I'm irritable. I decide that the only cure is chocolate, so I get up and follow the voice of the twisty that has been calling out my name from the fridge.

Sitting in Ed's recliner, I quietly undress my little friend, then suck the chocolate from its twisty body as I watch Charlie sleep on the sofa opposite. She's lying on her side facing me, her long legs tucked up and her arms cradling her pregnant belly. It's amazing to think that a few weeks from now a beautiful baby girl will be in her arms.

Will she be strong-willed and independent like her mother? Creatively talented and strikingly beautiful? Or will she be like her father – intelligent but gutless? Fiercely attractive but obnoxious, selfish and untrustworthy? And will she ever know him? Will he stay away in Scotland and never see her grow? It devastates me to even consider it.

Lost in thought, my eyes start to feel heavy, and my head heavier still. Not wanting to lose this drowsy feeling, I head back to bed, hoping to slip into a coma, but the moment my head hits the pillow, the anxiety about our money troubles resurfaces.

Desperate to regain control, my phone is back in my hand and I start scouring the internet looking for jobs while Stanley snores gently beside me. I visit all of the usual sites for musicians but there are no new teaching positions advertised, no auditions for orchestras – nothing music related at all. The birds have started whistling by the time I click on the jobs section of Facebook. There are a couple of local delivery jobs that require an LGV licence, one looking for a security guard for a nightclub on the Broadway, one for a quantity surveyor (whatever that is) and a post for a Japanese interpreter.

I might have been joking about it earlier with Charlie, but maybe a career in the sex industry is on the cards? Ironing in my underwear on a webcam might be an option? Or lunging with the hoover and dusting the skirting boards on all fours? Or I could avoid the camera altogether and answer dirty phone calls and talk filth to strangers? Thanks to the erotic novel, I now know half a dozen inventive terms for male genitalia, and if I ever finish it, I'll be able to expertly quote whole passages about 'throbbing love wands' and 'aching appendages' to whoever wants to pay to listen.

My phone starts vibrating just as my eyes close. Ed's name is flashing on the screen, and to avoid waking Stanley, I answer with a whispered, 'Hi.'

All I hear is the sound of heavy breathing on the other end of the line. I climb out of bed and run into the hall, closing the bedroom door behind me. 'Ed, what's going on?'

'It's …' He gasps, his breaths laboured and rattling in his lungs. 'It's my … heart. It—'

'Okay, okay. Stop talking. Just stop and breathe with me,' I say with forced calmness. I inhale deeply through my nostrils and exhale noisily and slowly through my mouth. I repeat it over and over again, breaking only to tell him to listen to and mimic the sound of my breathing.

'I ca-can't.'

'You can, love. It's okay. Just follow me. You're going to be okay. Just do what I do.'

And we keep breathing together, deeply and slowly, until he is able to speak.

46

One-Way Ticket

Ed arrived home three days later. It cost £789 for a one-way ticket from Melbourne to Heathrow, but that's what credit cards are for. For emergencies just like this. He had been mugged. He was in no fit state to continue the tour, and I was in no fit state to let him. He needed to be home, and it was down to me to make it happen.

The full details of his ordeal will probably never be known, but what he did tell me was enough to warrant taking immediate action. He'd gone out for a drink with the other band members after their gig as usual, but a few beers soon turned into trays of shots being passed around, and he ended up with his head in the toilet bowl. By the time he'd returned from the bathroom, the other guys had cleared off without him, and he was left to make his own way back to the hotel alone. He'd totally lost his bearings and had to ask a couple of local lads on the street for directions.

'They were nice guys,' he said, 'and they wanted to know all about the tour and get me to sign autographs and stuff.'

It didn't take much for them to persuade Ed to join them for one more drink at a bar en route to his hotel, but on their way they veered off the main road onto a dark side street where several men were waiting. They gathered around Ed and escorted him to the nearest cash machine, where he was made to withdraw the maximum allowance from each of his bank cards and hand it over.

'They didn't hurt me,' he said, but that brought me no comfort. The thought of him, my gentle husband, standing in the middle of a ring of intimidating thugs made me feel sick to my core.

Ed was too embarrassed to tell anyone what had happened. He suffered in silence for a few days until he decided to call me, by which point his anxiety had escalated to crippling levels.

'You're coming home,' I told him.

'I can't. I can't leave them in the lurch,' he spluttered breathlessly down the phone. 'I'll never work again.'

'Leave it with me, love. Don't worry, I'm going to sort it.'

After extracting the tour manager's number from him, I hung up the phone and ran straight to the living room to wake up Charlie. I was so upset that I could barely string a sentence together, but once I managed to tell her what had happened, she took control and came up with a plan to get Ed home as quickly as possible.

Pretending to be me, she called the tour manager in Australia and told him that there had been a major family emergency and Ed needed to be released from the last leg of the tour. The man wasn't happy. The words 'too short notice' were used at first, and as the conversation progressed, even worse words – 'breach of contract' – were being thrown around. Not one to back down, Charlie persisted, and when all hope seemed lost, she played her last card. She turned on the waterworks – Hollywood style – and within seconds, she had the manager eating out of the palm of her hand. He agreed to release Ed, and although the cost of flying him home early was to be met by me, Charlie managed to negotiate a free transfer to the airport. It was better than nothing. I called Ed and told him to pack his bags and then sat up the rest of the night with Charlie, necking coffee and frantically comparing flights from several websites to try and find the cheapest deal. By the time Stanley appeared looking for his chocolate pancakes, we'd found a flight and maxed out my credit card to pay for it.

The moment Ed emerged through the arrivals gate some thirty-six hours later, I burst into tears at the shock of his appearance. He was deathly white, his eyes heavy and bloodshot, his cheeks sunken and covered with wiry stubble so thick and overgrown that it almost qualified as a beard. He was so very thin too, a shadow of his former self. Walking towards me with a huge suitcase and a guitar on his back, he seemed so small. So vulnerable, so broken. We hugged for ages as I howled on his shoulder, then we walked to the car and drove home in silence. Charlie and Jen had been watching the kids, and by the time we arrived home, both boys were in bed and fast asleep. They gave me and Ed a massive hug and left us to it.

There was so much I wanted to do, so much to say. I wanted to stuff his belly with food to fatten him up a bit, to sit him down and talk it all out. But no matter how desperately I wanted to fix him, he was exhausted and fragile and clearly not in the right headspace to have a heart-to-heart over a king-sized portion of shepherd's pie. He just wanted to sleep, so he took himself off to bed.

Come 4.38 a.m., a little visitor was prodding his bald head. 'Daddy, is that you? Daddy, why do you have a big beard?'

Ed didn't even stir, but Stanley wasn't going to stop poking him until he had a response to his very important question. 'Daddy, Daddy, where is my new Australia puzzle? I said where is my new puzzle?'

I tried to explain in the dead of night that Daddy wasn't very well, that he couldn't buy Australia-map puzzles when he was away because he was too sick to walk to the shops. But this was the wrong thing to say. Stanley was promised a puzzle, and regardless of the condition of his father, he needed one promptly. As the emotion in his voice ramped up, I made a snap decision to tell a whopping black lie.

'There is one in Daddy's suitcase, but his suitcase is still at the airport and I have to go and pick it up. So you will get your new puzzle then, okay?'

'When?'

'Soon. Okay?'

'Okay. That is very okay,' came his reply. He climbed in between me and Ed, continuing to quiz me about his new puzzle, and eventually he fell asleep, granting me the opportunity to trawl through Amazon and see if they had one that could be delivered quickly.

I was woken the following morning in the usual fashion. Stanley had climbed out of our bed and was knocking on our door, only there was a very welcome adjustment to the script. 'Mummy, Daddy, Mum-EE, Dad-EEEE!'

I looked down at Ed, who was still dead to the world, and smiled, my heart oozing with love and beating steadily for the first time in ages. 'Okay, Stan. Me and Daddy will be there in a minute!' I called back.

Then came the countdown. 'Sixty, fifty-nine, fifty-eight, fifty-seven ...'

47

The Box

'Why does Daddy have a beard now?' Stanley asks again at dinner time.

'Because he forgot to shave.' I hold a spoon of peas up to his mouth and wait patiently for him to open wide. 'Don't forget that he has been on a plane all the way from Australia, so his beard will have grown a lot since he got on it.'

He pushes my hand out of the way. 'But he's been home for three sleeps and he *still* has a beard.'

'I know, Stan. I guess he is too tired to shave it off right now.'

'Is that why he has gone back to bed? Even if it is not night-time?'

'Yes, I suppose it is. And we have to try and keep quiet so that he can have a good rest.' The questions have been coming thick and fast for the last few days, and I've struggled to know how to answer them. Explaining why Ed hadn't brought him a new puzzle has turned out to be the least of my worries compared to the other enquiries that he has been making.

'Why does Daddy not want to play puzzles?' 'Why does Daddy not laugh at the Fart Blaster gun?' 'Why does Daddy not like the Superhero States game any more?' 'Why does Daddy smell bad?'

Poor Ed has been in a real state since arriving home,

and it doesn't take a genius to see that he is not well. Over the last few days, I've done my best to build him up and bring him back from the brink of turmoil. Stuffing him with home-made dinners and keeping the kids out of the way so he could sleep was the easy part. Helping him with his inner demons has proved more difficult. Having suffered from panic attacks at college, Jen made several suggestions, from taking medication to speaking to a counsellor and using mindfulness apps, and she also sent me a link for a local meditation group which had really helped her. Anxiety medication might be a good start, but I can't imagine Ed meditating. I can't imagine him even leaving the flat right now, let alone turning up to a hall full of strangers to sit cross-legged on a yoga mat and chant with his palms clamped together.

'Do you think Daddy is sad?' asks Stanley after he spits his peas out onto his plate.

'Why do you think that?'

'Because his face is sad. And he hasn't done a real smile yet,' he says. 'And he does not want to play puzzles or say, "Bah! Rain!"'

'Well, I guess you're right,' I say, deciding to give in and be as honest as possible. I can't have the poor child thinking that Ed's behaviour is his fault. 'Okay, I'll tell you what has happened to Daddy. But if I do, you have to promise to eat some more of your peas, okay?'

He nods and takes the spoon out of my hand.

'So, ever since Daddy was a little boy, just like you, he has had lots of things to worry about.'

'What worry things did he have?'

'Well, he felt like he had no friends and that he was different to everyone else in school. So every time he had a worry or felt sad, he put the worries and sad bits in a box inside his brain.'

'A box? Inside his BRAIN?'

'Yep. A big box that had lots of room in it. And as he got older, he kept on putting his worries inside it and the box got fuller and fuller until one day ...'

'It broke?'

'Yes, Stan. Exactly. His box became so full that it split open and all of his worries, hundreds and hundreds of them, came spilling out all at once.'

'Oh no!' he gasps.

'I know, it's very sad. So that's why Daddy is so sad right now. Because his box has just broken and his brain has lots of worries inside it.'

'How can he get them out?'

'Well, that's the hard part. Sometimes they just fall out of your ears, sometimes they come out of your eyes as tears, and sometimes they come out of your mouth when you tell people about them.'

He lays the spoon on the table, gets up and then begins to pace back and forth in a line. 'Is he going to tell his best friend?'

'Yep, that's what I hope. And then he will feel much happier and he'll want to play puzzles again.'

'But, excuse me,' he says, stopping in his tracks and turning to look me in the eye. 'Who is his bestest friend?'

'Me,' I say without hesitating. 'And you and Jack. Together we can all help him get rid of his worries, okay? But first, we have to eat our peas.'

Ed appears in the doorway moments later, having overheard our entire conversation. 'Hi, little man,' he says, his voice croaky and deep. 'Are you eating your peas?'

'Excuse me, Daddy, but yes. I have to eat them all because Mummy told me about your brain box.'

Ed smiles, parks down on the sofa and pats it, gesturing for Stanley to join him. 'Come and give me a hug, little man. I've missed you so much.'

Stanley points his index finger at Ed's face. 'You did a smile!'

'I did,' replies Ed, smiling again.

'Does that mean that one of your worry things has come out of your ears?'

'Um, yep.' Ed pokes his finger in one ear and shuggles it about. 'Definitely! I just felt one fall out, right as you pointed at me. So thank you.'

'That is okay,' Stanley says. He resumes pacing the floor. 'So do you want to play Africa puzzles now?'

'Of course I do. Let's do it.'

Stanley drops down to the floor and picks up the Somalia piece in one hand and Libya in the other. 'But, Daddy. Actually, can you take your beard away before we do it? My countries don't like beards.'

Ed laughs for the first time since he came home. 'Okay, I will shave it off, but only if you finish every single one of your peas. Deal?'

'Okay. That is very okay.'

48

Tails and Owls

Instead of going straight home after the school run, I decide to take Jack out for a few hours. We both need a break, and heading home to where Ed is cocooned inside a duvet isn't going to lift either of our spirits. I'm exhausted after another frantic sprint to retrieve Stanley, who had legged it at school drop-off. This time, he made it all the way up the stairs and into the library, so I had to lug the pram up three flights to retrieve him. The screaming was more shrill than ever and it lasted all the way back to school, by which point most of the residents of Ealing were at their windows having a nose at the drama.

Jack and I spend a while mooching around the shops buying knick-knacks, then I wheel him down the High Street to Walpole Park. The rain is spitting and I've forgotten my umbrella, but I don't care one bit. Listening to his cute giggles as I push him on the swings and his shrieks of delight as he jumps in muddy puddles make a welcome change from listening the torturous screams of his older brother.

On the way home, we stop at the bakery to pick up some of his favourite sticky buns. Just as I'm paying for our treats, a bony finger pokes me on the shoulder.

'Have you heard from Edward? Is he okay? Because he hasn't answered any of my calls!'

I fight the urge to sigh. 'Hi, Judith. What are you doing he–?'

'Has he called?'

'Yep. He's totally fine,' I say. I busy myself reorganising my shopping bags on the pram's handles so I don't have to make eye contact. 'He's just really tired, and he's looking forward to coming home. So nothing to worry about.'

'And when is he back?'

'Um, just, um, four more days to go,' I lie, hoping that Ed, who at this very moment is fifty or so yards from where this conversation is taking place, has kept the curtains drawn like I told him to.

I've been in two minds about whether to tell her that Ed is home early. I know that she has a right to know that her son is falling apart, but having her fussing around him is the last thing he needs. Endless cups of herbal tea aren't going to magically fix him, nor will stuffing him full of supplements from Holland and Barrett and bombarding him with difficult questions about his ordeal. Ed is in no state to be a husband or father right now, so playing the role of dutiful son is definitely too much to put on him. To stand a chance of healing, he needs time and space. And in truth, so do I. I decide to keep schtum. I've succeeded in keeping him hidden for most of the week, so a few more days won't hurt.

'Why don't you and the boys come over for a nice dinner later? I haven't seen them in ages,' she says, 'what with you having had period pains and diarrhoea.'

I played the period-pains card when she rang the buzzer on Monday. Then the migraine card came on Tuesday, then the diarrhoea one on Thursday.

'Okay. That would be lovely.'

Some hours later, I am sitting on Judith's armchair with Jack on my lap, praying that both he and Stanley are going to behave themselves long enough for us to get through dinner. I had to bribe Stanley with a large bag of Wotsits before he would agree to come, but I'm okay with that. It's better to keep his jaws busy munching than risk him talking and blurting out the truth of Ed's whereabouts to his grandmother.

'What would you like to drink, Lucy?' asks Judith. 'We have a lovely selection of cordials – lime and mint, blood orange and grapefruit, or elderflower? Or I can make you a cup of tea?'

What I want is a massive glass of wine, but it seems that's not an option. 'The lime and mint sounds nice. I'll try that, thanks.'

'No problem,' she says before turning to Alan. 'Darling, can you get the coasters out, please?'

'Of course,' he replies, already on his feet.

'And can you make sure the boys don't touch my owls, Lucy?' she says, eyeballing Jack. 'They are *very* expensive.'

I'm left behind to make idle chit-chat with Alan and keep Jack's paws away from all of her precious ornaments. I've worn a chunky beaded necklace, which seems to be keeping him occupied for now, and if I'm lucky, he might strangle me to death with it and spare me having to get through the next hour.

'I like what you've done to the place,' I say to Alan as I survey the interior of their velvet and mahogany love nest. I have no idea what it looked like before Judith moved in, but now it's almost an exact replica of her bungalow in Hertfordshire. Her gold-rimmed Royal Doulton plates are stacked neatly into a glass-fronted cabinet, and her ugly owl ornaments are perched on lace doilies, glaring at me with their black eyes from their new home above the fireplace. The lavender walls are decorated with old paintings of English landscapes that she inherited from her grandmother, and her maroon velvet sofa sits in front of the window, which is framed with the matching curtains from her former living room.

'Oh, isn't it nice and homely?' Alan replies. 'Judith really has added the womanly touch.'

'She has,' I say, smiling at the sight of the paisley sofa cushions that have all been plumped up and placed an equal distance apart. 'It's cosy, and *very* tidy.'

It's not just the flat that Judith has put her stamp on: Alan himself is noticeably neater. His unruly eyebrows are half their usual size, his nostril and ear hairs have vanished, and his cream trousers have perfectly straight seams down the front of both legs.

'Stanley, can you keep those dirty fingers away from my rug, please?' says Judith when she enters with a silver tray of drinks. He is sitting under the dining table, quietly eating his Wotsits. 'You shouldn't even be eating those. They will ruin your dinner.'

'Mummy said I could have them if I come to this house, because Daddy is—'

'It's okay, Stan,' I jump in. 'Let's go and wash your hands now. Quick, before dinner is ready. Come on.' I manage to get him out of there before he has a chance to disclose that his father is across the road watching *Thunderbirds* in his dressing-gown, as he has been for days. There was a brief moment where I thought he had turned a corner, but I was wrong. He has slipped back in to the abyss and shows no sign of returning to us any time soon.

Judith is at the table ready to plate up our dinner when we come back from the bathroom, and the smell of it causes

Stanley to gag, as it does me. He scurries under the dining table to escape.

'Here we are. Baked teriyaki tofu with cauliflower,' Judith announces proudly. She plunges the serving spoon into the baking tray to dish up the first portion, and as she lifts the spoon, a hot gush of cauliflower steam shoots into the atmosphere.

'It's all organic *and* vegan,' she continues, unfazed by the stench of her creation. 'Stanley, come up here and sit down, please.'

'It smells like farts!' he says. 'Bad, bad farts!'

'Don't be silly. And this isn't even for y—'

'Farts! Farts!'

'Stanley, come on now. It's just vegetables,' I say as I strap Jack in a high chair then wipe the cauliflower steam from my brow.

Alan doesn't appear to hear the racket. He takes his seat at the top of the table, and once he has filled each of our glasses with water, he lifts his napkin and tucks it under his chin, eager to get stuck in.

But Stanley isn't as keen. 'No farts! No farts!'

Bending down, I take his hand and gently encourage him to come out from under the table, then I pull him up on my lap. Any of my attempts to shush him only make him protest louder, and before long Jack joins in with his brother and starts to cry.

'Yours is coming now, Stanley! I've made you some chicken,' Judith barks, but her voice doesn't stand a chance of competing with the 'Fart!' chanting and the cries of a hungry toddler. 'Goodness! This is madness!' she huffs, flustered.

It *is* madness. Total, absolute chaos, but there is worse to come. Hanging over Judith's new antique dresser is a painting of a fox-hunting scene, which pictures several hunters galloping valiantly on white horses towards a couple of fluffy foxes with long bushy ...

'TAILS! TAILS!'

And without warning, a bellyful of Wotsits spew out of Stanley's mouth, smacking the mahogany table with considerable force and splashing onto the tapestry rug below.

'What a shitter of a day!' I sweep the chocolate-bar wrappers and empty beer cans off the coffee table to make room for Ed's glass of wine. 'I don't think your mother is going to invite us back any time soon. And I'm pretty sure she's going to slap us with a bill for a professional carpet clean.'

Ed doesn't even seem to notice that I'm in the room. He is lying in his recliner, still wearing his dressing-gown, still staring at the TV, still drumming his fingers absent-mindedly on the armrest, still hiding in his cave in the dark, a world away from where I am. Maybe that's where he wants to be, but maybe he's trapped in there and doesn't know how to get out?

I prise the remote out of his hands and pause the TV. 'Let's talk, love.'

'What are you doing?' His eyes don't shift from Darth Vader, who is frozen on the screen. 'I'm watching that!'

'You can finish it later,' I say. 'I'm worried sick about you.'

He sits in silence gazing at the TV. I put my glass down and kneel in front of him on the floor, taking hold of his hand to still his drumming fingers.

'Listen. I've been thinking about this loads, and I've done all sorts of research online, and I've come to the conclusion that you're in shut-down.'

'I'm not having a breakdown. I'm okay.'

'No, Ed. Not a breakdown, but a *shut*-down. And if you're ever going to recover, then you need to know exactly what it is you're recovering from,' I say softly. 'This is not just about the mugging.'

His voice is quiet, shaky. 'What is it, then?'

'Autism, Ed.'

He pulls his hand away from mine and reaches for his glass. 'But you can't just "recover" from autism,' he says, wincing as the tart wine hits the back of his throat.

'No, you can't. But you can make a start in undoing the damage that's been done from years of masking who you are. It's time to stop pretending. It's time to be *you*.'

'I *am* me,' he says, his eyes glazed with tears.

'No. You're who you think people *want* you to be. You're Mr Tipsy around your friends, Mr Guitar Hero around your colleagues, Mr Fun to your kids and Mr Perfect to your mother.'

'I'm not.'

'You are, Ed. In fact, I think you're only the *real* you when you're with me. I mean, aren't you tired of all this bullshit?'

His bottom lip starts to quiver.

'It's about time you embraced who you are. And time you showed the world too, because do you know what?'

'What?'

'You're pretty lush … a pain in the arse at times, but pretty damn lush.' I lean in and kiss his forehead. 'I think you need to know for sure if you're autistic. Don't you?'

He nods and opens his arms for a hug. Eventually, I pull away, get up and leave the room. When I return, Darth Vader is back in motion, so I lift the remote and pause the telly once again.

'What now?'

'Here,' I say, dangling a Tesco carrier bag in front of him.

'What's that?' he says, softening.

'A present … for you.'

He reaches into the bag and pulls out my gift. 'Uh, what is this?'

'She's Dr Ellen Jones.' I pause for dramatic effect. 'A top surgeon who left her post in a London hospital to join the army and serve her country.'

Ed rolls his eyes. 'It's a Barbie.'

'She's not just a Barbie, Ed. She's a *doctor*, and her specialty is sewing blown-off limbs back on. Come on, let's get her out of the box and introduce her to your army guys.'

He shrugs. 'Okay, why not?'

Once we are clear to come out of hiding a couple of days later, me and Ed walk down the street in plain sight towards the surgery. Hand in hand, we sit down, and Ed opens up and tells the GP everything about how he is feeling. Not only does she listen, but she agrees that it is likely that he is autistic. We leave with a prescription for medication to help take the edge off his anxiety and a referral letter to an autism clinic for adults.

It feels like a breakthrough. For the first time in his life, Ed is accepting help.

49

The Punch

'Where is he then?' says Judith breathlessly as she hurries up the stairs.

'Hi, Judith, how are y–?'

'Where, Lucy, where?'

'In the living room having a bit of lunch. Would you like a cup of tea?' I ask, but she barges in, thrusts a stack of letters into my hand and heads straight through to see Ed.

'Goodness me, you look exhausted!'

I follow, hot on her tail, ready to fire out excuses for his ragged appearance. 'It was such a long flight, wasn't it, love?' I say. 'It's no wonder you're so out of it.'

'Yep,' Ed replies. He puts his sandwich down on the coffee table and gets up to greet his mother. 'Thirty-odd hours door to door, I think.'

'It's such a long way to go.' says Judith. She hugs him and then withdraws quickly. Laying her hands on each side of his face, she tilts her head to one side, concerned. 'You look so terrible, my son. I really hope they are paying you properly for all of this?'

'They are,' I assure her. I look down at the letters in my hand and clock a large brown envelope poking out of the stack. 'Is this *our* mail, Judith?'

'Oh yes. I picked it up on the way in,' she says. 'There's a gas bill, a few junk letters and that big brown one is from the Inland Revenue.'

The colour drains from Ed's cheeks, as I'm sure it does mine. 'I'll just leave you two to catch up and I'll go and put the kettle on. What are you having, Judith? Peppermint tea?'

'Yes, please, Lucy. And you should make that three. You and Edward both look as though you could do with some hydration.'

'Not for me, I'm off out for a coffee with the girls.'

'More coffee?' she says, leaning in to inspect my dehydrated pores. 'Perhaps stick to decaf, then.'

'You're going to want to snog me so hard when you hear this, girls,' says Charlie.

I push my mug to one side and lean forward, positioning myself quite literally on the edge of my seat. 'What? What's happened?'

'Okay, before I tell you both, let it be known that I've had a shit ton of garlic for lunch, so snogging me is ill advised.'

'We'll try and control ourselves, Charls,' I say. 'Now spit it out.'

'Okay, so, I've got us a gig. It's next week and it's for a private party in a mansion in Surrey. And it's for … *multi*millionaires.'

Me and Jen 'Oooh!' in unison.

'Go on,' I say.

'Long story short, an actor friend of Stevie's knows a girl who is the PA for a *loaded* South African diamond merchant! Half of De Beers are going to be at this thing, and they want a string quartet to give a short recital of Mozart classics. Stevie told me to quote high, so …'

'How much?' Jen asks, her eyes bulging in anticipation.

'Nineteen hundred *each!*'

Jen and I squeal so loudly that the heads of everyone in Costa turn to look at us. We're both on our feet within milliseconds, breaking our promise as we smother Charlie's face in sloppy kisses.

'That ought to put a dent in Ed's tax bill, right?'

Ed's tax bill is far worse than I was expecting. Six thousand and forty-nine pounds and sixty-two pence to be precise. We didn't have nearly that amount saved in the first place, and with the mugging having drained our accounts almost completely dry, and Ed not well enough to take on any work, it's all on me to drag us out of the deep end of the shit pit.

'Back up! Get off me and I'll tell you the rest,' says Charlie, as she bats us away like we are irritating flies. 'There is one potential ball-ache, as there always is with these kinds of things.'

I sit back down. 'Let me guess. They want us to play naked?'

'Nope, nothing as bold as a naked recital, Luce. Let's leave that kind of thing for the twenty-year-olds, eh?'

'More boob-tube dresses?'

'Nope. And thank God for *that!*' she scoffs. 'But be warned, there is a theme.'

'Oh no. It's not a bondage party, is it? Or some kind of Playboy Bunny soirée?'

'It's "Diamonds are forever".'

'Great.' I tut. 'So they're wanting four sexy half-naked Bond girls?'

'No, Luce. Don't panic. They just want us in white gowns to match the sparkly decor. Which I said would be no problem.'

'But it *is* a problem,' says Jen. 'Where are we going to find white gowns? And ones fancy enough to dazzle a bunch of gazillionaires?'

'She's right, Charls. We'll end up spending our fee before we even get there.'

'Chill, girls.' Charlie exhales noisily. 'I've booked Maz on viola, and she's already got a white frock from TK Maxx that she thinks is posh enough, so that's her sorted. And I thought we could ask Clara from the Angels Quartet if she'll lend us a couple of her dresses for you two.'

'That's a bit of a gamble, isn't it?' says Jen. 'Why would she want to help us out if she's not even on the gig? She's not the most charitable of people.'

'Yeah, she's a total cow-bag. But if I promise to pass on all of my gigs to her when I'm on maternity leave then I reckon she'll play ball.'

'But you don't have any gigs.'

'She doesn't need to know that, though.' Charlie smiles wickedly. 'So, basically, that just leaves *me* to dress.'

'And her,' I say, eyeing her pregnant belly. 'So we do have a *massive* problem. Jen, have you got a king-size white sheet we can stick her in? Or, or … maybe we can borrow a marquee from somewhere?'

'You cheeky bitch,' huffs Charlie.

Jen plonks her latte down on the table. 'I've got it! What about your wedding dress, Luce? You've still got it, right?'

'I do. And it's a maternity one, so it'll definitely reach around those knockers. It'll need a dry clean, though. 'It's been in the wardrobe for over five years, and I distinctly remember you spilling a glass of champers down the front of it, Charls, so it'll be reeking by now.'

'Ah, yes. That was fun,' says Charlie, smiling, no doubt fondly recalling my wedding day where she got smashed and snogged Fit Ben, then fell on top of his drum kit and split the snare skin. 'Okay, maybe just dig it out when you get home and see what nick it's in. It shouldn't cost much to spruce it up, should it? And that's our problem solved. We're going to rake in the big bucks!'

I leave the girls eating cake, and with a spring in my step, I stride down the Broadway to pick up Stanley from school. It has been another dreary, wet January day, but as I turn the corner onto Oxford Road, the sun fights its way through a gap in the grey clouds, exuding a bright ray of light over the pavement ahead. Approaching the playground, I spy Marsha gassing with her mum chums outside the gate, and when she sees me, she breaks away from the pack and waves in my direction. I turn around expecting to see Heidi or some other figure of importance behind me, but there's just an old man putting his rubbish in a street bin.

'Lucy!' she calls out. 'Lucy!' She heads towards me, her pace quickening from a fast walk to a trot. 'Has Mrs Beard called you? About Stanley?'

'No!' I'm suddenly breathless, as if she has just karate chopped me in the windpipe. 'What's happened?'

She catches up with me and grabs hold of my forearm. 'He has had a *terrible* morning!'

'What? Is he okay?'

'I can't *believe* Mrs Beard didn't call you.' She cocks her head to one side and gives me a pitying look. 'She said that she would.'

'Just tell me what's happened!'

She lets go of my arm and steps back. 'Okay, so it was around eleven when it all kicked off. I was in the office printing off posters to advertise the PTA coffee morning next Thursday, and I was almost finished—'

'Marsha, please get to the point.'

'Stanley came running into reception screaming,' she blurts out, a twinkle of excitement in her eyes.

'Screaming?'

'Yes, screaming! He tried to get the door open, but he couldn't reach, thank God, or who knows what would have happened. Then Mrs Beard came running after him and he hit her!'

'He what?'

'Right in the face. It was more like a punch, actually. And Mrs Abel was in the thick of it too, but it was all so hectic so I'm not sure if she was clobbered—'

Without waiting to hear another word, I dash off, leaving Marsha standing behind in the sunshine.

Mrs Abel greets me with a stern expression, and I'm told to stay in reception while she collects Stanley from his classroom. She returns a few minutes later without him and tells me that Mrs Merryweather would like a word once the other children have left. Until then, I must wait.

The next ten minutes last forever. Pacing back and forth in front of Mrs Abel's desk, my mind tortures me with images of my son attacking Mrs Beard. I picture him clawing at the door trying to escape – distressed and tearful – then Mrs Beard runs out to help him, and his fists plough in to her as she cowers to protect herself. Hot sick splashes the back of my throat when I think of how frightened he must have been, how out of control, and what torments me most is that I wasn't here to rescue him. Mrs Abel and Marsha were. It should have been me, not those horrible bitches. I'm his mother, but I wasn't called.

Mrs Merryweather is stacking tiny blue chairs when I'm finally granted permission to go to the classroom.

'Where is he?' I scan the room but Stanley is nowhere in sight. 'Is he okay?'

'Please don't worry, Mrs Wright, everything is fine.' Mrs Merryweather lowers her voice to a whisper. 'He's drawing over there,' she says, pointing to a large green room divider in the far corner of the classroom. 'He's quiet for now, so let's have a quick chat before you take him home.'

I feel like I should hear her out, but I don't trust myself not to explode. I only want to grab my little man and make a run for it. *He hit Mrs Beard.*

Unlike Marsha, Mrs Merryweather keeps the drama to a minimum and chooses her words carefully. In her gentle, lilting Scottish accent, she tells me that Stanley had an 'episode' just after morning break. The children were all sitting on the carpet ready for story time, and out of the blue, Stanley 'became distressed' and ran out of the room. Mrs Beard went after him and caught up with him by the main entrance, but he was 'very distraught'.

'But I was told that he hit her?'

'Not on purpose,' she says reassuringly. 'It was an accident, and both Stanley and Mrs Beard are absolutely fine. So please don't worry.'

'How can I *not* worry?' I snap, trying but failing to keep my anger in check. 'Why hasn't anyone called me?'

'Mrs Abel did try, but she couldn't get through. Mrs Beard managed to calm him down pretty quickly, though, and he has apologised.'

I pull my phone out of my pocket, lay my thumb on the sensor and shrink back in my seat when I see the notifications on the screen: six missed calls, three voicemail messages and one email. All from the school. 'I am so sorry,' I say. 'My phone was on silent.'

'Honestly, it's okay.'

My voice starts trembling. 'I just, I just don't know why this has happened … He won't tell me how he's feeling, and I don't know how to help him.'

'He said that he didn't like the other children looking at him. That was why he became so upset. I spoke to the SENCO over lunchtime, and she suggested using a screen to give him some privacy.' She points over to the corner of the room and gestures for me to go and have a look.

I wind my way around the small tables and stacks of tiny plastic chairs, trying my best to control my wobbling limbs. My little boy is behind the dark-green screen, sitting in the shadows on a tiny chair, with his tiny legs tucked under a tiny desk, drawing maps.

'Hello, sweetie.'

He doesn't hear me because of the clunky noise-cancelling headphones that he is wearing, so to get his attention, I reach down and ruffle his hair. He looks up and says, 'Mummy, can we go home? I want to play alphabet with Daddy and Jack.'

I take him by the hand and pull him up. 'Let's get your coat and bag and we can get out of here. Come on. Let's go home.'

Mrs Merryweather beckons me out into the corridor to show me where Stanley's coat peg is. I don't need her guidance, as it's pretty hard to miss. His name is written very clearly on a white label just above his peg – 'Stanley Wright' – and underneath his name is a picture of a cloud. It's his writing, his picture, his design. I glance down the line at the other names on the labels: Paddy, Scarlett, Hugo, Imran, Katy, Ben, Yoshi. Then I look again and home in on the pictures, the messy, colourful pictures drawn by his young classmates: love hearts, cupcakes, a smiling sun, stars and moons, footballs, ice cream. But there's only one cloud. And it's dark grey with a thick black outline. My son's cloud.

Mrs Merryweather assures me that she'll let me know how it goes with the screen, and if there are any more problems, she will call me directly. She pats Stanley gently on the head, says goodbye and returns to the classroom.

We exit through the main entrance and cross the playground with no stress, no fuss, no tears. All of the other children have already gone.

We are all alone.

50

The F Word

'Why don't you just come home?'

It's Mum's answer to every problem. But I can't run to Wales for bacon and egg McMuffins every time something bad happens. Stanley's problems will still be here when we get back, as will mine and Ed's. No amount of hugs from my parents can save me from reality, nor can any barbecues in the rain with cans of Guinness or impromptu bagpipe recitals.

'I can't, Mum. I've got my teaching and a big gig for a diamond merchant coming up, and there's a rehearsal in the diary for it.'

Rachel takes control of the phone. 'She means come home for good. *Move* home, Luce.'

A shrill squeal shoots out of my mouth like a firework.

'Why not?' Her tone is serious. 'You could get rid of the insane interest-only mortgage on your poxy flat and buy a nice affordable house here. There's a three-bed going in Dunraven Oaks, and it's cheap enough that you'll probably have some cash left over to sort out the tax man and some of your debts.'

'Tell her about the size of the garden,' Mum says. 'And the airing cupboard and the range cooker.'

'Yeah, it's got a massive garden and one of those posh ovens. And it's a few doors down from—'

'Hold on,' I interrupt. 'You've actually been looking at houses?'

'Yep. For ages. I'm on Rightmove half my working day and I've done the maths. If you sell up and financially downsize, you and Ed won't have to work nearly as hard. You'll both be less stressed, and you'll be around more for the kids.'

She is deadly serious. The woman has done research. 'Um, you do know that I live *here*, Rach. My life's work is here and so is Ed's. Not to mention Stanley's school. And all of my friends. I could go on and on, but we'd be here for weeks. Our lives are *here*.'

'But your lives are shit, Luce.'

'They're not!'

'Yeah, they are,' she says matter-of-factly. 'Ed is having a breakdown, Stanley is miserable at school and is punching teachers, Judith is an asshole, and you are a fucking mess from trying to hold it all together.'

'Rachel! Wash that mouth out!' Mum barks in the distance.

'Sorry, Mum, but sometimes you've just got to say fuck. And this is one of those fucking times.'

'Roger! Sort your daughter out!'

Poppy, the Shih-Tzu, starts to yap, and rather than chastise Rachel for swearing, Dad takes on the dog instead and yells at her to shut up.

'I'm your sister,' Rachel continues, ignoring the racket, 'and it's my job to be straight with you. Mum and Dad are worried to death, and so am I.'

'About what?'

'*You*, you twat. We're all really worried.'

I'm momentarily mute. 'Me?' I eventually say. 'Why?'

'For starters, you don't sleep. You're always stressed about Ed and the kids, about work and money. I'm not trying to upset you, Luce, but your life is far harder than it needs to be, and it's not going to get easier any time soon.'

'And your life is so perfect, is it?'

'Pretty close, yeah. I have a nice affordable house, a regular salary, a lush son who goes to a lush school where everyone knows his name, and a family to help. And you could have it too, all of it … if you move home.'

'No way, Rach. This is where it's all happening for musicians.'

'You're not a musician, though. Not really.'

'I *am*!'

'Yeah, obviously you're still a musician. What I mean is, how many gigs are you really doing? Gigs that you actually *want* to do?'

'Plenty!'

'Like what? Other than the X *Factor*, which you hated, all you've done is teach and do weddings and parties for posh twats.'

My mind goes blank, all memories of any recent achievements suddenly wiped from my hard drive. 'I, um … There, uh, was,' I splutter pathetically, 'there was those orchestra concerts for the Philharmo—'

'Which you didn't do,' she cuts in. 'Because you got so stressed juggling kids with practising that you ended up hurting your back.'

'The … uh, the audition for The Fierce!'

'Which you didn't get.'

'Fuck off!' I screech. 'Just fuck right off!'

'Fine! If you're happy with your life as it is, just keep it. If not, change it,' she says coolly. 'That's all I'm saying … that and there's a four-bed detached house with a garage going on Kennedy Drive.'

'Tell her about the shutters on that one,' says Mum. 'And the cabin they've built in the garden. It'll make a great music room.'

'Both of you stop! I am *not* giving up. I haven't worked my arse off to make my mark in London only to throw it all away and run home with my tail between my legs.'

'No one's saying you've got to give it all up. There's orchestras here too, you know. It's Wales, not Middle-earth. And there's loads of bands for Ed. All the greats come from here,' she continues. 'The Manics, The Stereophonics, Tom Jones, Shirley Bassey, Bonnie Tyler ...' She blathers on listing every Welsh star that she can think of while hot blood surges through my veins. 'You've literally become a teacher, which is something you said you'd never do.'

'I'm hanging up.'

'You know I'm right,' she persists.

A scuffle follows and Mum commandeers the phone. 'Love, are you okay?'

'No, Mum. I'm not!' I say as Rachel chants, 'Move home! Move home!' like a brutish football fan.

'Just have a wee think about it,' Mum says softly. 'Stanley loves it here, and so does Ed. It'd be lovely to have you all around the corner.'

'So you're on her side?'

'No, no. There's no sides. We just think that Stanley might be happier at Tref Y Glaw Primary with George. It's a nice wee school, much smaller than where he is now, and Mike and Gwen's kids go there too, so he'll already know some friendly faces. There's also a fab Welsh nursery for Jack, and you'll have a garden and more space. Your dad and me will be here to help youse all, and you can play your cello more than you are now.'

'But my friends! Charlie needs me.'

'Sure, you hardly see her much as it is. And you can Boom her any time you want ...'

'Boom?'

'Zoom,' Rachel corrects her. 'It's *Zoom*, Mum.'

'Boom, Zoom, whatever, but she can come for a visit with her baby and you can take them to the beach and we can have a barbecue.'

The 'Move home! Move home!' continues, as does the yelping of the dog.

'Pack it in, Rachel!' Mum scolds. 'And Roger, shut that dog up too. I can't hear our Lucy.'

I'm rapidly losing patience. 'Look, Mum, I've got to go. The kids need a bath. We'll talk later when I'm in a better mood. Just go.'

'Just *come*,' she replies. 'Come home! Or rather, *fucking* come home. There, I can say "fuck" too.'

51

Going Backwards

'I don't know squat about Mozart, but it sounds gorgeous to me, darlings.' Stevie slurps his tea from a cup so large that it requires two hands to hold it. 'And the dresses look fabulous!'

Jen, the perfectionist, is not quite so convinced. 'Shouldn't we run the opening of the C major one more time and see if we can tidy it up a bit?'

'Nope,' says Charlie. 'They'll be so busy drinking Bollinger and staring at their diamonds that they won't notice a few duff chords here and there. I say that we're done for today.'

Dan barges in. His jogging bottoms and tight black vest are plastered in white paint and he looks to be in a right grump. 'You coming to help or what? I'm getting RSI.'

Stevie throws his hands up defensively. 'Cool your boots, babe! It's not my fault. I got waylaid by these bitches.'

'*Bitches?*' says Charlie. 'I'm the mother of your baby, you tool.'

'Not you, darling.' He flutters his eyelashes and smiles sweetly at her. '*You* are our queen. Obvs.'

'You bet your bony arse I am!' She hoists herself up and puts her violin down on the chair. 'Right, who's staying for pizza? I need a wee, so tell me what you all want and I'll order it on the bog.'

'No pizza for him,' says Dan, eyeballing Stevie. 'Not until

he's finished taping over the skirting boards.' He stomps out of the room, and when the coast is clear, Stevie asks Charlie to order him a large Hawaiian with extra pineapple and some buffalo wings.

Maz and Jen both have gigs to get to, and I really should go home to help Ed with the kids. He got dressed today, which is a big step, but he's still pretty fragile, and I'm not sure that he's ready to tackle the bed, bath and beyond routine all by himself.

'I'd best be off, Charls.'

'Not you. Sit your arse down, we've got stuff to discuss.'

I look across at the clock on the wall. It's only 5.55 p.m. 'Okay, fine. I'll stay for a quick drink. Half an hour tops,' I say. 'But maybe take *my* dress off before you wee. I've only just had it dry cleaned.'

'Help me out of it then. Quick, before I piss myself … again.'

I unzip my wedding dress and she steps out of it before waddling off in her bra and pants. Stevie doesn't budge from the sofa while the rest of us disrobe. Unfazed by the sight of three women stripping off in front of him, he sits and prattles on about the nursery colour scheme, and once Maz and Jen have left, he drags me down the hall to see it.

Until recently, the spare room was being used as a mini gym, but Dan has insisted that the baby will need her own room. Charlie's room will be big enough to accommodate a Moses basket, but when the baby moves on to a full-size cot, it'll be too much of a squeeze in there, so the decision has been made to sacrifice the gym and redecorate.

Dan is halfway up a stepladder, sweating profusely as he sands down a rough patch on the wall. 'It's about time,' he snips when we enter.

Stevie ignores him. 'So we're having white on these three walls, and this main one is going to be Lavender Mist,' he says, pointing at a tin of lilac paint sitting on the window sill. 'And there'll be a mural on it too. Something with birds.'

'What about the girls?' I ask, gesturing towards huge framed posters of Bette Midler and Barbra Streisand, which are leaning against the radiator. 'Are you throwing them out?'

'Good God, no!' Stevie is horrified. 'The ladies are moving up to our boudoir to join Prince and Kylie. It's all good. They'll be much happier up there, I think. The lighting is *very* complementary.'

I chortle away, but he glares at me, unimpressed. A quick recovery is essential. 'So, um, birds? On the lilac wall, right? That'll look lovely, guys.'

'Not birds,' Dan says, his back turned to us. 'Butterflies.'

'But we agreed on birds!'

'We didn't. *You* did, but me and Charls want butterflies. So suck it up, you've been outvoted.'

'This is how it's going to be, is it?'

'Yep.'

'So I suppose you'll both vote against me on everything else?'

Dan sighs. 'For the last time, we're not calling the baby Cher.'

Stevie sticks his bottom lip out like a petulant toddler. 'Fine! But we're getting a canopy for the cot. A hot-pink one with sparkles. I will *not* negotiate.'

'No pink.' Charlie walks in, still wearing just her underwear. 'You can have your sparkles, but strictly *no* pink.' Stevie lifts Bette Midler off the floor and storms out of the room. Charlie takes no notice. 'So, approve of the plan, Luce?'

'Definitely. It'll be light, but cosy at the same time. And what about furniture?'

'Most of it is in my room for now. We've splashed out on new drawers and a changing table. We're going to build them on the weekend after we've got this sodding gig out of the way.'

I subtly glance at the purplish stretch marks which are creeping up the sides of her belly like ladders in a pair of tights. I vividly remember this stage of both of my pregnancies, where every time I stood up, I felt like my insides were going to fall out. Where my days were spent sitting on the toilet and my evenings lying awake panicking about labour. 'Are you sure you even want to be doing this gig, Charls? Shouldn't you be taking it easy for the next few weeks while you've got the chance?'

'She won't be told!' shouts Stevie from the other end of the hall.

'He's right, she won't,' agrees Dan.

'I'm doing it,' she says assertively. 'I'm not sitting around here twiddling my thumbs. I want to keep busy. Now quit lecturing me and get the drinks sorted. The pizza is on its way.'

I end up staying for the rest of the evening. After pizza, the boys power on with the decorating and Charlie and I hang out in the living room, trying to have a respectable conversation over the racket of them bickering.

'Turn that down!' barks Dan over the Bluetooth speaker, which is blasting out the Bee Gees. 'Hand me the cutting-in brush!'

Stevie sings along to 'Tragedy' at the top of his lungs.

'Stop dicking about and give it! Right, that's it!'

A shrill scream penetrates the atmosphere. 'You bastard!'

'I did warn you! Brush, *now*, or you'll get the full tin!'

'Aren't you going to get in there and break it up?' I say to Charlie. She is sitting next to me on the sofa, her lips stained bright red with buffalo sauce, as she picks at the last few chicken wings. 'It sounds like it's getting messy in there.'

She shrugs. 'Nah. They'll be snogging each other's faces off within the hour. I'll let them get on with it.' One by one, she licks her fingers clean, then she pulls her legs up and awkwardly twists her body around to face me. 'So how's he doing?'

'Ed? Yeah, better. But he still has a long way to go. I can't see him on stage any time soon.'

'He'll get there. Once the drugs kick in, he'll start to feel loads better, then he can decide on his next move.'

The words 'next move' stick in my chest. Charlie picks up on it straight away. 'What's with the face?'

'What's wrong with my face?'

'Something's up. I can tell.' Through intermittent yawns she says something along the lines of 'Just spit it out … before I pass out.'

'Okay, fine.' I come clean about the fight I had with Rachel, telling her about all of the brutal things she'd said and how she and my parents are plotting to get me to move home to Wales.

'They don't get it,' I huff, the rage having resurfaced as I deliver my rant. '*None* of them have seen what it's taken to get to where we are. How we've busted a gut all these years to succeed. They just want me to ditch it all and run home to sit in a field full of sheep.'

I expect her to interject with a passionate 'Hell no!' or something with more expletives, but she sits there, not saying a word, not moving a muscle. Not a 'Fuck no!', a tut or even a frown. Nothing.

'Earth to Charls? Are you even hearing me?'

She reaches over to the coffee table beside her and grabs a slice of garlic bread. 'Yep, I am.'

'Where's the outrage?'

She folds the bread in half and takes a huge bite. 'I think they're right,' she says, munching. 'It's a genius idea.'

'How can you say that?'

'It's a no-brainer, Luce.'

'How so?'

'Moving home will literally put an end to all of your problems. You'll be financially much *much* better off, so you and Ed won't have to bust a gut doing the shit gigs that you don't want to do. Stan will grow up with George, who he idolises, and you'll have an amazing support network on your doorstep.'

'And who will *you* have? I can't just abandon you when you're about to become a mum.'

'Don't worry about me, you softie. I've got my boys in there. They've got my back.'

'You're seriously going to raise her with Dan and Stevie?'

She nods. 'Yep.'

'What if you meet someone else? You're not going to be single for—'

'Nope.'

'Obviously, it's the last thing on your mind right now, but at some point, you might want to get back out there, maybe meet someone and settle down.'

'Not interested. Men will come and go, Luce, but those boys in there are my family. They're my forever people.'

Stevie pops his lilac-speckled head around the door. 'I'm putting the kettle on, girls. Who wants a brew?'

'Me,' says Charlie. 'But Luce is off now. She's got to bath her babies and buy a house.'

Stevie doesn't pick up on the last part. 'All right. One cuppa and a Hobnob coming up.'

'More 'Nobs required.' She licks the garlic butter off her fingers. 'And some Jaffas if there's any left.'

'Obvs on the 'Nobs.' He smirks. 'I'm on it.'

'As long as you know what you're doing,' I say once he has left the room.

'I know exactly what I'm doing. I'm doing what's best for my baby. And so should you.'

I lean over and hug her.

'If you want to move forward, Luce, sometimes you have to go back.'

52

Village Life

When I get home at around nine thirty, Stanley and Jack are snoozing next to Ed in our bed. After quietly undressing, I pull on my nightie and squeeze onto the edge, then lie in silence listening to them breathe, all three of them immersed in the tranquillity of their dreams.

Snuggling up to Stanley's warm body, I watch his chest rise and fall. His heart is beating steadily, and the sound of it is comforting. Wherever his mind is right now, it's somewhere peaceful, somewhere happy. But hours from now, all of that will change when he wakes up to face the real world. The sun will rise and his anxiety will resurface, and it will take control of every part of him just so he can make it through the day. His heartbeat will accelerate, his breathing will become shallow and erratic, and his throat will be sore as he screams and kicks me at the school gates. And there's nothing that I'll be able to do but leave him sobbing in the arms of Mrs Beard and go to work.

I've told myself that it will get better in time, that one day he will walk through the gates smiling. But there's a dark cloud at the back of my mind saying the opposite, one that's been lurking there long before Rachel said what she did.

He hates school. He is miserable. He is punching teachers.

My childhood was nothing like Stanley's. I didn't grow up in a poky flat in London, and I didn't have to walk fifteen minutes just to access a patch of grass to play on. Our house might have been small, but we were hardly ever inside as we had the biggest garden on our street with a swing set and a climbing frame. Come rain or shine, kids from the neighbourhood were always calling over to play after school. If we weren't in the garden, we'd all be out on the streets chasing each other on our bikes, or we would take our dog Harry to run wild in the field behind our house. Our free time was spent climbing trees, making daisy chains and picking wild berries off the bushes, and in the summer, we would make perfume from flower petals, then sell it to our parents to raise money to buy ice lollies from the corner shop.

Unlike Ealing Primary, my school wasn't huge either, and it wasn't sitting in the centre of a commuter town on the outskirts of a major city, where cars constantly sit in gridlocked traffic and spew harmful fumes into the playground. Tref Y Glaw Primary School, where George is a student, is set in the middle of a huge field at the bottom of a mountain. You'd have thought they would've expanded it since I went there decades ago, but it's still as small as it ever was, with only thirty kids in each year group. The area is true country-bumpkinsville, and back in my day, sheep used to wander down from the mountain to graze on the grass, and Mr Morgan, our head teacher, was forever running out with a broom to chase them away.

When I was there, I knew everyone's names and they knew mine. Even now, I can remember so much about my fellow classmates. Dewi Jones was the kid who regularly got busted looking up the girls' skirts, and Leanne Hopkins, the daughter of the PE teacher, was a bossy little know-it-all, but we all did as she said because she was the only girl in the class who could do a backwards roly-poly. Harri Lewis was from a poor part of the village and he never had anything nice in his lunchbox, so we would always take it in turns to donate our crisps to him. Keith Hewitt was the naughty boy and an accomplished graffiti artist – a gift which always landed him on the green chair outside Mr Morgan's office. And Anita Adams was a wheelchair user but none of us ever knew why. Looking back on it, I think she had cerebral palsy, but it didn't make a difference to us. She was in my dance team, and we always came first or second in the school eisteddfod every summer. We were all very different kids, but we got along because we only had each other.

The highlight of the year was the summer fête, and all proceeds raised always went towards the 'Anita Adams fund', as she needed expensive surgery that could only be done in America. Everyone would muck in and help. All of the parents would be on hand to do face painting and run the raffles and the tombola, Uncle Ray would park his ice-cream truck on the yard and sell 99s (which were actually 99p!) and Auntie Betsi, who at the time owned the Greenacre village shop, would come down and sell penny mixes in paper bags. Bouncy castles and trampolines would be set up on the field, the recorder club would always give a recital on the yard, and the dance team would put on a little show too.

The annual carnival was another big event that our whole school looked forward to. We would make our own costumes in class weeks in advance, and on the day, we would ride on the floats and show them off, then end the carnival at the Tref Y Glaw rugby club with a disco and a fireworks display. I remember all of it so clearly – the time I won the three-legged race with Lisa Cartwright on sports day, the time I got hit in the face by a rugby ball and Mr Williamson had to mop up my tears with a tea-towel. Then there was the day me and Ellie Bryant got booted out of assembly for talking when we should have been singing 'Kum Ba Yah', and the concert where the choir sang 'Eternal Flame', but Mrs Mandell had altered the lyrics and we were all kicking up a stink about it. I remember every word, even now.

> *Close your eyes, give me your hand, my friend*
> *See the West and East meeting,*
> *Children tall and proud,*
> *Do you feel the same?*
> *Or am I only dreaming?*
> *Or is this feeling an eternal flame?*

I can't imagine Stanley and Jack having anything close to the wonderful childhood that my parents gave me. Our lifestyles are too chaotic, and Ed and I will never have the time, the money, the space or the support required. We'll always be chasing gigs, and one of us will always have to pack a suitcase and lug an instrument overseas to spend weeks away from our children's sides. We'll always have to watch the pennies, and we'll always panic about inflating interest rates and scary brown letters falling on our doormat. If things don't change, we'll remain stuck on the hamster wheel, running in circles and terrified about what might happen if we fall off.

It's not autism that's getting in the way of Stanley's happiness. It's London. And it's us. Ed and I.

I lean across and gently kiss Stanley on the forehead, then I roll onto my side, lift my phone and google Rightmove.

Hunters are delighted to bring to market this 3 BEDROOM DETACHED house found in the popular estate of DUNRAVEN OAKS, TREF Y GLAW.

Key features:

- Five-minute drive to M4
- Walking distance to train station
- Close to local schools (all rated OUTSTANDING by Ofsted)
- Large rear garden
- Conservatory

Diamonds Aren't Forever

'No parking!'

'What did he say?' In a fluster, Jen rolls down the window. 'Sorry, sir?'

'No parking!' the man repeats, charging towards our car with a face like thunder. 'Guests only in this area!'

Charlie leans across from the passenger seat to speak to him. 'We're the string quartet for the event,' she says sweetly. 'We just need to load out our gear.'

'No loading out. Not here,' the man insists. 'Staff park at back of house.'

'Are you Tau?' she asks.

He grunts and nods.

'Well, Tau. Your colleague at the front gate — Denzel, I think it was — said that we should speak to you about parking out front. I'm pregnant, you see, and we've got loads of heavy stuff to—'

'Roll it down,' he orders Jen, and once the window is down as far as it will go, he practically puts his entire head inside the car. 'How far?' he asks, eyeballing Charlie's belly.

'Eight and a half months.' She smiles at him, then strokes her bump for added effect.

He steps back and reaches into the top pocket of what

looks like a bullet-proof vest. He pulls something out, and for a split second, I fear it's a weapon. But it's not. It's a photo of a newborn baby. 'Amara,' he announces proudly. 'Three months old.'

The lion has been tamed.

Before we know it, two parking attendants are carrying our bags and instruments into the house, and Tau has taken Jen's keys, assuring us that he will park our car somewhere close to the main entrance.

Charlie's magic charm might have worked a treat on Tau, but when we walk into the house, there is absolutely *no* special treatment. Three security guards wearing the same vests as Tau wait by the entrance, the most menacing trio of burly brutes, and we are ordered to open our bags and instrument cases. A thorough inspection follows, where every item in our handbags is turfed into grey trays and examined, and once our baggage has passed inspection, the men move on to our bodies and pat us all down with their meaty hands.

'What are you looking for?' asks Charlie as she stands spread-legged with her hands on the wall.

'Guns, knives, explosives,' says her security guy. 'It is protocol.'

'You must be the quartet?' calls out a smartly dressed woman from across the lobby. 'Which one of you is Charlotte?'

'Me,' says Charlie, her hands still on the wall as the guard works his way down her legs.

'Okay. Can you sign in after security have finished? Then I can take you through to the ballroom.'

'Sure.'

I'm the last to get frisked, and once I've scooped up the shameful innards of my handbag from the tray (countless dummies, tubs of McDonald's curry sauce, unwrapped tampons covered in green eyeshadow, a few cold fries, a smashed foundation compact and Lord knows how many magnetic letters), we lift our instruments and cases and make our way across the lobby.

We've performed in some posh places in our lifetime, but in terms of grandeur, this house is right up there with Kensington Palace. The stately oak floors seem to go on for miles and miles, and the golden walls are absolutely dripping in works of fine art, one of which I'm certain is a genuine Rembrandt. Life-size marble sculptures of noble historical figures are dotted around, and hanging over our heads is a crystal chandelier the size of a double-decker bus. Afraid to mark the polished floors, we all instinctively lift our wheelie cases and follow the event organiser through to the ballroom, making sure to be extra careful as we pass the Ming vases displayed on mahogany tables either side of the doorway.

The ballroom is vast, and the fifty or so circular dinner tables that are laid out don't even begin to fill it. Dozens of people are scurrying around, some laying place settings and others hoovering, steaming upholstery or tying crimson bows on the chairs. In the far corner is a large team of young waiting staff who are being given instructions by an older man dressed in a white tux.

'So, here we are, ladies,' says the woman. 'One of you will be here, another there and another—'

Charlie interrupts. 'Um, sorry. But do you mean that you want us to play up there? On *those*?'

We all gawp at a row of cylindrical golden podiums that are each about six feet tall.

'Exactly,' says the woman. 'We'll want all four of you in a line on your designated podiums. Obviously, the cellist will have to sit, so hers is slightly wider, but the rest of you will be standing.'

Charlie is speechless. 'But how are we going to get up there?' asks Jen, taking control.

'We have a stepladder. So ten minutes before the guests arrive, the stage crew will be out to help you all get into position.' She unclips a walkie-talkie from her belt and saunters off towards one of the dining tables. 'Nigel. Come in, Nigel. It's Lissa. I've just noticed that some of these champagne glasses are marked. Send the girls out to sort it, please. Quickly!'

'What's going on, Charls?' Jen mutters discreetly. 'Podiums?'

'I'm fucked if I know.' She pulls her phone out of her bag and turns her back to us. 'Give me a sec, girls ... I'm just finding the contract.'

'What does it say?' I whisper as we all wait with bated breath to hear her out.

'Hold on ... um. Wait ... um ... Fuck it! "Artists will be required to play the first set on podiums." Great! We're all going to fall to our deaths! I'm so sorry, girls, I would never have agree—'

'Calm down!' I jump in. 'It's too late to kick up a fuss now. You just take mine, then at least you can sit down. We don't want you flattening that baby if you fall.'

'But what about you, Luce?' asks Maz.

'I'll stand ... I'll wing it. Don't worry, girls. It's all fixable,' I say, gulping with dread at the thought of losing my balance and ending up arse over tits on the cold marble floor.

'What about the music stands, though?' asks Jen. 'They'll never fit.'

Charlie has turned ghostly white.

'How good are your memories, everyone?' says Maz. A collective 'Bad' falls out of our mouths.

'Okay, so we're just going to have to play stuff that we know. What can we swing? Pachelbel's Canon? Some *Eine Kleine?*'

'I could rattle those off blindfolded,' says Jen. 'And maybe a bit of the *Four Seasons*, but only the slow movements. It's too cold in here for semiquavers.'

'Perfect,' I say, trying my best to sound confident. 'We just need to get through the first set, girls, then once we're back on the floor, the rest of it should be a breeze.'

'And can you send Daria to put out more napkins? We are eight short,' continues Lissa down her walkie-talkie. 'Eight. I said eight.'

We wait. She swivels around to face us. 'Let's get you all through to hair and make-up. The jeweller is already here to fit you, so I need you all in your dresses as quickly as possible.'

Charlie frowns. 'Jeweller?'

'Yes, from De Beers. You will be modelling our latest collection, which I've been told is nearly four million pounds' worth of diamonds, hence why security is so tight.'

'Fuck me,' mutters Charlie, reaching for her phone to read the contract once again.

'Come on through to the green room.' We follow Lissa down the never-ending corridors of the magnificent mansion where our diamonds are waiting for us.

'I feel like Julia Roberts in *Pretty Woman*,' I say, admiring a £249,000 diamond choker in our dressing-room mirror half an hour later. 'You know the bit where Richard Gere gives her the necklace before they go to the opera.'

'I'm livid,' Charlie huffs. 'It's ridiculous.'

'Well, I'm loving it!' says Jen, trying to lift the mood.

'Yeah, me too,' I chip in. 'Dressing up in diamonds and pretending we're loaded isn't all that bad, is it, Charls?'

'Yeah, it is, Luce. I mean, I started the day pissing my pants. And now I'm in a mansion, heavily pregnant and single, wearing *your* wedding dress and a diamond ring that I have to give back.' She leans forward in her seat and starts rocking back and forth. 'I just feel so sick.'

'Embrace it,' I say. 'It makes for a great story to tell the grandkids.'

'No, I'm serious …' She gets up abruptly, her eyes fixed wide open in blind panic. 'I'm literally going to—'

And right there, without any warning, my best friend's life changes forever when vomit *and* her waters explode all over the white marble floor.

54

The Text

 Charlie Danvers is at **Wokingham Hospital** with **Lucy Wright** and 3 others

11.32 a.m.

In the back of a limo yesterday afternoon, Veda Cher Danvers came flying into this world! Special thanks to **Lucy Wright** and **Marianne Acton** for preparing to catch her, to **Tau Ngwenya** for his expert driving skills, and to the folks at **De Beers** for not arresting us after making off with four million quid's worth of diamonds. Mother and baby doing well. x

'Maybe you should hold her a different way,' suggests Stevie. 'She might latch on better. Let me try.'

Charlie slaps him away. 'Hands off my tits!'

'But the book said—'

'Forget the book. They're my boobs. Just let me figure it out.'

Dan drags him back into his seat by his elbow. 'Stop fussing and just sit your arse down – I want to hear the rest of the story.'

'Oof! It's like getting stung by a hornet on the nips.' Charlie winces as she manoeuvres Veda to a slightly different position.

Stevie is back out of his seat. 'Want the nipple cream?'

'No, she doesn't!' Dan pulls him back again, only this time, he holds his hand to keep him there.

'Okay, that's better.' Charlie sinks back into her pillow. 'So, where did I get to?'

Dan leans forward. 'Your waters had gone and you were out the front of the house, and the African guard couldn't get to your car.'

'Yeah, yeah. So, anyway, our car had been boxed in by a load of catering trucks, and the drivers were off faffing around somewhere—'

'And you were sobbing by this point, Charls,' I add. 'You were having hardcore contractions and you couldn't stand up.'

'Yeah, that's right. So that's when Jen turned all badass and bollocked the security guard!'

'I did,' says Jen. 'I told him that we needed a car, right now. I didn't care what car, but if he didn't sort it then Charls was going to blow in front of all of their rich clients. And if that happened, I was going to sue their arses.'

'So *that's* how you ended up in a limo!' Dan is totally gripped by the drama. 'And what about the diamonds?'

'Are you hungry, Charls?' interrupts Stevie. 'Because there's a Costa on the ground floor.'

'No!' scolds Dan. 'Just sit.'

Charlie tells him how frantic it all was, and how Tau was so distracted getting the limo that no one noticed we'd made off with the diamonds until we were halfway to the M3. 'And by the time the De Beers lot had chased us down and pulled us over, I was full-on crowning!'

'Bloody hell! So did they take the diamonds back there and then?' asks Dan. 'On the hard shoulder? Right as you were about to blow?'

'No,' I say. 'Once they saw the state she was in, they climbed in the back of the car and took over. They basically delivered the baby and they were amazing. And so were you, Charls. You were a real warrior.'

Stevie is back out of his seat to hug Charlie, only this time Dan joins him. Both of them are in tears.

'Stop crying, you dicks!' Charlie laughs.

'You stop!' sobs Stevie.

I reach for the tissues and hand them all out, holding a couple back for Jen and myself, as they've set us both off too.

'I'm going to kick you all out in a minute if you don't get a grip!' says Charlie.

A while later, the boys head down to Costa and return with sandwiches, cakes and a tray of coffees for us all to share. Sitting on the bed next to Jen with her boobs out, Charlie gets stuck in to a tuna melt, and Stevie seizes the opportunity to have a hug with Veda. Walking back and forth with her in his arms, he sings 'Papa's Gonna Buy You a Mockingbird', stopping every few steps to kiss her on the forehead and tell her how perfect she is. Dan is busy on the phone sussing out prices for cabs to get his girls home when they are discharged, which, according to the midwife, might be later this afternoon.

Lying back in my chair, I take a long sip of coffee and soak up the beauty of my surroundings. My amazing friend, strong, brave and beautiful, is now a mum. She did it. And now her little girl is here, safe and well, cradled in an abundance of love.

'Want a turn?' Stevie asks me, but I'm lost in thought. 'Luce, hello?

'Sorry?'

'I said do you want a hug?'

'Uh, no, no, my darling. You enjoy her.' I smile. 'I've had plenty already. It's your turn now.'

He gazes down at the little bundle in his arms. 'She's so perfect, isn't she?'

Veda is so tiny, with an unusually thick head of dark hair and huge brown eyes, just like her mum.

'She is,' I say. 'She is all Charlie.'

'A real little heartbreaker,' Stevie says, welling up once again.

I see it now. It's all laid bare right in front of me. Charlie has found her tribe. They're all here, by her side when she needs them the most. Stevie and Dan love her. They will have her back no matter what, and Veda will have so much love that she won't know what to do with it.

I reach for my phone. Ed knows that I'm in Wokingham, some thirty or so miles from home. He knows that I've been waiting for Stevie and Dan to arrive to take over, and he isn't expecting me back any time soon. But I miss him. And I miss my little boys.

My phone goes nuts when I turn it on, buzzing persistently as my messages load. I wait for it to fully boot up, and when it finally does, there's a shocker of a text waiting at the top of my inbox.

> Hi, Lucy. A decision has been made to double up the strings for The Fierce tour. Rehearsals start mid-April and the tour starts in Geneva on 1 May. Fee is £2,000 p.w. plus all transport and accommodation covered. Are you still interested? SM.

'Where are you going, love?' asks Jen when I spring up and hurry towards the door. 'Is everything all right?'

'Yeah, yeah. It's all, um, it's all fine,' I stutter. 'I've just got to send a quick text. I won't be long.'

'Bring me back another one of these, will you, love?' mumbles Charlie, her mouth still full of tuna melt.

'Sure, you greedy bitch.' I wink.

I peg it down the long white corridor towards the elevator, and when I reach it, breathless and dripping in sweat, I slam my hand on the button and wait. It's taking too long, excruciatingly long, so I take to the stairs and bound down them two at a time, hoping that my jelly legs don't give way.

I make it to the reception and throw myself down on the nearest free seat next to an old lady. I take a brief moment to catch my breath before I compose the most important text message of my life.

> I want to go home. x

Ed replies a few minutes later.

> Hi, love. How is Charlie? Just come home and I'll pick you up from the station. What sort of time? Xxx

I write back straight away.

> I mean I want to go home to Wales. Forever. Will you move to Wales with me? xxx

This time, his reply is instant.

> Let's do it. xxx

The tears stream down my cheeks and I let them fall, because for the first time in a very long time, they are good tears. Happy tears. And they deserve to run free.

'What's wrong, dear?' asks the old lady next to me, her face a picture of concern.

'Nothing,' I say.

She lays her hand on my thigh and squeezes it lightly. 'Has something happened?'

'Yes.' I turn to face her. 'But it's something good. Something wonderful, actually.'

The lady keeps her hand in place, waiting patiently for all to be revealed.

'We're going to be with our tribe,' I say. 'We're going home.'

Epilogue

'Picture this, Luce. It's my lunch-break, and I'm sitting on the toilet with a tuna baguette in one hand and a breast pump in the other. There's only ten minutes to go until I'm due back in the studio …'

'Go on,' I say.

'There I am, pumping like fury to squeeze my milk out so I don't wind up squirting all over my violin. Then, out of nowhere, the door swings open and …' Charlie pauses for dramatic effect.

'And? For crying out loud, and what?!'

'And I'm busted!'

'By who?'

She pauses again, even longer than before. 'By Harry fucking Jarvis!'

'Nooo!' I roar with laughter. 'What was *he* doing at Abbey Road?'

'What was he doing in the girls' toilets, more like? The dirty perv.'

'Charls! I'm dying here … actually dying! What did you do?'

'What could I do?' she says. 'I just said, "Sorry, mate, this cubicle is taken," and kicked the door closed in his face. But d'you know what, he was properly checking me out.'

'Uh, are you sure about that? Maybe he was gunning for a bit of your baguette.'

'It was *not* my baguette that he was after, Luce. *Believe* me.'

I laugh so hard picturing the scene: Charlie. Abbey Road studios. Her massive engorged breasts. A tuna baguette. Her squeaky breast pump. Then, enter from stage left, the UK's hottest pop star, bursting through the door to catch her with her nips out. Ha! It's one for the memory books, that's for sure.

'Celebrity nipple-flashing aside, how's little Veda?'

'Perfection! Stevie has just taken her down to baby yoga, so I'm about to have a shower and then do a bit of practice for my gig later.'

'Baby yoga? Is that even a thing?'

'Yep. She loves it, or so he says, but me and Dan both think it's a crock of shit.' She pauses briefly and I hear her slurp a drink. 'Anyway, enough from me. How's it going there? Did you get any sleep?'

The truth is, I didn't. Not at all. I sat up past midnight freaking out to Rachel on the phone. She assured me that everything would work out, that I'd made the right decision and, no matter what happened, she and George would be there for us. But it didn't matter what she said. I still tossed and turned all night long, unable to escape the gnawing feeling that everything was going to fall apart come morning.

'No sleep was had,' I reply. 'I won't lie, I'm an anxious wreck here.'

'He'll be okay. You might not be, but he will. I've got a good feeling about it'

'Well, I can't do any more to prepare him. He'll either love it or he'll kick me in the shins and do a runner. Either way, it's in the hands of the gods now.'

We say our goodbyes and I promise to call later with an update. After hanging up the phone, I head down the hall, passing dozens of half-opened boxes, bulging black bags and mounds of bubble wrap. 'How are we getting on in there?' I call out, but no one answers. I lift Stanley's coat and bag off the floor and take them through to him. 'Are you ready, Stan?'

The living room appears empty, but the TV is on and the same old video about Pangea is blaring out at a deafening volume.

Is anyone in here? Yoo-hoo!' I ignore the muffled sniggering and play along. 'Come out, come out, wherever you are!' I sing as I tiptoe around the huge stack of empty boxes draped in old bed-sheets and towels. I kneel down and wait for my cue.

'Got you!' Stanley shrieks.

'Argh!' I squeal. 'You gave me a fright!'

'Mummy, we are all in here, silly! We are watching Pangea in the den, and Daddy said that it is now his favourite video, but Jack likes Peppa Pig more. But I don't like her because I don't like tails.'

Ed pokes his head out from behind the bed-sheet. 'Is it time?'

'It is,' I say. 'Come on, Stan, let's go and meet George.'

He crawls out from the den and springs to his feet. In the time that I've been gassing on the phone, Ed has nailed it. Stanley's shoes are on, his crisp white shirt is tucked neatly into his grey trousers and, miraculously, he is wearing the tie.

'Gosh, don't you look handsome,' I say without thinking.

'I am NOT handsome!'

'I know, I know.' I help him put his coat on then lick my thumb and wipe away a smear of chocolate from the corner of his mouth.

'Stop, Mummy!'

'All done.' I retreat quickly with my hands in the air. 'You're clean and ready. And don't worry, you don't look handsome at all. Okay, do we have everything we need, Stan?'

'Yes. I have got my bag and my Libya. He is in my pocket.'

'Great. Let's go then. Say goodbye to Daddy and Jack.'

'Goodbye to Daddy and Jack,' he shouts before charging off towards the front door.

'There he is! Stan!' Stanley's grip on my hand loosens ever so slightly when he sees his cousin bounding across the yard towards us. The other children aren't arriving for another twenty minutes, so it's nice and quiet, just as Mr Jones said it would be.

'Let's go!' shrieks George when he catches up to us. He grabs hold of Stanley's arm and tugs him free from my hand.

'Stop it!' Rachel scolds. 'You nearly pulled his arm off.'

'But you said to hold his hand, Mum, and that's what—'

'Shhh! Enough!' She presses her index finger over her lips, then leans down. 'Stannie, I've just spoken to Mr Jones and he is waiting inside for you. I told him how good you are at drawing maps and he can't wait for you to show him.'

'Does he like Libya?' asks Stanley. 'Because I have got him.'

Rachel smiles. 'Of course he does. You should take him inside and—'

'Can we go now? Can we, Mum?'

'Wait a minute, George. Auntie Lucy has to say goodbye to Stanley first.'

Now's my moment. My heart is pounding in my ears, my tear ducts swelling, but I must hold it together. I have to choose my words carefully – nothing too emotional, nothing too long-winded, just a simple goodbye and have a good day.

'Okay, little man. I'll see you late—'

'No, Mummy, I can't go!'

I'm straight down on my knees, my trembling hands taking hold of Stanley's. 'It's okay, Stan. Please don't be scared. George is going to take you inside and—'

'No! No!' He yanks his hands free and turns his back on me. 'I said no! Not yet!'

I look up at Rachel, desperately hoping that she'll know what to say or do next, but like me, she is lost for words.

'Come on, Stan,' says George, his patience rapidly waning. 'We're going to be late.'

'Not now!' Stanley shoves his hand in his pocket and rummages around for what feels like ages.

Suddenly, he turns around and totters over with his fist extended in my direction.

'This is for you, Mummy.' He opens his hand and lays his palm out flat for me to see.

'Libya? Are you sure?'

'I am.'

Wrapping one arm around his waist, I pull his small body close to mine. 'That's so kind. Thank you.' I blink away my tears. 'Do you know what? I have a great idea.'

'What idea?'

'How about George looks after you today, and I will look after Libya. Does that sound okay?'

He nods stiffly. 'That sounds very okay.'

George is bouncing up and down on the spot, desperate to get going. 'Come *on*, Stan!'

He grabs Stanley's hand and, without looking back, the two of them run off towards Mr Jones, who is waiting by the door.

Rachel puts her arm around me as I sob. 'Welcome home, Luce.'

Acknowledgements

Acknowledgements aren't an easy thing to write, especially as there are only so many ways one can say 'thank you' in English. I'll try my best to mix things up, but if I fail, please accept my apologies for the unavoidable repetition that might await you.

Writing a book is very much a team effort and I've been so lucky to have had an absolutely stellar team behind me on *The Mother Load*. First and foremost, a whopping thanks must go to my brilliant editor, Sarah Hodgson. You have taught me so much and I will be forever grateful to you for sharing your wisdom and expertise. What a woman!

Merci beaucoup also to my wonderful copy editor, Emma Dunne, and the fabulous team at Corvus (Kirsty Doole, Aimee Oliver-Powell and Hanna Kenne to name but a few)... you're all ridiculously lovely and first class at what you do.

To my lush agent, Katie Fulford. *Danke schön* for your never-ending support. You're a gem of a lady and an absolute joy to work with! I'm so happy that I met you, a fellow Katie.

To my wonderful children and my husband who inspire me daily, my gorgeous parents and my close friends (Jessica Feaver and Emma Parker in particular) who have spurred me on when the words wouldn't come... *muchas gracias*.

My sister Helen deserves a special mention. You might have been a royal pain in the arse when we were kids, but now, you are my number one hero. *Diolch yn fawr*, sis, for reading my manuscript a gazillion times, and for telling which bits were good, which were utter shite and which were 'okay-ish'. You're a clever old broad with a sharp eye for detail and I love you for it. I'm so grateful for your help that I've almost forgiven you for the time you defecated in the bath aged seven and blamed it on me. Almost.

Obridgada to the Muso Mums, the Bridgend Netmums and to the wonderful autism community online who have all shared their personal experiences with me.

Starting out as a debut author isn't easy in a world saturated with fabulous books and if it wasn't for the brilliant writers and bloggers who have read and reviewed my work, I doubt I would ever have found an audience beyond my gran and her neighbours. Your support has meant the world to me, and I can't express my gratitude enough. And speaking of audiences, *arigatou* to everyone who bought this novel or my first one, *M is for Mummy*. Without you all, my hard work would be for nothing.

I've come to the end, and I've just had a quick count and discovered that I managed to write two whole pages with only two 'thanks'. Truth be told, I didn't know I had it in me! If you've read this far, then may I express my appreciation for your patience.

Or in short, thanks.*

*doh!